CON

TONI M. CROSS, direc[tor of the Ameri]can Research Institute [in Turkey], [speciali...] classical archaeology and has participated in excavations in southeastern Turkey, on the Euphrates River, and in the Hatay. Resident in Turkey since 1975, she has written many articles about her travels throughout the country for *The Ankara Scene,* a bimonthly publication of the U.S. embassy. She is the editorial consultant for this guidebook.

ZEYNEP BAGANA-ÖNEN is account director for the printed materials produced for Turkey's Ministries of Culture and Tourism by the Yorum advertising firm in Istanbul. Born in Istanbul, she lived for several years in İzmir. She studied in the United States for ten years, earning a master's degree at the University of California at Irvine before returning to Istanbul in 1988. In 1989 and 1990 she was an editor of a daily English-language newspaper in Istanbul.

ANNE TURNER BRUNO has worked in Turkey for 29 years, writing about its history, politics, culture, and cuisine for magazines such as *Newsweek, Reader's Digest,* and *National Geographic.* In June 1991, Turkish president Turgut Özal presented her with an award of appreciation for informing Americans about Turkey.

ANTHONY BRYER has been haunting the Turkish Black Sea coast for more than 30 years. He is the author of *The Empire of Trebizond and the Pontos, Peoples and Settlement in Anatolia and the Caucasus,* and *The Byzantine Monuments and Topography of the Pontos,* and is director of the Centre for Byzantine, Ottoman & Modern Greek Studies at the University of Birmingham, England.

METİN DEMİRSAR, the editor of *Insight Guide: Turkish Coast* and the author of *Insight Pocket Guide: Istanbul* and other travel books about Turkey, is a Turkish journalist whose articles have appeared in *The Wall Street Journal, Barron's Weekly,* the London *Daily Express,* and *Global Finance* magazine.

ANNA G. EDMONDS was an editor at the Redhouse Press in Istanbul for 30 years and has observed Istanbul and Turkey since 1949. Her special interests have been the art and history of the country, and she has contributed articles on these subjects to various local newspapers and magazines.

GARY LEISER spent eight years in Ankara as an area specialist and interpreter for the U.S. Department of Defense and as a historian for the U.S. Air Force. Fluent in Arabic and Turkish, he has a doctorate in Medieval Islamic history and has led tours for the American Research Institute in Turkey to eastern Turkey. His translation of M. Fuad Köprülü's classic work *The Origins of the Ottoman Empire* has recently been issued.

PATRICIA TARBELL LEISER did graduate work in Islamic art and architecture and is fluent in French, Arabic, and Turkish. She lived in Ankara for eight years, where she coedited the American embassy newsletter, *The Ankara Scene,* and wrote various articles on the culture and history of Turkey. She has lectured for, managed, and guided numerous tours in Turkey and is a specialist in Turkish weaving.

SHERRY MARKER studied archaeology at the American School of Classical Studies in Athens and has participated in an archaeological dig on the Aegean coast of Turkey. She contributes travel articles to *The New York Times* and *Travel & Leisure* magazine.

SCOTT REDFORD is director of Georgetown University's McGhee Center for Eastern Mediterranean Studies in Alanya, Turkey.

PATRICIA ROBERTS lived in Istanbul and has written about Turkey for *The Wall Street Journal* as well as for other guidebooks.

JAMES RUGGIA, associate editor at *Travel Agent* magazine, has contributed articles on Turkey to such magazines as *MD* and *Pan Am Clipper.* He lived in Turkey for a year and has travelled there extensively.

DOROTHY SLANE has lived in Adana for six years, first as a Fulbright scholar and now as a lecturer for the University of Maryland extension at İncirlik Air Base. Dr. Slane holds a Ph.D. in Hittite archaeology of the Adana region as well as a master's degree in underwater archaeology.

JAMES WALLER was the news editor of a daily English-language newspaper published in Istanbul. He now lives in New York City, where he works as a freelance writer and editor.

THE BERLITZ
TRAVELLERS GUIDES

THE BERLITZ TRAVELLERS GUIDE TO TURKEY 1993

ALAN TUCKER

General Editor

BERLITZ PUBLISHING COMPANY, INC.
New York, New York

BERLITZ PUBLISHING COMPANY LTD.
Oxford, England

THE BERLITZ TRAVELLERS GUIDE
TO TURKEY 1993

Published by Berlitz Publishing Company, Inc.
257 Park Avenue South, New York, New York 10010, U.S.A.

Distributed in the United States by
the Macmillan Publishing Group

Distributed elsewhere by Berlitz Publishing Company Ltd.
Berlitz House, Peterley Road, Horspath, Oxford OX4 2TX, England

ISBN 2-8315-1782-6
ISSN 1057-1465

Designed by Beth Tondreau Design
Cover design by Dan Miller Design
Cover photograph © David Ball/Allstock
Maps by Diane McCaffery
Illustrations by Bill Russell
Copyedited by Cornelia Guest
Additional consultation by Bruno Blumenfeld, Charles Gates,
and Marie-Henriette Gates
Fact-checked in Turkey by Zeynep Bagana-Önen
Edited by James Waller

Printed in the United States of America
1 3 5 7 9 10 8 6 4 2

THIS GUIDEBOOK

The Berlitz Travellers Guides are designed for experienced travellers in search of exceptional information that will enhance the enjoyment of the trips they take.

Where, for example, are the interesting, out-of-the-way, fun, charming, or romantic places to stay? The hotels described by our expert writers are some of the special places, in all price ranges except for the very lowest—not just the run-of-the-mill, heavily marketed places in advertised airline and travel-wholesaler packages.

We indicate the approximate price level of each accommodation in our description of it (no indication means it is moderate in local, relative terms), and at the end of every chapter we supply more detailed hotel rates as well as contact information so that you can get precise, up-to-the-minute rates and make reservations.

The Berlitz Travellers Guide to Turkey 1993 highlights the more rewarding parts of the country so that you can quickly and efficiently home in on a good itinerary.

Of course, this guidebook does far more than just help you choose a hotel and plan your trip. *The Berlitz Travellers Guide to Turkey 1993* is designed for use *in* Turkey. Our writers, each of whom is an experienced area specialist or travel journalist who either lives in or regularly tours the city or region of Turkey he or she covers, tell you what you really need to know, what you can't find out so easily on your own. They identify and describe the truly out-of-the-ordinary restaurants, shops, activities, and sights, and tell you the best way to "do" your destination.

Our writers are highly selective. They bring out the significance of the places they *do* cover, capturing the personality and the underlying cultural and historical resonances of a city or region—making clear its special appeal.

The Berlitz Travellers Guide to Turkey is full of reliable and timely information, revised and updated each year. We would like to know if you think we've left out some very special place. Although we make every effort to provide the most current information available about every destination described in this book, it is possible too that changes have occurred before you arrive. If you do have an experience that is contrary to what you were led to expect by our description, we would like to hear from you about it.

A guidebook is no substitute for common sense when you are travelling. Always pack the clothing, footwear, and other items appropriate for the destination, and make the necessary accommodation for such variables as altitude, weather, and local rules and customs. Of course, once on the scene you should avoid situations that are in your own judgment potentially hazardous, even if they have to do with something mentioned in a guidebook. Half the fun of travelling is exploring, but explore with care.

ALAN TUCKER
General Editor
Berlitz Travellers Guides

Root Publishing Company
330 West 58th Street
Suite 504
New York, New York 10019

CONTENTS

MAPS

THE
BERLITZ
TRAVELLERS
GUIDE
TO
TURKEY
1993

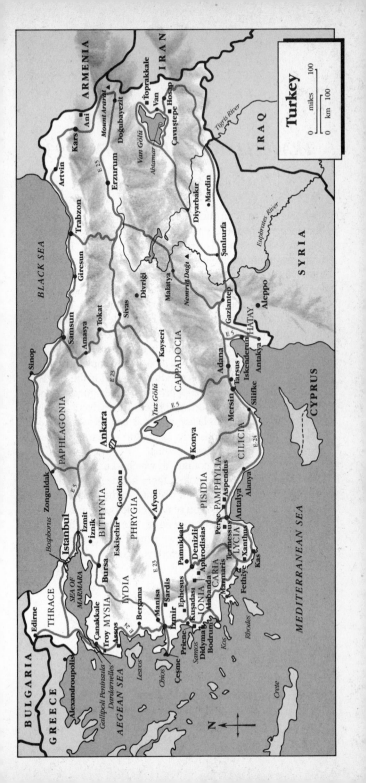

TRAVELLING IN TURKEY IN 1993

It's not cheap to fly to Turkey, especially from North America, but once you're there you'll probably find that you spend less on food and hotels than you had anticipated. Furthermore, travellers are largely insulated from Turkey's alarming rate of inflation. First of all, the exchange rates are extremely favorable. Second, hotels and restaurants here make a concerted effort to keep prices reasonable, to protect Turkey's burgeoning tourism industry. Stay in an international chain hotel and you'll pay international prices, but stay in the government-run Turban hotels, or in almost any of the small, privately owned hotels, and you'll have no complaints about the cost. In addition, those goods designed for the tourist market—kilims, carpets, copperware, leather goods, silks, and spices—remain reasonably priced. Turkey has a rapidly developing garment industry, and you can pick up good-looking clothes by Turkish designers for a fraction of what you'd pay for similar Italian clothing.

Turkey is a very safe country in which to travel: Crime is virtually unknown. Nonetheless, there has been a good deal of political unrest—some of it violent—in the southeastern-most part of the country. You're unlikely to become aware of these problems unless you venture into the southeast; if that's your destination, check with the U.S. Department of State or your Foreign Office before you go.

—*Sherry Marker*

OVERVIEW

By Toni M. Cross

Director of the Ankara branch of the American Research Institute in Turkey, Toni M. Cross earned a doctorate in classical archaeology and has participated in excavations in southeastern Turkey, on the Euphrates River, and in the Hatay. Resident in Turkey since 1975, she has written many articles about her travels throughout the country for The Ankara Scene, *a bimonthly publication of the U.S. embassy. She is the editorial consultant for this guidebook.*

Visitors to Turkey have had the trail blazed for them by some of the most famous European travellers, and travel writers, of the 18th and 19th centuries: Chandler and Tournefort, Leake, Hamilton, Arundel, Texier, and Fellows. Products of a classical education, these early travellers came to Anatolia to identify the cities and roam the countrysides described by Homer, Herodotus, Xenophon, and Strabo. They climbed the mound of Troy and swam the Hellespont, crossed more than 2,000 years before by Xerxes on a bridge of boats. They sketched the tomb of Gyges, traced the March of the Ten Thousand and the route of Alexander the Great, sought out the towns where Caesar conquered and Cleopatra bedazzled Antony. Equally well versed in the Bible, they devoted journal pages to the Seven Churches of Asia, Saint Paul of Tarsus, and the snowcapped peak of Ararat, supposed resting place of Noah's Ark.

Twentieth-century travellers, too, are drawn to Turkey by that same urge to muse on the seasons of man at Troy and to envision the theater of Ephesus filled with the mob chanting, "Great is Artemis of the Ephesians!" On pilgrimages to these old, familiar places you will discover the vestiges of ever more remote antiquity, back to the very beginnings of set-

5

tled life. And overlooking these ancient cities done to dust are Byzantine churches, Crusader castles, Seljuk caravansaries, and Ottoman palaces—for no other land on this earth has nurtured so many different civilizations.

In search of the ancient past, early European travellers were also responding to the exotic lure of the Ottoman Empire. Along with details of temple and tomb, they fattened their journals with descriptions of the landscape, its flora and fauna, and the character and habits of the people. Modern visitors with no qualms about seeking the exotic head straight for Istanbul and the palaces of the Ottoman sultans, though the harems no longer shelter odalisques. Present-day travellers drawn by the landscape are probably heading for the many fine beaches of Turkey's 5,000-mile coastline. But less than an hour's drive from the shore the landscape and scenery change dramatically: All the regional variations of the continental United States are here, squeezed into a country not much bigger than Texas. The coastline is backed by a ring of mountains that encircle the central, upland plateau. This explains why Turkey, almost alone among Mediterranean countries, has no tradition of the afternoon siesta: In summer the central plateau is hot in daytime but blessedly cool at night, while until recently the coastal inhabitants simply moved to second homes in the mountains from June through August.

Once in Turkey most of you, like your earlier counterparts, will discover the country's main attraction, for too long a well-kept secret: the people themselves. Since besieging Vienna in 1683, the Turks have suffered from an exceedingly bad press. The Ottoman Empire that so frightened Christendom was lost in World War I; the secular Republic of Turkey that arose in its place celebrates its 70th anniversary in 1993. But though the Western image of the "terrible Turk" lives on, the Turkish people have always found friends among European visitors. The English antiquarian Sir Charles Fellows began the account of his travels in 1838 with this frank statement: "It will be gathered from my Journal, that at the time of my arrival in the country I was strongly biased in favour of the Greeks, and equally prejudiced against the Turks; and it will be seen in the course of the narrative how this unfavourable idea of the Turkish character was gradually removed by a personal intimacy with the people, generally in situations where they were remote from every restraint but those which their religion imposes."

Despite the exotic images of "Orientalism," Turkish culture is just different enough to be interesting. You will discover that the manners and mores of the Turks resemble those of medieval chivalry and that hospitality to strangers is an integral part of the culture. Calm, dignified, and exceptionally slow to anger, the Turks exemplify the old Roman virtue of *gravitas* (except, it must be admitted, when behind the wheel of a car). Markedly fierce and brave when finally aroused, the Turks will literally die for their friends, as the Western allies learned in the Korean War.

The recent introduction of Western-style consumerism has filled stores with everything from Scotch to contact-lens solution. Sadly, it has also set a modern, hectic pace with little time for the old civilities. This is especially true in Istanbul, now drastically transformed into an industrial and commercial metropolis. But Turks of every class still take delight in the simple pleasures of life: a view of water (the Bosphorus or a tiny fountain), gardens (wild rather than formal), leisurely meals with an endless supply of good food and drink, the companionship of family and friends. Even fiercely mustachioed males expect to receive flowers as well as to give them. And Turks of both sexes and every age love children, the younger the better, making the country a haven for travellers with offspring in tow.

Of course, those who ruled the Ottoman Empire for 600 years did not lack sophistication. This is most evident at the Topkapı palace in Istanbul, begun in the 15th century and then enlarged and embellished by generations of sultans. With the decline of the empire in the 19th century, the sultans lost their confidence and with it their taste, abandoning Topkapı for new palaces in the European manner, which they furnished in a French/Levantine Rococo hodgepodge.

In a sense, every Turk could claim membership in the ruling class of the Ottoman Empire, a vast domain in which Greek, Arab, Jewish, Serbian, Hungarian, Bulgarian, Romanian, Circassian, Georgian, and Levantine subjects were permitted to retain their own customs, languages, and religions. Even the poorest, most backward Turkish peasant is therefore fully prepared for the foreigner to be "foreign." Visitors travelling to the most remote areas of the country need only conduct themselves as proper Americans, Canadians, Australians, or Britons to be treated with full respect. Even isolated villagers, however, have a fair idea of what constitutes proper behavior in Western terms (notwithstanding years of seamy American soap operas broadcast on Turkish TV). Attire unsuitable for church or synagogue is equally unsuitable for visiting mosques. And while a topless stroll across the beach at a Mediterranean resort will not lead to arrest, the local youths may respond with less than respectful attention.

Turkish Dining and Cuisine

Another pleasant surprise awaiting the first-time visitor is Turkish food, which, with the French and the Chinese, is one of the world's three main cuisines. The basis of Turkish cooking, and its strength, is the quality and freshness of the ingredients themselves. Although elaborate dishes requiring long and careful preparation do have a place in Turkish cuisine, sauces and spices are intended to enhance, not mask, the robust flavor of the basic ingredients. Given Turkey's wide climatic variations in its relatively small area, the major cities are easily supplied with the freshest of fruits and vegetables, meat, and fish. All this edible wealth is displayed with an artistic flourish in even the tiniest of shops, and it is not unusual to see a busload of tourists expending more film on the corner market than on the famous monument nearby. The restaurants of Istanbul are rightly famed for the richness and variety of their menus, and each region boasts its local specialty. But the true glory of Turkish cuisine can be found in the high-quality, low-priced meals served at even the humblest of bus-stop restaurants throughout the country.

Turkish restaurants fall into three basic categories: the *kebap salonu,* the *lokanta,* and the *restoran.* The ubiquitous *kebap salonu* (kebap place) serves quick, one-dish meals, mainly lamb grilled on a spit or cooked in a wood-fired oven, served on *pide* (pita) bread. Try the elaborate version of *döner* (lamb cooked on a vertical spit, like the Greek gyro) called *İskender kebap*—slices of *döner* laid on *pide* bread and covered with spicy tomato sauce, butter, and yogurt.

A *lokanta* is a restaurant too humble to call itself a restaurant. Here you will find *hazır yemekler* (cooked foods) such as soups and stews, green beans with meat, stuffed peppers, and that hearty standby of peasant and soldier, beans and rice. Most bus-stop *lokantas* are cafeteria-style. In small towns the waiter may lead you directly into the kitchen to have you inspect all the bubbling pots and point out your choices. If nothing appeals, you might ask for *menemen*—ranch-style eggs scrambled with tomatoes, peppers, onions, and perhaps a little cheese. Most *lokantas* serve nothing stronger than beer, if that. Here Turks will order *ayran,* a salty, watery yogurt drink something like buttermilk—but it is an acquired taste.

A true restaurant (*restoran*) offers a complete *rakı sofrası,* an endless stream and incredible variety of dishes traditionally accompanied by rakı, though wine is becoming increasingly popular. A colorless liquor flavored with anise, rakı is normally mixed with water and imbibed only with meals, to lessen its powerful effect. A *rakı sofrası* begins with cold, then hot, *meze* (appetizers), then proceeds to a main course of meat or fish, depending on the establishment. It draws to a close with dessert or fruit, and Turkish coffee. A meze is not merely an hors d'oeuvre; many are simply small portions of dishes that could form a meal in themselves. You should select three or four from the huge tray the waiter will bring to your table. Prominent among the choices will be *zetinyağlı,* vegetable dishes such as vine leaves or green peppers stuffed with a mixture of rice, currants, and pine nuts (these dishes are cooked in olive oil and served cold), and an eggplant dish called *imam bayıldı* ("the imam fainted"). Most typical of the hot mezes are *börek*—pastry leaves filled with meat or cheese.

The *kebap salonu, lokanta,* and *restoran* all have their regional variations. The spiciest food is found in the southeastern part of the country, and, not surprisingly, fish restaurants are most common along the coasts (although restaurants in Ankara, which is inland, offer fish that's delivered fresh daily).

Serious chefs should definitely buy a Turkish cookbook. Those concerned more with the end than the means may proceed directly from Atatürk airport in Istanbul to a seafood restaurant on the Bosphorus. Order your Turkish wine or rakı, then call for some of the specialties these establishments are so famous for: fried mussels and squid, tiny prawns marinated in a vinaigrette-like dressing, tangy little potato balls. If you choose carefully and eat slowly, you may even have enough room left for an entrée of bluefish, pulled fresh from the Black Sea just a few miles to the north.

Time spent over such a meal is not time wasted but a good occasion to decide what to see and do in the days ahead—not an easy task. You can choose from the beaches and spectacular coastlines of three seas—Black, Aegean, and Mediterranean. Then there are the remains of the many civilizations that have flourished here since 10,000 B.C. to be explored on site or in museums. Hard choices must be made, for it is truly impossible to see everything: Even if your antiquarian interest is restricted to castles you must choose from among the hundreds of Greek, Roman, Byzantine, Georgian, Armenian, Seljuk, Crusader, and Ottoman citadels scattered across the country.

History

You will, of course, enjoy your trip much more if you know at least a little about the history of the area you are visiting.

The problem is that there is simply so much of it. Civilization in Anatolia slowly evolved from the first settled communities based on domesticated plants and animals (10,000 to 5000 B.C.) to the small city-states of the Early and Middle Bronze Ages (3000 to 1750 B.C.). In the Late Bronze Age the Hittites established an empire among the city-states of Central Anatolia (fl. 1450 to 1200 B.C.), then moved southeast into the Levant to challenge Egypt, the dominant power of the time. Around 1200 B.C., for reasons that are still not entirely clear, the major states of the eastern Mediterranean, including that of the Hittites and their Mycenaean contemporaries in Greece, were utterly destroyed.

Some four centuries later Anatolia was divided among a number of different peoples, some indigenous and some newcomers—Urartians in the east, Phrygians in the central plateau, Carians and Lycians in the southwest, and Lydians in the west, with a string of Greek colonies established on the Aegean coast. All these peoples and their territories were destined to be taken over by and incorporated into large empires ruled by the Persians (545 to 333 B.C.), Alexander the Great and his successors in the Hellenistic age (333 to 33 B.C.), and the Romans (33 B.C. to A.D. 500). While the monuments erected during the latter two periods are traditionally, and conveniently, labeled "Hellenistic" and "Roman," these designations usually refer more to the dates of construction than the actual builders, for the native peoples did not disappear but, to a greater or lesser extent, adopted and assimilated the culture, religion, and language of their rulers.

In A.D. 330 Constantine the Great dedicated the newly enlarged city of Byzantium as the New Rome, although its name soon changed to Constantinople. With this city as its capital, the eastern half of the Roman Empire began its slow evolution into the Orthodox Christian state referred to today—although never by its rulers—as the Byzantine Empire. In 1071, the Seljuk victory over the Byzantines at the battle of Manzikert, near Lake Van, opened the way for Turkish migration and the establishment of the first Turkish state, the Seljuk Sultanate of Rum, in Central Anatolia. This and the fall of Jerusalem to the Turks in the same year provoked the European Crusades, most of which passed through Anatolia and in the long run did more damage to the Byzantine Empire than to the Turks. In 1243, however, a devastating Mongol invasion shattered the Seljuk state and ensured that the Turkish dynasty that was to rule Anatolia (and well beyond) for 600 years was not Seljuk but Ottoman. (The word *Ottoman,* by the way, is a European derivation of the Arabic name of the dynasty's founder, called Osman in Turkish. Though *Ottoman* is used throughout this guide on account of its familiarity, *Osmanlı* is the more accurate term and the one used in Turkey.)

Initially settled in the region of Bursa, which became their first capital in 1326, the Ottomans expanded across the straits into Europe (Thrace and the Balkans), moving their capital to Edirne (Adrianople) in 1361 and defeating the Serbs at Kosovo in 1389. Their own defeat by Tamerlane at the battle of Ankara in 1402 caused only a temporary setback, and in 1453 Sultan Mehmet II, called the Conqueror, captured the city of Constantinople and made it the capital of his empire. He then turned east to incorporate Central Anatolia and, in 1461, the tiny empire of Trebizond on the eastern Black Sea coast. In 1492 his son Sultan Bayezit II welcomed into the growing empire the Jews of Spain, expelled by the Catholic rulers Ferdinand and Isabella. Early in the 16th century Mehmet's grandson Selim I added the Arab lands to the Empire; the Muslim caliphate thus passed to the Ottoman sultans, who claimed to be the religious as well as the temporal leaders of the Islamic world. The Ottoman Empire reached its height under Süleyman the Magnificent in the 16th century, and at its greatest extent included much of Eastern Europe, the Crimea, the Caucasus, Mesopotamia, the Levant, Arabia, Yemen, Egypt, and North Africa.

Economic shifts following the Age of Discovery led to the decline of the Ottoman Empire, obvious by the later 17th century, and corresponded to the rise of the great empires of Europe—Russian, Austrian, British, and French—which stood poised to profit from Ottoman weakness. With the rise of nationalism in the 19th century, these European empires encouraged the separatist ambitions of the various minorities in the Ottoman domains for their own territorial advantage. Despite the efforts of reforming sultans, the century leading up to World War I saw an ever-shrinking empire across whose borders streamed Muslim refugees from the Caucasus, Greece, Crete, and the Balkans.

But this rising nationalism had affected the Turks as well, as the European powers were to discover at the moment of apparent victory. Having defeated the Ottoman Empire, which was allied with the Central Powers in World War I, the Western allies apportioned among themselves not just the empire's outlying provinces but also the bulk of present-day Turkey, intending to leave the Turks with only part of north-central Anatolia. Under the leadership of the young general Mustafa Kemal, who later took the surname Atatürk, the

Turks repelled the invading allied armies, then went on to establish the secular Republic of Turkey, whose motto was, and continues to be, "Peace at home, peace abroad."

Touring Turkey

Travellers with a week or ten days usually begin in Istanbul and then must choose between the seaside, with mainly classical antiquities, and the inland plateau, with predominantly medieval monuments. That any visit to Turkey must include **Istanbul** is fitting tribute to the Delphic Oracle, who first recommended the site to prospective Greek colonists in the seventh century B.C. Set on low hills overlooking three bodies of water—the Golden Horn, the Bosphorus, and the Sea of Marmara—and upon two continents, Istanbul was destined to be both beautiful and important. For 1,600 years it served as the capital of successive empires, the (eastern) Roman, the Byzantine, and the Ottoman, each of which rose to the challenge and adorned it with monuments of majesty and grace, which still dominate the skyline of the old city.

The present inhabitants accept the glories of Istanbul with aplomb, supremely confident that no city is more beautiful or more intensely alive than their own. They commute by ferry between Europe and Asia, sipping tea and reading newspapers. They shop in Istanbul's Covered Bazaar and modern boutiques, dine at the seafood restaurants lining its shores, and taste the pleasures of its nightlife, from belly dancers to jazz to opera. That the concert takes place in a sixth-century church and the floor show in a fourteenth-century tower is accepted as natural—just as natural as living beside (or in) a pasha's palace and working in a modern office building.

Though Ankara has been the capital since 1923, Istanbul is Turkey's business and industrial center and its largest city, with a population fast approaching ten million in the greater metropolitan area. The tremendous growth in population and industry has led to dramatic changes that now threaten the very character of the city. Every year old buildings are lost to fire or to hasty, unplanned construction, while winter smog and traffic gridlock try the patience of the most stoic *İstanbullu*.

This hectic pace has not yet eliminated the city's rather smug disdain for the provinces—meaning all of Turkey to the east beyond the Asian ramp of the Bosphorus bridge. Ignore this imperial attitude, for the various regions of the country offer so many attractions of such diversity that the most vexing question is not *whether* to go, but *where* in the time available.

The deep, narrow Bosphorus separates Europe from Asia and connects the Black Sea with the Sea of Marmara, immediately south of Istanbul. You can escape the pressures of the city for a day by hopping a ferry to the nearby **Princes' Islands** in the Sea of Marmara, where the leisurely pace is enforced by a ban against automobiles and the fastest means of transportation is the horse carriage.

A taste of the countryside can be acquired on a day or overnight trip west to Thrace, Turkey's only European province (bordering Bulgaria and Greece), or south along the Marmara shore. Close to the Bulgarian border is **Edirne**, the Ottoman capital before the conquest of Constantinople and the location of the great Ottoman architect Sinan's masterpiece, the Selimiye mosque. At the southwestern corner of the broad Sea of Marmara is the Dardanelles, or Hellespont, a narrow sea lane connecting the Marmara with the Aegean. Forming the western shore of the Dardanelles is the rugged **Gallipoli** peninsula, its battlefields now haunting memorials to the men on both sides who fell in the bloody campaign waged there in 1915 and 1916.

From Istanbul numerous boats and car ferries cross the Sea of Marmara to the pleasant cities on its southern shore: **Bursa**, the 14th-century Ottoman capital, known today for the production of silks and fluffy "Turkish" towels, and **İznik**, ancient Nicaea, where in A.D. 325 a church council promulgated the Nicene Creed. The latter city is also celebrated for the fabulous tiles its artisans created, which adorn the palaces and mosques of Istanbul.

After Istanbul, the most popular destination is the **Aegean coast**, in summer breezier and cooler than the Mediterranean for those in search of sun and sand. In his foreword to *Aegean Turkey* (1966), the classical scholar George Bean noted that the country was at last becoming "tourist-minded," with towns providing "a perfectly tolerable, though simple, night's lodging." The Aegean is now the most tourist-minded region in Turkey, with that "simple" lodging squeezed between luxury hotels. A host of companies offer package tours, but a private car gives much more freedom and car-rental agencies are easy to come by. Passenger, ferry, and cruise boats call at the major ports, and a number of coastal cities have direct ferry service to the closest Greek island.

While the scenery is lovely and the beaches sandy, the region's main allure is exerted by its ancient cities, a roll call of names that still resonate through Western culture. Most

evocative is **Troy**, the city of Homer, on the mainland opposite Gallipoli. The road south passes near **Assos**, home of
Aristotle after the death of Plato, and Bergama, ancient **Pergamum**, whose library rivaled that of Alexandria.

Tucked midway along the coast is İzmir, Turkey's third-
largest city, with a major airport (flights from Istanbul are
frequent and take less than an hour) and good boat and ferry
service to Istanbul and the major ports of Greece and Italy. A
morning's drive inland will bring you to **Sardis**, where
"money" was invented and Croesus was rich; the unspoiled
provincial capital of **Manisa**; and the pleasant **hilltowns of
the Bozdağlar** (Gray Mountains), where Turks from İzmir
escape the summer heat. Two hours south of İzmir are the
popular seaside resort of **Kuşadası**, a convenient base for
visits to **Ephesus**, capital of Roman Asia; **Priene**, a must for
historians of the theater; **Miletus**, where the philosopher
Thales first tried to "understand the world"; the gigantic
temple of Apollo at **Didyma**; the lakeside ruins of
Heraclaeia-under-Latmus and the rarely visited Carian sites
of **Alinda, Alabanda,** and **Labranda**. Well worth a day's drive
up the valley of the ancient Meander river (now the
Menderes) are **Aphrodisias**, its museum overflowing with
Roman sculpture, and **Pamukkale**, ancient Hierapolis, where
the by-now-weary traveller can restore body and soul with a
well-earned soak in pools fed by natural hot springs.

Travellers intending to concentrate on the Aegean coast
may fly directly to İzmir from Istanbul or Europe, then
journey out from the city to the north, east, and south (as
described in our chapter on the Aegean). Those with more
time may catch the steamer from Istanbul to **Çanakkale**, on
the Asian shore not far from Troy, then drive south along the
coast. An increasingly popular option is simply to follow the
coastline and traverse as much of the Aegean and Mediterranean shores as time allows. Just be aware that the coastline is
long—you'll need at least two weeks to travel along the
shore from Gallipoli to the Syrian border.

The southwest corner of Turkey is known as the **Turquoise Coast**, for here pine-covered mountains plunge into
the bluest of seas. Along this shore and enfolded within its
mountains are so many Carian, Lycian, Greek, Roman, and
Byzantine sites that several weeks would be needed to see
them all. First port of call for most travellers is **Bodrum**,
ancient Halicarnassus, where Herodotus was born and Mausolus buried; a Crusader castle still dominates the harbor. In
season this once-quiet village of sponge divers is a home
port of the international jet set and those who don't go on a
vacation to sit still.

From Bodrum you can drive or, better yet, sail along the deeply indented coastline, with stops at the Greco-Roman city of **Cnidus**, the popular resort and yacht harbor of **Marmaris**, and the ancient Carian city of **Caunus** before anchoring in the huge bay of **Fethiye**. Inland from Fethiye lie the major Lycian site of **Xanthus** (its sculptures now residing in the British Museum) and the **Letoön**, sanctuary of the goddess Leto and her children, Artemis and Apollo. On the coast directly south are **Patara**, birthplace of Saint Nicholas (a.k.a. Santa Claus), and the little ports of **Kalkan** and **Kaş**, both with yacht harbors and charming old houses. A flotilla of boats, large and small, plies between Kaş and the picturesque little towns of **Kekova bay**. Farther east are **Demre/Myra**, with its Lycian rock-cut tombs, Roman theater, and church of St. Nicholas; **Olympus**, home of the Chimera; and **Phaselis**, where Alexander the Great passed the early months of 333 B.C.

Beyond Phaselis the road winds down out of the mountains to the city of **Antalya**, at the western edge of a broad, fertile plain. For most travellers the **Mediterranean coast** begins at Antalya, a major tourist center offering accommodations in old Ottoman mansions and beach resorts as well as pensions and five-star hotels. In the mountains behind the city is **Termessus**, on a lofty perch so daunting that even Alexander did not besiege it. On the level plain to the east are ancient cities whose remains testify to the benefits of the *Pax Romana:* **Perge**, once adorned with sculptures that now crowd the Antalya Museum; **Aspendus**, its Roman theater standing almost complete; the mountain town of **Selge**, still reachable only by a Roman bridge; and **Side**, where visitors stay in hotels alongside the ancient ruins and spend the days on a broad, sandy beach, recovering from late nights at the disco. This beach continues another 64 km (40 miles) to the mighty Seljuk fortifications of **Alanya**, which now guard a harbor rimmed with little shops, favorite haunts of collectors of carpets and kilims.

Beyond Alanya the mountains again come down to meet the sea, the coastal highway presenting spectacular, if occasionally unnerving, views on its way to the Late Antique ruins of **Anamur**, the medieval **Mamure castle**, and **Silifke**, near which Holy Roman Emperor Frederick Barbarossa drowned in 1190, bringing an abrupt end to German participation in the Third Crusade. Farther east along the coast is **Tarsus**, where Saint Paul was born, Cicero governed, and Cleopatra conquered Antony.

Most coastal peregrinations end here, thus leaving the **Hatay**, that small wedge of Turkey jutting down the Mediterranean coast to Syria, blessedly free of both tour bus and backpacker. Under French mandate from the end of World War I until 1939, the Hatay retains a cosmopolitan, Levantine air reminiscent of Lebanon in the days before that country's civil war. In the north is the broad Plain of Issus, where in 333 B.C. Alexander the Great defeated the Persian army under Darius and, to commemorate his victory, founded the city of Alexandria, long called Alexandretta, now İskenderun. Immediately to the south, the formidable Amanus mountains bisect the Hatay, but an excellent highway now zigzags its way over the single pass and down into the fertile Amık plain, dotted with hundreds of ancient mounds. In the center of the plain is **Antakya**, ancient Antioch-on-the-Orontes, third city (after Rome and Alexandria) of the Roman Empire. To the early Christians Antioch was the epitome of sin and dissipation, and the splendid Roman mosaics now housed in the Antakya Museum are evidence of its inhabitants' wealth and luxurious mode of living. In summer the present-day residents, like their Roman predecessors, abandon the city for the laurel groves and tumbling streams of **Harbiye**, ancient Daphne, in the hills to the south.

Having traversed the coast from Istanbul to Antakya, you will have seen much less than half the country. The interior is not as developed (for either tourist or industry), and its monuments are mostly medieval and thus less familiar. Most general guidebooks devote no more than a third of their pages to central and eastern Turkey, and accurate equivalents of the detailed *Blue Guide* to the Aegean and Mediterranean coasts remain to be written. These regions, equally worthy of the attentions of tourists and guidebooks, are thus all the more rewarding for those who prefer to discover things for themselves. Travellers for whom all beaches look alike (and all ancient theaters are beginning to) are strongly advised to bear off the well-beaten tourist path and into the heartland of the country.

The vast plateau of **Central Anatolia** was home to very early civilizations as well as the later Romans, Byzantines, Seljuks, and Ottomans. The uninspired modern buildings of **Ankara**, the capital of Turkey, surround the old city and its citadel. Here the narrow streets are lined with tiny shops purveying such wares as spiked dog collars and reed bird cages; bags of pistachios, saffron, henna, and cinnamon bark; lengths of batik cloth; and arguably the best selection of carpets and kilims in the entire country.

The road west to **Eskişehir** and its Phrygian and Roman sites passes through **Gordion**, where King Midas rued his golden touch and Alexander sliced the knot. To the northeast are **Boğazköy**, capital of the Hittites (ancestors of the biblical Uriah), and the Ottoman towns of **Amasya** and **Tokat**, as notable for their hospitality to foreigners as for their late medieval Islamic monuments. Southeast is **Cappadocia**, a landscape of soft, volcanic tufa out of which the Byzantines hollowed not just churches and monasteries but entire cities, and **Konya**, 12th-century Seljuk capital and home of the Whirling Dervishes. To the east lie **Sivas** and **Divriği**, each with splendid Seljuk monuments in equally splendid isolation.

Travellers to the **Black Sea Coast** are advised to concentrate on the eastern half (the western being endowed with few amenities or antiquities), flying or cruising from Istanbul to **Samsun** or **Trabzon** and traversing the coast in between these two cities by car. This narrow coastal strip was once the tiny empire of Trebizond, a Byzantine offshoot that supplied Europe with goods of the East and that became the exotic locale of medieval romances. The scenery is indeed romantic, the fiercely green Pontic mountains rising straight up from the roiling sea. The coastal road winds its way between sea and mountain to Trabzon (ancient Trapezous, medieval Trebizond), passing through the small port of **Giresun**, where the Roman general Lucullus supposedly discovered the cherry.

Several days will be needed in Trabzon to wander through its narrow, twisting streets in search of the monuments of its medieval past. A morning visit to the Orthodox monastery of **Soumela**, clinging to the side of a mountain some 30 km (19 miles) south of Trabzon, is essential, an *après*-climb lunch of fresh trout highly recommended. From Trabzon the road continues east along the coast through **Rize** and **Hopa** to the town of **Sarp**, at the Georgian border. To get a taste of Georgia without crossing the border, which might be difficult to do, visit one of the "Rus" bazaars, the unofficial open-air markets that have sprung up in many of these Black Sea towns. Operated by budding Georgian capitalists from the trunks of their aged cars, these markets boast an unusual selection of merchandise, from car parts, dusty plastic toys, and the china from grandma's cupboard to microscopes and electric shavers. Serious antiques collectors should team up—and be prepared (mentally *and* financially) to fight it out with big-city dealers.

Not the least of the region's attractions are the natives themselves, a lively lot with distinctive folk music and dance, best appreciated in upland towns such as **Çamlıhemşin** and **Uzungöl**. Here the sturdy can arrange for hiking trips into the mighty Kaçkar range.

Both the Euphrates and the Tigris rivers flow through

eastern Turkey, a land of wild, natural beauty populated by villagers still following the traditional way of life. Scattered about this landscape are wonderful but little-known medieval monuments that, until recently, drew a mere handful of tourists. These few returned home so vocal in their enthusiasm that increasing numbers are following in their intrepid footsteps, and most towns here of any size now boast at least one decent hotel. Travellers coming directly from Istanbul should fly to **Erzurum**, while those following the Black Sea coast can drive south from Hopa.

Just 70 km (43 miles) south of the Black Sea port of Hopa, on the southern side of the Pontic watershed, is **Artvin**, the departure point for visits to the medieval Georgian churches and castles hidden safely away in isolated mountain valleys. On the high plateau to the southeast stands **Kars**, long the goal of Czarist armies, and near it medieval **Ani**, deserted now on its promontory, which juts into Armenia. A few hours south is **Doğubayezit**, where the romantic can wander through the ruins of İshak Paşa's dream-like palace while the energetic climb **Mount Ararat**. The road to **Lake Van** passes near **Manzikert** (now Malazgirt), where on August 26, 1071, "that dreadful day"—for the Byzantines, not the Turks—the victorious Seljuks opened the way into Anatolia. The city of **Van** is the proud possessor of a massive citadel, several good hotels, an airport, numerous carpet shops, and its own breed of cat. Between 850 and 600 B.C., Van was the center of the kingdom of Urartu, whose rulers built fortresses, dams, and irrigation systems (some still in use today) and were rivals of the mighty Assyrians of northern Mesopotamia. Easily reached from Van are the Urartian citadels at **Toprak-kale** and **Çavuştepe**, the 17th-century castle at **Hoşap**, and the Armenian church on the tiny island of **Aktamar**.

Visits to the **southeast** usually begin at **Adana**, the nondescript but agriculturally rich provincial capital with a busy airport and plenty of car-rental agencies. On day trips from Adana you may stroll through the imposing Roman remains at **Anazarbus** and **Castabala**, with only village children for company, en route to the Neo-Hittite city of **Karatepe**, its statues and reliefs almost hidden among the pines.

East of Adana the road passes through **Gaziantep** and crosses the Euphrates to **Şanlıurfa**, home of the biblical patriarch Abraham before his journey to Canaan and, a few thousand years later, seat of the Crusader county of Edessa. After feeding the massive carp thronging the pool alongside the Rizvanıye mosque, you can roam through streets lined with massive stone houses and search out that special kilim in the town's truly eastern bazaar.

No one who has come this far should pass up an overnight trip to **Nemrut Dağı**, the mountaintop burial site of a local first-century B.C. ruler, its huge, conical tumulus ringed by massive statues and reliefs. On the Tigris river to the northeast is **Diyarbakır**, its late Roman walls enclosing a warren of streets and ancient churches of the Eastern Orthodox sects. South of Diyarbakır is the city of **Mardin**, where the ascetically inclined can stay overnight in the cells of the Syriac monastery.

The southeastern corner of Turkey is dominated by the Cilo mountains, formerly known only to the most intrepid of hikers. Travel in this region had been discouraged for more than a decade because of armed Kurdish separatists—members of the P.K.K. (Kurdish Workers Party)—operating here and across the nearby Iraqi border. The 1991 Gulf War and its aftermath have introduced many Westerners to this region while, ironically, further reducing their chances of unrestricted travel within it.

During the war, Turkey aligned itself firmly with the West, immediately shutting off the pipeline between the Iraqi oil fields and the Mediterranean ports of the Hatay, then allowing hundreds of thousands of Iraqi Kurds to seek refuge across its border. Turkey's reward to date has been the loss of billions of dollars in income from the pipeline, an upsurge in separatist activity, and severe environmental damage to the once pristine area occupied by the refugees. A further blow to the Turkish economy was the drastic reduction in the number of Western visitors, even though the troubled southeast is many hundreds of miles from the regions commonly visited by tourists.

Those determined to visit the southeast in 1993 are advised to consult the latest travel advisories issued by the U.S. State Department and the Western embassies in Ankara, then decide for themselves. In any case, you should stick to the major routes and avoid travelling at night.

A Few Words about Mustafa Kemal Atatürk: Travellers unaware of his accomplishments may be forgiven for thinking the Turks a bit obsessed with a man now dead more than 50 years. But the Turks are an exceedingly loyal people, and Atatürk truly deserves the title Father of His Country, having saved it from foreign domination and then changed it into a modern nation-state. At the end of World War I, the victorious Western allies confidently set about apportioning the remnants of the Ottoman Empire, its subjects decimated by war and demoralized by defeat. Following the occupation of Istanbul in 1920 by the British, Italians, and French, a Greek army advanced from İzmir deep into Anatolia. While the sultan offered no resistance, Mustafa Kemal, the young hero of the Gallipoli campaign, rallied his countrymen to one last, supreme effort and pushed the invaders into the sea. At the moment of victory, Kemal retired his uniform and inspired his people to an even greater task, the transformation of his country into the democratic, secular Republic of Turkey.

Reforms initiated by Atatürk encompassed almost every aspect of life: The sultanate was abolished and a democratic, parliamentary system of government instituted; women were given equal rights; the Turkish language was purged of its Arabic vocabulary and script; traditional clothing was replaced by Western garb; and the Muslim "sabbath," Friday, was made just another weekday, with Sunday becoming the official day of rest. Although predominantly Muslim, Turkey was proclaimed a secular state, and special emphasis was placed on education and on the archaeology of Anatolia and the history of the Turkish people. Perhaps symbolic of this total metamorphosis from empire to nation was Atatürk's insistence that the church of St. Sophia in Istanbul, which had been converted to a mosque by Mehmet the Conqueror, be turned into a museum, open to all.

The Turks have reason to remember Atatürk with gratitude. The foreigner who can follow maps and signs because they are written in the familiar Latin alphabet; visit ancient monuments saved by their conversion into museums; mingle in streets, stores, and restaurants with Turkish women as well as men; loll on beaches in the briefest of swimwear; and shop on Friday, rest on Sunday, and lunch well during Ramazan, has cause to be grateful as well.

A Few Words about Turks and Greeks: Some visitors may arrive with the impression that Greeks and Turks dislike one another intensely and that passing from one country to the other will be difficult, if not distinctly unwise. Once in Turkey they may be surprised to discover that the Turks think it perfectly natural that tourists would want to pass back and forth between the two countries, "which God decided would be neighbors." Travellers should know that beyond the political rhetoric, Greeks and Turks understand one another very well—much better in fact than third parties understand either of them. Where do you suppose Greeks go on *their* vacations? According to statistics, tiny Greece sends more tourists to Turkey than any country other than Germany and England . . . and the Greeks know how to enjoy it.

A Few Words about Health and Safety: Turkey does have a (rather unfair) reputation as a "dirty" country. Most tourists never have the opportunity to judge the interiors of private homes (invariably spotless, even the tiniest cottage in the muddiest village). The cities, while not reaching Swiss standards of cleanliness, compare favorably with London and New York. The bad reputation stems from the condition of those spots most vital to travellers: public rest rooms. Most are of the *alla turca* variety—that is, set into the floor—requiring some practice and a certain amount of dexterity. Few are immaculate, and some are deplorable. Buckets of water are sloshed about (meaning wet toes for those in sandals) to compensate for the lack of hands-on cleaning and the inadequacy of the plumbing (not the Turks' strongest point). Happily, conditions are improving, notably in the fancy gas stations sprouting up all over the country, to the relief of Turk as well as tourist.

Your person and your belongings are far safer in Turkey than in Europe or the United States. Istanbul, like all big cities, does have its intentionally meandering cabdrivers and pickpockets after your wallet, but the latter usually rely on finesse rather than force. Elsewhere in Turkey even petty thievery is so rare that luggage is routinely left unattended at crowded bus stations and waiters dash after forgetful patrons with the left-behind handbag or package. The main danger you must guard against is becoming *too* careless with personal belongings. But if something untoward should happen, every Turk in sight will leap to your defense.

All travellers should be aware, though, that in Turkey it is definitely "live at your own risk." There are no lifeguards on those long, sandy beaches, no annoying barriers to stop you from clambering about that deserted castle perched on a cliff—and no guardrails to prevent you from falling off. Lone hikers in out-of-the-way places may meet up with a shepherd, if they get both lost and lucky. At even the most obscure and seemingly deserted archaeological site, however, a guard will suddenly appear out of nowhere to sell entrance tickets. Usually local villagers (don't be put off by the lack of uniform), these guards will offer their services as guides. You will do well to accept the offer in exchange for a tip. Most guards know enough English to point out "Roman temple" and "Bizans church"; some are distinctly well informed. All will lead you along the best and safest paths, hold your hand over the steep bits, and ward off any ferocious sheepdogs whose turf has been violated.

The old, formal hospitality to foreigners is strongest in small towns and villages—the more isolated the spot, the

warmer the welcome. Western travellers may be discon-
certed by the close scrutiny and frank stares, for guests, too,
have their roles to play in this traditional form of information exchange. Visitors may ignore mother's teaching and
stare back in turn, indulging that urge to observe a very
different and ancient way of life that will all too soon
disappear.

The best way to meet "the people" is to head inland by car
or bus (the cheaper the bus, the more interesting the ride).
Even calorie-counting and nonsmoking travellers might take
along some hard candy (*bonbon*) and a pack of cigarettes,
handiest of icebreakers with village children and wandering
shepherds. In small towns stop at the *lokanta* on the central
square, in villages the coffeehouse. Offer tea or a cigarette to
the wizened old gentleman in the corner and you'll be well
on your way to finding out that the people themselves are
indeed the best reason to visit Turkey.

USEFUL FACTS

When to Go

The months between April and October are the best for
visiting Turkey. That said, keep in mind that during July and
August the Aegean and Mediterranean coasts, and especially
the southeastern portion of the country, can be very hot.
Anatolia contains a wide range of climates, with coastal areas
being generally more temperate than the interior. Winters in
the central Anatolian plateau and in the mountainous eastern region of the country can be severe. Istanbul's climate is
basically similar to that of New York, though drier in summer and perhaps wetter in winter, with frequent light snowfall. On the Aegean coast, the "season" extends until early
October, though nights can by that time have become quite
chilly. July and August are good months to visit eastern
Turkey from Artvin south to Lake Van; August is the only
month during which the lake is warm enough for swimming. The Mediterranean coast is typically Mediterranean,
with mild winters and blazingly hot, humid summers. In the
far southeast, temperatures during even late spring and early
fall regularly soar to 110-plus degrees Fahrenheit.

You must also weigh your ability to deal with the swarms of
tourists that descend on Turkey during the months of July
and August. Istanbul is probably pleasanter, and more interesting, to visit during April, May, or September: The weather is
better; there are fewer contenders at the major tourist sites;
some hotel rates are lower; and the life of the city is intact

(many *İstanbullu*s flee the city during high summer, and Istanbul then lacks the vibrancy it has at other times of year).

If you are visiting Istanbul between October and March, you must prepare yourself (psychologically; there is no way to prepare yourself physically) for the intensity of the air pollution—a compound of motor-vehicle exhaust and smoke from the ubiquitous burning of soft coal for home heating. The ongoing installation of natural-gas pipelines in many areas of the city may, over time, ameliorate the problem.

Entry Requirements

Visitors from many countries of Western Europe and from the United States, Canada, Australia, and New Zealand do not need visas to enter Turkey. Visitors from the United Kingdom and Ireland do need visas, but these are given automatically upon entering the country. Note that visa requirements are subject to change—sometimes rapid—as Turkey's relations with other countries alter. A U.S. passport will, as of this writing, allow you to remain in the country for as long as three months. Medical shots are not required of Western visitors (but see Health, below, for more information on vaccinations you may wish to obtain).

Arrival at Major Gateways by Air

Turkish Airlines (Türk Hava Yolları, or THY) offers flights to such major cities as Istanbul, Ankara, İzmir, Antalya, and Adana from most European countries and from New York. (In the U.S., Tel: 212-986-5050 or 800-874-TURK; in London, Tel: 071-499-9240/9247/9248.) Many other major carriers—including Air France, American Airlines, British Airways, Delta, KLM, Lufthansa, Sabena, SAS, and TWA, among others—offer flights to Turkey. THY offers some nonstop flights from New York to Istanbul, but most of its flights include a stop for refueling in Brussels; flights on other carriers involve changing planes in Brussels, Copenhagen, Zürich, or elsewhere.

In addition to Turkish Airlines and the major carriers listed above, six private charter companies offer flights to Istanbul—Birgen Air, Bosphorus Airlines, Green Air, Istanbul Airlines, Onur Air, and Sultan Air. All have been adding new Western cities to their flight lists each year.

Coach fares on regularly scheduled flights from New York to Istanbul are more expensive than Turkey's geographical position might seem to warrant. It may therefore be worthwhile, if your travel dates are firm, to check newspapers for advertisements placed by small travel agencies that offer tickets on regularly scheduled flights at substantial discounts. (Such firms buy empty seats on underbooked flights and resell them. Tickets, though they may be ordered in advance, are generally not available until a few days before departure; neither are they generally refundable, but the significant savings offered may outweigh this option's disadvantages.)

The lengthiness of the New York–Istanbul flight (and the consequent fatigue you're likely to feel), coupled with the unfamiliarity of the culture if this is your first visit to Turkey, warrant your simply taking a taxi from Atatürk airport into the city. The drive is a long one, so the fare should be between US$15 and $20, depending on your destination.

Arrival by Ship

Turkish Maritime Lines (Türkiye Denizcilik İşletmeleri) operates a passenger-car ferry between Venice and Istanbul. (It can also be boarded at Piraeus [Greece] and İzmir.) The ferry service operates between March and November, though service is more frequent during the high season (July through September). For schedule information or reservations, call (London) (071) 623-7222, (Venice) (41) 520-8633, or (Piraeus) (1) 412-4315, 412-8161, or 412-4542.

The Crete-based company Minoan Lines offers a roundtrip cruise between Ancona, Italy, and the Aegean Turkish resort of Kuşadası, making stops at Corfu, Kefallonia, Piraeus, Paros, and Samos. For information, call (Piraeus) (1) 411-3819 or, in Istanbul, Minoan Lines' Turkish agent, Caravan Tourism, Travel and Shipping; Tel: (1) 248-3699 or 248-0691. The Turkish firm of Rinaldo Levante Turism Denizcilik, A.Ş., also books passage on Minoan Lines cruises; Tel: (1) 251-4739. In the U.S., Minoan Lines is represented by the International Cruise Center in Mineola, New York (Tel: 516-747-8880 or 800-221-3254), and in the U.K. by P&O European Ferries, Dover (Tel: 304-203-069).

Shorter crossings can be made from the Greek islands of Lesvos (to Ayvalık), Chios (to Çeşme), Samos (to Kuşadası), Kos (to Bodrum), and Rhodes (to Marmaris). Several privately operated ferry services compete for business on each of these routes; you may wish to comparison-shop before purchasing a ticket. Also note that travel between Greece and Turkey, though not difficult, is not automatic: You may be required to purchase your ticket one day before departure. If you are arriving on a Greek island from Turkey, you may be required to pay a "port tax" not included in the price of your ticket.

It is necessary to mention one other point concerning travel between Turkey and Greece, important only if your itinerary includes a visit to northern Cyprus (the Turkish Republic of Northern Cyprus, a state whose independence from the rest of that island has so far been recognized only by the government in Ankara). If your passport contains a stamp showing that you have visited the Turkish sector of that contested isle, you will *not* be permitted to enter Greece. Customs authorities in northern Cyprus will oblige you, however, by providing you with a separate document if you do not wish your passport stamped.

Arrival by Train

The Turkish Republic State Railroad (TCDD) operates trains between major European cities and Sirkeci station in Istanbul (near Eminönü square in the old city). The train ride through the Balkans and northeastern Greece has been described as uncomfortable and painfully slow by travellers who've chosen this route. You must obtain the required visas for the countries you'll be travelling through before setting out. The civil war in the former Yugoslavian republics made the train journey inadvisable during 1992.

Daily service is available between Athens and Istanbul, and there is regular service between Istanbul and Moscow.

Arrival by Car or Bus

Motor vehicles enter Turkey either from Bulgaria (near Edirne) or from Thrace in Greece. Public buses from Alexandroupolis in northeastern Greece will leave you off at the border, where you then walk across, go through customs at Kapıkule on the Turkish side, and board a Turkish bus to Istanbul.

A number of private Turkish bus companies are now offering service between major European cities and Turkey. The most reliable is Varan Turizm, based in Istanbul; Tel: (1) 251-7474. You can board a Varan bus bound for Istanbul in many major—and some smaller—European cities. For information on Varan routes and schedules outside Turkey, call (Athens) (1) 513-5768, (Berlin) (30) 694-3333, (Strasbourg) 88-81-02-32, (Vienna) (1) 65-65-93, or (Zürich) (1) 272-0477.

Around Turkey by Air

Turkish Airlines (THY) and its new spinoff company, THT (Türk Hava Taşımacılığı) provide domestic service in Turkey. Turkish Airlines flies between Turkey's three largest cities, Istanbul, İzmir, and Ankara, and it also offers regular service to 12 other Turkish cities: Adana, Antalya, Dalaman, Denizli, Diyarbakır, Erzurum, Gaziantep, Kayseri, Konya, Malatya, Trabzon, and Van. THT, whose planes are former THY cargo planes that have been refurbished for passenger service, flies shorter routes, including flights between Ankara and the cities of Batman, Elazığ, Erzincan, Kars, Muş, Samsun, Şanlıurfa, and Sinop. THT also runs an Istanbul–İzmir–Antalya–Dalman route and, like THY, flies between Ankara and Trabzon. Two of the private companies mentioned above—Green Air and Istanbul Airlines—provide service to Antalya and to Dalaman airport, which is near Bodrum, Kaş, and Kalkan.

Around Turkey by Ship

Cruising. A number of Greek cruise-ship lines offer trips through the Greek islands strung along Turkey's Aegean coast. Many of these journeys make stops (though usually for a day or less) in the towns of Dikili and Kuşadası (with visits to ancient Pergamum and Ephesus, respectively) and in Istanbul. The following lines have offices in both the United States and Greece: Epirotiki Lines (New York and Piraeus, Greece), Sun Line Cruises (New York and Piraeus), Royal Cruise Line (San Francisco and Piraeus).

Ferries. Turkish Maritime Lines (Türkiye Denizcilik İşletmeleri) operates boats along the Aegean, Mediterranean, and Black Sea coasts; most of these routes have Istanbul as their point of departure and final destination. There are routes between Istanbul and Trabzon (stopping at Sinop, Samsun, Ordu, and Giresun), Istanbul and İzmir, Istanbul and Avşa and Marmara islands, and Istanbul and Çanakkale, among others. Schedules change yearly; for schedule information, call (Istanbul) (1) 244-0207 or 249-9222 (the latter number is specifically for information regarding service to İzmir, Mersin, and Magosa in Northern Cyprus), or (İzmir) (51) 21-00-94.

Municipally operated ferries crisscross all the waterways in and around Istanbul; service is frequent and very inexpensive. For more information on these services and other boat travel in and around Istanbul, see Istanbul—Getting Around, below.

Around Turkey by Train

The Turkish Republic State Railroad (TCDD) offers service to almost everywhere in the country. The question is whether you have time enough to explore the pleasures—which range from the rustic to the glamorous—of taking a Turkish train, as this mode of travel is notoriously slow. Even though most trains are labeled "express" (*ekspres*), this designation remains nominal rather than actual. The train ride to İzmir from Istanbul, for instance, takes more time than travelling between those cities by bus, for passengers from Istanbul must first go to Bandırma by boat and then board the Bandırma Ekspresi to İzmir.

Those interested in travelling in style may, however, want to throw time considerations to the winds and schedule a trip on the Ankara Ekspresi, which features recently renovated *yataklı vagon*s (cars with beds), whose elegance and fine service evoke the romance of an Agatha Christie novel. The Ankara Ekspresi leaves Istanbul (from Haydarpaşa Garı) at 10:00 P.M. and arrives in Ankara at 7:45 the following morning.

Some of the routes from Istanbul are as follows: Toros Ekspresi goes to Adana and Gaziantep. Konya is served by both the Meram Ekspresi and the Mavi Tren. Pamukkale Ekpresi goes to Denizli, İsparta, and Karaman. From Ankara, Doğu Ekspresi goes to Kayseri, Erzincan, Erzurum, Sivas, and Kars; Güney Ekspresi follows the same route, but also stops at Malatya and Diyarbakır; Van Ekspresi goes to Elazığ, Muş, Tatvan, and Van. Almost every railroad station in Central Anatolia is served by the Anadolu Ekspresi.

There is one notable exception to the generally slow-paced train travel in Turkey: Service between Istanbul and Ankara is very rapid.

Trains to points in Anatolia from Istanbul depart from Haydarpaşa Garı; for information, Tel: (1) 336-0475 or 336-2063 (English spoken); for reservations, Tel: (1) 336-4470 or 337-8724 (English not spoken). The station is just north of Kadıköy on the Asian side of the Bosphorus. Trains to and from points west of Istanbul use Sirkeci station (Tel: 1/527-0051) near Eminönü square in the old city. In Ankara, the station (Gar) is in the Ulus district; information, Tel: (4) 311-0620; reservations, Tel: (4) 310-6515 or 311-4994.

Around Turkey by Bus

Excellent coach service is offered between all major cities and towns in Turkey. Bus companies are privately operated, and the service offered by the major lines—among them Varan Turizm, Pamukkale Turizm, Ulusoy, and Kamîl Koç—is more or less equivalent. (All of these lines have offices in Istanbul, Ankara, and İzmir, as well as at smaller depots.) Bus fares are inexpensive, and Turkish bus drivers are experts at keeping to schedules (sitting in the front seat, behind the driver, can be a bit hair-raising). Additional buses are added at peak times (the summer months and national holidays). Note that smoking is generally permitted on buses except double-decker buses, where the lower level is designated the nonsmoking section.

The main bus station in Istanbul is in the district called Topkapı, just outside the land wall on the western side of the old city (not to be confused with Topkapı palace). At busy times, the level of activity at Topkapı terminal can be night-marish and *very* confusing, especially if you are fatigued after a long journey. Many buses travelling to and from distant points, however, also make stops at Taksim square in the center of the new city, in and around which the major bus companies also have offices.

The main bus terminal in Ankara is currently moving to the suburban district of Söğütözü, though the move may not be completed in 1993.

Around Turkey by Car

Traffic in major Turkish cities has always been congested and chaotic, ever more so in recent years because of burgeoning population and ubiquitous construction and road repair. In Istanbul, the ongoing installation of natural gas pipelines is currently causing traffic disruptions, as is the subway con-struction in Ankara. Do not rent a car for use in Istanbul or Ankara: It is much easier and cheaper to use taxis.

It is expensive to rent a car in Turkey (though making arrangements in advance may save you some money). The rates offered by major car-rental companies like Hertz, Bud-get, and Avis can be much higher than rates in the U.S. or Europe. (Auto-Europe and Europcar also have rental offices in Turkey.) Check with car-rental firms concerning current rates and drop-off policies.

Note that driving in Turkey is not for the timid. Turkish drivers are aggressive and inconsiderate, and accidents are hardly a rarity.

The best road maps of Turkey are the "Western Turkey" and "Eastern Turkey" maps that are part of the series of Euromaps published by GeoCenter International.

Taxis and Dolmuşes

Nowadays all taxis in major metropolises are metered. Al-most all taxis are yellow, have lighted signs on the roof (the Turkish word is *taksi*), and are generally newer-model cars in good shape.

A *dolmuş* (the word comes from the verb *dolmak,* "to be filled") is a larger taxi that follows a particular route and serves several customers at once. Some dolmuşes are mini-buses; others are vintage Chevrolet or Ford clunkers (unfortu-nately these are disappearing). Dolmuşes operate in almost all towns and cities and have regular pick-up and drop-off points. They are convenient for travel to airports and other popular destinations and are significantly less expensive than taxis. They are also fun: Particularly in the older cars, drivers often decorate the interiors with colorful plastic flowers and photos of film stars, singers, and politicians. "Arabesque" music often blares from the radio or tape player (though Western music is becoming more popular). As a foreigner, you aren't likely to get closer than this to the lively—and kitschy—culture of the ordinary Turkish workingman.

Local Time

All of Turkey is in one time zone. The country is one hour ahead of Amsterdam, two hours ahead of London, seven hours behind Sydney, and, during most of the year, seven hours ahead of New York. Turkey goes onto and off of daylight savings time with the rest of Europe, so there are a few weeks each year when the country is only six hours ahead of New York or Toronto.

Currency

The unit of currency is the Turkish lira (TL). Bills come in denominations of 1,000, 5,000, 10,000, 20,000, 50,000, 100,000 and 250,000. Coins come in denominations of 500, 1,000, and 2,500 liras. The exchange rate, at press time, was about 8,250 TL per U.S. dollar. The exchange rate almost keeps pace with inflation, which has (unofficially) averaged between 65 and 80 percent annually in recent years.

Throughout *The Berlitz Travellers Guide to Turkey,* prices are always given in approximate U.S. dollar amounts, which have risen only slightly from year to year. The rise in prices as measured in TL is often so rapid that supplying prices as of press time would be meaningless. It's generally easy to find a place to exchange money; note that PTT offices (post offices) perform this service at the current official exchange rate. Also, since restrictions on Turks holding foreign currency have been lifted (and many people buy dollars or deutsche marks as a hedge against inflation) small money-changing establishments have cropped up everywhere. Changing money in one of these places is extremely easy and convenient.

Telephoning

Telephone booths where you can make long-distance and international calls can be found in PTT offices and near major tourist sites in big cities and elsewhere. Calls are paid for with tokens (*jetons*), which come in three sizes: The smallest, worth 400 liras, is for local calls; the medium-size token, worth 1,800 liras, is for long-distance calls within

Turkey; the largest, 5,000-lira jeton is for international calls (prices as of December 1992). It is also possible to purchase telephone cards from PTT offices and at some hotels. It is not always easy to find a telephone booth, so be aware that most shopkeepers will allow you to use their phones for local calls, though they may charge you a few thousand liras for the privilege. Although new fiber-optics communications systems are being installed throughout Turkey, intra- and intercity connections (especially to remote areas) are often of very poor quality—much less clear than international calls.

Turkey is continuing the arduous process of rationalizing its cumbersome phone-number system—a process that is expected to take several more years to complete. This can be an enormous headache for the traveller trying to book hotel rooms ahead of time, make restaurant reservations, and so on. Eventually, telephone numbers all over the country will have the same number of digits, but, for the moment, count on trouble. Telephone numbers in this book were the latest available at press time.

The country code for Turkey is 90; the city code for Istanbul is 1, for Ankara 4, for İzmir 51, for Antalya 31, and for Bodrum 6141. If you're calling between cities within Turkey, you must now dial 9 before entering the city code.

Staying in Turkey

The Turkish government uses its own system for rating hotels, ranging from five stars (the best) down to one star. Some contributors to this book have included these designations in their hotel descriptions.

Hotel room rates listed in this book are, unless otherwise noted, for double rooms, double occupancy. Rates are projections for 1993—something many managers find difficult to do because of the intense inflation that has afflicted Turkey in recent years and because the Turkish government, which regulates hotel prices, does not release its guidelines until early in the calendar year. As prices are therefore highly susceptible to change, always double-check before booking. Rates given usually include the 12 percent value-added tax; the rates may or may not include service charges and/or the cost of breakfast. In some cases a range of rates has been given. In resort areas (such as the Aegean and Mediterranean coasts), room rates are often much higher from July through September; in Istanbul, differences in rates often reflect the luxuriousness of the accommodations, including whether or not the room features a Bosphorus view (always more expensive).

Rafting, Trekking, and Bird-watching in Turkey

Faced with the "concretization" of Turkey's coasts and the increasing pollution of the country's coastal waters, the Turkish Ministry of Tourism has initiated a program to encourage foreign visitors to try "alternative" tourism activities such as rafting, canoeing, and trekking, whose ecological impact is minimal.

Many of Turkey's rivers are suitable for rafting. The most popular in the Black Sea region—the Çoruh Nehri—ranks as one of the top ten rafting rivers in the world. Half a dozen other rivers in the Black Sea region (and another four or five in the Mediterranean region) also provide sensational rafting routes. The undammed section of the Euphrates makes for good "white water" rafting. For more information on rafting in Turkey, call Istanbul's **Alternatif Turizm** (Tel: 1/369-8190), or write or call **Test Seyahat Acentası**, at Dikilitaş, Yeni Gelin Sokak, Meksan Binası 1/7, Beşiktaş 80700, Istanbul; Tel: (1) 258-2589; Fax: (1) 258-8732.

Turkey's phenomenal landscapes make trekking especially appealing. The Aladağ and Bolkar regions of the Taurus mountains and the Kaçkar mountains in the Black Sea area make excellent venues for a trekking adventure. One of the better firms offering guided treks is **Sobek Travel, Trekking, and Adventure**, with offices in the city of Niğde, in Cappadocia; write or call Sobek at İstasyon Caddesi 67, 51100 Niğde; Tel: (483) 121-17; Fax: (483) 206-63.

Turkey possesses an incredible variety of bird life, and there are numerous wildlife preserves all over Anatolia. For information on bird-watching possibilities in Turkey, contact the Turkey project office of the International Council for Bird Preservation at **Doğal Hayatı Koruma Derneği** (Society for the Protection of Wildlife), P.K. 18, 80810 Bebek, Istanbul; Tel: (1) 279-0139; Fax: (1) 279-5544.

Tipping

The Turkish tradition of generosity and hospitality impedes the easy social acceptance of the Western custom of tipping. Receiving money in the form of a tip still causes the recipient some embarrassment. This is not to say, however, that tips are not appreciated; they most definitely are. General guidelines for tipping follow.

In a restaurant, it's good manners to leave about 10 percent of the total bill, which already includes value-added tax. A service charge may or may not have been added (different restaurants follow different practices), but it's a good idea to leave an extra 10 percent in any case since Turkish waiters, like waiters almost everywhere, earn the minimum wage. When tipping cabdrivers, follow this rule of thumb: For long distances, such as trips between a suburban airport and a central-district hotel, tip about 25,000 TL; for short intracity trips 5,000 or 10,000 TL is sufficient. The etiquette is more complex when you're paying a site guide or when you're offering a tip, say, to the captain or crew of a boat you've rented. The most tactful way of transferring money is to get the person alone, offer effusive verbal thanks, and then, in as discreet a way as possible, press the money into the person's hand. A site guide should be given the Turkish equivalent of seven or eight U.S. dollars. If you've hired a boat, draw the captain aside at the end of the voyage and give him about 10 percent more than the cost of the trip; if there are additional crew members, don't forget to stress that the tip is to be divided "among everybody" (*herkes için*).

Newspapers and Magazines

Newsstands in the central districts of large cities and in coastal resort towns commonly sell *The International Herald Tribune* and European editions of newsmagazines such as *Time* and *Newsweek*. Many of the major European papers are also available (though generally a day or two late) as are financial dailies like the *Financial Times* and the European edition of *The Wall Street Journal*. Two English-language periodicals, both published in Turkey, may be especially useful: the *Turkish Daily News,* published Monday through Saturday in Ankara and widely distributed throughout the country, and *Cornucopia,* a glossy quarterly whose in-depth articles are well written and often gorgeously illustrated. *Cornucopia* can be found in a number of upscale boutiques as well as on newsstands.

Electricity

Electric current is 220 volts; North American electrical appliances therefore require a converter and adapter plug, which can be brought from home or purchased in almost any appliance shop in Turkey. Electric service in Turkey is improving but is still subject to occasional surges, brownouts, and blackouts. (The Turkish word for "candle," by the way, is *mum,* in case you should need to make an emergency purchase.) Sensitive electronic devices such as typewriters and laptop computers may react poorly to these shifts in the current's strength.

Business Hours

Government offices, including PTT offices, are open Monday through Friday, 8:30 A.M. to 12:30 P.M. and 1:30 to 6:00 P.M. Banks are open weekdays from 8:30 A.M. to noon and from 1:30 to 5:00 P.M. Shops are open Monday through Saturday, 9:30 A.M. to 1:00 P.M. and 2:00 to 7:00 P.M. (Many small shops selling groceries, toiletries, and so on stay open until late in the evening and have Sunday hours.) The Covered Bazaar in Istanbul is open Monday through Saturday from 8:00 A.M. to 7:00 P.M. Museums generally are open every day except Monday. Topkapı palace is closed on Tuesday.

Holidays

Official national holidays are as follows: New Year's Day (January 1), Children's Day (April 23), Youth and Sports Day (May 19), Victory Day (August 30), and Independence Day (October 29).

The dates of religious holidays change from year to year with the Islamic calendar. The most important religious holidays and their dates for 1993 are as follows.

Ramazan (Arabic, *Ramadan*) is the Muslim holy month, during which believers fast from sunrise till sunset. In 1993 Ramazan lasts from February 23 through March 23. Propaganda concerning the intolerance of pious Turkish Muslims toward non-Muslims during the holy month should not be believed: Tourists can easily find restaurants that serve alcohol, and you will be treated as courteously as at other times of year.

Şeker Bayramı (Sugar Feast) directly follows Ramazan and is sometimes called Ramazan Bayramı. Its dates for 1993 are March 24 to March 26. On these days, Turks visit relatives and friends and exchange gifts of candy and other sweets.

Kurban Bayramı (Feast of the Sacrifice, sometimes referred to simply as "Bayram") occurs from May 31 to June 4 during 1993. Although offices and many shops and restaurants are closed during Kurban Bayramı, it can be an interesting (if you are squeamish, unsettling) time to be in Turkey. Sheep and cattle are driven through the streets in the days leading up to the holiday—for sale to families fortunate enough to be able to afford the sacrifice. In cities, the slaughter and butchering of the sacrificial animals sometimes occurs on the street, though this is a much more graceful procedure than it might seem, with groups of men standing or kneeling around the doomed animal to comfort it and then, when the sacrifice has been performed, offering thanks to God with prayers and singing. The meat is distributed to needy families.

At both Şeker Bayramı and Kurban Bayramı, many offices close early in the afternoon on the day before the holiday begins.

Credit Cards

Most major international credit cards are accepted in many establishments, especially in the big cities. This is not true, however, of smaller towns and rural villages.

Health

Vaccinations and other shots are not required for visitors from the U.S. and Europe. Many travellers, however, take precautions against typhoid, cholera, tetanus, polio, hepatitis, and malaria. There seems to be no need to do so, but you may wish to consult your physician, especially if you are planning to visit the southeastern part of the country.

Tap water, though officially deemed safe, unfortunately is no longer so in Ankara, Istanbul, and İzmir. Antalya's tap water, however, is renowned for its refreshing flavor and softness and may be drunk. Bottled mineral and distilled water are available everywhere.

Turkish cities are crawling with feral cats and dogs. The dogs, which roam in packs late at night, are frightening enough that you won't need any warning to avoid them. The cats, however, often seem cuddly and friendly. Resist the urge—no matter how strong—to pet their little heads: Rabies is, unfortunately, a big problem in Turkey.

Regular counts of coliform bacteria are performed in the bodies of water around Istanbul. It is unclear, however, what action the municipality would take were counts so high as to render swimming unsafe. *Do not* swim in the lower Bosphorus; swimming in the Sea of Marmara near the Princes' Islands is, however, considered safe, as it is nearly everywhere along Turkey's Black Sea, Aegean, and Mediterranean coasts.

Medical care in Turkey is good to excellent. State-run hospitals operate in 67 cities and towns nationwide. Medicine is socialized, and care is free in public hospitals. The larger cities also have many private hospitals, some specializing in the treatment of specific diseases. Although you may receive treatment at any public hospital, you may not wish to deal with the overcrowded conditions that sometimes occur there or, more importantly, with a medical staff that speaks little or no English. The following private hospitals in Istanbul treat many foreign patients: **İtalyan Hastanesi** (Italian Hospital), Defterdar Yokuşu 37, Tophane, Tel: (1) 249-9751/9752; **Alman Hastanesi** (German Hospital), Sıraselviler Caddesi 119, Taksim, Tel: (1) 251-7100; **Amerikan Hastanesi** (American Hospital, also called Admiral Bristol Hospital), Güzelbahçe Sokak 20, Nişantaşı, Tel: (1) 231-4051. Ankara also has a superb private hospital, the **Bayındır Medical Center**, immediately behind the Ulusoy bus terminal in the Söğütözü suburb; Tel: (4) 287-9000.

With few exceptions, almost all drugs and pharmaceuticals are available over the counter (*eczane* is Turkish for "pharmacy"). Though the law prohibits the dispensing of many drugs without a doctor's prescription, it is rarely enforced. Drugs are sold under their Turkish brand names; pharmacists can be consulted for popular remedies for common ailments such as diarrhea, headache, and so on. An over-the-counter preparation called Streptomagma is effective against mild cases of diarrhea.

Eyeglass-wearers in need of emergency spectacle repair take note: **Emgen Optik**, at İstiklâl Caddesi 65 in Istanbul (very near the Taksim hotel district) performs quick, cheap repairs and offers a wide selection of new frames.

What to Wear

Dress practically. Light clothing is recommended for summer travel, as are good, durable shoes (preferably high-top shoes or sneakers that provide some ankle support). Middle- and upper-class Turks are smart dressers; if you intend to go to formal restaurants or chic nightspots, bring an appropriate wardrobe along. In cities and towns avoid shorts, especially if you intend to visit mosques. Women should come prepared with a shawl, scarf, or jacket to cover their arms when visiting mosques (although some of the more frequently visited mosques supply visitors with shawls at the door). At seaside resorts, anything—or almost anything— goes, but be forewarned that if you're a woman and decide to sunbathe topless, your photo may appear on the front page of the next day's edition of one of Turkey's tabloid dailies!

What to Bring/What to Take Out of the Country

Turkish customs law is always subject to change. Electronic equipment—from cameras to typewriters—being brought into the country is registered in your passport, so if you bring an electronic device into the country you must be carrying it when you depart. (Take this regulation very seriously.) Items valued at more than US$1,000 are also registered in passports. Sharp instruments, including camping knives and the like, may not be brought into the country without special permission.

When packing, don't neglect to bring two important items: a flashlight and a pair of binoculars. The interiors of many monuments are very poorly lighted, and some sites have no interior illumination at all, so a flashlight is essential. The binoculars will allow you to view the details of mosaics, frescoes, and tiles high up on the inner walls of churches and mosques.

Antiquities and other items deemed to have historical value may not be removed from the country. Penalties, including fines and imprisonment, for breaking this law can be quite severe, so you must obtain certificates for any items that might be construed by customs officials as having historical significance. For carpets and kilims, such certificates are generally supplied by the merchant. If the seller cannot verify the legality of your purchase, take the item to one of the following places, which have offices that can provide the necessary evaluation: For rugs and Ottoman furniture, the Topkapı palace museum in Istanbul (Tel: 1-512-0480); for paintings, the Resim ve Heykel Müzesi (Painting and Sculpture Museum) in Beşiktaş, Istanbul (Tel: 1-261-4298/4299); for icons, St. Sophia museum in Istanbul (Tel: 1-522-1750); for old coins or reproductions of artifacts, the Archaeological Museum in Istanbul (Tel: 1-520-7740).

There is no limit on the amount of foreign currency that may be brought into Turkey. However, not more than US$5,000 worth of Turkish currency can be brought into or taken out of the country.

Turkey's drug laws are harsh. It should go without saying that you should not attempt to transport illegal drugs into or out of the country (nor use illegal drugs while you are there).

Language

Turkish is not an Indo-European language, but a member of the Ural-Altaic family. (Its closest cousins among European languages are Hungarian and Finnish.) When Atatürk promulgated his modernizing reforms in the 1920s, the Latin alphabet replaced the Arabic as the medium of written Turkish. (Spelling in Turkish is almost perfectly phonetic.) Actually, the Turkish alphabet includes several characters that are modified forms of Latin letters and that are treated (e.g., in dictionaries) as separate letters. Without our attempting to supply even a minimal guide to Turkish pronunciation, take note of the following: The letter "c" is pronounced as an English "j" (*cadde,* "avenue," is therefore pronounced JOD-day). The character "ğ" is unvoiced and simply acts to lengthen the vowel that precedes it. The undotted "ı" (ı) has a sound—difficult for an English speaker to reproduce—like the vowel sound in "look." The characters "ç" and "ş" are pronounced, respectively, as "ch" and "sh." The letter "ö" has a sound equivalent to the same character in German. The letter "ü" sounds like the "u" in the French *tu*.

Turks appreciate it when foreigners attempt to use at least a few words of their language. The following words and phrases may be of some use: *merhaba* (MARE-ha-ba, "hello"); *teşekkür ederim* (tesh-shay-cur eh-der-im) or, more simply, *mersi*—both mean "thank you"; *lütfen* (LOOT-fen, "please"); *pardon* ("I'm sorry" or "pardon me").

The polite way to address an adult Turk is to use his or her first name plus the honorific *Bey* (pronounced "bay"), for a man, or *Hanım* (HAH-nuhm), for a woman. Use of these titles, which mean "lord" and "lady," respectively, was discouraged during the early Republican period, when Atatürk promulgated his linguistic and political reforms, but they gradually regained favor and are now commonly employed.

For Further Information

The Turkish Tourist Information Office is a good resource. In the U.S., 821 United Nations Plaza, New York, NY 10017, Tel: (212) 687-2194, or 1714 Massachusetts Avenue NW, Washington, DC 20036, Tel: (202) 429-9844. In Canada, the Turkish Embassy, 197 Wurtemburg Street, Ottawa, Ontario K1N 8L9, Tel: (613) 232-1577. In the U.K., 170–173 Piccadilly, First Floor, London W1V 9DD, Tel: (071) 734-8681.

—*James Waller and Zeynep Bagana-Önen*

BIBLIOGRAPHY

History and Archaeology

EKREM AKURGAL, *Ancient Civilizations and Ruins of Turkey* (1985). The most detailed guide to the ancient sites of Turkey, with historical essays on the ancient civilizations, site plans, drawings of many individual buildings, and some photographs; difficult to obtain outside of Turkey.

———, *The Art of the Hittites* (1962). Well-illustrated book by the dean of Turkey's classical archaeologists; still the best introduction to the subject, despite being somewhat dated.

American Journal of Archaeology. The AJA's annual report "Archaeology in Anatolia," although written by a scholar for scholars, is an excellent way to find out about the most recent discoveries at the sites you'll be visiting in Turkey.

M. S. ANDERSON, *The Eastern Question, 1774–1923* (1966). Comprehensive account of the decline of the Ottoman Empire in the arena of European power politics.

Archaeology. This bimonthly publication of the Archaeological Institute of America, meant for the nonspecialist, often has articles on excavations in Turkey. Book reviews of works of interest and ads for special-interest tours to Turkey make this lavishly illustrated magazine well worth reading.

GEORGE BEAN, *Aegean Turkey* (1966); *Turkey's Southern Shore* (1968); *Turkey Beyond the Maeander* (1971); *Lycian Turkey* (1978). Indispensable and engaging series of books by a scholar who lived most of his life in Turkey. Bean's books are dated regarding archaeological discoveries, but his ability to bring the ancient cities to life is unsurpassed.

EVERETT C. BLAKE AND ANNA G. EDMONDS, *Biblical Sites in Turkey* (1990). The fourth edition of this classic handbook provides up-to-date information on the events mentioned in the Bible that took place in Anatolia and the locales where they occurred.

CARL BLEGEN, *Troy and the Trojans* (1963). Good introduction to Troy and the controversies surrounding the Trojan War by an American archaeologist who excavated at Troy.

ROBERT BROWNING, *The Byzantine Empire* (1980). Good one-volume historical narrative enlivened by color plates and the author's interest in intellectual and social history.

ANTHONY BRYER AND DAVID WINFIELD, *The Byzantine Monuments and Topography of the Pontos* (1985). Well-written scholarly work, in two volumes, about the Medieval Empire of Trebizond on the eastern Black Sea coast, full of fascinating anecdotes as well as specialist detail.

CLAUDE CAHEN, *Pre-Ottoman Turkey* (1968). Scholarly study of Anatolia in the Seljuk and Mongol periods, based primarily on Muslim sources.

M. A. COOK, ED., *A History of the Ottoman Empire to 1730* (1976). Handy account of premodern Ottoman history by a group of noted specialists.

ANNA COMNENA, *The Alexiad of Anna Comnena.* Remarkable 12th-century epic account of the life and reign of the Byzantine emperor Alexius I (1081 to 1118), who ruled at the time of the First Crusade, by his bluestocking daughter.

FANNY DAVIS, *The Ottoman Lady: A Social History from 1718 to 1918* (1986). Chapters on all aspects of life, from marriage and divorce to intrigue and home furnishings, make this study of upper-class Ottoman society fascinating (despite its matter-of-fact, even dry, tone). Since Ottoman men spoke little and wrote less about their women, the author's research involved some detective work, including interviews with the elderly grande dames of Ottoman families.

CHARLES DIEHL, *Byzantine Empresses* (1967). Lively, occasionally titillating, portraits of the empresses by the great French Byzantinist.

KENAN ERİM, *Aphrodisias, the City of Venus Aphrodite* (1986). This lavishly illustrated volume is much more than a coffee-table book thanks to the text by the late Kenan Erim, who was excavation director at Aphrodisias. Erim traces the history of the city and its excavations and gives an incisive account of the important school of sculpture that flourished there under the Romans.

JACK FINEGAN, *The Archaeology of the New Testament: The Mediterranean World of the Early Christian Apostles* (1981). Finegan ranges widely around the Mediterranean, but his chapter on Saint Paul's third missionary journey (A.D. 51 to 54) and the Seven Churches of Asia will interest anyone curious about the history of the early church.

PETER GREEN, *Alexander of Macedon, 356–323 B.C.: A Historical Biography* (1991). Revised edition of one of the best treatments of the life of the world conquerer.

JOHN S. GUEST, *The Yezidis* (1987). The Yezidis, who are Kurds, live in eastern Turkey, Iraq, Syria, and the former Soviet Union. Guest gives a vivid picture of this small (150,000) religious sect that has been in the news since the 1991 Persian Gulf war.

O. R. GURNEY, *The Hittites* (1968). Good introduction to the Hittites, whose empire dominated central Anatolia from about 1700 to 1200 B.C.

W. K. GUTHRIE, *The Greek Philosophers from Thales to Aristotle* (1950). This survey of Greek philosophers includes many from the city-states of Asia Minor.

G. M. A. HANFMANN, *Letters from Sardis* (1972). This collection of letters from George Hanfmann, field director of the Sardis expedition, takes you behind the scenes at the excavation between 1958 and 1971. Hanfmann's enthusiasm makes this an appealing book for any armchair archaeologist.

HERODOTUS, *The Histories.* The fifth-century B.C. historian Herodotus of Halicarnassus (modern Bodrum) is often referred to as "the father of history." Herodotus traces the enmity of the Greeks and Persians, marvels at the strange customs of the peoples he visits, and seems particularly fascinated by the Lydian Empire and the fate of its last ruler, Croesus.

DAVID HOTHAM, *The Turks* (1972). Turkey has undergone enormous change since this concise and readable book appeared; still, Hotham provides a generally accurate picture of modern Turkey, although his occasionally sweeping generalizations about "the Turkish mind" are an irritant.

HALIL İNALCIK, *The Ottoman Empire: The Classical Age, 1300–1600* (1973). Description of the rise of the Ottoman Empire and its major institutions by a leading authority.

NORMAN ITZKOWITZ, *The Ottoman Empire and Islamic Tradition* (1972). Excellent introduction to the historical development, institutions, social structure, and intellectual foundations of the Ottoman Empire.

ESTER JUHASZ, ED., *Sephardi Jews in the Ottoman Empire* (1990). Lavishly illustrated volume with chapters on all aspects of Jewish life, from childbirth to burial. Although this book was published as the catalog accompanying an exhibit at the Jewish Museum in New York, you don't have to have seen the exhibit to enjoy the book.

M. FUAD KÖPRÜLÜ, *The Origins of the Ottoman Empire* (1992). Translated by Gary Leiser, this comprehensive account of the Turkish history of Anatolia in the 13th and 14th centuries challenges Western historiographical assumptions.

PATRICK BALFOUR KINROSS, *Atatürk: A Biography of Mustafa Kemal, Father of Modern Turkey* (1964). Probably still the best introductory biography of Mustafa Kemal Atatürk, the founder of modern Turkey and first president of the Turkish republic.

BERNARD LEWIS, *Istanbul and the Civilization of the Ottoman Empire* (1963). A fine description of Istanbul at the height of its glory.

———, *The Emergence of Modern Turkey* (1968). Excellent account of the origins of modern Turkey, focusing on the years from about 1850 to 1950, which saw the final stages of the Ottoman Empire and the early decades of the Republic of Turkey.

RAPHAELA LEWIS, *Everyday Life in Ottoman Turkey* (1971). Interesting behind-the-scenes account of family life, occupations, customs, and religious beliefs.

ROBERT LIDDELL, *Byzantium and Istanbul* (1956). Elegant and evocative portrait of Byzantine and Ottoman civilization by one of the best writers on Greek and Turkish life.

SETON LLOYD, *Ancient Turkey: A Traveller's History of Anatolia* (1989). If you are going to read only one book on ancient Turkey before setting off on your travels, this should be it. Lloyd, the first director of the British Institute of Archaeology at Ankara, covers a vast time span, from the Hittites through Saint Paul, and writes so well that you'll wish this book were twice as long. The photographs of landscapes and antiquities are excellent.

JAMES MELLAART, *Çatal Hüyük* (1967). The excavator's account of the discovery and excavation of Turkey's most important Neolithic site (about 6500 to 5000 B.C.), Çatalhüyük, some 40 miles from Konya. Mellaart's discovery of what has been called a planned urban development, with houses richly decorated with frescoes, forced scholars to rewrite the history of early Anatolia.

ALAN MOOREHEAD, *Gallipoli* (1956). Gripping account of Turkey's successful defeat of the allied attempt to seize the Dardanelles in the bloody campaign of 1915/16, in which the young Mustafa Kemal (later Atatürk) distinguished himself.

SIRAPIE DER NERSESSIAN, *The Armenians* (1979). Solid account of the Medieval history of one of the Ottoman Empire's most important minorities.

JOHN JULIUS NORWICH, *Byzantium: The Early Centuries* (1989) and *Byzantium: The Apogee* (1992). Lord Norwich, renowned for his works on Venice, has now taken on the Byzantine Empire. In the first volume, he looks at Byzantium's growth in the years between the foundation of Constantinople and the coronation of Charlemagne. In the second, he carries the saga to Byzantium's 11th-century apogee under the brilliant emperor Basil II (called "the Bulgar-Slayer") and beyond to the empire's crushing defeat by the Seljuks at Manzikert in 1071. Like other Byzantinists, Norwich is intent on showing that the history of Byzantium is far more than the "monotonous story of the intrigues of priests, eunuchs and women" that historians like W. E. H. Lecky and Edward Gibbon saw.

JOHN GRIFFITHS PEDLEY, *Sardis in the Age of Croesus* (1968). Pedley has succeeded in writing a book that he says is intended for "anyone who might chance to be interested in the cultural and historical events which surrounded the familiar and legendary Croesus."

F. E. PETERS, *The Harvest of Hellenism* (1970). Well-written account of the spread of Greek culture into Asia Minor and beyond during the period between the rule of Alexander the Great and his successors and the spread of Christianity.

PLUTARCH, *Life of Alexander.* Forty-six of the biographies written by Plutarch, the second-century antiquarian and priest of Apollo at Delphi, survive. This is one of the best, with a vivid portrait of the Macedonian who conquered the world and may have believed his own propaganda that he was a god.

PROCOPIUS, *Secret History.* Some scholars doubt that the sixth-century author of the sober *History of His Own Time* could also have written this salacious account of the scandals of the reign of Justinian and Theodora. Whoever the author was, his portrait of Empress Theodora is an unforgettable depiction of an energetically licentious woman.

MICHAEL PSELLUS, *Chronographia.* A lively, brilliant account of 11th-century Byzantium by a leading scholar and statesman of the period. This masterpiece of Byzantine literature makes a wonderful read.

STEVEN RUNCIMAN, *Byzantine Style and Civilization* (1975); *The Fall of Constantinople* (1955); *A History of the Crusades* (1951–1954). Always entertaining, often moving, Sir Steven's books are scholarship at its most enjoyable.

FREYA STARK, *Alexander's Path from Caria to Cilicia* (1958). Perhaps only Rose Macaulay and Patrick Leigh Fermor can compare with Dame Freya Stark, an indomitable traveller, acute observer, and breathtaking writer. Here Stark follows Alexander's path across the Hellespont and down the Aegean coast into Caria, Lycia, and Pamphylia. Stark also draws the reader into Turkey of the 1950s—where travellers were few and tourists were virtually unknown.

————, *Ionia: a Quest* (1954); *The Lycian Shore* (1956); *Gateways and Caravans: A Portrait of Turkey* (1971). More travels and history by the writer whom Lawrence Durrell called the "poet of travel." Stark went just about everywhere—often alone—in Asia Minor.

RICHARD STILLWELL, ED., *The Princeton Encyclopedia of Classical Sites* (1976). This comprehensive volume includes all the major and most of the minor sites in Turkey and provides a bibliography for each entry.

STRABO, *Geography*. Born in Pontus in northeastern Asia Minor, Strabo (63 B.C.–A.D. 21) travelled widely in the Mediterranean region. His historical geography provides a glimpse of the people and places of ancient Anatolia.

TAMARA TALBOT-RICE, *The Seljuks in Asia Minor* (1961). The Seljuks never seized Constantinople, but their empire included much of today's Turkey from 1071, when they defeated the Byzantine army at the battle of Manzikert, until 1242, when they were conquered by the Mongols. Talbot-Rice combines historical narrative with several chapters on Seljuk art and architecture, religious thought, and music.

MICHAEL WOOD, *In Search of the Trojan War* (1985). Attractively illustrated volume on the controversies surrounding the historical authenticity of the Trojan War and the site of Troy, issued in conjunction with the BBC television series of the same name. Contains vivid portraits of the early travellers to Troy and of the great archaeologist Heinrich Schliemann, as well as a lucid chapter on "the Homeric question."

XENOPHON, *Anabasis*. The Athenian Xenophon served with the Ten Thousand, the Greek mercenaries who fought for Cyrus the Younger of Persia against his brother, King Artaxerxes. After their defeat at the battle of Cunaxa near Babylon in 401 B.C. and the subsequent death of their commander, Xenophon led the retreat. Later he wrote this account of the Greek campaign and the long trek north from Cunaxa to the Black Sea and home to Greece.

EDWIN M. YAMAUCHI, *The Archaeology of New Testament Cities in Western Asia Minor* (1980). Although a scholarly book, Yamauchi's clear account of the historical framework and the archaeological remains of the cities will engage anyone with an interest in early church history. The site plans and black-and-white photographs of many monuments make this a useful volume for travellers.

Art and Architecture

OKTAY ASLANAPA, *Turkish Art and Architecture* (1971). Comprehensive and no-nonsense discussion of the subject, with the emphasis on architecture.

NURHAN ATASOY AND JULIAN RABY, *İznik: The Pottery of Ottoman Turkey* (1989). Lavishly illustrated, massive volume on the school of pottery that flourished during the 16th century in the city of İznik (ancient Nicaea).

ESIN ATIL, *The Age of Sultan Süleyman the Magnificent* (1987). A beautiful catalog of high Ottoman art produced in conjunction with the museum exhibit of the same name.

ESIN ATIL, ED., *Turkish Art* (1980). Essays on Turkish architecture, miniatures, ceramics, rugs, and textiles by specialists in each field.

ZEYNEP ÇELIK, *The Remaking of Istanbul: Portrait of an Ottoman City in the Nineteenth Century* (1986). Istanbul is filled with 19th-century buildings, but they tend to be overshadowed by Byzantine and earlier Ottoman architecture. This book redresses the balance. Worth looking at for the photographs alone.

FANNY DAVIS, *The Palace of Topkapı in Istanbul* (1970). Lively and thorough study of the architecture and history of the great palace, with numerous anecdotes about palace life.

JOHN FREELY, *Classical Turkey* (1990). This conveniently slim volume in the *Architectural Guides for Travelers* series has entries on all the major and many of the minor sites. Good site maps, building plans, photographs, a handy architectural glossary, and a helpful introduction on the world of the East Greeks make this a particularly useful book for travellers.

GODFREY GOODWIN, *A History of Ottoman Architecture* (1971). Not a book to read straight through but to dip into, a solid reference work with numerous plans and photographs. That said, the chapters on the great architect Sinan and a chapter on the Ottoman house do make enjoyable reading.

JOHN D. HOAG, *Islamic Architecture* (1975). Part of the same lavish series as Mango's *Byzantine Architecture* (see below), this volume has magnificent black-and-white photos. The chapters on the architecture of the Ottoman Empire and classical Islamic architecture of Anatolia will be of particular interest to travellers to Turkey.

RICHARD KRAUTHEIMER, *Early Christian and Byzantine Architecture* (1965). Perhaps only the great architectural historian Krautheimer could have written this comprehensive work, ranging from the origins of Christian architecture to the last accomplishments of the Byzantines—and you may feel that only he could have read it! As a reference work, however, it is unsurpassed.

ÖNDER KÜÇÜKERMAN, *Turkish House: In Search of Spatial Identity* (1988). Well-illustrated volume tracing the development of vernacular Turkish domestic architecture from the yurt to town and country houses.

APTULLAH KURAN, *Sinan, the Grand Old Master of Ottoman Architecture* (1987). Sinan was almost as prolific an architect as Titian was a painter: 120 of his buildings survive in Istanbul alone. This volume provides a good evaluation of the great 16th-century architect and his contributions to architecture.

CYRIL MANGO, *Byzantine Architecture* (1974). This handsomely illustrated volume covers practical details, such as techniques of brick making, as well as explaining the theories that shaped Byzantine architecture.

DAVID TALBOT-RICE, *Byzantine Art* (1935). Still the best one-volume introduction to the art of Byzantium.

PAUL UNDERWOOD ET AL., *The Kariye Djami* (1966). Non-scholars will appreciate the exquisite plates in the four lavishly illustrated volumes that make this the definitive work on the church of St. Savior in Chora (the Kariye Camii), which has the finest surviving Byzantine mosaics and frescoes in Istanbul.

CORNELIUS C. VERMEULE, *Roman Imperial Art in Greece and Asia Minor* (1968). This scholarly book contains a useful survey of Roman imperial architecture and sculpture in Asia Minor.

Travel Accounts and Guidebooks

GEORGE GORDON BYRON, *Letters* (published 1973–1982). Byron went nearly everywhere, including Troy and Mount Ida; his letters are among the best companions to travel in the former Ottoman Empire.

RICHARD CHANDLER, *Travels in Asia Minor and Greece, 1764–1765* (1817; reprinted 1971). Chandler led the expedition of the Society of Dilettanti to Turkey in 1764, visited the major sites, and wrote these observations, which include ruminations on the Turks he encountered in his travels.

DAVID CONSTANTINE, *Early Greek Travellers and the Hellenic Ideal* (1984). Delightfully written account of the English, French, and German travellers to Greece and Turkey during the 17th and 18th centuries.

GRACE ELLISON, *An Englishwoman in a Turkish Harem* (1915). As the author says in her introduction, this is "an Englishwoman's impression of Turkish harem life, written during a very happy and interesting visit amongst Turkish friends." Ellison spent a good deal of time in Istanbul, travelled widely, and was particularly interested in the nascent women's movement in Turkey.

CHARLES FELLOWS, *A Journal written during an Excursion in Asia Minor* and *Travels and Researches in Asia Minor, more particularly in the Province of Lycia*. Fellows brought the monuments of Xanthus back to the British Museum in London and recorded the preparations for his travels (he recommends taking a minimum of five or six horses) and the travels themselves in these two books, published in 1839 and 1852.

E. S. FORSTER, ED., *The Turkish Letters of Ogier Chisolm de Busbecq, Imperial Ambassador at Constantinople 1554–1562* (1968). Busbecq's letters are filled with keen observations made during his stint as the Hapsburg ambassador to the court of Süleyman the Magnificent. An ardent classicist and collector of antiquities, Busbecq was as fascinated by the rare birds he saw as by street life, holiday observances, and power politics.

PHILIP GLAZEBROOK, *Journey to Kars* (1984). Alternately insightful and irritating account of the author's trip through Turkey in search of the "menaces and dangers" faced by 19th-century travellers, who are listed in the bibliography so that you can pursue them yourself.

W. J. HAMILTON, *Researches in Asia Minor, Pontus, and Armenia* (1842). Another intrepid Englishman who discovered and described antiquities and wrote about the peculiarities of "abroad."

LAURENCE KELLY, ED., *Istanbul, A Travellers' Companion* (1987). A highly entertaining and informative collection of readings about Istanbul from its foundation to the 20th century.

W. M. LEAKE, *Journal of a Tour in Asia Minor* (1824). Leake went almost everywhere in the Levant and Asia Minor and wrote about his travels with methodical precision and tongue-in-cheek humor.

H. V. MORTON, *In the Steps of St. Paul* (1935). Personal account of what amounts to a pilgrimage retracing the travels of Saint Paul in Greece and Asia Minor; the chapter on Ephesus is particularly fine.

DERVLA MURPHY (INTRO.) AND CHRISTOPHER PICK (ED. AND COMP.), *Embassy to Constantinople, The Travels of Lady Mary Wortley Montagu* (1988). Lady Mary Wortley Montagu was a tireless traveller and the wife of the British ambassador to the Sublime Port from 1716 to 1718. She was fascinated by almost everything she saw and had a keen eye for detail; when she wasn't travelling she was writing about her travels.

ALEXANDER PALLIS, *In the Days of the Janissaries* (1951). English translation of selections of Evliya Çelebi's *Seyahatname,* describing Istanbul and the countryside, town and village life, and local customs during the time of Murat IV, when Çelebi (1611 to 1684) travelled throughout the Ottoman Empire to visit the tombs of Muslim saints.

MICHAEL PEREIRA, *East of Trebizond* (1971). Pereira and a companion explore northeastern Turkey by foot and local buses. Chapters on the history of the area alternate with chapters on Pereira's own experiences, which include crossing snowy mountain passes, avoiding snarling sheepdogs, and hiking the remote gorge of Tortum.

————, *Mountains and a Shore: A Journey through Southern Turkey* (1966). Pereira's awareness that towns like Kaş would not long remain undiscovered made him a careful observer of the traditional mountain and coastal life of rural Turkey in the 1960s.

MARY LEE SETTLE, *Turkish Reflections: A Biography of a Place* (1991). A description of the novelist's travels through Turkey, especially the Mediterranean coast and Central Anatolia.

RICHARD STONEMAN, ED., *Across the Hellespont: A Literary Guide to Turkey* (1987). Mark Twain's description of a Turkish bath, Herodotus's thoughts on King Croesus of Lydia, Rose Macaulay's dream of Trebizond—all this and more in this marvelous anthology. Stoneman's pithy introductions to the selections are part of the fun.

HILARY SUMNER-BOYD AND JOHN FREELY, *Strolling Through Istanbul* (4th edition, 1989). This well-written guide is organized geographically and takes you through virtually every quarter of Istanbul. A month in Istanbul would not be enough to see everything, but even if you're there for only a few days this will make your visit more enjoyable. The comprehensive index and many maps and plans make *Strolling Through Istanbul* particularly easy to use.

JOHN TUMPANE, *Scotch and Holy Water* (1981). Humorous (if you overlook the heavy drinking and sexism) account of experiences and travels in Turkey in the 1950s, by a man whose first sentence in Turkish was "There's a mouse in my bedroom."

Fiction and Poetry

ERIC AMBLER, *The Light of Day* (1963). The novel on which the movie *Topkapi* was based.

MARGOT ARNOLD, *Exit Actors, Dying* (1979). This mystery novel featuring archaeologists and corpses at ancient Pergamum is eminently suitable airport reading for travellers to Turkey.

MAUREEN FREELY, *The Life of the Party* (1984). Roman à clef set in an American college in Istanbul of the 1960s.

ROBERT GRAVES, *Count Belisarius* (1938). The poet/classicist's somewhat ponderous historical novel focusing on Justinian the Great's brilliant general Belisarius.

MOSES HADAS, TRANS., *Three Greek Romances* (1953). This selection of proto-novels includes Xenophon's *Ephesian Tale*, a richly romantic yarn of the trials and tribulations that separate, and the love and luck that reunite, two young lovers from Ephesus in the second century A.D.

HOMER, *Iliad* and *Odyssey*. The story of the Trojan War and its aftermath for Odysseus and his companions.

YASHAR KEMAL, *Memed, My Hawk* (1958). The best-known novel by Turkey's best-known living novelist, who has been nominated for the Nobel Prize. The novel is set in a poor village in southeast Turkey not unlike that in which Kemal himself grew up.

RICHMOND LATTIMORE, TRANS., *Greek Lyrics* (1970). Richmond Lattimore was a scholar, a poet, and a gifted translator. This anthology includes selections from the early Ionian poets, such as Anacreon of Teos, Hipponax and Callinus of Ephesus, and Alcaeus and Sappho of Lesvos.

GEOFFREY LEWIS, *The Book of Dede Korkut* (1974). This collection of 12 stories set in the heroic age of the Oghuz Turks (ninth and tenth centuries) was probably written down in the 13th century. The stories give a vivid picture of Oghuz nomadic life, princes and princesses, shepherds and infidels, and of the high priest and bard Dede Korkut.

ROSE MACAULAY, *The Towers of Trebizond* (1956). Hilarious and moving account of travels on camelback, the BBC, and love en route to Trebizond.

JOHN MASEFIELD, *Conquer* (1941). Leisurely historical novel about the sixth-century A.D. Nika Revolt, which almost cost Emperor Justinian and Empress Theodora their thrones.

NERMİN MENEMENCIOĞLU, ED., *The Penguin Book of Turkish Verse* (1978). Anthology including verse from the 14th to the 20th centuries.

ORHAN PAMUK, *The White Castle* (1991). Set in the 17th century, a strange tale of the capture of a young Italian intellectual by the Ottoman Turks. Reminiscent of the works of Calvino or Kafka, it becomes a meditation on the nature of history and self-identity.

MARY RENAULT, *Fire from Heaven* (1969); *The Persian Boy* (1972); *Funeral Games* (1981). There's simply no one better at historical novels set in classical antiquity, and these works focusing on Alexander the Great are among her best.

MARY LEE SETTLE, *Blood Tie* (1977). This novel describing the lives of natives and expatriates in fictional Ceramos (real-life Bodrum) won the American National Book Award.

IRVING STONE, *The Greek Treasure* (1975). Historical novel in rather purple prose (some of it Schliemann's own) based on the lives of Heinrich Schliemann, the excavator of Troy, and his Greek wife, Sophia.

GORE VIDAL, *Julian* (1964). Breezy and erudite historical novel focusing on the last pagan Roman emperor, the fourth-century soldier-scholar Julian the Apostate.

Cooking, Carpets, Nature, Daily Life

BELKIS BALPINAR ACAR, *Kilim, Cicim, Zili, Sumak: Turkish Flat-weaves* (1983). An authoritative discussion of the major categories of flatweave rugs and the techniques by which they are made. Color plates.

AYLA ALGAR, *Classical Turkish Cooking for the American Kitchen* (1991). More than just a collection of recipes, this book by the Mellon lecturer in Turkish at the University of California at Berkeley explores Turkish social and cultural history through what she calls "the mirror of food."

A. NACI EREN. *Turkish Handmade Carpets* (1988). This handy pocket-size book gives a good overview of what is available in the Turkish market today.

NEŞET EREN, *The Delights of Turkish Cooking* (1988). One of the best of the cookbooks that you'll see among the many on sale at bookstores and shops near ancient sites in Turkey. There are color pictures and step-by-step instructions; American measurements are used throughout.

JOHN FREELY, *Stamboul Sketches* (1974). Offbeat picture of Istanbul life by a former professor of physics at Robert College in Istanbul. Freely has also written a number of guide-books to Turkey and Greece.

RESAT NURİ GÜNTEKİN, *The Autobiography of a Turkish Girl* (1949). Tearjerker about a teacher's youthful days at the turn of the century.

IRFAN ORGA, *Portrait of a Turkish Family* (1950). Orga began life as the son of a prosperous Constantinopolitan family; after his father was killed in World War I, Orga's family lost almost everything. His account of their survival, and the contentious relationship between his mother and grandmother, is sometimes amusing and often heartrending.

OLEG POLUNIN AND ANTHONY HUXLEY, *Flowers of the Mediterranean* (1967). Lots of color photographs to help you identify the flowers you'll see in coastal Turkey.

CLAUDIA RODEN, *A Book of Middle Eastern Food* (1968). Many of the recipes in this clearly written cookbook are Turkish.

Turkey 1991. The General Directorate of Press and Information of the Republic of Turkey publishes this useful annual volume (sometimes available free from Turkish tourist offices). Brief essays and lots of facts and figures on the basics of Turkish history, government, and aspects of social life and culture.

Turkish Trends. Government-sponsored monthly newsletter with features on a variety of topics. To order, contact World News Features, Box 418, Wilmette, Illinois 60091 (Tel: 708-251-5009).

WILLIAM ZIEMBA, ABULKADIR AKATAY, SANDRA SCHWARTZ, *Turkish Flatweaves: An Introduction to the Weaving and Culture of Anatolia* (1979). Good introduction to the different kinds of contemporary flatweaves and how they are made.

KURT ZIPPER AND CLAUDIA FRITZSCHE, *Oriental Rugs,* volume 4, *The Carpets of Turkey* (1989). This would be an ideal book to read before you go to Turkey if you are thinking of buying a carpet. Chapters on the history of carpet weaving, techniques, classifications, and symbols, and a region-by-region survey of different patterns and techniques make this a very useful guide. Several chapters on the weavers themselves and the history of carpet making add a dimension of social history.

—*Sherry Marker*

ISTANBUL

By Anna G. Edmonds

Writer, editor, and former teacher, Anna G. Edmonds has observed Istanbul and Turkey since 1949. Her special interests have been the art and history of the country, and she has contributed articles on these subjects to various newspapers and magazines. She was an editor at the Redhouse Press in Istanbul for 30 years.

Istanbul, like a great work of art, is a city whose fascination grows with familiarity. The city's setting of hills and water, enhanced by its silhouette, its pomp and the historical circumstances that warrant that pomp, and its legends of intrigue and romance, only begin to outline the elements of its enduring spell.

Istanbul offers a mixture of Eastern and Western, ancient and modern, religious and secular elements. The customs of the city's residents are both deceptively familiar (you take flowers to your hostess, but they should be an uneven number) and frustratingly different (there are no corner mailboxes). A *hamal* (porter) bent double under a load of firewood waits patiently while a very important person drives past, one of his hands lightly on the steering wheel, the other holding his cellular phone. Some teenagers find their identity in the dress of the latest international pop artists, while their classmates are more comfortable behind waist-length headscarves. As in the centuries before alarm clocks, drummers parade up and down the back streets an hour or so before sunrise during the holy month of Ramazan, although the people they wake for the predawn meal are at ease with computers. When the snow lies on the ground in January, Gypsies on the street corners peddle wild red and purple anemones and paperwhite narcissus— welcome harbingers of spring. Everyone expects to have

51

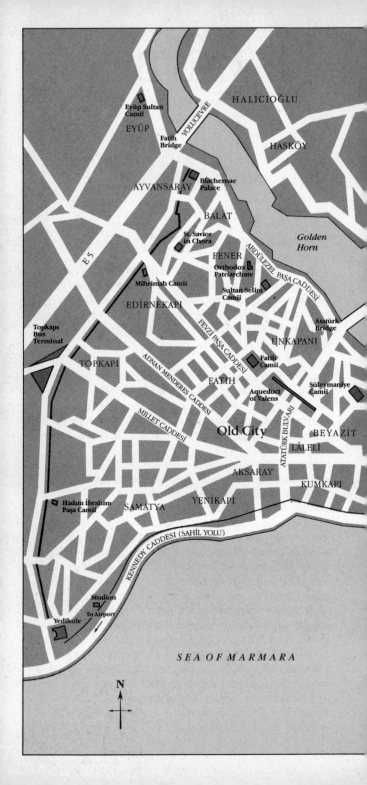

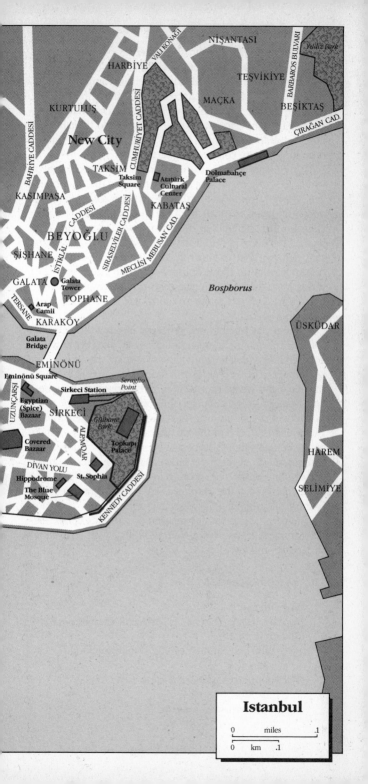

bread steaming fresh from the bakery for breakfast. And good friends greet one another with a kiss on both cheeks.

Writing to his friend Nicholas Michault, ambassador to Portugal, the Hapsburg ambassador Ogier Ghiselin de Busbecq described Istanbul in 1555: "It seems to have been created by nature for the capital of the world. It stands in Europe but looks out over Asia. . . . No place could be more beautiful or more conveniently situated."

The climate of the city is strongly influenced by two winds, the *poyraz* (ancient *boreas*), bringing the cold, bracing weather from the northeast, and the *lodos* (ancient *notus*), blowing warm air from the southwest. Some people maintain that Istanbul has only two seasons, controlled not by the revolution of the earth but by these winds. The *lodos* can melt two feet of snow in as many days. It can tie up heavy shipping in the Bosphorus from the violence of the waves it produces. It can also transform the usually phlegmatic *İstanbullus* (as the residents call themselves) into headachey grouches.

Summers in Istanbul are generally pleasant. While mild weather may continue on into December, sharp cold wind and rain often mark the end of the swimming season in early September. The recent stormy winters, with their heavy snowfalls and weeks of subfreezing temperatures, have belied Istanbul's reputation for mild winters. A solitary rose may bloom against a sunny south wall up till New Year's Day, and fruit trees do bud before the calendar says it's spring, but Istanbul is rarely at its best in February. The cloudy skies and muddy streets improve in late March, the storks return, and the blackbirds and nightingales whistle in thickets. Autumn colors along the Bosphorus are reminiscent of a 17th-century oil painting—burnt sienna, yellow ocher, Venetian red; in spring the technique recalled by the landscape is not oil painting but watercolor, with the hills awash in mauve, chartreuse, and fuchsia.

MAJOR INTEREST

The Old City
Topkapı palace, Harem, and Archaeological Museum
Church of St. Irene
St. Sophia's classical Byzantine architecture and mosaics
The Hippodrome, site of ancient racetrack
The Blue Mosque
Ancient cisterns and waterworks

The Egyptian (Spice) Bazaar
The Covered Bazaar
Süleymaniye Camii, Ottoman mosque
Old neighborhoods along the Golden Horn
St. Savior in Chora's frescoes and mosaics
The city walls and gates

The New City
Karaköy's Venetian and Genoese history, Whirling
    Dervishes' museum
Beyoğlu's foreign-consulate district
Dolmabahçe palace
Shopping, especially for clothing and shoes

Along the Bosphorus
Fish restaurants (both sides)
Rumeli Hisarı, 15th-century fortress (Europe)
Beylerbeyi Sarayı, 19th-century palace (Asia)

Asian Istanbul
Imperial mosques of Üsküdar

Lively folk and Oriental dances, the eastern rhythms of the janissary band, a labyrinthine bazaar, a world-famous cuisine—Istanbul appeals to almost every taste. The romance of the Ottoman palaces, the physical beauty of the land and the buildings, the sporting events, and above all the charm and hospitality of the residents—choose your own combination of the city's varied offerings.

Rich in art of the Middle East, Istanbul's museums contain significant works from periods ranging back as far as Hittite times (fl. 1450 to 1200 B.C.). There are masterpieces of art and architecture (St. Savior in Chora, St. Sophia, Süleymaniye Camii) along with bargains in the markets: copper, leather, carpets, icons, old books, meerschaum, and jewelry. Don't overlook smaller museums such as the Beylerbeyi palace on the Asian coast and the Sadberk Hanım Museum 20 km (12 miles) north of Istanbul proper, in the district of Sarıyer. Museum hours are given for the summer season: The times may be a little shorter in the winter. If you're a theater lover you may enjoy the stage plays during the winter season; the staging and acting often compensate for a foreigner's inadequate Turkish. Most large movie houses show foreign films in the original language with Turkish subtitles.

The City's History

The Seraglio point (Sarayburnu in Turkish), the tip of the peninsula formed by the meeting of the waters of the Bosphorus, the Golden Horn, and the Sea of Marmara, was settled, according to tradition, by 665 B.C., probably by fishers and/or pirates. (Pliny puts the date 200 years earlier; present-day archaeologists are adding another 500 years to that.) Strabo (?63 B.C.–A.D. 25) reports the legend that colonists from Megara in northern Greece, led by Byzas, were the first to stay here. He says their settlement took on its name—Byzantium—from this presumed leader. Its residents turned to commerce but left little mark on its history for centuries. Nonetheless, their obvious prosperity and strategic location eventually led several generals to covet the place: The Persian Darius (513 B.C.), the Athenian Alcibiades (408 B.C.), and the Macedonian Philip II (339 B.C.) all laid siege to the city.

The battle that caused Byzantium's citizens to suffer most occurred at the end of the second century A.D., when the Roman emperor Septimius Severus put the town to the torch. He repented his destruction a few years later, however, rebuilding the walls and constructing the Hippodrome (racetrack or sports arena), whose foundation is visible as you walk between the mosques of Sultanahmet and Küçük Ayasofya.

Byzantium remained small until Constantine the Great moved the capital of the Roman Empire here; he dedicated the city, which he called the New Rome, in A.D. 330. Constantine's contributions to the new capital were such that when people didn't speak of it simply as The City they called it the City of Constantine: Constantinople.

For more than a hundred years the Roman Empire remained split between Eastern and Western halves. Subject to increasingly frequent and devastating invasions from Germanic tribes during the fourth and fifth centuries, the Western empire disintegrated while the Eastern empire, relatively protected from barbarian onslaught, flourished. Encompassing the ancient centers of Greek civilization, it grew more Hellenic and less Latin in character—and more Oriental. Although the rulers of the Eastern empire considered themselves the heirs to Rome until the final downfall of Constantinople in the mid-15th century, we today call the culture over which they presided by a different name: the Byzantine Empire.

Byzantine history is complex and long—more than a thousand years passed between Constantine's founding of the New Rome and the city's fall to the Ottoman Turks. It is the story of emperors and empresses, power struggles and popular uprisings against authority, religious controversies, the expansion and diminution of territories. Many of the remains of that history and culture can be seen in Istanbul today.

When Ottoman Sultan Mehmet II, called the Conqueror, captured Constantinople on May 29, 1453, Byzantine history came to a close. Mehmet made the city his capital, opening a new period of grandeur—now Turkish and Muslim rather than Greek and Christian. Under the Ottomans, the city went through several name changes, among them Konstantiniyye, the Abode of Sovereignty, and, finally, Istanbul. (The city's name was officially changed to Istanbul in 1930.)

With the advent of the Republic of Turkey in 1923, Mustafa Kemal Atatürk, the republic's first president, moved the capital to Ankara, and Istanbul's importance was, for a time, in eclipse. But in the years following World War II an influx of people and a nationwide population explosion swelled the number of residents from about one million people in 1945 to something approaching ten million today. Now reinforced-concrete apartment blocks, high-rise hotels and office buildings, suspension bridges, and satellite dishes are changing the character and skyline of this ancient city.

Istanbul Today

Istanbul can be divided into the "old city" (enclosed by the fifth-century Theodosian walls), the "new city" (the lower European side of the Bosphorus), the upper Bosphorus (both European and Asiatic), and the lower Asiatic side of the Bosphorus (Üsküdar and Kadıköy—and be careful not to confuse Karaköy in Europe with Kadıköy in Asia). Today, the city continues to sprawl out, east and west, to ever-more-distant suburbs.

In rough outline, the European section of Istanbul resembles the back of your left hand placed palm down in front of you. Below your thumb (south) lies the Sea of Marmara. If you separate your thumb from your other fingers, you will create in the empty space the waterway of the Golden Horn, which divides the European city into old and new sectors. Your thumb represents the peninsula of the old, walled city, your thumbnail marking the Ottoman palace area known as the Seraglio point, or Topkapı (not to be confused with the city gate called Topkapı). The first joint of your index finger is the approximate place and relative size of the districts of Karaköy and Beyoğlu, in the new city. The Bosphorus surrounds the tips of your fingers, separating Europe from Asia, the indentations indicating the many bays and coves of its 20-mile coastline. The Black Sea stretches above your hand, to the north.

If you now place your right hand palm down opposite your left, you make an equally rough (but not proportional) map of Asian Turkey, or Anatolia. Together these lands provide a dramatic clasp connecting Europe, Asia, and, farther south, Africa.

Istanbul is deceptively similar to cities of the West. Most İstanbullus dress in Western garb (though you will notice some girls and women in conservative, traditional dress). Many of the shops have Western or Western-style goods; the signs are written in a phonetic, slightly adapted form of the Latin alphabet. (In recent years the once-forbidden Arabic has appeared again in the windows of shops catering to rich southern neighbors.) During the Christmas–New Year season stores are decorated with lighted evergreens. Most of the offices with which a foreign tourist would be likely to do business have a receptionist who speaks at least one European language, most often German or English. It is perhaps indicative of the difference that even the Turkish language seems a mirror-image of English: In Turkish, "I love you" comes out as *seni seviyorum,* which translates literally as "You, loving am I."

The residents of the old city tend to be conservative, lower-middle-class businesspeople. Over the past decade many areas of the old city that had become very run down have been cleaned up as people began to recognize the commercial advantages of building good hotels and other facilities near the major tourist attractions.

For decades Istanbul's population has been swelled by the migration to the city of peasants from the Anatolian countryside. These new residents re-created their villages in the form of the squatters' houses called *gecekondu*s (literally, "put up in one night") that circle the central area. Gradually these districts have been incorporated into the city, and nowadays the *gecekondu* settlements have paved streets, city water, electricity, bus service, and trees tall enough to top the apartment buildings that in many cases have replaced the original squatters' shacks.

As the city has grown, the fashionable districts have moved farther and farther northward in the European part of the city. In the 1890s Beyoğlu was the prime residential area for the foreign and Levantine population; by the 1940s Nişantaşı and Teşvikiye were the fashionable addresses. Today the choice residential areas are farther up the Bosphorus, in the bustling suburbs of Bebek and Emirgân, once sleepy coastal villages. As far back as the 1700s those with the means to do so escaped the city's summer heat (and sometimes plague) by moving to homes along the Bosphorus shore or to the shady **Belgrad Ormanı** (Belgrade forest) west of Sarıyer.

The majesty of Istanbul dates from Constantine the Great's choice of Byzantium as the site for the New Rome. Constantine likened the seven hills of his city to those of Rome. That somewhat superficial comparison is useful today as a quick reference to the geography of the old city: The first hill is the Sarayburnu (Seraglio point); the second is near the Kapalıçarşı (the Covered Bazaar); the third is at the Süleymaniye mosque complex; the fourth is the area around Fatih; the fifth is at the mosque of Sultan Selim; the sixth is around the church of St. Savior in Chora; and the seventh encompasses the large area generally south of Adnan Menderes Caddesi.

EUROPEAN ISTANBUL

THE OLD CITY
Topkapı and the
Archaeological Museum

When Mehmet the Conqueror took the city in 1453, he first built his palace on the third hill, now occupied by Istanbul University and the Süleymaniye complex. That remained his private residence (and that of his successors for the next hundred years) when he was in the city, but he soon moved his working quarters to a more strategic location on the first hill, or the **Seraglio** (Italian for "harem") **point**.

The Seraglio point had been the city's core in the time of Constantine. In addition to the Byzantine Great Palace (the administrative center), here were clustered St. Sophia and St. Irene (the religious center) and the Hippodrome (the entertainment center), an arrangement Mehmet did not change. Sometime between the reigns of Mehmet and Süleyman the Magnificent a military barracks for the crack

To Fener, Kariye Camii,
Ayvan Saray and Eyüp

Atatürk
Bridge

Golden
Horn

FATİH

RAGIP GÜMÜŞPALA CADDESİ

EMİNÖNÜ

ATATÜRK BULVARI

Rüstem
Paşa Camii

Egyptian
(Spice)
Bazaar

Aqueduct
of Valens

Süleymaniye
Camii

TAHTAKALE

SABUNCUHAN

İstanbul
University

FUATPAŞA CADDESİ

UZUNÇARŞI CADDESİ

MAHMUTPAŞA YOKUŞU

Şehzade
Camii

SÜLEYMANİYE

TAKVİMHANE

Beyazıt
Tower

AĞA ŞİR SOKAĞI

Old
Bedesten

BEYAZİT

VEZNECİLER

BAKIRCILAR

VEZİRHAN CADDESİ

LÂLELİ

CADDESİ

Covered
Bazaar

Nuruosmaniye
Camii

ORDU CADDESİ

Beyazıt
Camii

Çemberlitaş

MİTHATPAŞA CADDESİ

TİYATRO CADDESİ

GEDİKPAŞA CADDESİ

TÜRKELİ CADDESİ

MUSA

USTAF

KADIRGALİMANI

To Airport

KUMKAPI

Kumkapı
Square

KENNEDY CADDESİ (FLORYA SAHIL YOLU)

SEA OF MARMARA

The Old City

| 0 | yards | 250 |
| 0 | meters | 250 |

janissary troops (now the İbrahim Paşa Museum; see below) was added just south of the Hippodrome. When Ahmet I built his Blue Mosque he strengthened the religious importance of the point.

The qualities of administrative acumen, military power, and religious fervor have been reflected in the Western image of the Ottoman sultans. Missing in this is their cultural stature. *Yavuz* (cruel) Sultan Selim I was a skilled painter of miniatures. Süleyman the Magnificent was both legislator and goldsmith. Mehmet the Conqueror knew Persian, Arabic, and Serbian in addition to Turkish. (Some add Greek and Italian to the list of his languages.) "Bloodthirsty" Murat IV was a patron of men of letters and wrote commands to his general in verse. He's also reputed to have been a superb athlete, skilled in wrestling, boxing, polo, archery, and javelin throwing.

Mehmet's New Palace, encircled by a crenellated wall, was on the grounds of the fruit orchard of the old Byzantine Great Palace. Into the 19th century, two towers (similar to those presently at the entrance to the Second Court) flanked a gate in the seawall on Seraglio Point. There, a battery of cannons guarded the harbor entrance. The cannon (*top*) at that gate (*kapı*) so represented the thundering power of the Ottoman Empire that the entire complex came to be known as Topkapı. (Parts of this defense wall were pulled down to make room for the railroad tracks that now round the point.)

The Topkapı Sarayı (palace) complex (open 9:00 A.M. to 5:00 P.M. every day except Tuesday, when it is closed) is an oval area of about a half a mile across and a mile long. It contains groupings of buildings, mostly small, separated by function into five courts, including the Harem. Each court is surrounded by walls. The Second Court held most of the administrative buildings; the Third Court was reserved for the sultan and his private staff except on rare occasions, when he deigned to receive foreign ambassadors in the Throne Room. The buildings of the Harem, a secluded area west of the Third and Fourth Courts, were begun sometime in the late 16th century. Until the 19th century, when the sultans moved their residence to new palaces on the Bosphorus, these grounds were the center of the Ottoman Empire.

Besides being the seat of the government, Topkapı was the site of several ateliers under palace control. Perfume was distilled in a factory (no longer standing) below the kitchens. The looms that produced much of the cloth used in the palace and given as presents to foreign rulers were housed in buildings in the First Court, below the church of St. Irene.

The sultan's caftans, pillow covers, and curtains were woven here, and the weaving of costly fabrics using gold and silver thread was permitted only in the palace workshop, with the use of the precious threads carefully controlled.

One of the most successful schools anywhere was established at Topkapı by Mehmet the Conqueror. Its classrooms and dormitories were in the Third (private) Court, indicating the students' privileged status. The purpose of this, the Palace School, was to train men for service in the army and government. If the conscription system for this school seems cruel by 20th-century standards, entrance to its program (where space was limited) was actively sought by some, and the training it provided was potentially very rewarding. Boys of Christian parents were enlisted at a young age through what was called the *devşirme* (recruitment) system. They were chosen for their intelligence and physical perfection. (If there was only one male child in the family he was exempted from conscription.) The *devşirme* system was discontinued in the 18th century.

Topkapı was constructed piecemeal, often to meet a specific need. It was first conceived as a fortress; that impression lingers, particularly at the outer wall. One of the original defense towers (now called the Tower of Justice) rises with a tapering roof above the Divan (see below). Its base dates from the time of Mehmet the Conqueror; while the upper half was restored in the 18th century, the columns may be original.

The area enclosed within Topkapı's walls is enormous; the circuit of the walls measures more than three miles, and the complex occupies a total of 700,000 square yards. The usual tour of the palace allows for a glance at the china, the Divan (the council rooms), the Throne Room, the jewels, the rooms of sacred relics, and the Baghdad kiosk, although other displays are open, too: the miniatures and the fabrics, for instance. A separate ticket is needed for the Harem (open 10:00 A.M. to 4:00 P.M.), and it's a good idea to proceed directly there once you're inside the palace grounds. Buy your ticket, which specifies the time when you should return to the Harem to wait for your tour group to be assembled. On busy summer days, the time between purchasing your ticket and being admitted to the Harem may be up to several hours, which will give you plenty of time to explore the rest of the palace. Be warned that you should get to Topkapı early: If you arrive late, tickets for the Harem may be sold out for that day. The Harem tour is a crowded, hurried one, and it is often difficult to catch everything that the usually knowledgeable guide says. Museum officials are justifiably concerned about damage to the Harem by either random plundering or set fires. They've chosen to keep it open, but the haste with which visitors get pushed through doesn't allow for much in-depth viewing.

The **Birinci Avlu** (First Court), inside the **Bab-ı Hümayun** (Imperial Gate), enclosed several administrative buildings of the palace. The mint was here at one time, as were the offices of the chief architect, who oversaw the plans and execution of all major buildings throughout the reaches of the empire. Near the gate was the infirmary for pages from the palace school. One rule strictly enforced when the pages were well was relaxed here: During their illness they were allowed the indulgence of wine.

The areas of greatest general interest at Topkapı are beyond the First Court's Middle Gate and past the flamboyant Gate of Felicity. The somber **Babusselâm** (Gate of Peace, also known as the Middle Gate), with its dark entrance and twin towers, once caused even favored grand viziers to hold their breath as they walked through: It was here that the sultan's commands of summary punishment were often executed.

The neatly laid out walks of the **İkinci Avlu** (Second Court) speak of the discipline and order that prevailed on days of great ceremony. There is also evidence of the variety of artistic ingenuity and the sometimes almost freakish sensibility of which the sultans were apparently fond: In one particularly jarring instance, a fig tree grows out of the roots and trunk of a cypress next to the main walk.

It was in front of the **Babussaade** (Gate of Felicity) that the sultans accepted pledges of loyalty from their court, that they presided over the formalities of the great religious holidays, and that on one tragic occasion Sultan Murat IV witnessed the assassination of his closest friend.

The formal sittings of the council of ministers, the *Divan-ı-Hümayun,* or Divan, often took place in a rather small three-room building (also called the **Divan**) in the Second Court (to your left as you enter). From a distance the building can be readily identified by the square tower above it, called the **Divan Kulesi**, or **Adalet Kulesi** (Tower of Justice). Ottoman political theory held that the first business of the sultan, and therefore of his government, was to ensure that all his subjects received justice. In theory, and sometimes in practice, even the most insignificant subject could petition the sultan for the redress of wrongs.

The Divan comprised several viziers, including the grand vizier, along with a small supporting army of legal consultants, financial officers, and scribes. The sultan, around whom the color and ceremony circulated, rarely appeared at the meetings of the Divan. From the time of Süleyman the Magnificent in the 16th century, the sultan had a small loge above the room of the Divan that opened onto it through a curtained, latticed window. There he could sit and listen to his viziers' deliberations, ready to pounce on them if he objected; or he could be absent and retain the impression of an ever-watchful, all-knowing presence. Documents approved by the sultan were inscribed with his seal, or *tuğra,* in itself a work of art. The first sultans drew their own *tuğra*s, and some who were expert calligraphers even wrote out their own decrees. The sultans' *tuğra*s appear on buildings they repaired. Thus Mahmut II's *tuğra* is above the Middle Gate. Another oft-noted *tuğra,* that of Sultan Ahmet III, which he himself inscribed, is above the entrance to the Throne Room. A collection of *tuğra*s is displayed in the Museum of Turkish and Islamic Arts (see Palace of İbrahim Paşa, below).

Hidden behind the wall to the east of the Divan (directly across the courtyard) is the series of ten **kitchens** where the meals for the palace staff were prepared. On ordinary days at the height of the empire the cooks prepared food for four to five thousand people; when the janissaries (the sultan's private standing army) came three times a year to collect their pay, the meal count rose to about 15,000. Each and every one of those men expected his own loaf of bread to be equal in weight to all the others. One of the formalities of the Divan on those occasions was to weigh a randomly chosen loaf in front of everybody. If the scales tipped the wrong way the baker could lose his right hand. The kitchen staff made up a sizable establishment: cooks, butchers, candy makers, even men to carry the ice from the mountain behind Bursa (across the Sea of Marmara) for the sultan's summer refreshments.

The chimneys of the kitchens (which help identify the palace from a distance) were added by the great architect Sinan after the fire of 1574, which started here and spread to many other buildings.

The kitchens are nowadays used to display a fraction of the palace's more than 12,500 Chinese porcelains, ranging from 10th-century Tang light-green celadons through 15th- to 18th-century Ming. The celadons were the most prized dishes in the palace because they were believed to discolor if the food served in them had been poisoned. This is one of the world's finest collections of early Chinese blue-and-white porcelain, which was probably originally created specifically for export to the Muslim world. Some of the classic designs were copied in Ottoman pottery and are now appearing again in modern Kütahya ware. Japanese, Russian, İtalian, Delft, and Dresden porcelains and pottery, which would highlight most other collections, pale before the stupefying quantity and quality of the Chinese ware.

Immediately beyond the Gate of Felicity in the **Üçüncü Avlu** (Third Court) lies the **Arz Odası** (Throne Room). The room may not be spacious (it was too small to accommodate crowds of slaves), but when the sultan was ensconced there on his throne, even that seasoned 17th-century traveller Jean Baptiste Tavernier was overwhelmed by the grandeur of the rich jewelry and silks. The Throne Room is distinguished now by the large canopied area in one corner, where the throne was placed. Above the sultan's head were suspended some of the pendants now on display with the jewels in the Treasury. These spheres signified the world that the Sultan controlled and also accented and gave dimension to whatever room they were in. The cloth that covered his throne was chosen each day according to how much he wanted to impress his visitor: Gold brocade indicated that the ambassador's country was of little account, while black velvet studded with pearls was a mark of greater respect.

At the entrance to the Throne Room you'll notice a circular red stone in the floor; this marks the place where the body of the enlightened Sultan Selim III was hurled when his nephew Sultan Mustafa IV had him murdered (1808), thereby putting a stop to the restructuring of the Ottoman state that Selim had envisioned.

On the back side of the wall of the Gate of Felicity were the entrances to the white eunuchs' quarters. In the heyday of the empire, the white eunuchs formed a close coterie around the sultan and were responsible for maintaining discipline in the palace. During the reign of Murat III (1546 to 1595) the power delegated to the chief white eunuch reached its apogee, and the office wielded nearly the same degree of influence as that of the prime minister. A bit farther, past the white eunuchs' quarters, in the buildings now used for some of the museum displays, were dormitories for the pages of the Palace School.

The incredible wealth represented by the jewels now on display in the **Hazine** (Treasury) in the northeastern corner of the Third Court, appears rather dowdy under glass. But consider that Süleyman's daughter Mihrimah had a daily income that for most of us today would constitute the fortune of a lifetime. Emeralds and rubies and diamonds gain beauty when they glint against a living person. Lady Mary Wortley Montagu, wife of the 18th-century British ambassador, had a sharp eye for such glamour during her visit with Sultan Mustafa II's widow: "Hafisa Sultan's floor-length purple vest was edged with pearls and its buttons were large loops of diamonds. Her belt was completely covered with diamonds. She wore three necklaces which hung down to her knees, one of pearls, the others emeralds. Her earrings were large, pear-shaped diamonds."

Many of the priceless objects on view show signs of daily use—evidence both of the sultans' fabulous wealth and of their enjoyment of their treasures. Portraits also reveal the sultans' fancy for jewelry: All who wore turbans added jeweled aigrettes on the front. A profile view of Sultan Selim I shows him with both a necklace and a large drop-earring of pearls.

A few of the small, separate buildings in the **Dördüncü Avlu** (Fourth Court) are interesting in themselves. The **Revan Köşkü** and **Bağdad Köşkü** (Yerevan and Baghdad kiosks, or pavilions) were built by Sultan Murat IV to commemorate his victories over those cities in the first half of the 17th century. East across the Fourth Court is the **Konyalı** restaurant, a convenient corner for busloads of tourists to get a meal and fantasize that they are experiencing life in the 18th-century palace. The restaurant has an expansive view across the waters and up the Bosphorus.

For Muslims the place of greatest importance is the **Hırka-i Saadet Dairesi** (Pavilion of the Blessed Mantle), on the west side of the Third Court, where the sacred relics of the Prophet Muhammad are kept. Among them is the mantle of the Prophet, a simple black camel's-hair cloak that the Prophet took from his own shoulders and gave to a friend, Kâab bin Züheyir, who had written a poem that pleased him. Also in the room are the sword and the sacred standard of the Prophet. The standard, the symbol used to inspire soldiers to their greatest exertions, was carried by the Ottoman sultans and their grand viziers into battle from the end of the 16th century on.

A new sultan always repaired immediately to this pavilion after he had been acknowledged by his court, and it was here that he said his first official prayers. Each year on the 15th day of Ramazan the sultan, his family, and his highest officials paid a state visit to the Pavilion of the Blessed Mantle. During the days preceding this visit, the pavilion was subjected to a thorough ritual cleaning by the pages of the privy chamber. The handkerchiefs dampened with rose water that were used to clean the mantle itself were later presented as gifts to members of the court. On the 15th, the sultan opened the mantle's gold box, unfolding the many squares of cloth that encased it and at last exposing it to view for a few brief minutes.

Attention of a different kind focuses on the private quarters of the sultan, the **Harem**. Comprising about 300 rooms in the western part of the palace, the Harem was organized around three main areas: the quarters of the black eunuchs, those of the women, and those of the sultan himself. During some sultans' reigns, upwards of 1,500 people may have lived in this complex.

The women's quarters were arranged and furnished to maximize the residents' aesthetic pleasure. Embroideries, calligraphy, tiles, marquetry, and frescoes delighted the eye; the sounds of singing birds, running water, and chiming clocks charmed the ear. The swimming pools were especially amusing to at least one of the sultans—"Crazy" İbrahim—who enjoyed tossing his women into them.

The quarters closest to the **Araba Kapısı** (Carriage Gate), the main entrance of the Harem, belonged to the black eunuchs, who protected the residents. The chief black eunuch (who had come up through the ranks) directed the other eunuchs, was in charge of the princes' education, and held the lucrative position of the absentee governor of Mecca—the holiest city of Islam. At least one chief black eunuch actually made the pilgrimage to Mecca. The head eunuch was often the most powerful person in the Harem after the sultan.

The young concubines (*cariyes*) who were being trained for their roles in the palace lived in quite crowded quarters. Though these girls were slaves, several points should be noted: They were paid regular wages. Their position in society was not at all degrading. Though they were at the absolute command of the sultan and though their futures were tied to his desires (and to his continuance as sultan), their children were born free. They were permitted to hope that a son might some day become the sultan himself, elevating his mother to the coveted position of *valide sultan*—queen mother. The sultans considered themselves to be slaves also—slaves of God—and the wisest of them knew that they were in some ways more limited in their freedom than the humblest of their subjects.

The *cariyes* usually came to the palace between the ages of 12 and 14. They were prisoners of war, kidnapped children, or girls whose families' poverty had forced them to be sold. Each girl was carefully chosen for her beauty according to the standards of the day: clear skin; black hair; red lips; long arms and legs; wide forehead, bosom, and hips; fine nose and fingers; thick thighs and calves; and small ears, hands, feet, and breasts. Girls who appeared to be dullards were not wanted. Foreign girls were taught Turkish; all the girls learned to read and write—not all of them equally well, as is evident from their letters. They were taught the feminine arts of embroidery, dancing, playing musical instruments, and cooking. Some spent time concocting new recipes—summer drinks of water lilies, maybe, or violets—to excite the sultan's jaded palate.

The most famous *cariye* was Hürrem Sultan. In Turkish her name means "the joyous one"; in English she is called Roxelana, perhaps because she came from Russia (actually, Ukraine; she was given to Sultan Süleyman the Magnificent by a Crimean khan). She was not one of Süleyman's most beautiful slaves, but from her poetry, still extant, she seems to have been his most intelligent. As she grew in his favor she demanded increasingly exclusive conjugal rights, finally ousting her rivals and forcing Süleyman to free her and marry her legally. Süleyman had older children by other *cariye*s, but it was one of her several sons, Selim, who inherited his father's throne. Witty and shrewd, Hürrem was Süleyman's most trusted counselor; when she died in 1558 her daughter Mihrimah took over that role.

Another area in the Harem, the **Kafes** (Cage), naturally arouses visitors' curiosity. The Cage was the quarters of the school-age princes. Recent scholarship indicates that the boys lived in apartments facing away from those of the *cariyes,* but accessible through the Golden Way to their schoolrooms over the chief black eunuch's residence (not included in the usual tour of the Harem).

The meaning of the Cage is more melodramatic and is tied in with the succession of the sultans. From the beginning of the empire to the time of Sultan İbrahim (1288 to 1640), the question of who should succeed to the throne on the death of a sultan was usually resolved by the deaths of all but one remaining male in the immediate family. While some of the young men died in battle, and some because of disease, a number of deaths were dramatic instances of the application of the *kanunname* (code of laws) written by Mehmet II (d. 1481), which legalized the execution of the sultan's brothers in order to maintain the welfare of the empire. On his accession (1593), Sultan Mehmet III's 19 brothers were bowstrung (i.e., strangled with bowstring, a preferred method of execution among the Ottomans), an application of the law that shocked the usually unreproachful İstanbullus.

Then the seemingly more humane policy of keeping them under strictly supervised control was developed. The Cage, the rooms where brothers who were old enough to threaten the rule of the reigning sultan resided, probably was above the cloister-like **Cinlerin Meşveret Yeri** (Council Place of the

Djinns). These designations seem in themselves enough to stir up rumors of palace intrigue. The young boys probably weren't actually imprisoned, as the name "Cage" might imply; they must have been allowed exercise, and without question they were given lessons and employed themselves with various handcrafts. Sultan Ahmet III, for example, learned to be a skilled calligrapher before he came to the throne at the age of 30. But, with one exception, no prince was allowed to father children. That exception—who later became Sultan Abdülhamit I—somehow managed to spirit his baby daughter out of the palace without his older, reigning brother finding out about her birth.

The visitor to the Harem may be surprised by the absence of anything resembling a formal dining room. Although there were sometimes as many as 50 courses in a palace meal, there were no "groaning boards" with long rows of courtiers keeping track of who was seated above and who below the salt. The sultan's meals and those of the other residents were served on trays around which three or four might gather, sitting on low cushions. In the 18th century the walls of one of Ahmet III's rooms were painted with pictures of flowers and fruit; perhaps he ate here, but in general people set up their trays wherever it was convenient.

Below the Harem, in the **Beşinci Avlu** (Fifth Court) of the palace, are a cluster of other buildings: the Çinili Köşk, the Archaeological Museum, and the Museum of the Ancient Orient. Of these, the **Çinili Köşk** (Tiled Pavilion) is the oldest, built by Sultan Mehmet II in 1472.

Sultan Mehmet and many of the men who followed him studied religious law and theology: Their buildings were designed to give enduring symbolic substance to Islamic thought. The square plan of the building was intended to represent the four corners of the world. The dome, as in mosques, was the circle of heaven, and the ribs of the dome the wheel of law. The decorative tile patterns were chosen, in part, for their original mystical meanings. The sultan's throne in the center emphasized the axial symmetry of the whole and his place within it. The entrance to the Çinili Köşk is covered with Bursa tiles glazed with designs in the tradition of Central Asia. The pavilion contains a collection of rare tiles and ceramics from the Great Seljuk, Anatolian Seljuk, and Ottoman periods (12th through early 20th century).

In addition to the geometric symbolism, the building had another use: From here Sultan Mehmet II enjoyed watching games of *cirit* being played outside. *Cirit* is a Central Asian game in which horsemen ride hard against each other as they try to catch and return hurled javelins. The field in front of the Çinili Köşk was used for this game while the sultans lived at Topkapı. *Cirit* is not as popular today as it once was, but it is still played in eastern Turkey.

Across from the Çinili Köşk in Topkapı's outermost court is the **Archaeological Museum**. The first floor of the museum and the new, well-lighted annex are open, but only a small portion of the collection of more than 60,000 objects (not including more than 75,000 inscribed clay tablets) is on public view. The museum's hours are 9:30 A.M. to 4:30 P.M., except Monday.

The most famous item on display is the so-called **Alexander sarcophagus**, which was found in Sidon (Saida, in present-day Lebanon). The question of whose body the sarcophagus once contained (perhaps that of the king of Sidon?) has provoked debate. And who is it who is memorialized in the high reliefs that decorate its sides? The figure wearing the lion skin could be Alexander the Great portrayed as Hercules. About the only damage this work has sustained since it was carved in the fourth century B.C. is the fading of some of the paint on its reliefs.

On the lid of the 13th-century B.C. **sarcophagus of King Tabnit** (another highlight in the museum) is an inscription in Phoenician cursing anyone who disturbed the mummy inside. The inscription casts a shadow on the character of Tabnit because it has been incised over earlier hieroglyphics about the Egyptian general Peneftah, whom Tabnit himself had displaced.

The **Gezer calendar** (the earliest known Hebraic text) and the **Siloam inscription** (commemorating King Hezekiah's tunnel) are on view, as is the fraction of the gold discovered by German archaeologist Heinrich Schliemann at Troy that went into the Turkish museum's keeping rather than being spirited off to Germany (whence it disappeared from a Berlin museum at the end of World War II). The new annex currently features two displays. In the first, called Anatolia and Troy through the Ages, are baked clay tablets from Kültepe (near Kayseri in Central Anatolia) that detail the concerns of 19th-century B.C. Assyrian traders (debts, smuggling, slave trade) as well as incised stones from the Hittite site of Boğazkale (see Ankara and Environs, below) that record legal matters, including a soldier's oath. The museum's Syrian, Cypriot, and Philistine collections are displayed in the Neighboring Cultures of Anatolia exhibit on the annex's top floor.

Among the items of special interest in the **Museum of the Ancient Orient**—the third building of this cluster—is a copy of the **treaty of Kadesh**, discovered in the Hittite capital of Boğazkale, northeast of Ankara. The treaty was enacted in 1284 B.C. between Pharaoh Ramses II of Egypt and the Hittite king Hattusilis III. Written in Akkadian, the international language of the time, it reads: "Behold, as for the relationship between the land of Egypt and the Hatti land, since eternity the god does not permit the making of hostility between them because of a treaty valid forever."

This museum contains a number of homely objects that bring to life the people of the ancient Middle East: a child's multiplication table, a well-worn brass ruler, and a recipe for an antidote for poisoning (mustard, thyme, pistachios, barley, wine, syrup, and sagapenum—*Ferula persica,* an antispasmodic).

Gülhane Parkı (open every day from 8:30 A.M. to 11:00 P.M.), today an undistinguished zoo and amusement park, takes up much of the original Fifth Court; the usual entrance to Gülhane is off Alemdar Caddesi rather than through the palace proper. The **Tanzimat Müzesi** (Museum of the 1839 Reforms), a small building restored by the Turkish Touring and Automobile Association, halfway along the main road, houses items relating to the period of Ottoman political reform, 1839 to 1856.

Near the north end of Gülhane, and visible from the sea, is the **Gotlar Sütunu** (Column of the Goths). The inscription on the base, only just decipherable, says it was dedicated "to Fortune, who has returned because the Goths have been defeated." It may be the oldest monument still standing in the city: The date of its erection is between A.D. 268 and 337.

The Church of St. Irene

St. Irene (closed to the public except for special events), which is actually within the First Court of Topkapı, is thought to be on the site of a church that predates the time of Constantine. Dedicated not to a saintly woman but rather to the personification of Holy Peace, St. Irene (called Aya İrini Kilisesi in Turkish) was Constantinople's first cathedral. After St. Sophia was constructed, the two functioned together as one Great Church; the same clergy officiated in both places, and both buildings suffered damage in the same riots and fires. St. Irene played an extremely important role in the formation of Christian doctrine: It was here, in 381, that the Second Ecumenical Council condemned the Arian heresy (the doctrine that the Son and the Father—Jesus and God—are not the same substance) and reaffirmed the Nicene Creed.

Architecturally the building is interesting because it shows the transition from the basilica to the domed, cruciform church. (Originally a basilica was a large, long Roman public building frequently used as a law court.) The present structure dates in part from the sixth century (some of the capitals have the monograms of Justinian and his empress Theodora) and in part from the eighth century, when it was enlarged following an earthquake. Additions to the exterior were made during the Ottoman period.

In the semidome above what was the altar is a large mosaic cross on a pedestal, repaired in recent years. The Greek inscription arching above it is a somewhat inaccurate copying of Psalms 65:5, 6: "Happy is the man of thy choice, whom thou dost bring to dwell in thy courts; let us enjoy the blessing of thy house, thy holy temple."

The northwest atrium contains some large stone sarcophagi. Surprisingly plain, they are reputed to have contained the bodies of early Byzantine emperors. According to historian Edwin A. Grosvenor in his book *Constantinople* (vol. 2), they were at one time housed in the Church of the Holy Apostles. (That building was pillaged during the Fourth Crusade and, in the 15th century, was torn down and replaced with the Fatih Sultan Mehmet Camii.)

During the Ottoman period St. Irene was used as the palace armory. It was conveniently located next to the janissary barracks inside the palace grounds and close to the Imperial Gate. Toward the end of the Ottoman period and up until the 1960s, the building was a museum, almost never open, but obviously devoted to military history: The yard around it was littered with cannons. It has since been used for art exhibits, including the Eighteenth Council of Europe exhibition, The Anatolian Civilizations, in 1983, and part of the first Istanbul Biennial in 1989. Since the late 1970s St. Irene has served as a concert hall for classical music performances during the International Istanbul Festival each summer.

St. Sophia

Inspiration for architects and religious leaders, for generals and historians, the domed basilica of St. Sophia (called Ayasofya in Turkish; open 9:30 A.M. to 5:00 P.M. every day except Monday) is one of the great jewels of the diadem of the first hill of the city. Built as a great cathedral, St. Sophia became a mosque under the Ottomans and was deconsecrated, becoming a museum, under the Republic in 1935. It is situated before the entrance to Topkapı and across the park from the Blue Mosque.

The scale of the building—both outside and in—has

defined architectural limits ever since it was built. Its lines are *the* statement of classical Byzantine art; its form, that of a central dome supported by massive pillars and two opposing half domes, was the ingenious resolution of the problem of how to create a large, uninterrupted interior space.

Most people who are not art historians or architects will probably not have a positive first impression of the exterior of the building. The barnlike interior, too, demands more than a casual glance to reveal the wealth of the building's attractions. Discreet lighting has, however, helped mask the echoing, dusty walls. Writing in *The Innocents Abroad* in 1867, Mark Twain expressed the disappointment that many have felt in St. Sophia, saying, "The people who go into ecstasies over St. Sophia must surely get them out of the guide book."

Though there is some justification for this possibly philistine reaction, St. Sophia continues to reward those willing to give the time and energy necessary to understand it. Church, mosque, and, today, museum, St. Sophia is a focus of religious identification for both Orthodox Christians and orthodox Turkish Muslims, a symbol of political dominance, and a marvel of building skill.

The church was the third of that name to be constructed on the first hill. (The name "St. Sophia" may be a bit misleading. The church's name in Greek, *Hagia Sophia,* means "Holy Wisdom," and the church is dedicated to Divine Wisdom rather than to any female saint.) Constantine the Great built his St. Sophia in 326 on a site where a pagan temple had been situated. That church was reconstructed by his son Constantius and consecrated in 360. Constantine had intended the church of St. Irene rather than St. Sophia to be his cathedral, and throughout the Byzantine period the two churches were considered as one unit, the *Megale Ekklesia* (Great Church). Both buildings were burned in the Nika Revolt of January 15, 532, a political uprising against the harsh fiscal policies of Emperor Justinian in which the rallying cry was *Nika!*—Victory!

In expiation for the devastation that the riot caused, Justinian determined that he would rebuild St. Sophia on a scale surpassing all other places of worship. He wanted it to be magnificent in conception, decoration, image, and scale. His architects, Anthemius of Tralles and Isidorus of Miletus, created their masterpiece, and with it bequeathed to future generations of builders the knowledge of how to satisfy that desire for immense space. The dome was the strongest, most stable kind of roof that they knew of that was capable of covering a large area. In learning how to balance a dome on top of a square building, the Byzantines made their greatest contribution to the science of architecture. More than that, they contributed to architectural aesthetics in developing the pendentive—the graceful sweep of arches that begins at the right-angle corner of two walls and moves upward to blend into the curve of the dome. In the pendentive, both the transfer of weight and thrust from the dome to the ground and the visual harmony of line are superbly satisfied. Justinian expressed his jubilation over the excellence of the building when he threw up his arms during its dedication and exclaimed, "Solomon, I have surpassed you!"

You can get an idea of the power and wealth that Justinian commanded even after the Nika Revolt in the speed with which St. Sophia was built. The work began almost at once; Justinian laid the first stone in 533 and dedicated the building on December 27, 537—less than five years later.

Justinian is thought to have used columns from already existing buildings. Eight porphyry columns may have been quarried in Aswan and may once have stood in the Temple of the Sun in Baalbek; eight serpentine columns may have come from the temple of Artemis in Ephesus. Whether this is so or not, they and other columns are curiously uneven. You don't notice the discrepancy at first: Your attention is drawn commandingly upward when you enter the nave. It's only when you look at the bases of the columns that you're disturbed by their different heights and rough edges, which in the sixth century would have been obscured by the richness of the decor.

Another impressive indication of the speed with which the building was constructed is most visible in the gallery. As you look down the side aisles you may be startled by the elliptical curves of the arches and the way the walls lean outward. This condition was caused by the weight of the dome, which was constructed when the mortar was still green.

Among other elements of St. Sophia deserving your notice are the mosaics (more on these below); the marble revetment on the walls, whose Rorschach-like patterns suggest devils' (or angels', or animals') faces; the crosses on the floor of the nave indicating the plumb lines from the ribs of the dome; the *minber* (pulpit) and *mihrap* (niche), which were installed when the building became a mosque; the large alabaster urn that once held water; and the eight large painted-wood disks, or medallions, with the names of God, Muhammad, the first caliphs, and two of Muhammad's grandsons. Some years ago these disks were taken down to be removed to another museum. They were, however, much too big to go through any of St. Sophia's doors, and they were much too old (1650) and too valuable to be cut into pieces.

Graffiti in the gallery suggest that some services held at the church were long and boring: Two drawings of sailing ships scratched in the marble (at about eye level on the inside face of the north pillar) may have been executed over several Sundays. On the balustrade near the south marble screen are runic letters spelling the name of a Viking, Halvdan, probably a visitor to Constantinople in the tenth century.

The details of history, of use, of added decoration, and of legend surrounding the building are almost numberless, and they continue to grow. There is, for example, the ghost of the priest who is still waiting just outside to enter and complete the service that was broken off when Constantinople fell to the Turks on May 29, 1453, and the Cold Window where the Conqueror's religious counselor Akşemsettin spoke so refreshingly that a cool breeze has blown there ever since. There is the northwest pillar in the north aisle that is reported to exude a moisture good for curing eye diseases (the so-called Sweating Column), and there is a handprint high up on a southeast pillar supposed to be a bloody stain left when Mehmet's soldiers entered St. Sophia that Tuesday in 1453.

The mosaic in the conch above the altar/*mihrap* is of the Mother of God with the Christ child seated on her knees. The child has a scroll in his left hand and is holding his right up in blessing. Above the upper northwest balcony (visible from the floor of the nave) are mosaics of several bishops. As you look up, the man to the left is Saint Ignatius (d. ca. A.D. 110); the middle figure is Saint John Chrysostom (d. 407); on the far right is Saint Ignatius Theophorus (d. 877). All were powerful in determining the course of Orthodox Christianity; the latter two were patriarchs of Constantinople.

Other people are hidden in the stiff postures and clothes of several of the splendid **mosaics** in the balcony. In the south gallery is the 11th-century mosaic of the Empress Zoë. This mosaic was tampered with during Zoë's varied reigns, once probably by Zoë's adopted son, the emperor Michael V Calaphates, who tried to get rid of her. Following the death of Zoë's second husband, Michael V shut her up in a nunnery on the island of Prinkipo (now Büyükada, one of the Princes' Islands), gloating over his power as he fingered the shaven locks of her hair. His own fall came soon after Zoë was recalled by popular demand to reign in her own right, and he was disgraced, blinded, and exiled. At the age of 64

Zoë married her third husband (scandalous venery in the eyes of the medieval Byzantine churchmen), the man now represented beside her in the mosaic she restored.

The south side of the balcony is also the location of one of the most moving of Byzantine mosaics anywhere, the **Deesis**, an icon showing Christ enthroned between John the Baptist and the Virgin Mary. The mosaic was probably executed in the early 14th century; only the heads and shoulders of its three figures have survived the ravages of time. At the center is Jesus; to the right the Virgin Mary gazes down in humility. On the left an aged John—the pain and sorrow of humankind reflected in his face—leans pleadingly toward the figure of Jesus. Lifting his right hand in benediction, Jesus quietly gazes out, all-knowing and all-suffering. Here in this mosaic is the height of the Byzantine artistic representation of the human tragedy and the spiritual power of redemption.

Two ecumenical councils were held here: The Fifth Council, in 553, and the Sixth, in 680, struggled over questions of the nature of Christ and the political center of church power. By the 11th century the conflict between Constantinople and Rome came to a head. The rift was completed when the Roman emissary placed a letter of excommunication on the altar of St. Sophia in 1054. (The mutual ban was finally lifted by Pope Paul VI and Ecumenical Patriarch Athenagoras in 1965.)

During the Fourth Crusade in 1204, Latin Christian warriors sacked the capital and ravaged its treasures. The Latin Empire set up in Constantinople lasted until 1261; its emperors were crowned in St. Sophia, and its first leader, Henrico Dandalo, the doge of Venice, was buried here in 1205. His gravestone is in the floor opposite the Deesis mosaic.

Further plunder of the city and some damage to St. Sophia occurred with the Ottoman conquest. In short order Mehmet converted the church into a mosque (in Turkish it is known as Ayasofya Camii), and it became the royal place of worship for the city's new, Muslim rulers. In a gesture of good will, Mehmet gave Dandalo's sword to Gentile Bellini when the painter returned to Venice. He also is supposed to have stopped the Muslim soldiers from destroying the mosaics of the church; instead, the mosaics were whitewashed to protect them through the centuries. (The whitewash was removed from some of them in the early 1930s.) The great buttresses on the exterior of the church were added in the 16th century by the architect Sinan, and the minarets, of course, were also added during the Ottoman period.

The importance that St. Sophia continued to hold, even above the mosques built by sultans, shows in the number of royalty buried in its courtyard. The first was Sultan Selim II (1566 to 1574), buried with his favorite wife, Nurbânu Sultan, in a *türbe* (mausoleum) built by Sinan. Selim's son Murat III (1574 to 1595) and his favorite wife, Safiye Sultan, are in the next *türbe*. The *türbe* of Murat's son and successor Mehmet III (1595 to 1603) and his favorite wife, Handan Sultan, is the last one to have been built. All these, as well as a small *türbe* set against that of Murat, also contain graves of many children, some of whom died natural deaths, some of whom were executed on the accession of their brother to the throne. The baptistery of St. Sophia was used as a mausoleum for sultans Mustafa I (1617 to 1618, 1622 to 1623) and İbrahim (1640 to 1648). The *türbe*s and the baptistery are open from 9:30 A.M. to 11:30 A.M. and 1:00 P.M. to 4:00 P.M., except Mondays.

The Hippodrome

The heart of the Byzantine city was the sports arena, the Hippodrome (called Atmeydanı—"Horse Square"—in Turkish), which backed up against the Great Palace complex, lying between it and St. Sophia. The original racetrack of the Hippodrome accumlated debris over the centuries, and what you see today is a grassy park punctuated by several ancient monuments, the bases of which are several yards below today's ground level.

The Hippodrome has of course not always been as quiet a place as it is now: More than once during Byzantine history allegiances to a combination of sports, politics, and religion caused blood to be spilled here. In one of the first of these uprisings, during the time of Justinian, the circus (i.e., Hippodrome) factions known as the Blues and the Greens combined forces to produce the Nika Revolt, described above. (The factions, which took their names from the colors of teams of charioteers, had by Justinian's time developed into quasi political parties, with the Blues being conservative supporters of religious orthodoxy, the Greens, Iconoclastic reformers.)

Even by today's standards, the Hippodrome, begun in 203 by Emperor Septimius Severus and expanded by Constantine, was a big stadium, capable of holding perhaps 100,000 spectators. A football field in the United States has 100 yards of playing space; the racetrack for horses here was more than 500 yards long end-to-end. The structure, which has vanished, enclosed an area considerably larger than that now occupied by a park, and its bleachers rose in ranks high above the ground.

When Constantine decided to make his New Rome equal in grandeur to the old capital, he raided many of Rome's squares and public buildings to adorn the upper promenade of the Hippodrome. Among the treasures decorating the racecourse were four life-size bronze horses. Part of the Fourth Crusade booty, in 1204 they were shipped off to Venice where they stayed until Napoleon took them to decorate the Arc de Triomphe in Paris. With his downfall they were returned to Venice to grace the entrance to the cathedral of San Marco.

Constantine transported three large monuments, two obelisks and a column, to decorate the central divider of the track. He brought the **Dikili Taş** (the Egyptian Obelisk; itself dating from the 15th century B.C.) to Constantinople, but he left it to a later emperor, Theodosius I, to set it in place. The reliefs on the north side of the marble base show Theodosius helping with that engineering feat. The story goes that the engineer in charge managed to lift it to within a few inches of the upright position. The groans of the crowd witnessing his defeat turned to cheers the next day. All night long workmen had poured water on the scaffold so that in the morning the timbers swelled, raising the stone the needed distance.

A victory of a different kind is marked by the **Yılanlı Sütan** (Serpent Column), a stumpy bit of bronze that was once a statue of three intertwined snakes. An inscription no longer visible on its base identified it as the monument to the battle for freedom between an alliance of Greek cities and invading Persian forces, led by Xerxes, in Plataea in 479 B.C. The metal used for the column, which originally stood in front of the temple of Apollo at Delphi, was taken from the shields of the Persian soldiers who fell in the battle. The snakes' heads were knocked off in the 18th century.

At the southwestern end of the Hippodrome stands another obelisk, **Örmetaş** (variously called the Walled Obelisk or the Mortar-Built Column). The date of its original construction is unknown, but it was repaired in the tenth century by Emperor Constantine VII Porphyrogenitus. It is built of roughly cut limestone blocks and was once faced with gilt-bronze sheets, which disappeared during the time of the Crusades.

Palace of İbrahim Paşa

Facing the Hippodrome is the Türk ve İslam Eserleri Müzesi (a.k.a. İbrahim Paşa Sarayı or Museum of Turkish and Islamic Arts; open 10:00 A.M. to 5:00 P.M., except Monday), located in the İbrahim Paşa palace. After renovation, it won the Council of Europe's 1985 award for the "museum of the year."

İbrahim Paşa, for whom the building is named, was the close friend and adviser of Sultan Süleyman the Magnificent. When Süleyman became sultan in 1520, he made İbrahim his grand vizier and soon after awarded him the hand of Süleyman's sister, Hatice. Süleyman repaired a building that had originally been built as a janissary cadet school by Sultan Bayezit II and gave part of it to İbrahim. But Süleyman's wife, Roxelana, accused İbrahim Paşa of intending to overthrow his master. Süleyman believed his wife and had İbrahim executed, whereupon the building reverted to the state. Later it was used as a prison, and eventually it became a ruin. With the need for large display areas for the Anatolian Civilizations exhibition in 1983, some of the rooms were again repaired, and items from the Museum of Turkish and Islamic Arts, which had been in the *imaret* (public kitchen) of the Süleymaniye complex, were moved here.

The permanent collection includes the old and very large carpets for which that museum had long been famous. On the ground floor are ethnographic displays of typical Turkish rooms. In one, a group of women prepare the skeins of wool for the rug they will weave; next to this grouping is a description of methods used to obtain natural dyes.

The Blue Mosque

On the opposite side of the Hippodrome, on the site of the early Byzantine Great Palace, is the **Sultanahmet Camii**, more popularly known as the Blue Mosque. (Note that mosques are always open, but that it is considerate not to disturb the worshipers during the five daily *namaz* prayers. Prayer times vary according to the season; in general they come at sunset, bedtime, sunrise, noon, and afternoon. Note also that the Islamic day begins at sunset, not midnight.)

The Blue Mosque is the mosque most often visited by foreigners; because it's so near Topkapı and St. Sophia, it's easy to include in a quick tour. The mosque's distinctive features, besides its overall elegance of form, include its six minarets and the more than 20,000 17th-century İznik tiles that cover the lower portions of the interior walls. The mosque's six minarets—an unusually high number—have inspired several stories. One old chestnut is that the order for them to be made of gold (*altın*) was misinterpreted as being an order to build six (*altı*) of them. Another more likely factual story is that the mosque's builder, Sultan Ahmet I, had a seventh minaret added to the Great Mosque in Mecca in order to emphasize that holy place's uniqueness.

Work was begun on the mosque in 1609 by 19-year-old Ahmet, who is generally thought to have been an ineffective ruler because he hesitated to go to war against his eastern enemies. Instead, he spent his money and energies here, checking on the construction's progress every payday and sometimes helping with the building himself. Sultan Ahmet intended the pervasive blue color of the interior to help turn worshipers' thoughts to God. The mural tiles in the balcony (not open to the public) were designed to suggest the garden of paradise.

Ever since 1617, the year of the Blue Mosque's dedication, it has been the custom to mark religious holidays by suspending an illuminated sign between two of the mosque's minarets. (Today other imperial mosques do this as well.) This illumination, called a *mahya,* consisted of a message in Arabic that was created by suspending as many as 500 oil lamps on cables stretched from the balcony of one minaret to that of the other. It was a daunting task: The whole apparatus of wires, glass cups, and oil had to be carried up the twisting steps of the minaret without being tangled or spilled. Balanced on the balconies, workmen adjusted the lengths and intervals of the cables to create the pattern by which the words would be spelled, in firelight, in the air. The lamps had to be lit in the dark and sometimes in a stiff wind, and the lighting of the last cup had to be done before the first burned out. The *mahya* illuminations continue, particularly during the month of Ramazan, with such phrases as "Welcome," "Holy Month," and "Praise God"—but today they are written in electric lights.

The Blue Mosque is now undergoing extensive repairs both inside and out; it's expected that they will take several years to complete. (Too, the aesthetics of the Blue Mosque are not enhanced by the insistent hawkers of postcards and cheap souvenirs in the courtyard.) Because the mosque is so popular with tourists, they are often asked to enter it by a side door and to stay within a cordoned-off area. This interferes with a full view of the building, but it protects the Muslim worshipers to whom the building is not an exotic curiosity but a place of daily prayer. On summer evenings, beginning at 8:00, a sound-and-light show is presented between the Blue Mosque and St. Sophia. The languages of the show rotate, one each night, in the order of Turkish, English, French, and German.

Constantine's Imperial Palace (also called the Sacred Palace or the Great Palace in Byzantine records) once occupied the Seraglio point (extending from where the Blue Mosque stands today to the sea), where he and his soldiers could keep an eye on movements to and from the Black Sea and the Mediterranean (*Akdeniz*—the White Sea—in Turkish). It was a complex of residences, office buildings, kitchens, stables, and workshops that adjoined the Hippodrome to the south and looked east and north across the water. Mosaics from the site, perhaps the flooring of a colonnaded court of the Imperial Palace, dating from the Roman period, are being restored and displayed in the **Mozaik Müzesi** (Mosaic Museum; open 9:30 A.M. to 5:00 P.M., except Tuesday), east of and below the Blue Mosque.

In the garden between St. Sophia and the Blue Mosque is the building known as the **Ayasofya Hamamı**, also called the Baths of Roxelana (open 9:30 A.M. to 5:00 P.M., except Tuesdays). Built by Sinan for Sultan Süleyman's wife, it has been beautifully restored and now houses a display of handwoven, naturally dyed reproductions of old Turkish rugs and carpets, sponsored by the Turkish Ministries of State, Culture, and Tourism. These museum-quality pieces are for sale. (The same selection is for sale in the gift shop in the First Court of Topkapı palace.)

In the same general area is the **İstanbul Sanatlar Çarşısı** (Handcrafts Center; open 9:30 A.M. to 6:00 P.M. every day), next to the Turkish Touring and Automobile Association's Yeşil Ev Hotel, where you can watch artisans at work on calligraphy, bookbinding, embroidery, glass painting, doll making, and a number of other crafts. Paper marbling is taught in the **Cafer Ağa Medresesi** off Caferiye Sokağı immediately west of St. Sophia; similar Turkish handcrafts are available there at reasonable prices.

The City Water Supplies

Across Alemdar Caddesi from St. Sophia is a tall old **brick column**, one of several such around the city that date from Byzantine times. Its purpose was to equalize water pressure for the area. These "balances" are not the only means that residents here have had to adopt to meet the city's recurring water problems. The **Aqueduct of Valens** (called Bozdoğan Kemeri in Turkish), which crosses Atatürk Bulvarı near Şehzade Camii, was built by the Roman emperor Valens about A.D. 375 and is among the oldest evidence of the struggle to provide adequate water—a struggle that continued with the aqueducts built in the Belgrade Forest by Sinan during the Ottoman period. Three huge open cisterns, Roman in date, stored water inside the city: Mocius (on the seventh hill), Aetios (on Fevzi Paşa Caddesi not far from the Edirne Kapısı), and Aspar (the largest, next to the mosque of Sultan Selim I). Aspar and Mocius were kitchen gardens for a long time; Aetios is now a soccer field. When they were still used as reservoirs, the city's populace was sometimes entertained by mock sea-battles staged on their waters.

The city's water problems seem destined to haunt Istanbul's engineers and residents. With increases both in the population and in the age of the conduits, shortages are part of the city's routine.

Underground, the old city is riddled with ancient cisterns, built both for public and for private use. No longer used, the public cisterns are remarkable feats of engineering. Two covered cisterns are in the area near the Hippodrome. On Yerebatan Caddesi, across from St. Sophia, is the **Yerebatan Sarnıcı** (a.k.a. the Basilica Cistern; open 9:00 A.M. to 7:00 P.M. every day), which has been cleaned up and lighted so that visitors can explore its recesses. A delightfully cool, damp (dripping) place in summer, it presents an unusual sound-and-light show, with colored lights playing on the columns and strains of Mozart or Beethoven echoing against its vaults. When the water was drained, two Medusa heads were found to have been used as bases to the supporting columns in the far corner.

Another large covered cistern is **Binbirdirek**, the "Thousand and One Columns," whose Turkish name somewhat overstates its 224 columns. (Binbirdirek is open 8:00 A.M. to 5:00 P.M. every day.) It is also called the Philoxenus cistern, for the presumed builder, a fourth-century Roman senator. Binbirdirek is located off Divan Yolu in a small park across from the main entrance to the Law Courts (Adliye). The bases and capitals of the columns are marked with monograms; the multiple-arched ceiling is of brick. At present the adventure of exploring it is not for people with poor eyesight or weak knees, for the place is poorly lighted and the steps and floor are uneven.

A small cistern that *has* been renovated is on Soğukçeşme Sokak, behind St. Sophia and against the outer wall of the Topkapı palace. This is the **Sarnıç**, operated by the Turkish Touring and Automobile Association. The ninth-century cistern contains a restaurant and currently features live classical guitar music during the supper hour.

Sirkeci Station

The **Sirkeci İstasyonu** (a.k.a. Sirkeci Garı, the Sirkeci train station) stands on the site of one of Byzantium's harbors, which Constantine the Great filled in when he was glorifying his new capital. In 339 B.C. (700 years before Constantine), soldiers dozing in the garrison here were startled by a very bright meteor. That chance happening awakened them to repulse the surprise attack by Philip II of Macedon. In thanks to what they considered divine help, they added a symbol of torch-bearing Hecate—a crescent—to their coins.

Just northwest of Topkapı, toward the Golden Horn and the Galata Bridge, Sirkeci (the name means "vinegar seller") station is today the European terminal for both commuter trains and trains departing to and arriving from various European cities. It swarms with people at morning and evening rush hours.

The **Gar**, a clean, good restaurant with reasonable prices, is located in one of the old Sirkeci station waiting rooms (open noon to midnight). Another excellent restaurant catering to the tastes of the business executives whose offices are in this area is the **Borsa**, at 60/62 Yalıköşkü Caddesi (open from noon to 5:00 P.M., except Sunday; other branches of Borsa are listed in Dining, below).

Agatha Christie (*Murder on the Orient Express*), Graham Greene (*Stamboul Train*), and Ian Fleming (*From Russia with Love*) have all done their share to make the train trip from Europe to Turkey appear fraught with mystery and adventure, which, in fact, it sometimes was: The Orient Express's famous riders included not only fictional detectives (Hercule Poirot) but also real-life spies (Mata Hari).

The original Orient Express first pulled into the Sirkeci station on August 12, 1888, as part of the Berlin-to-Baghdad system. It was a model of late Victorian elegance and comfort, with plush seats, inlaid wood panels in the sleeping cars, linen tablecloths for the dining cars, and an air of international intrigue throughout. Until the airlines took over, it was *the* way to travel. The regular service of the Orient Express is finished; its final run was in 1977, after which the antiquated cars were put on the auction block. Its memory, however, has not died: A five-day sentimental journey was staged in 1988 to observe the line's centennial. (Now this extravaganza is continued on an occasional basis by a Swiss enterprise, Intraflug A.G. Orient Express Journeys. In the United States check with Nostalgic Istanbul Orient Express, 104 S. Michigan Avenue, Suite 802, Chicago, IL 60603, Tel: 312/782-1912 for up-to-date schedule information. The Turkish agent for Intraflug is VIP Turizm; in Istanbul, Tel: 1/241-6514.) Some of the art and the spirit of this elegant mode of transportation have also been preserved in the Orient Express restaurant of The Marmara Hotel in Taksim, the central square of the new (European) city.

The Sirkeci station was situated so as to be convenient for those who wish to continue on to Asia by the same means of transportation. It's only a short walk to the **ferries for Asia**, some of which transport passengers to the Haydarpaşa station across the Bosphorus. (See the Getting Around section at the end of this chapter for more information on the ferries.)

Eminönü Square

Yeni Cami (the New Mosque—it was new in the 17th century), Eminönü square, and the Mısır Çarşısı (the Egyptian, or Spice, Bazaar) are a cluster of important reference points in the old city at the foot of the Galata Bridge just west of Sirkeci where you can get your bearings for the next move. The square is also a major place to switch buses. Several hundred years ago it was the location of the customs and security (*emin*) buildings; an open area lay in front of (*önü*) them, hence the name. The approaches to the new Galata Bridge are still under construction, so Eminönü is even more chaotic, these days, than usual: Pedestrians struggle to make their way around the rubble, the underground pedestrian walkway debouches into the middle of traffic, and bus and ferry terminals make do in temporary locations.

Eminönü square and the steps leading into Yeni Cami are a pandemonium of pigeons (and their benefactors) and postcard salesmen. The square is the easiest place in the city to find shoeshine boys, sellers of cigarette-lighter fluid and flints, recycled brown paper envelopes for reporting value-added–tax returns, public scales (he who guesses his correct weight may win a cord with which to repair his string of prayer beads), street photographers (note that the women selling corn for the birds do not take kindly to curious attention), *simitçi*s (peddlers of sesame-seed–coated circles of bread), and Gypsy women toting cloth bundles of piecework.

Yeni Cami was begun in 1589 by the queen mother Safiye Sultan and completed in 1664 by another queen mother, Hatice Turhan Sultan. The first architect was Davud Ağa, the successor to the great Sinan. Davud Ağa's plans were used throughout the construction, but he was executed, probably for heresy, two years after work on the mosque was started.

The next architect, Dalgıç ("the Diver") Ahmet, got his soubriquet from the foundations that he built for the mosque—stone bridges reinforced with iron—which solved the problem caused by seepage from the Golden Horn.

The mosque was completed only as far up as the lower windows when Safiye Sultan died in 1603, and her grandson, Sultan Ahmet I, stopped the work. In 1660 the queen mother Hatice Turhan Sultan was persuaded of the economic wisdom of using the half-finished mosque for her "pious foundation" rather than starting another, brand-new project.

The first part of Yeni Cami to be completed was the Hünkar Kasrı (Imperial Pavilion) on the southwest corner looking out over Eminönü square. Incorporated into the Byzantine seawall, it sits above an arch for pedestrian traffic and at the end of a long, unattached ramp up which the sultan could ride his horse. The reason for the haste in building this part was to permit Hatice Turhan Sultan to oversee the construction of her complex. Such pavilions connected to mosques were often used from the 17th century onward as places where the sultan could both rest and conduct business.

A library, primary school, timekeeper's house, mausoleum, fountain, and market were included in the complex. A bank has taken the place of the library, and the primary school has disappeared. The mausoleum stands southeast of the mosque. In addition to the tomb of Hatice Turhan Sultan, it contains the tombs of her son, Sultan Mehmet IV, her grandsons who became sultans, and several other family members.

In keeping with the original plan, income from the **Mısır Çarşısı** (the Egyptian Bazaar or **Spice Bazaar**; open 8:00 A.M. to 7:30 P.M., except Sundays) contributes to the upkeep of Yeni Cami. The bazaar's own support originally came from taxes imposed on Egyptian imports, hence its name. The Mısır Çarşısı—the second-largest covered bazaar in Istanbul—is run by its own society, with an elected head. The shops are all of one size and built on the same plan, with a basement and an upper floor. A police station and a small mosque occupy two corners of the cross street; **Pandeli's** restaurant is above the north entrance (see Dining, below); and at the far southeast end is a public toilet.

Several shops purvey the spices for which the Mısır Çarşısı is famous. Other shops sell various Middle Eastern specialties: luffas (gourd sponges), strings of dried okra, tubs heaped high with green henna powder, embroidered slippers, colorful basketwork, sage leaves and linden blossoms for tea, slabs of *pastırma* (a kind of smoked beef bacon, identified in Turkey with Indian summer, the season when it's made), sweet *sucuk* (walnuts or pistachios threaded on a string and then dipped in grape syrup until they form something that looks like a lumpy brown candle), jewelry (both the valuable and the kitschy kinds), nuts and dried fruits, and a variety of concoctions that all go by the name of "the sultans' aphrodisiac."

That aphrodisiac is famous in Ottoman history. Some of the sultans were more highly sexed than others, but their prowess (or lack thereof) didn't cause a crisis until the 17th century, when only one male was left in the family. Because of Sultan İbrahim's long years of imprisonment, during which he constantly feared that he would be executed by his older brother, he had become impotent. All sorts of remedies were tried, to no avail. At last his mother found an herbalist named Cinci Hoca (she thought he was a charlatan, but she was desperate) who prepared a spicy paste that did the trick. From being the equivalent of a eunuch, İbrahim became notorious for his sexual marathons. Perhaps one reason that there are so many rooms in the Harem is that he had to find places to put all his children, three of whom were sultans after him.

(For more information on shopping at the Mısır Çarşısı, see Shops and Shopping, below.)

The street that begins at the uphill exit from the Mısır Çarşısı, Sabuncu Han, is an outdoor five-and-dime. Stands selling pencils and school notebooks, cheap toys, condoms, tape-radio combos, watches, pliers, and scissors give way toward evening to carts of in-season fruits and vegetables. The stooped porters and the many pedestrians compete with motorists, all of them apparently knowing to the precise centimeter where they are in relation to each other.

On the east side of the Mısır Çarşısı is one of the city's **flower markets**. New stalls were put up in 1988, organizing what has long been a bright attraction of the area. You will find sacks of seed onions and peat moss, garden tools, trees and shrubs in gunnysacks next to small pots of flowers in bud or bloom. In the fall, leeks and cabbages supplant the boxes of tomatoes, peppers, and eggplants set out in late spring and summer. The market is both an herbarium and a kind of mini-zoo: Here and there are pet shops specializing in fish and small birds. Occasionally one will have an exotic parrot or a scolding monkey for sale.

Down the street that begins with the coffee sellers at the west side of the Mısır Çarşısı is the **Rüstem Paşa Camii** (currently closed for repairs). Rüstem Paşa was twice grand vizier under Süleyman the Magnificent; the interruption of his political career came when it was discovered he had engaged in a conspiracy with Süleyman's wife Hürrem and daughter Mihrimah to establish one of Hürrem's sons as next in line for the sultanate. The plot resulted in the execution of Süleyman's eldest son, Mustafa, and the army, infuriated, demanded Rüstem Paşa's removal from office. It is a testimony to his prestige that he was able to regain the sultan's favor.

Rüstem Paşa was famous for his miserliness: Once, when relations came to the city to ask for his help, he turned them away empty-handed, and he was even known to sell the fruit and vegetables grown in the palace gardens to supplement the palace budget. The positioning of and use of space in the mosque may reflect its patron's parsimony. The mosque possesses only an abbreviated courtyard, without an ablution fountain, and the worship space was elevated above the street level to accommodate shops whose revenues were used for the mosque's support.

The mosque is noted for the beautiful 16th-century İznik tiles of floral design that completely cover the interior walls. Red tulips in many different stylized shapes are the main flower represented, but there are also pomegranates, artichokes, roses, hyacinths, and carnations entwined in acanthus leaves, as well as stylized zoomorphic designs, geometric patterns, and striking blue-and-white Arabic inscriptions from the Koran. It's hard to imagine why a miser would have been so lavish in ornamenting a businessmen's mosque in a grubby part of the city.

The street that continues up the hill from the mosque is called **Uzunçarşı** ("long market"). Uzunçarşı is the place to find wooden items: thin Turkish rolling pins (*oklava*) for making *yufka* or baklava dough, wooden cups, chess and backgammon boards (the slapping of dice against the side of a backgammon board is as characteristic a Turkish sound as is the clinking of glasses against the brass spigot of the water carrier's large, curvaceous urn), coat racks, and walking canes. It's also the street of vendors of old clothes, plastic dishes, hanks of rope, and photograph albums. Farther up, where the street widens out, are leather-goods stores and shops selling brass fittings, Turkish musical instruments, dog collars, glass beads, and hunting gear.

Before Uzunçarşı reaches one of the entrances to the Covered Bazaar, it crosses a street called **Tahtakale**, which gives its name to the area and is the informal financial market of the city. Here shady deals are presumably arranged and price changes on sensitive items may be determined. In years past the black market value of the Turkish lira in relation to foreign currencies was indicated by the price charged on the district's streets for a pack of imported cigarettes. Today the black-market rate is quoted in the daily papers. There is a slight advantage to changing your money here (about 1 percent), but the risk you face is that you have no guarantee that the money you get won't be counterfeit.

The Covered Bazaar

The enormous **Kapalıçarşı** (variously called the Covered Bazaar, Grand Bazaar, or Grand Covered Bazaar) has many entrances; it can be approached from the upper end of Uzunçarşı, from Mahmutpaşa, or by going through the court-yard of Nuruosmaniye Camii, among other routes. The bazaar is open from 8:30 A.M. to 7:00 P.M. daily, except Sunday, but note that many merchants close up shop before the outer gates are locked.

Begun by Sultan Mehmet II in the 15th century, the bazaar was at first a wooden structure. The market may originally have been part of a stable for the sultan's horses. The stalls on the east side between the market and the mosque were still used as stables until the turn of this century. The bazaar was extensively damaged in an earthquake in 1894 and has also suffered a number of fires, the most recent in November 1954. Today the refurbished bazaar houses more than 3,000 shops, making it the largest covered bazaar in the world.

While at first glance the Kapalıçarşı appears to be a maze, its 60 streets are laid out more or less on a grid plan, the center of which is the İç Bedesten (Central Bedesten), also called the Old Bedesten or the Cevahir Çarşısı (Jewelry Bazaar). A number of *han*s (inns) with inner courtyards are entered through the Kapalıçarşı: one such inn is the Zincirli Han off Acıçeşme Sokağı. Several smaller markets have been added to the covered area, including the Sandal Bedesteni, a place specializing originally in textiles, particularly silks. (The Sandal Bedesteni, perhaps the oldest part of the Covered Bazaar, was begun in 1457.) This became an auction room in 1914, by which time European mills had drained off much of the market for Turkish textiles; in 1988 the interior was refurbished. New stalls have been opened and the rug auction discontinued.

The bazaar is generally organized according to the areas occupied by the early guilds: The goldsmiths are mostly between the Mahmutpaşa and Nuruosmaniye gates; the rug and carpet merchants cluster around the Old Bedesten; the row of dry-goods shops is near the Örücü Kapısı (Gate of the

Knitters). Of course, the character of many of the bazaar's streets—and the merchandise available—has changed over the past four centuries: Guilds such as the fez-makers, quilt-makers, and slipper-makers survive only in the street names.

Furniture, leather goods, tourist trinkets, foam rubber, alabaster and onyx, shoes, *karagöz* shadow-play puppets, authentic and reproduction antiquities, and jewelry ranging in value from nearly nothing to a king's ransom can be found here by the eager, canny shopper. Though a working market, the Covered Bazaar seems more like a museum to many tourists, for whom the leisurely bargaining, the hospitality of cups of coffee or tea (including a delicious apple-flavored tea), and the quick banter of the shopkeepers make it fascinatingly "Oriental."

The **İç Bedesten** may predate the market surrounding it. It is a very solid structure, the roof of which consists of fifteen double domes that rest on the four walls and eight large pillars. Its shops are considered to be simple "cupboards" (*dolaps*); originally the merchandise was laid out on platforms, while the rest of the stock was kept in the cupboards behind the merchant, who sat cross-legged on the counter displaying his wares. At night, when the shoppers have been locked out of the bazaar, the place is patrolled by dogs, which are kenneled during the day on the roof.

(For information on shopping in the Covered Bazaar, see Shops and Shopping, below.)

Between the southwest corner of the Kapalıçarşı and the Bayezit Camii and at the east end of a street (Lekeciler Sokağı) of copper sellers is the **Sahaflar Çarşısı** (market of secondhand-book sellers). Vine-shaded in summer, always crowded, it is the place of first resort when looking for any book in any language and of any date (also see Shops and Shopping, below).

Instead of tracing your steps down Uzunçarşı, you can walk back to Eminönü and the Golden Horn via Mahmut-paşa Yokuşu (*yokuş* means slope). The merchants on this street specialize in clothing, particularly garments carrying name-brand labels.

The Golden Horn

The Golden Horn, one of the boundaries of the old, walled city, is an estuary shaped, roughly, like a cornucopia. Two almost insignificant streams empty into it at its western end. It separates the old city, to the south, from the newer city, which extends ever farther upward on the northern side of the Horn.

One explanation of the channel's name is that the sunset reflecting off its waters makes them sparkle like gold. Another is that the muck at its bottom is incalculably valuable because of the treasures that people have thrown into it to avoid enriching invading armies. Several foreign companies have offered to dredge the Horn for no payment other than being allowed to keep what they find; so far no one has been granted that franchise. (In Turkish, the Golden Horn is known by the less poetic name Haliç, "estuary.")

In years long past the oysters from the Horn were choice delicacies; people apparently immune to typhoid, jaundice, dysentery, and/or cholera still fish off the bridges. On good days enterprising cooks offer a quick-order supply of grilled fish out of rowboats tied to the Eminönü quay, but high levels of coliform bacteria found recently in the Horn should dissuade you from sampling this fare.

Almost nothing is left of the Byzantine seawall along the Golden Horn, although between the Atatürk bridge and Ayvansaray yon can still see short, exposed sections of it. One tower—**Zindankapı**—a dungeon-prison from the time of the Byzantines until 1872, was left standing in the Golden Horn beautification program of the mid-1980s, during which many of this quarter's old structures were razed. You can see it about 200 yards up the street from the Galata Bridge (you cannot enter, however).

An ancient custom that has been maintained up to today is that of the small-boat traffic plying the Golden Horn. Until about 30 years ago these were rowboats, propelled at times by a man standing erect in the stern; now open motorboats cross back and forth from just below the Zindan tower to the Galata side. When the stench of the Horn is not overpowering, a crossing as the sun is setting behind the Süleymaniye mosque can transform a day that had seemed unsalvageable.

Other larger but less romantic ferries zigzag up and down the Horn on a regular schedule between the Chamber of Commerce building and Eyüp, with stops along the way at Kasımpaşa, Fener, Balat, Hasköy, Sütlüce, and Ayvansaray. This line also includes service between Kasımpaşa and Üsküdar across the Bosphorus.

Süleymaniye Camii

The 16th-century Süleymaniye Camii (mosque of Süleyman the Magnificent) is supreme among the mosques of Istanbul and the masterwork of the great Ottoman architect Sinan. For Turkish Muslims, the Süleymaniye exercises a religious and aesthetic appeal similar to that exerted on Western

Christians by certain sculptures of Michelangelo or the orato-
rios of Bach.

Before going on to discuss some of the notable features of
this marvelous complex, however, it may be worthwhile to
discuss the basic structure of most Turkish mosques.

ABOUT MOSQUES

Islam originated on the Arabian peninsula. Muhammad, the
religion's founder, was born in Mecca, Islam's holiest city,
and mosques throughout the world are all oriented so that
worshipers, when praying, face Mecca. The *mihrap* in the
front interior wall (*kıble*) of the mosque indicates the direction of the holy city. As Islam began in a region where the
climate is hot and dry year round, the earliest mosques were
walled areas with porticoes for shade on one or more sides.
The primary portico on the *kıble* side contained the *mihrap*.
Later architectural sophistications led to a large basilical or
columned hall along the *kıble* with a domed or arched
eyvan over the space before the *mihrap*. In Turkey's more
temperate clime, the interior space expanded to become the
primary congregational area, with the courtyard becoming
simply a forecourt.

The Turks were expert adapters of other architectural
traditions, particularly Byzantine church architecture. Turkish
mosque architecture, in turn, was widely influential throughout the Muslim world. (The Turkish word for mosque is *cami*
[JA-mee], the same as the word for "assembly." Turkish words
for the various elements of the mosque and other Islamic
religious terms are used throughout this guidebook.)

Inside almost every mosque there is an Arabic inscription
over the *mihrap;* the inscription is nearly always from the
third *sura* (chapter) of the Koran, reminding worshipers
that in this sanctuary God will provide for everyone. The
minber rises to the right of the *mihrap*. The banisters shield-
ing the risers of the *minber* are often made of intricately
carved wood or marble. At the Friday noon prayer the *imam*
(preacher) delivers the sermon from the steps of the *minber*. The *imam* is not a priest or pastor in the Christian sense;
in Islam the belief is that each person may address God
directly—there is no need for an intercessor.

Near the center of the room is a raised platform (*müezzin
mahfili*), on which chanters sit. It is most commonly used
when a *mevlût* (recitation of the Birth Song of the Prophet)
is celebrated, often to commemorate a person who has died
or to mark other significant events. The *mevlût* is also part of
the service on the Night of Power (the night of the 27th day
of Ramazan), the occasion when Muslims commemorate the

revelation of the Koran to Muhammad. Many, many people attend the service, which begins with the evening prayer and continues long into the night. Across from the *müezzin mahfili* on the east side of the mosque is the raised *kursu* (*imam*'s seat), used on ordinary days.

Besides the many Arabic inscriptions that may decorate the mosque's walls, the interior often contains eight round name-plaques, hung at regular intervals around the mosque. To the right of the *mihrap* is the name of God; to the left is that of the Prophet Muhammad. The other plaques carry the names of Ebu Bekir, Ali, Ömer, and Osman (the first four caliphs), and Hasan and Hüseyin (the martyred sons of Ali). A long inscription from the Koran may encircle the building as a stringcourse just below the upper windows. The *mihrap* may be highlighted with tiles of floral or geometric patterns. (Representational art does not appear in a mosque.) The lower windows are usually clear, but the upper windows often have patterns of stained glass set in plaster (not lead). Both the outer doors and the window shutters may be carved with geometric patterns.

Originally mosques were illuminated by oil lamps. Now they are lit with electricity, but the large cast-iron hoops that carry the glass cups still create the effect of a ceiling of lacework. Süleymaniye and a few other mosques have huge beeswax candles flanking the *mihrap*. (They are no longer lit.) In other mosques these have been replaced by wooden candles capped with electric lights.

Muslims are not supposed to enter a mosque until they are ritually clean. The ablution fountain (*şadırvan*) beside the mosque or in its courtyard is for the men to wash their feet, hands, arms, and faces. Women worshipers must wash at home before attending. The floor of the mosque is covered with reed mats or rugs. Everyone—tourists, too—must remove their shoes when entering a mosque. (There is sometimes a rack just outside or inside the door where shoes can be left.) In some mosques the rugs are all the same and have been woven to mark individual worshipers' places; in others the rugs differ, each a gift from an individual donor.

For a Muslim, the ceremony of prayer (*namaz*) consists first of the announcement of intent and the statement of belief; there are several prescribed postures (bowing, kneeling) and at least one recital of a chapter of the Koran. If a prayer is interrupted (for instance, by an uninstructed tourist walking in front of a worshiper), it must be started again. While Islam prescribes only that the place of prayer be clean and although Muslims may say their prayers alone, prayers with a congregation in a mosque are considered more efficacious.

In the imperial mosques, the sultan's loge was usually in the balcony to the left of the *mihrap*. Although the loge separated the sultan from the public, and in later mosques allowed him to approach through his private pavilion, such areas were not equipped with any special furnishings.

Convention, now breaking down, dictated that only imperial mosques were entitled to have more than one minaret. The Süleymaniye has four. From the balcony of the minaret the muezzin gives the *ezan* (call to prayer), albeit now with the help of a loudspeaker (some mosques have dispensed with live muezzins and use tape-recorded chants).

A *külliye* (complex) usually includes the mosque itself, one or more *türbe*s (mausoleums), a *medrese* (school of Islamic law), and possibly other social-service facilities such as an *imaret* (public kitchen serving regular meals to the poor of the area), a *hamam* (bath), a hospital, a hospice or a caravansary, and a room for the timekeeper, who determined the hours of prayer and recorded the moment when the first sliver of the moon was seen, marking the new month. Many mosques are supported by the income from markets in or near the *külliye* or from other properties. (The loot from Süleyman's victories in Belgrade, Rhodes, and Baghdad helped pay for building this mosque. Caravansaries in Konya and elsewhere contributed to the costs of running Rüstem Paşa's mosque in Istanbul.)

The Süleymaniye mosque complex sits on a hilltop approximately in the center of the old city (follow the winding streets west—and up—from Eminönü square). Sinan sited and organized the complex so as to compose an architectural totality that culminated in the place of prayer.

Over the main entrance to the mosque is inscribed the following sentence from the Koran: "O Lord who opens all doors, open the door of felicity." The aesthetic felicity produced by the complex's many domes rising to the central height is undergirded by the symmetry of the structure's measurements. The central floor space of the mosque is half the total; the height of the dome is twice that of its diameter. These dimensions architecturally reaffirm the Muslim concepts of the centrality and unity of God. Sinan, the architect, was a geometrician, and thought of pure mathematics as a divine science. The structure's near-perfect balance has protected it against damage from the earthquakes that have occasionally shaken Istanbul.

According to the *Tezkiret ül-Bünyan* (the register of buildings attributed to Sinan), the inscriptions in this mosque "were traced by the greatest calligraphers of the day and were translated into stone by skilled masons and decorators in order that a page might remain from time, which passes as the wind."

In addition to its theological purpose, Süleyman conceived of his mosque as his political statement of the power of the Ottoman Empire. While the whole complex was not finished at once, the mosque itself took only a little longer to build than did St. Sophia, having been started in 1550 and completed in 1557.

Part of the greatness of the building is reflected in the number of legends that have become attached to it. One of them concerns an insult that a neighboring potentate directed at Sultan Süleyman. The potentate sent Süleyman a camel caravan of jewels with a letter saying that he was pleased to hear of the plans for a royal mosque but that since he was concerned that Süleyman might not have sufficient resources to complete it he wanted to contribute this gift. Süleyman accepted the jewels and returned the message that he had found the right place to use them: To make sure they would always sparkle in the sun he had had them ground up and mixed into the mortar for one of the mosque's minarets.

Other sources of building materials were closer to hand: Columns in the courtyard are supposed to have come from the Hippodrome; some columns inside were once in the ruined church of St. Euphemia in Kadıköy.

The *türbe* of Süleyman is in the yard just south of the mosque (open 9:30 A.M. to 4:30 P.M., except Mondays and Tuesdays). That of his wife Hürrem (Roxelana) is next to his, but never open. At a time when women were thought to exist only for men's gratification, this woman demanded and received enduring respect and love from the most powerful man of the time. If it was regrettable for the continuing growth of Ottoman power that Hürrem succeeded in her plot to discredit the most obviously able of Süleyman's sons, it's still possible to sympathize with a mother concerned that her own son survive his father's death and take his father's place.

Under Süleyman, the empire grew fabulously wealthy, and art flowered under the stimulus of his successes. But while in the West his name is coupled with magnificence, in Turkey he is known, like his namesake Solomon, as the Lawgiver. He himself considered his codes so important that he had a copy of them buried with him in his mausoleum.

Today, the Süleymaniye library contains one of the most important collections of medieval Arabic manuscripts in the world.

The architect Sinan is buried a short distance away from Süleyman and Hürrem in a more modest setting just within the northern end of the complex. Sinan was the chief court architect for Süleyman and his successors, Selim II and Murat III. Sinan's genius brought the expression of classical Ottoman architecture to a climax. In charge of the palace corps of architects for 50 years (1538 to 1588), Sinan is credited with at least 477 projects scattered from Mecca to Hungary and ranging from the transport carriers he is said to have built for the army at Lake Van to the imperial mosques of Istanbul. He also worked as a laborer on his own buildings—which may be one of the reasons they are of such greatness.

Fener

The area along the Golden Horn west of the Süleymaniye Camii and stretching to the Theodosian land walls contains some of Istanbul's oldest—and poorest—neighborhoods. Walking tours through their winding streets can be immensely rewarding: More of the old survives here than in most other areas of the city, albeit in ramshackle, dilapidated condition. But strolling through these neighborhoods can also be slightly dangerous. The rate of serious crime in Istanbul is insignificant as compared, for instance, with many large cities in the United States. Still, if you venture out into Unkapanı or Fener, don't go alone, be sensitive to the fact that as a foreigner you will stand out, and be wary of the various scams cooked up by some of the city's more desperate inhabitants to relieve you of your wallet. Don't be disarmed if you're suddenly surrounded by a horde of small children, all shouting, "Hello, good-bye! Hello, good-bye!" Most such encounters are innocuous, but it's wise not to let your guard down. The urchins, however, can be excellent, if informal, sources of information about the area, having poked into more holes than scholars have dreamed of.

Fener is particularly fascinating: The comparatively large number of old wooden houses, despite their decrepitude, gives you some idea of how Istanbul must have looked in the 19th century. The neighborhood is also the location of the **Greek Orthodox Patriarchate**. The ecumenical patriarch, who lives in this compound, is "first among equals" among the heads of the Eastern Orthodox church—a position roughly equivalent to that held by the pope in Roman Catholicism.

The patriarchate has been in this location since about 1600; today's patriarchal **church of St. George**—an unimposing building but one whose sumptuous interior makes it worth a peek inside—dates from 1720 (open 7:00 A.M. to 5:00 P.M. daily; Sunday service at 9:00 A.M.). Some say that the patriarchal throne in the church's apse has been preserved since the time of John Chrysostom, who was patriarch from 398 to 404. Much of the patriarchate's compound was destroyed by fire in the 1940s; a few years ago the patriarch was given permission by the Turkish government to rebuild, and the living quarters and conference facilities have been exactingly re-created imitating classic Ottoman style.

A slate-gray **Bulgarian Orthodox church** in Fener contrasts with the many brown stone and brick churches of the city. It stands alone in the park along the Golden Horn, an unmistakably different kind of structure. According to the story, the Bulgarian community was given permission to build its church in 1871 on the condition that the congregation could construct it within one week. Undaunted by this restriction, they had the walls cast in iron in Vienna, floated down the Danube and on to Istanbul, where they were bolted together in ample time to meet the challenge. The church has a caretaker (*bekçi*); if you'd like to see the interior, look for him in the neighborhood so that he can let you in. Services are still held in the church, once a month.

St. Savior in Chora

Farther west, near the Edirne Gate (Edirnekapı) and just inside the fifth-century land walls that defined the western extent of the Byzantine city, is the church of St. Savior in Chora (**Kariye Camii**; open 9:30 A.M. to 4:30 P.M., except Tuesday). The ruins of the late Byzantine palace of the Porphyrogenitus—known as Tekfur Sarayı—are also nearby (see A Tour of the City Walls, next). To get there, take a bus or *dolmuş* marked Edirnekapı, ride to the end, then—staying inside the city walls—walk about four blocks north.

Even if nothing else remained of Byzantine Constantinople, St. Savior in Chora, like St. Sophia, would alone be enough to justify Byzantium's reputation as a center of learning, artistry, and culture. The church is famous for its superb early 14th-century mosaics and frescoes.

After the fall of Constantinople, the church was made a mosque by the grand vizier Atik Ali Paşa, who held office from 1495 to 1511. Some of the mural decorations were painted or whitewashed over in the 15th century. Others were later damaged by weather and by earthquakes. In the late 18th century the Ottoman government became interested in preserving the church because of its art, but the real work of cleaning and restoration happened in the 1950s under the direction of the Byzantine Institute of America.

We can gather some idea of how long a church has stood on this site from the church's name: In Greek, *chora* means a woods outside the city proper. The first church built here probably dated to before the seventh century; the monastery, no longer extant, that was associated with it may have gone back to the time of Justinian. It was in this refuge that Theodore Metochites, the man who is responsible for the building as we see it now, spent his last days. His portrait, with his wildly flaring hat, at the right of the entrance to the nave shows him in the dress appropriate to his position as the grand *logothete* (prime minister) of 14th-century Byzantium.

Metochites became rich during his years in office, and using both his money and his scholarship, he set about restoring the church of the monastery of Chora, which had been despoiled during the Latin occupation. Work on the church began about 1316; it was dedicated in 1321.

Metochites intended the arrangement of the scenes in the mosaics of the outer narthex (which you step into as you enter the building) to parallel those of the inner narthex. Thus, the birth of Jesus, which you see ahead and to your left in the outer narthex, is echoed in the inner narthex with a scene of the birth of the Virgin Mary. On the north wall of the outer narthex is a depiction of Joseph dreaming; on the same wall of the inner narthex is a scene of Mary's father, Joachim, praying for a child. The similar scenes can confuse you if you don't realize that two stories are being told. In both, Christ's royal ancestry and the prophecies concerning his coming and his message to the world are central themes. Those same themes are expressed in the frescoes of the parekklesion, or side chapel, which was used as a mortuary chapel. The names of the artists are not known; scholars assume that one person was responsible for the masterful portrayals in both the mosaics and the frescoes, while that artist's assistants carried out the lesser details.

When you go to St. Savior, take your binoculars so you can get a close-up view of facial and other details. The story told in the church's mosaics is taken from the New Testament, supplemented by several apocryphal books—the Gospel of James, the Pseudo-Matthew, and the Nativity of Mary. The cycle of the life of the Virgin begins in the first three bays of the narthex: An angel appears to Mary's father, Joachim, promising him a daughter; God announces to Mary's mother, Anne, that her child will be known around the world. Anne's prayers are represented in the picture of a mother bird feeding the fledglings in her nest.

Mary's tender fondness for her parents is visible in a scene in which she is shown sitting on Joachim's lap and caressing Anne's face. The peacocks in the pendentives on either side of this mosaic are balanced by two pheasants in the next scene, in which Mary is presented at the Temple. From the time that Mary began living in the Temple she was fed by an angel, who also came to teach her. Her residence there lasted until she reached puberty.

A panel in the soffit of the arch between the second and third bays shows how Mary's husband was selected. The high priest, Zacharias, gathered together the widowers of the city and laid their rods on the altar. The rod of Joseph miraculously sprouted leaves, and Joseph, who, the story says, was a reluctant suitor, hurried Mary off. Her skirts are shown flapping around her legs, and Joseph seems to be straining to look behind him to make sure she is following properly.

Joseph then took a job that required him to go away. While Joseph was gone the priests decided that a new veil needed to be woven for the Temple. They called all the virgins to cast lots for the color of wool with which each was to work. Mary won the royal purple, and the expressions of the other girls show their jealousy and chagrin.

The annunciation of God's favor to Mary came while she was drawing a pitcher of water. The scene, portrayed in the southwestern pendentive of the dome in the first bay, shows her with one foot lifted off the ground as if the voice had made her jump in surprise. The annunciation was, however, followed by a misunderstanding: As a scene in the west lunette of the first bay shows, when Joseph returned from his time away he was ashamed to find that Mary was pregnant. Both were tried before the priest on a charge of adultery, and both were vindicated.

From here on the story follows the events recorded in the Bible but also includes the death of Mary (above the central door in the nave), when all the apostles, living and dead, came to be at her bedside.

The frescoes in the side chapel (probably a mortuary chapel) continue the theme of the Virgin Mary's importance in resurrection, judgment, and salvation. In contrast to other medieval scenes of resurrection, in which only Adam is pictured, the artist in St. Savior not only pictured Christ saving Adam (mankind) from the grave but also gave Eve (Mary, womankind) equal value.

The human touches visible in the mosaics (for example, the servant girl shown testing the bathwater of the baby Mary to see if it is the right temperature) can also be found in the frescoes. In the depiction of the Last Judgment, in the line of condemned souls being pulled into the fiery lake by a small black devil, one person is looking regretfully back at the scales where his deeds were weighed and another is offering his neighbor the chance to go first.

According to Metochites' plan, four Old Testament scenes in the western dome and bay of the side chapel symbolically prefigure Mary. Jacob (with his ladder to heaven) was the father of the chosen people; Mary, one of his descendants, was the one through whom the Messiah came. Moses' bush, which burned but was not consumed, represented Mary, because although she gave birth she remained a virgin. Solomon's temple as the dwelling place of God paralleled Mary, who contained the uncontainable. The angel who protected Jerusalem from being invaded (in the book of Isaiah) was like the inviolate Virgin.

By framing the scenes, the structural elements of the building—the arches and domes—increase the dramatic qualities of each picture. The scenes were, in general, conventionally drawn; books of illustrations of religious scenes were available at the time, and Byzantine artists frequently used these as cartoons to sketch out a painting. Thus many similarities can be seen among paintings done by 13th- and 14th-century Italian, Slavic, Greek, and Constantinopolitan artists.

In Byzantine church painting, scenes are often arranged to be read like a book: Within a single frame are found developments of the story. John's baptism of Christ and Christ's temptations are shown together in the vault immediately to the left in the outer narthex. (The Devil's hair looks as if it is being blown away by the force of Christ's "Get thee behind me, Satan!") When Mary appears in a scene she is accompanied by a knobby stick (Joseph's rod) that has returned to life with new leaves. The characterizations of saints Paul and Peter are consistent throughout the building.

Some realistic touches lighten the seriousness of the side chapel. Each of the faces—whether of angel, apostle, or warrior—is a portrait of an individual. Two warriors are wearing only one shoe each, and the sheep in Moses's flock are eating the twigs of the burning bush to show that they are not touched by its flames.

Metochites had a reputation for venality and overweening egotism, but above and beyond his faults stands his gift to Byzantine art. The genius of the unknown artist who painted these frescoes shines in the power, glory, and mystery in the expression on the face of the risen Christ above the apse of the side chapel.

A Tour of the
City Walls

Istanbul, like most early strategic cities, was conceived as a castellated fortress. Probably little or nothing is left of the land wall that the Emperor Septimius Severus built about A.D. 200; it may have been worked into the foundation of the Hippodrome, which he also built and which Constantine greatly enlarged. But many of the walls and towers that successive emperors constructed, repaired, and continued to add to, enclosing more and more land, are extant. The walls can be traced with a very long day's tramp that would encompass the old city. In the following description we start at the walls along the Golden Horn, cross the western limits of the old city with the land walls, and return via the Marmara seawalls, pausing for a few detours along the way.

The **seawalls** along the Golden Horn were the last of the city walls to be completed, because for centuries the emperors thought that the iron chain stretching across the estuary at the mouth of the Horn was sufficient to protect the city from invaders approaching by water. The walls were built as close to the water as possible; their distance from the water today shows how narrow the Horn has become over time.

The walls were twice attacked by military invaders. In 1204 the Crusaders ran their ships so close that they were able to lean their scaling ladders against the walls and thus surmount them. The second attack came when the fleet of Sultan Mehmet II surprised the Byzantines on April 25, 1453. The demoralized, beleaguered citizens awoke to find that enemy ships were riding on their "inland sea."

One other—perhaps the most destructive—"attack" on the walls occurred in the spring of 763 near the Seraglio point following an unusually severe winter. Spring ice floes from the Black Sea had packed the Bosphorus from Üsküdar to Galata and up the Golden Horn as far as Blachernae. As the floes broke up, two icebergs, so large that they over-topped the walls, dashed against the shore, shaking the entire neighborhood and destroying a large section of the defenses.

Near the western end of the Golden Horn the seawalls met those of the land in Ayvansaray. Here stood the **palace of the Porphyrogenitus** (Tekfur Sarayı) and the **palace of Blachernae** (Ayvan Sarayı, or Anemas Zindanları). Standing so close to one another, the two palaces were probably part of the same complex. The first imperial residences were built here about A.D. 500; under the Comnenis (11th and 12th centuries) Blachernae became the seat of government, eclipsing the importance of the Great Palace on the Seraglio Point. The Latin emperors of Constantinople (1204–1261) held court here. On his restoration of the Byzantine government, Michael Paleologus abandoned the Great Palace completely. It was from Blachernae that the last Byzantine emperor, Constantine XI, left to meet the challenge of Mehmet the Conqueror in 1453. While Blachernae is easier to view from just outside the walls, Tekfur Sarayı is easier to explore starting from Edirnekapı or Kariye Camii (St. Savior in Chora, see above). Tekfur Sarayı is today just the shell of a building; Blachernae's outlines aren't even that clearly defined.

One of the two towers of Blachernae is identified with Michael Anemas, an insurgent who plotted to overthrow Emperor Alexius I Comnenus. (Walk through the courtyard of the İvaz Efendi Camii to find the cement steps down into the base of the tower that was most likely Anemas's; note that you must procure the key from someone at the İvaz Efendi mosque.) Caught and condemned to be blinded, Anemas had his beard plucked out and his head shorn, and, crowned with sheep's horns and intestines, he was paraded around the palace and then up the main street of the city. The emperor's daughter, Anna Comnena, saw him, called her mother's attention to his misery, and together they intervened to save his eyes. He was imprisoned in the tower for a while, but unlike a few later emperors, who were brutally punished there, he was eventually freed.

By starting at the western corner of Blachernae, near the Golden Horn, you can climb around the seventh-century land walls built by Emperor Heraclius and the ninth-century additions of Leo V.

The district of **Eyüp** begins northwest of Blachernae outside the walls. It is named for the Muslim holy man Eyüp Ensari. (Buses and dolmuşes from Eminönü go to Eyüp; Eyüp Sultan Camii is about a mile from the walls.) Eyüp Ensari was a companion and the standard-bearer of the Prophet Muhammad. He was with the Arab forces that attacked Constantinople in the seventh century; he died when the army was encamped in this region, and was buried here. His tomb was rediscovered in 1458, after the conquest of Constantinople by the Ottomans.

The place of Eyüp's burial and Eyüp Sultan Camii, the mosque connected with it, comprise the fourth most holy place of pilgrimage for Muslims, after Mecca, Medina, and Jerusalem. The complex, which also includes a functioning hamam, is located somewhat away from the water and at the foot of a small hill. It was here that the Ottoman sultans were girded with the sword of Osman, a ceremony equivalent to the crowning of a king. Many, many valuable offerings have enriched the complex, including brass railings for the window of the mausoleum given by Sultan Selim III, embroidery on the covering of the catafalque donated by Sultan Mahmut II, and carpeting to cover the entire floor of the mosque given by the late Turkish prime minister Adnan Menderes in gratitude for having escaped unscathed from a plane crash in 1959.

Other buildings in Eyüp that interest Ottoman historians include two mosques (Zal Mahmut Paşa Camii and Defterdar Mahmut Efendi Camii, both Sinan works), the *türbe* of early 20th-century sultan Mehmet V, and the graves of a number of grand viziers, including Sokollu Mehmet Paşa.

Near the Golden Horn, a low, square building known as the **Feshane** (fez factory) has been renovated by architect Gae Aulenti to become the **İstanbul Büyükşehir Belediyesi Nejat Eczacıbaşı Çağdaş Sanat Müzesi** (Greater Istanbul Nejat Eczacıbaşı Contemporary Art Museum). Named for Turkey's great patron of the contemporary arts, the museum has a permanent collection that includes the works of modern Turkish artists. The new museum will provide the setting for the next Istanbul Biennial, scheduled for fall 1994.

An extensive **cemetery** stretches up the hill behind the Eyüp mosque complex, a desirable place for those who wish to be buried within hearing of the call to prayer from the minarets of the Eyüp mosque. At the top of the hill is the **Piyerloti Kahvehanesi** (Pierre Loti Coffee House; open 8:00 A.M. to midnight), where Loti, the 19th-century French novelist, sat and composed his sweetly poignant books *Aziyadé* and *Les Désenchantées* about the women of Istanbul. The present-day coffee house, much improved over its 19th-century predecessor, is a quiet place to pause and ruminate about the city.

Built largely by the Emperor Theodosius II in the fifth century, the **land walls** consisted of three parts: a high inner wall interrupted by 96 towers at fairly regular intervals; an outer wall, also with 96 towers located between those of the inner wall; and a deep, wide moat outside the wall. Wars, earthquakes, and city developers have caused the walls' present tumbledown condition. A recent project to restore them has been aborted, but in a few places new masonry provides a glimpse of how the walls once looked.

Between Blachernae on the Golden Horn and Yedikule near the Sea of Marmara—a stretch of about four miles—the land walls are pierced at irregular intervals by gates. A squeeze even for pedestrian traffic, the Edirne and Fifth Military gates have been changed very little over the years. The Eğri, Fourth Military, Silivri, and Yedikule gates are also about as they were; now they are used by cars, but traffic through them moves with difficulty. The Belgrade gate has been handsomely rebuilt; the Topkapı gate is marked by a marble plaque commemorating the Ottoman soldiers who overcame the Byzantine defenders here in 1453. Two broad avenues—Adnan Menderes (a.k.a. Vatan) and Millet—have been driven through the walls and are now jammed with traffic every workday.

A memorial to Adnan Menderes, prime minister of Turkey from 1950 to 1960, stands just outside the old walls and above Adnan Menderes Caddesi. Menderes was overthrown in a military coup in May 1960 and then tried for treason along with the entire National Assembly. He and two members of his cabinet were executed in 1961, but in recent years his memory has been rehabilitated.

Four mosques in the vicinity of the walls are of more than passing interest. **Mihrimah Camii** (near Edirnekapı) was founded by Sultan Süleyman's daughter. The **Kara Ahmet Paşa Camii** near the Topkapı gate and **Hadım İbrahim Paşa Camii** near the Silivri gate were built by two of Süleyman's grand viziers. These three are all Sinan buildings. About a quarter of a mile down the road that leads away from the city opposite the Topkapı gate is the late 16th-century wooden **Takkeci** ("felt-hat maker") **İbrahim Ağa Camii**. Among the decorations in it are some beautiful İznik tiles.

Outside the walls, south of the Topkapı gate, intercity and international traffic crowds the noisy, large, and very active Topkapı bus terminal.

Yedikule (the Castle of the Seven Towers, open 9:30 A.M. to 5:00 P.M., except Monday), almost at the edge of the Sea of Marmara, was given its fortress-like character by Sultan Mehmet II when he added the three inside towers in 1457. Previously there had been four towers, which defended the Golden Gate (see below). Yedikule got much of its notoriety as a prison for European ambassadors: Russians, French, Germans, and Venetians were shut up here, some of them cutting their names into the stone walls inside the East

Tower, also called **Kitabe Kulesi** (Tower of the Inscriptions). It was also here, in the South Pylon of the Golden Gate, that the janissaries executed Sultan Osman II in 1622.

The **Altın Kapı** (Golden Gate) was the Byzantine emperor's triumphal arch, first erected by Theodosius I toward the end of the fourth century. It was decorated by a number of statues, including a group of bronze elephants and a Roman eagle. Only victorious emperors and occasional distinguished visitors entered the city through the Golden Gate. The last emperor to do so was Michael IX Palaeologus, who recaptured Constantinople from the Latins in 1261.

A short distance east of Yedikule and about a block south of Samatya Caddesi is the oldest of the Byzantine church buildings still standing: **St. John the Baptist of Studius**, or the Studion, a basilica built in 463 by the Roman nobleman Studius. (In Turkish the Studion is known as İmrahor İlyasbey Camii.) The monastery connected with the church was built slightly later. The monks of the Studion lived under the Rule of St. Basil. Not allowed to feel sorry for themselves, they followed a vegetarian diet, softened by the allowance of two or three glasses of wine a day. No females—not even egg-laying hens—were allowed near. If a monk kissed his mother, no matter what the occasion, he was excommunicated for 50 days.

The monastery's thousand-year history continued for a while after the Turkish conquest, but by the end of the 15th century the church building was converted into a mosque. After its roof collapsed in 1910, it was abandoned.

Moving northeast toward the city, you will see the modern Sosyal Sigorta Hastanesi (Social Insurance Hospital), which dominates the skyline between Yedikule and Yenikapı. Yenikapı is the landing for the *deniz otobüsü* (sea bus, or hydrofoil) that connects Istanbul with the islands of Marmara and Avşa in the Sea of Marmara. Also at this crossroads is the **Gar Müzikhol**—one of the large, better restaurants where you can find a good floor show in the evening.

A number of fish restaurants are located in the district of **Kumkapı** along the Marmara here and in Kumkapı square, which has been turned into a pedestrian mall.

Between Yenikapı and Kumkapı is the Armenian Orthodox Patriarchate (on Şarapnel Sokak). The patriarchal church, **Surp Astvadzadzin** (named for the Holy Mother of God), is a relatively recent building, dating from 1913; the patriarch was recognized from the time of Sultan Mehmet II in 1461 as the religious head of the Armenian Orthodox *millet* (nation). Sunday service begins at 9:00 A.M.

As you reach the bend that leads to the Seraglio point you

will find, near the wall and just a few blocks south of the Blue Mosque, **Küçük Ayasofya Camii** (Little St. Sophia, also called the church of SS Sergius and Bacchus). It was begun by Justinian and Theodora in 527; those of their monograms that have not been defaced grace the capitals of columns in the nave. It was the first of Justinian's buildings, built to partially fulfill his vow to honor those saints who had interceded for him in a dream of his predecessor, Emperor Anastasius, who was about to execute him for treason.

Most of the similarities that have caused Küçük Ayasofya to be compared with the Great Church are superficial: Both have capitals with deeply incised monograms of the emperor and empress, both have Rorschach-like marble revetment, both possess an arcaded gallery, and both use paired columns beneath the semidomes. And, of course, both churches were founded by Justinian and Theodora. This church (now a mosque) is, however, the more human in scale and is actually much more comparable (in design, not decoration) to San Vitale in Ravenna, Italy, also built by Justinian. It is architecturally significant because of its ribbed dome, the (crooked) octagon inscribed in a square, and the delicately carved frieze of the architrave—all successful building experiments of the early sixth century. (The distortion in alignment is more noticeable in a floor plan than when you're actually viewing the building's interior; the differing distances of the eight pillars are visually insignificant.)

A short walk north from Küçük Ayasofya is **Sokollu Mehmet Paşa Camii.** Although this mosque carries the grand vizier's name, it was actually built by his wife, İsmihan Sultan, the daughter of Selim II. The design of the mosque is worthy of its architect, Sinan. Around the *mihrap* are beautiful turquoise-green 16th-century İznik tiles; above the door, the *mihrap,* and the *minber* are small bits of the black stone of the Kaaba in Mecca. "Penwork" style painted decorations embellish the lower surface of the wooden balcony to the right of the entrance.

On the seawalls beneath the Topkapı kitchens, running inscriptions in Greek identify Emperor Theophilus (829 to 842) as the man who built much of the walls after the destruction wrought by ice floes in 763. A section of Topkapı's land walls stretches up the hill not far from the Ahırkapı lighthouse (which was relocated closer to the palace treasury in the movie *Topkapi* in order to heighten the dramatic effect).

THE NEW CITY

The section of the city north of the Golden Horn between the Galata Bridge and the Atatürk Bridge was first known as Sykai ("fig-tree garden" in Greek) and then Galata (meaning uncertain). While the bridge retains the name Galata, the section is now more commonly called Karaköy. Like the old city, it was walled. The walls were extended five times between 1303 and 1453. Galata was originally a self-governing Genoese colony, and its population remained non-Turkish long after the conquest.

Foreign diplomats built their palaces beyond the last wall, north of Karaköy, in a place known as Pera (*pera* means "beyond" in Greek). They often headed their correspondence "among the vines of Pera," referring to the vineyards on the hill. Pera's name is now Beyoğlu—the son of the *bey,* or lord, perhaps after some then-famous but now-forgotten personage of the early 19th century, who may have been one of the first Turkish people to move into this newer city.

The bridges across the Golden Horn linking the new and old parts of European Istanbul are relatively new additions to the city. When the Horn served more as a defensive moat than as a commercial waterway, an easy crossing was not desired. The first bridge, a wooden one, was built by Bezmiâlem Sultan, mother of Sultan Abdülmecit, in 1845. It was a toll bridge and was closed at night. It was replaced in 1910 by a charming pontoon bridge. After several near-collapses, the 1910 bridge burned and was taken apart in May 1992. Work on the new **Galata Bridge**—which was even then under construction—was speeded up, and it opened to traffic a month later. Like its famous predecessor, it has a central section that is unhitched for an hour every morning at 4:00; that piece swings out to allow large ships into the drydocks just above the Atatürk Bridge (built in 1936 and also known as the Unkapanı bridge) a quarter of a mile upstream. Like the old, the new Galata Bridge will have shops on the lower level.

A short description of the main streets of the rest of the European part of the city may help in locating salient points. Until the divided highways and suspension bridges were built linking Europe with Asia across the Bosphorus, there were only two main roads running the length of the new part of the city north and south. One was along the winding coast; the other followed the crest of the hills. The placement of these streets determined how the city grew, particularly after World War II.

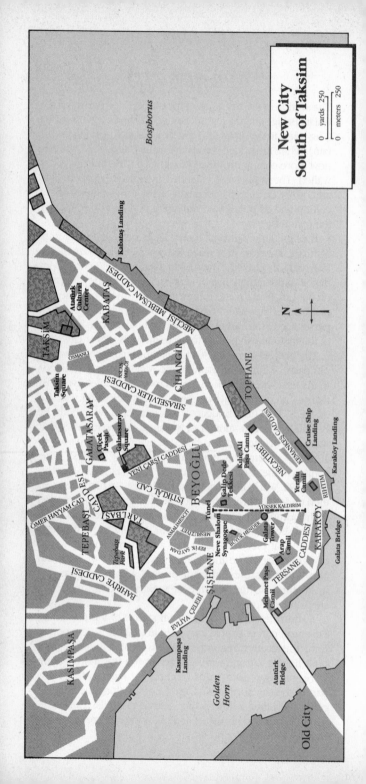

**New City
South of Taksim**

0   yards 250
0   meters 250

N

Bosphorus

Kabataş Landing

Atatürk Cultural Center

TAKSİM

KABATAŞ CADDESİ

MECLİSİ MEBUSAN CADDESİ

OSMANLI

Taksim Square

ASLAN YATAĞI

CİHANGİR

TOPHANE

GALATASARAY

SİRASELVİLER CADDESİ

İSTİKLÂL CADDESİ

Çiçek Pasajı

Galatasaray Square

YENİ ÇARŞI CADDESİ

BEYOĞLU

Galip Dede Tekkesi

Kılıç Ali Paşa Camii

Cruise Ship Landing

NECATIBEY

KEMANKEŞ CADDESİ

Karaköy Landing

Yeraltı Camii

ÖMER HAYYAM CAD.

TEPEBAŞI

TARLABAŞI

İSTİKLÂL CAD.

Tünel

YÜKSEK KALDIRIM

RIHTIM

CADDESİ

ASMALIMESCİT

REFİK SAYDAM

MEŞRUTİYET

Neve Shalom Synagogue

BÜYÜK HENDEK

Galata Tower

KARAKÖY

Galata Bridge

Tepebaşı Parkı

BAHRİYE CADDESİ

SİŞHANE

Arap Camii

TERSANE CADDESİ

EVLİYA ÇELEBİ

KASIMPAŞA

Mehmet Paşa Camii

Kasımpaşa Landing

Atatürk Bridge

Golden Horn

Old City

From Karaköy along the Bosphorus the sea road goes through what for convenience can be called the "lower" Bosphorus areas of Tophane, Kabataş, and Beşiktaş. Farther along this road, the "upper" Bosphorus districts include Ortaköy, Kuruçeşme, Arnavutköy, Bebek, Rumeli Hisarı, Emirgân, Yeniköy, Tarabya, Büyükdere, Sarıyer, and Rumeli Kavağı, among others.

Inland, the city expanded northward from Beyoğlu along İstiklâl Caddesi to Taksim, then along Cumhuriyet Caddesi to Harbiye, where it divided into Vali Konağı Caddesi, going to Nişantaşı, and Halâskârgazı Caddesi, leading to Osmanbey, Şişli, and Mecidiyeköy.

A boulevard, Barbaros Bulvarı, which goes up the hill from Beşiktaş, is a main connector between the sea road and the inland road. Where these meet it branches, with the north section going beyond Levent to Gültepe and Maslak and eventually joining the sea road at Büyükdere. The eastern section runs through Birinci Levent to Etiler, with streets connecting to the sea road at various points.

Karaköy

The **Galata Tower**, the most prominent building in Karaköy, was built as a watchtower for the Genoese community in the 14th century; it has been partly destroyed and rebuilt several times since then. (It is likely that there has been a tower in this location since the fifth century.) The present tower was at one time defended by a moat, one wall of which can still be seen at the tower's base. Still used as a fire tower, it has been renovated and contains a restaurant and nightclub (Galata Kulesi) on its top floors. There is a good view of the city from the balcony that encircles the restaurant. (There is a small charge to go up to the balcony, which is open from 9:00 A.M. to 9:00 P.M.)

The 17th-century observer Evliya Çelebi relates an account of a certain Hezârfen Ahmet Çelebi, who he says flew from the Galata Tower across the Bosphorus to Üsküdar. Sultan Murat IV watched the flight, granted the flyer a purse of gold, and then exiled him to Algiers, fearful of his considerable powers. (The distance between the Tower and Üsküdar is about two miles.)

Below the Galata Tower are several other buildings that recall the years when much of the commercial activity of Constantinople was in the hands of Venetian and Genoese merchants. One of the oldest of the buildings (the castle of the Holy Cross) is now **Yeraltı Camii** (Underground Mosque); its hard-to-find entrance is between the passenger ships and the ferry landings for Kadıköy. The famous iron chain that was stretched across the Golden Horn to protect the city from Arab invaders in 670 may have been attached to the castle. (A few pieces of that chain are now in the Harbiye military museum; see below.) The Muslim congregation gathers for prayers among the 54 square columns of the former castle's basement.

Close to the shore of the Horn, a little more than halfway between the Galata and Atatürk bridges, are the **Fatih Mehmet Bedesteni** and the **Rüstem Paşa Hanı**, places of business active since the 15th and 16th centuries. The han, built by Sinan, has an unusual arrangement, with a central staircase that begins in the courtyard and leads to both sides of the upper story.

A little farther up the Horn and across Tersane Caddesi, near the old market square of Galata (still enclosed by wrought-iron gates), is **Arap Camii** (Arab Mosque), its Italianate bell tower now a minaret. The date of the first building here is in doubt, but its location, like that of the Austrian **church of St. George** up the hill, may long ago have been a spring and a site of pagan worship. A marble pedestal beneath Arap Camii's minaret gives some credence to the identification of the site as once that of a temple to Aphrodite. Tradition says that the present building was originally a mosque built during one of the Arab attempts to conquer the city, hence its name. The Dominicans constructed its belfry about 1232; it was given as a mosque by Sultan Bayezit II to Moors who had fled from the Spanish Inquisition at the end of the 15th century.

A steep street (once a long flight of stone steps, hence its name Yüksek Kaldırım—"high steps") leads past Çerkezo, one of the city's best shops selling pork products. For those who don't relish the steep climb up Yüksek Kaldırım, there is the **Tünel**, reputedly the oldest—and certainly the shortest—subway in Europe. Built by French engineers in 1875, the Tünel offers a 90-second ride up the slope from just west of the Karaköy side of the Galata Bridge to the south end of İstiklâl Caddesi. At the crest of the hill, just below the beginning of İstiklâl, is the **Galip Dede Tekkesi** (also called the Divan Edebiyatı Müzesi; open 9:30 A.M. to 5:00 P.M., except Mondays), a museum of the Mevlevi dervish community. The Mevlevis (sometimes known as the Whirling Dervishes) are a Muslim mystical order founded by the poet/philosopher Mevlâna Celalettin el Rumi, who died in Konya in Central Anatolia in 1273. While the main observance of Mevlâna's death takes place in Konya the second week of December, the *sema töreni* (whirling dance) is performed occasionally in

this museum, once the order's lodge. There are also performances of the *sema* during the International Istanbul Festival
each summer. (For more on the Whirling Dervishes, see the
chapter on Central Anatolia, below).

Between Şişhane square and the Galata Tower on Büyük
Hendek Sokak is the **Neve Shalom synagogue**, an example
of the hospice offered by Sultan Bayezit II to refugees from
Spain. In painful contrast to that welcome and the 500 years
during which the Jewish community has lived peaceably in
Turkey, there was a terrorist attack on Neve Shalom on
September 6, 1986, when 22 people were killed by unknown assassins. Saturday service at the synagogue—on
which major restoration work was performed last year—
begins at 8:00 A.M.

East of the Galata Tower and just north of the Genoese
walls of Galata are several Ottoman buildings of note:
Tophane, now an empty shell, was the foundry where Ottoman cannons were cast. The Ottoman writer Evliya Çelebi
describes the excitement of the foundry when the viziers
and sheiks gathered in solemn ceremony to "throw some
gold and silver coins into the brazen sea as alms, in the
name of the True Faith,... great care being taken that not a
drop of water gets in, because a drop of water thrown into
the molten brass would burst asunder the gun-mold and
wipe out all those present."

Cater-corner across the divided street from Tophane is
the **Kılıç Ali Paşa Camii**, possibly designed by Sinan in his
old age, in 1580. Kılıç Ali Paşa (originally an Italian named
Occhiali) was a commander in the Ottoman fleet during its
defeat in the Battle of Lepanto (1571). Because of his action
in that battle, Sultan Selim II dubbed him Kılıç (sword). He
served as governor of Algiers, where he happened to pre-
side at the trial of a slave who had tried to run away from his
cruel Albanian master. The trial was unimportant except for
the fact that the slave, Miguel de Cervantes Saavedra, later
mentioned the kindness of his judge in his novel *Don
Quixote de la Mancha*.

Beyoğlu

Up to the 19th century most Turkish İstanbullus ventured
into Galata (a.k.a. Karaköy) and the regions north of it only
on necessity and shook the dust off their coats when they
returned to the old city. The regions beyond Galata were
called Pera; the main street was the Grand Rue de Pera
(today's İstiklâl Caddesi). At that time the high Levantine
society gathered in the patisseries of Lebon and Markiz at the

crossroads of the Grand Rue and Asmalımescit. The 19th-
century murals of the seasons are still visible through the
dust-blackened windows of Markiz, where once the French
ambassador toasted Sarah Bernhardt with champagne. (The
Lebon patisserie has been reopened.)

The length of İstiklâl Caddesi has been converted into a
pedestrian mall. Old-time streetcars, their bells clanging, ply
their way between the Tünel and Taksim. The street is no
longer congested with cars, so you can pause in the middle to
look at the Neoclassical architectural elements that were the
19th-century fashion. Acanthus capitals, pilasters, and egg-
and-dart and Greek-key stringcourses decorate the façades of
many buildings. Caryatids stand above the entrance to the
Çiçek Pasajı (Flower Passage, also identified as the Cité de
Péra) just beyond the Galatasaray corner. This passage is a
great place to enjoy a beer and an Istanbul specialty—mussels
on a stick.

In the immediate vicinity is the Balık Pazarı (Fish Market),
where choice fresh fish, fruit, and vegetables are found.
Much of it is an open-air market, but there are also shops
that sell pork products, game (sometimes wild boar), and
turkeys.

Farther along toward Taksim the façade of the former
Tokatlıyan Hotel (İstiklâl Caddesi 122, now identifiable by a
large sign marked SE-SAM above the main door) has been
cleaned up. A horned devil surrounded by cherubs leers
down at passersby while above the highest windows are
winged leonine dragons.

Patches of Europe can be found today in the former
embassies, now consulates, on and near İstiklâl. Most of
them, after several huge conflagrations, were built of stone
and set well back in their gardens. Bright orange tulips grace
the garden of the Palace of the Netherlands on Queen
Beatrix's birthday; the architect of the British consulate was
Sir Charles Barry, who also built the Houses of Parliament.
The courtyard of the Catholic church of St. Anthony of
Padua is like a little bit of Italy. In the chapel of St. Louis on
the French embassy grounds are engraved marble stones
commemorating the lives of soldiers who fell during the
siege of Rhodes in 1522, French diplomats (the first to live
here bought the property in 1634), and Capuchin monks.

Writing in 1895, Edwin Grosvenor (in his book *Constantinople*) complained that the United States embassy had no
fixed abode and "that its appropriate emblem is a carpet bag
rather than an eagle." The present location of the U.S. consulate in a palace built in 1873 by the Italian Ignazio Corpi is
one of the more distinctive of the 19th-century residences

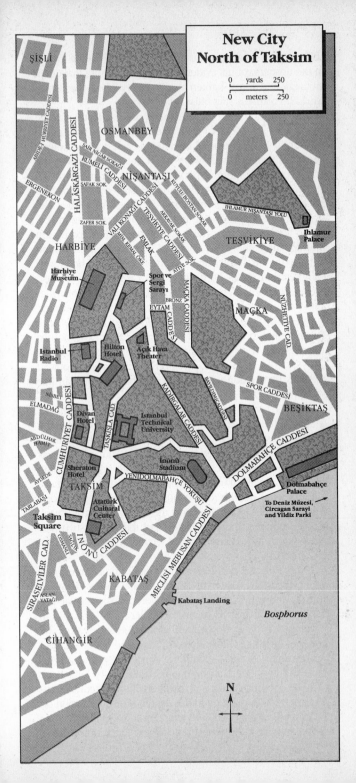

still standing. Statuettes and the banisters and ceiling murals in the upstairs rooms evidence the epicurean life that Corpi enjoyed, and today lighten the drudgery of all the paperwork the consular staff must suffer through.

North of the U.S. consulate, the **Pera Palas Hotel** was the *pied-à-terre* for General Mustafa Kemal before he was sent to Samsun in 1919. The hotel, a late 19th-century period piece, keeps his rooms as they were when, as Atatürk, he was the first president of the Republic of Turkey. A more recent guest was Agatha Christie; the hotel staff report that she always requested the same room (number 411) when she stopped in Istanbul during her frequent peregrinations between England and her husband's archaeological excavation in Iraq. After she died, some of her papers were found hidden in the floorboards of the room. The hotel was completed in 1892, and its main lobby is a fantasia of plush *fin de siècle* decor. The bar to the right of the lobby provides a very comfortable spot to relax after a day of hiking around the new city (see also Accommodations, below). The large Tüyap Exhibition Palace, just north of the Pera Palas, houses a succession of art and commercial exhibitions throughout the year. The third annual Istanbul Art Fair, with about 50 galleries participating, is scheduled to be held here in late September 1993.

What is now **Taksim square**—at the northern end of İstiklâl Caddesi—was a battleground in April 1909 when the repressive, spy-ridden government of Sultan Abdülhamit II was overthrown. The opposition army of Young Turks was led by men inspired by the works of such poets as Namık Kemal and Tevfik Fikret, who called for reforms. The sultan's soldiers were quartered in a number of buildings, among them the Taşkışla barracks, now the Faculty of Architecture, across from the Sheraton Hotel, and the Gümüşsuyu barracks, which now house another section of Istanbul Technical University.

The **Atatürk Kültür Merkezi** (Atatürk Cultural Center) is at the northeastern corner of Taksim square. Under construction for more than 30 years, it suffered a spectacular fire during a performance of Arthur Miller's *The Crucible* in November 1970, at the beginning of its second season. Restored to its former glory, it now hosts grand opera and solo performances, ballets, symphony concerts, special movies and exhibits—a gamut of cultural events. Every June since 1976 the opening concerts of the International Istanbul Festival have been performed in this center. (For information on the Istanbul Festival, see Entertainment and Nightlife, below.)

The **Spor ve Sergi Sarayı** (Sports and Exhibition Palace), the **Muhsin Ertuğrul Theater** (the winter theater season starts October 1), the **Açık Hava Tiyatro** (Open-Air Theater), and the new **İstanbul Belediyesi Concert Hall** (a.k.a. the Cemal Reşit Rey Concert Hall) are all near the big-name hotels around Taksim. Stores offering European- and American-style carpets, leather goods, and household furnishings; travel agencies and airline offices; high-class boutiques; nightclubs; and hospitals are concentrated here as well, particularly on Cumhuriyet Caddesi, which runs north from Taksim toward Şişli. Between Taksim and Şişli are also located most of the city's privately operated legiti- mate theaters and many cinemas. Nearer Şişli, along Rumeli Caddesi, Halâskârgazi Caddesi, and surrounding streets, is one of the city's most exclusive shopping districts, the stores of which purvey men's and women's apparel by Turkish designers, equal in quality to but generally lower in price than clothing produced by their American and European counterparts (see Shops and Shopping, below).

Cymbals, drums, bells, horns—the instruments of the janissary band (*mehter takımı*)—resound for an hour, begin- ning at 3:00 P.M., in the **Harbiye Müzesi** (Military Museum). (The museum is housed in the old Harbiye military school, north of Taksim, and is open 9:00 A.M. to 5:00 P.M., except Mondays and Tuesdays.) The band members perform in the costumes of the janissaries, who were the sultan's private standing army from about 1330 until Sultan Mahmut II abolished them in 1826. They were the men whose might sent shivers down the spines of their enemies (including occasionally the sultan), whose rhythms during battle in- spired the soldiers to daring acts, and whose music (known to 18th-century Europeans as *alla turca*) startled and in- spired Haydn (Military Symphony), Mozart (*The Abduction from the Seraglio*), Beethoven (last movement of the Ninth Symphony), Rossini, and Berlioz to enrich Western music with their themes and exotic instruments. At the height of the fad, piano makers in Vienna even added pedals for a "janissary stop" to imitate their percussion instruments.

The *mehter takımı* gave several daily open-air concerts, played for weddings and holidays, and accompanied royal processions. They acted as town criers, warning people of fires, and in given places around the city they played before sunrise (to wake the people for prayers) and at sunset (to announce the hour of curfew). While each janissary unit had its own band, the sultan's was, of course, the largest. His was a 15-fold band: 15 trumpets, 15 bells, 15 cymbals, 15 kettle- drums, 15 *zurna*s (oboe-like instruments), 15 brass drums, and 15 triangles.

The Lower Bosphorus

Although the Ottoman Turks disdained living in Galata or Pera among the Levantines, they enjoyed their waterside summer homes (*yalıs*) on both sides of the Bosphorus. Even before the final conquest of Constantinople itself the Otto- man sultan had a fortress at Anadolu Hisarı (on the Asian side); afterward there were palaces in a number of the vil- lages: Beşiktaş, Beylerbeyi, Çırağan, and Küçüksu. The "Sweet Waters of Asia," the two streams that emptied into the Bosphorus at Küçüksu and Anadolu Hisarı, were favorite picnic spots for the court and its followers. In good weather a colorful fleet of long, many-oared rowboats carrying the sultan and his advisers, the foreign ambassadors, and the women of the harem gathered at the docks in front of shady cafés. More than 15 of these gilded caïques, gigs, ship's boats, and rowboats are on view in one of the buildings of the **Deniz Müzesi** (Naval Museum; open 9:30 A.M. to 5:00 P.M., except Mondays and Thursdays) in Beşiktaş, just beyond Dolma- bahçe palace (see below).

When the sultans tired of living in Topkapı in the 19th century, they moved their main residence to new quarters up the Bosphorus. Built in 1853, **Dolmabahçe Sarayı** (Dolmabahçe palace; open 9:00 A.M. to 3:00 P.M., except Mondays and Thursdays) reflects the influence of French king Louis Philippe. It was a sultan's folly: Abdülmecit ex- hausted the resources of the treasury in building it. The ceiling of the central stateroom is 130 feet high; its chande- lier, which was made in London and was a gift from Queen Victoria, holds 750 light bulbs and weighs four and a half tons. The expense of turning those lights on for just a few minutes must make that earlier, miserly grand vizier Rüstem Paşa shudder in his grave. (The size of this and the palace's other chandeliers may give you the wrong impression about illumination inside Dolmabahçe today. Because of old and bad wiring, use of electricity within the building is strictly limited, and it is quite dark. Choose a sunny day to visit Dolmabahçe.)

Dolmabahçe holds a cherished place in the memories of staunch republicans because it was in one of its rooms that Mustafa Kemal Atatürk died. The anniversary of that time in 1938 is observed punctually at 9:05 A.M. every November 10, when people pause (and traffic stops) for one minute to honor the man and his reforms.

Just beyond Beşiktaş—once a village but now a bustling, highly urbanized area—is **Çırağan Sarayı** (Palace of the Torches). A palace has stood in this location since the 18th

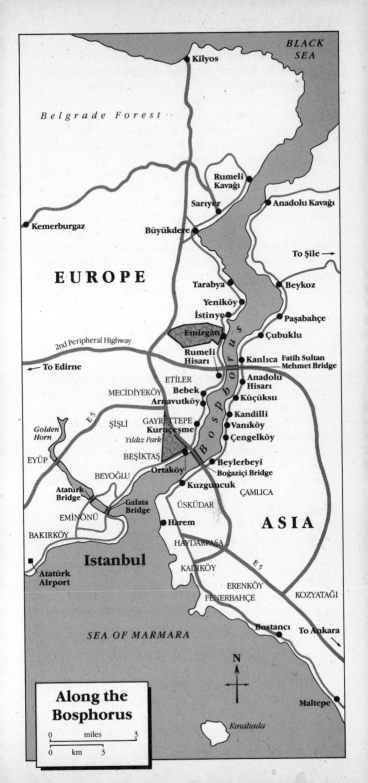

BLACK SEA

Kilyos

Belgrade Forest

Rumeli Kavağı

Sarıyer

Anadolu Kavağı

Kemerburgaz

Büyükdere

To Şile →

EUROPE

Tarabya

Beykoz

Yeniköy

İstinye

Paşabahçe

Emirgan

Çubuklu

2nd Peripheral Highway

Rumeli Hisarı

Kanlıca

Fatih Sultan Mehmet Bridge

← To Edirne

ETİLER

Anadolu Hisarı

MECİDİYEKÖY

Bebek

Küçüksu

Arnavutköy

Kandilli

GAYRETTEPE

Vaniköy

ŞİŞLİ

Kuruçeşme

Çengelköy

Golden Horn

Yıldız Park

BEŞİKTAŞ

Beylerbeyi

EYÜP

Ortaköy

Boğaziçi Bridge

BEYOĞLU

Kuzguncuk

ÇAMLICA

Atatürk Bridge

Galata Bridge

ÜSKÜDAR

EMİNÖNÜ

Harem

ASIA

BAKIRKÖY

HAYDARPAŞA

Istanbul

Atatürk Airport

KADIKÖY

ERENKÖY

KOZYATAĞI

FENERBAHÇE

To Ankara

SEA OF MARMARA

Bostancı

N

Along the Bosphorus

Kınalhada

Maltepe

0   miles   3

0   km   3

century, but the original wooden structure was torn down to make way for the marble structure begun during the reign of Sultan Abdülmecit, in 1855. The new Çırağan was completed in 1871 but was gutted by a fire started by faulty electrical wiring in 1910. The palace has been restored and now serves as an entertainment complex and convention center for the Çırağan Palace Hotel Kempinski Istanbul next door (see Accommodations, below).

A short distance past Çırağan and just across the road that travels north all the way up the western shore of the Bosphorus is **Yıldız Parkı** (open 8:30 A.M. to 8:00 P.M. daily). The park contains **Yıldız Sarayı** (Yıldız palace), built in 1875 and now being restored, and a number of small kiosks set amid charming gardens. These buildings have been rescued in recent years through the work of the Turkish Touring and Automobile Association, which has been responsible for saving—and restoring to Ottoman grandeur—many notable buildings in Istanbul. A wooded hillside, the **Şale Pavilion** (open for tea and light refreshments 9:30 A.M. to 4:00 P.M., except Mondays and Thursdays), teahouses, ponds, and the factory outlet of the Yıldız glassworks add to the park's attractiveness. The park itself is open every day, the palace only on special occasions. The pretty **Malta Köşkü** houses a café and is the venue for many special events (open 9:30 A.M. to 8:00 P.M. daily).

The **İstanbul Şehir Müzesi** (City Museum of Istanbul, open 9:00 A.M. to 4:30 P.M., except Thursdays), which houses a collection of paintings and ethnographic items related particularly to Istanbul, has recently been moved to one of the small palace buildings, approached from the entrance to the palace grounds near Yıldız University halfway up the hill and north off Barbaros Bulvarı.

The Upper Bosphorus

While some of the romance of the Bosphorus is in the palaces, some rests also with the people who have sailed its waters. Jason reputedly travelled north from Miletus in search of the Golden Fleece in Colchas; on his return he and Medea and his Argonauts anchored briefly in the Kuruçeşme bay. The Roman poet Ovid passed through this strait en route to his exile in Constanza, as did Pliny the Younger when he was governor of Bithynia.

Once each of the indentations along the coast of the Bosphorus sheltered a separate village. Communication among them was managed more frequently by boat than by horse carriage. Many were fishing villages; some, such as

Arnavutköy—the village of the Albanians—were settled by foreign colonies.

Travelling north along the coastal road (which is known by a variety of names as it proceeds up the Bosphorus), you come first to the villages of Ortaköy and Kuruçeşme. **Ortaköy** has a reputation among İstanbullus for its bohemianism, though that quality may be hard for a foreigner to discern. Around the square on the quay there's a handcrafts and books market (open-air in good weather) that's most active on weekends, especially Sundays. Several restaurants, some with tables outside, offer authentic Turkish cuisine and a perfect place to escape the heat on a sultry summer evening.

Kuruçeşme, just above Ortaköy, was for years little more than a dirty coaling station on the Bosphorus. Now it is undergoing a change in fortune, visible first in the new waterfront park. A number of discos, bars, restaurants, and nightclubs are located along the sea road, both on land and on boats tied to the quay. Notable are the Divan Kuruçeşme (see Entertainment and Nightlife, below) and the enormous **Kuruçeşme Pasha** discotheque, an open-air dance emporium that stays awake until the early morning hours and draws hordes of young people on weekends.

One restaurant in Kuruçeşme has an unusual menu. Called **Pafuli** ("popcorn"), it specializes in the distinctive cuisine of the Laz people, an ethnic group from the Black Sea region. Laz cooking has two staples, corn and sardines, and you'll want to try them in their many separate manifestations (a plate of sardines prepared in several different ways makes a delectable appetizer; an unusual corn-and-cheese fondue is a scrumptious accompaniment to any main course), or together in the restaurant's unusual fish-cornbread.

Arnavutköy (about four and a half miles as the crow flies from the Seraglio point) and **Bebek** (in the next bay north) are homes to two distinguished schools. (Both towns are stops on the Bosphorus ferry and both are served by frequent buses from Taksim and Eminönü.) Robert College, a private coeducational junior and senior high school for Turkish students, was founded in 1863 by an American philanthropist, Christopher Robert, and a vigorous, versatile educator, Cyrus Hamlin. Combined since 1971 with the American College for Girls (founded in 1871) and located in Arnavutköy, Robert College was previously atop the hill in Bebek. That campus is now occupied by **Boğaziçi Üniversitesi** (Bosphorus University), one of the six state-run institutions of higher learning in Istanbul. (The others are Istanbul

University, Istanbul Technical University, Yıldız University, Marmara University, and Mimar Sinan University.)

The campus of Bosphorus University extends into the next village of **Rumeli Hisarı** (European Fortress). The fortress (open 9:30 A.M. to 5:00 P.M., except Mondays) that distinguishes the village was built in 1452 by Sultan Mehmet II, the first foothold the Ottomans established on the European shore of the Bosphorus. With the smaller castle (Anadolu Hisarı; see below) that his great-grandfather Sultan Bayezit I had built directly across the Bosphorus, Mehmet was able to control the shipping here, the narrowest crossing of the strait. Mehmet parceled out the responsibility for the towers to three of his viziers: the north, or Black, tower, to Saruca Paşa, the east tower on the water to Çandarlı Halil Paşa (who was executed soon after for opposing the sultan's plans), and the south, or Rose, tower, to Zaganos Paşa. Mehmet himself took responsibility for the fortress's curtain walls. After Mehmet conquered the city the next year, the fortress served mainly as a dungeon for foreign prisoners. Some of their names are scratched in the wall of the Black Tower (not open to visitors). On fair summer evenings the fortress is sometimes used as a theater, where productions of, for instance, *Macbeth* (with soldiers manning the battlements) and folk dances blend with the backdrop of the strait and the hills of Asia. Tickets are on sale at the Atatürk Cultural Center in Taksim or at the fortress on the night of the performance.

The park above **Emirgân** (a ferry and bus stop about seven miles north of the Seraglio point) has been planted with thousands of tulips that make a brilliantly colorful display every April. Tulips came originally from the Middle East; Europe recognized them as a valuable species in the middle of the 16th century, when the Hapsburg ambassador Busbecq carried home some bulbs—for which he had had to pay a considerable amount. After tulips had become popular in Europe, they were reintroduced into the Ottoman Empire in the early 18th century, when they influenced much of the palace art. The Tulip Period was a time of interest on the part of the Ottoman court in French ways and Western ideas.

Like Yıldız park, Emirgân park contains a number of Ottoman *köşk*s (pavilions) beautifully restored by the Turkish Touring and Automobile Association. For special events, dinner is served and chamber-music recitals performed at the **Beyaz Köşk** (White Pavilion); the **Sarı Köşk** (Yellow Pavilion) offers breakfast, lunch, and cocktails; the **Pembe Köşk** (Pink Pavilion) serves tea.

The **Sadberk Hanım Müzesi** (open daily, except Wednes-

days, 10:00 A.M. to 6:00 P.M. in summer and 10:00 A.M. to 5:00
P.M. from September through May) in the district of Sarıyer
near the northern end of the Bosphorus contains a collection of archaeological artifacts and ethnological items in two
quite different housings. The rooms set up to represent
customs of Ottoman life are in a late 19th-century mansion.
In striking contrast, the adjoining building houses antiques
collector Hüseyin Kocabaş's outstanding accumulation of
items emphasizing the archaeology of Anatolia. The collection is highlighted against black marble floors and black
walls.

Sarıyer is about 12 miles north (as the crow flies) of the
Seraglio point; there are buses and ferries to it and beyond
to Rumeli Kavağı—for which see Anadolu Kavağı, below. If
traffic is moving smoothly the trip by private car from
Taksim over the Maslak road takes about half an hour. On
weekends and holidays, when many are enjoying the restaurants along the Bosphorus or the fresh air of the Belgrade
Forest, the only comfortable way to get to and from Sarıyer
is by boat.

ASIAN ISTANBUL

The Asiatic districts, in closer touch with the Anatolian heartland of Turkey, pulse to a more sedate rhythm than do the
European districts. Their distance from the city center has
helped preserve an attractiveness that contrasts with the
intensity of the European areas.

Kadıköy is a busy shopping and residential area, the
farthest south on the Asian side of the Bosphorus. It's served
by frequent ferries from the Seraglio point and from
Karaköy. It's also a terminal for buses and dolmuşes to other
city districts and to points east along the Sea of Marmara.
North across a small bay is Haydarpaşa, the station for trains
to Ankara and beyond. Harem, directly east of the Seraglio
point and a main terminal for intercity buses, took its name
from the harem of the sultan's palace that long ago stood on
the crest of the hill. Üsküdar was once the major city on the
Asiatic shore. The road into the interior began here; its
importance, however, had diminished some time before the
superhighways and the Bosphorus bridges diverted the traf-

fic away. Today it's a quieter, more conservative district than Kadıköy.

North from Üsküdar, the upper Bosphorus villages on the Asian side include Beylerbeyi, Çengelköy, Vanıköy (across from Arnavutköy), Anadolu Hisarı, Kanlıca (across from Emirgân, and known for its yogurt), Paşabahçe (the location of a well-known glass factory), Beykoz (with a large bay across from Tarabya), and Anadolu Kavağı. Buses go along the sea road; the car trip from Üsküdar to Beykoz takes about an hour if there's no traffic tie-up. There are occasional ferries between each of the villages and the Seraglio point, and there are also ferries that cross between many of these points and other points on the European side.

Although the first settlements in what is now Greater Istanbul appear to have been in Asia, and although many of the later events—Byzantine, Ottoman, Turkish—affected people living on the Asiatic side of the Bosphorus as much as they did those on the European, nevertheless Kadıköy, Üsküdar, and the other sections here do not generally hold the same fascination for tourists that the Seraglio point does. Or perhaps the fascination is there only for those who want to enjoy the city at a leisurely pace.

There are many palaces and mosques on the Asian side, but the early ones that the sultans built (Mehmet II's kiosk was west of Beykoz, Süleyman's palace was in Üsküdar) no longer exist, nor were these palaces ever the seat of government. There are few ancient walls or dungeons here, no Roman columns or Byzantine mosaics.

THE UPPER BOSPHORUS

Starting our Asian itinerary with the village farthest from the Seraglio point and travelling south, among the best (and most reasonably priced) fish restaurants anywhere in Istanbul are in **Anadolu Kavağı** and its corresponding European village, Rumeli Kavağı, almost at the northern entrance to the Bosphorus. Anadolu Kavağı can be reached by ferry (it takes a little less than two hours from Eminönü), by private boat, or by road. Ferries are scheduled so that they arrive in time for lunch or supper, and others depart about an hour and a half later.

On the hill above Anadolu Kavağı are the ruins of a **Genoese castle**. In early Byzantine times the point boasted 12 temples to the Olympian gods, including one to Zeus of the Favorable Winds said to have been built by Jason. In the early second century B.C., Prusias I (the king who sheltered

Hannibal and for whom the city of Bursa is named) placed a small fortress here commanding the entrance to the strait. Harun al-Rashid, the caliph of *Arabian Nights* fame, tried to take it (A.D. 789), and the Genoese captured and reinforced it about 1350. Russians also held the fort briefly before Sultan Bayezit I secured it for the Ottomans around 1390. (Note that the road from Anadolu Kavağı is open to foreigners to continue north about 8 km/5 miles to Anadolu Feneri, where there is a breathtaking view high above the Black Sea. Try this on a stormy day if you like the drama of waves crashing on rocks and foam spewing against your face.)

A few fishing weirs (*dalyan*s) are set in the shallow water in the large **Beykoz** bay south of Anadolu Kavağı. In earlier days the common catch here was swordfish. The north side of the bay is where the treaty of Hünkâr İskelesi was signed in 1833 between Russia and the Ottoman Empire. One of its clauses closed the Bosphorus to Russia's enemies during the eight years the treaty was in force. A road to Polonezköy (a former Polish colony) and to the beach towns of Riva and Şile begins in Beykoz. (See Istanbul Environs, below.)

The tall, tower-like summer palace on the **Çubuklu** hill (downstream of Beykoz) was built about 1900 by the last *hıdiv* (khedive, or viceroy, of Egypt), Abbas Hilmi Paşa. Restored to its early 20th-century glory (a strange blend of Ottoman and Art Nouveau styles) and turned into a hotel and restaurant by the Turkish Touring and Automobile Association, the **Hıdiv Kasrı** commands a spectacular view of the upper Bosphorus. Its shaded garden is an attractive place to sit and have a drink on a hot summer day (see Accommodations, below).

Sultan Bayezit I, great-grandfather of Mehmet II, built the fortress of **Anadolu Hisarı** (across the Bosphorus from Rumeli Hisarı) about 1390. Bayezit's desire was to conquer Constantinople, but before he was able to attack the city he was defeated by Tamerlane in Ankara in 1402, and the Ottoman power went into eclipse for 11 years. The conflict between those two leaders is one of the subjects of Marlowe's *Tamburlaine the Great*. During the heyday of the Ottoman Empire the two short streams that empty into the Bosphorus near Anadolu Hisarı were known as the **Sweet Waters of Asia**. A pretty little palace/museum, the **Küçüksu Kasrı** (open 9:30 A.M. to 4:00 P.M., except Mondays and Thursdays), stands on the shore here; it and a nearby marble fountain are favorites for photographers.

Someplace between Kandilli (the point opposite Bebek) and Çengelköy, Empress Theodora built the Convent of Repentance in the sixth century for the more than 500 prostitutes whom she rescued from her old stamping grounds of the Hippodrome (Theodora herself was a woman with a checkered past) and then tried to reform. Procopius remarks cynically that among them were girls who preferred suicide to chastity. No trace remains of the convent.

Beylerbeyi Camii in the town of the same name was built first by Sultan Ahmet I early in the 17th century. It disappeared, and Sultan Abdülhamit built another mosque on the site in 1778. He asked that it be named after his mother, Rabia Sultan, but the place name stuck instead. That mosque, which had only one minaret, was damaged by an earthquake. When Sultan Mahmut II repaired it, he added a second minaret.

South of the mosque and at the foot of the Bosphorus Bridge is the **Beylerbeyi Sarayı** (open 9:00 A.M. 12:30 P.M. and 1:30 P.M. to 4:00 P.M., except Mondays and Thursdays). Before the present marble palace was built, Sultan Murat IV had laid out its extensive gardens in the 17th century. (Into the late 19th century the gardens possessed a menagerie that included troops of ostriches and cages of Bengal tigers.) Sultan Mahmut II then built here what was considered one of the most beautiful palaces of the early 19th century. It burned down several years later, and a new one, a coronet among the more ostentatious of the imperial buildings, was built by Sultan Abdülaziz in 1865.

The spacious rooms, particularly the grand salon, are decorated lavishly with Japanese and Sèvres vases, Bohemian chandeliers, Venetian crystal columns, and frescoes by Italian artists. Of particular interest in the dining room is the furniture, which was hand-carved by Sultan Abdülaziz himself. The sultana's reception room has a writing desk with secret drawers and mirrors arranged so as to prevent anyone spying on the person seated at it.

The person whose visit to the palace of Beylerbeyi created the greatest spectacle was Empress Eugénie of France, in 1869. To honor her and her country, a room was furnished to duplicate her own at the Tuileries (the one at the Tuileries is gone).

THE LOWER BOSPHORUS
AND SEA OF MARMARA
Üsküdar

The ancient name of Üsküdar was Chrysopolis, meaning Golden City, possibly so-named because of the large tribute paid to the Persians by the inhabitants or because of the duties on shipping in the Bosphorus that were collected here. Later it was the first of the posts for couriers to Asia. Somewhere in the vicinity of Çamlıca ("hill with pines") east of the Üsküdar landing, Constantine the Great defeated Licinius in 324 to become the sole emperor of both the Eastern and Western Roman empires. Because it is the highest point visible from across the water, Çamlıca was a signal station, relaying messages from the armies in Asia Minor by firelight to the Byzantine emperors.

Up until the beginning of the 19th century, Üsküdar (Scutari in Byzantine times) was the point of convergence of the caravan routes through Asia Minor. The many caravansaries (long since gone) near its landing bustled with merchant princes and their camels. When the Ottoman sultan was also the caliph of Islam, the yearly sacred procession carrying the sultan's presents and the new covering for the Kaaba in Mecca started its Asiatic journey from Üsküdar.

In those years an hour's carriage trip from the Üsküdar landing up to the **Çamlıca hill** was considered a romantic outing. The romance was enhanced on moonlit nights in early spring, when nightingales warbled in every tree and shrub along the way. Thanks to the Turkish Touring and Automobile Association, the crest of Çamlıca is a pleasant park in which to enjoy the view of the city, the countryside, and the Bosphorus along with a cup of tea and light refreshments. Buses from the ferry landing go to Kısıklı, a short distance below the hilltop; the time of the trip has been cut to about 20 minutes.

Because of its height and its position, Çamlıca has become a favorite spot for bird-watchers. Most of the birds migrating between Asia and Europe do not fly across long stretches of water. Thus the two straits in Turkey—the Bosphorus and the Dardanelles—act as funnels for migrating flocks in spring and fall. Ornithologists gather here to observe the biannual flights of storks, kites, rollers, cuckoos, herons, and a host of other species.

At Bağlarbaşı, between Çamlıca and the ferry landing, the Üsküdar American School carries on the educational work of Protestant missionaries begun in 1820—the oldest American enterprise in Turkey. Farther down the main street, at Bülbüldere ("valley of nightingales") is a small mosque and cemetery for the community of followers of a 17th-century Jewish messianic leader, Shabbetai Tzevi, who converted to Islam.

The mosques of interest in Üsküdar are within walking distance of each other, although the Eski Valide and Çinili mosques are about a mile up a hill. (A point to note: All the imperial mosques on the Asian shore were built by or for women.) The oldest of the six imperial mosques in Üsküdar, İskele Camii (the Landing Mosque, immediately opposite the ferry boats) was built by Sultan Süleyman's daughter Mihrimah Sultan. The architect was the famous Sinan. The wide, double portico, the ablution fountain in the courtyard, and the marble sundial on the *kıble* (front interior) wall are interesting details. Also in the square south of the Üsküdar landing is the large Yeni Valide Camii (New Queen Mother's mosque), built at the beginning of the 18th century by Sultan Ahmet III for his mother. The bit pazarı across the boulevard from Yeni Valide Camii and behind the Mimar Sinan Çarşısı on Büyük Hamam Sokak is one of several outdoor flea markets around the city in which an unexpected treasure may catch your eye. This market is not active on Sundays, although some of the others are.

In the Toptaşı district, Eski Valide Camii (Atîk Valide, or the Elder Queen Mother's Mosque) is another of Sinan's buildings (to get there take Hakimiyeti Milliye Caddesi, then Toptaşı Caddesi up the hill). A more stately mosque than the İskele Camii of Mihrimah, it was built in 1583 by Nurbânu Sultan, the favorite of Sultan Selim II and the mother of Sultan Murat III.

Eski Valide sits on the slope of a hill, its quiet courtyard contrasting with the clutter of houses around it. The entire complex at first included the mosque, several schools, caravansaries, a hospice, a public kitchen, a hospital, and a residence for dervishes. The hospital and the public kitchen have been sadly altered by their use as a prison, but the mosque is still the beautiful building that Nurbânu Sultan desired and Sinan designed.

Mahpeyker Sultan was the founder of Çinili Cami (the Tiled Mosque, ca. 1650, about four blocks up the hill beyond Eski Valide). The favorite of Sultan Ahmet I, Mahpeyker Sultan played a deciding role in government during the reigns of two of her sons (Sultan Murat IV and Sultan İbrahim) and one of her grandsons (Sultan Mehmet IV) before her daughter-in-law murdered her. While the mosque is rather cramped for space, its interior is similar to that of Rüstem Paşa in that its walls are covered with beautiful tiles.

The fifth imperial mosque in Üsküdar is Ayazma Camii (the mosque of the Holy Spring; follow Doğancılar Caddesi south from the ferry to Enfiyehane Sokak, then turn toward the water). It was built between 1760 and 1761 in memory of Mihrişah Emine Sultan by her son Mustafa III. Mihrişah Emine died when Mustafa was only 15 years old, 25 years before he became the ruler. To the east behind the royal gallery is the cistern to which the mosque's name refers. The mosque's commanding height above the Bosphorus is an important element of the Üsküdar skyline.

One other imperial mosque in Üsküdar completes those that were founded in Asia to honor women: The Baroque-style **Selimiye Camii** (immediately north of the Selimiye barracks) was built between 1803 and 1804 by Selim III for his mother, Mihrişah Sultan. Its courtyard is shaded by an ancient plane tree.

The Turkish affection for birds is evident in the stone birdhouses high on the sides of the Yeni Valide, Ayazma, and Selimiye mosques. Some of them are modest shelters with only a shelf below their entrances for the birds to perch on. Some are as elaborate as the 18th-century buildings that they mirror. It is striking that these birdhouses are most commonly found on buildings erected in memory of sultans' mothers.

The large, yellow **Selimiye Kışlası** (barracks), with towers on each of its four corners, are prominent above the Harem ferry landing. The first wooden structure was built by Selim III—hence its name—who hoped to quarter his new army here. He was deposed before he got rid of the recalcitrant janissaries, but his barracks were rebuilt by Sultan Mahmut II, who did accomplish that reform in 1826. Later the barracks were enlarged by Sultan Abdülmecit. During the Crimean War (1853 to 1856) they became the army hospital where Florence Nightingale battled the diseases of cholera and mismanagement, dignifying the profession of nursing with her own stature and determination. The room in the north tower used by the "Lady with the Lamp" is now a small museum. Permission to visit Nightingale's room must be secured from the office of public relations at the barracks (open from 8:30 A.M. to 5:00 P.M., except Saturdays and Sundays). A prominent school of nursing in Istanbul carries Nightingale's name.

Üsküdar is the location of the biggest Muslim cemetery in Istanbul, the **Karacaahmet Mezarlığı**, which attracts Muslims because of their desire to be buried on the same continent as the holy cities of Mecca, Medina, and Jerusalem. It takes its name from a 14th-century holy man, Karacaahmet Veli, originally from Khorasan in Persia, who rode horseback throughout Anatolia curing the mentally ill. (His grave is claimed by six other places besides Üsküdar.) There are some old graves near Karacaahmet's reputed tomb and the canopied tomb of his horse. Many of the headstones are being replaced with markers of the newer burials.

Up to the 19th century, headstones identified the sex of the deceased, and, if he was a man, his profession and rank. The older women's stones have carved designs of flowers, fruit, and jewelry. You can estimate the date of a man's death by whether the stone is topped by a turban (up to about 1830) or a fez (Sultan Mahmut II made turbans illegal). Since 1926 the fez has itself been an illegal headgear; in consequence, recent tombstones—both men's and women's—are plain.

A lighthouse off the Üsküdar point has inspired several romantic fables. One by Jules Verne is typical of that writer of imaginary voyages: His hero escapes danger by means of a cable linked through the lighthouse from one continent to the other. A glance at the lighthouse gives a clue of how high Verne's imagination had to fly for him to have invented this tale. The lighthouse's Turkish name, Kız Kulesi (Maiden's Tower), comes from a story of a sultan's daughter who, like Sleeping Beauty, was destined to die on her birthday. A similar fable, but misplaced, has given rise to its English name, **Leander's Tower**. Leander is reputed to have swum, not the Bosphorus, but rather the much wider Dardanelles for his ill-fated tryst with Hero. The lighthouse's island served as a place of quarantine for plague sufferers in 1836. It is now the most prominent of the series of signal lights along the Bosphorus.

From the town of **Haydarpaşa**, two miles south of Üsküdar, trains go to Ankara, Kayseri, Adana, Van, and points in between. It's also Istanbul's harbor for container ships. The Byzantine church of St. Euphemia, where the Fourth Ecumenical Council was held in 451, may have been located at some distance inland from the train station, perhaps near Ayrılık Çeşmesi (Fountain of Separation), where the families of Ottoman soldiers bade goodbye to their menfolk as they left for war.

Kadıköy

Kadıköy (immediately across the bay from Haydarpaşa) in Byzantine times was called Chalcedon, perhaps meaning "new town." Originally a Phoenician colony, its first location was on the saddle between the Bosphorus and the Sea of Marmara about where the crossroads of Altıyol ("six roads") is now. There may have been a city gate here at one time, but its stones were used by Emperor Valens in Constantinople, and nothing of the old walls remains.

Kadıköy is a peninsula almost surrounded by water: to the north by Kadıköy bay, west and south by the Sea of Marmara, and east by the small Kurbağalı Dere (Valley of Frogs). Prehistoric settlements have been excavated along this stream and on Fikirtepe, the hill northeast of Altıyol.

During the Crusaders' attack on Constantinople in 1203 and 1204 Chalcedon was a campground used by Henrico Dandalo, the 90-year-old Venetian duke who instigated the attack. His chronicler Villehardouin writes with some enthusiasm about the palace of the Byzantine emperor Alexius V Dukas in Chalcedon, calling it "the most beautiful and delectable that ever eyes could see." He adds that "the country was fair, and rich, and well supplied with all good things, and the sheaves of corn (which had been reaped) were in the fields, so that all—and they stood in no small need—might take thereof." Three days later the Crusaders moved north to another of Alexius's palaces in Scutari.

Kadıköy means "judge's village," and there are several possibilities as to which Islamic jurist is responsible for the town's present name. The most likely is a certain Hızır Bey, one of two learned men to whom Sultan Mehmet II gave the responsibility of managing Constantinople immediately after its capture.

On a clear day the Kadıköy bluff gives a panoramic view of the Princes' Islands, the Sea of Marmara, the Seraglio point, and the Istanbul harbor. Seen from this vantage or from a ferry returning to Istanbul, the silhouette of the city often stands out dramatically against the sunset.

GETTING AROUND

Transportation to Istanbul takes all forms: sea, land, and air. International passenger ships land in Karaköy near the north end of the Galata Bridge. The frequent city buses that stop just south of the Customs Building on Kemankeş Caddesi take people to a variety of destinations farther north. For those who are not familiar with the city or who have too much luggage to hop a bus, most taxi drivers know a smattering of foreign languages.

Trains from Europe come into the Sirkeci station in the old city; from Asia the terminal is in Haydarpaşa across the Bosphorus. Travellers from Asia continuing to Europe can catch the ferry to Karaköy right at the Haydarpaşa station. The ferries depart every 20 minutes during the day—making this the most romantic way of approaching the Seraglio point; the ride lasts about 20 minutes. Both train stations are conveniently located for buses, and there are usually plenty of taxis available.

For people arriving by plane at the Atatürk airport (about 30 km/19 miles from the center of Istanbul), there are regular service buses that bring passengers either to Aksaray in the old city or to Şişhane in the new. The airport taxis are controlled by a dispatcher who will give you a slip with the taxi license plate number on it. Taxi fare from the airport to the Sultanahmet area should be about $12 during the daytime, or about $25 at night. From the airport to Taksim, the fares are about $18 in the day and $40 at night. The driver will most likely accept foreign currency if you haven't had the chance to change money.

The main European **bus** terminal is at Topkapı, just outside the city walls—an anthill of scurrying activity morning, noon, and night. From there you can find buses, minibuses, and taxis that will take you closer to your lodgings in the city.

Traffic can be a nightmare in Istanbul even at high noon. If you are willing to risk **driving**, you should drive defending all six sides of your car. Expect that a clearly marked one-way road will have two-way traffic, and that most drivers, given a fighting chance, will try to push you out of your lane. The streets are full of unmarked hazards, such as manholes minus their covers, and parking is quite scarce. In other words, leave your car at your hotel.

The best way to see the old city—and the central districts of the new city—is to **walk**. Wear sturdy, low-heeled shoes with soles that won't skid on wet, muddy cobblestones, and watch your footing. Don't expect to find sidewalks everywhere— you'll have to compete with cars, carts, buses, other pedestrians, and sometimes livestock, but if you don't mind getting splashed and jostled and if you can stand the foul bus and truck exhaust blown in your face, you'll see more and get to know the city better.

Bicyclists in Istanbul have a hard time of it. The drivers won't give you any space, the streets aren't smooth, and the city has many more than the proverbial seven hills.

The tiny **subway** line known as **Tünel** climbs the steep hill between the new-city foot of the Galata Bridge and the southern end of İstiklâl Caddesi. The ride, which is charming in a grimy, urban sort of way, takes about 90 seconds and is an essential way of transporting yourself between two points where you're quite likely to want to be.

The Istanbul municipality has installed an old-fashioned **streetcar** line on İstiklâl Caddesi, running back and forth from Taksim square to Tünel. Take it if your object is simply to get quickly from one end of this fascinating street to the other; otherwise you'll want to walk (the trip takes about 15 minutes by foot).

In the old city, the new **light-rail system** is now complete between Sirkeci and Aksaray. It's a good way to avoid having

to hike the long, winding hill up to Sultanahmet from
Sirkeci—*if*, that is, you have the stamina to endure the
crowds of people waiting to board (not to mention the
squashed conditions inside the cars). One reason things are
so crowded is that, at least for now, the ride is free; once the
route is extended you will have to pay a fare.

The **city buses** have regular routes; they, and the other
public transportation systems, run regularly from about
6:00 A.M. to near midnight. To find your bus you can look
for the two terminals (the point of departure and the
destination) given on the front of the bus (e.g., Emirgân–
Eminönü) or the bus number (e.g., 22), also on the front.
Or you can read the details of the route given on the left
side of the front door (e.g., Emirgân–R.Hisar–Bebek–
Ortaköy-Beşiktaş–Karaköy–Eminönü), which will tell you
whether the bus goes to your desired stop.

You will probably need to learn two of the main transfer
points in the European city: Eminönü (near the Galata
Bridge in the old city) and Taksim (in Beyoğlu in the new
city). A third point, in Mecidiyeköy (in the north of the new
city), serves buses between Europe and Asia.

In Asia buses connect with the Kadıköy and Üsküdar
ferries. From Kadıköy the buses run east to regions along
the Sea of Marmara. From Üsküdar buses go up the hill to
Çamlıca and farther inland, or north along the Bosphorus, or
south to Kadıköy.

Note that in both Eminönü and Taksim the bus stops are
spread out over some distance. Don't be afraid to ask where
your bus can be found. On the street, a "Sultanahmet bus?"
with a rising inflection—even spoken in English—should
see you safely on your way. But note also that Sultanahmet,
for instance, is not a terminal, so you may be looking for a
bus marked Bayezit or Aksaray, which makes a stop near the
Sultanahmet mosque.

Bus tickets should be purchased before you board. Prices
and routes are frequently changing, but a fare anywhere in
the city will probably remain under half a dollar. The colors
of the public buses have nothing to do with the prices or
routes.

Buses move in only a few major directions: either along
the water or through the center of the city. There are few
cross-routes. For instance, if you are in Rumeli Hisarı and
want to go by bus to Etiler, which is just at the top of the hill,
you must travel south as far as Beşiktaş and there find
another bus that will bring you back.

In addition, if you are looking for a specific bus to a
distant point you may have an hour's wait. Note that Topkapı

palace is not to be confused with the bus terminal of the same name, which is outside the walls on the western side of the old city. Buses marked "Topkapı" go to that terminal—about four and a half miles from the palace.

Prices of the **ferries** across the Bosphorus are the equivalent of about half a dollar. You must buy a *jeton* (token) for the turnstile. The most frequent ferries run between Eminönü and Kadıköy, between Eminönü and Üsküdar, and between Karaköy and Kakıköy/Haydarpaşa. While Eminönü square is being reconfigured, the names on the landings (*iskele* in Turkish) for the ferries will not necessarily correspond with the actual destinations of the boats. You should give yourself extra time to make your ferry because you may have to run from one landing to another to find the right one.

In Eminönü, moving in sequence east from the Galata Bridge, the arrangement has been as follows: Closest to the bridge is the landing for the ferries going north up the Bosphorus. In large letters it is marked both "Boğaziçi" and "No. 3." The next landing, "No. 2," is for those going to Üsküdar. Landing "No. 1," closest to Sirkeci, is the Kadıköy landing. Just beyond—in Sirkeci—is the unnumbered landing for the car ferry to Harem, which also takes foot passengers. Passenger ferries to Marmara and Avşa islands leave from the quay east of the car ferries for Harem. The trip takes about five hours. (A trip of half that time via the *deniz otobüsü* hydrofoils begins in Yenikapı on the Sea of Marmara.) Last in this series come the landings for ferries from Sirkeci to the Princes' Islands (*Adalar*) and for passenger ships bound for İzmir.

Ferries going up the Golden Horn start in the old city west of the Galata Bridge near the large Chamber of Commerce building. These include, in order, ferries to Kasımpaşa, Fener, Balat, Hasköy, Ayvansaray, Sütlüce, and Eyüp. Half the runs, both coming and going, extend the trip over the Bosphorus to Üsküdar.

Across the bridge in Karaköy, the first landing serves both Haydarpaşa and Kadıköy, while next is the *deniz otobüsü* for Bostancı (on the Asian coast southeast of Kadıköy) or Yenikapı. Farther up the Bosphorus there are also regular ferries going back and forth between Beşiktaş and Üsküdar, Bebek and Kandili, Yeniköy and Paşabahçe, and Rumeli Kavağı and Anadolu Kavağı. From Kabataş there are ferries to the Princes' Islands, Çınarcık, and Yalova, and also hydrofoils to Bostancı, Büyükada, and Mudanya (the seaport for Bursa).

Tickets for Marmara and Avşa are best purchased some time in advance (from the Denizcilik Bankası in Karaköy), although even on a summer weekend there always appears to be space for one more family and its cumbersome bundles to crowd onto the deck. One quirky aspect of Turkish travel is that return tickets for ships, trains, and buses cannot usually be obtained at the point of the journey's origin. The logic, presumably, is that passengers cannot be sure they'll want to reverse the trip until they've gotten where they're going.

In addition to the ferries run by the state-owned Denizcilik Bankası, there are the fast *deniz otobüsü* hydrofoils, which zip between Karaköy, Kabataş, the Princes' Islands, and Bostancı, and between Bostancı and Bakırköy for around two dollars.

Both on land and on water, the **dolmuş** (the word means "filled") adds another dimension to travel and a way to get from place to place that's somewhat quicker (and not much more expensive) than a bus or ferry.

A dolmuş taxi may come in one of several shapes—minibuses, station wagons, and grand old junkers from the heyday of the American automobile. Sadly, the last are gradually disappearing from Istanbul's streets.

Dolmuş drivers make the change for their fares while they drive; they keep in their minds who has paid what and very rarely forget or cheat. Dolmuş taxis travel between two fixed points; they have no schedule, and they charge a fixed rate no matter how far the passenger goes. Dolmuşes start when all the seats are taken (hence the name). If in the middle of the run someone gets out, that space may be occupied by a new passenger. Dolmuşes cannot be found everywhere, nor can they be quickly identified when they pass unless the dolmuş is a car that has been stretched to include a third row of seats or unless it has the identifying word written above the front windshield. A long line of people waiting at a dolmuş stand probably means that the line will move quickly. (Dolmuş lines are usually orderly and polite.) Dolmuş taxis are found during working hours. Dolmuş minibuses sometimes work in conjunction with the dolmuş taxis, and sometimes they have their own stands.

Dolmuş ferries go back and forth between Beşiktaş and Üsküdar and across the Golden Horn. They will sometimes travel in fog, when the big ferries must stay tied up at the dock. Neither kind ventures out when the *lodos* wind has churned up the waters.

Almost all **taxis** are yellow; they all have a black sign on their roof reading TAKSİ. Drivers are required to start their meters as soon as they take a passenger; they are obligated by law to take the customer wherever he or she wants to go. Because of the traffic congestion, it's difficult to get a taxi at rush hour, particularly in Eminönü. Fortunately, most taxi drivers are honest, most have an excellent sense of humor, and most are skillful drivers.

Taxi fares currently begin at 5,000 Turkish liras (about 65 U.S. cents) during the day. The price goes up 50 percent at midnight; if your trip begins in the evening, but goes into the "night" hours, the price is the night rate. If you wish to take a taxi across the Bosphorus you will be expected to pay the bridge toll (currently 10,000 Turkish liras, or about $1.50) in addition to your fare. Taxi fares are a bellwether of inflation in Turkey and are subject to sudden—often dramatic—raises.

For a romantic view of the city, a moonlit **evening cruise** on the Bosphorus is not impossibly expensive for a group if you hire one of the small dolmuş ferries. (You do need to make arrangements ahead of time.) If you start your cruise in the midafternoon you can sail north as far as the Black Sea, anchor in a quiet cove long enough to swim, and be sailing back in time to see the moon just above the mosques of the Golden City, Üsküdar. Or you can take your own picnic supper for the trip. Expect that the temperature on the water will be noticeably cooler than on the land—a welcome change in July or August.

ACCOMMODATIONS

In the 1960s and 1970s the Turks, with their consummate hospitality, would often apologize profusely for a $20 or $50 *hesap* (bill) for a night's lodging. They would protest, "We shouldn't charge you. You are our friend and guest." Then they would discount the total or deduct the food and beverage charges.

The Turks still feel as friendly toward their clientele. However, in the past few years, *patron* (owner) and cashier have managed to suppress their traditional values. Today they don't even blink as they levy luxury hotel rates up to $400 a night for a double room. This amounts (in 1993 terms) to more than three and a half million Turkish liras (TL), a wad of bills big enough to choke a camel—and about three times the monthly salary of the average İstanbullu.

Istanbul's deluxe hotels now number 14, with at least two more 300- to 600-room grandiose establishments scheduled to open later in 1993 and in 1994. The more luxurious hotels offer Western conveniences and Oriental delights to cosset the affluent traveller. The basics are air conditioning, direct-dial telephones, international satellite TV, radio news, taped music, double-paned windows where necessary, minibars, swimming pools, Jacuzzis and Turkish baths, saunas, and 24-hour room service. Additional amenities often include tennis courts, fitness rooms or health clubs, garages, boutiques, and bidets, telephones, and hair dryers in the marble-clad bathrooms—not to mention the casinos in many of the luxury hotels.

It is important to remember that Greater Istanbul—approximately 40 miles in breadth and with a population fast approaching 11 to 12 million—is divided into three parts. The city is cut into European and Asian halves by the Bosphorus, and European Istanbul is further divided into the "new city" and the "old city" by the Golden Horn.

The new city is the modern commercial, intellectual, and artistic center. It's where most of the high-fashion shops are and where the most varied entertainment can be found—which means it's also home to the most expensive hotels. Many of these are located near the hub of Taksim square, but some are in the districts (once fishing villages, now urbanized) that stretch up the western shore of the Bosphorus. In the new city it is relatively easy to take care of international and local travel plans and bookings, and from Taksim square you can get almost anywhere in the European city in under an hour. Major tourist sites in the old city are less than half an hour away.

The old city contains Istanbul's most important tourist attractions—St. Sophia, the Blue Mosque, the Süleymaniye Camii, Topkapı palace, and the Covered Bazaar. Here, though, there are only a few outstanding places to stay—the Ramada Hotel Istanbul, the President Hotel, the Hotel Akgün Istanbul, and the Kalyon Hotel. If you stay in the old city, you'll maximize your time for visiting tourist sites and museums—but you'll still want to cross the Golden Horn to sample some of the pleasures of the new city and the Bosphorus suburbs.

Asian Istanbul is slower and sweeter paced than the European side; it boasts some of the city's most elegant restaurants and private clubs, most located along the Bosphorus's eastern shoreline and the coast of the Sea of Marmara.

Istanbul's neighborhoods are small—go ten or, at most, twenty streets and you're in a different district. The names of individual neighborhoods are of vital importance in tracking down addresses, particularly for hotels. Among the best-known districts in the new city are Taksim, Harbiye, Nişantaşı, Şişli, and Teşvikiye; in the old city the district names you're likely to hear most often include Cağaloğlu (JAH-low-loo), Eminönü, Sirkeci, Sultanahmet, and Lâleli. Turkey's new postal codes are rarely used by Turks, who prefer the neighborhood designations. Some restaurants and other establishments don't even know their postal-code numbers. Of course, you're doubly safe when you use both the postal code and the district name when you write to a hotel.

All large tourist facilities and installations—hotels, motels, pensions, restaurants, shops, nightclubs—accept major credit cards, most often Visa, American Express, Access, MasterCard, and Eurocard. They do not usually accept Diner's Club, however.

In the past two years, Turkey has begun the arduous process of rationalizing its cumbersome telephone-number system. Some telephone exchanges in Istanbul changed during 1991 and 1992. Numbers given in the following pages are the most up-to-date available at press time. The telephone code for Turkey is 90, and the city code for greater Istanbul is 1.

The following hotels and other lodgings have been designated *deluxe* (usually from $200 to $400 per night for a double room), *expensive* ($100 to $200), or *moderate* (less than $100). The price range for a double room appears at the end of the paragraph giving the hotel's address; prices at hotels in Istanbul generally do not vary with the season (there are some exceptions), but rooms are more or less expensive according to how good a view they offer, the kind of amenities provided, and so on. Prices for suites are shown for some hotels. Unless otherwise noted, prices given here are the best estimates available for 1993 and include the 12-percent value-added tax and a 15-percent service charge. The cost of breakfast is not usually included in the price.

THE NEW CITY

Deluxe

Of all the posh new hotels around Taksim square (the heart of the new city, at the northern limit of the district called Beyoğlu, pronounced BAY-o-loo), the **Hilton International Istanbul** has for years been "Turkey's premier hotel," as its logo states. (It is, however, being outclassed by the even more luxurious and sophisticated Hotel Conrad Istanbul and the Çırağan Palace Hotel Kempinski Istanbul; see below.) Many world travellers consider this superbly designed nine-story hotel the Hilton chain's handsomest, most tasteful, and best run. The principal approach to the hotel is from Cumhuriyet Caddesi: Take it about a mile north, turning right at the driveway marked "Istanbul Hilton." The shopping arcade here includes upscale boutiques, a Tourism Ministry information office, and airline and rental-car offices.

The Hilton's lush, spacious grounds include a garden in back of the hotel facing the Bosphorus, replete with three tennis courts, two squash courts, and one of the city's largest and loveliest outdoor swimming pools, surrounded by cabanas and possessing an adjacent children's pool. As if these features weren't enough, there is an attractive, sizable indoor pool in the nearby **Hilton Health Club** (overlooking the garden) and a gambling **casino** in the separate Şadırvan (fountain) building; open 4:00 P.M. (for slot machines) and 5:00 P.M. (for tables) to 5:00 A.M.; Tel: 247-5902. In the front yard, which is surrounded by rosebushes that bloom almost year round, are the entranceways to the large, white-marble Hilton Convention and Exhibition Center and the separate underground garage.

The cool, ever-breezy terrace and adjoining indoor lounge on the main floor of the hotel feature live music at teatime. The lounge area and the adjacent **Lalezar Bar**, which has live music from 9:00 P.M. to 11:30 P.M. for its small dance floor, are gathering places for international royalty, celebrities, and captains of industry.

The Hilton boasts four very good restaurants—the **Rooftop Rotisserie**, the **Greenhouse**, the Chinese **Dragon Restaurant** (in the convention center), and the **Pool Terrace** (see the Dining section, below)—as well as **L'Expresso**, a café that serves Italian coffees, alcoholic beverages, and light snacks. L'Expresso's lovely garden leads through a passageway to the extremely luxurious 101 Club guestrooms, which are housed in a separate building. Along the passageway are two new meeting rooms. There is a sizable ballroom on the hotel's first lower level that opens onto the back garden, and, in the front garden, a helicoper landing pad lies beyond the entrance with its concrete "flying carpet" canopy.

In the main lobby, there are exclusive jewelry, leather, and men's and women's apparel *butik*s; a Godiva chocolate shop; antiques, rug, gift, and photo shops; a beauty salon and barbershop; an art gallery; and the hotel's own PTT (post office).

Within walking distance of Taksim square, the Hilton is convenient to the Sultanahmet area—about 20 minutes by taxi—and is approximately half an hour away from the airport by car (as are all Taksim-area hotels). Travel times may increase during rush hours—morning, midday, and evening—especially if you're crossing the first Bosphorus bridge to Asia.

Cumhuriyet Caddesi, 80200 Harbiye; Tel: 231-4646; Fax: 240-4165. In the U.S., (800) HILTONS (800/445-8667); in the U.K., (0800) 289-303 or, in London, (081) 780-1155; in Canada, (800) 268-9275 or, in Toronto, (416) 362-3771. $218–$334.

One long block south from the Hilton, down tree-lined Cumhuriyet Caddesi, is the **Divan Hotel**, located behind a gray stone obelisk (which helps equalize the flow of city water). The Divan is a prestigious European-style hotel with superior amenities and warm, personalized service provided by an English-speaking staff. It is patronized by Turkey's oldest and wealthiest families.

The hotel's 180 rooms are decorated in a pleasing peach color. The Divan has three bars, three very good restaurants (see the Dining and Entertainment sections, below), plus Istanbul's most famous pastry shop, the **Divan Pastanesi** (with eight other branches throughout the city). It has women's and men's hair salons and an exceptional jewelry shop. Perhaps the hotel's only disadvantages are that it has no on-premises swimming facility or garage.

The rooms on floors four through eight of the Divan's eastern side have views of the Bosphorus: the higher, the better. The hotel also possesses nine suites—with bedroom, sitting room with balcony (and Bosphorus view), kitchen, and bath—which, at $270 per night, are very good buys.

Cumhuriyet Caddesi 2, 80200 Taksim; Tel: 231-4100; Fax: 248-8527. $170–$190.

Diagonally across the street from the Divan is the **Istanbul Sheraton Hotel & Towers**, right on the northern edge of Taksim Parkı (the park just above Taksim square). Its 23 stories hold 429 rooms (including 19 suites) in a distinctive semirectangular tower—a major component of Istanbul's skyline. Its rooftop **Sultan Bar and Terrace** and **Revan** restaurant (see Dining, below) offer breathtaking 360-degree views of the Golden Horn, the old city, the Sea of Marmara, and the Bosphorus.

Public areas and private rooms on the lower floors are smaller and not as well decorated as those in the Hilton. The Sheraton's main lobby is crowded with several sections: There's a reception area, lounge, bar, tea and pastry shop (Café Vienne), and waterfall and rock garden, over which an ornately carved wooden staircase ascends to the mezzanine's restaurant, **La Coupole**, which features excellent international cuisine, delightful decor, and entertainment by a pianist-singer. On the top three floors of the tower, the private lounge, the check-in service, and the rooms (while not large) are of higher quality. Floors 12, 14, and 15 are now classified "executive" and have been redecorated. Every bathroom at the Sheraton has a bidet.

The Sheraton's outdoor swimming pool (small), large ballroom, three capacious meeting rooms, and underground garage are among the features that make it a favorite with conventions and trade fairs. The management is in the process of redecorating all the hotel's standard double rooms with new carpets and fabrics (competition makes for improvement). The Sheraton also operates its own boat, which makes open buffet and dinner cruises (each about four hours long) up and down the Bosphorus; these cruises are open to the general public.

The Sheraton's **casino** is one of Istanbul's largest and classiest; it opens at 2:00 P.M. and closes at 5:00 A.M.; Tel: 246-2021.

Taksim Parkı 80174, Taksim; Tel: 231-2121; Fax: 231-2180. In the U.S. and Canada, (800) 325-3535; in the U.K., (0800) 35-35-35. $230–$341.

Just across Taksim park and on the south side of Taksim square is **The Marmara Istanbul**, its 20-story rectangular tower topped by the **Panorama Restaurant**, a bar, and a nightclub, all with fantastic views. It has a sizable swimming pool, a sun deck, and a separate casino.

The long, two-way escalator running from the hotel's street-level Opera Pastry Shop–Café up to the first floor seems to fill the lobby. To the right of the lobby is the excellent open buffet of the **Brasserie**, serving international and Turkish dishes. However, The Marmara's 402 rooms and suites, as well as the bathrooms, are on the small side (although all rooms have been redone, with new upholstery and carpets). The Marmara is perhaps the place for those tireless travellers who are out all day touring and shopping.

Taksim Meydanı 80090, Taksim; Tel: 251-4696; Fax: 243-4342. $210–$230.

The **Swissôtel Bosphorus** in Maçka—northeast of Taksim and sitting on the hill above Dolmabahçe palace—is a huge, costly (reportedly it took $300 million to build) mixed metaphor. It consists of three buildings with modern exteriors and period interiors—a scheme that might have been better reversed. Designed and built by the Japanese, it is managed by a Swiss concern that also, apparently, was responsible for some of the interior decoration: A few walls have been painted with scenes of medieval Swiss towns and dreary alpine landscapes—uninteresting non sequiturs. There's nothing Turkish about the hotel except for its spectacular views of the Bosphorus. The Japanese gardens surrounding the buildings are, however, delightful.

The hotel's west wing opened in 1991. Besides 200 guest rooms, a ballroom, and a shopping arcade, it boasts the Presidential Suite, at $1,344 per night! The Suite Tower hotel of nine floors (in the center of the complex) and the 18-story east wing opened last summer. One- and two-bedroom apartments may be rented by the night ($174–$370) or on a longer-term lease. The east wing contains 300 rooms, including suites on the top four floors; it features a "native" Japanese suite with floor seating, futon bed, and wooden bathtub (price, $399 per night, and almost constantly booked). The hotel's nearly 600 rooms, suites, and apartments are served by 14 restaurants, plus a full-service business center and a health club.

The three buildings—all encased in sleek glass skins—are an imposing presence, which has raised a furor among İstanbullus, Turks and foreign expatriates alike. Rising above the romantic, resplendent Dolmabahçe palace, the glassy towers almost nullify the effect of this venerable landmark.

Despite the hotel's mixed-up aesthetics, the west wing does possess what is undoubtedly the largest lobby lounge in Istanbul—a vast, extremely high-ceilinged salon whose wraparound windows look out over the Bosphorus to Asia. More than a dozen comfortable seating areas are arranged around an elevated grand piano. There's a white marble fountain, 18th- and 19th-century bronze statues, handsome period furniture, and thick, rich oriental carpets underfoot.

The west wing's dining rooms are often full, although their food is less than top-notch. These include **Cafe Suisse**, with good service and continental cuisine; a Japanese and a Chinese restaurant; and the top-floor, open-roof garden grill, its sensational panorama framed by pink geraniums and white marble. In the cooler months, September through May, the hotel opens its **Swiss Farm**—built from a century-old, rustic wooden Swiss structure that was dismantled and shipped here—which offers great cheese fondues, raclettes, and Swiss provincial fare.

Rooms and baths throughout the hotel are satisfyingly large; the amount of marble in the floors and walls is awesome. But, aside from the lobby's quality period furniture, furnishings throughout the hotel are unimpressive, too often upholstered in banal "hotel green." In some of the more expensive rooms, the bathroom includes a bidet.

In the hotel's west wing, **Juliana's Night Club** has a bar, videos, and disco. The nightclub is open Wednesday through Saturday nights, the disco Thursday through Saturday; hours 8:00 P.M. to 4:00 A.M.; Tel: 259-0940.

The Swissôtel Bosphorus's refurbished excursion boat,

1,001 Nights, provides evening cruises during the summer and fall, Tuesday through Saturday. The cruise along the Bosphorus features a buffet-style dinner. A shuttle bus leaves the hotel at 7:30 P.M. for Kuruçeşme landing, from which the boat departs at 8:00 sharp. The cruises are open to the public; reservations must be made and paid for in advance at the hotel; cost, $35 per person. On Sundays the *1,001 Nights* makes a day-long (11:00 A.M. to 7:00 P.M.) cruise from Kuruçeşme to the Princes' Islands; cost, $50 per person. The boat is also available for hire by private parties.

The Swissôtel Bosphorus's **casino** is open from 11:00 A.M. to 4:00 A.M.; Tel: 259-0742.

The hotel is about a 20-minute walk from Taksim and at least half an hour by taxi from Atatürk airport.

Bayıldım Caddesi 2, 80680 Beşiktaş; Tel: 259-0101; Fax: 259-0105. West wing: $213–$319; suites, $285–$1,344; east wing, $174–$370 (value-added tax not included).

Expensive

Built in 1892 to house Orient Express passengers, the **Pera Palas** is the oldest operational Istanbul hotel, almost in the center of the new city. With its grandiose lobby of 20-foot-high coral marble walls and gray marble columns, white marble stairway, period furniture, ornate chandeliers, picturesque bar, and bird-cage elevator—all in Belle Epoque style—this is a place to savor Turkey's past. Royalty and ambassadors to the Ottoman court stayed here during the hotel's early days; later, President Atatürk was a frequent guest (in room 101, now preserved as a museum). Agatha Christie lived in room 411 while researching her book *Murder on the Orient Express.*

The Pera Palas's 145 high-ceilinged rooms and six suites have all been pleasantly renovated; each possesses a private bath, air-conditioning, double-pane windows, direct-dial telephone, satellite TV, and minibar. A spacious Ottoman townhouse across the street has been added as an annex (its 17 bedrooms, at $100 per double, are about 40 percent less expensive than rooms in the hotel proper). The main building's front rooms face the street and can be noisy; those at the back are often hot at sunset, but they do offer views of the Golden Horn. The large, gold-paneled restaurant has satisfactory food. An open-air tea garden and pastry café has been added to the hotel's east side, and on the west side of the ground floor there's a new pastry shop outfitted with period furniture including a pair of antique sedan chairs.

A 25-minute walk from Taksim square, the Pera Palas is about 30 minutes away from the airport. It's a very colorful place to stay on your first—or any—visit to Istanbul. At the very least plan to have a drink or coffee at the **Orient Express Bar**. One caveat: Even though this charming period piece is expensive, don't expect great food or service.

Meşrutiyet Caddesi 98–100, 80050 Tepebaşı; Tel: 251-4560; Fax: 251-4089. $180 (including breakfast).

An uplifting influence on the lower stretch of İstiklâl Caddesi is the gleaming **Richmond Hotel**, adjacent to the Russian consulate. Its graciously modern, mirror-fronted six floors (housing 117 rooms) surround a lovely old Ottoman townhouse. The casual, appealing **Café Lebon**—on the sidewalk extension—is immediately beguiling. Inside is the well-appointed lobby, filled with copper and brass artifacts and hung with original pastels of Ottoman-period buildings. The Richmond Hotel's large-enough double rooms are air-conditioned and have direct-dial telephones, minibars, TVs, safe-deposit boxes, and hair dryers (35 of the rooms have king-size beds).

This welcome addition to the lower part of the new city seems to have led the way in revitalizing the area.

İstiklâl Caddesi 445, 80670 Beyoğlu. Tel: 252-5460; Fax: 252-9707. $150.

Inter Hotels, a Turkish chain, is the proprietor of the Richmond Hotel and of the two-year-old **Hotel Mim** in the Nişantası district, north of Taksim. Unfortunately, the Mim has an awkward location, at the bottom of a hill; traffic around here is bad, and the hotel is difficult to reach. The building is a small, postmodern-ish structure whose design incorporates Greek columns, arches, and triangular forms. The lobby's decor is Mexican, as is the decor of the hotel's **Mariacchi** restaurant. This Mexican eatery (a rarity in Istanbul, to say the least) and the hotel's two bars—the **Jungle Disco** (on the roof) and the **Bar** (next to the restaurant)—are jammed on weekends, so reservations are necessary; Tel: 231-2807. Dinners are about $18 per, excluding drinks.

The Mim has 112 rooms equipped with air conditioning, hair dryer, direct-dial telephone, TV, radio, and minibar. It operates a shuttle bus service to Taksim.

Ihlamur Fulya Bayırı, Ferah Sokak 19, 80200 Nişantaşı. Tel: 231-2807; Fax: 230-7377. $140 (breakfast, $8 extra).

On the other side of central Taksim square, on the Maçka hillside, is the **ParkSa Hilton Istanbul**, opened in 1991. This extremely pleasant "boutique" hotel (small, exclusive, and stylish) has 122 units on seven floors, which the owner, the Sabancı Holding Company (that's where the *Sa* in the name comes from), has endowed with top-quality fixtures and attractive furnishings. The ground-floor restaurant is extremely attractive and has one of the best buffets in Istanbul.

The rooms are blessed with adjustable air conditioning, double-glazed windows for soundproofing, direct-dial telephones, radio news, taped music, satellite TV, minibars, and hair dryers and telephones in the bathrooms. Two suites have Jacuzzis. Managed by Hilton International, the ParkSa has already become a popular place to stay.

Maçka Caddesi, 80200 Maçka; Tel: 258-5674; Fax: 258-5695. In the U.S., (800) HILTONS; in the U.K., (0800) 289-303 or, in London, (081) 780-1155; in Canada, (800) 268-9275 or, in Toronto, (416) 362-3771. $146–$186.

Up the hill from the ParkSa toward Taksim is the **Maçka Hotel**. A long six-story building set in a garden, the Maçka is relaxed—maybe even sleepy—but the staff are wide awake and several speak English. The hotel sits on a tree-lined street opposite Maçka Parkı. Each of its 184 adequately sized rooms is provided with bath, air conditioning, direct-dial telephone, satellite TV, and minibar. The Terrace Restaurant and Bar is in the lobby. The hotel also has a ballroom that seats 200, a conference room, a sauna, a massage room, and a tanning salon. As of 1992, the bedrooms on the fifth floor had been fully refurnished; rooms on the lower floors were to be completely reoutfitted by summer 1993. Rooms on the east side of each floor have balconies. The hotel provides a satisfying experience overall—and should improve this year, with the additions of a swimming pool, two more floors, and a second Terrace Bar on the roof. A sauna and casino are also planned.

Eytam Caddesi, 80200 Maçka; Tel: 234-3200; Fax: 240-7694. $110–$130.

Moderate

Closer to Taksim, on Aydede Caddesi just west of Cumhuriyet Caddesi, is the very attractive **Riva**. The hotel's bar and restaurant are suspended over the lobby on an open mezzanine. Its 71 rooms and seven suites are all good-sized and have double-glazed windows, air conditioning, direct-dial telephones, satellite TV, taped music, and minibars. The restaurant here serves international and Turkish food, and there are a snack bar and two meeting rooms as well. The Riva has a money-changing office in the corner of the lobby (closed Sundays). The Riva's staff is very much "with it"; its style and range of facilities attract businesspeople, writers, and other purposeful travellers, who usually keep it full year round.

Aydede Caddesi 8, 80090 Taksim; Tel: 256-4420; Fax: 256-2033. $98.

On the southern side of Taksim, just a three-minute walk

away from the square, is a cluster of handy hotels along or off
Sıraselviler Caddesi. The best of these is the **Dilson Hotel**. Its
lobby floor of black-and-white marble, its sizable bar (with
live piano music), and the restaurant are decorated in classic
European hotel style. The appealing **Philadelphia Gourmet
Restaurant** (Philadelphia is the ancient Greek name of the
town of Alaşehir in southwestern Turkey, the owner's hometown) serves traditional and international cuisine. The Dilson
has 114 large-enough rooms, each with bath; a few on the
higher floors of the east side have good views of the
Bosphorus. All the rooms have air conditioning, direct-dial
telephones, satellite TV, and minibars. The service is considerate and efficient. There's also the Uncle Bar (with live piano
music), the Snack Bar, and the Patisserie Jasmine, which are
frequented largely by foreign travellers.

Sıraselviler Caddesi 49, 80090 Taksim; Tel: 252-9605; Fax:
249-7077. $70–$110.

The best hotel buy in Istanbul, at about $30 for a single
room or $50 for a double, is the 100-year-old, handsome
Büyük Londra (Grand London), just up Meşrutiyet Caddesi
from the Pera Palas. Its 54 rooms and eight suites, each with
bath and telephone, have been redecorated in Ottoman
style. Rich velvet drapes hang in the large, high-ceilinged
lobby, and the windows are etched with floral patterns—
even the pastel color scheme is Ottoman in tone. The place
is redolent of old Istanbul. The hotel's central location,
reasonable rates, large breakfast buffet, and Old World mi-
lieu attract families from the United States and Europe. Be
warned that if you're planning to do a lot of telephoning,
don't stay here: The hotel's ancient system is a veritable
instrument of torture.

Meşrutiyet Caddesi 117, 80050 Tepebaşı; Tel: 249-1025 or
245-0670; Fax: 245-0671. $50.

Down a side street from the Pera Palas is one of Istanbul's
small but simpatico hotels, the **Bale** (as in "ballet"), right on a
major thoroughfare that whisks you by taxi to the airport in 15
to 20 minutes. Recently modernized, it has 63 nice rooms,
each with bath, air conditioning, direct-dial telephone, satellite TV, taped music, and minibar. The Bale also has a restaurant, two bars, and meeting rooms. A good buy.

Refik Saydam Caddesi 62, 80050 Tepebaşı; Tel: 253-0700;
Fax: 250-1692. $60–$80.

On the north side of Taksim square opposite the Hilton
on a typical side street off Cumhuriyet Caddesi is the **Hotel
Konak**, reasonable and homey. The Konak's warm, wood-
paneled restaurant-bar, which serves good Turkish home
cooking, adds to the friendly atmosphere. The Konak has an

attentive, English-speaking staff, some of whom have worked here for as long as 20 years. The Konak has only 23 medium-size rooms, each with bath, direct-dial telephone, satellite TV, music, and minibar. Young Turkish and foreign business-people have found the Konak a great spot—near the deluxe hotels but offering very reasonable rates.

Nisbet Sokak 9, 80230 Elmadağ; Tel: 248-4744; Fax: 232-4252. $94 (including breakfast).

East of Taksim square on a side street off İnönü, or Gümüşsuyu, Caddesi is an even more reasonably priced option—the **Hotel Star**, with 26 small rooms on eight floors and a restaurant. Each wood-paneled room has a shower-bath and telephone. The first-floor lobby, also wood-paneled, is attractively decorated and has a game room. Another good buy, especially given its central location.

Gümüşsuyu Caddesi, Sağlık Sokak 11, 80090 Gümüşsuyu; Tel: 245-0050 through 245-0052. $39.

ALONG THE BOSPHORUS

Lying just above the Dolmabahçe palace, the district of Beşiktaş is the first—that is, the southernmost—of the series of waterside districts stretching up the western bank of the Bosphorus. Like the towns above it—Ortaköy, Bebek, İstinye, to name a few—Beşiktaş was once a fishing village, but in recent decades has become more and more heavily urbanized. Traffic along the road that hugs the Bosphorus all the way north (and that goes by different names depending on which district you're passing through) is often intense, so despite the fact that Beşiktaş is only a mile or two from Taksim, the trip by taxi from the center of the new city to Beşiktaş can, at peak times, take upwards of half an hour. The pleasures that accompany staying in one or another of the Bosphorus towns are substantial, but if your visit's a short one and seeing the major sites of the old city is your major reason for being in Istanbul, you'll want to figure in the inescapable traffic delays before deciding to stay in Beşiktaş or, especially, any of the more northerly suburbs.

With that caveat out of the way, it must be said that Beşiktaş offers two of the most glamorous and sophisticated of Istanbul's many new hotels: the Hotel Conrad Istanbul and the Çırağan Palace Hotel Kempinski Istanbul.

Deluxe

The stunning new **Hotel Conrad Istanbul** (operated by the international subsidiary of Hilton USA) is a strikingly hand-some round tower of 14 stories with 614 air-conditioned rooms, including 30 suites—for a total of 1,228 beds! Aspiring to become Istanbul's "most exclusive and deluxe five-star hotel," the Conrad is situated in the park just below Yıldız palace—a hunting retreat of the sultans. Special accommodations include nonsmoking guest rooms and rooms fitted out for disabled visitors. Many of the suites have their own gardens—and all the suites (and many of the rooms) have magnificent panoramic views extending north to Bebek and all the way south to the Golden Horn. The rooms at the back of the hotel look out over Yıldız park's terraced gardens and the palace's domed mosque and slender minaret.

The Conrad's luxurious columned lobby—under a domed ceiling and featuring a romantic, curving marble staircase—is hung with original paintings, its floors covered with colorful, sink-into carpets. Rooms are attractively decorated: The furniture is French Empire and contemporary Italian, the color scheme pale green and rose. Every room is provided with three phones, each with a two-line capacity. The regular double rooms are big enough, but not even the three-sided mirrors can make the bathrooms seem roomy. Rooms on the so-called Executive Floors (12, 14, 15) are larger, of course.

The Conrad has achieved state-of-the-art facilities catering to businesspeople and conferences. The Business Centre on the mezzanine stays open "extra-long" hours to provide secretarial, communications, and courier services, and some rooms come with fax machines and personal-computer modems. The hotel will also rent you a portable cellular phone if you wish—the whole place is rather a communications extravaganza. All rooms are equipped with radio alarm clocks and electronic safety locks.

The Conrad has two interesting—though hardly first-class—restaurants, the Gülizar Cafe, whose decor, furnishings, and food hearken back to Ottoman times, and the Monteverdi Room, whose charming, *intime* yet formal decor features black, pink, and gray marble.

The classic oval ballroom of the Conrad has five crystal chandeliers and partly mirrored walls. The hotel possesses a fully equipped health club with indoor pool, and there's an outdoor pool in the front garden below a wall of hanging gardens.

The Conrad's **casino** is open from 2:00 P.M. to 5:00 A.M.

Yıldız Caddesi PQ 203, off Barbaros Bulvarı, 80700 Beşiktaş; Tel: 227-3000; Fax: 259-6667. For advance reservations, call, in the U.S., (800) HILTONS; in the U.K., (0800) 289-303 (in London, 081-780-1155); or, in Canada, (800) 268-

9275 (in Toronto, 416-362-3771). $195–$295 (double rooms); $360–$1,550 (suites).

The Conrad will have to try hard if it is to surpass the spectacular **Çırağan Palace Hotel Kempinski Istanbul**, situated right on the Bosphorus about a mile north of central Beşiktaş. The complex, nearly one-third of a mile in length, consists of a new hotel building and the reconstructed Çırağan Palace (Palace of the Torches). The project is a joint venture of Turkey's Ministries of Culture and Tourism and the Kempinski Hotel Group of Berlin, which is managing the facility. The new building opened in 1991; the restored Çırağan (pronounced CHUR-ah-ahn) Palace, to which the new building is linked, celebrated its grand opening in summer 1992. This gorgeous Rococco marble and marble-trimmed structure, used by the sultans from 1874 until it was completely gutted by fire in 1910, has reemerged as a national treasure, which former U.S. president George Bush and Luciano Pavarotti, among other guests, have already enjoyed.

The palace part of the complex contains 13 "sultan suites," one of which, with a floor area of about 510 square yards, is undoubtedly the largest hotel suite in all of Europe (its price tag—roughly $2,900 per night—is enormous, too). All the suites have mesmerizing views of the Bosphorus.

The palace's architectural grandeur—its regal divided staircase with crystal balustrade, the ornate atrium lighted by chandeliers, the exquisite fabric wall-panels, the lavish ballroom overlooking the Bosphorus and Asia—is in elegant, marked contrast to the square, concrete sameness of too much modern hotel architecture. It's definitely a must-see for foreign tourists. (The only false notes in the decor are some ugly faux marbre columns and some ceilings painted in garish colors.)

About three-quarters of the new building's 312 large guestrooms have Bosphorus views; the remainder overlook enchanting Yıldız park. Despite the hotel's grandeur (there's marble everywhere in the hotel's public areas), some guests have complained that the room rates seem steep given the unimpressive decor of most individual rooms—dull fabrics, amateurish-looking chests and bookcases (painted dull gray), carpeting that's far from luxurious. That drabness, however, contrasts with the smashing decor of the lobby's soaring **Gazebo Lounge**, with its rustic Spanish wickerwork chairs, tall green metal lamps copied from ancient Roman braziers, and a row of blue and pastel-colored Ottoman windows just below the ceiling.

The Çırağan's business center offers secretarial and simultaneous-translation services and communications facilities. The corridor linking the new building and old palace displays a permanent exhibition of a sultan's *haman* (bath) and sitting rooms. There's a working Turkish bath in the hotel's **health club**, where you can lie down and sweat on a traditional hot *göbek taşı* (belly stone) before being given a scrub-down at one of the bath's seven marble basins.

Between the complex's buildings and the Bosphorus shore lie two long swimming pools, the upper pool (perhaps Istanbul's largest) spilling over into the lower; both are served by a spacious poolside bar. A pair of extremely large bright yellow wrought-iron sea gates set in richly decorated marble frames lead from above the Bosphorus pier to the palace; the gates are nostalgic, enchanting remnants of the past.

The hotel has four restaurants and a coffee shop; none of the eateries is adequate to the hotel's grandeur. Among the Çırağan's myriad amenities are an opulent **casino** (open 2:00 P.M. to 5:00 A.M. daily), travel agencies, limousine rental, valet parking in an underground garage, and men's and women's hairdressers. You can shop in a full range of boutiques for clothing, jewelry, and rugs.

Çırağan Caddesi 84, 80700 Beşiktaş; Tel: 259-6355; Fax: 259-6686. $235–$360.

Expensive

About 24 km (15 miles) north of Taksim, at the burgeoning commercial crossorads of Maslak, is the towering new **Mövenpick Hotel** (operated by the well-known Swiss chain). The Maslak district is about three miles (and three minutes by taxi) from the Bosphorus, directly west of İstinye. With its 30 floors, the Mövenpick is one of Turkey's highest structures, something that riles a lot of Turks, who much prefer their buildings to be low-rise, nestled into a rolling landscape. Neither are Turks enthralled by the slim tower's offbeat color (a sort of mustard–terra-cotta) or its overbearing plastic signage.

But everyone seems to like the hotel's comfortable, attractive interiors. The Mövenpick has 280 standard double rooms, 112 deluxe rooms on four executive floors, and 13 suites. Among the noteworthy details are the extra-large beds, the personal-computer and fax-machine hookups, and the hair dryers and heat lamps in the bathrooms. The hotel has 58 nonsmoking rooms, and every one of its rooms has its own safe-deposit box. It's a point of pride that all the (extremely good-looking) fabrics used throughout the hotel have been woven exclusively for Mövenpick.

The Swiss firm began as a restaurant chain, and thus the Mövenpick is very food-and-beverage oriented. There are four restaurants: the **Kazan**, with marvelous Ottoman fare; the **Orangerie**, surrounded by a large verandah with lush greenery; the **Baron**, a gourmet buffet; and the **Mövenpick International**. The best of the hotel's three bars is the **Maslak Bar**, in the lobby. The Maslak bar features live jazz and blues (closed Sundays). The Mövenpick also has the **Zodiac** disco (closed Sundays), a small cinema that shows foreign (mostly American) films, and recreational and beauty facilities that include an indoor swimming pool, a large Jacuzzi, two saunas, a Turkish bath, a tanning salon, a squash court, and a beauty center. The Mövenpick's business center is open 24 hours. Its shopping center sports 45 stores. The hotel runs a shuttle bus that will deliver you to Taksim in 20 minutes or to the airport in about 15.

Büyükdere Caddesi 49, Üçyol Mevkii, 80670 Maslak. Tel: 285-0900; Fax: 285-0951 or 285-0952. $165–$205.

Across the Bosphorus in Asian Istanbul is the **Hıdiv Kasrı**, built in the first years of the 20th century as a small palace for the last *hıdiv* (khedive, or viceroy) of Egypt. The Hıdiv Kasrı's tower dominates a promontory above the town of **Çubuklu**; its grounds comprise one of the last remaining thickly wooded areas on the formerly forest-covered slopes surrounding the Bosphorus. The mansion has only 15 rooms on two floors, including two suites, originally used by the *hıdiv* and his wife. Though the Khedive's Suite includes an enormous bath with silver fixtures, most of the other rooms must share baths (which makes the Hıdiv Kasrı a good place for families or groups of friends). It is a truly magnificent experience to stay in this historic structure, restored to all its Art Nouveau glory by the Turkish Touring and Automobile Association.

Summer dining is on the spacious, curving terrace set above the fragrant gardens and beyond the main restaurant on the ground floor. The marble salon has a café, and, outside, there's a beer garden surrounded by stone terraces. All these facilities plus the concert hall are for rent for large parties and performances. The garden and ground floor of the palace are open to the public. Travel note: Though public buses, dolmuşes, and some ferries stop at Çubuklu, the Hıdiv Kasrı sits atop a sizable hill at the end of a long, winding road and is accessible only by taxi or private car.

Hıdiv Kasrı, 81640 Çubuklu; Tel: 331-2651; Fax: 322-3434. $47–$86 (shared bath); $143 (suite with private bath).

Moderate

On the European side of the Bosphorus about 11 km (7 miles) from Taksim is the prestigious suburb of **Bebek** (the name means "baby"), perhaps Istanbul's favorite and most charming offspring, where affluent Turks and foreign businesspeople and consular-staff members live in seaside villas and apartments, their boats anchored in their back yards. Bebek is a delightful community of old mansions, a mosque, teahouses, and parks around a ferry landing—plus some good restaurants. It has become a little glitzy, though. You can now find gold-lamé bathing suits displayed in the windows of boutiques along its main street.

Right in the middle of the town, on Cevdet Paşa Caddesi, is the small, old, and well-established **Bebek Hotel**, whose water-level **Restaurant Ambassadeurs** is very highly rated (read: overrated). The hotel's main attraction is a large open terrace right on the water; its wide Bosphorus view attracts writers, artists, and a generally well-heeled clientele including some foreign visitors, who come here to take tea or cocktails. The hotel bar just inside serves sandwiches and light meals.

The hotel's five floors have 47 rooms of varying size, most with private bathroom, direct-dial telephone, and television. The back rooms (on the Bosphorus side) have glorious views. Last year, the Bebek created a fifth-floor suite (two bedrooms, bath, sitting room, and balcony); it's not well furnished, but it does overlook the strait. All the hotel's rooms are being refurbished. Do avoid the middle rooms in back; they surround the noisy elevator. The hotel's lounge features piano music at teatime, daily. Though it may seem a bit far from town (usually about half an hour to Taksim, 45 minutes to the old city), the Bebek is a grand place if having a room with a superlative Bosphorus view is one of your priorities.

Cevdet Paşa Caddesi 113–115, 80810 Bebek; Tel: 263-3000/01/02; Fax: 263-2636. $60–$110.

THE OLD CITY

Expensive

Probably the most architecturally compelling hotel in the old city is the **Ramada Hotel Istanbul**, notable for its masterful combination of graceful Ottoman elements and a modern arched glass canopy that covers its streets and walks. In the heart of the old city near Istanbul University and the Covered Bazaar, the Ramada is a 25-minute walk from the principal tourist sites of Topkapı palace, St. Sophia, and the Blue Mosque.

The hotel, which opened in 1988, features stunningly renovated, cream-colored apartments with winged Baroque roofs and elegant Ottoman-style interiors. The Ramada was converted from four apartment houses that, when they were constructed in the early 1920s, represented Istanbul's first effort at "multiple-floored concrete buildings for social purposes." Of its 275 rooms, 132 are deluxe, and many of the 143 smaller rooms are attractively situated on the interior balconied courtyard above the lounge and gardens.

The lobby is a delight of sienna-hued marble floors, down the middle of which runs a stream stocked with goldfish; thick oriental rugs are strewn about on each side of the stream. To the left is an invitingly open buffet under a glass-bubble cover. White marble steps lead up or down from the lobby to the hotel's four restaurants: the Lâle (Tulip), Dynasty Asian, Winter Garden, and Ocakbaşı Grill, plus the Babiali Wine Bar, named for Istanbul's "Fleet Street" of newspaper publishing in nearby Cağaloğlu. All the hotel's public rooms are furnished with period reproductions; the guest rooms had been looking a bit tired, but they're all being renovated, with new carpets and fabrics throughout.

The Ramada's **health club** has an indoor swimming pool, a Jacuzzi, two saunas (men's and women's), and a tanning salon. The hotel's **Lâleli Casino**—with mirrored walls and a wealth of overhead lights—opens at 4:00 P.M. and closes at 5:00 A.M.

Ordu Caddesi 226, 34470 Lâleli; Tel: 513-9300; Fax: 512-6390, for reservations, 512-8120. In the U.S., (800) 228-9898; in the U.K., (0800) 18-17-37; in Canada, (800) 268-8998. $139–$200; presidential suite, $333.

In the heart of the old city only two blocks from the Covered Bazaar is another find: the glass-fronted **President Hotel**, which opened in 1989. The President is roomy, nice-looking, and comfortable. It has 204 double rooms, each with a full range of amenities, including hair dryer, direct-dial telephone, satellite TV, minibar, and pants presser. Room service is 24 hours. There are eight suites plus two large President Suites (at $180 a night) with views of the Sea of Marmara. The President's top floor boasts an indoor heated pool, open terrace for sunbathing, poolside bar, and nightclub with live music and dancing—and a great view of the Istanbul skyline.

The President's **Pub Bar**—an English-style pub—features a guitarist each evening. Its **Ocakbaşı** restaurant is excellent, with a handsome, wrought-iron decor and outstanding Ottoman and contemporary Turkish menu. Two superb singer-musicians provide entertainment.

Tiyatro Caddesi 25, 34490 Beyazit. Tel: 516-6980; Fax: 516-6999. $135.

Another great surprise is the **Hotel Akgün Istanbul**, on the northwest side of the old city just seven minutes from Atatürk airport. The Akgün, which opened in March 1992, is very close to the major tourist sites. Its furnishings in the lobby and other public areas feature bold kilim designs and black-and-white marble patterns. The Akgün's 240 rooms are large and attractive enough, especially given the relatively low price tag of about $140 a night. There are eight suites, one per floor, and two "king suites" on the eighth floor (one has one bedroom, the other two bedrooms and two and a half baths). The hotel's fitness facilities (on the lower level) take up almost an entire floor; there's a gorgeous, all-marble Turkish bath, plus sauna and exercise and massage rooms. The sizable swimming pool is outside.

Food in the Akgün's **restaurant** is generally superior. Its master chef creates refined, delicious Ottoman dishes, including meat terrines, cold artichoke hearts with olive oil and vegetables, and tomatoes and green peppers stuffed with rice, pine nuts, and currants. The desserts are terrific.

The Akgün's operators, who together have 30 years' experience in the hotel trade, toured some of the best European hotels before opening their establishment—and incorporated some of the European hotels' latest features, including an air-conditioning system that shuts off when a room's windows or doors are opened.

The hotel's **Casino Emperyal**, on the lower level, is open from 1:00 P.M. to 5:00 A.M.

Adnan Menderes Bulvarı (a.k.a. Vatan Caddesi), 34270 Istanbul. Tel: 534-4879; Fax: 534-9126. $140.

Praised by visiting Swiss (who make up about 90 percent of its clientele) as well as by Germans and American businesspeople—not to mention local gourmets—the **Kalyon Hotel** (the name means "galleon") has been properly "docked" on the Sea of Marmara, just south of the Topkapı walls' southernmost extension, for some 20 years. This clean, modern, and blessedly peaceful hotel is set off with a row of flags that makes it easy to identify (so does the large Mobil gas-station sign, set among trees next door).

The Kalyon's view stretches all the way to the Princes' Islands and the twinkling Asian shore beyond. It's an easy ten-minute walk from here up a hill through a neighborhood of old wooden houses to the major tourist sites. The

Kalyon's two floors contain 110 ample-size rooms, each with bath, hair dryer, telephone, TV, and air conditioning. There's plenty of parking space, too.

The hotel has an attractive restaurant indoors, for winter dining, and a **terrace restaurant** outdoors (open from April to October), usually packed because of marvelous soup, seafood, salads, and desserts (including the best *krem karamel* in Istanbul) and magnificent sea vistas.

Sahil Yolu, 34400 Sultanahmet; Tel: 517-4400; Fax: 517-6770. $120 (taxes not included).

Over the past decade the Turkish Touring and Automobile Association, under Çelik Gülersoy's innovative leadership, has launched an impressive program of restoring and renovating Ottoman town houses and *köşks* (i.e., kiosks—the pavilions that dot Istanbul's parks and the hills around the Bosphorus). These charmingly rehabilitated treasures of past centuries have greatly encouraged tourism development.

One of Gülersoy's greatest successes is the **Yeşil Ev** (Green House), a four-story mansion between Sultanahmet Camii (the Blue Mosque) and St. Sophia. Here up to 41 guests can stay in 20 spacious rooms, each with "W.C." and shower. All of the Yeşil Ev's pleasantly decorated rooms feature 19th-century brass beds and carved wooden furniture upholstered in velvet or silk, and all are hung with old art prints recalling bygone days. There's a Rococo white-marble fountain in the dining room in which you can wash your hands; at five o'clock tea and at dinner a pianist plays an old Constantinopolitan piano in the drawing room. A major attraction of the Yeşil Ev is the **Terrace Restaurant** in its back garden, where about 150 can dine or take refreshments under huge old trees around a pink porphyry fountain (see the Dining section, below).

The Yeşil Ev's lodgings are among the most sought-after in Istanbul, so make your reservations early.

Kabasakal Caddesi 5, 34400 Sultanahmet; Tel: 517-6785 through 88; Fax: 517-6780. $125; $200 for "Pasha's Room," with private Turkish bath.

Moderate

Also restored and operated by the Turkish Touring and Automobile Association are the **Ayasofya** (St. Sophia) **Pensions**, a row of nine distinctively gracious pastel clapboard houses on cobblestoned Soğukçeşme Sokak just outside the Topkapı palace walls. These renovated Ottoman houses have a total of 61 rooms (including five suites), each with bath, direct-dial telephone, radio, and beguiling period furniture and Turkish rugs. (The rooms are not air-conditioned but are equipped with fans.) Two of the five suites have Turkish baths. Arrangements are made for guests to eat dinner at the nearby Sarnıç tavern.

The pensions' location couldn't be nearer the major tourist attractions of the old city. It's worth mentioning, too, that the street on which they sit is closed to motor traffic—a real boon in auto-clogged Istanbul. At prices more reasonable than those charged by the Yeşil Ev, the Ayasofya Pensions allow you to experience the lifestyle of upper-class Turks of the Ottoman era.

Soğukçeşme Sokak, 34400 Sultanahmet; Tel: 513-3660; Fax: 513-3669. $90–$100.

"Sultanahmet" refers to the tourist area around Sultanahmet Camii (the Blue Mosque), St. Sophia, and the Hippodrome (once the world's largest horse-race track, now an open oval area). In Turkish the Hippodrome is called Atmeydanı (Horse Square).

The old city has a new mode of surface transportation: a light-rail commuter train whose tracks cut through Sultanahmet—meaning that vehicular traffic is now prohibited around the Hippodrome. Therefore, everyone must walk across the light-rail tracks to visit the İbrahim Paşa Palace (see above). Past the palace is a sweet urban oasis—full of walnut, chestnut, and mimosa trees and relatively free of traffic noise and pollution—where a number of new small hotels have opened.

These include the **Hotel Alzer**, which offers surprisingly reasonable Ottoman-style housing for the dedicated traveller who wants to probe the old city close up. The Alzer offers 21 nice-size double rooms with period furnishings, private baths, telephones, satellite TV, and minibars. You enter the hotel by the attractive **Terrace Café**, offering excellent Ottoman and continental fare prepared by the owner's wife and daughter—truly accomplished cooks. Food is served from breakfast time till midnight, and the Terrace Café has become a favorite spot for night-owl diners.

There are a lot of nice touches at the Alzer—including five o'clock tea with *kek* (cake) and bowls of fresh strawberries and cherries in the rooms each night.

Atmeydanı 72, 34400 Sultanahmet; Tel: 516-6262; Fax: 516-0000. $85–$100 (including breakfast buffet).

Two doors east of the Alzer is an inn operated by another high-minded entrepreneur, Halit Özüdoğru, a former Fine Arts Academy student who turned his home into the **Optimist Guesthouse**, which his South African wife, Kutsi, runs for him. The ten rooms are simple—those on the lower floors tiny and with shared bath, those on the top floor larger and with private baths and views. The clever and simpatico Halit Bey wants to increase the number of the Optimist's rooms to 20—but still maintain his mid-1980s prices (he values the great friends he makes from all over the world more than money).

The Optimist has recently added a good **restaurant**—15 tables under the wild chestnut trees along the front pavement (in winter, just four or five tables indoors). Because of the Optimist's nearness to the Blue Mosque—with its nightly sound and light show—the sidewalk restaurant is a very romantic spot on a summer evening.

Atmeydanı 68, 34400 Sultanahmet; Tel: 516-2398; Fax: 516-1928. $30 (without bath); $35 (with bath); breakfast included.

—*Anne Turner Bruno*

DINING

There is a time-honored saying—enthusiastically endorsed by Ernest Hemingway, who worked in Istanbul as a correspondent—that Turkish cooking is one of the world's three great cuisines, along with French and Chinese. (Many do qualify this to mean specifically *Ottoman* Turkish cooking.)

Turkish cuisine certainly reflects the Turks' great love of food. Historically, it has incorporated distinctive dishes from the great number of ethnic groups that were embraced by the Ottoman Empire, which at its height ranged east to Baghdad, south to Cairo, and west to what is now Austria. No matter what the ethnic inspiration of a particular dish, the greatness of Turkish cooking resides, in part, in the use of the freshest garden-ripened vegetables, sometimes cooked with meat but always delicately spiced and lovingly prepared.

The Turkic nomads who ranged the Central Asian steppes are credited with the invention of yogurt as a method of preserving milk. Today Turkish cooks employ yogurt in dishes for every course of a meal, from soup to dessert. (The creamy, stiff, and pungent yogurt available in every corner grocery in Turkey bears only distant resemblance to its North American cousin, which usually has cornstarch and sugar added.) These nomadic tribespeople were also the originators of *şiş* (meat cooked on a skewer over an open fire) and what is now known as steak tartare—raw meat that, in those days, was tenderized under the saddle of a horse.

After the Ottomans captured Constantinople in 1453, they adopted many of the Byzantines' finest culinary creations, especially their vegetable dishes—stuffed green peppers, squash, eggplant, cabbage, and grape leaves. Also of Byzantine origin are the *pilav*s—hot or cold rice dishes embellished with spices, pine nuts, and ground lamb—and some desserts, possibly including the most "Turkish" of desserts, baklava (thin layers of pastry filled with chopped walnuts and sugar syrup).

The numerous other worthy acquisitions included Circassian chicken (*Çerkez tavuğu*), cold chicken breast slathered with a ground walnut and paprika sauce; and, from the Arabs, hummus, a salad made of spiced chickpeas.

Restaurants in Turkey are called by different names indicative of the kind of food served and the level of service provided. A humbler sort of establishment is likely to be called a *lokanta;* a fancier place may be known by the borrowed Western word *restoran*. Many restaurants stay open late into the night, and good, wholesome food is available almost everywhere. If you're on the run and in need of quick nourishment, don't make the mistake of settling for Turkish versions of American fast food: hamburgers are tough, french fries are greasy, and even the ketchup isn't great.

Instead of going for a poor imitation of American fast food, why not try one of the quick, delicious snacks readily available in neighborhood stores and sidewalk restaurants? For instance, in the shops known as *muhallebici*s you'll discover a variety of **puddings** that make the Western world's pudding seem a plain, sugary mass of empty calories. Turkish puddings aren't just sweets but nutritious and interesting food. Definitely try the pudding called *tavuk göğsü,* which is made with sweetened milk, rice flour, and finely shredded pieces of chicken breast. Another delicious pudding is *aşure,* also known as "Noah's pudding" for the supposed last meal on the Ark (which according to the story took place on Mount Ararat in Eastern Turkey) when Noah's family cooked up all the odds and ends they had left over. Pudding chefs claim *aşure* has a hundred ingredients; it does have at least 20, including cereals, nuts, and dried fruit, as well as fresh apricots, figs, dates, plums, or pomegranates. It's often sprinkled with rose water before serving.

In most countries rice pudding is hardly special, but wait until you try Turkish *sütlaç*. You'll beg for the recipe. Sometimes it's fired in the oven so that its surface is caramelized black. These and other *sade* (plain, that is, milk or vanilla), chocolate, or pistachio puddings can be found at shops within three blocks of one another in the central new city. **Sütiş** (meaning "milk work") at Teşvikiye Caddesi 137/A, Nişantaşı, and **Saray**, another *muhallebici* right down the street, have branches throughout İstanbul. **Keremoğlu**, at number 97 İstiklâl Caddesi, the main street of Beyoğlu, also offers omelettes and *menemen* (scrambled eggs with green peppers and tomatoes), as well as its many puddings, yogurt treats, *pilav* dishes, and ice creams. All these *muhallebicis* are open from 6:00 A.M. to midnight daily. One of the best quick foods is plain yogurt; every *bakkal* (mom-and-pop-type grocery store) stocks both 200-gram and 650-gram containers. Add a banana from a fruit seller and you've got yourself a light lunch.

Turkish **ice cream** and **sherbets**, which supposedly originated as delectable delicacies for the sultan, can be divine. They aren't usually as creamy as American ice cream, but ice-cream shops offer a range of interesting flavors, such as watermelon, Persian melon, raspberry, apricot, cinnamon, and caramel.

Many *kafeterya*s have hearty lentil, split pea, dried bean, or cream of chicken **soups** in every season. Small eateries serve staple **fast foods** such as *döner kebap* and *lahmacun,* a sprinkling of ground beef on a thick pancake that is known as Turkish pizza.

If you drink, don't leave Turkey without sampling the national liquor, **rakı**. Distilled from grapes and flavored with anise, rakı, like Pernod, clouds when ice or water is added. Nicknamed "lion's milk," rakı is so strong that it is almost never drunk except as an accompaniment to food. Try it, therefore, with a good selection of *meze* (Turkish appetizers): dips made from yogurt or white cheese and garlic; marinated cold green beans; eggplant purée; *çoban salatası* (shepherd's salad), a mixture of chopped onions, tomatoes, and peppers; hot potato balls; fried cheese; or *börek*—cheese, spinach, zucchini, meat, or mussels wrapped in little square, triangular, or rolled packages of dough and quickly deep-fried (to be eaten with the fingers). Other meze you'll want to sample include fried squid (*kalamar*) and *Arnavut* (Albanian) *ciğeri,* little cubes of liver fried with onions.

Turkish **bread** of all sorts is excellent. Many restaurants simply serve the loaves—whose weight and quality are strictly controlled by the government—that are available in every bakery and grocery store. But some restaurants have special kinds of bread—flat, pita-like loaves (called *pide* in Turkish), or big, puffy loaves that are hollow inside, covered in caraway seeds, and served piping hot. Most Turks prefer the common white loaves (with their chewy crusts) or *francala* ("French" bread), the superior quality of white that's sprinkled with poppy seeds, but it's not hard to find semidark *çavdar* (rye) or *kepekli* (bran) breads at specialty bakeries.

At dinner the main course often consists of **fresh fish** chosen from the tray displaying the day's catch. Unfortunately, fish is becoming scarce and expensive in Istanbul because of the overfishing and pollution of the Black Sea and the Sea of Marmara. But Istanbul's seafood—*levrek* (sea bass), *lüfer* (bluefish), *palamut* (tunny, or bonita tuna), *kılıç* (swordfish), and *kalkan* (turbot)—is renowned as the world's tastiest because of the mineral salts that fish ingest from the Black Sea.

Choice **meat** entrées are mixed grill, generally including a lamb chop, *köfte* (a wonderfully spiced meatball), and perhaps an organ meat; *köfte* alone; lamb or veal chops; lamb, veal, or chicken *şiş; tas kebap,* a stew of lamb, veal, or chicken with vegetables; tasty meat croquettes known as *kadın budu* ("woman's thigh"); and beefsteak—ordered as *bonfile* or *file minyon.* Steak is surprisingly flavorful, but is usually cut very thin, which makes it tough and overcooked for a North American steak-lover's taste. The entrée is accompanied or followed by a vegetable course, perhaps a mixed vegetable stew called *türlü,* very much like ratatouille.

Dinner almost always includes a rice or pasta (*makarna*) course, but, unfortunately, the latter is unfailingly overcooked—no pasta al dente here. The **salad** course highlights the freshness of Turkey's produce; for Westerners who've gotten used to tomatoes picked green or raised in hothouses, the taste of the vine-ripened Turkish variety can be a nearly religious experience.

Desserts are *sweet*—perhaps too cloying for the Westerner's taste—but invariably fresh. There's baklava, of course, and many other kinds of sugar-syrup–soaked cakes with names that translate as "lips of beauty," "woman's navel," and "nightingale's nest."

The meal may be topped off with **fresh fruit**: huge, ambrosial peaches, pears, sugary purple or green figs, chilled watermelon, or justly famous Persian melon. A demitasse of Turkish **coffee** brewed to order with the desired amount of sugar (*şekerli* means "very sugary," *orta* is "medium sweet," *az* means "a little sugar," *sade* means "plain") can settle the feast and your fortune as well—if there's a reader of coffee grounds around. **Tea** (*çay*), truly the national drink, is enjoyed all day long, sipped from little tulip-shaped glasses, so coffee is usually preferred after meals.

Even in humble establishments table service is likely to be fastidious, with a change of service between courses. Turks are also meticulously clean when it comes to food preparation.

If you choose not to accompany your meal with rakı, you might want to sample some local **wines**. Winemaking in Anatolia goes back at least to the time of the Hittites, circa 1300 B.C. Actually, the Bible and Judeo-Christian tradition credit Noah as the first winemaker: He is said to have created wine after docking the Ark on Mount Ararat. Though they're not yet well known abroad, Turkey today produces some fine wines.

As in all winemaking regions, the local vintages make wonderful complements to the local food. Turkey's reds are full bodied and dry and go marvelously with lamb and game. The light, dry whites are splendid with seafood. Turkey's great rosés—lively and refreshing—are often compared with the best produced by California or the Loire Valley. Labels to request include Villa Doluca's white, red, and rosé; the whites and reds of Doluca Nevşah, Doluca Antik, and Villa Neva; and the white demisec called Moskado. Equally desirable are the Kavaklidere Selection Premiere white and red, Fevzi Kutman Semillon white and red, Çankaya white, Yakut and Dikmen reds, and the lovely rosé called Lâl. Foreign wines are not for sale in Turkey, but French and German sparkling wine, Champagne, Cognac, Sherry, vermouth, and other aperitifs are readily available.

Turkish **beer** is delicious. Made in Turkey under German license is the superlative Efes (Ephesus) Pilsen, for decades a prizewinner in international beer competitions. Other beers are the slightly sweeter Tuborg, made in Turkey under Danish license, and Tekel, the beer produced by the Turkish state liquor and tobacco monopoly (also called Tekel).

Almost all kinds of **liquor** are available in Turkey; some are even produced in-country under government control. Turkish gin (*cin*) is, however, to be avoided. The better Tekel vodka (*votka*) is Binboğa, and the best vodka is probably İzmira, which is made with glycerine and resembles Russian vodka. It is hard to get as it is primarily made for export. Imported Scotch—always called *viski*—of several brands is to be found everywhere, and better establishments have bars well stocked with foreign libations at imported prices. Drinks can be expensive and—for a drinker—appallingly small.

Despite the Islamic prohibition against drinking alcohol, few İstanbullus are teetotalers. Those who do eschew liquor—as well as those who imbibe—have a range of some 500 sources for **spring and mineral water**. (Some Turks take pride in being able to identify a water's source from just a sip.) Turkish spring and mineral waters are rated by many travellers as Europe's finest. One warning is, however, in order: The great flavor of Turkey's mineral water reflects a high sodium content, so those on restricted-sodium diets may want to avoid it. (Distilled bottled water is available everywhere, however.)

It was true until very recently that tap water was safe to drink in Istanbul; sadly, that is no longer the case. The danger Istanbul's tap water poses is minimal, but it's probably safer to avoid drinking it. It is quite unlikely that you will get very sick; it is, however, possible that you will experience mild stomach discomfort and diarrhea, probably simply the result of changing continents and adjusting to new strains of bacteria. A preparation called Kompensan, for gas and acid stomach, and another called Streptomagma, for diarrhea, are available in pharmacies (*eczanes*) without a prescription.

Restaurants discussed below are categorized as *deluxe* ($50 to $100 per person), which often refers to decor and ambience as much as it does to price (reservations are recommended); *expensive* ($25 to $50 per person); and *moderate* (less than $25 per person).

The telephone area code for Istanbul is 1.

THE NEW CITY

Deluxe

Istanbul's most luxurious and Lucullan dining is to be found in the new city and its affluent suburbs, ranging about ten miles up the Bosphorus on the European side. The fast-developing Asian side also possesses a growing number of fine restaurants.

In contrast to what's usually said about hotel food almost everywhere, Istanbul's deluxe hotels currently offer some of the city's best dining. An imperative for any visitor is to experience the Ottoman-style **Revan**, the Sheraton Hotel's rooftop restaurant (Taksim Parkı; Tel: 231-2121). Its unmatched view feeds the eye before the actual feast begins. The Revan's special traditional recipes are a revelation. Try for starters one of the two *börek* specialties: *puf böreği,* a delicious cheese pastry, or the *Revan böreği,* with meat. Other delectable appetizers consist of swiss chard leaves stuffed with lamb and rice and topped with a dollop of yogurt and squash patties with herbs. The restaurant features superb entrées of eggplant kebap and chicken with eggplant purée. The baked fruit desserts—figs, apricots, or apples stuffed with double-rich *kaymak* (clotted cream)—are magical. Diners here are entertained by a musician playing the *ud* (a long-handled string instrument). The Revan also carries on the old tradition (elegant or irritating, according to your politics) of presenting female guests with unpriced menus.

From mid-April until October, the Sheraton's **private boat** sails up and down the Bosphorus every evening on dinner cruises four hours long, and the buffets are very good. Reservations—a must—can be made at the Sheraton desk (Taksim Parkı; Tel: 231-2121). These cruises are open to all tourists if space is available. A shuttle bus leaves the Sheraton for the dock at Kabataş, a short distance below the Dolmabahçe palace on the European side. Check current schedules.

The distinguished **Divan Restaurant** on the mezzanine of the Divan Hotel (Cumhuriyet Caddesi 2; Tel: 231-4100) is legendary for serving the finest in Turkish and international cuisine. A variety of well-heeled Turks and diplomats fills the Divan's long, attractive salon every evening except Sunday, when the restaurant is closed. The service is divine.

The Divan's ground floor features three interesting eating places. The reasonably priced **Divan Pub** has good food and service and is open from noon until 11:00 P.M. for lunch, light meals, and snacks. The Divan Pastanesi (pastry shop) sells unique pastries, sweets, ice cream, and chocolates, which can be consumed in the connecting open-air **Bulvar Teras** (Boulevard Terrace), which overlooks busy Cumhuriyet Caddesi and is, therefore, one of the new city's best spots for people-watching. Finally, there is the relatively new **Divan Soupé**, a friendly adjunct to the **Kehribar** (Amber Bar), where late-night snackers can satisfy their hunger while listening to the bar's jazz show (10:00 P.M. till 1:00 A.M.; also see Entertainment and Nightlife, below). The Soupé serves French onion soup, smoked salmon, spaghetti, and the like.

A few blocks up Cumhuriyet Caddesi from the Divan is the Hilton International Istanbul and its **Rooftop Rotisserie** (Tel: 231-4646), where maître d' İsa Bey will assist you (in perfect English) as you select from a sophisticated and large menu of traditional Turkish and international dishes plus an extensive wine list. The large room's chandeliers and candles echo the lights on the Asian shore, about a mile away across the Bosphorus.

On summer evenings Hilton guests may dine alfresco around the garden swimming pool, with flowers and colorful balloons afloat. On the Hilton's ground floor, the **Greenhouse**—complete with fig trees, singing birds, and green bamboo furniture—offers elaborate buffet breakfasts, lunches, and dinners. The Hilton's Dragon Restaurant is covered below in the Foreign Dining section.

Expensive

The **Bronz Brasserie** opened in 1991 at Bronz Sokak 5 in the heart of the Nişantaşı-Maçka-Teşvikiye district. Bronz's sizable ground-floor bar-and-dining salon holds 70, but everybody seems to want the 14 places on the front patio, where black armchairs are arranged around tables draped in orange-colored linens under the magnolia, fig, and linden trees.

Metin Sarier, the charming and knowledgeable restaurateur, has an extremely interesting menu with some unusual specialties. His spaghetti salad with cheese and tomato vinaigrette sauce is simply great, as are the *moules marinières,* melon and ham, crab cocktail with curry sauce, smoked meat with *marul* (romaine lettuce), or smoked fish platter. His unusual fish entrées include salmon with Champagne sauce, and sole and shrimp *en brioche.* Meat specialties include *escalope de veau* in red wine sauce, chicken and asparagus with béarnaise sauce, *blanquette de veau* with Roquefort sauce, and chateaubriand with three sauces. Among desserts offered are *poire belle Hélène,* strawberry pudding with pineapple, and a serving of Persian melon filled with ice cream or red wine.

If you want to eat where the young professional İstanbullus and elite businesspeople do, have lunch or dinner at **Park Şamdan** (Mim Kemal Öke Caddesi 18, Nişantaşı, facing Maçka park; Tel: 240-7523 or 240-8368). The Şamdan serves truly delicious Ottoman-influenced nouvelle cuisine and other innovative contemporary dishes. There's a day-to-day consistency in the quality of the food served here—you can always count on being served a tasty meal. It's also been characterized as the best-working restaurant in the city. The superiority of its food and efficiency of service guarantee that its 80 or so seats will always be full. (The Park Şamdan is open year-round every day except Sundays during July and August.)

The young chef, Hüseyin Gürsoy, who trained at Turkey's famous cooking school in Mengen-Bolu, has for the past five years been creating such memorable dishes as *piliç java* (sauteed young chicken with raisins, almonds, curry, and fresh cream), *piliç park* (young chicken stuffed with béchamel sauce, mushrooms, and peas), finely spiced ground veal and lamb *köfte* wrapped in chard leaves (served with homemade noodles), and *çin böreği* (a deep-fried Chinese roll of finely diced shrimp, chicken, veal, almonds, and spring onions), as well as interesting and substantial salads. Chef Hüseyin's desserts are like Ottoman fables come to life. The Park Şamdan (*şamdan,* by the way, means "candle holder") is only about ten minutes by car from Taksim and the major hotels.

Also in Nişantaşı is the rustic yet classy **Hasir** restaurant, at Valıkonağı Caddesi 117; Tel: 230-1636. Hasir, which has possibly the best meat dishes in Istanbul, is presided over by its extremely personable maître d', Abdullah, whose English is good and service impeccable. Each meal begins with Hasir's hallmark—enormous, steaming *puf pide* (i.e., "puff" pita bread). Then follows a series of great Ottoman dishes: *paçanga böreği* (a fried dough envelope enclosing minced meat, onion, pine nuts, currants, and cumin), *keşkek* (a cream of wheat–like dish consisting of pounded lamb and wheat served with butter and cinnamon), and *tandır kebap* (lamb or veal roasted in an underground oven). The unusual mixed grill—lamb chop, Wiener Schnitzel, fondu bourguignon, and filet mignon—is well worth trying, as are the special *köfte* (meatballs), to which Hasir adds cheese. All the desserts are mouth-watering, especially the profiterole with sesame oil and sugar syrup and the *künefe*—which is like sweet shredded wheat stuffed with cheese and dripping with sugar syrup.

At the other (southerly) end of the new city between the Tünel entrance at the foot of İstiklâl Caddesi and the foreign consulate district is **Dört Mevsim** (The Four Seasons; İstiklâl Caddesi 509; Tel: 245-8941). Here, in a corner four-story building with Victorian furniture and lace-curtained windows, you can enjoy the inventive, fresh food prepared by the Turkish chef, Musa Hiçdönmez, and his British wife, Gaye. Dört Mevsim offers such refreshing international dishes as prawns and chicken in a béchamel sauce au gratin, served in a grapefruit shell; crepes of tomatoes and meat topped with rich *kaşar* cheese; and tender breaded shrimp and snowpeas. The desserts here—sherry trifle, cheesecake, stewed quince in rosé wine, and fresh figs in raspberry sauce (when these fruits are in season)—also defeat your willpower.

A few restaurants in Istanbul have been around for a long time and remain at their classic best. At the head of that list is **Borsa**, whose latest dining salon opened in Osmanbey, at Halâskârgazi Caddesi 90/1, in 1987; Tel: 232-4200. Borsa has several branches, including one in Eminönü in the old city, at Yalı Köşkü 60; Tel: 527-2350 or 2351. The Eminönü branch is near the restaurant's original site, which opened in 1927; its menu features stews and other hearty foods.

Borsa also has two excellent fast-food outlets; the one at İstiklâl Caddesi 87 does not serve alcoholic beverages, but it has a superb salad bar and its three floors serve 3,000 customers a day. The other is near the Taksim bus stop (it's very noticeable) and offers beer and cocktails. What's particularly impressive is that the fast-food joints operated by Borsa serve the same high-quality entrées and desserts as the full-service restaurants—and charge about half the price. All the Borsa restaurants are air conditioned.

Borsa is famous for its Ottoman menu as well as the innovative dishes its chefs have created during the past two decades. Anything you order will please you, but try the appetizer of cold shrimp and asparagus arranged on an artichoke bottom cooked in olive oil. Other memorable Ottoman selections are *hünkâr beğendi* ("his imperial majesty liked it"), the most tender veal cubes atop smoky eggplant purée, and the simply superb desserts, such as *sütlaç* (a milky rice pudding heavy with vanilla), *tavuk göğüsü* (a milk pudding with chicken breast), and crème caramel. Reservations are recommended at all the full-service Borsa restaurants; for the Osmanbey branch, Tel: 232-4200.

Great new restaurants, pubs, and cafés are popping up all over the city. Certainly one of the biggest overnight successes is **Cafe Wien**, a *ganz echt* Austrian coffeehouse and restaurant in a handsome townhouse with a beguiling garden on Atiye Sokak 5 (Tel: 248-7860) across Teşvikiye Caddesi from the Teşvikiye mosque. This charmingly arranged coffeehouse features Austrian coffee, home-cooked breakfasts, hot breads and sweets made by an Austrian pastry chef, plus racks of Turkish, English, French, and German-language newspapers. Up to a hundred customers can imbibe fragrant coffee and the news in the café's four salons and two-level balcony. Cafe Wien is, however, best known for its delicious lunches, superb tea-time pastries, and light suppers of goulash, schnitzel, and crepes.

Turks love plays-on-words, so the name **Cafe-İn** (which in Turkish is pronounced just like the word for caffeine) almost guaranteed that this coffeehouse would be a hit. Cafe-İn is a one-room downstairs coffeehouse, bar, and light lunch counter at Abdi İpekçi Caddesi 17/1 in Nişantaşı. In addition to espresso and alcoholic drinks, the café offers croissants, sandwiches, salads, and other snacks; it's a good place for a light lunch in this prime shopping area. Its black bentwood chairs, black-and-white marble tables, and black bar are set off by attractive rust-colored walls.

Moderate

Halfway down İstiklâl Caddesi from Taksim square, just before the Galatasaray intersection, you'll see on the right an old cobbled street lined with flower sellers and, farther up, toward its crest, stalls selling fish, chickens, and general produce. This is the well-known Çiçek Pasajı (Flower Passage). A sharp turn to the right and under the wrought-iron gate marked "Cité de Pera" brings you into another narrow corridor parallel to the floral displays. About 25 years ago some American *roués* and regulars aptly nicknamed this the "Drunk Man's Passage," for it features a number of little taverns set side by side. Here, drinkers used to sit on stools around marble slabs atop upended beer kegs. In the old days vividly painted women were to be seen casing the scene below as they leaned from windows in the pastel façades of the buildings surrounding the courtyard.

This area of the Çiçek Pasajı was a real after-work equalizer, where laborers sat next to bankers and journalists, all quaffing draft beer or savoring a *rakı sofrası* (a spread of meze eaten to soften the impact of the powerful rakı). Together the men would sing along with a buxom accordion player or, sometimes, mount the tables to perform an impromptu dance. Such an evening's entertainment would cost only pennies; it's doubtful any of the customers dreamed that someday tourism would "clean up" this delightful place's act or that European prices would force out most of the colorful clientele.

But that, of course, is exactly what has happened. Now proper benches and booths flank the tiled tables that have replaced the beer barrels. Some of the old elements do, however, remain. The courtyard's drinkeries still draw a varied crowd. The erstwhile brunette accordionist is now a heavier bleached blonde, but many of the youths who once hawked mussels, tripe, and shrimp from table to table are still around—they're now the bar owners (and getting a little gray at the temples). Journalists still drink here, perhaps to take the public pulse.

Çatı (meaning "roof") is a cozy penthouse restaurant near the bottom of İstiklâl Caddesi, two blocks east of Pera Palas. Right in the heart of Beyoğlu, Çatı is on the top (seventh) floor of Baro Han on Orhan Adli Apaydin Sokak 20 (Tel: 245-1656 or 245-1642), which has the Dostlar Tiyatrosu (Friends Theater) on the ground floor. Here is a great place for cocktails where you can take in the sunset above the surrounding rooftops through the picture windows. Tables in the south corner look out over Istanbul's large, oval harbor where the Bosphorus empties into the Sea of Marmara. The innovative owner is always creating new recipes; try the golden-fried rounds of *kaşar* cheese, the cold spiced *işkembe* (tripe), the cold (but cooked) chard and onions, or the candied tomato with walnuts—an Ottoman dessert.

Catering to top international military personnel and diplomats during World War II, **Liman Lokantası** (Rıhtım Caddesi, on the third floor of the boat terminal, Karaköy; Tel: 244-1033 or 244-9349) is renowned as one of the best places in the city for lunch. (Actually, it serves only lunch, every day except Sunday.) Since it first opened as a training center for chefs working on the Turkish Maritime Lines' cruise ships, it has been known for its fresh fish as well as for its caviar; its cold buffets of chicken, lamb, and beef; a marvelous specialty consisting of fried eggplant and rice with slivered green peppers; and its sumptuous desserts. The service here is Old World and gracious. The Liman's long dining room overlooks the harbor.

ALONG THE BOSPHORUS

Dining out along the Bosphorus is an İstanbullu's favorite way to spend an evening. The headiness of the occasion is enhanced, early in the evening, by the sunset glimmering on the waters of the strait and, later, by the magical lights of the many boats cruising up and down this intercontinental waterway— in many cases literally the restaurant's front yard.

Fresh fish is the mainstay of Bosphorus restaurants, despite the fact that fish grow yearly less plentiful in the waters around Istanbul. Seafood restaurants take care of their regular customers, but the fish shortage leads some restaurateurs to try to get away with serving day-old fish to unfamiliar customers. When selecting a fish, make sure its eyes are bright, not clouded.

Every village and community fronting the Bosphorus has at least a few seafood restaurants, sometimes just a couple of tables outside a small kitchen. If you're in an adventurous mood, it can be great fun to dine at harborside in one of the minute fishing villages—often at a third the cost of a meal in one of the large, fancy establishments.

Deluxe

"S" may be Istanbul's most elegant restaurant. It's somewhat oddly positioned, though, spread out on a green lawn atop the B.P. gas station at Çamlıbahçe Caddesi, Vezirköşkü Sokak 2, in **Bebek** (Tel: 263-8326), just a few yards up from the western end of Bebek's yacht-lined harbor.

"S" is probably the only one of Istanbul's deluxe restaurants to be run by a woman, the young Leyla Akcağlılar, a graduate of the Cordon Bleu in Paris. The name of the restaurant is the initial of the late White Russian restaurateur Sureyya, who established an elite dining salon in this spot. Leyla Hanım has surpassed even Sureyya in her divine menu and wonderfully tasteful decor, in which meticulous attention has been given to every detail. She changes the menu every four months to feature different French, Russian, and Turkish dishes.

Maître d' Firat Vargönen assists you, in excellent English, in choosing from among the seemingly countless superb offerings: real Russian-style borscht, lamb karski, chicken kiev, sea bass on leeks with creamy caviar sauce, two-salmon terrine, sole soufflé, swordfish with Provençale sauce, or gratin of shrimp with mousse of fish. "S" is one of the rare restaurants able to prepare the traditional puréed eggplant salad in a truly Ottoman manner—the smoky taste is sensational. The desserts are sinful: ice-cream soufflé with fresh raspberries, fruit mousse ringed with kiwi slices, and so on and on.

Every evening except Sunday most of the 110 armchairs are filled in the handsome, long dining salon, backed by tall Empire mirrored panels and infused with *l'heure bleue* of the Bosphorus as a pianist or trio plays. Leyla Hanım serves *kokteyl*s, appetizer-preludes to the grand meal, and snacks in the **Pergola Terrace**, a delightful glassed-in garden with hanging vines. In winter guests can enjoy their drinks while settled in leather chairs before the fireplace in the wood-paneled library bar. In every room of "S," service is impeccable. Reservations are a must. The first Sunday of every month, "S" has an informal Champagne brunch/open house—the only time male guests aren't required to wear a tie. The brunch—an extravaganza of gourmet food—costs less than $20. Brunch is from 11:00 A.M. to 3:00 P.M.; reservations are a must.

A more informally elegant restaurant, just below Bebek, is **Ziya** (Mualim Naci Caddesi 109; Tel: 261-6005 or 261-6006). It occupies a square, white two-story mansion with a beautiful garden almost directly beneath the European foot of the first Bosphorus bridge in **Ortaköy**. Through the winter the indoor bar-restaurant is the watering hole of the smart set. In summer businesspeople and sophisticates flock to its white wrought-iron gazebo bar and covered terrace garden for Ziya's international fare—snails Bourguignonne, frogs legs Provençale, shrimp Ziya (lots of garlic), crepes Ziya (with shrimp and mushrooms), and avocado crepes with shrimp, onion, and tomato sauce. There are also caviar and smoked sturgeon, salmon, eel, and the world's best sea bass, from the Black Sea.

About 7 km (4 miles) farther up the Bosphorus is **Emirgân**, one of the most charming communities on the European side. Emirgân was long famous for its Poets' Park, where audiences gathered to listen to recitations beneath a grove of enormous trees—until traffic noise snuffed out these readings. On one of Emirgân's lush, gardened hills stands the chalet-style **Abdullah Lokantası** (Koru Caddesi 11; Tel: 263-6406), which grows its own produce. Because of its 60-year reputation with "old" Istanbul as a place to dine on the finest of Turkish cuisine, reservations are always necessary. It's a long taxi ride from anywhere up the winding hill to Abdullah's, so make sure the driver knows the way.

Istanbul's culinary cognoscenti as well as many foreign visitors rave about Ömer Salur's **Körfez** restaurant (Körfez Caddesi 78, Kanlıca; Tel: 332-0108 or 332-2223), on the Asian shore of the Bosphorus. Educated in London and the United States, Ömer Bey opened Körfez here in 1982, transforming his attractive modern *yalı* (waterfront villa) into a comfortable dining room and terrace with shipboard decor. Turkish yachters and the international set flock to the restaurant for Ömer's inventive dishes include morsels of tenderloin sautéed with shrimps. But the sorcery here is more scenic than culinary: The dramatic *levrek tuzda* (sea bass in salt) is presented to the table flaming, but it's not as spellbinding as the lights of the second Bosphorus bridge spanning the strait from Europe to Asia. If you telephone about 30 minutes in advance, Ömer will send his boat across the Bosphorus to pick you up on the European side. (He'll also provide the return boat trip.) One caution: if you plan to eat in the garden at night, bring along insect repellent, or you'll be dined upon as well as dining.

Expensive

The yacht cove at **Tarabya**, on the European bank of the Bosphorus north of Bebek, is a veritable horseshoe of eateries, which used to number some of Istanbul's best fish restaurants. Unfortunately, Tarabya's good restaurants have recently been slipping, and some of the others feature music so horrendously loud you feel you might be blasted out of your seat. So for good seafood and Bosphorus-side serenity, leave Tarabya behind. Proceed about a mile past the busy cove to **Façyo**, at Kireçburnu Caddesi (the Bosphorus shore road) number 6; Tel: 262-0024. Façyo's three large salons are designed to take superb advantage of its picture windows, which embrace a scintillating Bosphorus view. Façyo's Armenian owner, Tatyos Jamgöçyan, is a conscientious workaholic: He's at the restaurant nearly every day of the year, and his food shows it. The tasty meze here include grape-leaf *dolmas* stuffed with spiced rice, fried zucchini and green squash, fried mussels, (oh so tender) *kalamar,* and *tarama* (orange-colored roe in a mayonnaise dressing). The fish is fantastically fresh, but the meat dishes—chicken kiev, filet mignon, tournedos—are also wonderful. The desserts are splendid too, especially when Tatyos Bey finds out-of-season fresh raspberries and graces them with chantilly. The wine list is likewise outstanding.

Near the northern end of the inhabited part of the European shore is the district of **Sarıyer**, long a sizable fishing harbor and now a community burgeoning with visitors who come to enjoy its cool, straight-from-the-Black Sea breezes all summer long. (The trip by automobile from central Istanbul up to Sarıyer takes at least an hour.) The large fish restaurant called **Urcan** (Tel: 242-0367 or 242-1677), built right over the water to the north of the port, has been an "in" place for politicians, businesspeople, artists, and the public at large for three generations.

This is one of the very best seafood restaurants in Istanbul. Live fish and lobsters crowd the tanks in the Urcan's entryway. The huge red dining room is festively adorned with flowers, and suspended from its ceiling are mounted fish and fish skeletons, nets, and fishing gear. Urcan is the kind of place where you'll get caught up in the fun, finding yourself singing along with "Roll Out the Barrel."

Just before Urcan is the harbor, where fishing boats dock. The walkway along the harbor used to lead to a string of little, one-room eateries that served good (and cheap) fish at outdoor tables ringed by rickety chairs. They've been replaced by a line of fancy restaurants, and prices have more than doubled. The restaurants seem to be competitive enough, however, that bargaining over prices might be possible. The place called **Captain's Terrace** is good.

Moderate

On the European side of the Bosphorus at **Arnavutköy** (just below Bebek) is one of Istanbul's tried-and-true fish restaurants, **Kaptan** (also spelled **Captain**; Birinci Caddesi 53; Tel: 265-8487). Long a little wooden building with a porch that extended out over the water, it's been enlarged to seat 120 under a peaked pine roof. Once the exclusive hangout of local fishermen, the restaurant served such good food it attracted the notice of the Turkish and foreign students attending the preparatory school, Robert College, atop the village hill, then the school's staff and their families, and, finally, the allegiance of many of the Americans living in Istanbul. It is still one of the best buys for fresh fish, and it is happily informal.

Myott Cafe, only a year old, is acclaimed for having some of the best coffee in Istanbul, brewed from imported Italian beans for espresso, which is served with marzipan, and for cappuccino, which is accompanied by the Divan-made *mekik,* an almond cake with tapered ends. Open from 8:00 A.M. to 4:00 P.M. every day but Monday, Myott is at İskele Sokak 14 (Tel: 258-9317), along the "tourist's walk" to the quay at Ortaköy (about five miles north of Taksim).

Myott Cafe's enterprising owner is Rafi Bisar (who speaks excellent English); he finds customers waiting on his doorstep at 7:30 A.M. for breakfasts of imported cereals, salads, and fruits, as well as the famous coffee. The two-room café is the perfect place for a light lunch while visiting Ortaköy's art galleries in the charming quay area.

Just north of Bebek is the mammoth fortress of **Rumeli Hisarı** and the little town of the same name, which boasts two good, attractive, and semi-expensive fish and general cuisine restaurants opposite the picturesque wooden ferryboat landing: the Han and the Karaca. The **Han** is a warm and informal wooden building with red checkered tablecloths and a tree growing up through its roof terrace. It's a magnet for artists, members of the press, and foreigners—a desirable place to dine on the water and not too far from the city. The brick **Karaca** (open 11:00 A.M. to midnight) is more formal and expensive; its street-side terrace is a place to be seen. Try the restaurant's renowned meze and *güveç* (a clay pot filled with fish fillets or shrimp and cheese sauce or meat and vegetables). Reservations required; Tel: 263-3468.

At one of the most historic crossings of the Bosphorus is **Kale Restaurant**, about 100 yards north of the 15th-century **Anadolu Hisarı** (Asian Fortress) and facing the Rumeli Hisarı (European Fortress), which Sultan Mehmet II threw up in three months before conquering Constantinople. The Kale (Tel: 332-0409 or 332-0531) was established some 23 years ago by Cemil Barın, who welcomes guests at the side entrance, giving them a choice of eating in his comfortably rustic pine-paneled main salon or the more modern terrace at the back, which has a piano and a fireplace; both areas offer an excellent view of the Bosphorus.

Cemil Bey knows his fish. He specializes in flying-fish soup, fried stuffed mussels, fresh anchovies, sardines, marvelous *lakerda*—raw tuna cured in brine and served with red onions—as well as *kalamar* and octopus, fried and grilled sea bass, bluefish, fried sole or flounder, baked swordfish, and turbot. He makes special sauces like *tarator,* which he serves on fish, and *muhammara,* made of hot red peppers, tomatoes, and chestnuts.

Every night at about 9:30 a pianist or guitarist plays Turkish tavern songs or ballads for the evening crowd. The taxi from Taksim takes 30 minutes and costs about $12.

THE OLD CITY

Expensive

The **Yeşil Ev** (Green House; Kabasakal Caddesi 5, Sultanahmet; Tel: 517-6785 through 517-6789), an elegant mansion (now a hotel) situated between the Blue Mosque and St. Sophia, has a shady garden, a respite from the heat on summer afternoons and evenings. You may wish to dine at the **Terrace Restaurant** here or simply enjoy a light omelette, *börek,* sandwich, ice cream, fruit juice, or alcoholic beverage in the café section.

The Yeşil Ev's garden restaurant has a sizable menu of traditional Turkish and Continental cuisine, which, however, is of indifferent quality. The place's appeal is more scenic than culinary. Dishes you might enjoy include cold duck salad, seafood casserole, flambéed prawns or shrimp, or roast or grilled quail with saffron rice.

At the bottom end of Soğukçeşme Sokak just outside the wall of Topkapı palace and near the Ayasofya Pensions (see Accommodations, above) is an ancient Roman cistern that once housed the cold spring (*soğukçeşme*) for which the street is named. The Turkish Touring and Automobile Association cleared out about 20 feet of accumulated dirt and restored the cistern's six massive stone columns (which support its 30-foot-high arches) to create the **Sarnıç** (Cistern) **Tavern** here (Tel: 512-4291). Seating up to 110 guests at rustic tables, the tavern is lit by a wrought-iron candelabra; its flicker is reflected on the ancient Roman yellow-brick walls. In winter the tavern is heated by the only contemporary addition—an open fireplace where huge caldrons of soup and other foods are kept warm. Diners here are entertained nightly by a classical guitarist.

In Eminönü, one flight up in what was once the guardroom directly above the entrance to the main building of the Mısır Çarşısı (Egyptian, or Spice, Bazaar), is a very touristy but treasured restaurant, **Pandeli's** (Tel: 522-5534 or 527-3909). Established in 1891, the restaurant serves the highest quality fresh fish and appetizers, thick veal and lamb chops, magnificent Ottoman vegetable dishes, and excellent desserts. Pandeli's windows look down in back on the Spice Bazaar's main corridor—a hodgepodge of goods, including special cheeses; sun-dried meats, apricots, and prunes; and spices from around the world (for more on the bazaar, see Shopping, below). From the front, diners look down on the new Galata Bridge spanning the Golden Horn. Pandeli's is open only for lunch, from 11:30 A.M. until 3:00 P.M. every day but Sunday and holidays.

Moderate

There's such a thing as deluxe food at moderate prices. The recently opened **Dârrüziyafe**, near the mosque and tomb of Süleyman the Magnificent at Şifahane Caddesi 6 (Tel: 511-8414), deserves a "deluxe" rating even though a meal of half a dozen courses costs only about $17 (plus tip). Housed in a 500-year-old *imaret* and run by a religious foundation (so no alcoholic beverages are sold), Dârrüziyafe is open for lunch and dinner year round. The serenity of this walled oasis—the building is the work of Ottoman master-architect Sinan—feeds the spirit as the superb Ottoman cuisine nourishes the body. Every dish is based on an authentic Ottoman recipe; all are excellent, but some are not to be missed—including the Süleymaniye soup of red lentils and marvelously spiced little meatballs; the *sultan gözdesi* (the name means "in the sultan's eye, or thoughts"), a half-chicken stuffed with spiced rice, meat, and pistachios; and the "poor man's" pudding, actually a quite rich concoction of milk pudding with chopped pistachios, almonds, hazelnuts, and coconut.

Amid the hustle and bustle of the Kapalıçarsı (Covered Bazaar) is a refreshingly quiet, old-fashioned restaurant, **Havuzlu Lokanta** (the name means "restaurant with pool"; the pool is right in front). A few steps from the bazaar's PTT (post office), at Gâni Çelebi Sokak 3 (Tel: 527-3346), the high-arched dining room seems to have been created by blocking off one of the bazaar's streets. You are welcomed in soft, scholarly English by a Turkish gentleman of the old school, manager Ali Riza Savaşer. He squires in Turks and foreigners with the same gracious saying: "We prepare Turkish cuisine for the pleasure of gourmets." He advises customers to try the spicy homemade soup, the tender lamb on smoky-flavored eggplant purée, and the baked *sütlaç* (rice pudding). The Turks who lunch here drink *ayran,* a beverage made with yogurt beaten with water and a little salt; foreigners are more likely to quench their thirsts with beer. The Havuzlu is open for lunch only and is closed Sundays.

At number 12/A Divan Yolu Caddesi, the street that leads from the Covered Bazaar to Topkapı palace and St. Sophia, is the 70-year-old **Meşhur Halk Köftecisi** (People's Famous Meatball Maker), where workers, teachers, and knowledgeable foreigners gather in the simple large room to savor Turkey's tastiest *köfte*. A meal of six of these meatballs costs about two dollars. You can also get half an order (*yarım porsiyon*), served with cold white-bean and tomato salad, bread, and yogurt, for about three dollars. This meatball joint has several not-so-good imitators that use the same name, so make sure you choose the original, easily recognized by its bizarre logo: an outline of the Blue Mosque with three meatballs stuck on each of its six minarets.

FOREIGN DINING

The colorful **Dragon Restaurant** on the ground floor of the Istanbul Hilton Convention and Exhibition Center (Hilton International Istanbul, off Cumhuriyet Caddesi; Tel: 231-6200) offers the best Chinese cuisine in the city and a refreshing change from Turkish fare. The Dragon, which has been in operation for six years, features canopied private dining rooms studded with talismans, swords, shields, statues, and other Chinese accessories custom made in Hong Kong. Chinese mushrooms, lychee nuts, and other Oriental foodstuffs are imported to make the Dragon's delicious dim sum appetizers, soups, sizzling steak with fried rice, and other dishes. The knowledgeable, London-educated Cemal Turgut directs operations; presumably much credit must go to his Chinese wife, Cathy Cheng, who supervises the kitchen. Note that the Dragon is closed Mondays.

A third of the way up İstiklâl Caddesi toward Galatasaray in the new city (hard to find, between Beyoğlu Evim at İstiklâl Caddesi 246 and Eren Tikko at 244) is the seedy-looking but safe Olivo Geçidi (alley), which leads to the White Russian restaurant **Rejans** (Regency) at number 15–17 (Tel: 244-1610; closed Sundays). It was founded in 1930 by refugees from the Russian Revolution and staffed by White Russians, many of whom had escaped by rafting 300 miles across the Black Sea. (One of them reportedly said, "It was nothing. Everybody was doing it then.") Run today by relatives of the founders, the Rejans still offers good Russian borscht, piroshki, Caucasian shashlik, lamb karski, chicken Kiev, beef stroganoff, pork chops, game birds, and amazingly good desserts like meringue with chocolate sauce, chestnut purée, stewed or baked quince (*ayva*) with clotted cream, and pumpkin stewed with ground chestnuts. Top it all off with Russian lemon or black-pepper vodka, which they prepare themselves at Rejans.

Slightly down-at-the-heels, the restaurant might depress some, but others love it as a relic of the past. It was, for example, one of Atatürk's favorite drinking and dining haunts. Its simple half-paneled walls covered by aged wallpaper, its balcony for musicians, and—in winter—its pot-bellied stove all give you a feeling of what life was like in Istanbul during the 1930s. And it does provide a rare Russian repast at a reasonable price.

Ristorante Italiano in the arcade off Cumhuriyet Caddesi behind the Divan Hotel is probably the best Italian eatery in

Istanbul. It was created in 1966 by Afer Gümüştaş, an Italophile who married his Italian wife on one of his early trips to that country. Since then they have been cooking up a plenitude of pasta and preparing antipasta, *roka* (arugula) salad, beef rolls, steaks, seafood—calamari and scampi—and outstanding desserts of *tiramisù*, peach Melba, and other delights. So if you want true Italian pasta al dente, Italian aperitifs like Campari, or drinks like Fernet Branca and Strega in a setting with the spirit of Italy, come to this easy-to-find, cozy restaurant, which has seating outside on a patio. It's at Cumhuriyet Caddesi 6, Elmadağ; Tel: 247-8640 or 248-3444. Closed Sundays.

—Anne Turner Bruno

ENTERTAINMENT AND NIGHTLIFE

As in any large urban center that plays host to great numbers of foreign visitors, nightlife in Istanbul presents two faces: that of "authentic" ethnic entertainment contrived for the tourist trade and the kinds of entertainments devised—and indulged in—by the city's inhabitants themselves. The nightspots, bars, and diverse cultural events discussed below have been selected for their capacity to give the traveller a taste of those nuances of Turkish big-city life—subtly exotic yet very familiar—that can only be felt after the sun sets.

At the higher end, Istanbul's nighttime pleasures are Western in flavor; the city boasts a range of clubs, bars, and discos equivalent to that of any good-size European or North American city. The language you hear spoken at adjoining tables may be unknown, but the music will often be quite familiar.

Your range of possibilities is really quite extensive, however. On the tame side, you can always find a movie to go to: The theaters around Beyoğlu and Taksim (mostly on İstiklâl Caddesi and Cumhuriyet Caddesi) show plenty of first-run American pictures (in English), though they usually appear here a few months after their release dates in the United States. If losing money gives you a thrill, you can either check into one of the major hotels' casinos or pursue your pleasure more indirectly by visiting a *pavyon*. There are scores of these seedy clubs on the side streets of the Beyoğlu district. They typically feature banquette seating, tiny dance floors, watered-down drinks, *saz ve caz* ("saz and 'jazz,'" i.e., live Turkish "Arabesque" music alternating with piped-in disco), and a few scantily clad and heavily made-up "young" women whose job it is to make sure you run up as high a bar bill as possible—very likely to be collected, by force, by the bouncer! (To be fair, some *pavyons* put on a good floor show, with folk- and belly-dancing performances and lively music by competent singers and musicians.)

Istanbul even has an officially controlled red-light district, on and around Yüksek Kaldırım Caddesi in Karaköy, complete with legal brothels. Depending on how far your interest in the wilder side of Istanbul nightlife extends, you may also want to have a drink at one of the several establishments (mostly in Beyoğlu and Taksim) that cater to the city's sizable transvestite community. The offerings presented here, however, are mostly of a tamer variety.

The telephone area code for Istanbul is 1.

NEW CITY AND BOSPHORUS

One of Istanbul's very best supper clubs is **Günay** (Beytem Han 5, Büyükdere Caddesi, Şişli), about a mile and a half north of the Hilton hotel between Şişli and Mecidiyeköy. Günay has a large dining room with a stage in the center and a very long bar on the right as you enter. The club's patron, Günay Tuncel, is usually to be found at the bar chatting with his guests and many friends—often in English. His impeccable taste shines through in every aspect of the club, particularly in the extraordinary food. Günay continues a tradition sadly abandoned in other Istanbul restaurants: The meal is followed by platters of "sculpted" fresh fruit. The bar opens just after 9:00 P.M., and dinner is served beginning at about 10:30. Before dinner an excellent pianist plays relaxing renditions of standards like "Laura," "Misty," and "The Shadow of Your Smile."

Günay's faithful clientele is a mix of "old money" and "new money" plus some "just folks" people out to enjoy themselves. In front of the stage is a small dance floor, and after the floor show there's disco dancing until 4:00 A.M. Reservations are necessary; Tel: 232-3333 or 232-4444.

Günay's splendid cuisine goes out-of-doors up the Bosphorus from the beginning of June until late September. The club takes over the handsome and historic **Memduh Paşa Yalısı**, right on the European shore of the Bosphorus at Tarabya Caddesi 4/6, Kireçburnu, about 4 km (2½ miles) past Yeniköy. This grand old *yalı* and its large romantic garden provide a cool place for the hot summer evenings. Reservations required; Tel: 263-5168 through 263-5170.

The difficulty of finding **Club 29** is an indication of how well established and "in" it is. It's at Nispetiye Caddesi 29 in Etiler, about five miles north of the Hilton, but it has no sign, there's no street number in evidence, and a high hedge screens the building's façade. In spite of—or, more likely, because of—its apparent indifference, Club 29 (Tel: 265-2925) is a chic place to be seen. The decor here is in superb taste. The food is undistinguished, but eating isn't what it's all about here anyway.

In early June the Etiler branch of Club 29 closes for the summer and moves across the Bosphorus to Çubuklu. **Club 29 Çubuklu** (Paşabahçe Yolu; Tel: 322-3888, 322-2829, or 331-3978), which stays open until late September, features a good restaurant, a disco, and a *yüzme havuzu* (swimming pool) and provides almost round-the-clock entertainment in an enchanting setting.

During the day Istanbul's summer sunshine—as intense as that of the Mediterranean coast—highlights the club's sienna-hued "Roman" villa (complete with marble statues atop a white balustrade). The villa overlooks the huge, brimming turquoise pool and the Bosphorus, here two miles wide and teeming with boats. By night, Club 29's magically lit groves and flaming copper braziers lend atmosphere to an artistically presented buffet.

To get to Club 29 Çubuklu, take a taxi to the Asian side (fare about $18) or use the club's special shuttle boat, which leaves from the dock at İstiniye, above the foot of the second Bosphorus bridge on the European side. During the day the boat departs from the European side every 45 minutes from 10:30 A.M. to 3:30 P.M. At night the schedule is more flexible, with boats running back and forth from İstiniye to Çubuklu from 8:00 P.M. until the early morning hours.

Memo's sensational supper club (Muallim Naci Caddesi Salhane Sokak 10/2, Ortaköy; Tel: 260-8491) is one of the most talked-about of Istanbul's deluxe bars. A former disc jockey, Memo (a nickname for Mehmet) opened his double-terraced club in Ortaköy, on the European side of the Bosphorus, four years ago, and it quickly became the place where the elite meet to eat and compete in preening. The atmosphere is *intensely* see-and-be-seen; do not dress "down" if you come here. Feel free, though, to wear any color you want—as long as it's black. (A taxi here from Taksim costs about $5.)

Every night a crowd of chic, beautiful young professionals jams the wide open-air bar on the Italianate red-roofed terrace. Memo's spectacular site has a 180-degree view that takes in Topkapı palace on the far right, Beylerbeyi palace right across the strait, and, to the left, Ortaköy's Rococo-style mosque and the floodlit First Bosphorus Bridge in the distance.

The bill of fare at Memo's is ambitious (food is served on the smaller terrace above the bar, which shares the same panoramic view). Memo imports every possible delicacy: Russian caviar, smoked salmon from Norway, magnums of French champagne, pork to embellish the fresh asparagus, and Italian prosciutto to set off Turkey's nectar-sweet melon. But Memo plays up Turkey's great cuisine as well. The marvelous fish soup combines fish stock, sea bass, grouper, shrimp, Norwegian cod, baby mushrooms, and herbs. The lobster tails are fresh and sweet, while the *pazı dolması* of chard leaves wrapped around baby lamb, lamb shanks, and gelatin is a new taste to savor. There are up to 70 diners nightly, with tabs up to 7 million TL per repast. (Which translates to $1,000. Ahem.)

The **Divan Kuruçeşme** (Tel: 257-7150) is the new, lush out-of-doors club and recreational facility of the Divan Hotel. Overlooking the Bosphorus's Asian shore, it is built atop ancient stone walls where an Armenian community once flourished. The club's regal entrance, with double staircases, leads you to a huge yellow plastic tent surrounded by luxuri-ant greenery, where 450 people can dine alfresco in summer. A new, closed-in dining section opened in 1992, meaning the Divan Kuruçeşme now welcomes dinner guests in winter as well.

The first building north of the Hilton hotel's passage is the **Kervansaray** (Cumhuriyet Caddesi 30, Harbiye; Tel: 247-1630 or 246-0818), a nightclub that for decades has offered a satisfying dinner and fairly good floor show for the whole family. Happily, it is unlike the sleazier, more expensive places just a block or two south of the Hilton. The floor show at the Kervansaray changes, but might feature young, attractive Turkish male and female singers, belly dancers on their way up the terpsichorean ladder, a magician, and an excellent pair of comedians, or Turkish folk-dance teams in any of several varieties: eagle and wooden-spoon dancers from Konya, Arab-inspired dancers from the south, or Cos-sacks, descendants of Turkic tribespeople of the Russian steppes, who are show-stoppers. The show is about two hours long and is performed on a large stage that projects into the audience; the emcee announces the acts in both Turkish and English.

Turks are great music lovers, devoted listeners to both symphonic and popular music—including jazz and blues. Unfortunately, a number of first-rate jazz clubs in Istanbul closed their doors last year, but a new crop is certain to spring up. Piano bars are, however, legion. One of the best is the Divan Hotel's elegant **Kehribar** (Amber Bar), on the hotel's ground floor. Featured performers change, of course, but you may be lucky enough to catch pianist/crooner Ilham Gencer, who presents a sophisticated medley of old standards and newer tunes.

Istanbul's emergent cosmopolitanism has brought with it a new brand of nightlife—less refined (though no less sophisticated) and much edgier than the elegant supper-club tradition carried on by most of the nightspots listed so far. The new-style clubs, catering to the young (or at least the self-assured and vigorous), are concentrated in the central–new city districts of Taksim and Beyoğlu. Sartorial splendor isn't required; a sense of style, however, definitely is, as are a strong set of ear drums, the patience to wait in line at the door, and an attitude of staunch cool—so you won't be undone by the inevitable elbowing and jostling that the intense crowdedness of these places guarantees.

In Beyoğlu, you might want to poke your nose into **Rockbar**, on Sıraselviler Caddesi just below Taksim square. On a typical Saturday night, the number of people crammed into Rockbar's modest space is only exceeded by the number of decibels pumped out by the club's immodest sound system. It's likely you won't want to stay for very long— unless you get off on the churnings of Metallica, say, or Ozzy Osborne—but you may want to have a look. It's a kind of exotica-in-reverse: In Istanbul, one doesn't precisely expect to see such a gaggle of stringy-haired, leather-clad post-teens (imagine a suburban American shopping mall parking lot gone Oriental).

Much more tolerable (though perhaps a tad less interesting) is **Hayal Kahvesi**, at Büyük Parmakkapı Sokak 19 (off İstiklâl Caddesi across from the Beymen department store). Hayal is a rock and jazz bar with live (and listenable) music. Weekend crowds here are likewise sardine-cannish, but, since the bar's a little roomier, you may actually be able to light a cigarette, gingerly sip a drink, or even, if you are patient enough, secure one of Hayal's tiny tables. You probably won't be able to reach the bar, but there's a host of waiters working the crowd, improbably (and at times imperfectly) balancing drink-laden trays on arms extended above the patrons' heads. There's a cover charge at the door.

In the past couple of years, Istanbul has acquired a sizable African community, some of whose members gather for drink, good talk, and great dancing at the predictably named **Roots**, also in Beyoğlu. Though a little divey, Roots is a very comfortable place. The music is mostly (though not entirely) reggae; the dance floor is small, decidedly non-glitzy, and lively.

On the western edge of Taksim, on Abdülhak Hamit Caddesi, is a row of small buildings that (besides some retail shops) house a number of bars, each of which is known by its building number. "14" (less well known by its actual name, Ceylân) began life as a gay bar, though it now attracts a diverse, coed crowd. Once again, expect a smallish room that's overpopulated, especially if you go on the weekend. The piped-in music mixes Turkish and Western pop, and the lack of a dance floor doesn't prevent bargoers from shaking their booties. If the possibility of sexual adventure's your reason for venturing here, do be cautioned: The politics of cruising, not to mention meeting someone, in so crowded and (nowadays) anything-goes a place are ambiguous and, probably, difficult to learn. The club's oval bar, which dominates the room, and its cool-blue lighting, which exerts a subtle, visually calming influence on the commotion, are nice touches. On weekends, "14" doesn't close until 5:00 A.M. (Word has it that, since the persuasion of "14" has become less definite, some of its former habitués have migrated a few doors away, to the bar known as "19.")

At the end of this little block is "20," a disco that draws a mob of revelers of various sexual orientations. It's also open until 5:00 A.M. on weekend nights, and its tiny dance floor (the club holds only 70 to 80 people) is usually packed. There's often an intimidatingly long line at the door; the line moves slowly (given the space limitations inside), but the bouncer pursues a policy of first-come, first served, so you won't be turned away for lacking the de rigueur hauteur or haute couture. The club's small rectangular space, with raised platforms on two sides, features a disc-jockey's booth above the entryway and an elevated bar opposite. The decor is reminiscent of a subway station or industrial space—everything is black and gray. The atmosphere is unusual and refreshing for Istanbul.

More or less around the corner from this numerical series of boîtes is **Taxim**, at Nizamiye Caddesi 12 (Tel: 256-4431), a restaurant-cum-disco that aims for, and achieves, an entirely different level of quiddity. Designed by British architect Nigel Coates, the year-old, multi-spaced club possesses a postmodern decor that juxtaposes urban apocalypse and faux-Ottoman elegance. Housed in a former dye factory, Taxim has been dubbed a "temple to urban salvage." You can dine here (dinners average about $30 per), then dance till 5:00 A.M. (on weekends). The cover charge for the disco is about $15.

OLD CITY

When in Istanbul between September and June, do as some affluent Turks do and have your cocktails at the **Cağaloğlu Hamamı** (Cağaloğlu Turkish Bath, at Dr. Kazım İsmail Gürkan Caddesi 34, near Cağaloğlu Meydanı; Tel: 522-2424), open daily from 8:00 A.M. until 8:00 P.M. Here you can drink your cocktails in the 300-year-old bath's all-marble chamber while enjoying a scrubdown at the same time—men and women together, in bathing suits. After the bath, everyone gathers in the picturesque café courtyard for more cocktails; sometimes there's entertainment by Gypsy belly dancers and musicians. The *hamam* has long been a favorite with the celebrated: Reportedly, Kaiser Wilhelm, the English king Edward VII, and Florence Nightingale all bathed here, and, more recently, the place has been visited by Rudolf Nureyev and Tony Curtis. These days the hamam is often booked for "foreign group nights," so telephone ahead to make sure it's open for individual guests on the night you want to go. (If you haven't brought a bathing suit with you to Istanbul, don't worry; the hamam will outfit you in one of its towel creations.)

The prices are higher at Cağaloğlu Hamamı than at the other hamams that cater to tourists. A complete luxury-treatment bath with massage costs $20, but maybe that's a small price to pay for feeling reborn. A sauna is $10 extra.

About five blocks to the northwest of the hamam, just behind the Blue Mosque, are rows of wooden benches where you can sit and enjoy a free **sound-and-light show** every evening at 9:00 from June through September. The lights play on the magnificent Blue Mosque, illuminating its six minarets, while a narrator relates Istanbul's history. Performances are in Turkish, English, French, or German; the English version is performed once every four nights. Check with the sound-and-light show office for the correct night; Tel: 522-1516.

INTERNATIONAL ISTANBUL FESTIVAL

This year marks the 21st season of the acclaimed International Istanbul Festival, which was first organized by industrialist Nejat F. Eczacıbaşı in 1973 to honor the 50th anniversary of the founding of the Republic of Turkey.

Running from June 15 through July 31 this year, the festival has gained worldwide recognition as one of the most important cultural gatherings in Europe. It has such a splendid reputation that top artists from East and West vie to appear in it. Each year spectators and performers from around the globe come to Istanbul to hear and play symphonic music, opera, chamber music, folk music, and jazz.

The festival also features dance—ballet, folk, and modern. In addition to offering Turks the chance to see top-rated international performers (at ticket prices ranging from $5 to $60), the festival also provides foreign visitors with the opportunity to hear the best in Turkish classical, religious, and folk music.

The festival's approximately 200 performances are held at eight venues throughout the city, including the Atatürk Kültür Merkezi (Atatürk Cultural Center) on Taksim square, the huge Açık Hava Tiyatrosu (Open-air Theater) in Harbiye (just northeast of the Hilton), and the Gate of Felicity on the grounds of Topkapı palace in the old city. Tickets can be bought at the Atatürk Cultural Center or at the performance venue; the latter box offices open an hour before showtime.

In addition to concerts, recitals, and theatrical performances, there are always some special events that don't fit any category—like the Bolshoi Ice Ballet. Also, every year the Istanbul State Opera stages several performances of *Abduction from the Seraglio* as part of the festival. (The Mozart opera, as always, will be performed "on location" at the Gate of Felicity in the Topkapı palace; performance dates are June 22, 24, and 26 this year.)

As they do each year, Turkey's **Whirling Dervishes** will perform their spellbinding *sema töreni* (whirling dance ritual) at the 1993 festival. Also slated to appear during this year's festival are the Bucharest Philharmonic, Monserrat Caballe, the Lar Lubovitch dance company, Angel Romero, and the Israel Chamber Orchestra.

OTHER FESTIVALS

The twelfth **Istanbul International Cinema Festival** will be held from April 3 through 18, 1993, primarily in a number of large movie houses on İstiklâl Caddesi in Beyoğlu. Gaining in international recognition, the festival last year showed 130 films from 30 countries in both feature and documentary categories. This year, the festival will screen more than 180 films.

The fifth **Istanbul International Theater Festival** will take place from May 19 until June 5, 1993. Performances will be held in the Atatürk Cultural Center and other large municipal and private theater buildings, primarily in the Taksim area.

Akbank, Turkey's largest private bank, will host the third annual Istanbul **International Jazz Festival** from October 13 through 17, 1993. Although its schedule had not yet been set when this guidebook went to press, the festival will include at least a dozen concerts; American artists will predominate, but European and Turkish musicians will be featured as well. The 1992 festival brought appearances by such jazzmen as Nat Adderley, Don Cherry, and Cecil Taylor. (By the way, Akbank, the festival's sponsor, is aiming at becoming an all-around corporate cultural impresario: The bank's new **Aksanat Center**—with extensive gallery spaces, a concert hall, and a theater—was scheduled to open in February 1993 on İstiklâl Caddesi near the French consulate. For information on art exhibitions, musical performances, and plays at Aksanat Center, contact the bank's culture and art department; Tel: 252-0776 or 252-3315.)

Programs and ticket information for most festivals can be obtained by writing to or calling the Istanbul Foundation for Culture and Arts, Barbaros Bulvarı, Beşiktaş, 80700 Istanbul; Tel: 261-3294 or 258-7498; Fax: 261-8823 or 258-4307.

CASINOS

Every single day of the year you can play the slot machines and games of chance at any of 14 hotel casinos in Istanbul. (Specific information, including hours, on many of the city's casinos is given in the Accommodations section, above.)

The kinds of games available, the poshness of the decor, and the subsidiary entertainments offered differ, of course, from casino to casino. The **Casino at the Hilton**, on the lower level of the Şadırvan building at the Hilton hotel (Tel: 247-5902) is open every day from 4:00 P.M. until 5:00 A.M. Though the Hilton's casino is one of the most spacious in the city—and currently offers the greatest variety of games—the atmosphere is too casual for some, and there's little festivity or excitement.

Another much more enjoyable place to part with your hard-earned dough is the **International Casino Club Istanbul** at the Istanbul Sheraton Hotel & Towers, open daily from 2:00 P.M. until 5:00 A.M. (Tel: 246-2021). Its two attractively decorated salons feature tall palm trees and faux-marbre columns. The fringed Tiffany-style lamps over the gaming tables give a warm feeling to the place—an elegant ambience that's reinforced by the smiling hostesses and women dealers glamorously robed in evening gowns. There's a dress code, so dress up.

SPORTING EVENTS

If you see a crowd of young men shouting as they run along an Istanbul street or a noisy autocade wildly waving flags, don't get upset: It's not a revolution in progress, just a celebration by supporters of a winning local soccer team. If you're interested in attending a soccer match (the Turkish word for the game is *futbol*), inquire at İnönü Stadyumu, right off İnönü Caddesi east of (and down the hill from) Taksim square. The soccer season begins in late August, and local professional teams play on Wednesday, Saturday, and Sunday, with games generally beginning at 1:00 P.M. in winter, 5:00 P.M. in late spring/early summer. Tickets cost $8 to $25. Cup matches and games between Turkish and foreign teams are held in the evening, beginning at 7:30, and the entrance fee is a lot steeper—from $10 to $50.

Thoroughbred-racing fans will appreciate knowing that Istanbul has a decent track, the Veli Efendi Hipodromu, located in Bakırköy on the western outskirts of the old city, about half an hour from Taksim by taxi. The facility, which can hold up to 25,000 fans in its grandstand and pleasant clubhouse, features Western-style pari mutuel betting, including a full range of "exotic" forms of wagering such as doubles, triples, exactas, and so on. Foreign horse-owners are now permitted to enter their horses in the track's five cup races. This year, the racing season at Veli Efendi runs from mid-April through mid-November; racing days are Wednesday, Saturday, and Sunday. Veli Efendi's grandstand has two restaurants.

> —*James Waller, Zeynep Bagana-Önen, and Anne Turner Bruno*

SHOPS AND SHOPPING

Shopping in Turkey, especially in Istanbul, presents a wealth of prospects and a spate of challenges. The range of Turkish crafts seems inexhaustible: wool and silk handmade carpets, kilims (flatweave rugs), *cicim*s (embroidered rugs); jewelry, including everything from traditional Ottoman silver jewelry to the latest designer settings; leather goods; copper and brassware; ceramics; even Turkish musical instruments, belly-dancing costumes, and Ottoman women's velvet court-costumes called *bindallı* ("thousand branches"), which are embroidered with silver or gold thread. The challenges include the need to haggle and to resist the strong-arm tactics of some shop owners, especially in the Covered Bazaar.

You simply must spend at least part of one of your days in Istanbul investigating the Covered Bazaar—a shopping experience unlikely to be matched anywhere else on earth. But don't forget that there are plenty of other places to spend your money, ranging from neighborhood bazaars to the chic shopping districts of the new city.

THE COVERED BAZAAR

The Covered Bazaar (Kapalıçarşı), said to be the largest bazaar in the Muslim world, is centrally located in the old city, bounded on the east by the Nuruosmaniye mosque and on the west by the Beyazit mosque and the campus of Istanbul University. Some 10,000 merchants boisterously hawk their wares from the bazaar's 4,000 shops, some of which are mere slots in the wall. The bazaar—a rambling, multidomed structure housing about 90 interior "streets"— is organized, basically, according to the types of items sold. One covered street will house mostly gold-jewelry shops, another will contain mostly rug merchants, and so on. There's almost nothing you can't buy here, from shaving cream to souvenir fezzes to bedroom furniture. Usually open until 8:00 P.M. in the summer and 7:00 P.M. in winter, the bazaar is closed only on Sundays and holidays. Be sure to procure a map of the bazaar (English versions are available at major bookstores and hotel bookshops) before setting out on your adventure.

It's important to remember two things about the bazaar today: First, you'll never get as good a buy as you might have in the old days, and, second, despite the fact that the bargains that were to be had in years past are gone forever, you *must* haggle with the shopkeepers. (The old rule was that a merchant would probably be willing to sell you something for half the original asking price, but this isn't true any longer.) Bargaining is a major part of the fun, so dive in. You'll be enticed by merchants speaking at least half a dozen foreign languages, eager to try any trick to get you to enter their shops. (It's a great game for the merchants and the hawkers who ply the streets in front of the shops to try to guess prospective clients' nationalities correctly.)

If the price seems high to you, just say, "It's too much money for me," and make as if to leave. If the shop owner is willing to come down in price, he won't let you out of the door. And don't feel guilty for drinking the tea or coffee the shop owner offers you. These refreshments are simply part of his normal operating expenses. Speaking of money, many of the shops in the bazaar—and others throughout the city—accept major credit cards. And some are even willing to take personal checks for rugs and other items being mailed to your home.

İç Bedesten and Copper Market

In the heart of the Covered Bazaar is the **İç Bedesten**, the original bazaar dating from the late 1500s. The Bedesten is known for its precious and semiprecious jewelry (much of it still made by Armenian craftsmen), for its antiques, and for its meerschaum. It's a great place to browse. Be on guard for clever counterfeits, but if a merchant gives you his word that a piece is authentic, believe him. With each sale he should also provide you with a certificate identifying the object and specifying its material, age, and value (as is also the case with rugs and jewelry). (See Useful Facts, above, for information on what you can and cannot take out of the country.)

You can still make some real finds among the antique copper vases, vessels, bowls, and pitchers in the rambling **copper (*bakır*) market** spread out immediately behind the main Covered Bazaar, though nowadays there are very few copperware shops sprinkled among those selling clothing and gifts. Exit the bazaar from the west side and turn right (north) to Bakırcılar Caddesi (Coppersmith's Street), where the copper-goods shops are strung along the street between Istanbul University to the west and Uzunçarsı Caddesi (Long Market Street) to the east. Most of the shops here sell only modern cooking pots and utensils, but it's worth browsing. If you buy a cooking pot that hasn't been tinned inside, request that this be done; it usually takes a day or less and costs only a little extra (about a tenth as much as it would cost in North America).

Old Book Bazaar

Walk east out of the bazaar via the major interior street called Fesçiler Caddesi and directly across the street and up several steps to reach the **Sahaflar Çarşısı** (Old Books Bazaar). Most of the 40 or so bookshops here sell only paperbacks, textbooks, postcards, and mementos, and most of the books are in Turkish, but you'll also find volumes—including a good selection of guidebooks—in English, German, French, and Italian. Only a few purveyors of genuinely old and valuable books remain; these authentic wares are quite expensive, but the experience of poking around the booksellers' stalls is a delight for the collector. The better old-book sellers are İbrahim Manav in the **Dilman Kitabevi** at Sahaflar Çarşısı 20, **Turan Türkmenoğlu** at number 39, and **Sinan Gözen**, at number 27. Gözen's shop is the best; it carries wares suitable for any pocketbook, from well-done imitations of old miniatures (which, however, do lack the subtlety of the originals) starting at about $15, to pages from old Korans (a few hundred dollars apiece), to exquisite old miniatures and picture maps, which range upwards from $1,000. The shop's stock of old leather-bound volumes in European languages (and generally on Orientalist topics) is really phenomenal. The manager speaks flawless English and enjoys showing you what he has on hand.

The breakup of the Soviet Union and the consequent freeing-up of borders has released a stream of Russians (and members of the many other ethnic groups who live in the new republics) into Turkey, eager to sell whatever they can to muster the hard cash necessary for survival. Scores of peddlers from the former U.S.S.R. gather daily in the little square just outside the Sahaflar Çarşısı, setting up little tables on which they display the memorabilia and detritus of Soviet civilization—military medals, defunct currency, and so on— as well as tarnished keepsakes and all manner of fascinating junk. The scene is heartbreaking, somehow, but if you're able to swallow your sentiment you may find some intriguing souvenirs.

SPICE BAZAAR

Just north of (that is, downhill from) the Covered Bazaar, at the foot of the Galata Bridge in Eminönü, is the Mısır Çarşısı (Egyptian, or Spice, Bazaar). Walk past the Yeni Cami (New Mosque), always blanketed by pigeons thanks to the corn sellers who congregate there, and proceed straight on to the huge open metal doors of the medieval-looking stone building that houses the Spice Bazaar. Its main corridor is a schizophrenic mix of modern neon lights shining down on centuries-old shops selling a welter of products from electronics to linens. The food shops, these days, are fewer than you might expect, but in front of these you'll see mounds on mounds of cheese—white and yellow kaşar and creamy, salty *tulum* in lamb- or goatskin wrappings—fresh meat and sausages, and slabs of the spice-cured beef known as *pastırma* (the ancestor of pastrami). If you look like a tourist, the grocers will call out, vying for your attention and assuming that it's caviar you're shopping for. The caviar prices are, in fact, appealing, but the grocers' harassment can be annoying. Do your best to ignore them, and concentrate on the feast of sights and smells to be enjoyed here.

In front of some of the shops you'll find as many as a dozen burlap bags, knee high and filled to overflowing with a veritable painter's palette of ground spices and dried herbs: mustard-yellow turmeric, orange tea leaves, reddish yellow saffron, yellow and white dried daisies, dark red sumac, tan cumin, drab oregano, gray-green needles of rosemary, and the strong green broken leaves of henna, which is used by traditional women to tint their hair and the palms of their hands. On shelves overhead are jars of cinnamon sticks, little dark brown balls of allspice, ovals of nutmeg, star-headed pins of cloves, and pale green cardamom pods (used to flavor coffee). Note, too, the variety of white and red raisins and the interesting "bird grapes"—very small dried currants used in pilaf dishes, *dolmas,* and stuffings for roast fowl. You might want to take home a jar of crystallized lemon salt—a delicious flavoring.

From the end of the corridor to the right wafts the tantalizing aroma of fresh-ground and roasting coffee beans. One store (next to the coffee sellers) has locally made peanut butter mixed with honey. Other holes-in-the-wall sell jars of different kinds of honey—everything from cactus flower to pine blossom—and jellies, marmalades, and the best-selling *Manisa macunu,* a honey-and-sugar mixture, medicated with spices, that men buy for use as an aphrodisiac.

In the open courtyard on the eastern side of the Spice Bazaar are displays of packets of vegetable and flower seeds, flats of fruit and vegetable seedlings, small trees in pots, and cages of finches, parrots, and puppies.

HANDCRAFTS

Right next to the Yeşil Ev hotel in Sultanahmet is the **Istanbul Handcrafts Center** (Sanatçılar Çarşısı), which occupies an attractive restored *medrese,* originally a school of Islamic law. The school's portico and rooms (which surround a central courtyard) serve as workshops, each devoted to one of many centuries-old Ottoman arts and crafts. These include *ebru,* the difficult art of paper marbling (which involves transferring floating colored inks from the surface of a gum solution onto a sheet of paper); calligraphy and gold-leaf illuminations; traditional bookbinding techniques; the painting of ancient designs in colors or gold on silk scarves and handkerchiefs, china pitchers and vases; engravings; and hand embroidery and lacework. Other shops create and sell prayer beads of carved wood, amber, or semiprecious stones; items inlaid with mother-of-pearl; glass and porcelain objects; and dolls and puppets clothed in the costumes of the Ottoman Empire.

In 1985 Çelik Gülersoy, president of the Turkish Touring and Automobile Association, decided to renovate the old medrese. He created this center, giving Turks and visitors alike the opportunity to observe artisans practicing these nearly forgotten arts and young people the chance to learn these skills before they vanish entirely. The center is a quiet oasis in the midst of the busy, touristic Sultanahmet neighborhood.

LEATHER

Istanbul's renowned consumer items have long been the "three C's": carpets, cotton clothing, and copperware, but today the best buy may be clothing of leather and suede—made to order or off the rack—at about half to two-thirds the price you'd pay at home.

The Old City

The leather goods purveyed at the Covered Bazaar are generally of inferior quality—though the variety of leather items available there is astounding. There are more than a hundred leather-goods shops selling coats (some shearling lined), jackets, suits, trousers, dresses, blouses, skirts, hats, wallets, and purses. Some stores offer custom-made leather clothing (it can take anywhere from one to seven days to fill an order, and the workmanship will be better the more time you allow).

Clothing sizes in Turkey correspond to the number system used in Europe. Men's suits go from size 46 to 56, coats from 46 to 56. Women's suits and coats are usually sized from 36 to 48; larger overcoats might simply be sized 1, 2, and 3. To avoid mistakes, have the salesperson measure you, and try on sample garments.

Some of the best leather shops in the old city are on Nuruosmaniye Caddesi, which runs beside the Baroque mosque of the same name and into the Covered Bazaar's eastern gate. **Bazaar 54**, at number 54, is a large store that mostly sells its leather, copper, jewelry, and rugs (about which more below) to the numerous tour groups that visit it. This is one of five large Bazaar 54 shops (and 28 smaller outlets in hotels) throughout Turkey; the chain, operated by the NET group of companies, was begun in 1975. Bazaar 54 carries an extensive array of leather items, particularly at its Villa Bosphorus store on the Asian side (see below).

Diagonally across the street from Bazaar 54, at number 83 Nuruosmaniye Caddesi, is the prestigious **Galeri İstanbul**, which has been here for 30 years. Its seven floors offer a wealth of leather, souvenirs, jewelry, and rugs (for more on the store's carpets and kilims, see below). Galeri İstanbul also offers a selection of handsome silver chests and mirrors.

Around the corner to the left and just before you enter the Nuruosmaniye Camii's grounds is Vezirhan Caddesi, which has about 25 leather shops. The **Mona Lisa**, at number 78, and **Studio 33**, at 72–74, offer a range of clothing styles in leathers of different qualities (lambskin is first class; sheepskin, second class; and goatskin, third). You choose from a number of models: There are about five coat styles, 20 jacket styles, and six skirt styles. Prices for coats and jackets range from about US$120 to $350; skirts are about $60 to $100 (the skirts take only a day to make). At least three days are needed to fill an order for a jacket or coat, but Haydar Şentürk, the proprietor of both stores, emphasizes that allowing a week between placing your order and picking up the finished garment ensures a higher quality of workmanship. Haydar Bey is a master at choosing cuts and colors to suit the customer, and he's very proud of the elegant Armani-knockoff coats his shop produces. Both stores accept major credit cards.

New City and Bosphorus

In the Hilton hotel passage and lobby are two *butik*s offering leather apparel. These are the **Semiramis** (in the passage) and the **Lion Shop** (in the lobby). Istanbul's other deluxe hotels have similar shops. (Hotel boutiques are notoriously overpriced.)

Desa Leather, which sells beautifully cut leather and suede coats and jackets as well as luggage and accessories, has three new-city locations: **Desa Osmanbey** (Halâskârgazi Caddesi 216), **Desa Rumeli Caddesi** (Matbaacı Sokak 61, Osmanbey), and **Desa Beyoğlu** (İstiklâl Caddesi 140). Desa also has a shop in the Ramada hotel in the old city.

Koşar Deri Ltd., in Teşvikiye at Maçka Caddesi 38, features its own line of splashy, multipocketed jackets and coats (both men's and women's) in colored leathers, including an appealing deep-green shade. Koşar sells quilt-lined vests, too: good travel garments for when it's changing seasons, weatherwise. The leather Koşar uses isn't of the best quality, but the designs are innovative and the prices affordable. At **Teodem**, at Şafak Sokak 29 in Nişantaşı, the emphasis is on high-drama leather outerwear: lots of outlandishly bright colors (including fire-engine red) and lots and *lots* of fur and shearling trim. Prices here are on the high end, to match the quality of the leather Teodem uses; this is definitely the place to shop if you like your clothes to make a (loud) statement. (For instructions on how to get to the Nişantaşı-Teşvikiye shopping district, see below.)

At Beylerbeyi on the Asian shore of the Bosphorus is the stylish waterfront mart called **Villa Bosphorus** (İskele Caddesi 14). Operated, like Bazaar 54, by the NET Group, Villa Bosphorus is open seven days a week from 9:30 A.M. till 7:30 P.M. You can get here by private boat or, for a fare of less than US$10, by taxi from the old city or Taksim, and the trip is well worth it: The store stockpiles an enormous range of leather and woolen goods, cotton dresses, rugs, handcrafts, jewelry, copper, brass, and assorted gifts and souvenirs. In addition, Villa Bosphorus features a lovely garden where you can refresh yourself with tea, Turkish coffee, Nescafé, beer, wine, or liquor.

Just across the street inland from the Villa Bosphorus is the **Sultan Leather and Suede Annex**. Coşkun Gürel, the store's buyer and manager, insists on offering only top-quality goods, which accounts for the fact that the prices here are close to those you'd pay in North America or Europe. He also claims that he has the largest stock of leather clothing in Turkey—about 5,000 garments in 40 to 50 different styles for both men and women. The Sultan line gives a substantial discount on discontinued styles.

RUGS AND KILIMS

Getting a good deal on a top-quality wool or silk carpet or kilim (flatweave carpet) at the Covered Bazaar probably depends upon your having a personal connection with a merchant or a recommendation from someone who knows the reputable rug sellers. Unless you know whom to buy from, or at least have some knowledge of Oriental carpets, it's probably unwise to go carpet shopping at the bazaar. Instead, resolve to pay a little more and purchase your rug or kilim from one of the NET Group merchants (Bazaar 54) or Galeri İstanbul on Nuruosmaniye Caddesi; see below. Their offerings are pricier, but you'll know what you're getting, and these outfits will insure your purchases and mail them home to you.

Bazaar 54 (which, again, is at Nuruosmaniye Caddesi 54) boasts one of the city's largest collections of rugs of all types and sizes; the store regularly stocks as many as 1,200 silk carpets, 4,000 wool carpets, and a few hundred kilims. Prices range up to US$200,000 for an exquisite 2½-square-yard silk rug and $15,000 for the finest wool offerings; expensive, yes, but these prices are about half what you'd pay for comparable items in North America or Great Britain. Major credit cards are accepted, as are personal checks for items being shipped home.

Rug sales manager Ertan Sandıkçıoğlu speaks English and is happy to help. Bazaar 54 charges a fee of 11 percent of an item's cost for handling, which includes securing a certificate for the rug from the Chamber of Commerce that identifies the rug in terms of material, size, and design; clearing the rug through Turkish customs (it must be less than 100 years old to leave the country); and mailing it to your home.

(Frankly, the surcharge is high, since customs duties usually run no more than 5.8 percent of the purchase price.)

The seven floors of **Galeri İstanbul** (Nuruosmaniye Caddesi 83) are devoted mostly to rugs, probably the largest single commercial collection of rugs and kilims in Turkey. Galeri İstanbul also sells leather, jewelry, and souvenirs. Like Bazaar 54, Galeri İstanbul caters to the tour-group trade; it offers the same shipping and handling services as Bazaar 54, but at a significantly lower surcharge. If you go to either Bazaar 54 or Galeri İstanbul, try to avoid the late afternoon, when the tour buses are most likely to make their scheduled stops. It bears mentioning that tour-group guides collect commissions of as high as 20 to 30 percent on the merchandise sold to their groups. If you're part of a tour group, note that this commission is being tacked onto your bill.

One of the best sources in the old city for rugs, kilims, copperware, ceramics, miniatures, and souvenirs is the **Cevri Kalfa Bazaar** (Divan Yolu 14, Sultanahmet), about half a mile due east of the Covered Bazaar and opposite the Hippodrome and Blue Mosque. The bazaar's setting is a restored Ottoman school; handsome white marble fountains are set into the walls, and one showroom features a long marble trough where Muslim students used to wash before prayers. The bazaar stocks 2,000 kilims, ranging in price from about $50 up to $2,000. Kilims from the eastern, Kurdish region of the country are thought to be the best looking and are made of the most durable material. Prices on wool and cotton-warp rugs range up to $5,000. (Some of the rugs here come from the city of Tokat, where weavers have taken to copying designs from the old rug-making center of Hereke.)

Cevri Kalfa Bazaar also sells smart kilim pocketbooks and suitcases. Besides rugs and related items, the bazaar offers a selection of antique copper items—pitchers, kettles, bowls, vases, candlestick holders, braziers, and samovars—from Russia, Iran, and the Kurdish and Armenian regions of Turkey. It also has a fine collection of porcelain vases, hand-painted miniatures, brooches, and boxes.

BOOKSHOPS, GALLERIES, AND GIFT SHOPS

Until a few decades ago the fashionable shopping district in the new city was along İstiklâl Caddesi in Beyoğlu. From the late 1800s on, İstiklâl was Istanbul's version of Fifth Avenue, serving the wealthy European communities of the district (then called Pera) with its fur and jewelry shops and custom haberdashers and bootmakers. After the 1960s, as the city expanded and its wealthy inhabitants moved into new neighborhoods north of Taksim, İstiklâl declined. Happily, that process has begun to reverse itself. Over the past two years, the Istanbul municipality has poured a great deal of money into revitalizing İstiklâl Caddesi, and the project appears to be achieving its aim. The street is now closed to motor traffic and has been beautifully repaved in pinkish-gray cobblestones. The city has also installed a streetcar line running from Taksim square south to Tünel (the fare, which like everything else rises with inflation, is paid in ordinary coins, not tickets or jetons).

The shopping along İstiklâl Caddesi is now much better than it was even two years ago. Major clothing stores such as Beymen and Vakko (see Clothing and Shoes, below) had never left the area, but their presence is now complemented by numerous boutiques selling fashionable, good-quality clothing.

Tünel

In the little district known as **Tünel** (named after the subway whose upper entrance is here), at the southern end of the main stretch of İstiklâl Caddesi, are a number of shops selling old books, postcards, maps, prints, and the like. If printed matter is an interest of yours, they're certainly worth browsing through. The side streets also hold a scattering of antiques shops and stores selling new copper- and brassware. Also in Tünel, at number 34 Sofyalı Sokak (two short blocks northwest of İstiklâl Caddesi and the Tünel entrance), is what may be Istanbul's best scholarly bookshop, **Eren** (Tel: 251-2858). The shop isn't only scholarly: Muhittin Eren, its affable proprietor, also carries an impressive range of art books (some of which are published under the Eren imprint). This is the place to come for gorgeously printed, large-format books on the traditional arts of Anatolia, or, if your bent *is* of a scholarly kind, for a full selection of books on Middle Eastern society, culture, and politics. Of course, many of the books here are in Turkish, but there is a truly impressive range of titles in English, French, and German. (Eren also has a small outlet in the Sahaflar Çarşısı, at number 16.)

If you're in need of English-language newspapers, magazines, or just a good murder mystery (to curl up with and take a vacation from your vacation), the Tünel end of İstiklâl Caddesi is also the place to look. The large **ABC Kitabevi** at number 241 offers a fairly good selection of periodicals and books in foreign languages, especially English.

Teşvikiye–Nişantaşı Area

In spite of İstiklâl Caddesi's recent renaissance, the city's art, antique, and fashion center is still concentrated (to use the word loosely) in the "uptown" districts of Maçka, Nişantaşı, Teşvikiye, Osmanbey, and Şişli (all adjacent to one another). If you're interested in exploring what Turkey's expanding art scene and burgeoning fashion industry have to offer, the following itinerary may be useful: Travel north from Taksim along Cumhuriyet Caddesi until you reach the fork in the road, a few blocks past the headquarters of TRT (Turkish Radio and Television) and the Hilton hotel. Here Cumhuriyet Caddesi splits into Vali Konağı Caddesi (which continues northeast into Teşvikiye) and Halâskârgazi Caddesi (which continues north into Şişli). The fork is marked, in the triangle formed by the road's division, by a beautiful, recently restored marble Art Nouveau building now owned by Türkbank. If you're travelling by bus or taxi you may wish to be deposited here and to continue on foot. Take the right-hand branch of the fork and walk down Vali Konağı until you reach Rumeli Caddesi, then turn left. Take Rumeli Caddesi west (while making sure to do a bit of exploring of the surrounding side streets) until you reach the intersection with Halâskârgazi Caddesi. Then turn right (north) on Halâskârgazi, which leads directly to Şişli. You'll be astonished at the sheer number of galleries, clothing boutiques, and antiques shops and by the high quality of their merchandise.

While shopping in this area, take the opportunity to have lunch at **Cafe-İn** or **Cafe Wien**, discussed under Dining, above, or at the **Saray** franchise at Teşvikiye Caddesi 105), a clean, well-lighted place whose (Turkish) fast-food offerings are of a far higher quality than what you'd expect at an American fast-food joint. (For better or worse, there is now a McDonald's franchise on Rumeli Caddesi, and even a 7-11 store, which, unlike its American cousins, features a sit-down café and a salad bar stocked with fresh-looking veggies.)

There are now more than a hundred art galleries in Istanbul, many of them clustered in and around the new city shopping area of Maçka–Nişantaşı–Teşvikiye–Osmanbey. Many of the new galleries are underwritten by major banks and holding companies, which have apparently discovered the value of showcasing culture. If you visit a number of galleries you're quite likely to see works by the same artists; it seems that Turkish galleries don't have exclusive contracts with the artists they show. If you happen to be in Istanbul in late September, you can get a good overview of what the city's galleries are showing by attending the **Istanbul Art Fair**

(İstanbul Sanat Fuarı) held annually at the Tüyap Exhibition Palace just north of the Pera Palas Hotel. Though the more cutting-edge galleries aren't likely to be represented at the fair, you can gain some idea of the range of media and styles in which Turkey's more established painters and sculptors are currently working. Otherwise, just try your luck by wandering around the Nişantaşı-Teşvikiye circuit. The galleries listed below (some of which are in the adjacent district of Kurtuluş, just west of Halâskârgazi Caddesi) represent a necessarily rather random selection.

The Istanbul art scene—not unlike those of New York, Paris, or Cologne—is extremely heterogeneous, which means, among other things, that there's a lot of bad (derivative, cloying, or just plain poorly executed) work to be seen. If your pockets are deep (and you're interested in acquiring Turkish painters' work), you may want to constrain your attention to searching for something by one of the certified masters of Turkish modernism: Fikret Mualla, Komet, Abidin Dino, or perhaps one of the quasi–social realist/quasi-mystical villagescapes of İbrahim Balaban.

For almost two decades, **Galeri Baraz** (Kurtuluş Caddesi 191/B, Sinemköy, Kurtuluş; Tel: 240-4783 or 241-1861; Fax: 231-6258) has been one of Istanbul's most important art galleries. The owner, Yahşı Baraz, "followed his bliss" after working in a New York City art gallery in 1974, returning to Istanbul at just the right time to establish the city's, and incidentally Turkey's, most significant art gallery. Yahşı Bey turned his family's large, corner, seven-floor building into an outsized gallery. Currently he specializes in top contemporary painters, some of whom work abroad and have earned considerable reputations in North America, France, Germany, and other European countries as well as their native Turkey.

In the lobby of the Hilton hotel is a branch of **Galeri Baraz**, which presents an extensive collection of paintings and other works by Turkish artists. On display at the Hilton are the gorgeous satin scarves, evening purses, and eyeglass cases hand-embroidered by Nihide Küçük. Her exquisitely crafted, Ottoman-inspired floral designs make special—and expensive—gifts.

If you want to see fanciful figurative works, try **Teşvikiye Sanat Galerisi** at Abdi İpekçi Caddesi 48/1, Teşvikiye; Tel: 241-0458. Owner Doğan Paksoy shows his impressionistic figurative paintings here, along with the works of about six of his young painter friends.

In the eight years it's been in operation, **Galeri Nev** (Maçka Caddesi 33/B Teşvikiye; Tel: 231-6763) has hosted scores of exhibitions—a new show nearly every month. This simpatico downstairs gallery is run by Haldun Dostoğlu and his assistant, Megi Bişar, whose aim is to promote the best in new Turkish painting and sculpture. Much of the work they show is abstract, though some figurative Expressionist paintings do appear on the gallery's walls, and the gallery has begun to feature occasional photography shows as well. Galeri Nev also makes it a point to show the work of women artists, including, for example, Nazlı Damlacı and İnci Eviner; Galeri Nev's catalogs are in English.

Almost every street of the upscale shopping area of Nişantaşı–Maçka–Teşvikiye has a number of gift and antiques shops. This is no place to bargain hunt, but the quality of the goods in many of these shops is outstanding.

A large, impressive, and reputable collection is that of **Rafi Portakal** at Kemal Mim Öke Sokak 19/1, Nişantaşı (Tel: 241-7181). Rafi Bey represents the third generation of his Armenian family to sell antiques and is considered the city's, and perhaps the country's, most knowledgeable antiques dealer. He holds auctions about twice a year, usually in May and November, of such prized items as Islamic silver; rare Russian silver samovars and porcelain or enamel eggs; silver rose-water sprinklers; and gilded copper incense boxes and burners. He and his assistant, Fatoş Türkmen, both of whom speak good English, can show you authentic treasures from old Ottoman families—an array of magnificent pieces in excellent condition.

Nearby, **Vip Antik**, at Eytam Caddesi 16 (fifth floor), Nişantaşı (Tel: 241-4048 or 230-4954), crowns its sizable collection of period furniture in many fine woods with 17th-century İznik porcelain plates and tiles in a rare tomato red color that has not been duplicated since.

The stylish shop and art gallery of **Urart** (Abdi İpekçi Caddesi 18/1, 80200 Nişantaşı; Tel: 246-7194) displays large Expressionist canvases by Bedri Baykam and other trendy Turkish painters, plus some original and reproduction statuary and vases. It's Urart's jewelry, however, that's likely to be of greatest interest to foreign visitors.

Urart (which takes its name from the ancient Urartian culture of eastern Turkey) has for almost two decades been making magnificent jewelry in designs that interpret the treasures of the gamut of cultures that have flourished in Anatolia over the past ten millennia. These include reproductions of necklaces and earrings of silver and semiprecious stones from 2,500 B.C.; gold necklaces and pendant earrings from the Ionian Greek period; and distinctive designs of the

Greco-Persian, Hellenistic, Roman, and Byzantine periods, as well as the striking geometric designs of the Seljuk Turks and the more ornate curved designs of the Ottomans.

Urart feels that re-creating something new from ancient designs honors Turkey's almost overwhelming inheritance. Depending upon your selection of historical period, any of Urart's sets of necklaces, earrings, bracelets, pins, and rings can be one of the most meaningful souvenirs or gifts you can buy. Prices on the silver pieces are surprisingly low.

Very centrally located, right off Halâskârgazi Caddesi in Osmanbey, is Muzaffer Eren's **BiZe Art Gallery** at Rumeli Caddesi 81 (fifth floor). Here Muzaffer Hanım has ample space to display old and new oil paintings and sculpture, a bar and snacks for winter cocktails, and a tea room that also offers lunch; it's open from 10:00 A.M. until 7:00 P.M. In winter it is closed only on Sundays; in summer, on Saturdays and Sundays.

Muzaffer Hanım has a fascinating collection of unusual items, particularly Ottoman memorabilia, that are far from cheap. But it's the sort of place where you can find, for example, old mosque candles, copper charcoal braziers, old Russian brass trays, Ottoman cigarette and tobacco cases, and other exotica. You might want to telephone first (Tel: 246-7025) to ask if there are any special art openings at the gallery while you are in town.

The **V-22** gift shop (Vehbi Bey Apartments, Maçka Caddesi 22, Teşvikiye), is known as one of the best shops in Istanbul for old Ottoman silver jewelry and artifacts at reasonable prices. The shop is operated by Ülker Germen, who has kindly marked the prices of all the items in her shop clearly and not in that secret hodgepodge of number codes that's so typical of antiques dealers. At V-22 you might find porcelain vases and pitchers, silver medallions set with turquoise, harem rings with gems dangling from each of their four to six bands, antique wooden bath clogs exquisitely set with mother-of-pearl, old water pipes, Ottoman stained glass, and worry beads set with semiprecious stones. This small store has an amazing selection of jewelry and household items jammed onto shelves and hanging from the walls.

On Atiye Sokak, at number 6/A (just across the street from Cafe Wien), is a modest-looking storefront concealing one of Istanbul's real treasure troves. This is **Gönül Paksoy** (Tel: 261-9081), whose proprietor, Gönül Hanım, and her brother travel all over Anatolia and (now that the Turkic republics of the former U.S.S.R. have opened their borders) Central Asia hunting down jewelry, carpets, and other items of rare quality. The shop's Ottoman-era silver earrings, bracelets, and necklaces, some set with semiprecious stones, are superb pieces of workmanship; the delicate patina that age has conferred on some of the pieces heightens their beauty. Gönül Hanım also carries a small but carefully selected stock of textiles, including *cicim*s (embroidered flatweave rugs) whose complexity, subtlety, and worth far exceed anything you'll find in the Covered Bazaar. Lately, the shop has begun commissioning traditional craftspeople to produce a line of superb sweaters and other knitted outerwear in handspun yarns colored with natural dyes. These good-looking garments—some of which feature bold archaeological motifs—are hardly cheap (sweaters begin at about $400), but their superior craftsmanship and dramatic one-of-a-kindness make their price-tags understandable.

Perhaps the best buys you might find in Istanbul are the original silver earrings, necklaces, brooches, pins, bracelets, and rings, sometimes embellished with semiprecious jewels, for about $40 to $300 at the **Ayşe Takı Galerisi**, at Sakayık Sokak 62/5 in Nişantaşı; Tel: 247-4746. Ayşe is a young Turkish jeweler who worked in New York City for more than ten years. Her mother, Gül Önet, is running this unusual shop displaying the interesting work of ten young Turkish sculptors and jewelry designers, including her daughter Ayşe.

Elsewhere in Istanbul

Though many of Istanbul's best gift shops, antiques shops, and art galleries are concentrated in and around the Nişantaşı-Teşvikiye circuit mapped out above, there are certainly treasures to be found elsewhere throughout the city. The central new-city district of **Çukur** (southwest of Taksim square, along and around Tarlabaşı Bulvarı), for example, has a slew of interesting antiques shops. Galleries have been springing up everywhere, including some relatively out-of-the-way places; the delightful works of the painter Balaban, for example, are sold through the Bilim Sanat Galerisi, at Mühürdar Caddesi/Akmar Pasajı number 70/1–2 in Kadıköy, on the Asian side near Haydarpaşa train station; Tel: 347-4443.

The Bosphorus district of Ortaköy (near the European foot of the first Bosphorus bridge), which has long had a reputation for Bohemianism and which, like İstiklâl Caddesi, has been experiencing something of a renaissance of late, is also an interesting place to shop. During the summer, there's a street fair here every Saturday and Sunday.

CLOTHING AND SHOES

A number of first-rate clothing stores have branches on İstiklâl Caddesi and in the Taksim area. Among these are Beymen and Vakko—the Turkish equivalents of Saks Fifth Avenue or Bergdorf Goodman. Prices at these stores are steep, and the slick fashions they market are imitations of the latest American and European styles. Vakko, founded 50 years ago, is the oldest and biggest manufacturer of fashionable clothing in Turkey. The company produces two lines and sells them in separate outlets: **Vakko**, at İstiklâl Caddesi 123–125, sells traditional, well-made garments to a conservative, affluent clientele. **Vakkorama**, at Osmanlı Sokak 13 (near The Marmara hotel just off Taksim square), sells casual clothing designed for younger, hipper customers.

Beymen also produces two lines aimed at different audiences. The more traditional garb is available at Beymen's stores on İstiklâl Caddesi (Vakıf Göknek İşhanı 2) and Halaskârgazi Caddesi (number 230, just a few blocks north of the intersection with Rumeli Caddesi). **Beymen Club**, with branches at the Beymen store on İstiklâl Caddesi and at Rumeli Caddesi 81, sells "weekend" and casual clothes that are highly reminiscent of Ralph Lauren's designs.

Other purveyors of chic casual wear include Mudo Collection, Cottonbar, NN Club, and Polo Garaj. Mudo and Cottonbar have outlets on İstiklâl Caddesi (at numbers 162 and 151, respectively), and all four of these stores have outlets along the Nişantaşı-Teşvikiye route that's been laid out above. **Mudo Collection**, with two stores in Nişantaşı-Teşvikiye (at Rumeli Caddesi 197 and Teşvikiye Caddesi 143) sells casual wear that's American in tone; its menswear line is more interesting than its women's clothing, and features a range of beautifully cut and tailored sport and dress shirts in fine cotton. **Cottonbar**, with a Nişantaşı outlet at Teşvikiye Caddesi 156, specializes in shirts and neckties (the ties are terrific). **NN Club**'s clothing is more Italian in flavor (again, some wonderful shirts); the store is on Abdi İpekçi Caddesi, at number 2. **Polo Garaj**—at number 47/2 Şakayık Sokak, off Akkavak Sokak—offers a full range of American-style casual wear for both men and women, including outdoorsy overshirts and sweaters and a range of well-made denim garments.

Also on Şakayık Sokak, just off Akkavak Sokak, is **Zeki Triko**; in season, Zeki Triko sells a fantastic variety of women's swimsuits, which are (justly) internationally famous. It's a "must" stop, especially if you're heading toward the Aegean or Mediterranean beaches after your sojourn in

Istanbul. (If you forget, don't despair: There are branches in İzmir and Antalya.)

Derishow, hard by NN Club at Abdi İpekçi Caddesi number 2, sells superb (mostly women's) sport and dress clothing on its three floors. Derishow first made its name in leather garments, and it still offers a selection of extraordinary leather coats and jackets, as well as interesting shoes, handbags, belts and other accessories, but now it sells lots else besides. The store's main level features moderately priced, clean-lined women's clothing. Unlike that of too many other Turkish designers, Derishow's women's clothing is simple, tasteful, and elegant: There's not a hint of the glitzy, ersatz sexiness that ruins other Turkish womenswear collections. The palette of colors explored by Derishow's designers is equally understated—with black, gray, beige, and subtle purples and burgundies predominating. Downstairs at Derishow, you'll find the store's casual line, including an appealing selection of men's shirts. Upstairs from the main level is Derishow's top-of-the-line womenswear, including luscious, superlatively well-cut silk blouses.

Relaxation of tariff and import regulations has meant that American and European clothing—once difficult to find and prohibitively expensive in Turkey—is now readily available and affordable. The Nişantaşı-Teşvikiye district now possesses outlets of Sisley, Bennetton, New Man, Naf-Naf, Lee's Jeans, and a host of other boutiques selling foreign-made garments. Note that in general the prices are no better than what you'd find at home. Stick instead to the Turkish manufacturers (and note that the Turkish word for sale is *indirim,* since end-of-season sales, especially, can be bargain extravaganzas, with markdowns of at least 50 percent being typical).

There are several excellent men's haberdashers along Rumeli Caddesi. **Mithat**—to choose just one—features Italian-nuanced suits and outerwear (Rumeli Caddesi number 26/28).

If you're looking for sweaters of 100-percent Angora, Shetland, or lambswool at reasonable prices, stop in at the **Penyelux** outlet in Osmanbey (at Şair Nigar Caddesi 60) or look for the Penyelux label on sweaters for sale in other shops. Styles and colors are contemporary. If you don't mind spending a little more money, your best bet is **Karaca**, at Matbaacı Sokak, Bekiroğlu İş Merkezi 38 in Osmanbey or Bekiroğlu İş Hanı 76, off Rumeli Caddesi in Nişantaşı. Karaca's classically styled sweaters are made of wool that's almost as durable as cashmere, and though the items are expensive by Turkish standards, Western customers will find them significantly cheaper than equivalent goods in Europe or North America.

On Şişli Meydanı (Şişli square), about a mile north of the Rumeli Caddesi–Halâskârgazi Caddesi intersection, is **Doğu Tekstil** (Abide-i Hürriyet Caddesi 251/10, fifth floor), a factory showroom for hand-painted or -printed scarves and shawls made of pure silk or polyester of an Angora-like softness. The designer of these lovely creations, Ayla Sepik, runs the show-room. Her pieces, which are marketed throughout Europe, make marvelous and inexpensive gifts.

On Kuyulu Bostan Sokak, three blocks past the intersection of Vali Konağı Caddesi and Teşvikiye Caddesi, are a number of designer-owned boutiques that offer sensational women's apparel. **Neslihan Yargıcı**, at number 11/1, offers unique outfits that manage skillfully to blend Western fashion innovation with traditional Eastern designs. Black is Neslihan's favorite color, though she does mix it (sparingly) with white once in a while. Her daring evening gowns are particularly interesting (and expensive). **Zeynep Tunuslu**, at number 46/A, is a younger, bolder designer (she herself is notorious for the scandalous outfits she's seen in at fashionable parties). Zeynep Hanım draws some of her inspiration from the geometric patterns of Seljuk and Ottoman art, and she's very fond of chiffon, sequins, and embroidered fabrics.

If you want to get an idea of the distinctive styling of Turkish haute couture, just drop in or, better, make an appointment between 10:30 A.M. and 7:00 P.M. with Bilge Mesçi in her **Artizan** (Zafer Sokak 42, running perpendicular to Rumeli Caddesi, one street north of Vali Konağı Caddesi, Nişantaşı; Tel: 234-3740).

Bilge Hanım has specialized for 20 years in creating stunning, original evening, cocktail, and dinner gowns plus elegant suits made out of raw or pure silk chiffon and taffeta in delicious colors like coral, shrimp, old rose, champagne, and turquoise. You won't see such understatedly feminine high fashion anywhere else in the world. If you buy only one special outfit this year, consider the ones here.

For style and quality, Turkish shoes are second only to those produced in Italy. When shopping for shoes here, keep in mind that shoes made in Turkey have a European last, which is much wider than the American last. Also, the sizes are European; North Americans—both men and women— should add 31 to their usual size (e.g., an American size 8 is 39 here; note that it's difficult to find women's sizes larger than 40, the American size 9). Here are a few stores you might want to check out in the Nişantaşı–Teşvikiye–Osmanbey neighborhood.

At Akkavak Sokak 15, just off Vali Konağı Caddesi a block past its intersection with Rumeli Caddesi, is **La Botte**, a small store with a limited but exquisite collection of women's shoes. The design of the boots and shoes is Turkish, but the top-quality leather is imported from Italy. More conservatively styled but extremely well made women's shoes are sold by **Ertuğrul**, at Vali Konağı Caddesi 101/A. This is the kind of footwear that never goes out of fashion; Ertuğrul sells beautifully crafted handbags as well. A wide selection of relatively inexpensive shoes can be found at **Elle**, at Rumeli Caddesi 12. Elle's footwear ranges from high-heeled patent-leather pumps to traditional loafers and oxfords.

For both men's and women's shoes, look in at **Demirel**, at Akkavak Sokak 13. Its shoes are as reasonably priced as they are fashionable, and its clientele is drawn from the ranks of those who can't quite afford the ultra-chic footwear they nonetheless crave.

Hayri, at Halaskârgazi Caddesi 226 (just a few doors down from Beymen), is the oldest, most reputable men's shoe store in Turkey. Its slogan, "Float around the world in our footwear," really reflects the comfort and durability of the shoes Hayri sells.

*—James Waller, Zeynep Bagana-Önen, and
Anne Turner Bruno*

ISTANBUL ENVIRONS

By Metin Demirsar and Patricia Roberts

Metin Demirsar, the editor of Insight Guide: Turkish Coast *and the author of* Insight Pocket Guide: Istanbul *and other travel books about Turkey, is a Turkish journalist whose articles have appeared in* The Wall Street Journal, Barron's Weekly, *the London* Daily Express, *and* Global Finance *magazine. Patricia Roberts lived in Istanbul for three years and has written about Turkey for* The Wall Street Journal *and other publications.*

After you have tasted all that Istanbul has to offer, set your sights beyond the city limits to discover the treasures of the neighboring countryside, towns, and cities. Istanbul is surrounded by intriguing places, located within three distinct geographic areas—the Black Sea coast (immediate vicinity), the southern coast of the Sea of Marmara (Asian environs), and Turkish Thrace (European environs)—all easily reached by ferry, bus, car, or train from Istanbul.

The main areas of interest are the Black Sea beaches, the Princes' Islands, Termal spa, Bursa and the nearby mountain of Uludağ, İznik, Edirne, and the Gallipoli peninsula. Istanbul is a convenient base from which to set out on day-long or weekend excursions.

MAJOR INTEREST

Black Sea coast's wide sandy beaches
Princes' Islands—quaint and traffic-free
Mineral-bath spas of Termal
Bursa's spas, Ottoman architecture, and bazaars
Ski slopes of Uludağ

İznik's walls and ceramics works
Edirne's Selimiye Camii
Gallipoli battlefield

You can never feel landlocked in Istanbul. It's easy—by car or even municipal bus—to reach the Black Sea coast beaches to enjoy a day, a weekend, or a week of sun, fresh air, and brisk breezes. The seaside towns of **Kilyos**, with its broad sandy beach, an hour's drive from Istanbul's center on the Thracian (European) side of the Bosphorus, and **Şile**, with its clean sea, fishing harbor, and long beach, two hours away on the Asian side, are two favorite getaway spots—and both generate the weekend traffic to prove it.

Dotting the Sea of Marmara just southeast of Istanbul are the nine **Princes' Islands**, which on a clear day seem to float on the horizon beyond the mouth of the Bosphorus. Each island has its own character, yet they share a common history: In Byzantine times they were used as places of exile where banished royalty and condemned clergy were deposited. Today the islands are desirable spots for self-exile. Sipping tea atop the open-air deck of a ferry from Istanbul, you can reach the islands in an hour (or half an hour by *deniz otobüsü,* or sea bus). Cars are forbidden on all the islands, and transportation is by horse-drawn carriage or bicycle, a welcome restriction after the bumper-to-bumper crawl of Istanbul.

You can visit the islands in a day and return to the city on an early evening ferry, or you can continue an hour farther by ferry (again, only half an hour by sea bus) to the Sea of Marmara port of **Yalova**, where you can then board a minibus for the 15-minute drive to the spa-resort of Termal.

Romans, Byzantines, and Ottomans, in turn, all retreated to **Termal** for therapeutic immersions in its mineral baths—purported to cure anything and everything. The spa complex is sheltered by a thick pine forest, and its open-air thermal pool and three public baths are surrounded by landscaped flower gardens and exotic shrubbery (lots of palms) remarkably well tended for a public resort. You can visit Termal in one day, but since the spa's purpose is relaxation, it warrants at least a weekend stay. Only if you're travelling by ferry can you visit the spa and return to Istanbul the same day (the drive overland takes three hours). Or you can continue on to Bursa, an hour to the southwest by car or bus (buses leave from Yalova's quay).

Bursa, or Yeşil Bursa (Green Bursa), as the residents refer to their city, should appear on every traveller's itinerary. The city was founded on the site of rich mineral springs on the

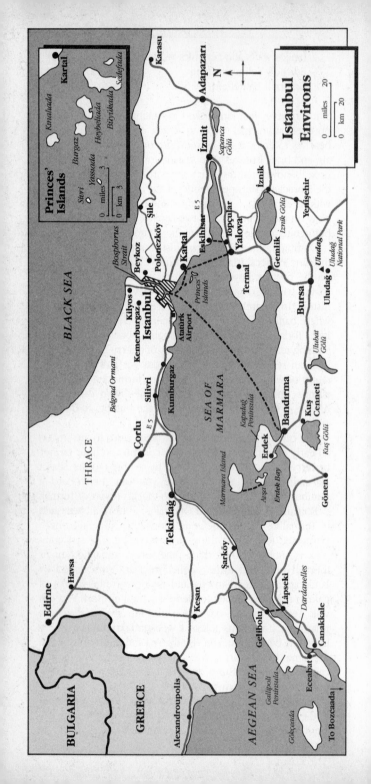

wooded foothills of Uludağ (Great Mountain). Many of the city's present-day baths lie on the original sites of spas made famous by such imperial bathers as Byzantine emperor Justinian I and empress Theodora. Perhaps it is this intimate connection to soothing water that makes Bursa's pace so relaxed and unhurried.

Leave plenty of time to roam Bursa's covered bazaars and *hans* (inns); you'll find them a welcome relief from Istanbul's more touristy and frenetic markets. Within their meandering passages hundreds of shops will tempt you with such affordable treasures as plush terry-cloth robes, "Turkish towels," and brightly printed Bursa silks. And the prices here are generally lower than those in Istanbul.

Bursa has some of the most beautiful examples of early Ottoman architecture. The powerful presence of the Ulu Cami (Great Mosque) and the splendidly decorated Yeşil Cami and Yeşil Türbe (Green Mosque and Green Mausoleum) serve as unforgettable reminders that Bursa reigned as the first imperial capital of the Ottoman Turks and was the beneficiary of unabashed civic spending by the sultans. You will need a full day to see all the city's monuments. A good map and a pair of walking shoes are all that's required to locate the sites since Bursa is small and conveniently laid out. The *dolmuş* system is also quite good, making travel fast and inexpensive.

As soon as the first snows fall, Turkey's downhill crowd heads to **Uludağ National Park**, where the country's largest ski resort is located. The ski slopes are situated just 37 km (23 miles) up the mountain from Bursa's city center. Smart skiers bypass the mountain traffic (and the higher mountain prices) by staying in Bursa and riding up on the city's *teleferik* (cable car).

From Yalova it's also possible to board a minibus to İznik, ancient Nicaea, about an hour and a half inland at the eastern end of İznik lake. This walled town played an important part in the evolution of church doctrine during the early centuries of Christianity. İznik is certainly worth a day trip from Istanbul (via Yalova) or a side trip from Bursa just to see its Roman-Byzantine city walls and to tour its Archaeological Museum, where a fine collection of İznik tiles—remnants of the city's artistic past—is on display. İznik ceramic production reached its height in the 16th and 17th centuries; tiles from İznik decorate many of Istanbul's Ottoman-era buildings.

West of Istanbul, Turkish Thrace—Turkey's foothold on European soil—stretches from the Bosphorus to the borders of Greece and Bulgaria and south to the Sea of Marmara and Aegean Sea coasts. A gateway between East and West, the region is characterized by rolling farmlands.

Edirne, the region's largest city and the second capital—after Bursa but before Istanbul—of the Ottoman sultans, sits near Greece and Bulgaria, about four hours west of Istanbul. Today Edirne remains much as it was centuries ago—a living museum of Ottoman architecture. Anyone with an interest in the evolution of the Ottoman building style should not miss Edirne's Selimiye Camii, the masterwork of the empire's most famous architect, Sinan.

Edirne is bisected by the ancient Via Egnatia, a Roman-Byzantine road that begins a mile outside Istanbul and heads southwest along the northern shore of the Sea of Marmara until reaching Kumburgaz, where it veers northward toward Edirne and then onward across the Balkans to Italy. According to one ancient source, "The Via Egnatia was carefully planned and engineered. Stone pavement in two rows as far apart as the wheels of a Roman chariot wound over the gently sloping plains of Thrace." The plains of Thrace still slope and the road is still only as wide, it seems, as the wheels of a Roman chariot, but the "chariots" are now transport trucks and Mercedes Benzes waging constant battle for space on the Via Egnatia's modern incarnation, the highway known as the E 5. (The E 5, by the way, travels the length of Turkey, beginning at the European border and traversing the country in a generally southeasterly direction until finally reaching the Hatay, the little strip of land between the Mediterranean Sea and Syria.)

In Thrace the E 5 was once scenic, with cliffs and farmland running down to the sea. Lately the disease of development has spread well outside Istanbul's limits, however, and for two hours the view takes in little but cluttered seaside towns with rabbit-hutch architecture. In summer the roads are congested, and it's advisable to leave early (meaning 6:00 A.M.) for trips southwestward.

The E 5 cruises past the town of Silivri, then forks, the E 5 turning north to Edirne and a secondary road continuing straight toward Keşan—and passing through the city of Tekirdağ, home of the Turkish government's Tekel distilleries, which produce the Turkish national drink, *rakı,* as well as the region's delicious wines. Past Tekirdağ the road continues on to the **Gallipoli** (Gelibolu in Turkish) **peninsula,** which juts from the southern shore of Thrace into the Aegean Sea. For 40 miles the peninsula closely parallels the Asian shore, forming the strait known as the Dardanelles, historically an immensely important strategic waterway and the first leg of the sea trade route that leads from the Aegean, through the strait, across the Sea of Marmara, and up the Bosphorus to the Black Sea.

To reach the Gallipoli peninsula, you can turn left after Tekirdağ at the signpost for Şarköy (this is the scenic route) or drive straight to the small city of Keşan and there catch the E 24 south. Both ways take about the same amount of time, but the 45-minute meander toward Şarköy takes you through fields planted with corn and sunflowers and up dramatic rocky ridges that overlook the Thracian plain.

The Gallipoli peninsula is a privileged piece of land, preserved from development and, hence, ruin. Of course, as the site of one of World War I's most brutal battles—the Gallipoli Campaign mounted against the Ottomans by the allies in 1915—it has paid a heavy price for survival. The tiny harbor town of Gelibolu greets you briefly, then sends you 30 minutes farther south to the Gallipoli War Memorial, a parkland created in tribute to the soldiers who fought the nine-month battle. The park offers spectacular views of the Aegean to the west and across the Dardanelles to Asia.

IMMEDIATE VICINITY

BLACK SEA BEACHES

There's something exciting about swimming off the beaches of the Black Sea. Thrashing breakers pull in strong, unforgiving currents; ships of many nations ply the dark waters; and on the western horizon float the outlines of the hills that stretch westward toward Bulgaria. What you might not expect are the miles of fine white sand beaches, lively cafés, and the crowds of people who drive for miles, with tents and kids in tow, to settle in for a day or two of rest, relaxation, and *raki*. Black Sea beaches are usually crowded on summer weekends and religious holidays.

An hour north (34 km/21 miles) from the center of Istanbul on the European side of the Bosphorus strait is the resort town of **Kilyos**. En route you pass the **Belgrad Ormanı** (Belgrade Forest) and the village of **Kemerburgaz**, popular spots for picnicking and recreation.

The sea here has the cleanest water around Istanbul—that is, reasonably unpolluted and safe for swimming. The beach is split into private and public areas, and if you walk far enough west along the beach you will likely find a spot all to yourself. It's worth paying the fee for the lifeguarded beach, however, as the Black Sea undertow is notoriously dangerous. Although it's not an especially pretty or quaint village and is populated largely by military personnel, Kilyos does offer a respite from Istanbul and claims a few enjoyable hotels and cafés. The **Kilyos Kale Otel** and **Yonca Hotel**, perched on a steep cliff overlooking a small bay, both have terraces where you can enjoy a fish dinner while watching the sunset. The **Turban Kilyos Tatil Köyü** (open from May to October) is right on the beach and has bungalows and a disco. The Turban's parking lot and beach are available for public use, for a daily fee.

Nightlife in the tiny settlement revolves mainly around the charming restaurants along the pier, of which **Şanzelize Lokantası** (Tel: 1882/1013), built on a wooden platform above the water, and the **Berlin** (Tel: 1882/1411) are the best. The Şanelize (Turkish for "Champs Elysées") was named by the French patrons who congregate there in the summers. The Berlin is a favorite hangout for German travellers. Both restaurants serve a good mix of tasty Turkish kebaps and seafood, with an array of *meze* (appetizers), *rakı,* and beer.

About 70 km (43 miles) northeast from Istanbul, on the Asian shore of the Black Sea, is the resort town of Şile, a popular seaside retreat for *İstanbullus* and foreign tour groups alike. The scenery leading to the shore is spectacular: Rolling green hills, red clay cliffs, and lavender-covered fields lie alongside the two-hour route (in normal traffic— sometimes much longer in summer). There are two ways to reach Şile: Once you're on the Asian side of the Bosphorus (crossing either bridge) you can take the leisurely, scenic route that goes through the small village of **Polonezköy** (30 minutes from Istanbul center), inhabited by descendants of immigrant Poles who earned their livelihood raising and selling fresh pork. With its many pleasant guesthouses and small hotels, Polonezköy is an excellent setting for a weekend outing. You can stroll in the woods or go horseback riding in the countryside. (Horses can be rented in the village square.) Istanbul's wealthiest families have summer villas in Polonezköy. Şile is 45 km (28 miles) past Polonezköy. The alternate route, by way of Beykoz after reaching the Asian shore, is a much more winding drive but just as scenic.

Şile's population of 15,000 swells in summer as people head to its string of beaches, beginning with **Kumbaba Plajı,** a sandy stretch with cafés and teahouses that turns into **Ayazma Plajı** farther east toward the town's harbor. Şile has a **Genoese fortress** (probably of Byzantine origin), which stands in ruins on small Ocaklı island just off shore. The harbor is always busy with fishing boats hauling in the day's catch. To the east of the town, high on a rocky ridge, is the black-and-white Şile lighthouse, standing watch over the area's prettiest beach, **Fener Plajı** (Lighthouse Beach), with massive rocks—good for sunbathing—ringing a tiny cove with turquoise water. The balcony at the **Fener Restaurant**, perched high above the cove, is a wonderful place to pull up a chair and take in the scenery. (The restaurant has an excellent selection of *meze*.) Nearby is the **Şato Oteli**, Şile's best hotel, which has a spectacular view of the rocky beach below. Heading east from Fener Plajı you come to **Ağlayankaya Plajı**, a wide public beach with refreshment stands nearby and what looks like a smuggler's cave at the western end. Farther on are Uzunkum Plajı and Eşekadası (Donkey Island), a rocky outcrop that can be walked to by sandbar at low tide. Along these last two beaches are camping facilities that are packed in summer.

Around 400 B.C. Xenophon and his Ten Thousand marched through Şile (then Kalpe), and in honor of his trek the locals have named a sea cave after him. The cave, called **Onophon Mağarası**, is about an hour's walk eastward along the dirt road paralleling the sea.

Besides its clean beaches, Şile is known for *Şile bezi*—gauze-like cotton cloth used by local women to make Şile's famous embroidered blouses, caftans, and *şalvar* trousers. Many shops sell *Şile bezi* clothing, so shop around to find the style you desire at the best price. **Boutique Uyum**, which offers a wide selection, is located just across from the Fener Restaurant.

There are two other good hotels. The **Değirmen Hotel** sits on a small hill at the end of Ayazma beach and looks straight across to the harbor. The hotel is a family-run establishment, with a lovely wide terrace for dining and an outside garden bar. The Değirmen is open year round and accepts credit cards. The **Motel Kumbaba**, to the west on Kumbaba beach, has a terrace restaurant and is open between May and October.

Scores of makeshift discotheques mushroom along the beaches of Şile in the summer months. But the best live music in town in the evenings can be found at the Şato Oteli, where a Turk performs a host of popular Western songs combined with *alla turca* tunes. Visitors can dine, drink, and join in the belly-dancing till past midnight.

THE PRINCES' ISLANDS

This nine-island archipelago in the Sea of Marmara could well be named the "Exile Isles," because each island possesses a history rife with tales of forced and self-imposed exile from the times of the powerful and sometimes paranoid Byzantine emperors. The islands welcomed many personages to their cloistered monasteries and convents, among them Empress Irene (widow of Leo VI), who ruled Byzantium aggressively from 797 to 802, when she was overthrown by her successor, Nicephorus I, and was sent to a convent on Prinkipo (present-day Büyükada), and the tenth-century Byzantine emperor Romanus I Lecapenus, just one of many deposed monarchs sent to the monastery on Proti (present-day Kınalıada) to live out his life as a monk.

Centuries later Leon Trotsky, banished from Stalin's Soviet Union, gathered his family together and sailed from Odessa to Istanbul to live in exile on the coast of Büyükada (the biggest island). Unable to obtain a visa from any other European country, Trotsky remained on the island, "a guest of the Turkish government," for four and a half years, writing his three-volume *History of the Russian Revolution* here. In those years Trotsky moved residences often, out of fear of murderers and spies. He lived in the Savoy Hotel on Büyükada (since burned down), then in Moda, on the Asian side of Istanbul, before returning to the İzzet Paşa Villa, Çankaya Caddesi 52, in Büyükada's Nizam district. To pass the time Trotsky fished and swam (with guns and guards close by), and was rumored to have held many secret meetings with revolutionaries behind his shuttered windows. Before Trotsky finally obtained a French visa, his daughter committed suicide at the villa, ending his stay in Turkey on a tragic note.

For centuries the islands were inhabited mainly by Greeks, Jews, and Armenians; today many of their descendants remain, lending the villages a cosmopolitan cast. You will undoubtedly hear Greek spoken and might be asked if you are *Rum* (Greek) by residents who notice you're not Turkish. On Burgaz you may even hear people speaking Ladino, a variety of Spanish—with Hebrew, Portuguese, and Turkish mixed in—used by Sephardic Jews whose ancestors began arriving in the Ottoman Empire from Spain 500 years ago.

The Princes' Islands (known in Turkish as Adalar—the Islands) are only an hour from Istanbul by ferry, yet they seem worlds away. Only four islands—Büyükada, Burgaz, Heybeliada, and Kınalıada—are serviced by ferry; the rest are accessible only by private boat. (See the Getting Around section at the end of the chapter.) The islands can be enjoyed for a day, a week—even an entire summer. There is no better, and no faster, escape from Istanbul. No cars are allowed on the islands; transportation is by bicycle or horse-drawn carriage. Since the late 18th century people have come to the islands to breathe the fresh pine-scented air, which, in combination with steady breezes that keep the curtains of island houses flapping, is an invitation that's hard to pass up on a hot, polluted day in the city.

Büyükada (Big Island), called Megale in antiquity and Prinkipo by the Greeks, is the most crowded and lively of the islands. It's been a popular summer residence for İstanbullus since the late 1700s, when wealthy French and British families left their summer villas in the Belgrade Forest near the Black Sea coast and built new mansions on the island's four hills. An island tour by horse and carriage climbs winding lanes lined with gardens that conceal 19th-century wooden mansions adorned with Victorian gingerbread. Many of the gardens outdazzle the residences themselves, with imported palms, jasmine, mimosa, and Judas trees mingling their fragrances with the island's native pine trees.

When you arrive at Büyükada's harbor, walk straight to the village center, past the newly restored Büyükada Princess Hotel (with a small pool, dining room, outdoor terrace, and air conditioning), and hire a phaeton for an island tour. Be sure to verify the price quoted by the driver against the price posted on the list at the nearby carriage stop. There are two tours to choose from: long (büyük tur, one hour) or short (küçük tur, half an hour). You can take the long tour and combine it with a walk to the monastery, described below, while your carriage waits.

On the tour you pass the Splendid Otel, a fading beauty from the turn of the century and one of the few wooden hotels to survive island fires. From the sea, the Splendid's twin white domes, which copy those of the Hotel Négresco in Nice, dominate the hillside. Open from April to November, the Splendid also has a restaurant and terrace, and a pool is under construction. Ask for a room with a view of the sea. The new Şütte delicatessen, across from the Splendid, is the place to buy food for your picnic. Mangals (grills) are provided on the hilltop if you wish to barbecue, and you'll find beverages on sale there.

Near the fire tower on the island's highest hill, Yücetepe, is the monastery of St. George (a functioning Orthodox monastery). Visitors trudge the 20 minutes to the top in hopes the monastery will be serving its homemade wine.

Each April 23 faithful pilgrims wind up the trail to pay homage to the sainted dragon-slayer. The monastery comprises six buildings, including three chapels and an *ayazma* (sacred fountain) believed to spout healing waters. (Note the iron rings set into the marble pavement of the chapel: The insane were chained to these when the monastery served briefly as an asylum.)

Yörük Ali Plajı, a beach on the west side of the island, is open to the public and has a restaurant open in the summer. There are two other public beaches, Kumsal Plajı and Aile Plajı (Family Beach), both on the northeastern side of the island, but these have fallen victim to coliform-bacteria pollution and are not recommended. (Ask the local municipalities about the results of the water-testing, which is performed frequently in the summer. Many island beaches passed the safety tests in 1992.) After an island tour, end the day at the quay in one of the restaurants off the square or take tea on the terrace of the Splendid.

The tavernas of **Zorba** and **Akasya**, across from the exclusive Anadolu Club about 300 yards to the right of the Clock Tower near the center of town, serve cocktails and *rakı* with light appetizers. The two pub-restaurants offer authentic Turkish and Greek taverna music. **Milto Restaurant** (Tel: 1/382-5312) and **Neptün Restaurant** (Tel: 1/382-6398) are excellent seafood restaurants on the shorefront promenade, off the boat landing. They both specialize in bluefish, mullet, lobsters, and a delicious local crabmeat dish known as *pavurya*.

The second-largest island, **Heybeliada**, is home to the Turkish Naval Academy, which welcomes visitors with a huge green mural depicting a mosaic of stylized sailing vessels. Heybeliada (Saddlebag Island) was formerly known as Halki and was famous for its copper (*chalkos* is Greek for "copper"), which used to be mined at Çamlimanı (Pine Harbor) on the southwest side of the island.

As on Büyükada, you can hire a horse and carriage and tour the island, although the 40-minute *büyük tur*—unlike that on Büyükada—uncovers little in the way of grand homes and gardens. Most of Heybeliada's mansions are on the hills above the harbor and can be reached only by walking. Historically, this island was more a place of higher learning than a site of exile, and so was the final resting spot for revered religious scholars rather than banished royals and politicos.

The first five minutes of the carriage tour take you past the red-tiled roofs and chapel cross of the **monastery of the**

Panaghia, which sits on Ümittepe (Hope Hill), on the present grounds of a Turkish naval high school. The monastery was long considered an important center of Greek Orthodox theology and has a tumultuous history, beginning in the twilight years of the Byzantine Empire, when it is believed to have been founded by Emperor John VIII Palaeologus (r. 1425 to 1448). Its role as a center of religious learning was interrupted often. It fell victim to destructive fires and an earthquake, and over the course of time has served as a convent, a camp for Russian prisoners of war (1828), and a commercial school founded by wealthy Greeks (1831). In 1916 the monastery was sold to the Ottoman government to be used as part of the imperial naval academy. It briefly returned to Greek ownership and housed orphaned girls before becoming a permanent part of the Turkish Naval Academy in 1942. A visit to the monastery and chapel requires permission from the academy's commander: Ask the guard at the entrance to lead you to him.

Off the street running parallel to the monastery grounds is a white tomb with a carving of an angel bearing a double-headed eagle. This marks the long-forgotten entrance to a **cemetery** where 300 Russian prisoners of war were buried during the Russo-Turkish war of 1828. The grave of Edward Barton, Queen Elizabeth I's young ambassador to the sultanate, is said to lie here as well. Barton may have died of plague, which in the late 1500s was besieging Istanbul. He escaped to Heybeliada for fresh air, but it was too late. People still believe in the island's curative powers: Down the street, on the southwestern side of Heybeliada overlooking Çamlimanı beach, is a tuberculosis sanatorium, still admitting patients.

Most of Heybeliada's beaches are rocky; the best ones are on the north side of the island at the foot of Değirmen Tepesi (Windmill Hill) and out near Değirmen Burnu (Windmill Point). The swimming club near Değirmen Burnu is private. Don't bother to explore the bathing possibilities at Çamlimanı; its sand shores are dirty and uninviting—a deserted hotel and the sanatorium add little to the scenery.

Kınalıada was originally called Proti (which means "first") by the Greeks, as it is the first island reached by boat from Istanbul. The Turks named it after its red cliffs, *kınalı* meaning "dyed with henna." Kınalıada was a place of exile for many unfortunates during the Byzantine Empire. Most never again knew freedom after entering one or the other of its two monasteries. Kınalıada is not a green island—its neighbors are blessed with far more wooded land—but instead it has lavender fields and windswept lookout points, such as Manastır Tepesi (Monastery Hill), from which the surrounding islands seem to float in space.

The ferry from Istanbul services Kınalıada a few times during the day, the only link to the island other than private boats. It's hard work to find someone willing to ferry you over, so coordinate the ferry schedule correctly to ensure that you can arrive and depart on the same day. There are no hotels on the island, only private homes that pale in comparison to those on Büyükada, Burgaz, and Heybeliada. If you arrive by boat you can swim to one of the small rocky coves that are the only beaches on the island.

Between Heybeliada and Burgaz is emerald green **Kaşık Adası** (Spoon Island). It appears to have only one building hidden in its forest. The island is accessible only by private boat.

Sandwiched between Heybeliada, Kınalıada, and Kaşık Adası is **Burgaz**, called Antigoni in Byzantine times and Pyrgos (tower) by the Greeks. Burgaz is populated mainly by Jewish and Greek families, who have been spending summers here for generations. The year-round population of fewer than 1,000 swells to nearly 17,000 in summer. A sign at the harbor urges, "If you love your island, come for the population count in WINTER!" (A higher count enables the island to benefit from tax breaks.) The island has a small harbor, dominated by the dome of the church of St. John the Baptist, one of three Greek Orthodox churches on the island. (There are also a mosque, a synagogue, and a Catholic church.) The present structure was built in 1867 and stands on the site of an older chapel. A visiting priest holds masses every Sunday morning. You may visit its subterranean sanctuary and light a candle, perhaps to ask Saint John for a little help in catching the right ferry at the right time. The church custodians keep a pretty garden across the street, but it's cordoned off with barbed wire. Behind the garden is the home and museum of storyteller and poet Sait Faik Abasıyanık, a sort of Turkish Mark Twain. The museum, in a run-down state, exhibits bits of Sait Faik's works; it is closed Sunday and Monday.

These days there are no accommodations at all on Burgaz for overnight visitors; the Greek-looking white wooden building at the ferry dock used to be the Yordan hotel, but it was turned into private apartments and has acquired a lonely, forlorn look. There are a number of restaurants on the quay; **Çardak** is a good bet. At the far northern end of the quay, past the horse carriages, is the **İdeal Restaurant**, a local favorite.

Both restaurants specialize in seafood; try the *kalamar* (fried squid). If time permits, take the 45-minute carriage ride to Kalpazankaya (on the southwest side of the island) for lunch or dinner at the **Kalpazankaya** restaurant. If you call in advance to special order it, the restaurant will prepare an authentic *tandır* meal for you; Tel: (1) 381-1504. *Tandır* is a special way of barbecuing, in this case whole lamb, in which the meat is cooked in a pit oven. You can also reach Kalpazankaya by special dolmuş boat, so ask for information when making reservations at the restaurant. Burgaz is ringed by stone beaches and has a private Sea Club and Sport Club, both located south of the harbor.

Tavşan Adası (Rabbit Island) is a tiny speck of land, as is **Sivri Adası**, which at one time held a monastery. Sivri is also called Köpek Adası (Dog Island) from the time, years ago, that feral dogs were rounded up in Istanbul and banished here. **Sedef Adası** (Mother-of-pearl Island) is the home of smart İstanbullus who enjoy the summer on its quiet shores. **Yassıada** suffered a tragic past. The island was the setting for the mass trials against the leaders and 2,000 senior officials of the ousted Democrat party following the 1960 military coup. Deposed prime minister Adnan Menderes and two of his top ministers, found guilty of attempting to establish a dictatorship, were executed, and hundreds of party officials served long prison sentences at Yassıada—a period of recent history Turks rather prefer to forget. The island today is a naval base and is off-limits to visitors.

If you would like to rent a private home or rooms on one of the islands, contact an *emlakçı* (real estate agent); offices are usually located on the harbor. Many families are willing to rent their houses during both summer and winter.

ASIAN ENVIRONS

Across the Sea of Marmara from Istanbul, on the gulf of İzmit, lies the tiny town of **Yalova** and its busy harbor. Every day hundreds of travellers pour off the Istanbul ferries, wave a quick hello to the town, then board buses or taxis for better-known inland destinations—Termal, Bursa, and İznik.

TERMAL

Many people, especially İstanbullus escaping city life and people searching for cures for sicknesses, board a minibus in Yalova and head 15 minutes (12 km/7½ miles) to the spa-resort of Termal, inland among the wooded foothills. Termal, known for its rich, medicinal mineral waters, has lured bathers since Roman times with its promises of relief for ailing bodies.

Termal's self-contained resort is located in a pine-forested valley. Three public baths stand on beautifully landscaped grounds with exotic gardens and shrubbery carefully tended by the government-run Turban hotel chain. The **Valide and Sultan baths** offer individual cabins with deep gray-marble tubs for "taking the waters." The **Kurşunlu bath** is the largest, and its lead-domed building and large open-air thermal swimming pool are the focal point of the grounds. The Kurşunlu also has individual cabins as well as a covered mineral pool and sauna with massage. Each service is purchased separately.

Turban operates two good hotels on the premises. The pink, fairy-tale **Turban Çınar Hotel** sits snugly under the tremendous boughs of a 300-year-old plane tree (*çınar*). Up on a ridge, with a view of the grounds, is the **Turban Çamlık Hotel**, whose location makes it a bit quieter than the Çınar. The hotels offer roughly the same accommodations for the same price. The Turban Çınar's private baths are much like those at the Sultan, with deep gray-marble tubs; the Turban Çamlık's tubs are of the modern, white-tile variety. Both hotels have restaurants, and there are shopping boutiques on the grounds.

Looking up through the forest from the Kurşunlu bath, you will see a white house, embellished with gingerbread trim, and a sign pointing the way to the **Atatürk Museum**. The white house is not the museum but a private house used by Atatürk's aides-de-camp whenever he visited the resort. The museum—which was Atatürk's lodging—is across the road. The plain building was constructed in 1929 in the Republican style—the quasi-Modernist, functional architectural style characteristic of many Turkish buildings of this period. A tour of the house reveals Atatürk's penchant for Baroque furnishings. The café on the side of the museum overlooking a stand of fir trees is a lovely place for tea.

Since everything at the resort is within walking distance of everything else, no cars are needed. From morning till night minibuses can be found waiting in the parking area at the base of the resort for the return trip to Yalova. From Yalova you can catch a public bus to İznik, Bursa, or Istanbul, or board a ferry or hydrofoil sea-taxi for Istanbul.

BURSA AND ULUDAĞ

Its nearness to Istanbul does Bursa a great disservice, allowing the easy assumption that Bursa is just another big city, lacking the charm of the city on the Bosphorus, and one that could be easily omitted from a busy itinerary. Nothing could be further from the truth.

Bursa fares well in comparison with its sister city across the Sea of Marmara: It is easily explored, has a casual air, and exudes an undeniable pride, perhaps carried over from its glory days, when it reigned as the first capital of the Ottoman dynasty.

It was King Prusias of Bithynia (a small monarchy) who, with a sharp eye for real estate, founded Bursa on the pine-forested slopes of Uludağ in the late third century B.C., naming it Prusia after himself. Bursa's attractions were most likely its seemingly impregnable citadel, rich water and food supplies, thermal spas, and proximity to trade routes.

Surviving the evolution from Roman bath to Byzantine spa to Turkish *hamam,* Bursa's famous mineral springs, which dot the hillside in affluent Çekirge (a western suburb), are now mostly disguised as pampering hotels that use their coveted baths as bargaining chips in the tourism market.

Bursa may owe its gift of natural springs to Mother Nature, but it remains indebted to the Ottomans for its legacy of exquisite religious architecture. It was the Ottomans who, under the command of Orhan, son of Osman I, the father of the Ottoman dynasty, seized Bursa from the Byzantines in 1326 after a seven-year siege. Orhan installed himself as sultan and proclaimed Bursa the capital. The city prospered under the reigns of six sultans, who spared no expense in building splendid mosques and monuments—testaments to their growing power. It is here that the architectural styles of Persian, Byzantine, and Seljuk cultures intertwined, emerging as a distinctly Ottoman style.

Bursa's architecture and baths are not its only temptations: Bargains can still be found in the labyrinths of its covered bazaars and open-air markets. The "Turkish towel" is made in Bursa and is, along with thick terry-cloth robes, priced to sell. Handwoven textiles, crafted by local women, are still true finds, as is diaphanous Bursa silk, advertised by the hundreds of jewel-toned scarves in every shop.

A visit to Bursa is not complete until you sample the city's famed *İskender kebap,* thinly sliced *döner* heaped atop chewy bits of *pide* (Turkish pita), slathered with a sauce of tomato and yogurt, and dribbled with brown butter. (You can hold the butter by ordering your kebap *yağsız*— "without oil.") For dessert try Bursa's *kestane şekeri* (candied chestnuts similar to marrons glacés), which are sold in local *pastahane*s (pastry shops).

In winter skiers flock to Uludağ in maddening numbers to ski the intermediate slopes or just to hang out at the foot of the mountain comparing tans and equipment. Many skiers stay in Bursa so they can enjoy a revitalizing thermal bath after a hard day on the slopes; they travel up the mountain via the city's *teleferik,* which begins in the district called Namazgâh. (For more discussion of the mountain resort, see below.)

The color green (*yeşil* in Turkish) is particularly revered in Bursa: Its residents proudly refer to their city as Yeşil Bursa, not so much on account of the many monuments decorated with green tiles, but because of the city's abundance of parks, gardens, and trees. Few streets, mosques, and courtyards are without a shady *çınar.*

Bursa's love of green is also reflected in its politics. The city's emerging Green party has recently begun to address the environmental consequences of the city's prosperity. With nearly 1,200 companies and 800 factories located here, Bursa has one of Turkey's highest concentrations of industry, and air pollution often reaches dangerous levels.

Bursa is about a four-and-a-half- to five-hour drive (363 km/225 miles) from Istanbul via the E 5 highway southeast toward İzmit and then west toward Yalova. A hectic visit can be attempted in one day, but Bursa really deserves a minimum stay of two nights. The most enjoyable way to reach the city is by ferryboat from Istanbul. (See Getting Around, below, for more information on getting to Bursa.)

Around Bursa

Upon arrival at Bursa's bus station you have several options for getting around. Dolmuşes are very convenient and plentiful in the city; they look like yellow cabs but have their pickup points and destinations posted on the roof and cost little compared to taxis. Bursa's bus system runs regularly along Atatürk Caddesi (the main east–west street), which turns into Altıparmak and then Çekirge Caddesi on the west side of town and Namazgâh Caddesi on the east side. Most sites can be reached by foot; if your time is limited, however,

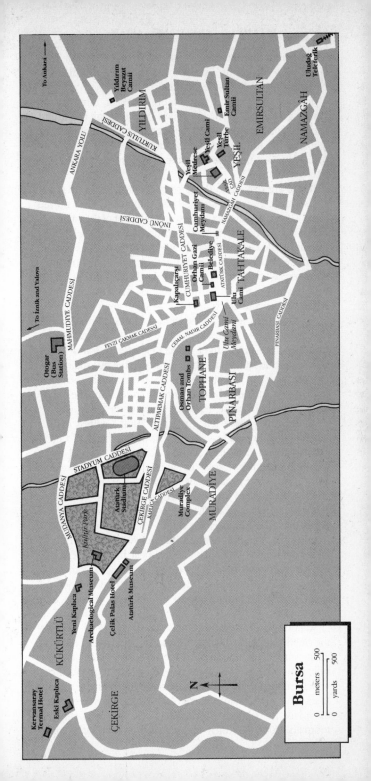

a whirlwind tour arranged by one of Bursa's travel agencies is the best bet. Yontur Turizm offers a number of different package deals; Tel: (24) 20-91-32.

You can also rent a car in Bursa. Major international automobile rental companies have offices facing the Kültür Park fairgrounds, including Avis (Çekirge Caddesi 139; Tel: 24/36-51-33) and Hertz (Çekirge Caddesi 93; Tel: 24/36-37-19 or 36-06-04). A taxi ride from the bus terminal can take you to them.

If you are driving to Bursa by car, you will end up at the city's garage district with the bus station (Oto Gar) on the right. The garage district is the terminal point of the Istanbul–Bursa Highway. Turn right at the roundabout and then left on Fomora Caddesi, immediately after passing the bus station, and drive about 1½ km (1 mile). At the next roundabout, take the overpass toward the Şehir Merkezi (city center), which brings you to the Altıparmak–Atatürk Caddesi, the main street, and eventually to the Ulu Cami, the great mosque.

Setting out from the bus station, take a dolmuş to Ulu Cami or walk five minutes straight up Fevzi Çakmak Caddesi to the rotary. On the right is the **Kervansaray Bursa Hotel**, whose chief asset is its location near both the bus station and market areas. If you stay here, book a room at the back; traffic noise can be unbearable on the street side. The bar by the rooftop pool has a 360-degree view of the city.

At the rotary, bear left up Cemal Nadır Caddesi until it reaches Atatürk Caddesi. To the left on the bend of Cemal Nadır Caddesi is **Roman's Bursa Kebapçısı**, a good place (recommended by locals) to sample the famous *İskender kebap*. To be able to say you've eaten at the original *İskender kebap* house, head for **İskenderoğlu Kebapçısı** (İskender's Son's Kebap House), at Ulu Cadde 7, where İskender Jr. has taken over the trend-setting eatery from his father. A third option is the centrally located **Hacıbey Kebapçısı** at Taşkapı Sokak 4/11, just off Atatürk Caddesi near the Atatürk statue. On the corner next to Hacıbey is the **Karagöz** confection shop, which sells *lokum* (Turkish delight) and wonderful *cezire,* a chewy candy made of carrots, nuts, coconut, and lots of sugar.

Walking west on Atatürk Caddesi you pass cliffside cafés; the **Sebil Café** has tables hidden in stone alcoves built into what were once the walls of Bursa's *hisar* (castle). On the hill above the cafés is the area known as **Tophane**, from which centuries of residents watched as Persians, Byzantines, Crusaders, Seljuks, Mongols, and Ottomans swept over the plain in conquest. Tophane is reached by a winding footpath from the cafés or by taking a right on Kaplıca

Caddesi, just beyond the cafés. Entering from Kaplıca Caddesi you'll see a sign marking the **tombs of Osman and Orhan**, father-and-son founders of the Ottoman dynasty. They are buried inside the small mausoleums on Tophane's grounds. Beyond the mausoleum is the **clock tower** that be seen from many points throughout the city and a black cannon (*top*), from which the hill takes its name. Teahouses edge the cliff on three sides, and on a clear day Uludağ seems to tumble straight onto the city's rooftops.

The **Ulu Cami** (Great Mosque), to the left of the large public square (Ulu Cami Meydanı) off Atatürk Caddesi, is the most spectacular example of the kind of mosque—sometimes called a "Friday mosque"—that was built for the townspeople for use on prayer day. It was commissioned by Sultan Bayezit I (called Yıldırım, "Thunderbolt") after his rousing victory at Nicopolis in 1396, when he turned back the Hungarian-Venetian Crusade. As legend goes, Bayezit promised to build 20 mosques if he won at Nicopolis, but was talked out of his idea by his adviser, the dervish Emir Sultan, who urged the sultan to spend his money on this 20-domed mosque instead. It was completed in 1399.

The Ulu Cami is an imposing, though pretty, sight. Its massive walls were built of honey-colored stone from Mount Olympus (i.e., Uludağ), and, inside, each of its supporting pillars is faced with medallions with dramatic black calligraphy. Note the incongruous trompe l'oeil drapery on some of the pillars: According to Ottoman-architecture expert Godfrey Goodwin, this is the handiwork of an Italian painter who in the 19th century left his Baroque touch on many mosques throughout Turkey. The mosque's carved wooden *minber* (pulpit) is believed to be one of the finest in the Islamic world.

The Ulu Cami plays a part in the folk legend of Karagöz, Turkey's shadow-puppet theater. Karagöz plays star two characters, Karagöz and Hacivat, who are the Turkish equivalent of Punch and Judy. According to the tale, the common, black-eyed Karagöz and his somewhat pretentious upper-class sidekick, Hacivat, work on the building of the mosque. Most of their time is spent clowning around and stirring up trouble, until the sultan has them executed. Rich social and political satire is played out with a lively cast of puppet characters: old women, witches, professionals, politicians, opium addicts, dwarves. The movable puppets were traditionally made of dried camel skin that was stretched and colored. The tomb of the real Karagöz, after whom the shadow play is named, is in Çekirge, discussed below.

Şinasi Çelikkol, a businessman who owns a Karagöz paraphernalia shop in Bursa's Covered Bazaar, organizes shadow-theater performances for large tour groups in different parts of the city. If you are interested in seeing a Karagöz puppet play you should contact him at his shop: **Kapalı Çarşı**, Eski Aynalı Çarşıiçi number 12; Tel: (24) 21-87-27.

Next to the Ulu Cami is Ulu Cami Meydanı (Great Mosque Square), also called Koza Parkı (after nearby Koza Hanı), whose centerpiece is a large marble water fountain. Under the sidewalk café here is a **tourism office**, one of several in Bursa; you might inquire about the local markets and fairs; Tel: (24) 21-23-59. Across from the tourism office is the folksy municipal hall, a crazy quilt of timber and red brick. Next door is **Orhan Gazi Camii**, the first mosque built in Bursa (1339) and the first to be constructed using a T-plan characterized by four *eyvan*s (wings with raised floors) built off the central court, a plan widely associated with the city. It is thought that these eyvans were used as teaching rooms or hostels for visiting dervishes. Unlike the spacious Ulu Cami, which accommodated many people on prayer day, the Orhan Gazi Camii was a "court mosque," smaller and with private sections for visiting dignitaries.

Behind Orhan Gazi Camii (and between it and Ulu Cami) the city's **market district** unfolds and seems never to end as one bazaar meanders into another. The interior *bedesten* (market) and surrounding bazaar burned down in 1955. The bedesten was perfectly restored, but critics complain that the bazaar was hastily repaired in the interest of resuming business quickly. Surrounding the bazaar are Bursa's hans—square, two-story stone buildings with individual merchants' stalls arranged around courtyards. Hans were centers of Ottoman commerce and trade.

The **Koza Hanı**, right off the square, is devoted to Bursa's thriving silk industry. It's the scene of haggling in June and early July as the silkworm farmers arrive bearing the "fruit" of their mulberry trees: bulging sacks of white cocoons, ready for spinning. Savvy buyers from the local textile companies drive a hard bargain, and the gesticulation can be as colorful as the scarves hanging in the shop windows.

The Koza Hanı is the place to buy silk; before purchasing, though, browse in all the shops to compare quality and prices. **Batica** has a selection of fashionable scarves, ties, blouses, and fabric (there are three locations within the han). Hasan Bey at **Elegant İpek** will gladly tell you the story of silk (*ipek*), demonstrating by pulling flossy threads from a broken cocoon. If you're lucky you will get to see live silkworms as well as the product of a "bad" cocoon—a chalky-white butterfly.

Sericulture has played a part in Anatolia's history since the sixth century, when, to the displeasure of the Chinese, silkworm eggs found their way to the Byzantines, who figured out the secret of spinning the gossamer threads. The Ottomans continued the industry and during the glory days of the empire were known throughout the world for their lavish silk brocades. Today Bursa is Turkey's silk capital, producing silk not only for fabrics but for the world-famous silk Hereke carpets, which come from the town of the same name about two hours northeast of Bursa on the gulf of İzmit.

Bursa's **Covered Bazaar** (Kapalıçarşı), which is adjacent to the Koza Hanı and behind the Ulu Cami, is as much fun to explore as Istanbul's but is a bit more relaxed (hardly anyone will try to guess your nationality or try to separate you from your wallet). Walking through the bazaar's meandering halls, you will notice that your shopping companions aren't tour-bus contingents, but locals. What's even better, you'll pay local prices, not those concocted for the *yabancı* (foreigner).

Many of the markets and hans in this district are close together and interconnect, through passageways, with the Covered Bazaar. Shops in the outer passages of the Covered Bazaar and in the restored **Emir Hanı** specialize in "Turkish towels," white cotton bedspreads, Bursa-made knives, and cotton fabric decorated with *yazma* (hand-block) designs from Tokat in Central Anatolia. The Tokat dyes usually bleed when the fabric is washed, so many shops now sell a pseudo-Tokat material that looks the same but doesn't bleed. Ask about washing in any case. The interior bedesten is where the gold merchants are housed. In the **Eski Aynalı Çarşı** (Old Mirror Bazaar), once a Turkish bath, **Karagöz** (shop number 22) has a fun collection of embroidered village hats as well as antique hamam towels, copper, and hand-loomed textiles bearing the imprint of Bulgarian craftswomen. (Bursa accepted many of the ethnic Turkish refugees who fled Bulgaria for Turkey in 1989.)

At shop number 13 in the **Turistik Eşya Pazarı**, in the Kuyumcu Çarşısı (Jeweler's Bazaar), just behind the Ulu Cami and past what appears to be the *tesbih* (worry bead) passage, **İbrahim Özin** sells village handwork and antique fabrics. Check out the crocheted pocket-watch and money holders. A mountain climate calls for woollen underwear, and Bursa is known for its superb winter long johns. On the western edge of the Covered Bazaar look for **Hasyün**, (Ulucami Caddesi 75) for a good selection. The shop's business card proclaims that its woollies will cure any disease or malady.

When you have shopped yourself into starvation, walk to the square behind the municipal hall and find the small sign for the **Çiçek Izgara**. Open the door and climb the stairs to the dining room. This pleasant restaurant offers grills— meat, chicken, and thick slices of tomatoes—that are delicious on the homemade rolls. Next door is another branch of **Roman's Bursa Kebapçısı**.

On Saturdays a huge open-air market springs up behind the municipal hall and loops around for what seems like miles of fruits, vegetables, baby chicks, and household gadgets. Pine nuts and spices are a bargain; look especially for saffron. Right off Atatürk Caddesi, opposite the Ulu Cami, is İnebey Caddesi, which leads to the **Otel Çamlıbel**, a low-priced alternative accommodation centrally located for easy access to all Bursa sites. At the corner before the hotel, at Küçük Tahil Sokak 1, is **İbrahim Güneş**, a purveyor of hand-spun woollen yarns. This area, called **Tahtakale**, has a lively open-air market every day except Sunday. It's a good place to buy Bursa's wonderful fruits (quince, peaches, cherries) in season, as well as herbal teas, bay leaves, and bark-handled fruit baskets made by mountain villagers.

The Yeşil Complex

After allotting the first part of the day to shopping, spend the afternoon touring the hilltop grounds of the Yeşil complex, a splendid triad of religious monuments built during the days when Bursa was the Ottoman capital. Walk east up Atatürk Caddesi and turn left onto Yeşil Cadde (a 15-minute walk from the market area) or take a dolmuş or taxi toward Yeşil Cami. On the way you will cross a small bridge and pass the statue of Atatürk (known simply as Heykel, or "statue") at Cumhuriyet Meydanı (Republic Square). Heykel is also a dolmuş stop and is very close to the market area.

The Yeşil complex includes the Yeşil Cami (Green Mosque), Yeşil Türbe (Green Tomb), and Yeşil Medrese (Green Islamic Law School), all dating from the 15th century. The area has been well restored, with a cobblestoned square replacing dirt roads. The **Hünkâr Café** hugs the edge of the cliff behind the mosque; in addition to refreshments it offers a great *manzara* (view) of the terra-cotta–tiled rooftops scattered in the valley. The **Yeşil Cami** rests in a tranquil, shady garden to the right as you walk down Yeşil Cadde back toward the town center. This magnificent mosque was commissioned by Sultan Mehmet I in 1419. The portico was never built because the sultan died, and, according to tradition, all work on a mosque had to stop when the commissioning sultan passed away. In 1855 the mosque was damaged in an earthquake and subsequently restored by Leon Parvillée, a French architect. Its present dome is made of lead, a tradition dating from the 15th century; research, however, indicates that it may well have been covered with green tiles up to the 17th century. The carved niches to the left and right of the stairs leading to the prayer hall are called *pabuçluk* and are for storing sandals.

Inside, the mosque is a dizzying display of turquoise, blue, green, and white İznik tiles (some in star and circle shapes), arabesque brushwork, and calligraphy. If you think you will never see anything more beautiful, ask the mosque assistant to show you the sultan's loge upstairs. The mosque's elaborately tiled *mihrap* (niche) is breathtaking, perhaps best described by Godfrey Goodwin as "more than the gate of paradise: it is paradise itself." An inscription on the right side reads, "The work of the masters of Tabriz."

Across the cobblestoned street is the **Yeşil Türbe**, which Murat II, son of Mehmet I, built for his deceased father, using nothing but the best court artists and İznik tiles. (After an earthquake the original İznik tiles were replaced with those you see now, which come from Kütahya.) Inside, Sultan Mehmet's tomb, ornamented in yellow, blue, green, and turquoise tiles and gilded inscriptions, rests on a platform like a delicate piece of cloisonné.

The **Yeşil Medrese**, the third building of the complex, was once a school of Islamic law, built from 1414 to 1421 by Mehmet I. It has been the home of Bursa's **Museum of Turkish and Islamic Arts** since 1975. In small stone rooms arranged around a courtyard, the ethnographic collections include such diverse displays as an entire cast of Karagöz puppets and a circumcision room dominated by a wildly festooned four-poster bed. Carpets, silver, religious items, Ottoman clothing, weaponry, Kütahya ceramics, and the somewhat grotesque green Çanakkale pottery from the early 19th century are also on display. Next to the museum is a small Ottoman **cemetery** noted for the large number of celebrated poets buried there, each of their gravestones marked by the *gül* (rose) motif carved on its *turban*, or face.

On the opposite side of the street tourist shops housed in quaint pastel buildings sell silk scarves, Karagöz shadow puppets, and carpets. However, save your money for a visit to **Minnatur** at Yeşilemir Caddesi 20. (Yeşilemir is the street between the Yeşil Türbe and the Emir Sultan Camii.) Here you will find the best in Turkish-style miniature painting (by an accomplished Iranian artist), Çanakkale pottery, new handmade tiles, antique fabric, and Turkish jewelry. An Istanbul antiques shop would charge twice the price for these items.

The 15th-century mosque of the mystic and holy man Emir Sultan is perched on a hill about a 10-minute walk southeast down Yeşil Cadde from the Yeşil Cami. **Emir Sultan Camii**, along with many of the city's monuments, was fairly badly damaged in the earthquake of 1855; its foundations have since been restored.

Bursa's **teleferik** up to Uludağ is at this end of town. Catch a dolmuş marked "Namazgâh," the name of the neighborhood where the teleferik begins. (To reach the teleferik from the city center you can catch a dolmuş on Başak Sokak, about a block away from the Heykel.) Don't try walking to the *teleferik;* even from the Yeşil complex it's about an hour's walk up steep cobbled streets. Plenty of dolmuşes service the route. The *teleferik* operates year round, every half hour (weather permitting) from 8:00 A.M. to 9:00 P.M. daily. There are two stops on the mountain, neither of which is the resort town of Uludağ. At the second stop, Sarıalan, you can catch a dolmuş to the resort, where the hotels and lifts are located. Round-trip *teleferik* tickets cost roughly $5. The *teleferik* ride is particularly enjoyable in autumn when the mountain foliage is most colorful. If you're heading up the mountain just to hike around, pack a lunch and be sure to wear comfortable clothing and appropriately sturdy shoes.

Çekirge

From the *teleferik* station follow Namazgâh Caddesi back toward Heykel and take a dolmuş west for Çekirge (which translates as "locust"), one of Bursa's affluent neighborhoods. This is where the Romans founded their baths; Justinian continued the ancient tourism trade into Byzantine times by building even better spas. In modern times hotels have sprung up along a two-mile stretch in the hills. The best-known and perhaps the nicest spa (for both sexes) is at the **Çelik Palas Oteli**. Atatürk commissioned the restoration of this bath, which was built on the original site of a Byzantine spa. Çelik Palas means "Steel Palace," so named for the large gray lead dome over the marble pool. The public is welcome to use the pool for a small fee; hotel guests are admitted free. A newly restored and terribly romantic private spa (with pink marble) can be reserved for about $33 an hour for hotel guests and $66 for visitors. A look out the back of the hotel reveals the beginnings of a second Çelik Palas hotel, even more massive than the original. Next door is Atatürk's house, now a museum (because of restoration, the house is currently closed to visitors).

The **Kervansaray Termal Hotel** is the Disneyland of Bursa hotels, with a large indoor swimming pool, four restaurants, a disco, and a fitness center. The hotel's domed baths, known as Eski Kaplıca (Old Bath), are built on the site of a Byzantine spa, and the Roman-style men's bath is one of the nicest in the city, with three rooms—the *camekân* (dressing room), *soğuk-luk* (cold room), and *hararet* (hot room). The women's bath is of the later Ottoman period, with one domed room containing a narrow thermal pool. An escalator ferries guests to a physical therapy and massage center. The **Gönlüferah Termal Hotel**, also in Çekirge, is popular because of its reasonable prices and nicely tiled Turkish bath. It's set back off the main street (1'inci Murat Caddesi), and its discreet sign makes it a bit hard to find.

Bathing in a Turkish hamam is one of the pleasures you shouldn't miss in Bursa. Because of the region's natural hot waters, the spas of Çekirge have long attracted visitors from all over the world seeking remedies for ailments such as rheumatism. Bathing in a public hamam is a favorite pastime of many Turks, who find in it a few hours of relaxation away from the tensions and stress of modern city living. Admission to the Kervansaray Termal's public bath costs only $5. For an additional fee of about $10 you can get a private room (and bed) and a massage-bath by a *tellak,* (masseur). (Admission is free for those staying in the hotel.)

After undressing in your cubicle or room, you don a coarse, knee-length waistcloth known as a *peştemal* (if, that is, you're a man—women don't wear them), and put on wooden sandals known as *takunya*s to prevent you from falling on the slippery marble floors of the bath. Note that, if you're a man, it is considered improper ever to appear nude in the bath; try to keep the *peştemal* on, even while you're being scrubbed. You should spend a few minutes acclimating yourself in the cold room (which actually is much warmer than the dressing room) before entering the hot room, where the temperature can get to 100° Fahrenheit. In the misty, domed hot room, you can swim in the small pool or wash at a basin in one of the niches, which have both hot-and cold-water fountains. Some Turkish baths have a *göbek taşı* (belly stone), a wide, raised hexagonal slab of marble where you can lie down, sweat, and have sweet dreams. The best part of the bath is being scrubbed and massaged by the (probably muscular) *tellak,* who wears rough gloves and uses a special scented soap to remove dirt. After your first scrub-down by a *tellak* you're likely to feel cleaner than you've ever felt before.

Return to your room after the bath, lie down, and have the attendants cover you with a blanket of "Turkish towels." Don't venture out for a while: Just relax in bed and sip tea till you're ready to return to the outside world.

Bursa's **Kültür Park** is a pretty, green area at the bottom of the foothills. A small lake, an open-air theater, and outdoor coffee houses draw local crowds on weekends. Signs everywhere beg visitors "Please Not To Steal The Heritage." Bursa's small and well-intentioned **Archaeological Museum**, on the park grounds, is worth a visit. A chronology of ancient coins (Mysian and Bithynian, as well as Roman and Byzantine imperial gold and silver coins), Roman and Byzantine glass, and five heads of Zeus are the stars of the collection.

The Muradiye Complex

If given only one hour in Bursa, many would choose to visit the Muradiye complex, where the 15th-century Murat II Camii and the decorated tombs of sultans and family members stand in one of Bursa's prettiest gardens. To reach Muradiye from Çekirge, walk east down Çekirge Caddesi past the Atatürk Museum and take the right fork up Kaplıca Caddesi to Muradiye (there's a sign). Here, under magnolia, fir, and palm trees, are 12 tombs holding members of the Ottoman imperial family. (The tombs are often locked; tip the guard and he'll be happy to open them so you can look inside.) Each tomb is a spectacular work of art, combining 16th-century İznik tilework, frescoes, calligraphy of verses from the Koran, stained glass windows, and natural light. The tomb of Prince Mustafa is exquisite, with blue and tomato-red İznik tiling and paintings of cypress trees. The solitary tomb of Murat is somber and open "under the stars" like that of a common man, as he wished. The most outstanding tomb is that of Prince Cem, the favorite son of Mehmet II, the Conqueror. When Mehmet II died, his sons Bayezit and Cem wrestled for control of the sultanate. To Cem's anger, Bayezit reached Constantinople first and installed his regime. Cem set up a rival sultanate in Bursa before fleeing Bayezit's armies. For years he eluded Ottoman search parties, living the life of a fugitive, until he was poisoned in Italy. Bayezit, now grieving, had his brother's body returned to Turkey and interred here.

Down the street from Muradiye (back toward the park) is a restored **typical Ottoman house**. It illustrates how a household's public and private functions were separated—the *haremlik* was the family's private quarters; men were permitted to move between the family quarters and the *selâmlık,* where visitors were received. The carved wooden cupboard and the upholstery fabrics are authentic.

From Muradiye you can take a dolmuş or walk 25 minutes north on Kaplıca Caddesi toward Tophane and, after paying respects at the tombs of Orhan Gazi and his father Osman, settle in at a cliffside café to watch the red sun set on Green Bursa. You can also eat dinner here: The cafés have little grills (*mangals*) where you can charcoal-broil the meat you order.

Uludağ National Park

Uludağ, with the tallest peak (8,300 feet) in northwestern Turkey, is actually a series of peaks and valleys skirting the eastern border of Bursa and sending spurs and forested slopes down to the city. In any season Uludağ offers pleasant relief from crowded cities. Wildflowers blanket the slopes in spring and summer, and autumn brings a burst of brilliant foliage.

Most people come to Uludağ in the winter; many—if not most—of the hotels are closed during the summer. Many of the winter visitors stay in the village called **Uludağ**, a ski resort (Turkey's largest and most popular) consisting of a collection of hotels that realize they've cornered the market on accommodations and feel no guilt charging five times the usual price for local beer. The mountain's 30 intermediate and beginner trails (there is one expert run) are crowded from November to April. It's common to see an entire family clomp all the way up the hill just to see brother Mehmet off on the lift. Uludağ is not without its critics, who complain that the winter resort is overrun with would-be gods and goddesses of this former Mount Olympus (there were many peaks so named in the ancient world) who work hard only at "being seen." With Day-Glo ski suits, fur accessories, and gold jewelry, they're hard to miss.

Uludağ's slopes are serviced by six T-bars and five chair lifts (new lifts are under construction). Ski-rental shops are located at the base. Have a travel agent call and reserve your equipment; two good Istanbul agencies are Renk Turizm (Tel: 1/230-5068 or 230-5162) and Kontuar Turizm (Tel: 1/230-0282 or 231-1546). Lift tickets are not inexpensive and are sold on a per-run, per-lift basis. As a rule, ski here during the week; on weekends the slopes are simply too mobbed.

The biggest hotel in Uludağ village is the **Grand Yazıcı Hotel,** which has a sprawling lobby, mini ice rink, pool, and game room. Its disco is crowded on weekends, and the

Greek-style taverna might keep you awake until the early hours if your room is directly above it. The **Kervansaray Uludağ Hotel** has a health club, indoor swimming pool, squash courts, and direct access to a ski lift. The **Beceren Oteli** has a solarium, sauna, and game room, and the **Büyük Hotel** has an outdoor heated pool.

In warmer months hikers trek three hours from the hotel area to the summit of Uludağ to enjoy the view and walk around the alpine lakes. If you have a car it is worth taking a trip outside Uludağ, among the hills and valleys of the range, to country villages such as **Soğukpınar** (one hour) and **Keles** (two and a half hours), where you can walk through quiet forests. The turnoff for Soğukpınar and Keles is on the Bursa–Uludağ road.

Uludağ is beginning to be discovered by foreign skiers. For arrangements from the U.K., call Ski Turkey, agents in London for the Uludağ resort (Tel: 081-461-5701).

İZNİK

İznik, the ancient city of Nicaea, sits on the shore of İznik Gölü (İznik Lake), surrounded by green mountains and farmland, a one-hour drive (60 km/37 miles) southeast of Yalova and one and a half hours (85 km/53 miles) northeast of Bursa. Visitors to the city are pleasantly surprised to discover a sleepy, relaxed town of 15,000 people living within a crumbled, four-mile-long ring of Roman-Byzantine walls.

Originally, İznik had four main entrance gates, one at each of the cardinal points of the compass. (One of these, the Göl Kapısı, or Lake Gate, at the western end of town, no longer exists.) In addition to the three extant main gates, the walls possess a number of smaller gates and the remains of many towers; if you wish, you can spend half a day walking the walls' circuit and exploring the ancient fortifications. Arriving at İznik from Yalova, you enter via the **Istanbul Kapısı**, which incorporates the remains of three Roman arches. İznik is laid out on a cross plan; its main north–south street, Atatürk Caddesi, leads from the Istanbul gate at the northern end of town south to the **Yenişehir Kapısı** (New City Gate), built by the Roman emperor Claudius II (A.D. 268 to 270). At the center of İznik, Atatürk Caddesi is intersected by the main east–west street, Kılıçaslan Caddesi, at whose eastern end stands the best-preserved of the gates, the **Lefke Kapısı**. The Lefke gate was constructed in A.D. 123, during the reign of Hadrian. Its central portal bears the inscription of its builder, the proconsul Plancius Varus. From the Lefke gate you can see a Roman aqueduct in the fields beyond—still in use for irrigation.

In addition to the entrance gates İznik has one other major gate, the **Saray Kapısı** (Palace Gate), this one within the walls in the southwestern quadrant of the city. The Saray gate was the monumental entryway to a 14th-century palace—no longer standing—built by Sultan Orhan; to find it, follow the signs for the Roman theater off Atatürk Caddesi. The gate is just past the site.

İznik's relatively small size and the basic grid pattern of its streets make it easy to find your way about. If you need help with your itinerary, call at İznik's **tourism office** (Tel: 2527/ 1933), located about midway between the center of town and the western entrance to the city on Kılıçaslan Caddesi. For a peaceful lunch of fresh fish, head toward the lake, just west of the city. The **Çamlık Motel and Café** is located to the left of the western entrance (where the Lake Gate once stood). The motel sits beneath pine trees and has a small outdoor restaurant and sparsely furnished but comfortable rooms. It's quiet during the cooler months, but in the summer your sleep might be disturbed by noise from the *gazino* (outdoor nightclub), a minute's walk to the left. To the right of the western entrance to the city on the lakeshore is the **Kırık Çatal Restaurant**, which specializes in trout (*alabalık*) and sheathfish (*yayınbalığı*) caught in İznik Lake and serves an array of *meze* (appetizers).

İznik's gates and walls are mostly of Roman origin, though they were extensively rebuilt and added to during Byzantine times. The city's history extends back well before the Romans, however. Evidence of the area's inhabitation reaches back to 1000 B.C. (there are a number of ancient mounds just a few miles outside town). The city was formally founded in the fourth century B.C. by Antigonus, one of Alexander the Great's generals, and called Antigoneia after him. It was renamed Nicaea in 305 B.C., taking its new name from the wife of Lysimachus, another of Alexander's generals. Nicaea served as the capital of Bithynia, a small monarchy, until 264 B.C., when that honor was taken by Nicomedia. In 74 B.C. Bithynia became a Roman province, and Nicaea was adorned with the requisite temples, baths, and other monuments. The city's Roman buildings—including many added by Hadrian—were mostly destroyed by invading Persians and Goths in the third century, but Nicaea continued to prosper.

In 325 Nicaea was chosen as the site of the First Ecumenical Council, called by Emperor Constantine I to settle the controversy between the Arian and Athanasian interpreta-

tions of the Christian faith. Arianism's main tenet—that
Christ was not the equal of God—was rejected by the
council, which promulgated the Nicene Creed. The creed,
one of the major statements of Christian belief, emphasizes
the co-equality of all three persons of the Christian godhead:
Father, Son, and Holy Spirit. Arius, the Alexandrian priest for
whom the heresy is named, was subsequently exiled. The
council did not succeed in finally squelching the heresy,
however: Near the end of his life Constantine became more
disposed toward Arianism. When he was baptized on his
deathbed, the emperor had the sacrament performed by an
Arian priest. Arius himself was recalled from exile, and his
brand of Christianity continued to exert great influence,
especially in the Eastern Empire and among the Germanic
tribes who played such an important role in late Roman and
early Byzantine and European history.

During his reign (527 to 565), the Byzantine emperor
Justinian poured attention on the lakeside city, building new
walls, churches, and baths. In 787 the Seventh Ecumenical
Council met here, this time in the **church of St. Sophia**,
which today stands in ruin at the junction of Atatürk Caddesi
and Kılıçaslan Caddesi in the center of town. Here the
Iconoclast controversy that had wracked the Byzantine Empire was settled, at least temporarily (a second period of
Iconoclasm—"image breaking"—did occur in the ninth century). The council accepted the legitimacy of icons, with the
understanding that believers who prayed before religious
images were worshiping what the icons stood for and not
the images themselves. The church's remaining fresco and
floor mosaic, depicting Jesus, Mary, and John the Baptist, are
protected by glass. A minaret, added when the church was
converted into a mosque by the Turks, now houses a stork
nest among its broken bricks.

Nicaea was three times lucky. Under the Romans the city
flourished, benefiting enormously from the lavish building
program of Hadrian. Then, from 1204 to 1261—when the
Crusaders grabbed Constantinople from the Byzantines and
established their own "Latin Empire" there—the Byzantine
emperor Theodore II Lascaris fled to Nicaea and ruled a
small territory from within the city's walls. Once again
Nicaea was the beneficiary of civic funds—resulting in the
construction of a moat and new outer wall with 100 towers
(adding to the 240-plus towers that had already existed by
the 11th century).

The city's third great period came in the centuries following its capture by the Ottomans in 1329. It was during this
period that İznik—as it was renamed by its Turkish

conquerors—became celebrated for its superb ceramic tiles and faïence. Indeed, people mostly know of İznik because of its legendary ceramics, which were produced in their most glorious form in the 16th century. In the last half of the 15th century Ottoman artisans were merely copying the blue-and-white patterns of Chinese porcelain. Gradually, however, the Ottoman potters began to create their own exotic, elegant style. To the blue and white they added turquoise, green, and red glazes, with motifs of carnations, roses, tulips, pomegranates, and grapes. Sultan Selim I, having conquered northwestern Persia, was so taken with the ceramicists of the city of Tabriz that he "resettled" 500 potters in İznik and put them to work in the empire's pottery kilns.

What emerged was some of the most prized faïence in the world; much of the tile was used to adorn the mosques and monuments of the Ottomans, and a great deal was exported. Today, after a long period of misidentification (as, for example, Damascusware or Rhodesware), İznik pottery has regained its artistic and historical importance. Following a 1989 exhibition in Istanbul of İznik pottery and the subsequent auction of pieces by Sotheby's, anything "İznik" is virtually untouchable.

No one to this day has been able to re-create methods or recipes used by the 16th-century artisans to glaze their exquisite wares; the so-called İznik red remains especially elusive. However, a few souls are valiantly attempting to solve the mystery. Eşref Eroğlu, a local artisan, can be found at his *çini fırını* (porcelain kiln) on Eşrefzade Mahalesi Çınar Sokak constantly testing new techniques aimed at capturing the glories of the past. You can find samples of Eroğlu's work at his shop: **İznik Çini** at Beyler Mahalesi, Orhan Sokak 3 (Tel: 2527/2446) in the center of the town across from Garanti Bankası, a commercial bank. (Beware: Most of the floral pottery on sale in other shops in İznik is actually new Kütahya ware.)

If you walk to the end of Salimdemir Can Sokak and turn right, you will find Professor Ara Altun and fellow archaeologists from Istanbul University digging at the site of the original İznik ceramics works. Their finds, which include İznik tiles and household vessels along with kiln materials, are on exhibit in the **Nilüfer Hatun İmarethanesi**, once a caravansary for dervishes and now the town's museum (follow the signs left off Kılıçaslan). (Nilüfer Hatun was the Greek wife of Sultan Orhan, the son of the founder of the Ottoman dynasty.) The museum holdings also include a collection of Roman and Byzantine glass and jewelry, as well as finds dating from the Paleolithic period. Its garden is a jumble of statuary, fragments, and gravestones.

The British Museum in London and the Musée de la Renaissance at Ecouen in France have excellent collections of İznik ceramics. For further reading, *İznik: Pottery of Ottoman Turkey,* by Julian Raby and Nurhan Atasoy, is sold at the Museum of Turkish and Islamic Arts (the İbrahim Paşa palace) in Istanbul.

İznik's **museum** is a lovely building (it's an *imaret,* a former soup-kitchen), with a terrific collection of İznik tiles. Across the street is the **Yeşil Cami** (Green Mosque), built in 1492. Its elaborately tiled minaret is Seljuk in style and one of the prettiest in Turkey. (The green-and-black tiles are not the originals from İznik, but replacements from Kütahya installed years ago after an earthquake.) İznik also has the distinction of having the oldest dated Ottoman mosque, the unpretentious, single-domed **Hacı Özbek Camii** (1332), located off Kılıçaslan Caddesi just east of the municipal building.

Roughly 6 km (3½ miles) north of town (leave from the Istanbul gate) is a 1,600-year-old Roman tomb (**Yeraltı Mezarı**) of a man and woman, painted with a scene of colorful peacocks, pheasants, and quails in Paradise. Its arched ceiling is a mosaic of sunny red, gold, and green designs. The tomb is always locked, but if you ask at the Nilüfer Hatun museum someone will accompany you there (for a price) to open it. It may be hard finding a taxi to and from the site, but it is worth the effort.

İznik Gölü (İznik Lake) has no real beach, but diehard swimmers head in anyway, despite the constantly chilly water. If you are similarly foolhardy but haven't brought a suit, you can undoubtedly find a swimsuit seller among the lakeside vendors hawking pistachios and confections. In September the town hosts its annual Grape Festival—a tribute to the local *müşküle,* a variety of table grape. A Grape Queen and folkdancers provide entertainment.

İznik is best visited as a day trip, and you're better off staying in Termal, Yalova, or Bursa. If you miss the minibus, however, your best bet is the aforementioned Çamlık Motel and Café, on the lakeshore road.

EUROPEAN ENVIRONS

EDİRNE

You could enter Edirne riding a camel, carried on a litter in a sultan's procession, or even rolling in at the controls of an army tank and you would not look out of place.

A lively border town, Edirne stands guard at Turkey's boundaries with Greece and Bulgaria on the banks of the Tunca and Meriç rivers and has the frenetic character of a frontier outpost. Centuries-old buildings look out onto cobblestoned streets, military zones ring the edge of town, and travellers speaking myriad languages join hundreds of *asker* (soldiers), who mill about 15th-century mosques and teahouses, looking for diversions.

Despite its somewhat tattered aspect, Edirne provides a vivid, unforgettable introduction to the Islamic world; its unparalleled showcase of Ottoman architecture is a reminder that Edirne was once a capital of the Ottoman domain. The four minarets of the Selimiye Camii command the skyline from every direction, marking the psychological gateway between East and West. Not a single high-rise building mars the city's silhouette because of a restriction forbidding tall structures.

Edirne is 245 km (152 miles) northwest of Istanbul in the northwestern corner of European Turkey, the eastern portion of Thrace. Legions of Greeks, Persians, Romans, Goths, Byzantines, Bulgars, Crusaders, Turks, and Russians have marched through here. Edirne's roots go back to 4000 B.C., but today's city was established by the Roman emperor Hadrian in A.D. 125. Originally Hadrianopolis, the city's name was later changed to Adrianoupolis under the Byzantines and was shortened to Edirne by the Ottomans, who, under command of Sultan Murat I, captured the city in 1362 and proclaimed it the capital (replacing Bursa). It remained the capital for 91 prosperous years, until Mehmet the Conqueror, a native son, plotted the fall of Constantinople from Edirne's palace and set off, with Edirne-made cannons (built by a Hungarian), to bring Constantinople to its knees. Edirne lost its title to the city on the Bosphorus, but maintained its cultural stature nevertheless.

For 400 years the city enjoyed relative peace, until the 19th century, when Russia invaded Thrace in 1828 and again in 1878. The Balkan Wars again disrupted the peace in 1912 and 1913. In 1922 Mustafa Kemal (later Atatürk) repelled the Greek invasion of Anatolia, and in the Treaty of Lausanne, which settled that conflict, Turkey was permitted to keep Edirne and the southeastern part of Thrace.

It's a bit difficult to imagine that at one time Edirne was one of the world's largest cities. During the Ottoman centuries the city swelled with travellers from both East and West who sought help from the city's world-renowned Bayezit II hospital—the largest charitable organization in the world at the time.

Edirne was reported at its height to have had 24 caravansaries, 56 convents, 285 mosques, 16 baths, 8 bridges, and 124 fountains, and its palace rivaled Istanbul's Topkapı in size and beauty (and was favored over Topkapı by some sultans because of Edirne's superb hunting). Süleyman the Magnificent spent many summers on the city's riverbanks. As a contemporary account puts it, "When each August the sultan moved his court (and harem) to the more bracing climate of Adrianople he ... spent days ... engaged in falconry, hunting ... wild geese, heron, hawks, eagles, ... only returning to Constantinople when the frogs began to be a nuisance with their croaking."

Edirne is 19 km (12 miles) from Kapıkule on the Bulgarian border and a mere 5 km (3 miles) from Pazarkule, Turkey's border gate with Greece. By car it is four hair-raising hours from Istanbul. The drive is anything but pleasant: Careening transport trucks crowd the way. Part of a new, faster ring road (Paralı Geçis) has opened, running from the Maslak road in Istanbul to Selimpaşa, an hour past the Atatürk airport. Taking this new road on weekends is advisable despite its toll (about $3). The lane running from west to east seems to be a continuous caravan of Mercedes Benzes with top-heavy luggage racks: Turkish guest workers returning from host countries in Western Europe.

People visit Edirne for two quite different reasons (aside from a simple border crossing): to see the early Ottoman mosques and monuments and to witness a cruder art form—grease wrestling—at the mid-June Kırkpınar grease-wrestling championships. It is somewhat incongruous that a city with such a noble past should have this sport, called *yağlı güreş*, as one of its main attractions. Each year contestants of all ages slather themselves with diluted olive oil, slip on thick leather breeches, and go one-on-one on the field of Sarayiçi.

What is a sport without a legend? According to the folktale that purports to give its history, in 1360, 40 soldiers, after successfully laying waste to a castle of Rumeli (what the

Ottomans called Thrace), celebrated by doing what they did best—wrestling. The contest dwindled to two unflagging fighters who continued into the night. They were found the next morning frozen in a literal deadlock. As their bodies were taken away, 40 springs spouted from the parched field, turning the site into a green pasture and giving the site its present name of Kırkpınar, meaning Forty Springs. Today's crowd of spectators, a mixture of government officials, soldiers, townspeople, fellow wrestlers, tourists, and Gypsies, reaches fever pitch when the highest-class athletes take to the field to the beat of the *davul* (drum) and blare of the *zurna* (shrill pipe) to fight for the meager purse and enormous prestige as *baş pehlivan* (head wrestler), an honor that is good for one year. Purchase tickets at Edirne's town hall, at Mimar Sinan Caddesi 10 (Tel: 181/111-28), on the west side of the street across from the tea garden leading to the Selimiye Camii (see below).

Around Edirne

Edirne is conveniently laid out and easy to explore. Begin at central **Hürriyet Meydanı** (Freedom Square) at the intersection of the two main streets, Saraçlar/Saraçhane Caddesi and Talatpaşa Caddesi. (Brochures and information are available at the **tourist office**, located at Talatpaşa Caddesi 17; employees speak English, French, and German.) At the central square you can fortify yourself with strong Turkish tea at the outdoor café while planning your ascent to the **Selimiye Camii**, which appears to float on the northern hill. Mimar Sinan constructed this magnificent mosque between 1565 and 1575, when he was well into his eighties. Sinan was pleased because he had finally achieved the construction of a dome that was higher (by a little more than eight feet) than that of Istanbul's St. Sophia (Selimiye's dome is almost 80 feet high). For the master architect, this was his best work.

The Selimiye is one of the most beautiful buildings in Turkey, each detail more exquisite than the last. The *minber* is a delicate piece of work, carved from one piece of Marmara marble. Red sandstone, quarried locally, is used with constrasting white stone in the arches. The tiles in the sultan's quarters are said to be replacements, installed after a Russian colonel spirited the originals off to Moscow in 1878. The intricate brushwork, intertwining calligraphy, and circular webbing of twinkling lights are dizzying.

Enter the mosque through the lower bazaar, called the **Kavaflar Arasta** (Cobblers' Market), and head up the thick stone stairway to the mosque's courtyard. The *arasta* now mainly sells religious items as well as Turkish dolls, towels, and onyx. Before entering the courtyard, walk to the right and visit Edirne's **Museum of Turkish and Islamic Art**, located in the old *medrese*. One of the displays is a photographic roundup of the area's great wrestlers. Don't miss the tombs of the janissaries. Behind the Selimiye is the **Archaeological and Ethnographic Museum**, where you can see examples of Edirne's famous embroidery as well as Thracian jewelry and weapons.

Across from Hürriyet Meydanı is the **Eski Cami** (Old Mosque), finished in 1413. The mosque pales in comparison to the Selimiye, yet it should be appreciated as an example of early Ottoman architecture and for its interior calligraphic decoration. Edirne's 14-domed **bedesten** is next to the Eski Cami; you can't miss examples of Edirne's famous fragrant *sabun* (soap), shaped like fruits and vegetables. In general, Edirne's bazaars are not on a par with Istanbul's or Bursa's. Ethnic handcrafts, like the area's much-heralded embroideries, have given way to stalls jammed with knockoff designer shirts, musical instruments, towels, and onyx. The famous painted Edirne *sandık*s (trunks) can be found only in the best antiques shops in Istanbul and abroad.

At the intersection of Talatpaşa Caddesi and Saraçlar Caddesi is a statue of Atatürk. Across the way, past a teahouse, the red sandstone arches of the **Üç Şerefeli Cami** (Three-Gallery Mosque) catch your eye. The mosque's name derives from the three balconies (with a separate stairway leading to each) on one of its minarets. Three of the minarets are good examples of Seljuk-influenced architecture. Built between 1438 and 1447, the mosque had the tallest minarets in the Ottoman Empire until Sinan added an extra ten feet to the minarets of his beloved Selimiye. The airy courtyard has fading decoration in need of restoration, but water still flows from its center *şadırvan* (fountain).

Across the street is another of Sinan's jewels: the **Sokollu Hamamı**, the 16th-century bath built for grand vizier Sokollu Mehmet Paşa, one of many baths Sinan built in Edirne. The bath is still used, and the men's side has been restored (the original İznik tiles are no more). Order *ekstra* (extra) to get the works—a one-and-a-half-hour session that includes six latherings of soap, a *kese* (a kind of luffa) scrub-down, and a pummeling massage. You won't know what hit you. The women's side is a bit dingy, but worth a look.

On the street behind the bath is a lonely-looking tower, the last remnant of Edirne's castle, now a fire station.

The city's dolmuş terminal is located in a small parking lot between the bedesten and **Rüstem Paşa Kervansarayı**, a sprawling, 100-room, domed caravansary also built by Sinan in the 16th century. Today it serves as a government-run hotel with a young and sincere staff. The hotel is not inexpensive, but it's worth a try if you want to experience life in a real Ottoman caravansary. Rooms vary in size and all have high, cantilevered ceilings and (nonworking) fireplaces. Some rooms are better ventilated and, hence, noisier than others. The courtyard, with a spreading *çınar* tree and flowers, is pleasant, but it is often the venue for a wedding or circumcision party. Inquire to see what's on to avoid a sleepless night. The hotel now accepts credit cards.

The most upmarket hotel you will find in Edirne is the **Balta Oteli**, on the main highway entering town. It boasts a casino in addition to a restaurant (where you'll pay hotel prices for basic Turkish food). On the same side of the street is the **Kervan Hotel**, with spartan but adequate rooms (insist on a room at the rear). The Kervan also has a restaurant and tea garden. Across from the tourism office is the **Sultan Hotel**, offering sparsely furnished but adequate rooms (almost double the price of the Kervan), a backyard tea garden, and a good restaurant.

Edirne does not rate high on culinary lists; in fact, some would warn you to bring your own food. Don't panic; there are a few spots of refuge. **Çatı** (The Roof) restaurant is the easiest to find (one block past the tourism office on Talatpaşa Caddesi and across from the Sultan Hotel). This restaurant accepts credit cards, a rarity in Edirne. Most hotels have adequate restaurants (which, however, charge higher prices than the Çatı). Following the length of Ali Paşa Kapalıçarşısı on Saraçlar Caddesi you'll find **Met Pizza** (number 108), a good alternative to the fried liver and greasy grilled chicken offered in the local *lokanta*s.

From the Atatürk statue in the center of town you can take side tours to visit two fascinating early Ottoman structures, Yıldırım Camii and Bayezit Külliyesi, in separate parts of the city, by taking a taxi or by walking. By taxi it is a five-minute ride to either destination. It takes 25 minutes to walk to each site. To walk to **Yıldırım Camii**, once a Crusader church and now the city's oldest mosque, head west along Talat Paşa Asfaltı, cross the Tunca river, and take the second right at the old fountain. Built in 1400 by Sultan Bayezit I, known in the West as the "Thunderbolt," Yıldırım Camii (Mosque of the Thunderbolt) has a single-balcony minaret. In its garden are the ruined tombs of two Ottoman princes.

To reach **Bayezit Külliyesi** from town, take Imaret

Caddesi, turning left immediately after Sokullu Hamamı.
Walk past the fire station and head straight for 20 minutes.
You'll pass a military zone and cross the six-arched Bayezit
bridge, which spans the trickling Tunca.

The Bayezit Külliyesi, with 100 gleaming domes, is an
unforgettable sight, almost eerie in its silent magnificence.
The complex includes a mosque (still in use), medrese,
hospital, *imaret* (soup kitchen), printing press, water mills,
and baths. The complex was once noted for its advanced eye
clinic and employed some of the best surgeons in the world.
The most fascinating room is the octagonal domed *tımarhane*
(insane asylum). The pampered patient would be sent to the
sanctuary of its cool interior, where treatment consisted of
water therapy (from a central fountain), music (an orchestra
played three times a week), and the fragrance of fresh flowers. According to 17th-century Turkish traveller Evliya Çelebi,
"Patients were given daffodils, jasmine, roses... in whose
fragrant benediction the sick people found health.... Some
of them stamped the blossoms underfoot, others ate them,
and still others made uncouth noises.... The youth of Edirne
would come to watch."

The new Thrace University holds art classes in parts of the
medrese; it's nice to see life returning to this astonishing
place. (Bring your own water: There is no place to buy
refreshments. It may also be hard to find transportation back
into town, so a 20-minute walk may be unavoidable.)

If you follow the river dike west from the Bayezit complex
you will come to a large field near an intersecting road. You
are looking at Sarayiçi, once the site of the Edirne palace,
now claimed by the grease wrestlers. The palace was home
to the sultans during the years Edirne was the Ottoman
capital. The Russians demolished some buildings in 1829;
what was left was accidentally shelled by the Turks during a
second invasion of the Russians in 1878. Carpets, tapestries,
paintings, and old Korans went up in smoke.

The surrounding wood, full of thistle and willow, is called
Söğütlük forest, a favorite picnic spot for locals. An amusement park here flaunts its neon spectacle nightly during the
summer. Edirne's raucous side emerges when the sun goes
down and the streets around Hürriyet Meydanı fill with
vendors pushing festive carts stuffed with grilled corn, steaming chestnuts, and *döner*. From nowhere miniature tables
and chairs appear, cluttering the gutters and sidewalks, offering true roadside dining under the minareted skyline.

GALLIPOLI PENINSULA

History has singled out the Gallipoli peninsula for an uncommon fate. The moment you reach the first miles of its wind-blown shore along the Dardanelles, you know this is no ordinary place. The peninsula, whose name derives from its original Hellenic name, Kallipolis, is the southernmost point of Thracian Turkey, located four hours from Istanbul southwest along the Sea of Marmara coast. It is a serene and beautiful land, noticeably spared the clutter of modern towns and villages. The peninsula stretches 52 miles into the Aegean Sea, with the 40-mile-long strait of the Dardanelles coursing between its European shores and those of Asian Turkey.

The strait is four and half miles across at its widest point and only 1,600 yards at its narrowest—a point marked by the heart-shaped 15th-century Kilitbahir castle on its western (European) bank and Sultaniye castle in the town of Çanakkale on the eastern shore. Long before Sultan Mehmet II built these two fortresses to protect his valuable waterway, the strait was the object of desire for many. In 480 B.C. the Persian king Xerxes on his way toward Greece crossed the Hellespont (the ancient name of the Dardanelles) on a bridge made of boats. During the Peloponnesian War, Athens was brought to its knees by the Spartans' clever blockade of the Hellespont. The Athenians were defeated by the Spartans, led by Lysander, in 405 B.C., at the battle of Aegospotami on the peninsula. Alexander the Great crossed the Hellespont in 334 B.C., entering Asia for the first time and immediately defeating a Persian force at the river Granicus. In the 14th century the Venetians and Genoese defeated the first assembled Ottoman navy in a brief battle in the Dardanelles.

In recent times the peninsula was the stage for one of World War I's fiercest battles. Known to the allies as the Gallipoli Campaign and to the Turks as the Çanakkale War (after the town on the Asian shore of the strait, where Turkish defenses lay), the battle lasted 259 days and claimed the lives of nearly half a million men.

The Gallipoli Campaign

In August 1914 the Ottoman government—then in the hands of the Young Turks—allied itself with Germany, prompting the British to impound two warships that were being built for Turkey at British yards. The Germans swiftly countered with a gift to the Turkish government of two warships—the *Goeben* and the *Breslau*—which eventually made their way, with German crews, to Constantinople and from there to Odessa, where they fired on Russian ships in port.

In December Lord Kitchener, the British secretary of state for war, received a message sent from St. Petersburg by Grand Duke Nicholas stating that the Russians needed a diversion to draw the Turks away from the Caucasus. After much debate, Kitchener, Winston Churchill (then lord of the admiralty), and the British war cabinet decided to launch a naval campaign to force open the Dardanelles, with the capture of Constantinople as its final objective. Only one member of the cabinet, Admiral Fisher, objected to the plan, which was unaided by military support on land. His words, "Damn the Dardanelles, they will be our grave," are still remembered. He was overridden.

The British began the campaign convinced that the Dardanelles would fall in a month's time. On February 19, 1915, twelve allied battleships were deployed and cruised into the strait. The Turks quickly entrenched along the strait, installing major defenses at Gelibolu, Çanakkale, and several spots at the tip of the peninsula. Their troops were largely untrained boys who knew little about war or military maneuvers, yet they doggedly hampered the allied warships, which tried over and over to make a successful pass through the strait. On the night of March 8 the Turkish minelayer *Nusret* emplaced 20 mines, which went unnoticed until the allied warship *Suffren* blew up, sinking in two minutes. The warships *Inflexible* and *Irresistible* were hit soon after. None of the allies' vessels ever made it farther north than six miles into the strait.

On March 10 Lord Kitchener announced that land support would be given, and on March 23 the naval assault ended. The allied land forces destined for Gallipoli included 30,000 troops from the Australian and New Zealand Army Corps (ANZAC), 17,000 men from the 29th British Division, 10,000 from the Royal Naval Division, and 16,000 French troops. On April 14, 1915, 200 allied ships left Cairo and Alexandria, full of supplies and eager soldiers who knew next to nothing about the terrain they would encounter. On the morning of April 25, the landings began. Nature was not on the side of the allies. Strong, unexpected currents and tricky weather hampered mobility; when added to a general state of confusion and poor communications, these factors spelled defeat for the first expeditions. Nearly half the British were killed trying to land at the southern end of the peninsula; the *River Clyde* landing was another disaster, with the allied soldiers sitting ducks for Turkish snipers on shore. To the northwest, on "Y" beach, 2,000 allied soldiers had to climb a steep cliff before receiving further orders, which, after 11 hours, still hadn't come. But the Turks did come, and Turkish bullets killed almost half the men.

That same morning, the ANZAC forces waded ashore at what they thought was Kabatepe. It was not. Their boats had drifted a mile north during the night, and they landed instead at the bottom of the treacherous Sarıbahir ridge. Many soldiers were killed or drowned before they reached shore. A few groups did manage to scale the ridge up to Conkbayırı, where they met Colonel Mustafa Kemal, just arriving with his troops from the area near Kilitbahir. Kemal, seeing the ANZAC soldiers, ordered his frightened men "not to fight, but to die," and they did, successfully putting off the first few ANZAC troops and gaining valuable time—time that may have cost the allies the battle.

And so the battle went on, a nine-month-long struggle, with fatal trench warfare fought along the rocky, spine-like ridge that marches down the peninsula. Sometimes the opposing trenches were almost next to one another, as reflected in this account by a Turkish officer: "The trenches were just five meters apart. The soldiers could see each other clearly and started to make jokes. . . . The ANZACs gave their buttons as souvenirs and the Turkish soldiers threw things like coins to the other side, . . . but later when the corpses arrived, the chocolates were thrown back."

On December 20 the withdrawal of allied forces began; the last soldier left on January 16, 1916. Casualty figures vary, but many estimate the number of dead at half a million, 250,000 on each side. Today the peninsula is a site of pilgrimage for many nations.

The War Memorial

The Gallipoli War Memorial, south of the town of Gelibolu, was designed by Sir John Burnett and is meticulously managed by the Commonwealth Wargraves Commission. It is forbidden to camp, light fires, or pick flowers within its boundaries. (You can, however, swim in the Aegean here.) First-time visitors are always surprised at the sheer magnitude of the memorial, which includes 31 cemeteries. With names like Shrapnel Valley and Lone Pine, the graveyards are hidden in pine forests, scattered along thorny ridges, or laid out on desolate beaches.

The road to the memorial park is 20 minutes south of the small town of **Gelibolu** on the eastern side of the peninsula. Gelibolu offers little except a **tourism office** (across from the harbor), which sells an English-language guide to the site. A car ferry leaves hourly for the town of Lâpseki across the strait on the Asian side.

The memorial is set in two parts, a reflection of the major landings: Cape Helles at the tip (the location of the massive four-pillared Turkish Memorial) and the west coast between Kabatepe and Suvla bay and inland to the hilltop ridge. Each area takes about three hours to tour, and you must have a car or minibus. Private tours are recommended: Troyanzac, with offices near the clock tower in Çanakkale, is one reputable agency (Tel: 196/5047 or 5049) that conducts daily tours of the memorial. Many travel agencies in Istanbul will arrange your visit to the area; however, this is more costly than driving yourself or travelling by bus and finding a guide at Gallipoli. Istanbul's Viking Turizm (Tel: 1/243-5347 or 249-9678) can help with arrangements year round. (Chances of finding special group tours from Istanbul to Gallipoli increase from April to June, when many visitors from Britain, New Zealand, and Australia make the trip.) Don't venture out without good walking shoes and snacks and water (there are no refreshments for sale at the Conkbayırı site).

Head first to Kabatepe/Arıburnu and visit the small war exhibit (shrapnel and photographs) at the **Kabatepe Tanıtma Merkezi**. A bronze wall plaque here, hung during the 75th anniversary observances in 1990, explains that the visitor will see ten other bronze plaques at the main sites throughout the war memorial. Cast in Melbourne, the plaques were donated by a private source and give descriptive accounts of each site. Begin your tour of the battlefields at Arıburnu, also called **Anzac Cove** in commemoration of the battle fought there, a beautiful stretch of sandy beach with a grassy knoll and shade trees—not exactly what you'd imagine a war zone to look like. On the higher ground of the beach, next to the road, is a large, white memorial stone, inscribed with the letter Atatürk wrote to the Australian people in 1934. In English translation, it reads in part, "Those heroes who shed their blood and lost their lives—you are now lying in the soil of a friendly country. Therefore rest in peace. There is no difference between the Johnnies and the Mehmets; to us they lie side by side, here in this country of ours. . . . You, the mothers who sent their sons from far-away countries, wipe away your tears; your sons are now lying in our bosom and are at peace. After having lost their lives on this land they have become our sons as well."

Each site has its own gripping story. **Johnson's Jolly cemetery**, named after an Australian soldier, holds the graves of the Australian troops who on August 6, 1915, emerged from the trenches on the northern side of Walker's Ridge and ran the 60 yards across flat ground to the Turkish trenches. For five days fierce fighting ensued, as the Australians attempted to draw fire away from the allied troops engaged in battle with the Turks at Conkbayırı and Suvla bay. In the end 4,000 Turks and 2,200 Australians died. Across from Johnson's Jolly some trenches can still be seen, grim reminders of the hideous battle. Just south of Johnson's Jolly is the **Lone Pine cemetery**, where a towering white monument carries the names of Australian and New Zealand troops killed. At Conkbayırı, **Twelve Tree Copse** and **Hill 60** are the resting places of New Zealand troops. The **Cape Helles** memorial carries the names of British, Australian, and Indian troops. All the gravestones are white, and many carry poignant inscriptions commissioned by family members of the dead.

The town of **Eceabat** lies on the east coast of the peninsula between Gelibolu and Cape Helles. It offers little except two hotels—the **Saros Oteli** and the **Ece Hotel, Bob Hawkes' Café** (beer and burgers), and the car/passenger ferry to Çanakkale on the Asian side. Three miles farther south is **Kilitbahir** (Sea Lock), the 15th-century castle built on the narrowest part of the strait by Mehmet the Conqueror.

There are few places to stay on the peninsula besides the Eceabat hotels mentioned above and the **Boncuk Otel** (with a swimming pool) on the Dardanelles shore just 20 minutes north of Eceabat. The Kabatepe campground is well maintained and has a lovely beach on the Aegean. Most people cross the Dardanelles and stay in Çanakkale (see the Aegean Turkey chapter, below). From the ferryboat en route to Çanakkale, you can see a giant inscription on the hillside just north of Kilitbahir. It begins, "Dur Yolcu" (Stop, Passerby), and continues, "This earth you thus tread unawares is where an age sank. Bow and listen; this quiet mound is where the heart of a nation throbs."

Gökçeada and Bozcaada

The offshore islands of Gökçeada and Bozcaada are lovely retreats for swimming, picnicking, and touring if time permits. Mountainous Gökçeada (Sky Island) is the larger and is located closer to the mainland, just off Kabatepe at the southwest end of the Gallipoli peninsula. Originally called Imroz (the Imbros of Homer), this green island welcomes visitors for excellent fishing, hiking, sunning, and swimming. Ferries leave daily from Kabatepe and Çanakkale.

Bozcaada, once called Tenedos, is farther south and is reached by ferry from Odunluk İskelesi, south of Çanakkale. It was used as an allied base during the Gallipoli Campaign. A fortress on the northeastern side of the island, next to a little harbor, was restored by Sultan Mehmet II after being occupied by Venetians, Genoese, and Byzantines over the centuries. Its well-kept appearance is due to restoration efforts by the Turkish Ministry of Culture in the late 1960s. A sandy beach in the Ayazma area is quite popular, as are Bozcaada's *çok meşhur* (very famous) white and red wines—to be found at the beachside cafés. The **Zafer Motel** is located near the ferry dock and offers decent accommodations for low prices. It's open between April and October, as are many of the island's other establishments.

GETTING AROUND

Black Sea Beaches

Kilyos is 34 km (21 miles) north of Istanbul's center, about an hour's drive along the Maslak highway following signs directly to Kilyos. The road is winding and slow going in many places. It's also fairly easy to reach by bus: From Beşiktaş, just in front of the fruit market on Barboros Bulvarı, you can board a bus (number 25) for Sarıyer and other destinations.

Şile, northeast of Istanbul, can be reached from the European side of the city (distance about 70 km/43 miles) most quickly by taking the Fatih Sultan Mehmet Köprüsü (the second Bosphorus bridge) over to Asia, then following signs to Beykoz and beyond to Şile. The drive in normal traffic takes about two hours. The Şile Ağva bus company services Şile daily, leaving every hour from Üsküdar (Tel: 1992/3000 in Şile, 1/334-1124 in Üsküdar). The first bus leaves at 6:30 A.M. from Üsküdar, the last at 7:30 P.M. The last bus back to Üsküdar departs Şile at 7:15 P.M. (To reach Üsküdar from European Istanbul, take one of the frequent ferries from Eminönü or Beşiktaş.)

Princes' Islands

Regular ferries leave Istanbul from the Sirkeci and Kabataş quays on the European side, and the Bostancı pier on the Asian side. Schedules are posted on the docks. The Turkish Maritime Lines publishes ferry schedules in English twice a year; these are available at the tourism office near the entrance to the Istanbul Hilton, north of Taksim square. The following telephone numbers provide ferry schedule information: for Sirkeci, 526-8659; for Kabataş, 243-3756; on

Büyükada, 382-6006; on Heybeliada, 351-8437; on Kınalıada, 381-4020; on Burgaz, 351-8126.

By regular ferry it takes about an hour to get from Kabataş (the most convenient departure point if you're staying in the new city) to Büyükada. You can cut that time in half if you take the *deniz otobüsü*, which makes frequent runs between Kabataş and Büyükada. The trip costs about three times as much as regular ferry service. Ferries between Büyükada and Heybeliada are frequent, with a few stops scheduled at Kınalıada and Burgaz throughout the day. Sea-bus service is available only to Büyükada, though some of these boats continue on to Yalova. You can try your luck at hiring private fishing caïques to the other islands. Also, if you're adventurous and can gather a large enough party to make the per-person cost reasonable, it is possible to hire a private boat for a day trip through the islands and back to Istanbul. Inquire at major hotels and tourism agencies, or ask around on the dock at Beşiktaş.

Bursa, Uludağ, and Termal

Ferries for Yalova leave Istanbul's Kabataş and Sirkeci docks daily, almost hourly. Schedules are posted at the docks or, as was mentioned above, are available in an English version at the tourism office near the Istanbul Hilton. The regular ferry to Yalova takes about two hours. (Snacks and refreshments are available on board. Most ferries have open-air decks fore and aft. Smoking is forbidden inside the boats. You are likely to be pestered by shoe-shine boys during the trip—even if you are wearing canvas sneakers!) Some ferries make stops at Büyükada and Heybeliada in the Princes' Islands. Sea buses leave from the town of Kartal on the Asian side and deliver passengers to Yalova in about 45 minutes. Car ferries operate between Eskihisar (near Gebze) to Topçular (just east of Yalova), and the crossing takes about 30 minutes.

The *deniz otobüsü*, which has frequent departures from the Sirkeci quay, takes only an hour. You cannot sit outside, but the ride is very pleasant. At the Yalova dock buses wait to take passengers to Bursa (a scenic one-hour trip), Termal (a 15-minute ride), or İznik.

Many bus companies offer regular service between Istanbul and Bursa. Bursa Uludağ Turizm bus lines offers hourly service from the Trakya terminal at Topkapı bus station just outside the walls of the old city in Istanbul (Tel: 1/567-1988) or from the Harem terminal on the Asian side of the city (Tel: 1/334-6954).

Sönmez Havayolları, a private airline (Tel: 1/573-9323), has two daily flights to Bursa from Istanbul's Atatürk airport (be sure to ask the taxi driver to take you to the *domestic* terminal).

Dolmuşes leave Bursa's bus station frequently for Uludağ National Park, 22 km (14 miles) away, or from the main road leading up to Tophane from Atatürk Caddesi. The *teleferik* leaves every half hour in good weather from the eastern end of Bursa and drops passengers at Kadıyayla (first stop) or Sarıalan (second stop). From Sarıalan you can catch a dolmuş to the hotel area at Uludağ resort. Uludağ is a five- to six-hour drive from Istanbul in good weather. Tire chains or snow tires are recommended in winter.

İznik

To get to İznik take the *deniz otobüsü* from Istanbul's Kabataş dock (look for the dolphin logo) to Yalova. The first leaves at 8:35 A.M. on weekdays, 9:15 on weekends. (There are six sea buses per day in each direction.) The last sea bus returns to Istanbul from Yalova at 7:30 P.M. (The Kabataş–Yalova trip takes about one hour.) Regular ferries, which take about two hours, leave frequently, beginning at 9:30 A.M., each day from Kabataş and Sirkeci.

Once in Yalova, board the minibus for İznik that's parked in the lot to the left of the ferry-station exit. The 60-km (37-mile) drive from Yalova to İznik takes about an hour, and minibuses depart on the hour. The last minibus back to Yalova from İznik is at 5:00 P.M. There is regular bus service to other cities (Istanbul, Ankara, Bursa) from İznik's bus station. Bus tickets can be purchased at İznik Seyahat; Tel: (2527) 1517.

Edirne

Buses of the Edirne Birlik lines (Tel: 1/576-5732) leave every half hour from the Trakya terminal of the Topkapı bus station in Istanbul. It's a 15-minute walk from Edirne's bus station to Hürriyet Meydanı. Dolmuşes from the bus station will drop you at the parking lot across from the Rüstem Paşa Kervansarayı.

The Istanbul–Edirne train leaves Istanbul's Sirkeci station (Tel: 1/520-6575) daily at 3:40 P.M. for the four-hour trip.

Gallipoli Peninsula

Çanakkale Seyahat (Tel: 1/576-7334) bus lines runs coaches to Gelibolu and Çanakkale every hour from the Trakya terminal at Istanbul's Topkapı bus station. Buses take approximately five hours to Gelibolu, six hours to Çanakkale. Passengers may specify whether they wish to get off the bus at Eceabat or continue on to Çanakkale—a 30-minute ferry ride across the Dardanelles (waiting for the ferry brings the crossing time to an hour).

It's a four-hour drive from Istanbul to Gelibolu by private car via the E 24 highway toward Keşan. Instead of driving to Keşan, you can also take a left for Şarköy just after Tekirdağ. You'll neither lose nor gain time via this second route, but you'll be driving through scenic countryside and leaving the heavy traffic behind.

The car ferry between Lâpseki and Gelibolu leaves every hour around the clock, as do the ferries from Eceabat and Kilitbahir to Çanakkale. Arrive 30 minutes before departure time and buy a ticket.

ACCOMMODATIONS REFERENCE

Rates given below are for double rooms, double occupancy, and represent projections for 1993. Where a range in rates appears, this reflects the difference in price between the high season and the low season. In cities and along the coasts of the Black Sea and the Sea of Marmara, the low season is (generally) from November through March; the high season is from April through October. In the ski resort of Uludağ, however, the high season is from mid-December through the end of March. All prices are subject to change and should be checked before booking. Some hotels and pensions include breakfast. When telephoning between cities in Turkey, dial 9 before entering the city code.

▶ **Balta Oteli.** Talatpaşa Asfaltı 97, Ayşekadın, 22110 **Edirne.** Tel: (181) 152-10; Fax: (181) 135-29. $28.

▶ **Beceren Oteli.** Uludağ Oteller Bölgesi, **Uludağ,** 16355 Bursa. Tel: (2418) 5111; Fax: (2418) 5119. $86 (includes three meals; open from Dec. 15–Mar. 31 only).

▶ **Boncuk Otel.** Fener Ovası Mevkii, **Gelibolu.** Tel: (1891) 1452. $48.

▶ **Büyükada Princess Hotel.** İskele Meydanı 2, **Büyükada** 81330 Istanbul. Tel: (1) 382-1628; Fax: (1) 382-1949. $80–$100.

▶ **Büyük Hotel.** Uludağ Oteller Bölgesi, **Uludağ,** 16355 Bursa. Tel: (2418) 5216; Fax: (2418) 5220. $41–$77 (high season, Dec.–Mar.).

▶ **Çamlık Motel and Café.** Göl Kenarı, **İznik.** Tel: (2527) 1631. $16.

▶ **Çelik Palas Oteli.** Çekirge Caddesi 79, 16080 **Bursa.** Tel: (24) 35-35-00; Fax: (24) 36-19-10. $91.

▶ **Değirmen Hotel.** Değirmen Turizm Sanayı ve Ticaret A.Ş., Plaj Yolu 24, **Şile,** 80801 Istanbul. Tel: (1992) 1048; Fax: (1992) 1248. $34–$44.

▶ **Ece Hotel.** İskele Meydanı, **Eceabat**, Çanakkale. Tel: (1964) 1770. $20.

▶ **Gönlüferah Termal Hotel.** 1'inci Murat Caddesi 24, Çekirge, 16090 **Bursa.** Tel: (24) 36-27-00; Fax: (24) 36-77-96. $41.

▶ **Grand Yazıcı Hotel.** Uludağ Oteller Bölgesi, **Uludağ**, 16355 Bursa. Tel: (2418) 5050; Fax: (2418) 5048. $57–$85 (includes three meals; high season, Dec.–Mar.).

▶ **Kervan Hotel.** Talatpaşa Caddesi, Kadırhane Sokak 134, 22200 **Edirne.** Tel: (181) 113-82, 113-85, or 111-67; Telex: 37194. $23–$32.

▶ **Kervansaray Bursa Hotel.** Fevzi Çakmak Caddesi 29, **Bursa.** Tel: (24) 20-00-00; Fax: (24) 20-00-15. $69.

▶ **Kervansaray Termal Hotel.** Çekirge Meydanı, Anatolia Oteli Karşısı, 16080 **Bursa.** Tel: (24) 35-30-00; Fax: (24) 35-30-24. $128.

▶ **Kervansaray Uludağ Hotel.** Uludağ Oteller Bölgesi, **Uludağ**, 16355 Bursa. Tel: (2418) 5187; Fax: (2418) 5193. $36–$91 (includes three meals; high season, Dec.–Mar.).

▶ **Kilyos Kale Otel.** Kale Caddesi 78, **Kilyos**, 80905 Istanbul. Tel: (1882) 1054 or 1295. $30.

▶ **Motel Kumbaba.** P.O. Box 4, **Şile**, 80801 Istanbul. Tel: (1992) 1038. $57.

▶ **Otel Çamlıbel.** Ulucami Karşısı, İnebey Caddesi 71, **Bursa.** Tel: (24) 21-25-65 or 22-55-65. $14.

▶ **Rüstem Paşa Kervansarayı.** İki Kapılı Han Caddesi 57, **Edirne.** Tel: (181) 121-95, 204-62, or 269-18; Fax: (181) 204-62. $70.

▶ **Saros Oteli.** İskele Meydanı, **Eceabat**, Çanakkale. Tel: (1964) 1770. $30.

▶ **Şato Oteli.** Feneryolu 9, **Şile**, 80801 Istanbul. Tel: (1992) 1075 or 1345; Fax: (1992) 1511. $32.

▶ **Splendid Otel.** 23 Nisan Caddesi 71, **Büyükada**, 81330 Istanbul. Tel: (1) 382-6950. $81.

▶ **Sultan Hotel.** Talatpaşa Bulvarı 24, 22100 **Edirne.** Tel: (181) 113-72 or 133-33; Fax: (181) 157-63. $33.

▶ **Turban Çamlık Hotel** and **Turban Çınar Hotel.** c/o Turban Yalova Termal Tesisleri, **Termal**, 81890 Yalova, Istanbul. Tel: (1938) 1400; Fax: (1938) 1413. $52.

▶ **Turban Kilyos Tatil Köyü.** **Sarıyer**, 80905 Istanbul. Tel: (1882) 1480; Fax: (1882) 1028. $79.

▶ **Yonca Hotel.** Kale Caddesi 3, **Kilyos**, 80905 Istanbul. Tel: (1882) 1045. $25.

▶ **Zafer Motel.** Bozcaada, **Çanakkale.** Tel: (1965) 1078 or 1113. $19.

AEGEAN TURKEY

By Sherry Marker

Sherry Marker first visited Turkey when she served as assistant recorder for the Sardis Excavation in 1964. After studying archaeology at the American School of Classical Studies in Athens she did graduate work in ancient history at Harvard and the University of California at Berkeley. She travels regularly in Aegean Turkey and has published articles in Travel & Leisure *magazine and* The New York Times.

Even the most experienced travellers have been dazzled by Aegean Turkey. Pausanias, the second-century A.D. antiquarian who journeyed through Greece, Italy, Palestine, Egypt, and Asia Minor, said that Ionia, in the heart of Aegean Turkey, enjoyed "the finest of climates, with sanctuaries unmatched in the world." The superb climate and the well-preserved Greek and Roman antiquities are as likely to enchant you today as they did Pausanias. Furthermore, that ideal climate lets you take advantage of the perfect complement to all those antiquities: Aegean Turkey's superb sand beaches.

When you set out, keep in mind that Aegean Turkey stretches 300 miles from Çanakkale in the north to Bodrum, where the Mediterranean begins, in the south. Although a good asphalted road runs all the way along the coast, heavily laden trucks travel slowly, buses stop unexpectedly, and progress is leisurely. And when you work your way inland through the mountain ranges that wall off the irregularly indented coast of western Anatolia from the Anatolian heartland, progress grows even slower.

It is possible, though not advisable, to see the major

archaeological sites in one very vigorous week. If you base yourself in İzmir you can take in a number of sites on day trips and reserve overnight jaunts for Troy, Pamukkale, and Kuşadası. However, if you want to see some of the smaller sites, enjoy the seaside, and take in the pleasures of today's Turkey, try to allow at least two weeks.

MAJOR INTEREST

The Seven Churches of Asia

İzmir and Vicinity
İzmir, Turkey's third-largest city
Çeşme's port, fortress, sand beaches, and resort
  hotels
The harbor town of Sığacık
The temple of Dionysus at Teos
Manisa's well-preserved Ottoman mosques
Sardis, the capital of the Lydian king Croesus
The hilltowns of the Bozdağlar

North of İzmir
Greco-Roman ruins at Pergamum and Assos
Seaside villages of Foça, Çandarlı, Ayvalık, and
  Babakale
The mound of Troy

South of İzmir
Greco-Roman ruins at Ephesus, Priene, Miletus,
  Didyma, and Aphrodisias
Kuşadası, Aegean Turkey's liveliest resort town
The calcified springs of Pamukkale and the remains
  of ancient Hierapolis
Carian mountain sites of Alinda, Alabanda, Labranda,
  and Gerga

No matter how carefully you plan your route through Aegean Turkey, you'll find you must do some time-consuming backtracking in order to cover the entire coast *and* visit the major inland archaeological sites. If you head north from İzmir—the hub of Aegean Turkey—you can take in the seaside resort towns (and fine beaches) of Foça and Çandarlı before heading inland to the important Hellenistic site of Pergamum, with its spectacular setting and vertiginous theater. Then rejoin the coastal road and work your way north into the Troad, stopping at the resort town of Ayvalık, the magical seaside village of Behramkale, and the temples of Assos and Chryse before arriving at Troy itself.

From Troy you'll have to retrace your steps back toward

İzmir before heading inland to visit a cluster of important archaeological sites: Sardis, the capital of King Croesus's Lydia; Aphrodisias, an important Greek and Roman cult center of the goddess Aphrodite; and Hierapolis (the modern Pamukkale), the ancient city that grew up around an extraordinary sulfur-spring spa that still draws visitors today. After your inland detour you can rejoin the coast south of İzmir to visit the important Ionian sites of Ephesus, Priene, Miletus, and Didyma, as well as the spirited resort town of Kuşadası. By now you may be feeling the need for a vacation from your vacation, which makes an excursion to the Çeşme peninsula southwest of İzmir, with its fine beaches and good resort hotels, an ideal last stop before heading home from İzmir airport.

All those beaches make it tempting to visit Aegean Turkey in the summer, when you can be assured of clear skies and temperatures in the 80s and 90s Fahrenheit. Still, if you can possibly visit in the spring or fall, do. In April, May, September, and October the sea will be delicious and the restaurants, hotels, and ancient sites will be considerably less crowded— and less hot. If you visit Aegean Turkey in the winter, bring rain gear and, especially if you're heading inland, warm clothes: Snowfall can be heavy in the mountains.

Whenever you visit Aegean Turkey, be aware that once-tranquil spots along the Aegean coast like Kuşadası, Ayvalık, and Foça are becoming riddled with hotels and holiday apartments, souvenir shops, and discos. In addition, ever-increasing numbers of Turks from rural villages are moving to such provincial capitals as İzmir, Manisa, Aydın, and Denizli in search of jobs, so these cities are being rapidly enveloped in new districts with rows of anonymous apartment buildings. But don't despair: Many wonderfully deserted coves remain, and some small villages, like Çandarlı and Behramkale, have yet to become major tourist destinations. And in the cities, the Ottoman mosques, bazaars, and street markets you want to see are still there—only now they're usually found in the "old" quarter of town.

If you're a woman travelling alone, most Turks *will* think it odd—and then probably do everything they can to help you (including accompanying you to the restaurant or archaeological site you can't find). Once you're where you wanted to be, your volunteer guide will usually disappear as quickly as a genie—often only after thanking you for allowing him to practice his English! If you find yourself with someone who speaks, reasonably enough, only Turkish, you'll be surprised at how patient and ingenious most Turks are when you produce halting phrases and flail your map about for help. (One thing to remember, especially if you're not a woman: Don't photograph or even stare as much as you might like at the brightly costumed Turkish women working in the country-side. It's considered rude and improper.)

With so many ancient sites to visit and so many beaches to relax on, it's easy to forget that one of the great pleasures of visiting Aegean Turkey is the everyday Turkey of today: An hour in a sweet shop surreptitiously spying on families enjoying plates of cream-covered pastries, a glimpse of a wedding party arriving for a banquet at a country restaurant, or a stroll through towns like Salihli and Çanakkale to see what's for sale in the *non*tourist shops can be every bit as memorable as time spent in more traditional touristic pursuits.

So, try to make haste slowly, allowing time for the ancient sites, the beaches, the mosques, the markets—without neglecting the fields of poppies and wild irises, stands of poplars, groves of cherry and peach trees, or the sight of storks and herons overhead, lizards underfoot, and tortoises lumbering through olive groves (and, all too often, across main roads). You may even spot a camel or two—but if you don't, remember that they always *were* more common inland.

GRECO-ROMAN AEGEAN TURKEY

Even though you may have been drawn to Aegean Turkey by such famous ancient sites as Troy, Ephesus, and Pergamum, once you start travelling here you may be startled at just how thick on the ground the Greek and Roman ruins are. That's because Aegean Turkey was such an integral part of the Greek world that scholars refer to it as "East Greece" (despite the fact that numerous non-Greek peoples, such as Hittites, Mysians, Trojans, Carians, Lydians, and Phrygians lived here).

Many myths give a good idea of the bonds that linked the Greek mainland and the western coast of Anatolia. There's the story of Auge, a slave from Arcadia in southern Greece, who married a king of Mysia and founded the first ruling dynasty of the city of Pergamum. There's Endymion, possibly a king of Elis in the Peloponnese, who fell in love with the goddess of the moon on distant Mount Latmus in Aegean Turkey. And there are the legends that settlers from Crete founded Chryse and Miletus, and that the first settlers at Sardis were the descendants of the greatest hero in the Peloponnese, Heracles.

Some of these legends seem to have a basis in fact. Minoans from Crete did explore the coast of Aegean Turkey and may have founded Miletus, where evidence of a Mycenaean settlement (ca. 1600 B.C.) has been found. Homer tells us that Agamemnon led the Greek host to Troy to recapture Helen, but it was probably not until about a hundred years after the fall of Troy (ca. 1250 B.C.) that a considerable number of immigrants from mainland Greece, fleeing the upheavals of the Dorian invasion, arrived to stay. They seem to have settled first on the island of Lesvos and then moved across to the Troad (the region around Troy). According to tradition, these first Greek immigrants were the Aeolians, and the area north of İzmir (ancient Smyrna) and south of the Troad where they lived was called Aeolis.

In the tenth century B.C. an even larger group of Greeks, the Ionians, also fleeing unsettled conditions in Greece, emigrated to the area south of Aeolis, soon known as Ionia. The Ionians believed that they were descended from Ion, a grandson of the legendary Athenian king Erechtheus. In a sense, descent from Erechtheus gave the Ionians a certain cachet, by making them honorary Athenians. Athens was to honor this tie when it assisted the Ionian cities in their revolt against Persia in the fifth century B.C.

By the eighth century B.C. the 12 cities of the Greek Ionian League, of which Miletus, Samos, and Ephesus were the most powerful, were more than a match for anything on the Greek mainland. The Greeks' first poets, including Homer, lived in these cities; their first philosophers, scientists, and town planners worked here; and some of the finest temples in the Greek world were built not in mainland Greece but in East Greece. Two architectural orders—the Aeolic and the Ionic—were born here. The Aeolic order never attained enormous popularity, but the Ionic order, with its spreading scroll-shaped column capitals, flourished here by the sixth century B.C. and spread to mainland Greece in the fifth century B.C. You'll see examples of the Ionic order at almost every site you visit, with some of the finest examples at temples in Ephesus, Sardis, Priene, and Didyma.

In the mid-sixth century B.C. the Persian Empire conquered Anatolia, ruling the Greek cities with what was by all accounts a light hand. Still, in 499 B.C. a number of the cities revolted against their Persian rulers in what the fifth-century B.C. historian Herodotus called "the beginning of the troubles": the Ionian revolt. The revolt was quelled in 494 B.C., but the troubles continued when the Persians invaded Greece, first in 490 B.C. and again in 480 to 479. Their motive was simple: revenge for Athens's support of the revolt and the Greeks' destruction of the Persian headquarters at Sardis. Against enormous odds, Athens and its allies repulsed the Persians;

thereafter, the balance of power in the Greek world shifted from the cities of Ionia to Athens and Sparta.

Although the eastern cities had lost much of their political clout, they continued to prosper, and after Alexander the Great conquered Persia in 331 B.C., they again surpassed the cities of mainland Greece in wealth and influence. Alexander died too soon to rule his empire, which was quarreled over and dismembered by his generals, one of whom, Lysimachus, brought stability to much of the Aegean coast by financing the establishment of the kingdom of Pergamum in 281 B.C. As a result, the Hellenistic era—the roughly 300 years from the reign of Alexander the Great (336 to 323 B.C.) to the Roman emperor Augustus (31 B.C. to A.D. 14)—so chaotic throughout much of the empire amassed by Alexander, was something of a golden age in Aegean Turkey. You'll see superb Hellenistic remains at Pergamum, and almost everything at Priene dates from the period after 350 B.C..

In 133 B.C. King Attalus III of Pergamum bequeathed his kingdom (which included most of Aegean Turkey) to the Romans, whose territorial ambitions had led them to intervene in the incessant quarrels that raged throughout the Hellenistic world. The Romans organized most of the territory of the kingdom of Pergamum as their province of Asia—and sent generations of officials off to administer it. For the third time—first under the Persians, then under the kingdom of Pergamum, now under the Romans—the cities of the Aegean coast were embraced within an empire.

During the Roman republic, and especially during the terrible years of the civil war in the first century B.C., Rome systematically fleeced the province of Asia for taxes; during the first three centuries of the empire, however, Rome began to give as well as take. Most of the libraries, gymnasiums, stadiums, fountain houses, monumental gates, and refurbished temples you'll see as you travel up and down the coast date, in fact, from the first and second centuries A.D., when the Romans benignly administered the Greek cities of Aegean Turkey. Edward Gibbon considered the second century A.D., the period of the *Pax Romana,* to have been the happiest period in human history.

This was when the cities of Ephesus, Pergamum, and Nysa were important centers of culture and learning, just as Miletus had been in the sixth century B.C. Even at Miletus the most impressive monuments—the theater and the baths of Faustina—are Roman, as are four other beautifully restored buildings in Aegean Turkey: the temple of Trajan at Pergamum, the Marble Court at Sardis, the Tetrapylon at Aphrodisias, and the library of Celsus at Ephesus.

This happy period of culture and prosperity ended for many of the East Greek cities not because of war or famine but because of nature. Almost all the Ionian cities had been built on or very near the sea, many in seemingly ideal sites in the fertile delta of the Cayster and Meander rivers (the modern Küçük Menderes and Büyük Menderes rivers). Yet, as Seton Lloyd points out in his delightful *Ancient Turkey: A Traveller's History of Anatolia,* the cities' "ultimate fate was already sealed when their sites were chosen . . . for each was soon to discover its own evil genius in the river whose favours it had at first so eagerly courted and beside whose mouth its temples and warehouses had so unsuspectingly been built."

Over the centuries the coastal Ionian cities were buried beneath alluvial deposits. So it takes something of a leap of faith, when you sit in the theater at Ephesus or Miletus, to visualize what you would have seen from that seat in antiquity: ships sailing into harbors that are now broad alluvial plains. Many cities (Ephesus, Miletus, Teos, Alexandria Troas) declined when their harbors silted up. Another, Heracleia, was left marooned inland when silt from the Meander transformed its harbor into an inland lake. Small wonder that the ancients called the Meander "relentless."

After you've visited the remains of several ancient cities (armed with the good site maps that can be found in the guidebooks sold at most ancient sites), you'll start to get the hang of deciphering what the 17th-century traveller Edmund Chishull once despairingly called these "venerable heaps of rubbish." You'll notice that each city contains, from its Greek period, an acropolis, some temples, a theater, a central agora (marketplace), one or more gymnasiums, a stadium—and, of course, houses. From the Roman period there will be more houses and temples and a number of new kinds of buildings: baths and monumental gates, at least one *nymphaeum* (fountain house), an odeon (concert hall), and perhaps a library. From the period of the Byzantine Empire there will probably be the remains of a church or two as well as massive fortification walls, built in an ultimately vain attempt to hold invaders at bay. And from the Turkish period, more houses, some fortifications, and perhaps a mosque and a caravansary.

The Byzantine and Ottoman remains of Aegean Turkey are reminders of the centuries when the once-proud cities of Asia Minor were at best frontier outposts. Surviving Byzantine monuments here are few: The sixth-century church of St. John at Selçuk is the most impressive. In some cities, such as Aphrodisias and Miletus, an ancient theater was converted into a Byzantine fortress. In others, such as Heracleia and

Assos, Hellenistic defense walls were incorporated into Byzantine and Turkish fortifications.

Through the period of the Byzantine Empire, Aegean Turkey's history is a weary catalog of invasions and campaigns. The coast was raided by the Arabs in the seventh century and fought over by the Byzantines and Seljuk Turks in the 11th century. In the 14th century its remaining good harbors were occupied intermittently by the Venetians and Genoese, and much of the area was buffeted by Tamerlane's armies in the early 15th century. After Sultan Mehmet II seized Constantinople in 1453, Manisa flourished, and its Ottoman monuments are well worth a visit. Yet only one of the cities of Aegean Turkey—İzmir—was again to attain the wealth and prominence that a cluster of cities on this coast had held in antiquity.

When the first European antiquarians began to travel to Aegean Turkey in the 17th century in search of the region's Greco-Roman past, most based themselves in İzmir. One of the most famous was the Englishman Richard Chandler, who was sent out by the London-based Society of Dilettanti to note "every Circumstance which could contribute towards giving the best Idea of the ancient and present State" of the ancient sites within a ten-day–journey's radius from İzmir. Like Chandler, you may well base yourself at İzmir, although it will only take you an hour or two to reach sites that took him days to reach.

İZMİR

With 2.7 million inhabitants, İzmir (the former Smyrna) is Turkey's third-largest city, after Istanbul and Ankara, and, after Istanbul, its second-largest port. The capital of the province of the same name, İzmir is the focal point of the entire Aegean coast, and highways into the city are clogged with open trucks loaded with entire households bringing villagers in search of work.

You'll see more new arrivals (the women in headscarves and baggy flowered pants, the men in somber suits, the children looking dazed) if you stand at the Basmane railroad station, the intercity bus station by the Atatürk stadium in Halkapınar, or at the *dolmuş* stop at Turgut Reis park. If you drive into İzmir, you'll probably be looking pretty dazed

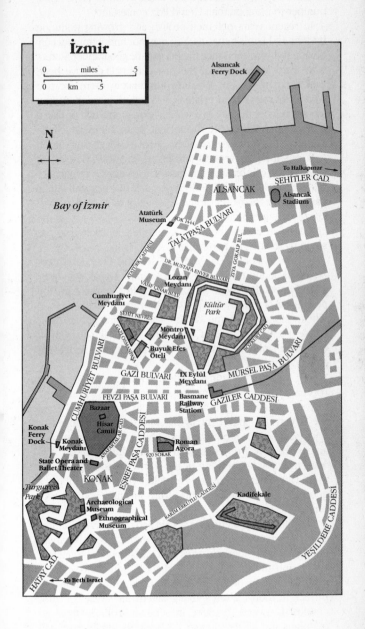

İzmir

0   miles   .5

0   km   .5

N

Bay of İzmir

Alsancak
Ferry Dock

To Halkapınar →

ŞEHİTLER CAD.

ALSANCAK

Alsancak
Stadium

Atatürk
Museum

SOK 1441

TALATPAŞA BULVARI

DR. MUSTAFA ENVER BULVARI

ZIYA GÖKALP BUL.

ATATÜRK CADDESİ

VASIF ÇINAR BULV.

Lozan
Meydanı

Cumhuriyet
Meydanı

Kültür
Park

ŞEHİT NEVRES

GAZİ OSMAN PAŞA

Montro
Meydanı

Buyuk Efes
Oteli

BOZKURT CAD.

MÜRSEL PAŞA BULVARI

CUMHURİYET BULVARI

GAZİ BULVARI

IX Eylül
Meydanı

GAZİLER CADDESİ

FEVZİ PAŞA BULVARI

Basmane
Railway
Station

Bazaar

Hisar
Camii

ANAFARTALAR CAD.

EŞREF PAŞA CADDESİ

Konak
Ferry
Dock

Konak
Meydanı

State Opera and
Ballet Theater

Roman
Agora

920 SOKAK

KONAK

*Turgutreis
Park*

Archaeological
Museum

Ethnographical
Museum

RAKIM ERKUTLU CADDESİ

Kadifekale

YEŞİLDERE CADDESİ

HATAY CAD.

← To Beth Israel

yourself by the time you reach your hotel: Street signs are few and far between, and many locals seem to drive faster, bumper to bumper, than Grand Prix contestants.

In recent years pell-mell growth and growing pollution have muted İzmir's charms. You may not find it immediately obvious why visitors since the peripatetic geographer Strabo, who lived at the turn of the first century B.C., have been captivated by the city's beauty. Fortunately, there are two wonderful ways to appreciate İzmir's superb location *and* get an overview of the city as a whole. First, grab a taxi or take a dolmuş up to **Kadifekale**, the ancient Mount Pagus, which the Turks call the Velvet Fortress because of its soft glow at sunset.

If possible, go around sunset, when locals (known as *İzmirli*s) stroll through the grounds inside the remains of the medieval fortress. Children play and fly kites while their parents sip cool drinks or glasses of tea at cafés. Join them to enjoy the superb view from the ramparts down across the city and out across the 30-mile-long bay, bracketed to the south by the Çeşme peninsula.

On the water below you can see the little ferryboats plying back and forth from İzmir's central Konak square or the Alsancak ferryboat station across to Karşıyaka on the north side of the bay. If you walk down from Kadifekale (on whose slopes sit some of the few remaining old İzmir houses) and catch one of the ferries at Konak square, you can enjoy İzmir's second great view: the city and Kadifekale as seen from the sea.

On summer evenings, when İzmir's beloved *imbat* (breeze) sweeps in from the sea and night shrouds the legions of unfinished buildings, the city is at its best. Then the street and apartment lights shine from the slopes of Kadifekale, itself often illuminated at night. The view back across the bay from Karşıyaka is splendid, and you may want to enjoy it from one of the many seafood restaurants there (the **Palet**, where you can select your own fish, has a good reputation among locals). Thus fortified, you can take on İzmir.

Despite İzmir's increasing sprawl and dense traffic, almost everything you want to see—the museums, the lively bazaar, elegant shops, sidewalk cafés and restaurants, the ancient agora, and the green expanse of the Kültür Park—is centrally located on or just off Atatürk Caddesi (also known as Birinci Kordon), İzmir's main waterfront street. (Atatürk Caddesi is closed to traffic in summer from 7:00 P.M. to midnight and all day Sunday.) A brisk 30-minute walk will take you from the Atatürk Museum on Atatürk Caddesi south through Cumhuriyet Meydanı (Republic Square) along the waterfront to Konak square and then uphill past Turgut Reis park to the Archaeological and Ethnographical museums.

Then, in about an hour (that is, if you ignore the tempting distractions en route), you can head back to Konak square, walk through İzmir's bazaar to the ancient agora, thence head north past the Basmane railroad station into the Kültür Park, before strolling back to the sea at Cumhuriyet Meydanı. In short, İzmir is easy to explore on foot, although the somewhat confusing traffic roundabouts may make you wish that İzmir had been laid out according to a proper fourth-century B.C. Hippodamian grid plan. (Many İzmir streets are numbered, but in the absence of a grid pattern, the rationale behind this system is elusive at best.)

A few words of caution before you set off: Do *not* assume that crossing at one of İzmir's infrequent traffic lights guarantees a safe passage. Striped pedestrian crossways are evidently used merely to decorate the otherwise monochrome surface of the streets—not to assist pedestrians. Proceed with caution. And don't be too busy looking left and right at the traffic not to look down: Many of İzmir's curbs are inordinately high.

Atatürk Caddesi, lined with slender palm trees, is interrupted by two important squares: **Konak**, with its 1901 Moorish-style clock tower (İzmir's unofficial symbol), and **Cumhuriyet Meydanı**, with the prominent equestrian statue of Mustafa Kemal Atatürk, known as the **İstiklâl Anıtı** (Independence Monument). Atatürk is shown pointing out to sea in commemoration of the Turkish liberation of İzmir in 1922, which proved to be the decisive event in the Turkish War of Independence.

The war began in 1919. In 1920, Greece, encouraged by the major European powers, invaded Ottoman Anatolia. On August 26, 1922, the Turkish offensive, led by General Mustafa Kemal, who became the first president of the Republic of Turkey in 1923, routed the Greek forces in the hinterlands of Anatolia. As the Greek army withdrew to İzmir to escape by sea, Greeks living in Anatolian villages fled ahead of the advancing Turkish army, which took İzmir on September 9. By early September more than 150,000 Greek refugees were camped out on İzmir's quay.

On September 12, in the midst of a ferocious heat wave, a fire broke out in İzmir's Armenian quarter. The fire raged through the narrow streets crowded with half-timber buildings with overhanging upper stories. Like the Great Fire of London in 1666, the İzmir fire could not be extinguished; after three days it burned itself out, leaving three-quarters of the city in ashes. The old Frankish, Armenian, Greek, and

Sephardic Jewish quarters were almost entirely destroyed, and an unknown number of people (estimates range wildly from 2,000 to 50,000) died. In the following year, under provisions of the Treaty of Lausanne, Turkey and Greece undertook a massive exchange of populations. When it was done, almost all ethnic Greeks were removed to Greece and ethnic Turks to Turkey.

Before 1922 İzmir had had such a large foreign population that the Turks had called it "Gâvur İzmir" (Infidel Smyrna). Jews migrated here from Thessaloniki in the late 16th century, and there was also a sizable Armenian community. In 1581 the English Turkey Company established itself in İzmir, and its trade activities drew numerous merchants, including many Greeks, to the area. After 1922 Infidel Smyrna was no more; the new İzmir rose quite literally from its ashes. Today, although İzmir's Greeks and Armenians are gone, the **Beth Israel synagogue** at Mithatpaşa Caddesi serves the city's remaining Jewish community.

It's a short stroll north from Atatürk's statue to the **Atatürk Museum**. The museum occupies the high-ceilinged house Atatürk used whenever he was in İzmir after 1923. Atatürk did not spend a great deal of time in İzmir, and the house gives much more of a sense of a state residence than of an actual home. It is furnished throughout with heavy Victorian furniture, including dark tables, massive chests, and ornate lamps.

To get to İzmir's cheek-by-jowl Archaeological and Ethnographical museums, head south along Atatürk Caddesi. On the way, you may want to browse through the exquisite kilims at **Dağtekin**, on 1382 Sokak, or the silk scarves and fabrics with Ottoman and Anatolian *yazma* (hand-blocked) motifs at **Vakko**, at Atatürk Bulvarı 226. Ignore until later the temptations of the bazaar, and head resolutely for Turgut Reis park. The modern Archaeological Museum (built in 1984) looms above the park; just to the left of its entrance is the handsome gray stone 19th-century Neoclassical mansion housing the Ethnographical Museum. Handily, the Archaeological Museum has a small café.

The **Archaeological Museum** has an extensive collection of artifacts found throughout İzmir province, from a reconstructed grave pit dated to circa 3000 B.C. to Byzantine pottery found in Smyrna and dating to the 14th century A.D. (labels in English and Turkish). A walk through the museum will give you a preview of the sites you will visit outside İzmir: There are portrait heads from Pergamum, column capitals from Didyma, a number of Roman copies of Greek statues from Ephesus, and a marvelous gallery of statues and busts of the important gods and goddesses worshiped throughout ancient Aegean Turkey. The exhibits are exceptionally well organized, some chronologically (Greek and Roman pottery), some by type (statuettes and busts from various periods), others by site (finds from Miletus, Smyrna itself, and elsewhere).

Although some legends say that Homer was born in Smyrna, it was not one of the more important Ionian cities, even though it certainly was one of the most ancient: The earliest known settlement here (at Bayraklı on the northeastern side of the bay of İzmir) dates to the third millennium B.C. You'll see some pottery from this site in the museum's Old Smyrna room, where an explanatory text on the wall suggests that the name Smyrna may have come from Tismura, the name of the settlement here during the Hittite era (ca. 1900 to 1200 B.C.).

Around the tenth century B.C. immigrants from Aeolis settled here, although Smyrna later became one of the Ionian cities. In 600 B.C. the powerful Lydian king Alyattes razed Smyrna and destroyed the temple of Artemis, which its excavator, Ekrem Akurgal, says must have been "the earliest and finest religious building of the eastern Greek world in Asia Minor." Alas, little remains except some architectural fragments, including some possible forerunners of the Ionic volute capital, now in the museum.

After its destruction by Alyattes, Smyrna became an insignificant town until Alexander the Great (who had an eye for such matters and was urged to act in a visionary dream) realized that Mount Pagus would make a splendid acropolis. He ordered a new city to be built beneath the hill, and this new Smyrna, overlooking the bay, must have been exceptionally lovely. This was the city that Strabo called the most beautiful in the world, with more than 100,000 inhabitants and broad streets paved with stone. The Archaeological Museum has several fine statues from a Roman altar that stood in the agora that Strabo visited.

If the Archaeological Museum is educational, the **Ethnographical Museum** next door, focusing on life in 19th-century Smyrna, is enchanting. (Again, labels are in both English and Turkish.) One exhibit, with life-size mannequins, follows a couple from marriage (the bride in cloth of gold) to the birth of their first child (the young mother watches the cradle while the father smokes his water pipe and looks on indulgently). The infant in the ornate wooden cradle appears next as a boy in a silk gown, looking understandably apprehensive, on the eve of his circumcision ceremony. (Observant Muslims are circumcised not shortly after birth but between ages 6 and 13.)

Another room has a diorama of a camel wearing the ornate trappings suitable for the sport of camel-wrestling, still popular in Selçuk (modern Ephesus), the site each January of a camel-wrestling festival. (The camels fight rather like swans, attempting to throttle each other with their long necks.)

Just beyond the camel diorama, a figure of a potter from the town of Menemen (north of İzmir) is shown making jugs on a potter's wheel, a method the label says was first used around 3000 B.C. Yet another exhibit shows glassworkers producing the blue "evil-eye" beads believed to ward off trouble by reflecting the malevolent glance back at the would-be spell-caster. (Those interested in pursuing this topic may wish to purchase the Turkish Touring and Automobile Association's volume *Glass Beads,* on sale at **NET Kitabevi,** a bookstore at Cumhuriyet Bulvarı 142/B.)

If you want to buy and not just read about evil-eye beads, head into İzmir's **Kemeraltı bazaar** (closed Sundays), best reached by following the waterfront past a string of warehouses, cafés, and simple seafood restaurants to Konak square before heading inland along Anafartalar Caddesi, which hooks through the bazaar area. (Before you head into the bazaar, check at the State Opera and Ballet Theater on Milli Kütüphane Caddesi to see what's on. Even if there's no performance scheduled during your stay in İzmir, the Baroque-style theater is worth a glance.)

If you manage to keep on Anafartalar Caddesi and don't get lost in the bazaar, you'll emerge near the ancient **Roman agora.** Archaeologists think that the commercial agora was nearer the harbor; the second-century A.D. agora you see here was Smyrna's state agora, which had a number of civic buildings, such as law courts, as well as shops. The agora, with its large central courtyard flanked by stoas, was largely rebuilt after the catastrophic earthquake of A.D. 178, which leveled the city and reportedly brought tears to the eyes of Emperor Marcus Aurelius when he learned of it. Probably the most impressive remains in the agora are those of the well-preserved vaulted basement of the north stoa.

With so many more impressive antiquities to see outside İzmir, it's forgivable to turn away from the agora and yield to the temptations of the bazaar—especially if you're not going to Istanbul. İzmir's bazaar is considerably less impressive than Istanbul's, with many shops simply selling everyday necessities such as clothes, electrical appliances, and china and glassware. This bazaar is still more a city market than a tourist attraction, and that is its charm. If you follow your eyes into the bazaar, your nose will take you from Anafartalar Caddesi to the side street with the fish market, and your ears will lead you on to where songbirds are for sale.

Look up from time to time and you'll see the minarets of a number of mosques, including the **Hacı Mehmet Ağa Camii** (1672) and the imposing single-domed **Hisar Camii** (1598), İzmir's oldest mosque, originally a church. The 17th-century han next to Hisar Camii is being restored and should be open to visitors in 1993. The mid-17th-century **Kastane Pazarı Camii** (Mosque of the Chestnut Market) and the late-17th-century **Sadırvanaltı Camii** (Mosque of the Fountain)—the latter currently closed for restoration—are both built on raised platforms above shops. At Kurban Bayramı (Feast of the Sacrifice), May 31 through June 4 in 1993, sheep are sold from pens outside the mosque and slaughtered in a make-shift butcher's shop tucked between a bookstore and a latrine.

It's hard not to stop at one of the first shops you pass on Anafartalar Caddesi as you enter the bazaar: the **Ali Galip Pastanesi** (pastry shop), with delicious confections and past-ries. If you don't want to begin your visit to the bazaar with a sweet, you'll have no trouble finding stalls and shops selling pastries, as well as *döner* and *şiş kebap, portakal suyu* (orange juice), and *ayran* (a watered yogurt drink) through-out the bazaar.

You'll also find whatever fruits and vegetables are in season, the inevitable rug and leather shops (virtually all the "designer" leather goods are knockoffs), and sacks of herbs and spices—from henna and hot peppers to apple, cherry, lemon, and orange tea. You may even encounter vendors of medicinal leeches walking along clanking glass jars filled with their offerings. (İzmir has a number of excellent hospi-tals, by the way, including the **American Hospital**, (at 1375 Sok, number 10, near the Hilton Hotel; the hospital is staffed by NATO physicians.)

Staying and Dining in İzmir

It's a good idea to have a decent hotel lined up before you reach İzmir—and it's vital to have a reservation if you plan to be in town during the trade fair held in the vast Kültür Park during the last week in August and first two weeks in September. If you do arrive in İzmir without a hotel reserva-tion, try checking at the **tourist office** in the Büyük Efes Oteli complex just behind the Atatürk statue; Tel: (51) 22-02-07 or 21-68-41. This is also a good place to find out what's on in İzmir, including concerts, theater, and the frequent modern-art exhibitions in local galleries and banks. The tourist office has a comprehensive list of İzmir's hotels, among which the comfortable **İzmir Palas** and the slightly more spartan and less modern—but recently renovated—**Hotel Karaca** are good choices. The new İzmir Etap, highly touted as a luxury hotel, is gloomy, with substantial cracks already appearing in its walls. A longtime favorite, the **Hotel Kısmet**, run by the same family that owns the Kısmet in Kuşadası (see below), has recently been redecorated; like its counterpart in Kuşadası, the İzmir Kısmet has excellent food.

Distinctly not inexpensive is the massive **Büyük Efes Oteli**, with swimming pool, Turkish bath, sauna, cafés, and shops. For years this was İzmir's only grand hotel, and it is still the city's only hotel with real style, as opposed to those hotels that go in for splashes of ostentation in the lobby and, all too often, signs of rapid deterioration in the rooms. Whether you stay at the Büyük Efes or not, try to have an afternoon drink in the garden terrace café, where you will see businessmen entertaining women obviously young enough to be their daughters (and equally obviously *not* their daughters). The Büyük Efes's pool is open to nonguests for a fee of about $12. The new **İzmir Hilton**, located just behind the Büyük Efes Oteli, may challenge its position as İzmir's premier hotel. The Hilton includes an upscale shopping complex.

If you do splurge and stay at the Büyük Efes, you can assuage your guilt and honor both your budget and Turkey's ancestral links with the Mongols with a reasonably priced dinner at the succinctly named **Chinese Restaurant** behind the hotel at 1379 Sokak 57/A. Better yet, have a splendid outdoor meal of mixed hors d'oeuvres and grilled meat and onions just around the corner at the **Cevat Dev** restaurant at Kazım Dirik Caddesi 3/CC, 2'nci Kordon. Eating at the Cevat Dev is almost as good as being in the country—which is where you'll probably soon head from İzmir.

If you want seafood, try the İzmir Palas hotel's elegant **Deniz** restaurant, which has a good reputation for fresh fish. A few doors away is the **Sirena**, whose sidewalk tables are favored by İzmir's *jeunesse dorée*, who sit sipping beers or toying with plates of fresh fruit. The traffic along Atatürk Caddesi can be bothersome, and you may find it more congenial to head inland to one of the streets where cars are not allowed, such as Sok 1444 in the Alsancak district, where the pleasant **Altın Kapı Döner Salonu** (Golden Door Döner Salon) sets up outdoor tables in fine weather. On the same street, **Pandora's Pub**, with a small garden, sometimes attracts an American contingent from the nearby NATO headquarters on Atatürk Caddesi.

SIDE TRIPS FROM İZMİR

Although you'll spend most of your time in Aegean Turkey travelling up and down the coast, you may want to consider several side trips from İzmir. Tours of all the Seven Churches of Asia, mentioned in Revelation, the final book of the New Testament, are possible from İzmir, although most visitors will visit only the better-known sites at Ephesus, Sardis, and Pergamum. It is possible, though not ideal, to take in Sardis, the capital of the ancient Lydian Empire, 76 km (47 miles) east of İzmir in the fertile valley of the Hermus river (the modern Gediz Nehri), as a long day trip from İzmir. And the town of Çeşme, at the end of the peninsula of the same name, is only 80 km (50 miles) west of İzmir. However, because the pleasures of the peninsula are considerable—beaches, seaside towns, and the splendid temple of Teos—a day trip onto the peninsula would be terribly rushed.

The Seven Churches of Asia

On your travels through Aegean Turkey you'll probably visit the sites of at least some of the Seven Churches of Asia (Smyrna, Ephesus, Laodicea, Philadelphia, Sardis, Thyatira, and Pergamum). The churches are associated both with Saint Paul and with Revelation (or the Apocalypse), a letter to the Seven Churches written around A.D. 95 by a visionary called John (not the Apostle John), who lived on the Greek island of Patmos.

There were considerably more than seven cities with substantial Christian congregations in Asia Minor at the time that John wrote, and it's not known why he addressed only these seven. Possibly they were the most important at that time; possibly letters to other churches have been lost. The "churches" were not church buildings, but congregations; in fact, these early congregations usually met in private homes, because Christians did not begin to build actual churches until the third century A.D.

Saint Paul had probably founded some of the Seven Churches on his travels in Asia between A.D. 47 and 57; he quite possibly visited all seven cities. Most of the churches

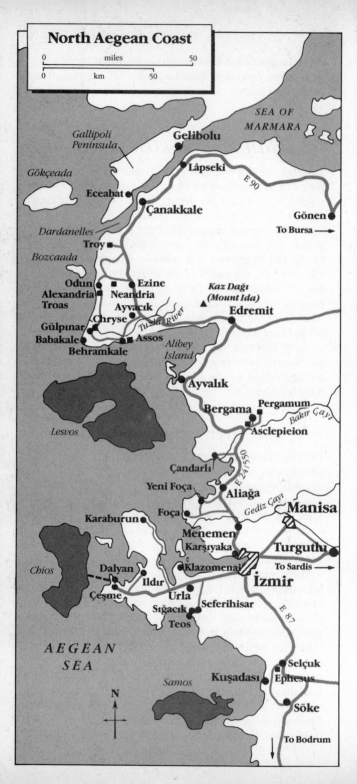

that Paul visited were in substantial cities, as Christianity had spread fastest among the urban poor. In fact, the new religion was initially such an urban phenomenon that the early converts scornfully called non-Christians *pagani* (pagans), the Latin word for country-dwellers.

Two of the Seven Churches were in cities that have not yet been properly excavated and are largely hidden under modern towns: Philadelphia, today's Alaşehir, east of Sardis, and Thyatira, 56 km (35 miles) southeast of Pergamum, now the town of Akhisar. A third, Laodicea (discussed below), once one of the most prosperous cities in Phrygia, has considerable scattered remains but is seldom visited today because most travellers head instead for nearby Hierapolis (modern Pamukkale).

A tour limited to the Seven Churches will appeal most to those with a serious interest in the history of the early church. Information on tours of the Seven Churches is available from travel agents or at the İzmir tourist office.

Çeşme

People used to go to Çeşme (80 km/50 miles west of İzmir and signposted on the E 24/550) primarily to catch the ferry to the Greek island of Chios some six miles offshore; in recent years the town itself, with its Genoese fortress, tumbledown houses, old mosques, and nearby stretches of sand beaches, has begun to draw visitors. If at all possible, try to stay in Çeşme for a few days: That way you can enjoy both the town and the peninsula, with its varied landscape of seaside coves and crescent-shaped beaches, wheat fields and bleak plateaus, pine-covered hills and groves of fruit trees, the tiny port of Sığacık, and the temple of Teos.

It's a good thing that Çeşme and the surrounding countryside are so enticing, because the drive here from İzmir is grueling, though the new İzmir–Çeşme highway, which opened in August 1992, should make the journey less wearying. En route to Çeşme (the name means "spring") you'll pass the turnoff for the so-called **baths of Agamemnon**, 10 km (6 miles) out of İzmir. Legend has it that Agamemnon sent soldiers wounded at Troy here to recuperate; today the simple bath facilities attract a local clientele as well as a good number of Scandinavian visitors.

Swimming—or floating—in Çeşme's thermal springs is rather like being immersed in warm champagne. If this seems too sybaritic, there's more than enough to see to keep you busy with excursions. You'll want to begin with Çeşme town, which has somehow avoided the excesses of tourism so

evident farther south (at Kuşadası) and north (at Ayvalık).
Along the harbor are some fine 19th-century buildings with
overhanging wooden balconies and pediments ornamented
with painted flowers. If you explore side streets you'll find
unexpected fountains and two fine 18th-century mosques,
Hacı Memiş Camii and Hacı Mehmet Camii. In short, despite
its popularity, Çeşme does not seem to be a place that exists
solely for tourists—except, perhaps, during the Çeşme Sea
Festival, a regatta held during the last week in June and the
first week of July. (If you want to stay in Çeşme town proper,
the serviceable **Rıdvan Oteli** and **Ertan Hotel**, both on the
harbor, are the best choices.)

Çeşme town is dominated by a 14th-century **Genoese fortress** with massive triple defense walls. The fortress overlooks
the offshore Greek island of **Chios**, itself a possible day trip
from Çeşme. The excellent Karavan travel agency on Çeşme's
harborfront, with branches in İzmir and Kuşadası, usually has
up-to-date information on the ferry schedule to Chios, an
hour away. The nearby tourist office (Tel: 549/216-53) across
from the Caravansary hotel on the dock sometimes has schedule information as well. The tourist agency and certain hotels
sometimes have information on how to hire a boat for an
excursion to **Eşek Adası** (Donkey Island), a nature preserve
with wild donkeys offshore from the town of Ildır.

The fortress's **museum** (with a meager collection of terra-
cotta figurines and coins from ancient sites on the peninsula) won't detain you for long, but the building itself is
splendid. Beneath the fortress is a 16th-century caravansary
(now a hotel) built during the reign of Süleyman the Magnificent. Like most of these wayfarers' hostelries, the Çeşme
caravansary is a thick-walled square building with an open
courtyard where shade trees are planted around a fountain.
This should be a wonderful place to stay, but isn't because of
the pop music piped into the courtyard by day and loud
entertainment by night. (As at the Club Caravansérail at
Kuşadası, the entertainment features the inevitable belly-
dancing.) Still, it's worth taking a walk around the courtyard
just to see the restoration.

Two harborside restaurants, the **Sahil** and the **Körfez**
(both a short walk from the caravansary), get good reviews
from the locals for their fresh fish. Locals also try to avoid
tourists by heading out of Çeşme proper to the little village
of **Dalyan** on the tip of the peninsula, north of Çeşme; the
village has a number of good, simple seafood places such as
the **Liman**. As many Çeşme hotels require demipension
(usually breakfast and dinner), you'll have ample opportunity to sample several local restaurants for lunch. Çeşme also

has a number of fast-food *büfe*s (snack bars), with Turkish pizza (*lahmacun*): chopped onions, minced lamb, and tomato sauce on a pita-bread crust.

If you don't want to stay in town, two of the hotels on the beaches at Ilıca, only 6 km (3½ miles) outside Çeşme, are particularly tempting. If you're arriving on your own boat, you may want the **Çeşme Altın Yunus** on the Boyalık Koyu beach, with its private marina; if not, the smaller **Turban Çeşme Oteli**, which avoids the impersonality and occasional chaos of the enormous Altın Yunus, is the better choice. Both hotels have all the creature comforts, including carefully tended sand beaches, attractively landscaped grounds, large pools, excellent massage facilities, and Turkish baths that take advantage of the local thermal springs. Either would be a good place to begin a trip along the Aegean coast (to recover from jet lag) or to finish up a holiday (to recover from all those ancient sites).

One final note concerning staying in Çeşme—and in some other places on the Aegean coast—is unfortunately necessary. The demand for water created by expanding tourist facilities outstrips local supply, and water must be trucked in. Your shower may end abruptly in the middle of your shampoo if your hotel's water tank chooses that moment to run dry. Do be mindful of the need to conserve water here and throughout the country.

Out on Çeşme Peninsula

One of the great delights of the Çeşme peninsula is its miles of sand beaches. You may want to pack a picnic and head out of Çeşme toward Karaburun on the northern tip of the peninsula that protects İzmir's deep harbor. It's overly optimistic to expect to find a deserted beach during the summer months, but out of season you may find yourself almost alone. The farther you go from İzmir, the less likely you are to encounter day-trippers. The beaches are so good that you may find it difficult to think about more vigorous sightseeing, but there are several ancient sites that you can visit on day trips from Çeşme town.

Of these, it has to be admitted that two (Klazomenai and Erythrai), though relatively easy to reach, are not irresistible. **Klazomenai**, near Urla, has remains of the sort usually described as "of interest only to the specialist." It is also often off-limits for military reasons. **Erythrai** (outside Ildır) has some fine Hellenistic defense walls, but as these are not in short supply along the western coast of Turkey you may want to pass on them and head for ancient Teos. It's an hour's drive from Çeşme town to Teos, but the peaceful setting of the second-century B.C. Ionic temple of Dionysus makes the journey well worth the effort.

To reach **Teos**, take the turnoff south from the main road for Seferihisar and then follow signs to the harbor hamlet of **Sığacık**, which is built almost entirely within the walls of a **Genoese fortress**. With its minuscule harbor, fishing boats, and several cafés, Sığacık is an enchanting spot. As yet there's no hotel here, but there are several *very* simple pensions near the harbor on the road to Teos.

In 1991 the **Teos Holiday Village** opened several miles outside Sığacık on the Teos road. This is a charming place, doing a brisk package-holiday business, attracting many Austrian and German tourists. Guests stay in a dozen attractive red-tile-roofed, pastel buildings scattered along cobble-stoned paths. No cars are allowed into the "village," where ducks and chickens wander about clucking at guests heading off for scuba, tennis, and windsurfing lessons.

To reach Teos from Sığacık, follow the road that skirts the town and runs over pine-covered hills to the **temple of Dionysus**. If you want to picnic, stop at one of the picnic tables in the Sığacık pine park, a popular weekend destination for locals, or spread out your picnic by the temple itself. If you choose the temple, bring bug repellent and keep an eye peeled for the cows—some of which are bulls.

This was the largest temple to Dionysus in the ancient world, designed in the second century B.C. by Hermogenes, whose innovations in proportion and design led the Roman architectural historian Vitruvius to consider him the most influential Hellenistic architect. Hermogenes' fame brought Richard Chandler and the Society of the Dilettanti here to excavate and sketch the temple in 1765; unfortunately, much of what they studied was later quarried and used as building material by local entrepreneurs.

Today fragments of several columns have been re-erected and a number of column capitals have been placed on bases to give a sense of the temple, which had six columns at each end and eleven along each side. Some of the capitals and many of the architectural fragments date from the temple's restoration during the reign of the tireless Roman emperor Hadrian, who toured Asia Minor in A.D. 123, founding new cities and restoring old buildings.

Teos, like Priene to the south, is magical. Freya Stark, the indomitable 20th-century adventurer and writer, who travelled almost as widely in Ionia as Herodotus, wrote that "Teos is where I should live if I had the choice of all the cities in Ionia." It's easy to see why: Perched on a pine-clad ridge and bracketed by two harbors, Teos enjoys a lyrically lovely set-ting. And that's just as it should be for the birthplace of the sixth-century B.C. lyric poet Anacreon, who wrote of love's fleeting pleasures. Fittingly, the only known representation of the poet shows him, as George Bean puts it in his *Aegean Turkey,* "singing in his cups." If Anacreon had stuck to the wine he might have gone on forever; instead, he choked to death on a grape pip when he was in his 80s.

In the second century B.C. Teos was the home of the Asian chapter of the society of actors and minstrels known as the Artists of Dionysus—the god Dionysus, of course, being the patron of the theater. Doubtless members of the society sometimes gave performances in Teos's own **theater,** carved into the slopes of the acropolis west of the temple of Diony-sus. The theater was begun in the second century B.C. and modified during Roman times; it is often cited as a good example of the Greek type, which blends harmoniously with its natural setting. With the temple on your right, head across the farm fields and then uphill to reach the theater. If you scramble farther uphill past the ruins of the Roman stage building and theater seats you'll be rewarded with a fine view down across the remains of ancient Teos and out to sea. When you come back downhill, stop at the remains of the Roman **odeon,** with 11 preserved rows of seats, a little to the south-east of the theater by several farm buildings.

With its two harbors, Teos was one of the most prosper-ous Ionian cities—far wealthier than nearby Smyrna. The Teians clearly enjoyed the good life: In 190 B.C. a Roman expeditionary force detoured to Teos upon learning that the citizens had stockpiled 5,000 jars of wine. It is pleasant to report that Teos's ally, the powerful Seleucid king Antio-chus III, got wind of the Roman scheme, trapped their ships in Teos's north harbor, and, one hopes, made them give back the wine.

If you have the time, you may want to head south from Teos to visit one or more of these sites: Colophon, Notium, and Clarus. **Colophon** has some sections of Hellenistic walls; **Notium,** which was the port of Colophon, has indeterminate scattered remains on an acropolis from which there are fine views out toward the Greek island of Samos. There's also a good beach below Notium. **Clarus,** the site of an important oracle, has the remains of the late fifth-century B.C. temple of Apollo, one of the few Doric temples surviving in Aegean Turkey. As at Miletus (see below), the ruins at Clarus are sometimes submerged when the water table (always high in this marshy area) rises.

INLAND FROM İZMİR

Manisa, the capital of the Manisa district, is 39 km (24 miles) northeast of İzmir, with Sardis, the capital of the ancient Lydian Empire, another 60 km (37 miles) inland. To reach Manisa from İzmir, take the E 24/550 north to route 565, signposted Manisa. If you don't plan to visit Manisa en route to Sardis, take the E 96/330 to Ankara, which passes the site. If you do stop at Manisa—or if you want to see Sardis at an enjoyable pace—don't attempt this excursion as a day trip from İzmir. If you do, you may find yourself having to battle your way back into İzmir after dark.

Instead, try the **Hotel Arma** or the **Atlas Hotel** in Manisa, (both somewhat gloomy but acceptable). The new **Büyük Saruhan** has a swimming pool but seems overpriced and has a dull location on the İzmir–Ankara bypass. Another possibility is the **Alkent Tesisleri Motel**, 10 km (6 miles) east of Sardis at Salihli on the main İzmir–Ankara highway (ask for a room in the new section, opened in 1992). The motel's roadside setting is charmless, but the motel has a decent restaurant—or you can head into the energetic town of Salihli (whose astonishing number of jewelry shops cater mostly to locals, not tourists) for a simple kebap dinner and a stroll.

If after seeing Sardis you're planning to go on to Pamukkale and Hierapolis, consider spending the night in the mountains above Sardis, either at the mountaintop **Bozdağ Turistik Oteli** at Bozdağ-Ödemiş or in the village of Gölcük, which has several very simple pensions, including the **Kavaklı Pansiyon**, on the main road (and looking across the road onto Lake Gölcük). Allow 45 minutes for the drive. In summer this will get you out of the fierce heat of the Sardis plain into the mountains, where snow flurries are not unknown in May (see Hilltowns of the Bozdağlar, below).

Manisa

Most travellers bypass Manisa, which is unfortunate for two reasons: First, Manisa has perhaps the finest collection of Ottoman monuments in Aegean Turkey, and, second, this energetic provincial capital that runs up the side of Mount Spil couldn't be more unlike the tourist meccas of the Aegean coast. (Going from one ancient Greek site to another, many with adjacent villages where you often hear as much German and English spoken as Turkish, it's astonishingly easy to lose sight of the fact that you're in Turkey.)

Manisa is a good corrective, but only if you're willing to allow several hours to negotiate your way in and out of town, find a parking place, take in the sights, and perhaps have a snack.

The sprawling outskirts of Manisa are growing rapidly, but the center of town is unusually green, with open parks and tree-lined streets around the principal mosques. If you ask for directions to the Sultan Camii or Muradiye Camii you'll end up in the right part of town. You probably won't run into many other travellers here, and you'll almost certainly find everyone you encounter so pleasantly surprised that you're visiting their town that they'll steer you to a favorite restaurant, walk you to an out-of-the-way mosque, or help you find the poorly marked **tourism office**, hidden away on an upper floor of Doğu Caddesi, number 14 (worth finding for its handy tourist brochure and map of Manisa).

During the 13th and 14th centuries, according to the changing fortunes of war, Manisa, which dominates the fertile plain where the Gediz Nehri (the ancient Hermus River) and Kum Çayı (the ancient Hyllus River) meet, was held variously by Byzantines, Crusaders, and Turks. In 1313, Saruhan Bey, the leader of the Saruhan Turkmen, captured Manisa from the Byzantines; but its real period of glory began in 1405 when Sultan Mehmet I captured Manisa from the Saruhanids and it became an important training ground for future sultans—hence its important Ottoman monuments. Many of the finest monuments date from the 16th century, when the future sultans Süleyman the Magnificent and Murat III served as governors here.

In 1522 Süleyman's mother, Ayşe Hafize Hatun, built Manisa's largest mosque, the **Sultan Camii**; the mosque is also known as the Valide Camii (*valide* is the term for a sultan's mother). The mosque, with a massive dome resting on an octagonal drum, is rather severe inside, but has enchanting exterior wall paintings of town views and landscapes. The mosque once had a flourishing *medrese* (school of Islamic law) and hospital, now a medical museum. Crowds gather here to catch the sweets flung down from the minaret during the Manisa Sweet Festival (Mesir Şenlikeri), which in 1993 is held between March 22 and March 25.

According to one legend, the festival originated when Süleyman's mother was cured of a mysterious illness by eating Manisa *mesir macunu*, a sweet paste made with 41 different spices. *Mesir macunu* may be something of an acquired taste, with some of those 41 spices warring with others. Still, aficionados say that Manisa paste is so delicious that it resembles the ambrosia that the gods washed down with nectar on Olympus; others suggest that the Manisa paste has not merely restorative but also aphrodisiac qualities.

Cater-corner from the Sultan Camii stands Murat III's **Muradiye Camii** (built between 1583 and 1585), with an elaborately carved wooden entrance door that opens on a splendid wall ornamented with blue floral İzmir tiles surrounding jewel-like stained glass windows. If you're in luck, the custodian will take you through the mosque, pointing out delicately painted floral motifs in the window frames and the elaborately carved wooden ceiling (whose gilt is still visible) under one gallery. The great architect Sinan may have designed this mosque, which was finished by Mehmet Ağa, the architect of Istanbul's Blue Mosque. In the little park beside the mosque is the small, domed 14th-century tomb and a modern statue of Saruhan Bey, who captured Manisa from the Byzantines in 1313. In the evening, small children play tag and hide-and-seek around the statue. Two other Manisa tombs worth a visit are the **Yedi Kızlar Türbesi** (Tomb of the Seven Maidens) in the Dere Mahallesi (Dere quarter) and the **Yirmi İki Sultanlar Türbesi** (Tomb of the 22 Sultans) at 55 Birinci Sokak off Mustafa Kemal Paşa Caddesi. The latter is one of the largest Turkish tombs in Asia Minor—although it still looks as if it must have been a tight fit for the graves of the sultans Murat II and Murat III and 20 of their wives and children.

The Muradiye Camii's former medrese houses the **Ethnographical Museum**, with splendid Ottoman costumes and weapons; its former *imaret* (soup kitchen) houses the **Archaeological Museum**, with finds from ancient Lydia, especially Sardis. The exhibit on how gold was refined and coins were made will help you understand what went on at the Lydian smelteries, the remains of which you'll see at Sardis. The museum also has some finds from Magnesia-under-Sipylus, the ancient city on whose site Manisa stands. In 190 B.C. the Romans defeated Antiochus III here and gave virtually all of Asia Minor to their Pergamene allies, greatly increasing Pergamum's strength.

If you're lucky enough to be in Manisa on a Thursday you can wander from the Muradiye Camii into the lively **market** that snakes its way through town. Turkey is one of only six agriculturally self-sufficient countries in the world, and much of that food (apricots, peaches, melons, beets, and eggplants in season, as well as spices, baby chicks, quarters of lamb, and pyramids of eggs) seems to be on sale in the Manisa market.

There'd be many more mosques to see in Manisa if the Greek army, retreating ahead of Atatürk in 1922, had not

virtually leveled the town. Only 500 of Manisa's 18,000 buildings were left standing. One mosque the Greeks missed, the
14th-century **Ulu Cami** (Great Mosque), sits on the slopes of
Mount Spil, with a pleasant old teahouse nearby; it's best
found by asking for directions. The Byzantine capitals on
some of the Ulu Cami's columns are a reminder that the
mosque—Manisa's oldest—incorporated architectural fragments from a church that was its predecessor.

From Manisa you can easily visit two nearby monuments:
the **Weeping Niobe Rock**, on the road to İzmir about half a
mile east of Muradiye square, and the Cybele Rock Relief, 6
km (3½ miles) east of Manisa at Akpınar. According to
legend, Niobe boasted that her seven children made her the
equal of Leto, who had produced only two children. Leto's
children, however, were Apollo and Artemis, and the two
gods took offense at Niobe's remark and slew her children.
Niobe herself was frozen in stone, forever weeping for her
lost children. This was not a happy family: Niobe's father,
King Tantalus, was condemned to spend eternity reaching
for cool water and refreshing fruits always just beyond his
grasp—hence the word "tantalize." The Greek traveller
Pausanias and others identified the rock near Manisa as
Niobe's petrified remains. The rock, though more weathered than when Pausanias saw it in the second century A.D.,
still does suggest a woman's profile.

Pausanias also saw the **Cybele Rock Relief** (the Taş Suret),
which he identified as "the most ancient of all statues of
Cybele, the Mother of the Gods," the principal female deity
of Anatolia. Later during your trip you'll see the remains of a
shrine to Cybele at Sardis. The Cybele relief, badly eroded,
shows the seated goddess wearing an elaborate headdress.
Traces of Hittite hieroglyphics in a panel to the right of
Cybele's head have allowed archaeologists to date the monument to the second half of the 13th century B.C.

Sardis

If you've been clinging to the Aegean coast, travelling from
site to site and harbor to harbor, the drive from Manisa to
Sardis through the rich agricultural plain around the Hermus (the modern Gediz Nehri) and Pactolus (Sart Çayı)
rivers may give you your first sense of Turkey's enormous
interior. (From Manisa, follow signs for Turgutlu and Ankara to rejoin the E 23/300, the main İzmir–Ankara highway
that runs through the site of Sardis.) Few places are
greener and lovelier than Sardis in spring, when snow
crowns Mount Tmolus (Bozdağ), or more parched and sere

in summer, when the fields around the excavation are dotted with women in baggy trousers tending the mounds of sultana grapes that the sun bakes into raisins.

Sardis, the capital of ancient Lydia, stood between the vast interior and the coast, blocking Greek expansion inland. Lydia was the heart of Asia Minor, bounded to the north by Mysia, to the east by Phrygia, to the south by Caria, with Aeolis and Ionia to the west. The Lydians themselves are somewhat mysterious: They spoke their own language but adopted the Greek alphabet and were more similar to the Greeks in their customs than were the other peoples of Aegean Turkey. The fifth-century B.C. historian Herodotus of Halicarnassus (modern Bodrum) noted one difference: Lydian maidens earned their dowries by prostitution.

If even half of what Herodotus has to say about the Mermnad dynasty of Sardis is true, it's no wonder that he found them so fascinating. According to Herodotus, the Mermnad dynasty began with an act of voyeurism and ended in philosophy. It seems that King Candaules of Sardis, besotted with his wife's beauty, invited a friend, Gyges, to hide behind a curtain in the palace to see the queen naked. The queen discovered Gyges and offered him a choice: Die for dishonoring her or kill Candaules and marry her. Gyges chose life, the queen, and the throne, and founded the dynasty, which lasted from about 680 until 547 B.C.

Under the Mermnads, Sardis was one of the richest and most sophisticated cities in the world, capital of the powerful Lydian Empire, which extended from the Aegean to what is now Iran. According to legend, Sardis's Pactolus river became rich in gold when King Midas of Phrygia washed upstream to rid himself of the golden touch that was turning his food (and everything else) into the precious metal. The Lydians simply put out fleeces in the river shallows (the origin of the term "fleecing"), collected the gold, and, not surprisingly, went on to invent coinage.

The Athenian statesman and philosopher Solon visited King Croesus, who reigned here from 560 to 547 B.C. Croesus gave Solon the grand tour and then asked him whom he considered the happiest man he had ever met. Croesus (whose name is still a synonym for "plutocrat") clearly expected to hear his own name, but Solon named the unknown Tellus of Athens. Tellus, Solon remarked, had not only had a long and happy life but a good death as well.

For years, Croesus probably thought Solon something of a crank. In 547 B.C., however, the Persian king Cyrus II conquered Lydia, captured Croesus, and ordered him burned on a pyre. As the flames rose, Croesus called out Solon's warning that no man could be called happy until he met a good death. Evidently this was more than enough to make Cyrus consider his own mortality; he ordered the pyre extinguished and saved his enemy. At any rate, that's what Herodotus says, although it must be admitted that spoilsport scholars doubt both that Solon visited Croesus and that Croesus was saved by Cyrus.

After the defeat of Croesus, which ended the Mermnad dynasty, Sardis continued to prosper under the Persians and during the Hellenistic, Roman, and Byzantine eras; the most impressive remains date from the Roman and Byzantine periods. The site, beneath Sardis's jagged acropolis and bounded to the west by the bed of the Pactolus river, is bisected by the main İzmir–Ankara road. Sardis also straddled a main road throughout much of antiquity: Today's İzmir–Ankara highway follows the course of the Persian Royal Road, which ran from Ephesus to Sardis and then on to Susa in today's Iran. You can't see any remains of the Persian road, but you can glimpse a stretch of the marble Roman road and some of the mosaic paving of its flanking colonnades between the ancient synagogue and the modern highway.

North of the İzmir–Ankara highway, Roman and Byzantine ruins—notably the massive **Roman bath-gymnasium complex** covering five and a half acres—dominate the excavation site. The bath-gymnasium complex was begun after the earthquake of A.D. 17, which destroyed much of Sardis; the complex's ornate **Marble Court** was added in the early third century A.D. The richly ornamented, multistoried Baroque façade of the Marble Court was reconstructed by the Sardis Excavation between 1964 and 1973, although the original marble veneer was not replaced. The niches in the façade held statues of gods and emperors.

The bath-gymnasium (largely excavated, but not reconstructed) is a complex of symmetrically arranged rooms flanking an enormous *caldarium* (warm pool) and fronting on a colonnaded *palaestra* (exercise hall). Patrons—both men and women, who usually bathed separately—would have entered from the east through the *palaestra,* where they would have taken some light exercise. Then they would have moved on into the heated changing rooms flanking the marble court and had a soak in the *caldarium* before taking a plunge in the *frigidarium* (cold pool). Finally, they would have enjoyed a massage and some chat with friends in two domed central halls.

In the late third century A.D. a hall on the south side of the gymnasium was converted into a **synagogue** for Sardis's prosperous Jewish community. The Sardis synagogue—the largest known ancient synagogue—was richly decorated with frescoes and mosaics. There were Jews at Sardis as early as the sixth century B.C. Under the Persians, Sardis was the capital of the satrapy of Sfarda (biblical Sepharad); some scholars think that the term *Sephardic* comes from the Jewish community at Sardis.

South of the İzmir–Ankara road and just east of the Pactolus river stand the ruins of the **temple of Artemis**. With the acropolis framing the temple to the east and the Pactolus river just below it to the west, the temple of Artemis enjoys a particularly lovely setting. (To visit it, take the road through Sartmustafa opposite the mosque on the İzmir–Ankara highway along the east bank of the Pactolus. En route, you'll pass the small **Artemis** café-restaurant, a good place for light refreshments.)

The temple of Artemis was one of the seven largest temples in the ancient Greek world, with eight columns at each end and twenty along each side; two entire Ionic columns and a number of column bases remain in place. Like virtually all the temples you'll see in Aegean Turkey, the Artemis temple was built in stages: Begun around 300 B.C., the temple was still not finished when it was added onto circa 175 to 150 B.C. or when it was remodeled in about A.D. 150; only four columns were ever fluted and a colonnade was never completed.

When the excavators began work here—and you can see how much earth they had to clear by looking at the hillside at the temple's east end—they expected to find a temple of the important Anatolian goddess Cybele. Instead, they found the temple of her successor, Artemis. (A shrine to Cybele has been unearthed beside the Pactolus in the excavation section known as Pactolus North, discussed below.) Like the temples to Artemis at Ephesus and Magnesia-on-the-Meander, this temple faces west, toward an altar that predates the temple itself and may originally have been dedicated to Cybele.

In the mid-second century A.D. the temple was remodeled to accommodate the Roman imperial cult: Sometime later an image of the recently deified Empress Faustina (wife of Marcus Aurelius) joined the cult image of Artemis here. You can see how the temple was divided to give each divinity—the venerable Artemis and the newcomer Faustina—her own quarters. In the fourth century A.D. a small Christian church (one of several discovered at Sardis, which was the home of one of the Seven Churches of Asia) was built in the northeast corner of the temple using many ancient blocks.

From the temple, near which sheep often graze, those

with good walking shoes may want to climb the **acropolis**. Alexander the Great considered the ascent no more than a pleasant stroll when, after conquering Sardis in 334 B.C., he decided to have a look at the acropolis fortifications. Most of what you'll see on the acropolis dates from the Byzantine period, although on the north side of the summit there are traces of the pre-Hellenistic fortifications that Alexander saw. You may be less nimble than that youthful empire-builder, however, and should allow two hours for the ascent and descent. Be *very* careful when peering over the edge, as the rock is friable and it's a *long* way down.

Before you leave the temple precincts, have a look at what the Sardis archaeologists call "the functionally anonymous Lydian building," north of the temple in the excavation compound. You'll have to ask the guard's permission to see it; in Turkish, it's called the **Lidya Evi** (Lydian House). This small rectangular reproduction of a Lydian building is enchanting, decorated with gaily painted terra-cotta tiles showing flying horses, goddesses, fruits, and vines. As so little remains of Lydian Sardis, this one building goes a long way in helping you imagine what modest buildings in Croesus's Sardis looked like. By all accounts, the Lydians enjoyed the good life, making and exporting perfumes, enjoying their distinctive music—the plaintive so-called Lydian mode was one of the three main musical scales of the ancient Greek world—and shrugging off accusations of softness from their (doubtless envious) neighbors.

For all this, most Lydian dwellings were simple brick and wood houses, roofed with straw and reeds (the royal palace, presumably grander, has yet to be found). When Cyrus II in 547 B.C. and then the Ionians in 499 B.C. sacked Sardis, the place went up like a tinderbox, leaving little but foundations. Not surprisingly, little has been found of the Lydian agora and residential quarters—the Lydian city center, in fact, has yet to be established—although excavations just south of the İzmir–Ankara highway, across from the Byzantine shops that line the gymnasium-bath complex north of the road, have uncovered the foundations of houses and other structures, including a fortification that excavators have named the "Colossal Lydian Structure." Evidence suggests that the fortification was destroyed in the mid-sixth century B.C.—quite probably when Cyrus II seized Sardis from Croesus.

You might easily walk right past one of the most important finds at Sardis: the **smelting factory** in Pactolus North, along the river back toward the main road. Here the Lydians turned the gold found in the Pactolus into the first known coins. The American excavator G. M. A. Hanfmann described his thoughts when the refinery was discovered in 1968: "To stand where the wealth of Croesus was made; to watch his craftsmen squat at little fires, pumping at the bellows, purifying the gold in dupels, pouring it out of crucibles—this could happen only in a dream. Yet this is the scene we have discovered and can prove by tiny but telling clues."

Excavators have hoped in vain (so far) to discover an untouched Lydian burial chamber in one of the mounds that dot the plain around Sardis. These burial mounds— "enormous molehills," as one archaeologist called them— were thrown up over the royal chamber tombs. Alas, grave robbers in antiquity got there first, although there is a chance that the tumulus known as Karnıyarık Tepe (Split-Belly Mound), once thought to be the tomb of Gyges but recently redated some 50 to 100 years after his reign, may have an as yet undiscovered and unplundered burial chamber. To visit the **Bin Tepe**, or Thousand Mounds, take the Alaşehir–Salihli road approximately 10 km (6 miles) north of Sartmustafa. From atop the mounds you'll get some fine views north to the swampy Gygean lake (Marmara Gölü) and south to Mount Tmolus.

Hilltowns of the Bozdağlar

If you're heading from Sardis to Pamukkale, the route through the austere Bozdağlar (Gray Mountains) allows you to see superb mountain scenery, speculate on what it would be like to live in the Shangri-La–like mountain villages you'll see on remote peaks, and visit several small villages en route. You'll be leaving tourist Turkey behind once you follow the road west of Salihli, signposted Ödemiş, off the road that bisects ancient Sardis (the E 23/330.)

The winding road climbs into the mountains that divide the fertile plains of Manisa and Ödemiş. As you crest the mountain, you pass the **Bozdağ Turistik Oteli** (with spartan rooms and a small, not particularly clean pool), but if you want to stay in a Turkish summer resort continue along the Ödemiş road and take the turnoff for Gölcük, whose inhabitants move here during the summer months to farm and escape the heat in Ödemiş. The village sprawls along the shores of a small lake whose reedy shoreline fortunately discourages swimming: Although the lake is shallow, it has dangerous currents and whirlpools.

On summer weekends, İzmirlis camp out along the lakeshore and do some serious all-day picnicking, working their way through substantial meals cooked on Sterno stoves and slaking their thirst with segments of watermelon cooled in the lake. Gypsies set up stalls selling everything from screwdrivers to embroidered cushions, and lakeside restaurants like the **Gölcük Sönmez** serve up fresh fish. If you stay at one of the small pensions in town, like the lakeside **Kavaklı Pansiyon** (open June through September), you'll almost certainly be the only foreigner there—and have a wonderful chance to watch Turkish families enjoying their holiday while they watch you enjoying yours.

From Gölcük, it's easy to visit the village of **Birgi**, a 20-minute drive south along the Ödemiş–Salihli road. Nothing seems to have been built in this tumbledown village perched on a steep hill for at least a hundred years. Wooden houses with crazily cantilevered balconies overhang a gorge and line streets leading up to a small square flanking the 14th-century **Ulu Cami**, with its red-tile minaret and turquoise-tile *mihrap*. (In 1992, a handsome house, decorated with wall and ceiling frescoes and traditional furnishings, opened as a **museum**.) Nearby there's a ruined medrese and bath and the tomb of İmam ı Birgivi Mehmet Efendi, a local 16th-century notable. There are also several teahouses and the **Çamlık** restaurant, shaded by tall trees, where you can eat the local specialty, *güveç*: onions, tomatoes, and lamb cooked in a clay casserole. (The diligent may want to stop en route to Pamukkale in Ödemiş, where a small **museum** of archaeology and ethnography on the road into town partially compensates for the intense summer heat.)

NORTH FROM İZMİR

The road north from İzmir (E 24/550) crawls through the city's seemingly interminable suburbs for about 30 km (19 miles) before reaching the town of Menemen (now virtually an İzmir suburb itself). **Menemen**, like so many of the ancient and modern towns of Aegean Turkey, was once much closer to the sea; an early 18th-century map shows it virtually on the seashore, whereas today's town lies 14 miles inland. Disappointingly, the name "Menemen" has nothing to do with the popular Turkish dish made with eggs, cheese, tomatoes, green peppers, and whatever other vegetables are in the kitchen, but rather may commemorate the Phrygian lunar god, Men.

A good deal of wine comes from Menemen's vineyards in the alluvial plain formed by silt laid down by the Gediz Çayı. The river's banks have excellent clay, and Menemen produces much pottery. A number of roadside stands sell unglazed brown jugs and pots, bottles of wine, and—especially when there are Gypsies in the neighborhood—wickerwork. The objects that look like enormous coolie hats are, in fact, rushwork beach umbrellas.

In antiquity the Hermus marked the unofficial boundary between Ionia to the south and Aeolis, which extended north to Pitane (modern Çandarlı). The fact that Smyrna was originally one of the Aeolian cities but later joined the more influential Ionian League, and that powerful Phocaea, located squarely in Aeolian territory, belonged to the Ionian League suggests that there was considerable flexibility in these matters.

The Aeolians had a reputation for enjoying the simple life, no doubt because they lived in this exceptionally lovely countryside. For whatever reason, the 12 cities of the Aeolian League seem to have lapsed from relative insignificance into obscurity by the time the Romans arrived in the second century B.C. Earthquakes (particularly a massive one in A.D. 17) and pillage finished off what was left of most of the Aeolian cities: In the fourth century A.D. stones from the ruins of a number of Aeolian sites, including the poet Hesiod's ancestral hometown of Cyme, were carted off to be used in the construction of Constantinople. Still, the Aeolian countryside is alluring whenever you escape the nasty İzmir–Çanakkale highway. (If you have time to spare here, get a copy of George Bean's splendid *Aegean Turkey* and follow his travels through Aeolis.)

Foça

Some 42 km (26 miles) north of İzmir, beyond Menemen, a turning to the left off the E 24/550 leads 25 km (16 miles) across the broad knob of a peninsula, through several villages and olive groves and fields producing wheat, tobacco, and artichokes, before entering the town of Foça, the site of ancient Phocaea, on the northern extremity of the bay of İzmir. Just outside Foça, beside the old main road into town, is **Taş Ev**, an elaborate, stepped, rock-cut tomb beside the main road. The Turkish archaeologist Ekrem Akurgal has suggested that this may have been the fourth-century B.C. tomb of a tyrant who ruled part of this area for the Persians.

Until recently a small harbor town that drew some Turkish tourists, Foça now gets its share of foreign visitors, many of whom stay in the **Club Mediterranée** on the beach three miles outside Yeni Foça (New Foça), 12 km (7½ miles) north of Foça. (French is the language of choice at the Club Med, which has simple seaside bungalows and good water-sport facilities.) In season Foça can be crowded, both with İzmirlis, who bemoan its despoliation, and with foreigners, who, not having known the town in its better days, don't know what they've missed.

This is a nice spot to visit off-season, when the hubbub along Foça's double harbor with its cobbled side streets is minimal (and sleep in one of the harborside hotels is possible). Then you can enjoy visiting the ruins of the **Genoese castle** and gazing out at the islands that the Phocaeans evidently thought looked like seals (seals appear on Phocaean coins, and the name "Phocaea" is close to the Greek word for "seal").

Little has been found of ancient Phocaea, which dominated trade throughout the Aegean and Mediterranean in the sixth century B.C. Massive Phocaean ships, powered by 50 oars, could probably carry 500 passengers. (The *Mayflower,* by contrast, held 102 passengers.) Usually, however, Phocaean ships held cargo: The Phocaean trade route extended as far south as Naukratis in Egypt, north into the Black Sea, and west to Italy, Corsica, France, and Spain. Wherever the Phocaeans went they established trade stations and colonies, of which the most prosperous was Massilia (Marseille). As Herodotus said, "The Phocaeans were the pioneer navigators of the Greeks, and it was they who showed their countrymen the way to the Adriatic, Tyrrhenia, and the Spanish peninsula as far as Tartessus."

Some fragments, presumably of the sixth-century B.C. temple of Athena mentioned by Xenophon, have been found near its putative site near the town school. (Because everything found here has been taken off to the Archaeological Museum in İzmir for safekeeping, this site is hardly worth a pilgrimage.)

From Foça you can drive to the hamlet of **Yeni Foça**, at the tip of the northern peninsula, passing through lovely rolling countryside dotted with several newly constructed tourist villages and the melancholy ruins of Greek villages evacuated during the Turkish War of Independence. In Yeni Foça itself, several small pensions and hotels, of which the inexpensive **Motel Çatlatan** is the most substantial, attract Turks out of season and many Germans in season. Out of season Yeni Foça, with some handsome stone buildings with corbeled edges and fishing boats coming and going, has its charm. Yet here, too, in the olive groves just outside of town, the condos creep closer.

Çandarlı

Beyond Yeni Foça the road leads through a landscape gutted and marred by cement works and other factories until it rejoins the E 24/550 north to Bergama/Pergamum. After some 15 km (9 miles), a left turn leads in 10 km (6 miles) to the impressive 13th- or 14th-century **Genoese castle** at Çandarlı (ancient **Pitane**, the northernmost city in Aeolis). Much of ancient Pitane went into building the castle, and you can recognize blocks from the Greek city walls in the lower courses of the fortification. Still, the castle is so splendid that it's hard to resent the Genoese. Fortunately, they missed a fine marble *kouros* (youth) now on view in the İzmir Museum.

Despite increasing development, Çandarlı is still a sleepy harborside hamlet, little visited by foreigners except for the ubiquitous Germans. There are small pensions, as well as the comprehensively named **Martı Motel-Café-Restaurant** overlooking the beach. The Marti would be a tranquil spot to spend a few days enjoying Çandarlı's superb sand beaches— *if* you could persuade the management to turn down the radio that constantly blares in the outdoor restaurant.

BERGAMA

The modern town of Bergama (pop. 60,000) and the site of ancient Pergamum (pop. 300,000 in the second century A.D.) are 107 km (66 miles) north of İzmir. The ancient site occupies a terraced peak that the geographer Strabo improbably compared to a pine cone; the modern town spreads out across the plain below. Small wonder that Pergamum was so powerful: Protected by its superb defensive acropolis, it controlled an exceptionally well watered plain where the rivers Cetius (Kastel Çayı) and Selinus (Bergama Çayı) meet and flow into the Kaikos (Bakır Çayı). The rivers still bring prosperity to Bergama, and it takes a severe drought before local farmers have to resort to trucking in water for their crops.

Most of Bergama's touristic effluvia is confined to the dreary main road (route 240) into the new part of town, where leather shops, campgrounds, and hotels are proliferating. Happily, the old part of Bergama is a delight, with winding side streets, several fine mosques, hillside teahouses, and traffic jams of brightly painted horse-drawn carts. As ancient Pergamum itself is flamboyantly spectacular, what better place to spent a night or two? (Because most Bergama hotels do a brisk tour-group business, it's best not to arrive without a reservation between May and October.)

The nicest place to stay here is the **Tusan Bergama Motel**, in a shady pine grove beside tobacco fields about a mile outside Bergama. (You'll probably be driving east to Bergama from the İzmir–Çanakkale road, so keep an eye out for the inconspicuous Tusan Motel sign to the left of the road. The motel itself is not visible from the road, but the pine grove is.) If you want to be closer to town, continue on the main road to either the **Hotel İskender** or the **Hotel Berksoy**. The slightly down-at-the-heels Tusan has only a wading pool—usually empty—whereas the Hotel Berksoy has a decent-size swimming pool. On the other hand, the Tusan has a homelike atmosphere and helpful staff, while the Hotel Berksoy's emphasis on package tours makes for bland food and haphazard service. There are a number of less appealing hotels in Bergama—also often full in summer. (The simple **Park Otel**, with a small garden, on a quiet side street on your right as you enter town, and the **Pension Pergamon** near the police station are good choices in the pension category.)

Bergama's **tourist office** (Tel: 541/11862 or 11858), which has information on accommodations, is easy to miss: As you enter town, it is on the left side of the main street in a building that's signposted both "Restaurant" and "Information." A bit farther into town you'll come to the **Archaeology Museum**, which would have a stupendous collection if much of Pergamum's finest sculpture had not been taken off and put in the Pergamon Museum in Berlin in the 19th century. Still, the Bergama museum is worth a visit for its votive offerings from the Asclepieion, architectural and statuary fragments from the acropolis, a handsome ethnographical room, and a welcome café in its courtyard, where tea and cold drinks are served.

Take a minute to look at the model of the second-century B.C. altar of Zeus in the museum courtyard. The altar was decorated with some of the finest sculpture in the entire Hellenistic world. The actual altar is in Berlin, but the model will help you understand what it looked like when it sat on Pergamum's acropolis. It's possible that future visitors here may not need the model to appreciate the altar of Zeus: In 1990 the Turkish Ministry of Culture and the mayor of Bergama asked the United Nations for assistance in persuading Germany to return the altar to its original site. (Not much progress has been made, however.)

One of ancient Pergamum's oddest remains, the temple of

the Egyptian gods (second century A.D.), is in the heart of old Bergama. This vast, crumbling red-brick edifice straddling the Selinus was originally faced with marble, but the marble was pillaged over the centuries, and the complex became known as the **Red Courtyard** (Kızıl Avlu). The central three-story hall, with walls still standing to a height of 62 feet, is well preserved, as are the two flanking domed towers, which house a mosque and an excavation storehouse. Excavations have revealed underground chambers beneath the towers; these presumably were used in religious observances of the cult of the underworld deity Serapis, who was worshiped here along with Isis and Harpocrates (Horus). The atlantes and caryatids (male and female column-figures) now standing in the courtyard may represent these deities.

Much of the enormous courtyard (200 yards long) in front of the great hall has disappeared beneath the shops and houses of modern Bergama. In antiquity the courtyard was probably used for religious processions; the Byzantine era saw religious processions of a different sort here, when the central hall of the sanctuary was converted into the church of St. John. Pergamum was the location of one of the Seven Churches of Asia, and this church was the cathedral of a bishopric between the fourth and fifteenth centuries. This is just the sort of place that Piranesi might have enjoyed sketching; today children scamper about playing soccer and flying kites.

From the Red Courtyard it's pleasant to wander along the river and across a small bridge to the 14th-century **Ulu Cami** (Great Mosque). The mosque was built on the foundations of a Roman gymnasium; a number of ancient blocks are visible in the exterior walls. It has an enviable collection of locally crafted rugs. Head back across the bridge and hazard the narrow side streets, and you may end up at the pale green Şadırvanlı Cami, with a bubbling fountain, across from the fruit and vegetable market. A number of small *lokanta*s (restaurants), like the **Adıl Lokanta ve Kebab Salonu** and **Kemal Döner Kebap Salonu** by the mosque, offer a pleasant change from more tourist-oriented places like the Bergama Restaurant on the main street.

As you wander Bergama's back alleys, catching glimpses of saddlers and metalworkers and probably acquiring a retinue of small boys demanding *bonbon*s, you may find your thoughts going back to those wonderful deep red rugs in the Ulu Cami. There are lots of rugs for sale in old Bergama, which has always been an important center of rug production, but many are now made with synthetic dyes on machine looms.

If you want to see carpets being made by traditional methods (from the dyeing of the wool with plants and herbs to the actual double-knot weaving), stop at the **Anadolu Halı** carpet shop on the main road, near the Tusan Bergama Motel. From the road this looks like just another tourist trap, but in fact it's the outlet for a cooperative that sells rugs from Bergama and numerous villages throughout Anatolia. Most of the rugs are made of wool, but the most expensive are the tiny silk rugs, with 100 double knots per square centimeter—just the thing for a sultan's wife to place under a bejeweled bowl of bonbons.

ANCIENT PERGAMUM

Despite its superb natural site, Pergamum (Greek, Pergamon), in the region of western Asia Minor known in antiquity as Mysia, was a relatively unimportant city before the Hellenistic era. The historian and soldier Xenophon tried to help the Pergamenes cast off Persian rule when he passed by here in 399 B.C.; he failed. It was not until the murky aftermath of Alexander the Great's death, when his general Lysimachus inherited both Pergamum and 9,000 gold talents, that Pergamum's centuries of glory began. Lysimachus entrusted the money to one of his officers, the eunuch Philaterus, and when Lysimachus died, Philaterus held onto both Pergamum and the money. In 230 B.C., the Pergamene king Attalus I defeated the Gauls, then ravaging Asia Minor, and earned the support of Rome. The infusion of money and, later, the attention accorded the city by Rome transformed the insignificant city into the capital of an extensive realm.

The kingdom of Pergamum had its heyday in the second century B.C. under Eumenes II. When the Romans defeated the Seleucid king Antiochus III at the battle of Magnesia in 190 B.C., they gave Antiochus's lands—which stretched as far east as Cappadocia and even included the distant island of Aegina in the Argo-Saronic Gulf off the coast of Athens—to Eumenes.

Eumenes, his kingdom vastly expanded and at peace, turned his efforts to beautifying Pergamum. Much of what you see on the crest and slopes of the acropolis, including the palace foundations, the massive stepped platform of the altar of Zeus, and the library, dates from the reign of Eumenes II. Eumenes also rebuilt Pergamum's spectacular theater, which the Romans later altered.

The last Pergamene king, Attalus III, an eccentric scholar

rather like the Roman emperor Claudius or the English monarch George III, willed his entire kingdom to Rome when he died in 133 B.C.—probably because he suspected that Rome already had designs on Pergamum. Administered by the Romans as part of the province of Asia, Pergamum was badly damaged in the earthquake of A.D. 17 but largely rebuilt with the usual assortment of aqueducts, baths, gymnasiums, city walls, and temples during the reigns of the two great emperors of the second century A.D., Trajan and Hadrian.

The rediscovery of Pergamum occurred in 1871, after several workmen on the Istanbul–İzmir railway found some ancient blocks and brought them to Carl Humann, the German engineer in charge of the railroad. Humann recognized the importance of the blocks and asked where they came from. Within days he had virtually forgotten the railroad and was busily poking around on the ancient acropolis at what later proved to be the great altar of Zeus. When Humann took some architectural fragments back to Germany with him, scholars there immediately realized that they must have come from ancient Pergamum. In 1878 German archaeologists began to excavate the site, and they are still at it today.

Only 2 or 3 percent of Pergamum has thus far been uncovered—and after you toil up and down the acropolis, you may find yourself grateful that the Germans are working so slowly and methodically. The best way to see the site is to take a taxi to the top and walk down through the ancient town from the summit. As you walk past the ticket booth on your way to the top of the acropolis, you'll see on your left the low remains of the **heroön** (shrine to a hero), which probably honored Attalus I and Eumenes II. The *heroön* had cult rooms surrounded by a colonnade and would have been richly ornamented with statues.

Beyond the *heroön* on your right are the disappointingly meager remains of the royal palaces of the Attalids, the Pergamene kings. The palace complex, which included barracks for soldiers, sprawls along the eastern side of the acropolis almost to its northernmost point, where courses of the city wall and a defense tower are preserved. From the walls you can see out to the hills beyond, where stretches of the aqueducts that once supplied Pergamum with water are preserved.

As you retrace your steps south you'll pass some of Pergamum's most important civic buildings, which were built along the western side of the acropolis. Pergamum was the most powerful city in the Roman province of Asia before the growth of Ephesus in the first century A.D. Even then Pergamum remained important and received honors and edifices

from several emperors. In fact, Pergamum's **acropolis** is dominated by the Corinthian **temple of Trajan**, the finest monument to that emperor erected in Anatolia. The temple is currently undergoing restoration and, at least until it weathers a
bit, looks rather like an overgrown garden folly. The temple
stood in the center of a *temenos* (sacred enclosure) flanked
by colonnades with the lavish palm-leaf capitals known as
"pergamene" because of their extensive use here.

Just south of the temple of Trajan are the nondescript
ruins of Pergamum's famous **library**, which housed one of
the most impressive collections known in antiquity. Scholarly envy is no new phenomenon: It's not surprising to learn
that the Pergamene library owed its great size to a quarrel
between Alexandria and Pergamum. The Ptolemies, the dynasty that ruled Egypt after the death of Alexander the Great,
held a monopoly on the papyrus used for book scrolls, and
when they feared that Pergamum's library would surpass
their own, they cut off the supply to Pergamum. King Eumenes II ordered that a substitute be found and the result was
pergamene, or parchment, made of specially treated animal
skins. Parchment had two great advantages over papyrus:
First, the sheets were substantial enough to take writing on
both sides, and, second, they could be bound into codices—
the first books—which were infinitely easier to read than
the cumbersome scrolls.

With the proliferation of parchment, the Pergamene library
grew rapidly, but Alexandria may have had its revenge: According to Plutarch (though he's the only ancient author to tell this
story), after the Alexandria library burned in 41 B.C., Marc
Antony looted Pergamum's 200,000 volumes for replacements to please his inamorata, Cleopatra. Still, enough books
remained for the future emperor Julian the Apostate to spend
a year at Pergamum studying philosophy in the fourth century
A.D. One wonders whether Julian was allowed to pluck volumes from the shelves or had to wait until librarians fetched
him his choices; the low bench still visible along the library
wall was probably built not as a seat for readers but as a
barrier to keep them from getting too close to the books. (The
German excavators here plan to restore the library when they
finish work on the temple of Trajan.)

Pergamum's most stunning ruin is its theater, which cas-
cades down the western side of the acropolis. Only the
foundations remain of the **temple of Athena** that stood on
the terrace above the theater, but the low remains of its
colonnade give an idea of the extent of the temple precincts.
The precincts contained a number of bronze statues commemorating Attalus I's victory over the Gauls in 230 B.C.,

including the famous *Dying Gaul,* known to later times only from its marble copy in the Museo Capitolino in Rome.

Walk along the colonnade past the temple foundations and you'll come to the sheer drop of Pergamum's 10,000-seat **theater**. The remains of the little Ionic **temple of Dionysus** (the god of the theater) are clearly visible at the north end of the long terrace that stretches below the theater's stage. The terrace would have been roofed and must have provided a lovely spot along which to promenade and enjoy the spectacular view out across the plain toward the Asclepieion (about which see below).

If you take a close look at the temple of Dionysus, you'll see that the local andesite walls of the original second-century B.C. structure are faced in marble. The donor of the marble facing was the Roman emperor Caracalla (A.D. 211 to 217), who recuperated from injuries received in a ship accident off Gallipoli at Pergamum's Asclepieion and later lavished gifts on both the Asclepieion and Pergamum itself. A monumental head of Caracalla from a statue he gave to the Asclepieion is on display in the Bergama museum. You'll notice marble facing elsewhere at Pergamum, for example on the temple of Demeter and the gymnasiums. The Romans were fond of doing this; in fact, the emperor Augustus once boasted that he found Rome "a city of brick and left it a city of marble."

If you like, you can plunge down the steep theater to enjoy the view from the terrace, but it's less unnerving to follow the path that descends along the southern end of the acropolis, skirting the ancient agora. En route you'll pass the remains of the **altar of Zeus**, most of which was carted away by the first German excavators here. Looking at the remains still at Pergamum, you might think that the monument was simply a stepped altar; in fact, what you see was flanked on three sides by an Ionic stoa, itself standing on a sculptured frieze almost 400 feet long. This monument, the largest known altar, commemorated the victories of both Eumenes II and Attalus I over the Gauls. The frieze, a masterpiece of Hellenistic relief sculpture, depicted a gigantomachy, or battle of gods and giants, an often-used symbol of the triumph of civilization (in this case, Pergamum) over barbarism (the Gauls). It was the discovery of one of these sculpted panels that made Carl Humann turn from engineering to archaeology.

If you retrace your steps to the upper agora, you can follow ancient Pergamum's broad, paved main street down the slopes past the extensive ruins of the middle city. Many of the buildings here originally date from the Hellenistic era but were extensively rebuilt by the Romans. Nothing that you'll see is as spectacular as the theater or as well preserved as the temple of Trajan, but recent excavations and restorations make clear the considerable remains of an extensive third-century B.C. complex of three **gymnasiums**, each occupying a separate terrace, as well as several shops, a latrine, and a partially restored *heroön*.

Inscriptions have revealed that the highest terrace held the gymnasium for adult men; the middle, the gymnasium for youths; and the lowest, the facility for boys. Baths were added to the gymnasiums during the Roman period; the bath at the northern end of the uppermost gymnasium is particularly well preserved. You'll also see some marble washbasins and a latrine. This impressive complex, with its libraries, temples, meeting halls, baths, and classrooms would be the envy of any modern Olympic training team: There was even an indoor track so that practice could go on during rainy weather.

If you continue down the acropolis slopes, which each spring are covered with flowers (and each summer with tall, spiky thistles), you'll eventually find yourself back in Bergama—but if your car is in the parking lot near the acropolis summit you'll have to toil back up. And don't think you're done with Pergamum: The Asclepieion, a very important site, is about a mile out of Bergama and must be visited separately.

The Asclepieion

The easiest way to get to the Asclepieion is to follow the signposted road by the tourist office on Bergama's main road. You may be asked to stop to gain permission to enter at the army base you pass en route, as the Asclepieion is technically inside a military zone.

It's best to visit the considerable remains of the Asclepieion (the sanctuary of the healing god Aesclepios), visible from Pergamum's theater, after a decent interval to avoid archaeological indigestion. A good plan of attack is to visit the acropolis in the early morning and the Asclepieion in the late afternoon (or vice versa). This plan has the added benefit that you'll avoid the heat and the tour groups and be able to enjoy the soft light that makes Pergamum's andesite bedrock almost pink. Come at twilight and you may be serenaded by band practice at the nearby army base, punctuated by the bleating of the sheep that roam the site.

The Asclepieion comes as something of a relief after the citadel of Pergamum. On level ground, shaded by pine trees, with only a scattering rather than a day's worth of remains, this is an ideal spot to relax. This shrine to Aesclepios was founded here on the outskirts of ancient Pergamum in the fourth century B.C., evidently by a local who had been healed at the great shrine of Aesclepios at Epidaurus in Greece and wished to spare others the long journey. By Roman times, Pergamum's Asclepieion was one of the god's most important shrines.

This is where the great second-century A.D. scholar-physician Galen (who was born at Pergamum) studied and worked and where his contemporary, the peripatetic hypochondriac Aelius Aristides, spent happy hours discussing his ailments with the temple attendants. Some of Aristides' accounts of his "cures" raise the possibility that Aesclepios was not without a sense of humor: On one wintry occasion, he appeared to Aristides in a dream and told him to rise and bathe at the sacred spring—frozen at the time.

You'll enter the Asclepieion along the colonnaded Sacred Way, just as ancient pilgrims did—although they may have walked barefoot along the marble road to demonstrate their piety. The entrance to the Asclepieion was marked by a massive gate whose finial, in the form of a winged Victory, is on display in the courtyard of the Bergama museum.

After pausing for prayers at the round temple of Zeus-Aesclepios, pilgrims might have proceeded to the hospital to discuss their course of treatment with staff physicians. Then they could have headed through the vaulted passageway from the hospital to the sacred pools near the theater. The pools were fed by the still-running **sacred spring** where Aristides tried to bathe in winter. After hydrotherapy, mud-packs, and some massage and exercise, pilgrims probably relaxed at lectures and performances held in the **theater,** which seated 3,500. Then, it would have been off to bed in one of the sleeping rooms, perhaps to have the healing god reveal himself in a dream. Small wonder that Aelius Aristides spent the better part of 13 years here, enjoying the medicinal and spiritual benefits of this spa.

If your sense of adventure is strong—and if you find the thought of skittering through dark, damp places to be weirdly appealing—ask the site guard to show you the entrance to the tunnel that runs under the *cavea* of the theater at the Asclepieion. Such tunnels were ordinary parts of the substructures of many ancient theaters, but that unglamourous bit of scholarly information shouldn't affect the bit of slimy fun you'll have crawling through. Bring a flashlight.

AYVALIK

The road from Pergamum/Bergama (route 240) runs west through flat tobacco fields before rejoining the main İzmir–Çanakkale road (E 24/550) and heading north to the resort town of Ayvalık, 60 km (37 miles) away, across from the Greek island of Lesvos. Located just north of Pergamum on the coast and about halfway between İzmir and Çanakkale, Ayvalık suggests itself as a logical stopping place—and so it is, if you concentrate on the side streets lined with old houses, the good beaches, and the olive groves (the area around Ayvalık produces three-quarters of Turkey's olive oil) and not on Ayvalık's sprawling touristic developments. If you visit Ayvalık the last week in April, you may get to see the Gypsies and *yörüks* (Turkmen nomads) who assemble here for their annual *panayır* (festival).

A recent Turkish Ministry of Tourism pamphlet, *Ayvalık and Environs,* says that "The harmony in the architecture, the blending of the colours and the layout of the streets make the city unique." Ayvalık and the village on the nearby island of Alibey (formerly Cunda island) have a large number of handsome stone houses and Neoclassical pedimented buildings dating from the days before the Greco-Turkish exchange of populations, when the inhabitants here were largely Greek. (The Turks during this period tended to build more in wood than stone.) In addition, the road running south along the cove toward Sarımsaklı beach has a string of quite mad "Victorian Gothic" villas. Formerly the summer homes of Greeks from Smyrna, an increasing number of these villas have been converted into pensions filled in summer with families from İzmir escaping the heat. The **tourism office** (Tel: 663/121-22) is on the same road, as is the appealing **Belediye Çamlı Restaurant**, set on a hill among pine trees.

The Ayvalık waterfront has lovely views of more than 20 wooded offshore islands, of which **Alibey** is the largest. In summer little boats ply back and forth on excursions around the islands; you can take a sunset trip across to Alibey, have dinner, and then return to Ayvalık. (Information on boat trips is available at the quay and at the tourism office.) The boat trip is infinitely nicer than the drive along the slender causeway linking Alibey to the mainland. That road passes through a maze of ugly new condos before reaching the small harbor village with the restaurants.

In the morning fishing boats put in with their catch at Alibey harbor. On summer evenings the harbor is lively, but often the village side streets seem melancholy, with too many fine stone houses and buildings, including the church of St. Nicholas (with some decent frescoes), in a state of advanced decay. You may hear some Greek spoken on Alibey, either by Turks who grew up on Lesvos or by Greeks whose families once lived here and who are visiting their ancestral home. Recently there have been signs that some of the old buildings in the village may be restored, and it is possible that Alibey may trade melancholy for chic in the near future, especially if the superb beaches on the island's north shore begin to draw more visitors.

Right now you can spend a pleasant evening having dinner on Alibey's waterfront, which is closed to traffic (if you come here for your seafood dinner you won't have to inhale exhaust fumes, as you might on Ayvalık's harborfront). You'll probably still have to listen to the war of the boomboxes (one restaurant plays Greek ditties on a radio picking up a station on Lesvos while another blasts out Madonna). And, on both the Ayvalık waterfront and Alibey island, you may well be served frozen fish—a disappointment that's not all that rare on the Aegean coast in summer.

If you stay in Ayvalık, the **Clup Hotel Murat Reis**, south of town on Sarımsaklı beach, is rather tranquil, despite doing a substantial package-tour trade, with rooms with balconies overlooking the sea and a good beach and swimming pool. The hotel is at the foot of a wooded hill called Şeytan Sofrası (Devil's Dinner Table), from which there are fine views over the dozens of islands in the harbor and out toward Lesvos. Sunsets here are memorable. If you want to visit **Lesvos**, check at the Ayvalık marina. From June to mid-September there's daily round-trip service for day-trippers. Off-season service is irregular.

INTO THE TROAD

North of the turnoff for Ayvalık, the İzmir–Çanakkale road begins to climb steeply as it winds around the western slope of Kaz Dağı (5,610 feet), Homer's Mount Ida. At the highest point, roadside stands offer delicious pine honey, various herbal teas, cold drinks, and snacks under the shade of pine trees. It's a good spot to take a rest from driving and to recall Mount Ida's importance in Greek mythology while sipping some mountain herbal tea. In antiquity this mountainous district in the northwest corner of Asia Minor overlooking the Hellespont was known as the Troad.

Zeus first saw the beautiful Trojan prince Ganymede as

the boy tended his flocks on Mount Ida, and carried him off to Mount Olympus to be his cupbearer. Helen's seducer Paris also spent part of his youth as a shepherd on Mount Ida (dallying with both maidens and fellow shepherds), and Lord Byron was mindful of both Ganymede and Paris when he visited the Troad. Byron complained that the shepherds he saw were a distinct disappointment, and he had to console himself by bagging snipe, not shepherds.

After Paris's shepherd days on Mount Ida, he was chosen to settle the famous dispute among the goddesses Hera, Aphrodite, and Athena. Each goddess claimed possession of a golden apple engraved with the words "For the most beautiful." Each offered Paris a reward if he would say she was the most beautiful goddess, and Paris chose Aphrodite's bribe: The most beautiful woman in the world, the fair Helen. With Aphrodite's help, Paris abducted Helen from her husband, Menelaus, in Sparta and brought her to windy Troy. Menelaus and the Greek host followed, and the Trojan War ensued.

The gods often watched the fighting at Troy from Ida's peaks, and Aphrodite had several dalliances here. The first, with the mortal Anchises, produced the child Aeneas, whose descendants went on to found Rome after the fall of Troy. With the god Hermes, Aphrodite had a second child here who was a most improbable half-brother (sister?) for the stolid Aeneas: Hermaphroditus, the bisexual god often depicted in Greek art.

Assos and Behramkale

The drive down Mount Ida toward Ayvacık (not to be confused with Ayvalık) on the E 24/550 affords splendid views out across the bay of Edremit and off to Lesvos. At Ayvacık— a lively town of 5,000, whose Friday farmers' market is well worth the visit—a signposted left turn leads 25 km (16 miles) through hills and valleys to ancient Assos and the modern village of Behramkale. Just outside Behramkale a steeply pitched 14th-century Ottoman bridge crosses the Tuzla river; village women do their washing here, heating the river water in caldrons blackened by fires, whacking their wash with wooden mallets, and stretching their rugs and clothing out to dry on the shrubs that line the riverbanks. On the massive acropolis beyond the bridge ancient Assos and the modern village of Behramkale tower over the landscape like an aberrant Tuscan hilltown with a mosque in place of the cathedral. (The mosque did, however, begin its life as a church; it was converted in the 14th century.) Below

Behramkale is its handsome port, where a handful of stone buildings line a crescent harbor. The port is very popular with both Turks and foreigners and, while delightful off-season, is crowded in summer.

To get to the temple of Athena at Assos (discussed below), drive up as far as you can, stop, and walk the rest of the way. To get to the port, drive down as far as you can, stop, and walk the rest of the way. If you want to avoid the steep harbor road altogether, a left turn at Behramkale will take you 4 km (2½ miles) to the good beach at Kadırga and the new **Assos Eden Beach Hotel**. The Assos Eden Beach is pleasantly landscaped, with serviceable motel-like rooms and a restaurant. In summer the hotel does heavy tour-group business, but off-season independent travellers will not feel outnumbered.

The modern village of Behramkale, straggling up the ancient **acropolis**, is experiencing change. The children mentioned in the *Blue Guide* as "shyly" proffering embroidery and knitting now line the steep path to the acropolis like so many little Scyllas and Charybdises. The embroidery is lovely, but the overkill sales approach is wearying. If you visit the acropolis in the early evening you'll be able to score a double coup: avoiding most of the sales pitches and enjoying the sunset over Lesvos from the recently restored sixth-century B.C. **temple of Athena,** with five standing Doric columns. Before you leave the acropolis, take a (cautious—there's no guardrail) look at the two massive cisterns to the left of the site entrance.

Assos was probably founded by settlers from Lesvos in the seventh century B.C. and had its moment of glory in the fourth century B.C., when its tyrant Hermias persuaded Aristotle to spend three years here. When not preoccupied with suggesting a model constitution for Hermias to put into effect, Aristotle found time to court and marry the tyrant's niece. It would be nice to relate that they all lived happily every after, but it was not so. In 344 B.C. the Persians, always lurking just over the horizon in those days, overthrew Hermias despite Assos's splendid fortification walls (the best-preserved fourth-century B.C. walls in Aegean Turkey). The Persians then crucified Hermias, and Aristotle took off to Lesvos, where he sensibly turned from political to scientific theory.

On the slopes below the temple of Athena, Turkish archaeologists have been excavating the **necropolis**, with its stone sarcophagi. The Assos sarcophagi, exported throughout the Greek world, were made of the local limestone, known, according to the first-century B.C. Roman naturalist Pliny, as "body-eating stone," because its high lime content made speedy work of mortal remains. It's possible that the noun "sarcophagus" (from the Greek for "body-eater") derives from the word originally applied to the particularly caustic stone used in the Assos tombs.

Excavations are also underway at the third-century B.C. **theater**, until recently only a dim impression on the acropolis slopes. This is the sort of place Freya Stark had in mind when she wrote of sites where "the splintered earthenware, the soft black shiny Hellenistic glaze, the red both ribbed and plain, whisper with tiny toneless voices, lying thicker or thinner about one's feet according to the ancient crowding of the streets and markets." This is also the sort of place where it will take all your willpower to keep in mind that removing potsherds from a site is *very much* against the law in Turkey. Many important finds from Assos were taken to the Boston Museum of Fine Arts in the 1880s.

If you're staying overnight in Behramkale's port, don't stay too long after sunset at Assos: The road is genuinely exiguous and makes you feel that if you miss a turn, you'll make a meal for the fish. The road down dead-ends at the Hotel Behram, for years the only hotel here. Unfortunately, the Behram has both rested on its laurels and become a favorite of travellers attempting to drink and disco their way across Turkey.

Fortunately, there are several alternatives to the Behram. The **Motel Yıldız** is on the main street and thus potentially noisy. The **Hotel Assos Kervansaray** has a small swimming beach, but the rooms overlooking the parking lot are to be avoided. Although the Kervansaray is a modern building, its architectural style blends unobtrusively with the other buildings. Like the Yıldız, the Kervansaray has a large *şömine* (fireplace) in the lobby, which is cheering when summer winds blow in from the sea and as warming as a fire in a New England or Scottish inn in winter. The **Hotel Assos** next door, in a newly restored harbor warehouse, has slightly smaller rooms and a good restaurant. The seaside rooms in the **Otel Nazlı Han** at the other end of the quay, also in a restored harborside building with an inner courtyard, are usually the quietest of all.

In short, Behramkale, until recently a decayed harbor village, has become a strip of hotels, cafés, and restaurants. Still, the harbor, the fishing boats, and the cluster of restored buildings make this a lovely place to visit, especially with the **Uzun Ev Café** (next to the Hotel Behram) playing classical music as well as more mundane Muzak on summer afternoons and evenings. Reservations are recommended in Behramkale, as the hotels do a brisk business both in and out of season. Try to go out of season, when there are few day-trippers. As at Çeşme, water must be trucked in to Behramkale, and so the taps in your hotel may occasionally run dry—until the next shipment arrives.

Ancient Chryse

A partly asphalted road (signposted "Apollo Smintheon") leads the 20 km (12 miles) west from Assos to Gülpınar (ancient Chryse), site of the Ionic temple of Apollo Smintheus. The drive from Assos to Gülpınar would be lovely even without a temple to look forward to. The road runs past lush olive groves, over hillsides redolent with oregano, and across a bleak plain that smells like an enormous barbecue pit: The plain is dotted with the low mounds of ovens used for making charcoal from the velonia oak that grows thickly in the hills.

At Gülpınar (the sort of village often described as "fly-specked"), the **temple of Apollo Smintheus** is signposted down a steep dirt track. Little remains of the temple, which had eight columns at each end and fourteen columns along each side, except its platform, scattered column drums, and some acanthus-leaf capitals. The ongoing Turkish excavations here may eventually give us a better picture of the sanctuary; for now, sheep graze around the temple, and a shepherd is sometimes on hand to shoo away the sheep and point out the fallen columns (some with scenes of the Trojan War) and architectural fragments.

The present temple dates only from the mid-third century B.C., but there must have been a shrine to Apollo here for centuries before that. According to Homer this was the home of Chryseis, the daughter of the priest of Apollo, whom Agamemnon captured and added to his mistresses but later grudgingly returned to her father. When Agamemnon took Achilles' mistress Briseis to compensate for the loss of Chryseis, Achilles withdrew "to sulk in his tent." You'll find the story of Chryseis in the first book of the *Iliad*—and what better place to read it, before heading on to Troy, than beside the temple where Chryseis's father entertained the Greeks with a lavish banquet when they returned his daughter?

The structure is known as the temple of Apollo Smintheus (Apollo the Mouse God) from one of Apollo's more improbable attributes. Apparently, when the first settlers (led by Teucer, later the first king of Troy) came here from Crete, they were set upon by mice, which nibbled their leather armor. As an oracle had advised the immigrants to settle where they would be harassed by the "earthborn," they interpreted this to mean the mice and stayed.

The locals already worshiped Apollo, so the newcomers erected a temple dedicated to Apollo Smintheus in the hope that he would deal with the rodents. Evidently he did, for in the fourth century B.C. the people of Chryse commissioned the famous sculptor Scopas to make them a statue of Apollo—with, we are told by Strabo, the figure of a mouse under his foot.

Babakale

Babakale, which is signposted off the Behramkale–Gülpınar road and lies on a point projecting into the sea, is as far west as you can go in Aegean Turkey. The village is minuscule, although the harbor is being extended with a new quay in an attempt to create a marina. For now, the greatest excitement in town is watching fishermen mend their nets; little seems to have changed since "this place was a deserted quiet one," to recall the words of an inscription on the 18th-century **Turkish fort** above the harbor.

If you really want to get away from it all, stay at Babakale's one simple hotel, the **Ser-Tur Motel Restaurant**. Babakale also offers several *very* simple pensions, including the **Karayel Pansiyon**. (These lodgings' telephone numbers appear in the Accommodations Reference at the end of the chapter; be aware that all phone calls into Babakale go through a central operator, who then attempts to reach the person being telephoned. You will most likely have to request the extension and attempt to make a reservation in Turkish.)

Alexandria Troas and Neandria

The site of Alexandria Troas (best reached by following the secondary road from Behramkale to Gülpınar and then bearing left at the Kaplıca thermal bath and sanitorium) gives new meaning to the phrase "a site probably of interest only to the professional archaeologist." Heinrich Schliemann, the discoverer of Troy, thought that the circuit of the city walls here was at least six miles; little of note remains except one admittedly splendid arch from a Roman bath.

Still, if you're heading north to Troy you can have a pleasant picnic in the shade beside the ruined baths, built by the great philhellene Herodes Atticus in the second century A.D. You can even scramble through fields for several miles around, discovering various recumbent architectural fragments and the occasional snake.

Despite its minimal remains, Alexandria Troas was a thriving city in the Hellenistic and Roman periods and controlled a good deal of sea trade. Saint Paul put in here twice in the hope of making converts; on Paul's second visit his preaching was so soporific that a young man named Eutychus, listening from a third-floor window, fell asleep and tumbled to the ground. Eutychus (the name means "fortunate") was sufficiently relaxed that he survived the fall.

Constantine the Great even toyed with the idea of making Alexandria Troas, not Constantinople, his capital. Instead, he and his successors simply quarried the site for marble, carting off shiploads of columns and blocks. As late as 1609 stones were transported from Alexandria Troas to Istanbul to be used in constructing the Blue Mosque. Even then enough remained that a number of early travellers to Turkey thought that this must be the site of Troy; Schliemann himself, of course, was not deceived.

Neandria makes Alexandria Troas look overdeveloped. The site is best reached by going from Ezine toward Odun İskelesi via Geyikli, looking for the signpost to Neandria and hoping to find a local person for more precise directions. Neandria's mountainside site is impressive, as are its fifth-century B.C. city walls. Perhaps the Neandrians tired of the stiff climb: In the fourth century B.C. most moved to Alexandria Troas. Little remains of Neandria's sixth-century temple of Athena, but you can see some of the temple's fine Aeolic capitals in the Istanbul Archaeological Museum.

TROY AND ÇANAKKALE

You can head north to Troy from Assos (64 km/40 miles on the main road) either by rejoining the main İzmir–Çanakkale road (E 24/550) at Ayvacık or by taking the secondary road along the coast and rejoining the main road just below the site of Troy. The coastal road is slightly longer and considerably slower, running through rolling hills crisscrossed with low stone walls topped with woven branches, which look like so many woolly caterpillars snaking their way through the countryside. Make the trip in late summer and you'll see workers harvesting hay with long scythes and gathering buckets of bright red tomatoes from seemingly endless fields.

It's not a good idea to arrive at Troy without a hotel reservation: The few hotels near the site are simple and noisy, and the **Tusan Truva Motel** (in a pine grove, with its own beach) between Troy and Çanakkale is often fully booked. If you can't get in the Tusan, there are several hotels in Çanakkale (see below). Most tourists seem to ignore the modern hamlet of **Truva**, a five-minute drive from Troy, which makes it a good spot to stop for a cold drink.

Troy: The Legend

A 19th-century French traveller, when asked why one should visit Athens—then a sleepy provincial town of no particular distinction—replied, "Mais Athènes s'appelle Athènes!" That's as good an explanation as any of the allure of those places that live in the imagination long after they have become, as one writer said of Troy, "a ruin of a ruin." No, there's *not* much to see at Troy—some fine walls, part of a *megaron* (palace), some dwellings, a massive ramp, and some inconsequential Hellenistic and Roman remains—but there's much to remember here. You can visit Ephesus and be so overwhelmed by what you see that you almost forget to wonder what happened there. It's just the opposite at Troy, where the romance of Homer's city is almost equaled by the saga of its rediscovery in 1871 by Heinrich Schliemann. As for the Trojans themselves, scholars disagree as to their origins, language, and culture.

Still, almost everyone wants to know what happened at Troy. Homer, of course, sang of the Trojan prince Paris's abduction of Helen, the wife of Sparta's king Menelaus, and the efforts of the Greek host, led by Menelaus's brother Agamemnon, to reclaim Helen and destroy Troy. The campaign took ten years, and when it was done, both Achilles, the greatest Greek hero, and Hector, the greatest of the Trojans, were dead. Troy was sacked and Helen returned home to Sparta. That's the story. But Homer seems to have lived about 700 B.C. What could he possibly have known of a war that may have taken place more than 500 years earlier?

According to many scholars, the answer is: not very much. The German scholar Friederich Wolff was one of the first to deprecate Homer, "proving" in his magisterial *Prologomena ad Homerum* (1705) that there never was a Trojan War, a Troy—nor, for that matter, a Homer! Today many of Wolff's scholarly descendants still see the *Iliad* and *Odyssey* as pastiches of charming legends, assembled from the work of generations of poets, riddled with anachronisms and inconsistencies, and at best preserving some faint outline of a dimly remembered conflict.

One of the best of these scholars, Sir Moses Finley,

thought that the *Iliad* had no more historical accuracy than the *Song of Roland,* which describes the battle at Roncevaux in 778 between Charlemagne and the Saracens. That "battle," Finley pointed out, was actually nothing but a skirmish between Charlemagne and a Basque raiding party. No Saracens were involved at all. Similarly, Finley said, Homer's poems may have a minor basis in fact but no real historical accuracy: If anything happened at Troy it was probably no more than a skirmish between locals and a marauding party, perhaps made up of the mysterious "peoples of the sea" known from Egyptian sources to have roamed the Mediterranean as pirates in the late 13th century B.C. There was no Helen, no Paris, no Trojan horse—and no Trojan War.

Whatever scholars say, the ancients certainly believed in the Trojan War, and that belief shaped a good deal of actual history. When the Persian King Xerxes invaded Greece in 480 B.C., he had in mind not just to punish the Greeks for the Ionian revolt but to avenge the fall of Troy. He made a point of stopping here and sacrificing a thousand oxen before he continued on to Greece. And when Alexander the Great (who slept with two things under his pillow: a dagger and the *Iliad*) invaded Asia in 334 B.C., he, too, stopped at Troy to offer sacrifice and to honor Achilles by running three times around the low mound out on the Trojan plain that's still known as the tomb of Achilles.

Nor was Troy's significance confined to antiquity. After Mehmet II conquered Constantinople in 1453 he stopped at Troy, where he announced, "It is to me that God has given to avenge this city and its people. . . . Indeed it was the Greeks who devastated this city, and it is their descendants who after so many years have paid me the debt that their boundless pride had contracted then—and often afterwards—towards us, the people of Asia." Mehmet's remarks bring home the significance of what people thought happened here, even if what actually happened is obscure.

Troy and Schliemann

In 1868 the self-made German millionaire and autodidact Heinrich Schliemann, who had become obsessed with finding Troy when he read Homer as a sickly child, visited the Troad and was shown around possible sites of Troy by the American consul at Çanakkale, Frank Calvert. Schliemann left convinced that the mound at Hisarlık hid Troy, and wrote that the site "fully agrees with the description Homer gives of Ilium [Troy], and I will add that, as soon as one sets foot on the Trojan plain, the view of the beautiful hill of Hisarlık grips one with astonishment. The hill seems designed by nature to carry a great city. . . . There is no other place in the whole region to compare with it."

Schliemann returned to Hisarlık in 1870 and cut a 130-foot trench through the mound from north to south. What was revealed was not one but many Troys, layered like a *mille-feuille* pastry, with the first settlement dating from about 3000 B.C. and the last to about A.D. 400. During the next ten years, Schliemann thought he found what he was looking for—Homer's Troy—and earned considerable enmity from later scholars for destroying so much of the evidence by his brutal excavation methods. In 1992, archaeologists here were reexcavating Schliemann's trench in the hopes of learning more and preserving exposed house remains.

Schliemann named the lowermost habitation layer Troy I. When he discovered a hoard of gold jewelry in the next layer, which he called Troy II, he concluded that this must be Homer's Troy. (It's not: Troy II antedates the Trojan War by as much as 1,000 years.) Afraid that his workers might make off with the gold, Schliemann announced a spurious holiday in honor of his birthday, which he said had slipped his mind. As the workers departed, Schliemann's Greek wife, Sophia, took the jewels, concealed in her shawl, to the excavation house.

Never one for understatement, Schliemann sent off telegrams thanking "Providence for rewarding my faith, and my wife for saving the treasure in her shawl." Not everyone was convinced: Rumors swept the world that the Schliemanns had bought the jewels in the bazaars of Istanbul and then hid them on the site to be "discovered."

Most scholars today accept that the gold was found at Troy, but many suspect that Schliemann made a good story better by adding the details about Sophia and the shawl. According to Schliemann's own diary, Sophia may have been in Greece when the jewels were found. (Matters are not helped by the fact that Schliemann spirited most of the hoard off to Berlin's Museum für Völkerkunde, whence it disappeared in the last days of World War II. A few pieces survive in the Istanbul Archaeological Museum, and at least part of what disappeared from Germany has recently resurfaced in a Russian museum.)

Troy: The Site

The first thing you see at Troy, just beyond the inevitable cluster of tourist shops and the ticket booth, is a modern rendition of the Trojan horse, perhaps better suited for Disney World than Troy. You can climb up into the horse, peer out, and remember the story of how Greek warriors hid in the horse, which the gullible Trojans pulled up a ramp into their city. That night, when the Trojans were sleeping, the Greeks leapt out and took Troy. Just behind the horse, the former excavation house has site exhibits and a video (English or Turkish) about Troy.

The American archaeologist Carl Blegen, who excavated at Troy in the 1930s, identified Homer's Troy with Troy VIIa (ca. 1275 to 1240 B.C.), which seems to have been destroyed by siege and fire. Others, including the Turkish archaeologist Ekrem Akurgal, have suggested that Homer's Troy was Troy VI (ca. 1900 to 1275 B.C.), which was destroyed not by siege but by earthquake.

Some scholars have proposed that the legend of the Trojan horse (which appears not in the *Iliad* but in the Epic Cycle, a group of non-Homeric poems on the fall of Troy) recalls an actual wooden horse that the Greeks erected here. The horse, they suggest, was erected as a thanksgiving offering to Poseidon, the god of earthquakes, when an earthquake destroyed the city after the Greeks had failed to do it by siege. In time the legend grew up that the horse itself had brought about Troy's destruction.

Beyond the replica of the horse, through a grove of pine trees, is the low mound of Troy. Although you'll probably be most interested in seeing "Homer's Troy," there are some remains from Roman Troy, including a **theater**, currently undergoing excavation, and the foundations of the **temple of Athena**. The construction of the temple of Athena caused at least as much damage to Troy VI and VII as Schliemann did, as the Romans leveled much of Troy to build the sanctuary.

Throughout much of antiquity housekeeping methods seem to have been simple: When the dirt floor of a dwelling became littered, a new dirt floor was laid down over the old. In time the roof of a dwelling would be raised. Periodically, a settlement would be destroyed by war or an earthquake and the inhabitants would level the wreckage of the old settlement and build anew. Over millennia these successive layers of settlement created a layered mound. The site plan posted near the entrance gives a good idea of the outlines of the various Troys, with Troy II encircling Troy I and Troy VI projecting well beyond its predecessors. The plan will also help you unravel Troy's habitation layers, from Troy I (ca. 3000 to 2500 B.C.) through Troy IX (350 B.C. to A.D. 400).

The remains at Troy are excellently marked in Turkish and English, and the site is so compact that visitors are led around the citadel in a counterclockwise direction to minimize congestion. Go at midday and you'll feel that you're on an anthill, with tourists taking the place of ants. Go first thing in the morning or late in the afternoon and you may find yourself almost alone. Then you can see the rough field-stone walls of Troy I, take in the cracks caused by the great earthquake in the massive walls of Troy VI, and see the scorched walls of Troy VIIa, which was destroyed by fire. (If you're lucky, you may encounter the site guide who speaks excellent English—and knows his Homer.) The buildings of Troy VIIa are considerably smaller and simpler than those of Troy VI; if Troy VI was destroyed by an earthquake, perhaps the inhabitants rebuilt hastily, as best they could—only to have their new city destroyed yet again.

As you explore the site, keep in mind that this was Troy's citadel; most of the houses would have been on the plain below. Along with the walls of Troy VI, Troy's most impressive remains are the great tower, also from Troy VI, in the southeast and the ramp from Troy II in the northwest, near which Schliemann found the hoard he mistakenly named "Priam's Treasure." Schliemann thought that the Trojan horse was pulled up this ramp; alas, it, too, antedates the Trojan War.

When you visit Troy you'll probably come away agreeing that Homer was right to call this "windy Troy": A parching wind usually whips in off the sea. This is a place where the whole is infinitely greater than the sum of the parts. Small wonder that the ancients thought Troy was haunted by the spirits of the dead heroes or that Homer's Troy catches the imagination more than any other site in Aegean Turkey. Perhaps a poet, not a scholar, should be allowed the last word on Troy. In *Don Juan,* Byron wrote

> . . . I've stood upon Achilles' tomb,
> And heard Troy doubted; time will doubt of Rome.

Çanakkale

After the coastal resort towns, Çanakkale (27 km/17 miles north of Troy) has a certain gritty appeal, with ships unloading and trucks jostling for position as they rush on and off ferryboats. This is where the ferries from across the Dardanelles—the strait between Europe and Asia—dock. Boats from Eceabat, near the southern end of the Gallipoli peninsula, dock in Çanakkale itself, while boats from the town of Gelibolu, north of Eceabat, dock at Lâpseki, just north of Çanakkale. It's perfectly possible if you're driving from Europe to the Aegean coast (or vice versa) to bypass Istanbul altogether and cross over by ferry. Even if you're coming from or bound for Istanbul, you might prefer the shorter drive to one of the ferry points rather than taking the more round-about route via Bursa.

Çanakkale's hotels are on the waterfront and are, there-fore, potentially noisy. Better to head south 15 km (9 miles) to the Tusan Truva Motel outside Troy (mentioned above). If you can't get a reservation there and have to spend the night in Çanakkale, try the **Anafartalar Hotel**.

Among Çanakkale's redeeming features are two fine old seafood restaurants, the **Şehir** and the **Yalova Liman**, both on the waterfront to the left of the tourism office. (Which office, by the way, has a metal-grille door, usually closed. The office often appears empty even when staff is within.) You can eat indoors or out at the Şehir, but with the heavy traffic along the waterfront the outdoor tables are a mixed blessing.

In any event, the view across the Dardanelles to the 14th-century fortress of Kilitbahir (Key of the Sea) from the Yalova's second-floor dining room is superb—as are the fried mussels (*midye tava*). At lunch you'll be surrounded by businessmen and dockworkers, all tucking into enor-mous portions of soup, vegetables, and seafood—most of them washing down their meals not with beer or wine, but *rakı*. (The Yalova has a branch on Yalı Caddesi, the street that runs to the right behind Çanakkale's clock tower; the food is just as good, but there's no view.)

Çanakkale is a good place to pick up English-language newspapers, at the stands where the boats dock. Go a few more streets back from the waterfront and you'll see some of Çanakkale's old one-story houses and shops, which have survived an earthquake in 1912, the Gallipoli Campaign of 1915 to 1916, and even Turkey's recent frenzy to demolish and rebuild.

It's hard to escape reminders of Gallipoli in Çanakkale. The collection in the military museum in **Sultaniye Kalesi** (the fortress twin to Kilitbahir, on the Çanakkale waterfront) con-centrates heavily on the Gallipoli campaign. Almost all the labels are in Turkish only, and most of the Turkish sailors on duty as guides understandably speak only Turkish. Still, lest visitors should forget just who won at Gallipoli, a replica of the minelayer *Nusret,* credited with undoing the allied fleet, is anchored at the foot of Sultaniye Kalesi. (If you'd like to visit Gallipoli, Troyanzac, with offices near the clock tower in Çanakkale, is a reputable agency that conducts daily tours of the memorial; Tel: 1969/5047 or 5049. For coverage of the

Gallipoli peninsula and its extensive battle monuments, see Istanbul Environs, above.)

Just outside Çanakkale on the road to Troy is the new **Archaeological Museum**, which gets so few visitors that the staff may have to turn on the lights for you. The museum collection includes finds from throughout the Troad, with pride of place given to objects from Troy. There's a splendid black-glaze *skyphos* (a small two-handled cup) decorated with an alert owl found at Troy VIII, impressive gold wreaths, a tiny ivory dolphin, and the fretboard of a musical instrument found in the Hellenistic tomb known as the **Dardanos tumulus**. (A short detour signposted from the main road to Troy leads to the tumulus itself. Although entry to the tomb is barred by an iron grille, you can peer inside and see the handsome stone masonry.)

A photographic exhibit that was mounted a few years ago at the museum and pointedly entitled Plundered Anatolian Civilizations illustrated why the collection is no larger than it is. The photos showed the treasures that Schliemann took from Troy; the reconstructed altar of Zeus from Pergamum, now in Berlin; the sculptures from Mausoleum of Halicarnassus, now in the British Museum; and various treasures plundered from Anatolia and now in the Metropolitan Museum in New York.

SOUTH FROM İZMİR

Ephesus is only 80 km (50 miles) south of İzmir on route 525, with the modern resort of Kuşadası another 20 km (12 miles) down the road, but you should allow at least two hours for the journey. It's not easy to extricate yourself from İzmir's sprawl, and when you do, you're on a two-lane highway clogged with cars, trucks, and tour buses. The scenery en route to Ephesus in the alluvial plain formed by the Küçük Menderes (the ancient river Cayster) is pleasant enough but hardly arresting, and there's no reason to stop.

Still, keep an eye out for the 13th-century Byzantine fortress known as **Keçi Kalesi** (Goat Castle), on a steep hill to the right of the road just before the town of Belevi. The castle got its nickname when the Seljuk Turks, who were laying siege to the garrison here, strapped torches to an

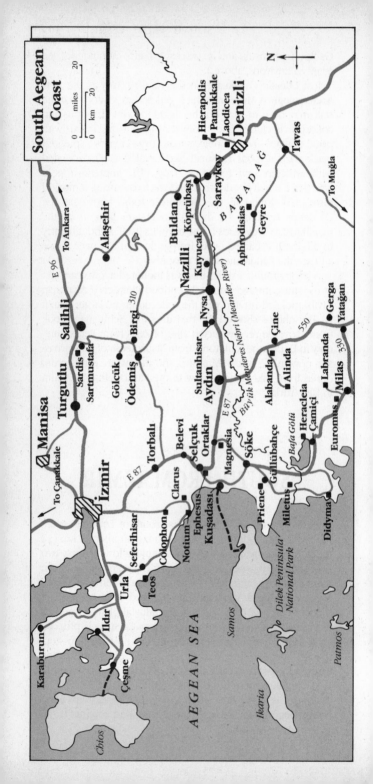

enormous flock of goats and herded them up the hillside in the middle of the night. When the Byzantine defenders saw the sea of lights, they thought that an enormous army was advancing, and surrendered.

If you're visiting Ephesus and then heading south to the ancient Ionian cities of Priene, Miletus, and Didyma, you'll probably stay at Kuşadası. The small **Tusan Efes Moteli** is the only attractive hotel at Ephesus itself, and at present there are no appealing hotels near the other sites. (The beach resort at Altınkum, about five miles south of Didyma, is as crowded as Kuşadası in season, with none of its charms.) In fact, you may want to bypass Ephesus and head straight for Kuşadası. That way you can get settled, have a swim, and then take on Ephesus—which is enormous, often crowded, and shadeless—in the late afternoon or early morning. If you don't have a car, or simply want to avoid the drive, the İzmir tourist bureau has information on day trips to Ephesus and to Priene, Miletus, and Didyma. (See the Kuşadası section, below, for hotel recommendations there.) The İzmir and Kuşadası tourist bureaus can also give you information on the Ephesus Festival held in the first week of May, with concerts and plays in the ancient theater, and on the occasional concerts held at Ephesus each summer.

EPHESUS

Everything about Ephesus (called Efes in Turkish) seems larger than life: As capital of the Roman province of Asia, Ephesus had a population of 300,000 and acres of baths and brothels, stoas and gymnasiums, private houses and public latrines, the largest theater in Asia Minor, a handsome library—*and* the temple of Artemis (Diana), which was one of the Seven Wonders of the World. Mark Twain visited Ephesus and described it in *The Innocents Abroad* (1869): "It was a wonderful city, this Ephesus. Go where you will about these broad plains, you find the most exquisitely sculptured marble fragments scattered thick among the dust and weeds; and protruding from the ground or lying prone upon it are beautiful fluted columns of porphyry and all precious marbles.... It is a world of precious relics, a wilderness of marred and mutilated gems. And yet what are these things to the wonders that lie buried here under the ground?"

Since Twain's visit much of Ephesus has been excavated, much has been restored; with so much of what was underground now above, visiting Ephesus can be daunting. And no matter how early or late in the day or season you come, you'll probably never be alone at Ephesus, where the throngs of visitors make the streets almost as crowded as they must have been in antiquity.

Ephesus draws an unusually diverse group of visitors. First, of course, are the travellers visiting the ancient sites of Aegean Turkey, of which Ephesus is easily the most extensive and, many think, the most impressive. Second, almost every Aegean cruise ship docks at Kuşadası and then buses its passengers to Ephesus. Finally, Christians (and a surprising number of Muslims, who also honor the Virgin Mary) from throughout the world come here to see the **house of the Virgin Mary** (the Meryemana), 5 km (3 miles) up the mountain road from Ephesus's Magnesian Gate. To reach the Meryemana from Selçuk, take the road signposted Germencik/Aydın at the traffic circle in the center of town.

Legend has it that the Apostle John brought the Virgin Mary here to live after Jesus's death. In 1818 an Austrian peasant woman, Anne Catherine Emmerich, had an eerily precise vision that led to the discovery of what many Christians believe was the house in which Mary lived. More rebuilt than restored, the house (dating from perhaps the sixth century A.D. but with foundations that may go back to the first century) is now a major pilgrimage shrine, where signs urging visitors to respect the holy spot are outnumbered in the summer by souvenir stands.

After visiting Mary's house, all those pilgrims join the crowds at Ephesus, itself an important Christian site. The Third Ecumenical Council met in the city's so-called Council Church (the church of the Virgin Mary) in A.D. 431 and affirmed that Mary was the mother of God (*theotokos,* "Godbearer," in Greek), not merely the mother of the *man* Jesus, as some had held. The church, partly restored in honor of the visit of Pope Paul VI in 1967, is north of the Harbor Gymnasium and Portico Verulanus.

Selçuk and the
Ephesus Museum

There's so much to see at ancient Ephesus that many visitors neglect Selçuk, 4 km (2½ miles) from Ephesus itself. That's too bad, because the town has the best-preserved Byzantine monument in Aegean Turkey: the sixth-century **church of St. John** on the south slopes of Ayasuluk hill. By the time the church was built, Ephesus's once-splendid harbor had silted up and many Ephesians had moved inland to the slopes of Ayasuluk, which was the acropolis first of a Byzantine settlement and then, as the fortress on its summit reveals, of the Ottomans. According to one tradition, Saint John died at Ephesus and the sixth-century emperor Justinian built this enormous church on the site where the saint was buried. The Justinianic church was exceptionally lavish, with mosaics, frescoes, and ornately carved column capitals; you can see some of the mosaics in the treasury, which adjoins the baptistery.

When you leave the church of Saint John, try to visit the **İsa Bey Camii**, lower down the slopes of Ayasuluk hill and also recently restored; you get a fine view of the mosque— and, incidentally, of the temple of Artemis—from the southern edge of the plateau where the church stands. The mosque, which was built in 1375 by İsa Bey, a member of the ruling family in this district in the 14th century, is often locked. Still, even if you can't get in and see the architectural ornament and mosaics, you can admire the mosque's western façade, which is covered with fine marble and has a monumental entranceway decorated with inlaid black-and-white marble geometric designs. This is the earliest known example in western Asia Minor of a mosque that has an arcaded courtyard and pool. The mosque was converted into a caravansary in the 19th century, and its *mihrap* was removed and taken to the Kestane Pazarı Camii in İzmir.

The superb **Ephesus Museum** (open most days from 8:30 A.M. to 6:00 P.M.) is also in Selçuk at the foot of Ayasuluk hill. (The museum and ancient site are signposted at the traffic circle. There is a small tourist bureau in the parking lot across from the museum.) According to legend, Ephesus was founded by one of the sons of Athens's legendary King Codrus, and there certainly was a Greek settlement here by about 1000 B.C. Nonetheless, most of the museum exhibits reflect Ephesus's greatest periods of prosperity during the Hellenistic and Roman eras—although some of the finest pieces, such as a small sixth-century B.C. bronze statue of an Egyptian priest are earlier. (This statue may have been a treasured family heirloom: It was found in one of the Roman houses at Ephesus. There's a reproduction of the statue in the house itself.)

The museum is well laid out, with finds from houses, sculpture, architectural fragments, and early Christian and Byzantine relics, all neatly organized in separate galleries. Labels in English make it easy to know whether you're looking at a bust of the poet Menander or the philosopher Socrates (who also appears in a fine second-century A.D. fresco).

The museum's hall of Artemis contains a number of votive offerings found in the temple of Artemis, of which two tiny seventh-century B.C. figures of priestesses (one gold, one ivory) are particularly fine. They're not the first things you'll notice, however, as the gallery is dominated by two marble statues of the goddess herself: the first-century A.D. *Great Artemis* and the second-century A.D. *Beautiful Artemis.*

Scholars disagree as to what exactly the rows of ovoids on the goddess's chest are meant to be: Breasts, eggs, bulls' testicles, and bees are the leading contenders. People in antiquity may not have known the answer either—these cult statues were probably clothed in elaborate costumes.

The Temple of Artemis

The remains of the temple of Artemis are just outside Selçuk on the Ephesus road, beside an army base. The temple, which in antiquity overlooked the sea, was linked to Ephesus by a splendid road ornamented with statues. (A fine description of a procession from Ephesus to the temple appears in the delightful romance *An Ephesian Tale,* by the second-century A.D. writer Xenophon.)

On January 1, 1869, after six years of excavating (and several bouts of malaria), the English engineer and amateur archaeologist J. T. Wood found the remains of the temple, buried beneath the mud laid down by the Küçük Menderes. One of Wood's colleagues wrote that trying to find the temple was like "groping for jewels amid mud and slime." The temple precincts are often flooded even today, and ducks sometimes paddle about in the water. On dry ground peacocks wander about shrieking, and you may also see soldiers from the nearby army base practicing grease wrestling beside the temple.

Only one of the temple's 127 massive Ionic columns remains to give a sense of the immense scale of this building, one of the largest temples of the ancient Greek world. Three times the size of the Parthenon, larger even than the Heraion of Samos (itself so large that it was nicknamed "the Labyrinth"), this marble temple must have been a stupendous sight. The cella (interior chamber) was encased in what Pliny called a "forest of columns"—a double row of Ionic columns along each side, with a thicket of columns at each end. In 356 B.C. the temple was set afire by a lunatic called Herostratus, who wanted to do something to make his name live on in history. Over the course of the next century the temple was rebuilt, and Herostratus was forgotten by all but scholars and trivia buffs.

The temple of Artemis probably drew as many tourists in antiquity as the site of Ephesus does today, and many Ephesians, especially the jewelers who crafted votive offerings for pilgrims, benefited handsomely. One visitor was Saint Paul, who spent two years here trying to woo converts away from Artemis to Christ. Never tactful, Paul finally provoked a riot, with the Christians shouting out imprecations against Artemis while most townfolk chanted, "Great is Artemis of the Ephesians." The Roman governor called a town meeting in the theater, where, according to the Acts of the Apostles, "some cried one thing and some another." Finally the governor restored order, but tempers were still so high that Paul hastily left Ephesus to pursue his missionary work in Macedonia. Later, Ephesus was the home of one of the Seven Churches addressed in Revelation.

Ephesus: The Site

Ephesus is often compared to Pompeii because the remains are so extensive that you can walk along ancient streets lined with actual buildings, peer into houses, and get a three-dimensional sense of what the city looked like. What's more, at Ephesus you don't have the uncomfortable feeling of being a voyeur at the scene of a disaster: Ephesus flourished well into the Christian era and was abandoned only in the sixth century A.D., when its harbor had completely silted up.

Ephesus sprawls across the valley between Panayır Dağı (the ancient Mount Pion) and Bülbül Dağı (the ancient Mount Coressus) in the valley of the Küçük Menderes. Much of the city runs up Panayır Dağı, and you can enter the site either near the Vedius gymnasium at the bottom or through the Magnesian Gate at the top of the hill. Beginning at the bottom has the distinct advantage that you pass the most impressive monuments when you're fresh—and it's downhill all the way when you finish your visit. Spend half a day here and you'll see almost everything, but it takes several visits to digest the site thoroughly and to take in the fine details of Ephesus's lavish architectural ornament. A good site map (maps and site guides are sold at the stalls outside the entrances), sturdy shoes, and a sun hat are vital, and bringing drinking water is a good idea. If you don't want to carry your own water, several small booths on the site sell cold water and soft drinks at inflated prices that you will probably be only too happy to pay.

As you enter the site, passing the indeterminate ruins of the **gymnasium of Vedius** and the Roman **stadium**, with its arched entrance, you may wonder what all the fuss is about—until you reach the **theater**. (You may also want to visit the restored **church of the Virgin Mary**, which is signposted to the right of the site entrance.) If you stand with your back to the theater, you're looking out toward Ephesus's lost harbor, originally about half a mile away. Ahead stretches the paved road that ran from the theater to the harbor. The street was flanked with covered porticoes that would have provided welcome shade; you can get an idea of what the porticoes were like from the columns that remain in place. At night the harbor road was lit by torches, making Ephesus, along with Rome and Antioch, one of the three ancient cities known to have had street lighting.

Walk down the harbor road away from the theater to explore the remains (to the right) of several enormous gymnasium-bath complexes and the open courtyard of the **Portico Verulanus**, a palaestra that was the largest structure in Ephesus. It's easy to lose your way in the sprawling baths, whose crumbling brick walls rear up over the level plain. The walk back along the harbor road offers a superb view of the theater, built into the slopes of Panayır Dağı. The original Hellenistic theater was adapted and expanded by the Romans until it reached its present capacity of 24,000 spectators. The ground floor of the Roman stage building is well preserved, but you'll have to imagine its flamboyant three-tiered façade: You won't be too far off if you conjure up something even more elaborate than the marble court at Sardis or the Celsus library just up the hill.

From the theater you begin the steep ascent of Ephesus's main street (known as the Marble Way), passing the main agora, which lay between the Marble Way and the harbor road. Ahead looms the ornate façade of the partially restored second-century A.D. **library of Celsus**. Celsus was a governor of Asia, and after his death his son built this library, which not only held 12,000 scrolls but also served as Celsus's mausoleum. If you peer through the low opening in the apsidal wall of the library façade you'll see Celsus's sarcophagus still in place. The library was squeezed into its site, and the architect used several tricks to give an impression of greater size. For example, the columns at the sides of the façade are smaller than those at the center, creating the illusion that the columns are farther apart than they actually are. In turn, this makes the entire building seem wider than it is. Ephesus's Austrian archaeologists are currently engaged in a frenzy of "site enhancement," and restoration is underway on Hadrian's Gate, the agora gate, and the long stoa of Nero, which extends from the harbor road to the agora gate. This project will take years, but when it is done (and the construction cranes are gone) an important section of Ephesus will have been restored.

From the library of Celsus (after casting a glance at the house opposite, signposted "Roman private house/so-called brothel") you'll follow the Marble Way as it skirts the side of Panayır Dağı. On your right there's a Byzantine fountain, a reminder of Ephesus's postclassical period. Farther up on the left are the **baths of Scholastica**, a Christian matron who restored the baths in A.D. 400. Nearby are the public latrines, usually easy to locate by the sound of nervous titterings from tour groups photographing themselves *in situ*. Just up the hill on the left is the delicate Corinthian temple of Hadrian, with its lovely arched porch and fine architectural ornament.

The recently restored complex of elegant **Roman houses** across from the temple of Hadrian offers the welcome chance for a break before taking on the last of the buildings lining the road to the Magnesian Gate. The Roman houses are at the top of a short, but dishearteningly steep, hill, so you may even find them relatively uncrowded. These houses—many of them three stories high—had rooms arranged around a central courtyard, open to the sky, often with a central fountain. Cool in summer but comfortably (and centrally) heated in winter, the houses' rooms are windowless and would have been quite dark. Their delicate frescoes and splendid mosaics show scenes from Greek mythology and drama. How pleasant it must have been to sit here, perhaps sniffing a bouquet of flowers of the sort shown in the mosaics, while outside others toiled along the Marble Way. (The houses were closed in 1991 and remained so in 1992 due to damage to the mosaics; check to see whether they've reopened when you visit.)

By the time you rejoin the Marble Way you'll have gotten some idea of the enormity of Ephesus—and there's much more to come. Ahead lie more temples, more baths, and an entire complex of civic buildings and monuments, several built by the Roman emperors Trajan and Hadrian, who seem to have left buildings behind them the way some people leave calling cards. In addition to his temple, Hadrian was honored here by a **monumental gate**, while Trajan gave an elaborate **nymphaeum** (fountain house), which has been partly restored.

Just beyond the fountain house of Trajan, the **gate of Hercules** (easily identified by the two relief figures of a round-faced Hercules in his lionskin garment) marks the farthest point where vehicles were allowed on the Marble Way; after this the steep road was for pedestrians only. You'll pass the foundations of a first-century B.C. arch, known as the **Memmius Monument** (named for its donor), and (just off

the Marble Way on your right) the scant remains of the
temple of Domitian (first century A.D.) before arriving at a
heavily restored second-century A.D. **odeon**, which seated
1,400. The odeon was used both for theatrical performances
and civic meetings; it fronts on the **state agora**, which was
used for both governmental and religious assemblies.

The Marble Way continues past the remains of the **Varius
baths** to the **Magnesian Gate**, which is flanked by yet another
gymnasium beyond the upper site entrance, known simply
as the **East Gymnasium** (second century A.D.). Although not
as large as the gymnasium complex beside the harbor road,
this was an impressive structure. Ancient gymnasiums were
centers of education as well as sport, and the East Gymnasium had classrooms as well as baths and exercise areas.
Archaeologists have suggested that the baths of the East
Gymnasium may have been used by weary travellers who
arrived at Ephesus after journeying through Asia Minor.
From the gymnasium the travellers could stroll down the
Marble Way, which is what you would do to retrace your
steps and bring your visit here to a close.

Before you leave Ephesus and Selçuk, you may want to
head north about 20 km (12 miles) on the İzmir road to the
village of Belevi and ask for directions there to the **Belevi
mausoleum**, just out of town beside the new İzmir–Aydın
road. The tomb chamber of this somewhat mysterious monument (perhaps the tomb of Antiochus II of Syria, who died at
Ephesus in 246 B.C.) was carved out of the hillside. The
entire monument resembled a small temple, with ceiling
coffers lavishly decorated with carved reliefs and a Corinthian colonnade (You'll see some of the Corinthian capitals
scattered near the tomb.) This is the most elaborate known
funeral monument in Asia Minor, with the exception of the
Mausoleum at Halicarnassus. From the mausoleum you can
see a nearby tomb-mound with a retaining wall of handsomely worked ashlar masonry.

KUŞADASI

The İzmir–Söke road bypasses Kuşadası (pronounced KOO-
shah-deh-suh), which you enter by one of the two access
roads, marked "Centrum/Şehir Merkesi," north and south of
town. Cars are not allowed on several streets (notably Barbaros Hayrettin Caddesi) leading down to the harbor, which
you'll probably find by trial and error. When you get there,
pick up the excellent town and environs map usually available from the **tourist office** (Tel: 636/111-03) on the harbor

at İskele Meydanı (Harbor Square), where cruise ships dock. This is also the place to find out about the several companies offering boat trips to the Greek island of Samos (daily in summer, irregularly the rest of the year). If you arrive during the Ephesus Festival, held during the first week of May, the tourist office is also the best place to inquire about the special events scheduled.

The tourist office is just below Kuşadası's splendid 16th-century Öküz Mehmet Paşa Kervansarayı, also called the Club Caravansérail Hotel-Restaurant. When you see the caravansary you'll want to stay here—but do so only if you conclude that rooms decorated with traditional weavings and old copper can compensate for the reverberations of the nightly floor show, so loudly amplified that it's a miracle that the walls haven't yet come tumbling down.

The nicest place to say in Kuşadası is the Hotel Kısmet, which is actually just out of town to the north, on the hooked Akyar peninsula. The hotel, owned by a descendant of the last Ottoman sultan, and situated in a cool, green garden shaded by palm and pine trees and scented with night-blooming jasmine, looks out over a marina toward Kuşadası. There's no beach, but there's good swimming off a pier. This is the place to go if you want peace and quiet—and the chance to forgo *rakı* for a dry martini. The sunsets here are spectacular, as are the delicate pastries served in the excellent hotel restaurant. In Kuşadası itself, the Hotel Atınç on Atatürk Bulvarı (on the harbor) has a rooftop pool—a nice plus, as Kuşadası's best beach, known as Lady's Beach, is outside town and often crowded. At the reasonably priced Hotel Efe on Güvercinada Caddesi (the southern extension of Atatürk Bulvarı), also on the harbor, most rooms have balconies overlooking the harbor and Pigeon Island (Güvercin Adası), but there's no pool. All these hotels are modern, clean, and perfectly acceptable, but the Kısmet is the sort of place where you can stay a week and be sorry to leave.

If you haven't been to Kuşadası for 15 or so years, you'll probably spend a fair amount of time waxing nostalgic over the charming little village that was: a seaside hamlet crouching by a harbor where fishing boats bobbed, with one or two simple hotels and seaside restaurants, quiet side streets to wander, and perhaps a shop or two selling rugs.

So much for nostalgia. Kuşadası has since become *the* tourist center of the southern Aegean coast. Almost everyone visiting the major Ionian sites of Ephesus, Priene, Miletus, and Didyma stays here, and almost every cruise ship that stops in Turkey docks here. Furthermore, many Europeans come here every summer, staying in the clusters of condominiums that have encircled the old Kuşadası, turning a village into a city (population 40,000).

It seems that every shopkeeper on Barbaros Hayrettin Caddesi, old Kuşadası's pedestrianized main street, is either a jeweler or a rug merchant. Few shop owners believe in keeping a low sales profile, and walking along B. Hayrettin is a bit like running the gantlet, as merchants call out invitations (orders, almost) to stop, look, and buy. Nor does it help to walk firmly down the center of the street looking neither right nor left: That's where the spice vendors have set up a row of barrows.

As you're not going to get a sense of the "real" Turkey in Kuşadası, the sensible thing to do is to take advantage of what the town has to offer: First, there's **Pigeon Island**, a pine-clad islet linked to the mainland by a short causeway. Locals sometimes come here for their evening constitutional, walking past the island's small Ottoman fort, now a café, and stopping at the tomb of Mehmet Efendi, a Whirling Dervish and local hero. The tombstone is usually festooned with bits of paper and cloth, which visitors leave as one might leave flowers at a grave.

The island possesses several pizza restaurants and discos, but for seafood you should head back to the harbor. It's hard to know which restaurant to choose; all do a heavy tourist business, and none is distinctive. The **Diba** and the **Toros Canlı Balık** restaurants usually have fresh fish—the *çinakop* (bonito) and *lüfer* (bluefish) are tasty. Both restaurants have gardens off the street that are pleasant in fine weather. If the harborside restaurants are too crowded, head inland and you'll find some small kebap places that are usually less congested, such as the **Konya** restaurant and **Loretta's** restaurant.

At some point you'll probably decide to stop running the merchants' gantlet and have a look at some of the rugs on display throughout Kuşadası. Two good places to begin are the **Bazaar 54** shop in the Club Caravansérail hotel and the **Lapis** complex (selling rugs, jewelry, and leather) on the harbor. Expect to bargain; prices are inflated so that you can do just that. If you start to succumb to a rug at the Lapis (which caters to the cruise-ship crowd) but then wonder aloud how on earth you'll get it home, a salesman will demonstrate by neatly folding the rug into just the right size to fit into a complimentary carry-on bag. Irresistible.

As for the jewelry stores, you may find them more resistible, as gold prices are no bargain—and not all the gold is of the advertised quality. Several shops along B. Hayrettin, however, do have nice necklaces of onyx and other stones, some incorporating old Turkish coins.

Dilek Peninsula
National Park

Whatever else Kuşadası is, it's not restful. If you're visiting all the ancient sites nearby, you may find yourself wishing guiltily to get away from it all—to read something other than a guidebook and see something other than a ruin. Why not pick up a newspaper or book at one of Kuşadası's two foreign-language bookshops, the **Art Kitabevi** on B. Hayrettin, or the **Kuşadası Bookstore** on the street above and parallel to Hayrettin (best reached through Kuşadası's self-styled "oriental bazaar," a sort of touristic mini-mall).

Once you have something to read, head out of Kuşadası to the Dilek Yarımadası Milli Parkı (Dilek Peninsula National Park), 28 km (17 miles) south of Kuşadası. When you stop to pay the small entrance fee, pick up the park's brochure (with map), available in English. This large nature preserve stretches along a thickly wooded peninsula that almost touches the island of Samos and reportedly is the home of bear, wild boar, jackals, and even leopards. You almost certainly won't see any of them (although you may see hawks overhead), nor are you likely to see many other tourists, except in high season, when there's a boat and dolmuş service here from Kuşadası.

A good road runs to the tip of the peninsula, where there's a fine sand beach and several small restaurants. Side roads run to smaller beaches with no restaurants, so this is a good place to bring a picnic. One thing to keep in mind: Forest fires are a constant threat, so dispose of matches and cigarettes carefully.

INLAND FROM KUŞADASI

If you want to head inland to see the ancient sites of Aphrodisias and Hierapolis, the calcified waterfalls at Pamukkale (Turkish for "Cotton Castle," because of its white mineral deposits), or any of several smaller sites, you have several choices as to your route. Whichever you select, expect to put in some long days in the car: It's about 180 km (112 miles) from Sardis to Pamukkale/Hierapolis and 220 km (136 miles) from Kuşadası to Pamukkale. Even the main roads are only two lanes wide, with so many trucks and buses that you're periodically slowed to a crawl. Plan on progressing at an average of 60 kilometers an hour (about 37 mph), and be pleasantly surprised if you do better.

From Sardis: If you're starting off from Sardis, you can head south from Salihli to Denizli (the city nearest Hierapolis and Pamukkale) via Alaşehir, Buldan, Köprübaşı, and Sarayköy. This route skirts the Bozdağlar range.

If you want a more mountainous route, take the secondary road through the mountains from Salihli to Ödemiş and continue east along route 310, then south to Denizli. This is a beautiful drive, passing through mountain hamlets and upland plains with flowering fruit trees, but there is no point in going this way unless you want to travel slowly and enjoy the scenery. If you want to break your journey, try the **Bozdağ Turistik Oteli** between Sardis and Ödemiş or the **Kavaklı Pansiyon** in Gölcük off the Salihli–Ödemiş road.

From Kuşadası: If you're heading to Pamukkale from Kuşadası go first to Söke, and then take the E 87 from Ortaklar via Aydın and Nazilli to the turnoff for Denizli at Sarayköy. Both Aydın (pop. 60,000) and Denizli (pop. 185,000) are capitals of provinces by the same names, but there's no real reason to stop at either unless you're making a very leisurely tour of Turkey and want to visit provincial capitals.

The trip from Kuşadası to Pamukkale along the Menderes river valley is speedier but less beautiful than either of the two routes from Sardis. Travelling along the twisting Menderes (the ancient Meander) will show you why "meander" means "to wander." This is the route followed below, with possible stops at Magnesia-on-the-Meander and Nysa suggested en route.

Magnesia-on-the-Meander

Stopping for a lemonade at the café beside the ancient site of Magnesia-on-the-Meander, just off the road between Söke and Ortaklar, will let you easily take in this site. Not many people bother visiting the ruins of Magnesia's Ionic **temple of Artemis**, which Strabo considered finer even than the temple of Artemis at Ephesus. If you wander onto the site, the guard may well give you a private tour of the scattered remains of the temple, a small theater, the gymnasium and stadium, and the Byzantine fortifications.

It's not easy to believe from these scattered ruins, but this Ionian site was one of the most important cities in the

Roman province of Asia, drawing much of its wealth from the rich agricultural plain watered by the Meander. Figs from Magnesia were particularly prized, and fig trees still dot the plain here.

Although Magnesia was most important during the Roman period, it was already a provincial center under the Persian Empire. The great fifth-century B.C. Athenian statesman Themistocles lived here in exile after his victories during the Persian Wars—a welcome guest of his old enemy, the Persian king Xerxes. According to Plutarch, when the Persians sought Themistocles' assistance against the Greeks, the Athenian chose suicide rather than abetting his former foe. The Magnesians, impressed, erected a monument to Themistocles in the agora, as yet unexcavated.

Nysa

Ancient Nysa is signposted in the village of Sultanhisar, about 30 km (19 miles) past Aydın. If you come here on the first Sunday in May, when the Nysa Festival takes place, you won't need any signs: Just head toward the source of the amplified music and you'll find yourself at Nysa's **Roman theater**.

Scholars disagree as to whether Nysa was in ancient Lydia or in Phrygia, but agree that it was an important center of learning during the Roman period: The geographer Strabo studied here, as did a number of philosophers. The city enjoyed a particularly lovely setting, which Strabo described as "divided by a torrential stream that forms a gorge." In the gorge beneath the theater are the considerable remains of a hidden underground passage (a vaulted Roman tunnel) that Strabo says served as a conduit for the stream; the site guard can show you the tunnel's entrance near the theater. Scattered through olive groves are the remains of a number of Roman civic buildings, including the **library** where Strabo studied and the second-century A.D. **bouleuterion** (council house), with a number of its seats preserved. You'll also come across the foundations and walls of several small Byzantine churches. When the festival is going on you'll encounter a great many picnickers; at other times Nysa is one place you'll probably have to yourself, although there's usually someone selling soft drinks at the Nyssa Kafetyria by the theater.

Off in the hills are the remains of the **Plutonium**, a shrine to Pluto, Roman god of the underworld. The Plutonium, located near a cave and springs, has virtually no remains and is not easy to find; if you want to track it down, go to the village of Çiftekahveler and ask for directions.

Aphrodisias

"Imagine coming upon a city of antiquity so rich in archaeological treasure that choice sculptures roll off the sides of ditches, tumble from old walls, and lie jam-packed amid colonnaded ruins." Those are the words of the late Kenan Erim, who directed the New York University excavation at Aphrodisias, the city of the goddess of love, Aphrodite (the Roman Venus). Aphrodisias was in the ancient district of Caria, a mountainous region in southwest Asia Minor. The site lies in a fertile valley cut by the Büyük Menderes (the ancient Meander) and is framed to the east by the Babadağ range (the ancient Salbakos), which supplied the marble that made this city such an important center of the arts that some have compared it to Renaissance Florence. To get to Aphrodisias from Nysa continue east on E 24/320, then turn south just after Kuyucak to Geyre, 2 km (1¼ miles) from the site; allow two hours for the drive.

Just as the temple of Artemis drew pilgrims to Ephesus, the shrine of Aphrodite drew worshipers to Aphrodisias, where finds indicate that there may have been a Bronze Age (ca. 2900 to 1200 B.C.) shrine to Ishtar, Aphrodite's local predecessor, on the low hill-mound known as Pekmez Hüyük. At some point the earlier fertility goddess yielded to Aphrodite, and by the Roman period Aphrodisias was one of the goddess's most important sanctuaries.

It makes sense that the Romans honored Aphrodite—after all, the goddess was the mother of Aeneas, whose descendants founded Rome. Official patronage—from the dictator Sulla, Julius Caesar, Augustus, and later emperors—brought considerable wealth to Aphrodisias beginning in the first century B.C. The Romans adorned not merely the shrine but the entire city, building the splendid gates, baths, theaters, and other public buildings, whose remains you see today.

During the last two summers, one of the city's most imposing monuments, the second-century A.D. **Tetrapylon** (a monumental gateway with four rows of columns, some fluted, some spiral), near the temple of Aphrodite, has been restored. Ongoing excavations beside the Tetrapylon are revealing a wide, marble-paved, colonnaded street. The Tetrapylon, like a number of Aphrodisias's public monuments, was decorated with "peopled scrolls." Both in the museum and at the theater baths you'll see examples of these architectural reliefs with little figures of gods and men peeking out from vines and acanthus leaves.

"Peopled scrolls" were only one characteristic of the

stonecarving produced by the important school of sculpture here, now known as the School of Aphrodisias. Sculpture was so important that this city—and only this city, as far as is known—held contests for sculptors at festivals honoring Aphrodite. Between the first century B.C. and the fifth century A.D. artists here produced an astonishing amount of high-quality architectural ornament and statuary in a somewhat florid and Baroque style. Artists who worked here were fortunate that the nearby Babadağ (Salbakas) range produced a superb white and blue-gray marble that took polish particularly well. As a result, many statues have the kind of silky patina usually associated only with individual works of genius, such as the Hermes of Praxiteles found at Olympia in Greece.

Although most of the sculpture, much of it signed by individual artists, was exported throughout the Roman world, enough remained to make the **Aphrodisias Museum**, near the entrance to the site, particularly fine. Just as the cult statue of Artemis dominates the Ephesus Museum, the cult statue of Aphrodite takes pride of place here—but don't miss the exquisite little seated Aphrodite whose gracefully crossed legs make you wish that her torso and head had survived. (The Aphrodisias Museum is open from 8:00 A.M. to noon and 1:30 to 5:30 P.M.)

There's an immense amount to see in this museum. Exhibits are arranged thematically, not chronologically, with busts in one gallery, decorative sculpture in another, religious sculpture in a third, and so forth. The **Zoilos Frieze** is as interesting as a document of social history as a work of art. Zoilos, a slave born in Aphrodisias, gained his freedom from Octavian (the future Emperor Augustus) and became wealthy enough to be a benefactor of his hometown, which honored him with the monument ornamented with this frieze, which shows him being crowned by a deity personifying the city.

As you walk through the museum, keep in mind that in ancient times almost all the sculpture you see was on public view, making the city a virtual sculpture garden. Photographers will be disappointed by the signs warning them not to photograph most of what they see; the museum shop sells postcards and a site guide (with a well-illustrated section on the museum) that offer some consolation.

When you leave the museum and head into the site, directly across from the museum, you'll encounter more signs forbidding photography. In fact, in contrast to most sites in Aegean Turkey, where discreet labels help you figure out what you're looking at, many signs at Aphrodisias merely command you not to enter or not to photograph. It's all perfectly reasonable: The excavators want to protect the ancient remains from tourists and the unpublished finds from sneaky scholars bent on stealing their thunder. Still, it's more than a little irritating that the newly discovered **sebasteion** (a shrine dedicated to the Roman imperial cult and packed with impressive sculptural reliefs), highly touted in excavation reports and Kenan Erim's own useful site guidebook, is virtually impossible to see: One view is blocked by a high wall, while access from other directions is cut off by barbed wire.

Fortunately, most structures—including the **Roman theater**, which seated 10,000; the **temple of Aphrodite**, with 14 standing columns; a well-preserved odeon; and the largest and best-preserved **stadium** in the classical world—are not off-limits. And, as Aphrodisias also has the usual complement of imperial baths, gymnasiums, and monumental gates flanking the enormous Roman agora, there's more than enough to see. Even if you can't photograph all the ruins you'd like, the landscape is easily worth a picture or two.

Two kilometers (1¼ miles) west of Aphrodisias is the village of Geyre, which, until recently, sprawled over the site itself. En route to the village you'll pass several small pensions and restaurants. The **Chez Mestan Pension** (the proprietress is French) on the main road is quite charming, with a small boutique selling good quality rugs. Just down the road toward Geyre itself is the new **Aphrodisias Hotel**, run by the same family. Over the years the Aphrodisias excavation purchased land from Geyre and was eventually able to relocate the entire village so that excavation could proceed unchecked (the museum stands in what was formerly the village square, and the theater was formerly almost hidden beneath the village). The theater, by the way, is not cut into a natural hill but into the habitation mound of Bronze Age Aphrodisias. In 1990 Aphrodisias acquired all the remaining land within the ancient city walls. Beneath that land lies yet more of the ancient city, its hidden treasures now safeguarded from damage from farmers' plows until they can be excavated.

Pamukkale and Hierapolis

The provincial capital of **Denizli**, southeast of Saraköy, is busily bursting at the seams. It's ferociously hot in summer, and you'll probably dodge through it on the E 24/320, following the yellow tourist signs for Pamukkale, and head straight up to the plateau topped by Pamukkale and ancient Hierapolis, 19 km (12 miles) away. The first hint of Pamukkale is the distant sight of odd, whitish cliffs towering above the plain of Denizli. Atop the cliffs stand the modern spa resort of Pamukkale and the ancient spa city of Hierapolis.

As you approach the cliffs you'll see that they have been formed—and are still being formed—by running water. The calcium in the water solidifies as the water flows from countless underground springs over the cliffs, forming shallow basins and deep pools flanked by gnarled and twisted stalagmites. According to scientists who calculate these matters, if the water has always flowed at its present rate, Pamukkale's cliffs began forming more than 14,000 years ago.

Most of the cliffs are as white as the cotton that gives Pamukkale its name, which in Turkish means "Cotton Castle," but some sections are naturally yellow, amber, or pinkish. The cliffs are at their best out of season: In high summer they take on a dusty beige tint and look like snowdrifts long after snowfall. Still, at night, when the cliffs are floodlit and visitors scamper and splash about in the warm pools, the entire panorama looks like a scene from Walt Disney's *Fantasia* that ended up on the cutting-room floor because it was just a bit *too* fantastic. The considerable ruins of Hierapolis—with its marvelously eerie necropolis—begin on the plateau just behind the watery cliffs and extend up the steep hill to the north.

Pamukkale is also a good place to see Turks enjoying themselves. This is a popular Turkish resort and a favorite spot for weddings and honeymoons. Some travellers, however, may find the summertime crowds simply too intense, what with 50 or 60 tour buses arriving every afternoon—and the threat of a new helicopter service for day-trippers from Antalya.

Not surprisingly, Pamukkale has a number of hotels, most with pools fed by the springs and cliffside views. That's the good news. The bad news is that the hotels are very hot in summer since they face west and are baked by the afternoon sun. Furthermore, since most visitors spend only one night here, service tends to be cursory and prices are absurdly inflated: In 1992, the Mistur Motel charged $5 for a bottle of water.

The **Pamukkale Motel** clearly wins the swimming-pool sweepstakes: Marble columns from ancient Hierapolis are submerged in the palm-shaded pool, which may be the former sacred pool that reportedly lay near Hierapolis's temple of Apollo. On the other hand, the motel's location at the entrance to the ancient site means that a lot of tour buses disgorge passengers here, many of whom pay the small fee to swim in the motel pool. A better choice might be the **Palmiye Motel**, with a number of rooms with individual soaking pools overlooking the cliffs and the plain below, or the **Tusan Motel**, with a large pool, also overlooking the cliffs and plain, and nice landscaping. The **Koru Motel** also has good rooms and pools—but Muzak is insistently piped into its lobby, bars, and shops, which include one of the outposts of Benetton's retail empire. Farthest away from the hubbub, the **Mistur Motel** has attractive domed rooms, some with spectacular views.

All of these hotels have their own restaurants, and almost all offer the standard evening buffet dinner. If you tire of this, try the small pizza and kebap place on the road to the Palmiye Motel. You won't find the wide selection of the hotel buffets, but the food is cheap and good, and it's pleasant to sit outside on the restaurant's shaded terrace and listen to the croaking of the frogs that inhabit the water channels and shallow pools on the cliffs. (There are also a number of modest small hotels, pensions, and restaurants at the foot of Pamukkale's cliffs and in nearby Denizli.)

You'll need no help in figuring out how to enjoy Pamukkale: Wander on the cliffs, wade in the natural hot springs, and float in your hotel pool. (Don't fret about the sludge in the bottom of the pool: It's only the springs' characteristic calcium deposit.) If, at some point, your conscience reminds you of ancient Hierapolis, here are a few pointers for visiting the site.

Hierapolis is here for the same reason that you are: the springs, which made this a popular resort and spa in antiquity. Unlike Aphrodisias, which seems to have existed virtually since time immemorial, Hierapolis is a relatively young city. Eumenes II, the energetic king of Pergamum responsible for so much building in that city, developed Hierapolis in the second century B.C., although there was probably already a settlement here. (The city's name seems to mean "The Holy City" but may instead derive from Hiera, the plucky Trojan woman who led an attack against the Greeks and was a legendary ancestor of the Pergamene kings.)

As usual, when the Romans arrived they rebuilt everything in sight and added a fuller-than-usual quota of baths because of the springs. (Hierapolis's small **museum** occupies the segment of the Roman baths across from the tourist information center.) Both the **theater** and the **temple of Apollo** at the foot of the hill Hierapolis occupies are Roman, as are the city's splendid **defense walls** and sprawling **agora** south of the theater.

Like Nysa, Hierapolis had a **Plutonium**, a shrine to the god of the underworld. The shrine, constructed over a crevice that emitted noxious vapors, was beside the temple of

Apollo. (The crevice is now blocked up.) When the second-century A.D. Roman historian Dio Cassius visited Hierapolis, he was fascinated by the Plutonium, whose vapors purport-edly felled mighty bulls and tiny sparrows—but spared eunuchs!

Farther up the hill, and a number of centuries later in time, is the fifth-century A.D. **martyrium of the Apostle Philip**, built, legend has it, on the spot where the saint was stoned to death.

From the martyrium, Hierapolis's **necropolis** spills down to the base of the hill, extending along a long avenue above the cliffs. More than 1,200 tombs have been found and exca-vated here; almost all were robbed in antiquity. Some of the tombs look like little temples, others like elaborate round bunkers; still others are mere depressions in the ground.

Laodicea

A signposted dirt road runs from the Pamukkale–Denizli road to the mournful site of Laodicea, which sprawls over low hills some 17 km (11 miles) from Pamukkale and 8 km (5 miles) from Denizli. As at so many of the smaller sites in Turkey, it's easy to imagine here that you are discovering, not just visiting, an ancient city. In spring brilliant yellow-and-black birds swoop over the hills where sheep graze, and shepherds are often willing to show you the scattered and elusive remains of two theaters, a *nymphaeum,* a gymna-sium, and civic buildings scattered through the wheat fields. The sheep are more than appropriate: Hellenistic Laodicea was famous for the excellence of its wool, said to be softer even than wool from Miletus. The wool was a distinctive jet black, the color supposedly resulting from the minerals in the water the sheep drank. Roman Laodicea was an impor-tant provincial center that boasted it was the "metropolis of Asia."

The few visitors who come here probably do so because Laodicea was the site of one of the Seven Churches of Asia, castigated in Revelation 3:15–17 for being "lukewarm" in its observance of Christianity. Perhaps John's words struck home: Laodicea went on to become an episcopal see and was the scene of an ecumenical council in the fourth cen-tury. A severe earthquake about 100 years later left the city in ruins, and it never recovered its former importance.

As you leave Pamukkale, you may want to head east about 8 km (5 miles) on the Denizli–Afyon road to see a 13th-century caravansary, the **Ak Han**. (The caravansary is on the left-hand side of the road, so you'll have to make a U-turn to

see it.) The caravansary's name, which means "white inn,"
derives from its marble facing. Numerous ancient blocks are
incorporated in the building's fabric. In the spring, you may
well find sheep stabled in the large vaulted chamber beyond
the courtyard.

SOUTH FROM KUŞADASI

You can, of course, visit the major sites of Priene, Miletus,
and Didyma on a day trip by car, coach, or dolmuş from
Kuşadası (the tourist office there has information on bus and
dolmuş service). It makes for a *very* long day, however, with
a round-trip drive of some 180 km (112 miles), and should
be avoided if at all possible. If a day is all you have, you may
want to head first to Didyma—the farthest away—and then
work your way back to Kuşadası via Miletus and Priene, to
minimize your drive home at the end of the day.

If you can spare two days, you might combine Priene and
Didyma with a swim or visit to the Dilek Peninsula National
Park (discussed above) and take on Miletus (again rewarding yourself with a swim) on the second day. Bafa Gölü, a
pine-surrounded lake, and the ancient site of Heracleia-
under-Latmus, are best visited as a separate day trip from
Kuşadası or perhaps on the way to Bodrum and the Mediterranean coast (covered in the following chapters).

While it is physically possible to visit the Carian sites of
Alinda, Alabanda, and Labranda in the same day, it is not a
good idea. Alinda and Alabanda involve a good deal of
climbing and are so remote and beautiful that a visit should
not be rushed. As for Gerga, the most remote of the lot,
allow at least half a day for the walk to the site. If you visit
these sites, you might consider spending one night in Aydın
and another in Milas.

Priene

The road from Kuşadası to Priene (40 km/25 miles) runs
through fertile farmland watered by the Meander; in antiquity
most of this was not land at all, but the Aegean Sea. To reach
Priene, take the road from Kuşadası to Söke (route 525), then
follow signs for Milas. South of Söke, along a stretch of road
whipped by fierce winds, are ancient Priene and the pleasantly named hamlet of Güllübahçe (Rose Garden), which,
with its several small shaded cafés and fountains, seems to
have earned its name.

From the village, drive up Priene's steep **acropolis**, park, and walk up a final, yet steeper stretch before passing through Priene's defense walls and entering the city itself. The climb is worth it: Priene's site on Mount Mycale (the Turkish Samsun Dağı) is spectacular. Priene has been compared to Delphi in Greece. Both cling to the slopes of a lowering mountain and look over a plain, with Delphi the more majestic and Priene the more magical. If at all possible, come here late in the day, when twilight softens the austere blue-gray marble of the temple of Athena.

Little is known of Priene's history, except that the Pan-Ionian sanctuary was located in its territory—perhaps because the other members of the Ionian League realized that Priene was not powerful enough to influence its meetings. Legend has it that a grandson of Athens's King Codrus founded Priene; this first settlement was probably nearer the sea and had to be abandoned in the fourth century B.C., when silt from the Meander threatened to bury it.

In a triumph of town-planning over natural terrain, the new fourth-century B.C. city followed a regular grid plan of the sort popularized by the Milesian architect Hippodamus: All the streets intersect at right angles, with the north–south streets running almost straight up the mountain. Most of the civic buildings front on the east–west streets that run above the agora. The residential district stood just west of the agora, with the major temples on the slopes above the agora and the larger of two gymnasiums lower down.

In 334 B.C., while the Prienians were rebuilding their city, Alexander the Great spent some time here and was sufficiently impressed with what he saw to finance the new temple of Athena. (The house Alexander is believed to have stayed in, on the western periphery of Priene, just inside the city walls, is known as the **Sacred House** or the temple of Alexander the Great.) In addition to the new Athena temple, Priene built shrines to Demeter, Zeus, and the Egyptian gods; little remains, but the **temple of Demeter** has a particularly lovely location on a plateau slightly above the rest of the city.

The insistent Meander, which had threatened to engulf the first Priene, finally destroyed the new Priene's harbor at Naulochus and, hence, Priene's prosperity, which depended on sea trade. By Roman times the town was a backwater and largely ignored. As a result, the site is not a palimpsest of history like Ephesus and Miletus, but the time capsule of a small Hellenistic city whose population probably never exceeded 4,000.

Freya Stark wrote of Priene's "intimacy," and if an ancient site can seem cozy this one does. How pleasant it must have been to live in a city where you could have gotten everywhere by a short, albeit steep, walk—everywhere, that is, except to a public latrine: Priene seems to have had none, and there was only one latrine for every three or four private houses. Still, the scale throughout is human, untouched by the "bigger is better" mentality of the Romans. Everything, from the **temple of Athena**, with five standing Ionic columns, to the little **bouleuterion**, which could seat only 640, is just right. The temple of Athena, in fact, became the classic model for the Ionic temple, largely because its architect, Pythius, wrote an influential book on architecture. (Pythius was also the architect of the Mausoleum at Halicarnassus, one of the Seven Wonders of the ancient world.)

A short walk up the hillside brings you from the temple to Priene's lovely **Hellenistic theater** with its well-preserved stage building and seats for dignitaries. While theater performances originally took place on the level ground of the orchestra, at some point during the second century B.C. performances were transferred to the **proscenium**, a raised platform above the orchestra. The proscenium at Priene is the best preserved in the Hellenistic world. The theater seated perhaps 5,000, allowing locals to invite a few guests to performances. On one occasion Marc Antony imported actors from the Society of Dionysus, based at Teos, to perform here for Cleopatra.

Those with *really* sturdy shoes and strong legs may want to climb the **acropolis**, from which there is a fine view of the sea nine miles away. The vertiginous descent will prove alarming to all but the most experienced climbers.

Miletus

It's an easy 25-km (16-mile) drive from Priene to Miletus on either the main İzmir–Bodrum road or a secondary road. (The secondary road is less heavily trafficked and runs through wetlands where many migratory birds rest in winter and storks congregate in summer.) The excavation **museum**, just outside the site, is modest in comparison to the grand museums of Pergamum, Ephesus, and Aphrodisias. Still, the exhibits, including pottery ranging from Mycenaean times through the Turkish Emirate period, give a good idea of just how long people have lived here. In fact, there was a settlement here until an earthquake in 1955 destroyed the village of Balat, which was subsequently relocated half a mile south of the ancient site.

The museum's Mycenaean pottery collection is more important than it looks. Excavations conducted between 1955 and 1957 near Miletus's temple of Athena, south of the theater, revealed that there had been a Mycenaean settlement here, the only one presently known on Turkey's Aegean coast. Elsewhere along the coast—as at Troy—mainland Greeks raided settlements and headed home, often with slaves. (Tablets found at Pylos in Greece mention the "women of Asia" imported to work in the flax fields there.) Some scholars think that Miletus was "Millawanda," the troublesome town that Hittite records mention as dominating Achaia (Greece). Millawanda was enough of a threat that the Hittites destroyed it around 1350 B.C.

Across the road from the museum the İlyas Bey Camii, a mosque built by İlyas Bey—the regional Ottoman military commander—in 1404 to celebrate his escape from Tamerlane, is now in a pleasant state of disrepair. A number of sizable storks—and, in the late spring, their chicks—nest on its dome. The mosque lost its minaret in the 1955 earthquake.

Unlike Ephesus, which seduces almost every visitor with its massive ruins, and Pergamum, whose sheer mountain-top site is dazzling, Miletus seems to be a place that visitors either love or loathe. For Michael Wood, author of *In Search of the Trojan War,* Miletus, with its massive theater looming above the plain, is the "most dramatic" of all the coastal sites in Turkey. To the laconic *Blue Guide,* Miletus is "not one of the most attractive sites in SW Turkey." Whether you thrill to the "immense ruins of the classical city," or are disheartened by the "profound melancholy" of ruins partially submerged in "an unpleasant morass" by spring rains but stretching across a "drab brown wilderness" in the heat of summer probably depends on how well you can conjure up ancient Miletus. Why should you bother? Simply because this was one of the most important cities in the ancient Greek world.

In antiquity Miletus occupied a peninsula a mile and a half long (and blessed with four superb harbors) and guarded the entrance to the deep bay of Latmus; today Miletus is five miles from the sea, and all that remains of the bay is Lake Bafa (discussed below), landlocked by silt carried seaward by the Meander. The two stone lions that once guarded Miletus's Lion Harbor still stand in their original positions on either side of the harbor's entrance, but now they look not on, but only toward, the sea.

Miletus was the largest and most important of the Greek colonies along the Aegean coast from the beginning of the first millennium B.C. until the fifth century B.C., when its preeminence sealed its doom: When the Greek cities of Ionia rose against their Persian overlords Miletus was the obvious leader—and the principal target of Persian vengeance. In 494 B.C. the Persians leveled Miletus, sending a shock wave of sympathy throughout the Greek world. Herodotus reports that when the Athenian playwright Phrynichus's drama *The Capture of Miletus* was performed the next year in Athens, "the whole theater burst into tears, and the people sentenced him to pay a fine of a thousand drachmas." The play, no longer extant, was never again performed.

After its destruction Miletus was rebuilt on a strict grid plan, with streets intersecting at right angles according to the principles of the Milesian town planner Hippodamus. Still, Miletus never regained its former stature but was overshadowed by Ephesus—as, indeed, it is today. Nothing here can compete with Ephesus's Marble Way; instead, individual monuments stand in isolation on the alluvial plain. Future excavations may reveal Miletus's extensive residential section, still hidden under the plain; until then, the site of Miletus gives little sense of the city that was once here.

To get an overview of Miletus, climb to the top of the **theater** (near the entrance to the site), which seated 5,300 spectators in the Hellenistic era and was expanded by the Romans to accommodate 15,000. In summer, it's cooler to climb to the top by the vaulted stairs on the left of the orchestra. The present theater dates from about A.D. 100. You'll see some fragments of the egg-and-dart molding from the earlier theater as well as lion's-head spouts from the Roman theater on the ground near where you'll start your climb. When you reach the top and look past the snack bars and souvenir shops, you see the low remains of much of Hellenistic and Roman Miletus: the west agora, the temple of Athena, a stadium, and a gymnasium. In antiquity these buildings were separated from the theater by the Theater Harbor; now they are overgrown by scrub and largely shielded from your view by trees.

The principal remains of Miletus are in the civic center behind the theater: the north and south **agoras**, connected by the Sacred Way and flanked by Miletus's most important temples and civic buildings. From the highest seats in the theater spectators would have seen the Theater Harbor directly in front of them and, over their shoulders, the Lion Harbor and the sea as well as Miletus's principal shrines and public buildings. The hill that you see about four miles west of the theater is all that remains of Lade, once an island in the sea; in 494 B.C. the Persians trapped and set fire to the Ionian fleet off Lade before sacking Miletus.

As you scramble down the back of the theater, past some walls from the **Byzantine citadel**, built onto the theater itself, you'll pass a round **heroön**, a monumental tomb similar to some found at Hierapolis. Presumably the man buried here was famous in his day; now his name is forgotten, unlike the names of the clutch of Milesian scientists and philosophers who made this city famous in the sixth century B.C. One of the most famous was Thales, the first scientist to plot solar eclipses; his gnomic utterance "Know Thyself" was carved on the temple of Apollo at Delphi. Thales' contemporary Anaximander is credited with drawing the first map of the world, spurred on, no doubt, by Milesian voyages of discovery. (The Milesians often sailed uncharted seas, and founded more than 100 colonies.)

These Milesians, as well as the philosopher Anaximenes, laid the groundwork for later thinkers like Aristotle, just as the Milesian geographer and chronicler Hecataeus, who travelled widely in Egypt, prepared the way for Herodotus's research on the Greeks and barbarians.

All in all, Miletus seems to have produced genius the way Aphrodisias produced sculpture: Yet another famous Milesian, Aspasia, mistress of the great fifth-century B.C. Athenian statesman Pericles, was as famous for her shrewd wit as for her physical charms. Finally, in the sixth century A.D., when Miletus was a wretched provincial backwater, it produced an architect at least as great as Hippodamus: Isidorus, one of the designers of Istanbul's St. Sophia.

From the *heroön* of the unknown Milesian, you'll want to make your way northeast toward the heart of the ancient city. Two Roman harbor monuments stood here, the larger rising 25 feet above its circular base. A drawing on the site near the monuments' foundations gives a good idea of what they looked like, lavishly ornamented with sculptured ship prows and reliefs of dolphins and Tritons (of which one fragment remains), and topped by caldrons supported by tripods. Miletus's early German excavators spirited the caldron from the larger monument off to Berlin.

From the harbor monuments you'll walk past the remains of Miletus's harbor gate, flanked by the north agora, the first-century A.D. **Capito baths**, and the remains of an important shrine to Apollo known as the **Delphinium**. The shrine seems to have consisted of an unroofed temple bounded on all four sides by stoas; only low foundation walls remain, and even these are often flooded by the Meander. Both Apollo and the dolphins (*delphin* is the Greek for "dolphin") sacred to him were particularly honored at Miletus, where it was believed that the god, in the form of a dolphin, had guided the first settlers when they sailed here.

The most important shrine to Apollo in Aegean Turkey was also in Milesian territory, at nearby Didyma (see below). The 12-mile **Sacred Way**, a marble road flanked by statues of priests, priestesses, sphinxes, and lions, ran through Miletus's civic center toward Didyma. Four of the 35 original columns of a first-century A.D. Ionic stoa and part of its entablature have been restored just south of the harbor gate; behind the colonnade were 19 shops, bounded to the rear by a Hellenistic gymnasium, whose *palaestra* was also bordered by stoas. You'll see some of the Ionic and Doric column capitals from the stoas scattered on the ground here.

Just beyond the Ionic *stoa,* the second-century B.C. **bouleuterion** and a monumental **nymphaeum**, built in the second century A.D. and rebuilt in the third, face each other across the Sacred Way. Miletus's *nymphaeum,* fed by an aqueduct, rose three stories, with statues of gods set in niches and water spouting from the mouths of bronze fish. The fountain house's paltry remains give no sense of its original splendor, but you can make out the shape of the *bouleuterion's* meeting hall, where a number of the semicircular seats are preserved.

The *bouleuterion* lay just outside Miletus's enormous **south agora**, which was 196 yards long by 164 yards wide. Like the theater, the south agora was begun in the Hellenistic period but was extensively remodeled by the Romans. Three massive gates marked the north, south, and west entrances to the agora; none remains. The north gate is in Berlin, the south gate was destroyed when the mosque of İlyas Bey was built, and the west gate was torn down and its stones reused in the Byzantine walls. All you'll see of the shops and stoas that lined the south agora are the scattered architectural fragments on the ground, overshadowed by the walls of the baths of Faustina.

The **baths of Faustina**, along with the theater, are Miletus's most imposing ruins. The baths were financed by, and named in honor of, the philosopher-emperor Marcus Aurelius's wife Faustina in the mid-second century A.D. They were lavishly ornamented with statues; you'll see the figure of a reclining river god (probably a personification of the Meander) in the *frigidarium.* You can wander through the remains of the rooms where bathers would have disrobed and proceeded from warm soaks to hot tubs, the steam room, and cold-plunge pools. The three large boiler rooms discovered near the *caldarium* would have supplied the heat that circulated through flues in the bath's walls and floors.

Perhaps one building more than any other shows how Miletus adapted to changing times, repeatedly incorporating old buildings into new ones: the early seventh-century A.D. **church of St. Michael** (now covered by a roof to protect those of its mosaics not removed to the museum), which was built on the foundations of the Roman temple of Dionysus. By the time the church was built all four of Miletus's harbors had silted up, leaving the city first marooned, then buried. For centuries only the theater remained above ground to remind travellers of Miletus. *Murray's Handbook for Travellers in Asia Minor, Transcaucasia, Persia (etc.),* published in 1895, dismissed Miletus as a "fever-stricken spot, which should on no account be selected as a sleeping place."

In fact, most of the early travellers in southern Ionia preferred Didyma to Miletus. Don't be surprised if, after you visit Didyma, you find that its solitary temple leaves a more lasting impression than Miletus's sprawl. If so, you'll be in good company: The intrepid 18th-century traveller Richard Chandler said of Didyma, "The memory of the pleasure which this spot afforded me will not be soon or easily erased."

Didyma

The Ionic **temple of Apollo** at Didyma, 20 km (12 miles) south of Miletus on route 525, startles the onlooker with its size, like a whale rising unexpectedly from beneath the waves. The temple is considerably below the present-day ground level of the small village of Didim. Ancient Didyma was probably even smaller than the modern village: It was the sanctuary of an important oracle, not a city. Overlooking the temple are a number of cafés, restaurants, and rug and jewelry stores; one shop, **Anatolian Handicrafts**, has nice wood carvings, ceramics, old copper, and old and new handcrafted silver jewelry, some pieces incorporating old Turkish coins.

If you arrive at Didyma feeling hungry, and find the temple-side restaurant seats taken, the **Mis-Mis 66 Kebap Salonu**, by the fruit market in the nearby village of Yenihisar, has excellent kebaps and salads—and few, if any, tourists. All in all, this restaurant is a good place to take a break from touring, enjoy the bustle of the fruit market, and bone up on Didyma. Then put your book aside and wander around the temple, the third largest in the ancient Greek world (only the temples of Artemis at Ephesus and Hera on Samos were larger).

The temple's great size is not its only noteworthy characteristic; many of its features are unusual, possibly even unique. If you climb up the steps at the temple's east end near the stairs leading down to the site you'll see several of them. The first is the antechamber with its steep five-foot-high doorsill, better suited for gods than for mortals. Such an antechamber is an oddity in a Greek temple, and some archaeologists have suggested that this was the *chresmographeion,* or oracle office, where copies of the oracles were stored. A flight of stairs leads from the antechamber down into the cella (the main chamber of the temple where the cult statue usually stood). The cella can also be reached by two tunnels—another unusual feature. If you walk through the tunnels into the cella, you can make out the foundations of yet another of Didyma's idiosyncrasies: At the west end of the cella is a temple-within-a-temple, the small Ionic shrine that probably housed the cult statue of Apollo. There seem to have been at least three sacred springs within the cella; the priestess of Apollo evidently inhaled the vapors of the spring before prophesying.

Even in antiquity Didyma's site, in a shallow hollow in the ground, must have been pretty; Zeus chose it for his tryst with Leto, which produced Apollo and Artemis, the Didyma (Twins), after whom some think the shrine was named. The temple is also sometimes called Apollo Branchidae; Branchidae was the family name of the early shrine's hereditary priests, descended, legend had it, from the youth Branchus, one of Apollo's many loves.

Didyma seems to have had a shrine even before the Ionians arrived in the tenth century B.C., but the sanctuary's real importance came after the Lydian king Croesus (also a great benefactor of Delphi) financed a new temple here. After Croesus's munificence, Didyma's oracle gained in prestige and rivaled Delphi's until 494 B.C., when the Persians destroyed first Miletus, then Didyma, just as the Delphic Oracle had prophesied.

The oracle was silent until the day Alexander the Great was born, when the sacred spring flowed once again. This was the more benign of the two omens in southern Ionia that greeted Alexander's birth: At nearby Ephesus the temple of Artemis burned, an event later interpreted as signifying that Alexander would destroy Asia.

While Miletus was quickly rebuilt after the Persian destruction, the temple of Apollo at Didyma lay in ruins until Alexander himself ordered it rebuilt. The new temple (actually begun around 300 B.C. by Seleucus, one of the successors to Alexander's empire) was so immense—with a platform 358 feet long by 167 feet wide and girdled by 120 Ionic columns—that it could not be roofed and was never finished. As George Bean remarks in *Aegean Turkey,* the temple of

Apollo at Didyma "serves as a reminder that vastness in architecture was not purely a monopoly of the Romans."

In the first century A.D. the Roman emperor Caligula did attempt to finish the temple, suggesting that it be rededicated in his honor. In the fourth century A.D. Julian the Apostate, the last pagan emperor, also had a go at completing Didyma, but he died before much progress was made. There matters rested for the next 100 years, until the Byzantine emperor Theodosius II had a church constructed within the temple courtyard, silencing the oracle so thoroughly that it is no longer known where the priestess sat and prophesied.

If you find Didyma too crowded for your taste, try to remember what it would have been like when the sacred precincts were thronged with pilgrims waiting to consult the oracle. The third-century B.C. poet Theocritus described pilgrims' reactions to the hubbub they encountered visiting major shrines like Didyma in this imaginary dialogue:

—For goodness sake, don't knock me down. What a mercy
    we left the baby at home!
—How will we manage to get inside?
—Everything is done by trying, dearie. It was by trying
    that the Achaeans got into Troy . . .
—What a crowd! They're all shoving like pigs!

Sitting beside the temple under the gaze of the colossal Medusa head fallen from the frieze, watching cats (and dusky lizards almost as large as cats) sun themselves, it's pleasant to imagine this temple as it once was, when every one of its 120 columns was standing. In the 15th century an earthquake brought Didyma down, leaving the columns, as one 19th-century traveller put it, "like shattered icebergs" on the ground.

If you want to combine your visit to Didyma with a swim, follow the road you took into town 8 km (5 miles) south to **Altınkum beach**, which is *very* crowded in the summer.

Lake Bafa and
Heracleia-under-Latmus

The drive (50 km/31 miles) from Kuşadası to Bafa—the inland lake formed when the Meander silted up the gulf of Latmus—passes through the town of Söke and over several steep hills. Once you reach the lake itself, the road runs through dense pine groves where there are several small restaurants beside the lake. At the southern end of the lake a

dirt road leads from the village of Çamiçi through farm fields
and olive groves before twisting up the rugged slopes of
Mount Latmus to the village of Kapıkırı, 8 km (5 miles)
farther on. As you drive up into the village you'll see ancient
Heracleia's most impressive remains: the exceptionally well
preserved **Hellenistic defense walls** that run for almost four
miles along the slopes of Mount Latmus to a small Byzantine
castle on a steep promontory above the lake.

Kapıkırı straddles a small valley and is built on top of
much of the site of Heracleia-under-Latmus, whose **agora**
was where the village schoolyard is. The foundations of the
Hellenistic **temple of Athena** are located on a spur of the
mountain beyond the schoolyard (to the left as you walk
uphill). Originally, of course, the temple looked down on
the Latmian gulf and out toward the sea itself.

As you walk uphill through Kapıkırı past the school and
temple, you'll see ancient blocks built into the houses that
cluster around an olive grove to the right. Scattered through
the grove are the low remains of Heracleia, difficult to spot
because many buildings were made of the local stone and so
blend into the gnarled, twisted boulders and outcroppings.
You'll make out the foundations and some seats of the small
bouleuterion, which was about the same size as the well-
preserved *bouleuterion* at Priene. The marble seats of
Heracleia's small **theater** were plundered long ago, but you
can still see the theater's semicircular impression on the hill.

Heracleia was never very important, as it existed under
the shadow of its powerful neighbor, Miletus. It was best
known as the scene of the myth of the shepherd Endymion's
love for Selene, the goddess of the moon. The remains of
the small temple on a low plateau above the lake have been
tentatively identified as a **sanctuary of Endymion**. Shaded by
pines and a short walk from several fish restaurants serving
the lake trout and eels that also nourish Bafa's waterfowl, the
sanctuary is an idyllic spot to pitch a tent. **Selena's** restaurant
and campground across from the small island with Byzantine remains gets the best breezes, but the nearby **Kaya** and
Zeybek campgrounds and restaurants are also pleasant.

In summer boats can be hired locally for excursions to
several small islands, some with ruins of **Byzantine chapels
and dwellings** built by monks who came to Bafa in search of
the contemplative life. If there are no boats around, you can
still visit the ruins of one chapel on an island joined to the
shore by a slender causeway.

In a sense, Heracleia's history is the history of Aegean
Turkey itself: a Greek city, later occupied by the Romans (the
remains of the inevitable bath are to be found near the

bouleuterion), fortified by the Byzantines, seized by the Turks, and finally all but absorbed into the walls and houses of a farming village, whose mosque overlooks the fallen temples and churches.

If you continue east about 16 km (10 miles) from Lake Bafa on route 330, you can take in the exceptionally well preserved second-century A.D. Corinthian **temple of Zeus** at **Euromus**, virtually all that remains of that extensive city, one of Caria's most important. (For more on Caria, see the chapter on the Turquoise Coast, following.) Farther down the 330, the site of the Greek city of **Iasos**, signposted about 16 km (10 miles) off the road, on a small peninsula, looks across a bay to the village of Güllük. Iasos is a nice spot for a swim, a picnic, and a stroll past the remains, which include a number of rock-cut tombs, a Roman mausoleum, and stretches of the Hellenistic defense walls.

Alinda, Alabanda, Labranda, and Gerga

Three euphoniously named sites—Alinda, Alabanda, and Labranda—are tucked away in the harsh mountains of Caria, with locations that rival any in Turkey. If you encounter anyone at Alinda or Alabanda, it's likely to be a shepherd or the site guard, startled but pleased to have company; visit Labranda in the summer and you may see Swedish archaeologists at work. A fourth site, Gerga, involves several hours of hiking through rough terrain. Your reward: the mountain and valley views as you walk to Gerga and a well-preserved Carian temple at the site itself.

The town of Aydın (ancient Tralles) is a good base for visiting Alinda, Alabanda, and Gerga; Labranda is best visited either as a separate excursion or from Milas. **Aydın** is an energetic town built on the southern slopes of the Aydın mountains; if you're there in July and August, you can taste the famous Aydın figs. The small archaeological and ethnographical museum is worth a visit, as are the 16th-century **Ramazan Paşa Camii** and the **Bey Camii**. The modern **Turtay Otel** (with a swimming pool) just outside town on the Aydın–Yatağan road (route 550) is the quietest place to stay, and there are several small hotels in town.

Alinda (signposted 25 km/16 miles off route 550 along the road to Karpuzlu) is perched on its steep acropolis on the eastern slopes of Mount Latmus above Karpuzlu. Fortunately, you can drive a good way up the acropolis, park, and then walk past old houses with wooden balconies to a terrace with a well-preserved Hellenistic **market building** overlooking the fertile plain below. Keep climbing and you'll find yourself at the arched entrance to Alinda's **theater**, shaded with pine trees. Even farther above is a fine Hellenistic **watchtower**, the entrance to a mysterious tunnel, and the remains of a small *nymphaeum* or odeon.

For some ten years, Alinda was the home-in-exile of Queen Ada of Halicarnassus, the sister of the grecophile King Mausolus, and it is pleasant to imagine her strolling here plotting her return to power. When Alexander the Great arrived in Caria, Ada welcomed the young king and plied him with rich delicacies, which he refused, remarking that his usual breakfast was a night march and his customary lunch a light breakfast. When he seized Halicarnassus in 334 B.C., Alexander restored Ada to her throne, and she left this mountain fastness. Perhaps someday the site will be located and Ada's royal palace unearthed; for now, Alinda's untouched remains make this one of western Turkey's most romantic sites.

The ruins of **Alabanda** sprawl across fields planted with wheat and piquant green peppers and up the slopes of the ancient acropolis, now the village of Araphisar (signposted off route 550 some 10 km/6 miles north of Çine). Alabanda has neither the dramatic setting nor the striking remains of Alinda and Labranda, but it's certainly worth a detour to see the scattered remains of the agora, Roman baths, and **temple of Apollo**, and to recall that Strabo mentions that the inhabitants of Alabanda were known for their debauchery: He cited Alabanda's reputation for numerous lyre-playing singing girls.

The drive from Alabanda along route 550 to Çine is one of the most beautiful in western Turkey, twisting through the gorge formed by the Çine Çayı (the ancient Marsyas river). Along much of the road, springs bubble forth from the mountainsides, shepherds sell honey and cheeses, and the air is scented with herbs. Marsyas was the satyr who challenged Apollo to a contest on the flute; Athena judged Apollo the winner and the god promptly flayed Marsyas alive; the river was formed from his tears.

About 10 km (6 miles) south of Çine, a yellow sign points 15 km (9 miles) off to **Gerga**. The road ends, essentially, in the village schoolhouse of Ovacık, and the schoolteacher will probably appoint one of the pupils as your guide for the trek to Gerga. If you go alone, you'll never find the site, so be grateful for a guide (and give about a $5 tip when you finish the hike). Just as you begin to despair of ever reaching Gerga, your guide will point out several massive stones inscribed, in Greek, with the name *Gerga* and a recumbent monolithic statue. All around, cut into the hills, are cisterns and rock-cut tombs, and on one hill stands the squat, fully roofed, gray limestone **Carian temple**, probably of the Roman Imperial period. Gerga is mysterious: Archaeologists are uncertain whether Gerga was the name of a Carian deity, or simply a town name. Whatever, the spot is magical.

At Yatağan, route 330 leads west to the market town of **Milas** (ancient Mysia), which is worth a stop to see the handsome, well-preserved two-story **Roman tomb**, perhaps modeled on the far grander Mausoleum of Halicarnassus. The tomb, which dates from the first or second century B.C., is known as the Gümüşkesen, or Silver Purse, in Turkish because of persistent legends that it contains undiscovered treasure. The tomb is not signposted and you'll find it most easily by getting a local to guide you there—and, if you desire, to Milas's two other significant ancient remains: the second-century A.D. Roman Gate of the Axe (Baltalı Kapı in Turkish) and the single extant column from a first-century B.C. temple of Zeus.

The site of **Labranda** is signposted 13 km (8 miles) up a narrow, winding dirt road, so deeply rutted that locals may try to discourage you from taking it. The dirt road follows the ancient sacred way from Milas to Labranda, and one reason to take the drive slowly is the occasional marble paving stone that protrudes from the hard-packed dirt road. (This is not a road to attempt in the rain, when the dirt becomes a sea of mud.)

Like Didyma in Ionia or Olympia in Greece, Labranda was never a city, but rather the site of an important cult: in this case, the Carian **sanctuary to Zeus Stratios** (Zeus of the Army). The terraced sanctuary was of great antiquity, but in the fourth century King Mausolus and his brother Idrieus rebuilt the temple and added a number of the surviving sanctuary buildings, including several guest houses (marked Andron A and B; *andron* is the Greek word for a men's sleeping/banqueting hall). Farther up the acropolis are the remains of several rock-cut tombs and—for those who undertake the very stiff climb to the summit—spectacular views across the hills and down to the plain below.

Labranda, shaded by pine groves and plane trees (there was a grove of sacred pine trees here in antiquity) and cooled by delicious breezes in the summer, is a wonderfully peaceful spot. It's hard to imagine that this was the scene of fierce fighting when the Carians, driven back to this remote site, went down to defeat before the Persians during the Ionian revolt (499 to 494 B.C.). Perhaps some were buried in the rock-cut tombs you'll pass in the olive groves on the slopes of the hill when you leave Labranda and drive back into the plain outside Milas.

(From Milas, if you're continuing on to Bodrum and Caria's southern coast, take route 330 south.)

GETTING AROUND

It's a good idea to contact the Turkish Ministry of Tourism well in advance of your trip to request maps and brochures on Aegean Turkey. Be persistent. Also ask for these two useful booklets, both containing general information: *Turkey: Travel Guide* and *Gelisim Tourist Passport to Turkey: A Pocket Guide to Turkey for the Tourist*. In the United States, the Ministry of Tourism has offices at 821 United Nations Plaza, New York, NY 10017 (Tel: 212/687-2194), and 2010 Massachusetts Avenue, NW, Washington, D.C. 20036 (Tel: 202/429-9844). In the United Kingdom, the office is at 170–73 Piccadilly, London W1V 9DD (Tel: 071/734-8681).

Arrival by Air

If you want to fly directly from the United States to Aegean Turkey, you have a number of choices: Delta, TWA, and THY (Turkish Airlines) will all route you to İzmir via Istanbul. If you fly a non-Turkish carrier to Istanbul, you'll have to transfer from the international to the domestic terminal at Atatürk airport (there's regular shuttle-bus service) and take THY to İzmir. Note that if you do fly THY from the United States, your connecting flight from Istanbul to İzmir is free, and making the connection is a much simpler matter.

If you want to avoid the inconvenience of changing terminals, your best option is to take Lufthansa, flying from New York to Frankfurt and from there directly to İzmir. If you begin your trip in London, your options multiply: Both THY and British Air have direct service from London to İzmir, and the London Sunday papers advertise numerous charter flights from London to İzmir.

Arrival by Sea

If you intend to travel to Aegean Turkey by sea, your best bet is to get information from your travel agent as well as from the Turkish Ministry of Tourism. Schedules for ships of the Turkish Maritime Lines, which offers service from Venice to Istanbul and İzmir, and for car ferries from Brindisi, Italy, and Piraeus, Greece, fluctuate greatly from season to season and month to month. Schedules from the Greek islands of Lesvos, Chios, and Samos seem to fluctuate from day to day. If you are approaching Aegean Turkey from Istanbul, keep in mind that you can take a ferry from there to Çanakkale or İzmir. If you're driving from Europe and want to bypass Istanbul, you can take a ferry across the Dardanelles from Gelibolu (Gallipoli) to Çanakkale. Again, schedules vary a great deal, and it's best to inquire of your travel agent or the Turkish Ministry of Tourism for specific information.

Getting Around by Car

By far the easiest way to travel around Aegean Turkey is by car. That said, certain warnings are in order. Do not drive at night: Cars and farm vehicles without lights are not uncommon. Take seriously the road sign showing an umbrella, rain, and skid marks: The surfaces of many roads are treacherous when wet. Slow down for villages and towns. Often the highway cuts right through a town, and local traffic crosses constantly from one side to the other. At certain times of day schoolchildren are thick on the road. Traffic lights are infrequent.

If you intend to fly into İzmir and pick up a rental car there, you can do so either at the airport or in town, where Avis, Hertz, Budget, Eurocar, and several local companies have offices. Make your rental arrangements before you leave on your trip; rates are usually somewhat less expensive when cars are booked in advance, though be warned that renting a car is never cheap. It's worth noting that Avis has more offices in Aegean Turkey than do the other agencies—which can be very useful if you need a replacement car in the event of a breakdown. (Breakdowns, sadly, are not infrequent.) Even if you have booked ahead, expect to spend at least an hour doing the paperwork when you pick up your car. If you're not actually heading into İzmir, picking up your car at the airport is a distinct plus. The airport is next to the main north–south coastal highway and only minutes away from the main İzmir–Ankara highway. If you're ending your trip in İzmir you may prefer to drop off your car in town the day before your departure and take a taxi to the airport. Driving in İzmir is unpleasant, and the drive to the airport is nerve-racking. Also, when you return your car the paperwork is likely to be even more time-consuming than when you picked it up, and you don't want to chance missing your flight.

Getting Around by Bus and Train

You can get almost everywhere in Turkey by bus, and this is a good way to travel. A large number of private companies offer intercity service. Local tourist offices usually have bus schedules for their areas. Travel by rail is less efficient than by bus; however, there is rail service from Istanbul to İzmir and from İzmir inland to Ankara.

If you're travelling without a car you'll probably use a good many dolmuşes and taxis. Both are cheap (dolmuşes, which carry a number of riders between set destinations, are of course cheaper) and provide an efficient way to get from a major center, like Kuşadası, to a nearby beach or historical site.

Tours

If you don't want to do your own driving and can't face the prospect of travelling alone, you may want to choose a one- or two-week tour of Aegean Turkey, leaving from Istanbul or İzmir. One- and two-day coach tours of major sites such as Ephesus, Priene, Miletus, and Didyma are offered by agencies in İzmir and Kuşadası. The Turkish Ministry of Tourism can give you information on these tours, as can major hotels in Istanbul, İzmir, and Kuşadası. Many tour companies advertise in the English-language *Turkish Daily News*.

Finally, there are a number of special-interest tours of Aegean Turkey. Among the many study-cruises, those offered by the long-established Swan Hellenic Art Treasures Tours, 77 New Oxford Street, London WC1A 1PP (Tel: 071/831-1616), are clearly the best. Wildlife enthusiasts may want to contact Turkish Wildlife Holidays, 8 The Grange, Elmdon Park Solihull, West Midlands B92 9EL, England (Tel: 21/742-5420 or 922/478-289), although their tours generally head deeper into Anatolia.

ACCOMMODATIONS REFERENCE

Rates given below are for double rooms, double occupancy, and represent projections for the high season (mid-May through September) of 1993. Many hotels offer discounts of 20 percent or more during the low season. Prices usually include breakfast. When telephoning between cities in Turkey, dial 9 before entering the city code.

▶ **Alkent Tesisleri Motel.** Ankara–İzmir Karayolu Üzeri, **Salihli**, İzmir. Tel: (644) 42400 or 16069. $38.

▶ **Anafartalar Hotel.** İskele Meydanı, 17100 **Çanakkale**. Tel: (196) 144-54/55/56; Fax: (196) 144-57. $27.

▶ **Aphrodisias Hotel.** Aphrodisias-Karacasu, Aydın. Tel: (6379) 8132. $15.

▶ **Assos Eden Beach Hotel.** Kadırga Koyu, Behramkale, **Assos**, Ayvacık, 17860 Çanakkale. For reservations contact the Istanbul office: Halâskârgazi Caddesi, Günaydın Apt. No. 64,

D2, Harbiye, 80220 Istanbul; Tel: (1) 248-4259, 248-9112, or 240-6441; Fax: (1) 247-5933. $30.

► **Atlas Hotel.** Dumlupınar Caddesi 22, **Manisa**. Tel: (55) 519-97. $12.

► **Bozdağ Turistik Oteli. Bozdağ-Ödemiş**, 35773 İzmir. Tel: (545) 370-06 or 370-28; Fax: (545) 372-38. $25; full pension, $40.

► **Büyük Efes Oteli.** Gaziosmanpaşa Bulvarı 1, Alsancak, 35210 İzmir. Tel: (51) 84-43-00; Fax: (51) 41-56-95. $120 (street side)–$130 (pool side).

► **Büyük Saruhan. Manisa.** Tel: (551) 32380; Fax: (551) 32648. $75.

► **Çeşme Altın Yunus.** Boyalık Mevkii, **Çeşme**, İzmir. Tel: (549) 312-50; Fax: (549) 322-52. $80.

► **Chez Mestan Pension. Aphrodisias-Karacasu**, Aydin. Tel: (6379) 8046. $8.

► **Club Mediterranée.** 3'üncü Mersinaki, **Yeni Foça**, İzmir. Tel: (543) 11147 or 11607; Fax: (543) 12175. In the U.S., Tel: (800) 258-2633; in the U.K., Tel: (071) 581-4766. Weekly rates for double rooms range from $619 (early June) to $995 (August); includes full board; shorter stays (not always available) are prorated based on weekly rate.

► **Clup Hotel Murat Reis.** P.K. 39, Altınkum Mevki, Sarmısaklı, 10400 **Ayvalık**, Balıkesir. Tel: (663) 414-56 or 417-32; Fax: (663) 414-57. $40; half-pension, $60.

► **Ertan Hotel.** Cumhuriyet Meydanı 12, **Çeşme**, 35310 İzmir. Tel: (549) 267-95 or 267-96; Fax: (549) 278-52. $35.

► **Hotel Arma.** Doğu Caddesi, **Manisa**. Tel: (55) 31980 or 36297; Fax: (55) 24501. $25.

► **Hotel Assos. Behramkale**, Ayvacık, Çanakkale. Tel: (1969) 7071 or 7034. $22.

► **Hotel Assos Kervansaray.** Behramkale Köyü İskele, **Behramkale**, Ayvacık, Çanakkale. Tel: (1969) 7093; Fax: (1969) 7200. For reservations contact the Istanbul office: Kefeliköy Caddesi 92, Tarabya, Istanbul; Tel: (1) 262-8182. $37.

► **Hotel Atınç.** Atatürk Bulvarı, **Kuşadası**, Aydın. Tel: (636) 176-08; Fax: (636) 149-67. $30; demipension, $45.

► **Hotel Berksoy.** P.O. Box 19, **Bergama**, 35700 İzmir. Tel: (541) 125-95 or 153-45; Fax: (541) 153-46. $40; demipension, $50.

► **Hotel Efe.** Güvercinada Caddesi, **Kuşadası**, Aydın. Tel: (636) 136-60 through 136-63; Telex: 58502 EFET TR. $35.

► **Hotel İskender. Bergama**, 35700 İzmir. Tel: (541) 321-23; Fax: (541) 312-45. $28.

► **Hotel Karaca.** Necatibey Bulvarı, 1379 Sokak 55, **İzmir**. Tel: (51) 84-44-45 or 84-44-26. Fax: (51) 84-57-84. $68.

► **Hotel Kısmet.** 1377 Sok 9, İzmir. Tel: (51) 63-38-50. $50.

▶ **Hotel Kısmet.** Akyar Mevkii, **Kuşadası**, Aydın. Tel: (636) 120-05; Fax: (636) 149-14. $70; demipension, $90. (open Apr.–Nov. only).

▶ **İzmir Hilton.** Gaziosmanpaşa Bulvarı 7, 35210 **İzmir.** Tel: (51) 41-60-60; Fax: 41-22-77. In U.S., Tel: (800) HILTONS. $108.

▶ **İzmir Palas.** Atatürk Bulvarı, 35210 **İzmir.** Tel: (51) 21-55-83; Fax: (51) 22-68-70. $73.

▶ **Karayel Pansiyon. Babakale**, Ayvacık, 17860 Çanakkale. Tel: (1969) 1429, then ask operator for 4 (*dört*) or 5 (*beş*). $10.

▶ **Kavaklı Pansiyon.** Gölcük, **Ödemiş.** Tel: (545) 35090 (Ödemiş); (545) 315-16, then 142 (Gölcük). $15.

▶ **Koru Motel. Pamukkale**, 20210 Denizli. Tel: (6218) 2429; Fax: (6218) 2023. $50.

▶ **Martı Motel-Café-Restaurant. Çandarlı**, İzmir. Tel: (5415) 1441. $20.

▶ **Mistur Motel.** Ören Mevkii, **Pamukkale**, 20210 Denizli. Tel: (6218) 2421; Fax: (6218) 2013. $33; demipension, $50.

▶ **Motel Çatlatan.** Fevzi Çakmak Mahallesi, **Yeni Foça**, İzmir. Tel: (5434) 5681. $20.

▶ **Motel Yıldız.** Behramkale, **Assos**, Ayvacık, 17860 Çanakkale. Tel: (1969) 7025 or 7169. $18.

▶ **Öküz Mehmet Paşa Kervansarayı** (Club Caravansérail Hotel-Restaurant). Atatürk Bulvarı 1, **Kuşadası**, Aydın. Tel: (636) 141-15. Fax: (636) 141-19. $63.

▶ **Otel Nazlı Han.** Behramkale İskelesi, **Assos**, Behramkale, Ayvacık, Çanakkale. Tel: (1969) 7064; Telex: 52596. In İzmir, Tel: (51) 83-14-00; Fax: (51) 86-50-73. $28 (street side)–$30 (harbor side).

▶ **Palmiye Motel.** Belediye Tesisleri, **Pamukkale**, 20210 Denizli. Tel: (6218) 1014 through 1017; Fax: (6218) 1018. $43 (without private pool)–$50 (with private pool).

▶ **Pamukkale Motel. Pamukkale**, 20210 Denizli. Tel: (6218) 2024, 2025, or 2026; Fax: (6218) 2026. $52.

▶ **Park Otel.** Park Otel Sokak 6, **Bergama**, İzmir. Tel: (541) 112-46. $15.

▶ **Pension Pergamon.** Bankalar Caddesi 3, **Bergama**, İzmir. Tel: (541) 123-95. $8 (without shower)–$10 (with shower).

▶ **Rıdvan Oteli.** Cumhuriyet Meydanı 11, **Çeşme**, 35310 İzmir. Tel: (549) 263-36 or 263-37; Telex: 51916 ERIT TR. $40.

▶ **Ser-Tur Motel Restaurant. Babakale**, Ayvacık, 17860 Çanakkale. Tel: (1969) 1429, then ask operator for 3 (*üç*). $10.

▶ **Teos Holiday Village. Teos** (Sığacık), İzmir. Tel: (5448) 7467; Fax: (5448) 7475. $75 (includes half board; open Apr.–Oct. only).

▶ **Turban Çeşme Oteli.** Şifne Caddesi 35, **Çeşme-Ilıca**, 35940 İzmir. Tel: (549) 312-40 through 312-48; Fax: (549)

312-88. $108 (includes demipension, which is compulsory June–Sept.)

▶ **Turtay Otel.** Aydin–Muğla Karayolu 3 km, *Aydin.* Tel: (631) 33003; Fax: (631) 30351. $38.

▶ **Tusan Bergama Motel.** Alaçatı Mevkii, **Bergama**, İzmir. Tel: (541) 111-73; Telex: 52599; Fax: (663) 119-38. $30.

▶ **Tusan Efes Moteli.** Efes Yolu 38, **Selçuk**, İzmir. Tel: (5451) 1060; Fax: (636) 474-79. $24.

▶ **Tusan Motel.** Pamukkale, 20210 Denizli. Tel: (6218) 2010; Fax: (6218) 2011. $50.

▶ **Tusan Truva Motel.** Güzelyalı, 17100 **Çanakkale.** Tel: (1973) 8210; Fax: (1973) 8226. $45.

THE TURQUOISE COAST
CARIA AND LYCIA

By Toni M. Cross

Those who have travelled along the Aegean coast are certain to have enjoyed its pleasures in the company of others, for nearly as many tourists now jostle one another on the main street of Ephesus as did Ephesians in its ancient heyday. But continue along the Turquoise Coast—southwestern Turkey from Bodrum to Antalya—and you can look forward to visiting any number of ancient sites with only the guard for company. "There is great excitement and pleasure in discovering these cities, once so splendid, and whose sites even have been for twenty centuries unknown"—so Sir Charles Fellows noted in the journal recording his travels in 1840. Because most of these ancient cities are off the main road and rarely visited and those on isolated headlands or tiny islands are reachable only by boat, the modern traveller, too, can experience the thrill of discovery.

MAJOR INTEREST

"Blue Cruises"
Ancient Carian and Lycian cities and tombs
Byzantine churches and monasteries
Roman theaters, baths, and temples
Isolated mountain villages and spectacular scenery

Bodrum
Mausoleum of Halicarnassus

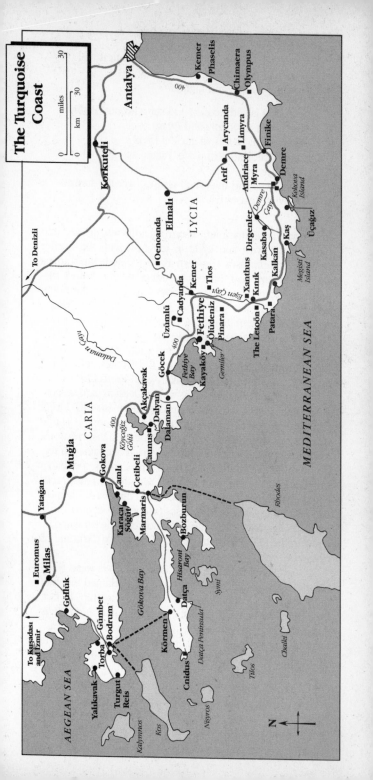

Castle of St. Peter and museum of nautical
  archaeology
Boating, dining, and nightlife

Secluded islands, coves, and ruins around Fethiye
Beaches at Ölüdeniz and Patara
Xanthus, major city of ancient Lycia
Saint Nicholas's birthplace, Patara, and church at
  Demre
Tiny towns and inlets and cruises over the sunken
  city at Kekova bay

In classical antiquity southwestern Anatolia was divided into
Caria in the west and Lycia in the east, with the border
roughly at Telmessus (modern Fethiye). Both the Carians
and the Lycians had their own languages and distinct customs, and according to Homer both took part, on the losing
side, in the Trojan War. While the origin of the Carians
remains obscure, much more is known about the Lycians.

The Lycian language appears to be closely related to
Luwian, itself closely related to and contemporary with the
Indo-European tongue spoken by the Hittites, who ruled
much of Anatolia in the Late Bronze Age (1400 to 1200 B.C.). It
is now assumed that the Lycians were, at least in part, descendants of the Lukka, the inhabitants of western Anatolia during
the time of Hittite rule. The Lukka appear in the Hittite
records mainly in connection with revolts and insurrections,
while the Egyptians and the king of Cyprus complained of sea-
borne raiders from the Lukka lands. The Carians, too, had a
reputation as warriors and seafarers, and the ancient Greeks
could establish only a few colonies along this coast. The most
famous of these was Halicarnassus (modern Bodrum), birthplace of Herodotus, who carefully recorded the Persian conquest in the mid-sixth century B.C. of his native Caria and its
neighbor Lycia.

Though taken by force, both Caria and Lycia were ruled
for the Persians by local dynasts and thus retained much of
their internal independence. Persian overlordship, in fact,
may have brought about their political unification. It is
therefore no surprise that a century later the dynasts, at least,
showed no eagerness to exchange the Persian yoke for the
"freedom" of the Delian League of Athens. The monuments
erected by these dynasts naturally reflect both Persian and
Greek influence, but most of all they reflect the character of
the people themselves, who for so long resisted foreign
domination. Resistance to Alexander the Great was futile,
however, and during almost two centuries of rule by his

successors both Caria and Lycia were fully Hellenized and their native languages replaced by Greek. Yet even centuries later, as a province of the Roman Empire, Lycia at least still retained some distinct characteristics of its own.

One notable characteristic of both Caria and Lycia was the attention lavished on their tombs by both dynasts and common people. The funerary monument of the Carian dynast Mausolus—the Mausoleum of Halicarnassus—provided the ancient world with one of its Seven Wonders and the English language with an appropriate word for a monumental tomb. This monument was only the most grandiose of many, and indeed Lycia has been called the "Land of Tombs." Those who have visited the British Museum will already be familiar with the works of sculpture that adorned the most elaborate: the Mausoleum itself and the Nereid monument from Lycian Xanthus. These were brought to light—and then to England—in the 19th century by C. T. Newton and the aforementioned Charles Fellows, who set out to discover the Carian and Lycian cities described by the ancient authors. (They were both knighted for their efforts.)

That travelling to these ancient sites is a pleasure in itself was appreciated by Fellows, who stated simply, "I know no scenery equal in sublimity and beauty." You won't find the pleasant, rounded hills, olive groves, and sandy beaches that characterize the Aegean coast: Here long, jagged peninsulas, pine covered and mountainous, enclose fjords of the deepest blue. This Turquoise Coast is normally mild in winter, hot in summer. The mountains immediately behind the shore offer relief from the summer heat, but beginning in October tremendous storms can suddenly arise here, covering the peaks in snow and sending torrents of water cascading down upon the valleys and coastal towns. The distances between modern towns and ancient sites are not great, but the coastline is so indented and the terrain so difficult that until very recently the few roads were passable only by jeep, and both native and visitor relied on the weekly steamer. The coastal road, completed in the 1970s, is an engineering triumph—but not of the sort to attract the giant buses of package tours.

The entire region has but a single major airport at Dalaman (about 55 km/34 miles west of Fethiye), the only plain here large and flat enough to serve the purpose. Charters from Europe and domestic flights from Istanbul and İzmir bring tourists here for seaside holidays, but upon arrival these scatter to a number of small towns and villages along the coast. Pleasant accommodations can be found everywhere, but large luxury resorts are so far blessedly confined to the outskirts of Bodrum and Marmaris.

This is definitely the region in which to travel by rental car or, if at all possible, by boat. The Turks call a voyage along this coast the Blue Cruise (*mavi yolculuk*) because of the color of the sea (it really *is* blue). For Westerners the name might more appropriately evoke the incredible calmness, serenity, and peace of mind such a trip induces. Passengers are removed from all the hassles of the modern world, not just traffic and telephones but such mundane concerns as outfits and hairdos, which, after a day or two on board, cease to have any importance. The only thing you need fear is a reluctance to return to civilization, a reluctance that is sure to grow as the end of the trip nears.

Visitors coming directly from Istanbul can fly to İzmir, then travel by rental car or bus the 220 km (136 miles) south to Bodrum. Those coming from Kuşadası (161 km/100 miles) will continue south past Lake Bafa and the ruins of Heracleia (discussed in the Aegean Turkey chapter, above). Clearly visible from the main road 18 km (11 miles) north of Milas is the second-century A.D. **temple of Zeus at Euromus**. Sixteen of its Corinthian columns still stand, some bearing inscriptions recording the names of the prominent citizens who donated them. While driving through Milas take note of its old Ottoman mansions—and, if there's time, its elaborate Late Hellenistic tomb and Roman gateway—before heading southwest down the peninsula to Bodrum, the starting point of our tour of the Turquoise Coast.

CARIA

BODRUM

About halfway along the peninsula from Milas the road turns south, and then suddenly you're looking down at Bodrum, ancient Halicarnassus. The city in antiquity was described as being shaped like a theater curving about its orchestra; today small, whitewashed houses cover a hillside that curves around the perfect circle of its harbor. Although Halicarnassus had been colonized by Dorian Greeks from the Peloponnese about 1000 B.C., the Carian satrap Mausolus

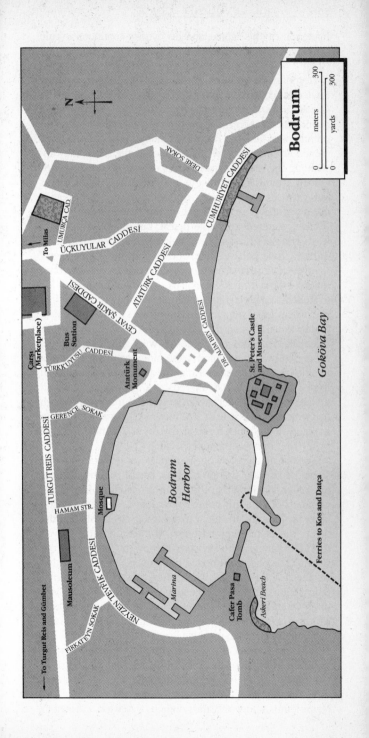

made the city his capital, and his dynasty continued to rule here even after the area was conquered by Alexander the Great.

Herodotus, born in Halicarnassus about 484 B.C., gives the town due recognition in his history of the wars between the Greeks and the Persians. In recounting how Xerxes raised contingents of men and ships from his subjects for the attack on Athens in 480 B.C., Herodotus mentions "a certain leader named Artemisia, whose participation in the attack, notwithstanding she was a woman, moves my special wonder." This Queen Artemisia, it turns out, not only ruled Halicarnassus but gave Xerxes "sounder counsel than any of his other allies." At the great sea battle off the island of Salamis the Persians suffered a terrible defeat, but Artemisia's ship, at least, was seen to ram and sink another. "My men," said Xerxes, "have behaved like women and my women men."

An even more famous ruler of Halicarnassus was Mausolus, satrap of Caria from 377 to 352 B.C. Mausolus devoted his life to Hellenizing his territory, enlarging its cities, and extending its borders, but is remembered only for his tomb. The **Mausoleum** was actually constructed (or at least finished) by another Artemisia, who was his sister, his wife, and his queen. As described by ancient authors, the monument consisted of a temple-like structure on a high podium, ornamented with friezes and statues and topped by a stepped pyramid on which stood a marble chariot drawn by four horses. Though the structure was at least 140 feet high, it was admired in antiquity not so much for its size as for its decoration, carved by the four best sculptors of the day.

The Mausoleum, having stood more or less complete for some 1,500 years, was probably in partial ruin by the time the crusading Knights of St. John arrived in 1402. These members of the (truly militant) religious order of the Hospital of St. John in Jerusalem had as their ostensible aim the protection of pilgrims travelling to the Holy Land. Driven from Jerusalem by the Saracens, then by the Ottomans from Cyprus, Anatolia, and Rhodes, the knights eventually settled on the island of Malta, where they remain today. During their century at Bodrum, the knights built the mighty castle of St. Peter. The toppled Mausoleum provided them with a handy source of construction material, and they burned some of its marble to produce lime.

In 1846 a number of relief slabs from the Mausoleum were removed from the walls of the castle and sent to the British Museum. Their arrival inspired a young museum assistant, C. T. Newton, to seek and discover the actual site of the Mausoleum. Among the finds dug up by Newton and sent to the British Museum are the greater-than-lifesize statues of a man and woman identified by some scholars as Mausolus and Artemisia. Whether they are, and, if so, whether they actually stood in the chariot at the top of the monument, are still matters of debate. Scientific excavations by Danish archaeologists, begun in 1966, have now completely revealed the subterranean burial chamber that lay beneath the monument. At the base of the staircase leading to the chamber, excavators found the bones of cattle, sheep, goats, hens, and pigeons, presumably slaughtered as part of Mausolus's funeral rites, along with more than two dozen eggs.

As long as you are prepared to find a broad, deep hole instead of a 20-story monument, the site of the Mausoleum is well worth a visit (in the center of town, a few blocks up from the harbor; open 8:00 A.M. to 5:00 P.M., except Monday). The exhibits in the small hall and open gallery, especially the tiny model of the Mausoleum set to scale on a plan of the ancient city, give a true sense of the enormous size of the monument and the wealth of its decoration. Walking about the excavated area you can see the broad stairs that led to the burial chamber of Mausolus as well as the staircase of a slightly earlier burial, then pass through a rock-cut tunnel to a sixth-century B.C. tomb.

The archaeologists have moved on to Çoban Yıldız Sokak, on the west side of town, where construction workers had discovered a substantial ancient building (the developers lost this round: the site will be preserved as an open-air museum). The structure is a large, multiroomed villa with mosaic floors of the Roman period, but parts of the house, as well as the ancient street alongside it, date back to the fourth century B.C. The excavators think that a section of this same villa was unearthed in 1856 by Newton, who packed off the best mosaics to the British Museum.

The **castle of St. Peter**, on a rocky promontory at the eastern arm of the harbor, is a marvelously well preserved example of Crusader architecture. Within the double curtain walls are separate towers of the French, English, Italian, and German Knights of St. John, who carved their coats of arms, inscriptions, and other graffiti into the stones. During World War I the French shelled the castle but did not cause enough damage to prevent the Italians from occupying it at the end of the war, during their attempt to claim southwestern Anatolia. Today visitors walk up a ramp, across a moat, and through seven gates to reach the inner castle. The courtyard here is now planted with representative local flora and is home to numerous birds (drop your donation to the protection society in the box provided). The freestanding chapel in

this courtyard was built with ancient blocks (those from the
Mausoleum are identifiable by their characteristic green
hue).

The castle is also the regional **museum**, housing within its
walls objects found on land and, most notably, during underwater excavations conducted by the Institute of Nautical
Archaeology. The chapel in the inner courtyard contains
Bronze Age material, including objects from the Cape
Gelidonya shipwreck (1200 B.C.) and some of the items
recovered from the Institute of Nautical Archaeology's current excavations at Ulu Burun, just east of Kaş. One of the
oldest wrecks excavated so far, the Ulu Burun ship was
transporting a rich and diverse cargo when it sank in the late
14th or early 13th century B.C. Among the objects recovered
to date are a gold chalice; the earliest diptych (two hinged
wooden panels with a now-lost writing surface of wax);
ostrich eggs; ivory; ebony; gold medallions; copper, tin, and
glass ingots; bronze weapons and tools; a faïence scarab of
Thutmose I; and a tiny gold scarab of Nefertiti. This last item
is possibly the most significant, for it may be evidence that
Nefertiti, the wife of the Egyptian pharaoh Akhenaton (and
mother-in-law of King Tut), herself ruled as pharaoh for a
short time.

Across the courtyard is the gallery sheltering a restored
11th-century ship from Serçe Limanı, near Marmaris, and
some of its cargo, including a collection of iron weapons.
(Because the climate in this gallery must be strictly controlled, it is only open 10:00 to 11:00 A.M. and 2:00 to 4:00
P.M., with a maximum capacity of 20 persons.) The ship's
cargo included about three metric tons of glass, most of it
painstakingly sorted and restored over the last decade. A
selection is now exhibited in the nearby Glass Gallery.

To the right of the chapel is a 19th-century Turkish bath
(*hamam*), just restored and now used, most appropriately,
to display the museum's collection of bathing paraphernalia.
In the open courtyard nearby is the newest (summer 1992)
exhibit, a representative selection of ancient amphoras.
These large, two-handled clay vessels were used throughout
the Greco-Roman period for transport and storage; many
still bear stamped impressions stating the merchant's name,
the city of origin, or the type and quality of the contents.

The castle and the museum galleries are open from 8:00
A.M. to noon and from 1:00 to 5:00 P.M. year round. A fine
guidebook to both town and castle, *Bodrum, Ancient Halicarnassus,* written by the museum's director, Oğuz Alpözen,
can be purchased at the ticket booth. A few steps from the
castle is the **Bodrum tourism information bureau,** open

every day from 8:30 A.M. to 7:00 P.M., with an experienced and exceptionally helpful staff.

Most of ancient Halicarnassus lies under the charming whitewashed houses of Bodrum, which rise up the slope from the harbor to the main road along the top of the ridge. Originally a quaint, isolated village of sponge divers and orange growers, Bodrum now attracts windsurfers, disco-goers, and a whole range of Turkish and international vaca-tioners eager to have a good time with a vengeance. Life in Bodrum follows a definite pattern: breakfast at ten, a quick swim, then back to bed until three. Afternoons from three to seven are devoted to water sports—windsurfing, boating to nearby islands, napping on the beach. Everyone then gussies up for dinner, served between eight and ten, then it's off to the music bars until midnight and the disco until at least three in the morning. The night winds down at quiet bars and clubs until five and is brought to a sobering close with a bowl of soup, preferably tripe, at six.

Dining and Staying
in Bodrum

This lifestyle assures you an enormous number of restau-rants, bars, and clubs to choose from. Almost all are within walking distance of the harbor square, the town's center. The street bordering the harbor, Neyzen Tevfik Caddesi, is lined with restaurants, most offering seafood (the waiters at the **Mausolos** are good at convincing you to indulge in that second helping of squid, called *kalamar*). For an intimate, elegant meal served in the garden of an old Bodrum house, try the **Sapa Restaurant**, Külcüoğlu Sokak 6, not far from the mosque in the Türkkuyusu district near the top of the hill. On a narrow street in a quiet residential neighborhood and identified only by the most discreet of signs on its garden gate, the Sapa—"Off the Beaten Path"—truly lives up to its name. As reservations are recommended (Tel: 6141/2553), you might want to make them in person during the day—and hope to find the place again after nightfall. No need to worry about finding your way home, though, as all streets in Bodrum lead downhill to the harbor.

Visitors longing for an evening of traditional Turkish mu-sic and dance are certain to love the **Han** on Kale Caddesi, one street back from the harbor and a block from the square. Dining is on trestle tables set up in the courtyard of the old *han* (inn), but the food is good and the entertain-ment excellent, especially when the place is crowded with

Turks who join in. The evening begins at nine with music and song, slowly proceeds to the belly dancer, and finishes up with authentic folk dancing. Those who have visited Greece (or seen the film *Zorba the Greek*) may be surprised to see how closely this dancing resembles what goes on in a Greek taverna, but half the native population of Bodrum is descended from Cretan refugees, resettled here after that island broke away from the Ottoman Empire. In any case the folklore of the region is much older than the present national boundaries.

Most popular of the postprandial music bars these days are **Hadi Gari** (regional patois for "Come on, let's go"), the **Veli Bar**, and **Sancy's Bar**, all on Dr. Alimbey Caddesi just off the square. At disco time nothing can compete with the **Halikarnas**—probably the world's largest, gaudiest laser-light outdoor disco, on the seafront a few blocks east of the castle. A hefty entrance fee barely holds down the crowds (the disco holds 2,000), and the action begins here at midnight and continues until dawn, when the rock music mingles with the muezzin's call to prayer. The Halikarnas also has a small hotel, presumably patronized by dedicated clientele of the disco.

Those staying in hotels or pensions in town, especially within range of the Halikarnas (that is, the entire neighborhood), and desirous of sleep should invest in a set of earplugs. An alternative is the **Hotel Manastır** at the crest of the hill, with a swimming pool and panoramic view of all Bodrum (nonresidents can catch the sunset while indulging in the hotel's excellent buffet dinner).

Those inclined toward regular hours may prefer to stay in one of the many little seaside towns on the peninsula and take the pleasures of Bodrum in controlled doses. The farther from Bodrum the slower the pace, with the north shore less developed than the south. Only three minutes' drive west of the city center is **Gümbet**, with a sandy beach and calm, protected water. Top of the line here is the five-star **Club M**, with a nice pub and good buffet dining. Among the many medium-range hotels are the **Baba** and the **Hotel Sami**. Both are three-star, right on the beach, and equipped with swimming pools. The Sami has a fancy lobby, English-speaking staff, evening parties on its own boat, and moderate prices—so don't be surprised when all the trappings of luxury end at the door to your room. Also in Gümbet is the **Kervansaray Restaurant**, offering Turkish entertainment as an alternative to the ubiquitous discos.

At **Torba**, on the north shore of the peninsula about ten minutes from Bodrum, is **Milta Torba Holiday Village**, on its own little cove and with full sporting facilities. For an (almost) unspoiled village, continue west past Torba on the northern coastal road another 20 minutes to Türkbükü and the very simple **Motel Kaktüs Çiçeği** (Cactus Flower). At the very western end of the peninsula are the **Club Monakus** at **Yalıkavak**, with villa-type accommodations perfect for families (but with lots of stairs), and the rather luxurious **Club Kadıkale** (Velvet Castle) at **Turgut Reis**, both with private beach, pool, and free transportation to and from Bodrum.

The entire peninsula is dotted with little towns and villages, each with a stretch of ancient wall, Byzantine dockyards, or medieval tower, mainly of interest to serious antiquarians. The surefooted might attempt the promontory of **Aspat** on the southwest shore, opposite the Greek island of Kos. This is probably the medieval site off Strobilos, which overlooked the narrow shipping lane between the peninsula and the island; from the little fortress on the summit you will have a bird's-eye view onto Kos town.

In addition to drives and cruises to nearby towns and beaches, there are daily boat trips from the harbor to the ancient city of Cnidus at the tip of the Datça peninsula to the south (described below). Bodrum harbor is also a major port for yachts offering Blue Cruises, with trips ranging in length from three days to three weeks. The marina at the west side of the harbor now has moorings for 300 private yachts. On the east side of the harbor is the Customs Building, departure point for car ferries to **Kos**, little more than an hour away (daily 9:00 A.M. from Bodrum, 2:00 P.M. from Kos). From here other car ferries now make twice-a-day runs to Körmen bay on the north shore of the Datça peninsula (at 9:30 A.M. and 5:00 P.M. from Bodrum, at 9:00 A.M. from Körmen). Depending on the weather, it's a two- to three-hour trip from Bodrum to Körmen, then half an hour by car to Datça and another hour and a half to Marmaris.

MARMARIS

Visitors coming directly to Marmaris, on the next peninsula southeast of Bodrum's, can fly to Dalaman airport, 110 km (68 miles) farther east. Those driving from Bodrum should head east back along the peninsula and through Milas to Yatağan, then 75 km (47 miles) south via Muğla to Marmaris. Near Çetibeli village, just 15 km (9 miles) before Marmaris, take a break at the **Çağlayan Pınarbaşı Restaurant**, a refreshing little haven with trees, flowers, and a natural spring tumbling into pools filled with live trout (highlights of the menu), plus spotlessly clean rest rooms.

Marmaris lies near the head of a long, straggling peninsula that divides into two, resembling the pincer of some enormous sea creature (the peninsula's two prongs enclose the Greek island of Symi). Mainly a little (about 8,000 inhabitants) fishing and market town, Marmaris lacks the antiquities of Bodrum—and the nightlife. But it no longer lacks tourists, who come here for summer vacations of swimming and boating. Along with mountains, pines, and clear, calm water, nature has endowed Marmaris with a wonderful harbor. Big enough to have held the fleets of Süleyman the Magnificent and Lord Nelson, the harbor is now home port for a flotilla of yachts and is the best place to charter a Blue Cruise heading east along the Lycian coast, the most spectacular in all Turkey.

The appeal of Marmaris is not the works of man but those of nature, and life here is a deliberate contrast to that of Bodrum. The *kordon* (the street that runs along the shore, officially called Atatürk Caddesi) is closed to traffic, no loud music is permitted after midnight, and the most exciting activity for both tourist and local is a stroll along the harbor to admire the yachts. Immediately behind the village square is a **castle**, now a museum. The **caravansary** nearby has been restored and is again filled with shops. Besides the standard tourist offerings you can find hand-embroidered table linens and local honey produced by bees of the pine forests.

Of the dozens of cafés and seafood restaurants bordering the kordon, the **Zuhal Restaurant** is notable for its purple decor (from table linens to flowers), its delicious French and Turkish cuisine, and its exceptionally high prices. Kısayalı Mustafa Sokak, one block in from the kordon, is lined with less-expensive restaurants catering to tourists, mainly British (fish and chips on the menu, ketchup bottle on the table). Beyond the restaurants the street changes its name to Hacı Mustafa Sokak and becomes quiet and residential. At number 71 is the small and charming **Hotel Begonya,** a restored Ottoman house where a few lucky guests breakfast in a flower-filled courtyard.

Medium-size hotels stand shoulder to shoulder along the beach for about five miles from the southern end of town to the district of Siteler, where there are a number of older hotels and several holiday villages (use the town's special form of tourist transport—open trailers pulled by tractors, slower but cheaper than the minibus *dolmuş* and certainly cooler). The best of the older establishments at Siteler is the three-star **Hotel Lidya**, with beautiful flower gardens bordering the sandy beach, 266 rather simple rooms, and a loyal Turkish clientele. Right next door to the Lidya is the **Gazan Motel**, a distinctly unpretentious place almost smothered in flowers and greenery, with a small seafront restaurant that is a good place to watch the sunset. Just a bit farther south of the Lidya is the **Turban Marmaris Tatil Köyü**, the oldest of the holiday villages. The Turban's architect relied on the beauty of nature rather than glitz, and accommodations are in plain but comfortable bungalows scattered beneath the pines.

On previously unspoiled little coves along the peninsula south of Siteler, enormous hotels are springing up like mushrooms after rain, each more grandiose and architecturally fantastic than the next. At the entrance to the Turban holiday village the road jogs across a headland to the new district of İçmeler, with a perfect sandy beach and clear water. Hotels, restaurants, and cafés line the shore, but a broad pedestrian walkway between hotel gardens and the beach ensures the general public equal access. Travellers in the mood for luxury accommodations and five-star pampering can proceed directly to İçmeler and take their pick— one of these vast new palaces is sure to have room.

Ferries regularly make the two-and-a-half-hour crossing from Marmaris to the Greek island of **Rhodes**, and local boats at Marmaris harbor offer numerous day trips: tours of the entire bay, with stops for swimming and lunch; an hour's ride to Kumlubük (a.k.a. Holland Beach) for a day on the beach and lunch at **Hollandalı Ahmet'in Yeri** (Dutch Ahmet's Place); and visits to the the ancient site of Caunus and nearby Dalyan (see below).

On Gökova Bay, northwest of Marmaris, are a number of little towns and ancient sites that can be visited on day trips by car. Boats from the tiny ports of Çamlı, Bucakbaşı, and Taşbükü, on the northernmost cove, carry day-trippers to the little offshore island known as **Sedir** (or, alternately, Sideri or Şehir Adası). On the eastern half of this island are the unexcavated remains of ancient **Cedreae**, with a fourth-century B.C. fortification wall along the shore, a half-buried theater, and the ruins of a Byzantine church lying over the Doric temple of Apollo that preceded it. The hundreds of people who visit each day during the season are drawn not by the antiquities, however, but by the island's minuscule beach. Known locally, and incorrectly, as **Cleopatra's Beach**, it is famous for its incredibly fine, reddish sand (oolite), the grains as round and smooth as fish roe. The island is uninhabited and under the protection of the Turkish Forestry Department, which operates a small restaurant/snack bar and each day performs the herculean task of returning the beach to pristine condition after the day-trippers depart. This exodus is usually complete by 4:30 P.M.; so by renting your own little boat (about $15) and visiting in the afternoon, you can explore ancient Cedreae, then enjoy the beach in comparative solitude.

On the next inlet south is **Karaca Söğüt**, with a complex of seaside villas alongside another unexcavated site with fourth-century B.C. fortification walls and at least one tower still standing intact. A rough road (not signposted; turn south at Söğüt village, about a kilometer inland from the villas) will take you to **İngiliz Limanı**, a charming port with two little restaurants (the field nearby is littered with fourth-century B.C. Greek pottery). Right next door to İngiliz Limanı is the seaside home of Turkey's president, Turgut Özal.

The long, forked peninsula stretching south from Marmaris has numerous lovely coves for picnicking and swimming, but not much else. The only town of any size is **Datça**, about midway along the western fork, with Cnidus, at the very tip, the sole ancient city of importance in the area. The paved road to Datça is so picturesque (narrow and winding, with hairpin bends) that a cautious driver should allow an hour and a half to cover the 75 km (47 miles). At Datça you will find pristine beaches, some simple but adequate accommodations, and a few seafood restaurants. Beyond Datça the dirt track covering the final 35 km (22 miles) to Cnidus is best left to jeeps. The most enjoyable way to see the peninsula is by boat (from Marmaris harbor to Datça, from Datça to Cnidus), but you will need at least a day and a half, including overnight mooring in a sheltered cove, to reach Cnidus from Marmaris.

Cnidus

The ancient city of Cnidus (Knidos) was one of the few colonies established by Dorian Greeks on the coast of Caria. Together with three cities on Rhodes, the island of Kos, and Halicarnassus, Cnidus formed the Dorian hexapolis (six cities), and every four years the city hosted the Dorian Games. The city lay both on the mainland and on a small island, with a causeway joining the two parts. To the north of this causeway was the naval harbor, to the south the much larger commercial harbor. The two harbors were necessary, for given its location at the farthest tip of a long and almost impassable peninsula, the city must always have relied on the sea. The English Society of Dilettanti paid a visit to Cnidus in 1812, and C. T. Newton later came from Bodrum, did a little digging, and added a few more statues to the British Museum's collection. Excavations conducted by an American team in the late 1960s and early 1970s revealed the tidy grid plan of the city's streets as well as the remains of its temples, theaters, concert halls, stadium, and Byzantine churches. The director of these excavations had the most appropriate surname of Love, for in antiquity the city was famous for its statue of Aphrodite.

In the fourth century B.C. the Athenian sculptor Praxiteles carved two statues of Aphrodite. One depicted the goddess of love properly clothed, the other totally—and daringly—nude. The city of Cnidus purchased the nude version, and, with it, fame. Though the sculptor's mistress had served as model, the goddess herself was said to have wondered how Praxiteles had managed to catch her at her bath. The Aphrodite of Cnidus, judged in antiquity to be the most beautiful piece of sculpture ever carved, made Cnidus a required stop on the ancient version of the grand tour.

The American excavators discovered a round building on a high terrace that they identified as the **temple of Aphrodite**, known to have been open and circular so that the statue could be seen from all sides—but no certain trace of the statue itself was found. Excavations were resumed by Turkish archaeologists in 1989. The results to date support the identification of this round building as the Temple of Aphrodite that housed the statue. But, if so, it was not the statue's original home: The temple, with Corinthian columns, dates to the second century B.C., as does the large altar of Apollo on the Middle Terrace. Just below this terrace the excavators have been uncovering the remains of a monumental gateway (*propylon*) that was probably constructed in the fourth century B.C.

The results of all this digging have made Cnidus well worth a visit by those seriously interested in classical archaeology and willing to spend an entire day on the trip (by boat from Bodrum or Datça or by jeep; there are no accommodations, but a few restaurants are open during the summer season). The site is barren and is not signposted. Take a hat and a site map with you.

Dalyan and Caunus

By land it is only 146 km (91 miles) from Marmaris to Fethiye to the east, so there is ample time to visit modern Dalyan and the site of ancient Caunus on the way. Take the main road east, which passes north of Lake Köyceğiz, about 75 km (47 miles) to Akçakavak, then follow the signposted road south another 7 km (4 miles) to the little town of

Dalyan (Fishing Weir) on the east bank of the Dalyan Çayı. While remaining a hospitable community of farmers and fishermen, Dalyan has lined its riverbank with neat little cafés and restaurants in hopes of gaining some tourist revenue. Along with cooling drinks and quite good seafood, many of these, notably the **Denizatı** (Seahorse), at the southern end of the quay, offer a view of the Carian tombs, some in the form of Ionic temples, cut into the face of the cliff on the opposite bank.

With a few small hotels and some pleasant pensions, Dalyan appeals to Turks and Europeans seeking an inexpensive beach vacation in a pastoral setting. The fanciest accommodations to date are in the three-star **Antik Hotel**, with a swimming pool, situated outside of town. To the dismay of the villagers, the vast majority of tourists only stay in Dalyan long enough to hire a boat for a visit to ancient Caunus (see below) or a day at **Turtle Beach** (this long, sandy spit where the river enters the sea acquired its name after a national campaign to protect an endangered species of sea turtle, *Caretta caretta,* which uses the beach as a nesting area). Hiring a boat in Dalyan is refreshingly free of hassles: The boatmen have formed a cooperative, with a single dispatcher handling arrangements and assigning boats.

The site of ancient **Caunus** lies on the western bank of the Dalyan Çayı, just a mile or so downstream from Dalyan. This ancient Carian city died a natural death in the Byzantine period, its harbor cut off by the silting of the river, which now enters the sea two miles from the ancient port. Those travelling by yacht along the coast must therefore moor at the cove of **Ekincik**, where villagers provide boats small enough to cross the sandbar and putt through the reeds upsteam to Caunus.

Herodotus tells of the stiff but futile resistence of Caunus to the Persians during their conquest of Caria in the mid-sixth century B.C. Later references to the city in classical antiquity are almost uniformly negative: Caunus was "sold" to Rhodes by Egyptian generals in 190 B.C.; a century later the city allied itself with Mithradates VI, the eventual loser in that Pontic king's wars against Rome; malaria was endemic; the silting of the harbor was a problem centuries before the city was finally abandoned; and, perhaps as a result of all these woes, Caunus's citizens had a reputation as worthless, untrustworthy rascals.

Two long stretches of Hellenistic fortification wall still stand at Caunus, complete with a tower and a fine gateway that once gave access to the harbor. Annual excavations by Turkish archaeologists have revealed a Hellenistic stoa and fountain house, a *palaestra* (exercise ground), a theater, a Byzantine church, and the so-called **Terrace Temple**—an unusual round building of uncertain date and purpose, surrounded by porticoes. Plans are being made to restore this temple as well as the stage building of the theater, where statues of Apollo and Aphrodite were found. New soundings in the ancient city dump have yielded thousands of objects, including many terra-cotta figurines.

Caunus is a beautiful and deserted site, and it is pleasant to walk up from the landing stage to the Terrace Temple and gaze across the ancient harbor, now a lake, from beneath its shady trees. But Caunus can be unbearably hot and muggy in July and August, and now, as in antiquity, mosquitoes swarm out of the marshes at dusk.

Returning to the main road, head east across the plain of Dalaman. Not far past Dalaman airport, prepare yourself for 50 km (31 miles) of spectacular scenery—and a few jitters—as the road swoops through the pines and around the mountains encircling the huge gulf of Fethiye.

LYCIA

FETHİYE

The modern town of Fethiye covers the site of ancient Telmessus, with only the tombs as reminders of its distant past. Scattered about town are a number of distinctly Lycian sarcophagi, each mounted on a base and covered by an arched, "Gothic" lid with a crest, resembling the keel of an overturned boat. The most famous example, which formerly stood partly immersed in the shallows of the harbor, was the subject of romantic drawings by early travellers. After a devastating earthquake in 1957, the ruins of the old town were bulldozed and the present esplanade constructed along the harbor; thus, the sarcophagus stands again on dry land, alongside the parking lot of the town's municipal building. If the location of the sarcophagus is no longer quite so picturesque, it is certainly more convenient for those wishing to examine its carved reliefs.

The town's small **museum** (a few blocks farther along the main street and one block north) consists of two large rooms, one devoted to the ethnography of the area, the other to archaeology. The latter contains pottery from the eighth through sixth centuries B.C., Hellenistic terra-cottas, a few classical marble heads, some Roman bronze utensils, and the "Letoön Trilingual," a fourth-century B.C. inscription in stone recording in Greek, Aramaic, and Lycian versions the establishment of a religious cult at the Letoön, not far from Xanthus (see below). Discovered by French excavators in 1973, the Trilingual advanced the decipherment of the Lycian language. Among the Roman funerary monuments in the museum garden is the lid of an earlier Lycian sarcophagus from Xanthus, with carved reliefs of warriors and riders, one of whom is shown falling backwards from his horse. The museum is open every day from 8:00 A.M. to 5:00 P.M., notwithstanding the shorter hours posted on the door.

The hill behind Fethiye is encircled by a strong wall, all that remains of a medieval **castle**, probably, like the one at Bodrum, the work of the Knights of St. John. Cut into a rocky hilltop on the southeast edge of town is a group of fine **Lycian tombs**, reached by concrete steps from the street. Most of the tombs are of the "house type," so called because they presumably imitate typical Lycian houses built of wood. The three largest, however, have the façade of an Ionic temple. The most elaborate is the fourth-century B.C. **tomb of Amyntas**, and all who climb up the stairs to its porch will be rewarded with a marvelous view of the gulf of Fethiye.

Since the construction of Dalaman airport, Fethiye has become popular with Europeans, particularly British tourists, for beach holidays and yacht cruises. During the day and early evening, tourists roam the **bazaar** area, just behind the main street bordering the harbor. Along with grocers, fruit stands, spice shops offering local sage, and the ubiquitous vendors of beach paraphernalia and souvenirs, are stores selling silver jewelry, carpets, and leather, many of them blessedly air-conditioned.

Mixed in with the shops of the bazaar are dozens of little restaurants, their menus in both Turkish and English (or just English) and conveniently posted on boards. The best is the **Meğri Restaurant** on Hamam Sokak, with tables set up in the street and alongside the minuscule park (if you have had enough *kalamar,* try the octopus, fried or in a cold salad).

The restaurants bordering the harbor tend to specialize in seafood and to be fancier than those in the bazaar. Of these, the **Rafet**, tucked between the esplanade and the park, is a favorite of locals as well as visitors. In season the residents of Fethiye cede the choice tables to the foreigners and willingly congregate in a back corner of the garden, but the waiters

honor their year-round customers with the best service—
and probably food as well. For good seafood at moderate
prices try the **Yat Restaurant**, situated (as its name implies)
just opposite the entrance to the yacht harbor. Vegetarians,
luckless throughout much of Turkey, are advised to head for
the **Rainbow Restaurant and Bar** at Hisarönü, 6 km (3½
miles) south on the road to Ölüdeniz beach. Owned by a
British-Turkish couple, the Rainbow has a mountaintop setting, outdoor dining in a charming, vine-covered courtyard,
and no fewer than ten vegetarian entrées on its menu. The
British (and vegetarian) half of the management team has
recently given in to her Turkish spouse and now serves meat
and chicken dishes as well.

After dinner you can join the locals as they stroll back and
forth along the esplanade, with stops for a cool drink, coffee,
or ice cream in a seaside café. Those who prefer a bit more
excitement in the evening can travel five minutes by car or
taxi to the **Cennet Pansiyon & Restaurant**, at Fevzi Çakmak
Caddesi 109 in the İkinci Karagöz district, which offers lively
Turkish music along with dinner.

Fethiye is cluttered with small hotels and pensions, but
these can be noisy and there is no place in town to swim. Just
across the street from the main pier and immediately beside
the tourism information bureau is the three-star **Dedeoğlu
Hotel**, with a fine rooftop restaurant and unobstructed views
across the harbor. At the northern, and thus quieter, end of
the esplanade is the new **Hotel Kemal**, with a charming
outdoor dining terrace and immediate access to Fethiye's
famous Lycian sarcophagus (the hotel's main entrance is at
the rear of the municipal parking lot). If you prefer to be right
on the beach, head 4 km (2½ miles) north to **Çalış Plajı**,
where there are one five-star hotel and about 30 small hotels
to choose from. Among the most pleasant is the **Letoon
Motel**, with flower-covered bungalows and a nice pool. Just
be lavish with the mosquito repellent before retiring—and
keep your earplugs within easy reach.

Those approaching Fethiye by yacht will sail past the new
Club & Hotel Letoonia, looking more like a deluxe housing
development than a holiday village. Its superb location—on
a narrow, pine-covered spit of land separating Fethiye harbor from the gulf—is certain to charm its guests (and create
anxiety in yachters who were hoping to escape from civilization). Separated into deluxe "hotel" (with its own beach and
pool) and "club" accommodations in simple but air-
conditioned rooms in white, wood-trimmed houses, the
Letoonia offers secluded beaches in tiny coves, tennis courts,
swimming pools, and its own yacht harbor. But anyone

staying in the club section had better be both hearty (Club Med–type atmosphere) and hale (lots of stairs, at least a 15-minute walk from one end of the grounds to the other, and no vehicles allowed).

Around Fethiye

Within the gulf of Fethiye are dozens of little islands, secluded coves, and isolated ruins of ancient settlements to be explored by boat. Lining the quay at Fethiye harbor are numerous large boats offering both day and evening tours. A nicer, and less expensive, alternative is to hire one of the little open boats moored in front of the Dedeoğlu Hotel, many sporting "rent boat with lunch" signs on their masts. (Lunch consists of meat or fish grilled on the beach by the *kaptan,* plus food from his own home.)

Tucked into the northwest corner of the bay is **Göcek,** on the cove nearest Dalaman airport and thus convenient for those heading straight from plane to yacht. Though still a hamlet, Göcek now has a troop of local girls assigned to keep track of the many yachts tied up at its single, long pier. It also has several sportswear and leather stores, numerous markets, and the **Göcek Restaurant.** Located at the entrance to the pier, the Göcek offers an exceedingly wide menu, from full dinners with seafood specialties to breakfast, both Turkish (egg, cheese, olives) and English (egg, fried bread, sausage). On the far side of the cove is the **Club Marina,** with mooring for 150 yachts and full facilities for both passengers and crew, including a Turkish bath and toilet facilities masquerading as Lycian tombs.

You can enjoy both the cooler upland scenery and a solitary wander through an ancient city on a day trip by car to **Oenoanda** (go east to Kemer, then drive 35 km/22 miles along the Fethiye–Korkuteli road to the village of İncealiler). Though known since the mid-19th century and meticulously surveyed by British archaeologists within the last decade, Oenoanda has never been excavated and is rarely visited. Here are the remains of Hellenistic and Roman city walls, a theater, an aqueduct, a colonnaded street, baths, several Byzantine churches, an agora, and a second open area known as the Esplanade. Most important, however, are numerous fragments of the so-called **inscription of Diogenes.** A second-century A.D. native son and Epicurean philosopher, Diogenes had lengthy quotes from the works of Epicurus plus his own maxims and moralizings inscribed on a stoa of the Esplanade for the edification of his fellow citizens.

If you desire exercise as well as solitude you can drive a

mere 29 km (18 miles) north from Fethiye to the village of Üzümlü, then climb 1,300 feet to the site of ancient **Cadyanda**, at the summit of the nearby hill. As the classicist George Bean pointed out in his book *Lycian Turkey,* "The ancient Greeks, like the modern Turks, made light of a thousand-foot climb at the end of their day's work." Your reward will be an undisturbed look at Cadyanda's Lycian tombs (several with carved reliefs), city walls, theater, temple, stoa, and well-preserved baths dating to the reign of the Roman emperor Vespasian (A.D. 69 to 79).

Just 8 km (5 miles) south of Fethiye is the ghost village of **Kayaköy**, a mainly Greek settlement deserted since the 1923 exchange of populations between Greece and Turkey. Such empty villages can be found elsewhere in the country, their churches still carefully locked, as if neither side really believed the move would be permanent. For both the Greeks of Turkey and the Turks of Greece, this compulsory exchange was bitterly painful, ending at one stroke not only intercommunal strife but centuries of settlement and friendship as well.

Ölüdeniz

A regular stop on the Blue Cruise, Ölüdeniz, 15 km (9 miles) south of Fethiye, has in recent years become the beach of choice with visitors staying in Fethiye. The name Ölüdeniz— "Dead (in the sense of calm) Sea"—actually refers to a lagoon, almost totally cut off from the sea, at the northern end of a long cove. For environmental reasons yachts can no longer enter the lagoon, and it has only a single hotel, the 75-room **Merih Hotel**. While not luxurious, the hotel has a sandy beach on the lagoon shaded by pines and bungalows marching up the hillside (the higher up the bungalow, the more spectacular the view—and the more stairs to climb). Stretching from the lagoon to the southern end of the cove is a long, sandy public beach especially popular with young Europeans (the locals already seem inured to the display of flesh). A few campgrounds, some cafés and restaurants, and numerous pensions have sprung up around the beach; all are "backpacker" quality in every way but the price (try **Harry's Bar** for drinks, a little dancing, and so-so food). At the opposite end of the scale—and at the far end of the cove—is the **Belceğiz Holiday Village**, with 126 rooms and a swimming pool.

A few nautical miles offshore is **Gemiler Adası** (Island of Boats), possibly known in medieval times as St. Nicholas Island, with the remains of an Early Byzantine monastery and its town. Quays and house foundations are submerged near the shoreline of this small, hilly island, and farther up are the remains of five churches, some with fragments of wall paintings and mosaic floors, a huge cistern, and a long covered walkway.

Rarely visited for perhaps a thousand years, in the last decade the island has become a popular anchorage for yachts. From the landing stage, their passengers scrambled up narrow goat paths winding through the rocky scrub in search of the Byzantine remains or just the spectacular view from the heights.

Endangered by the loss of its protective obscurity, in 1992 the island at last began to receive official attention: A scientific survey is to be carried out by Japanese archaeologists, a rough path to the various monuments has been cleared, and a site guard now collects entrance fees at the landing stage. The opportunity for exploration and discovery has not been totally removed, however; it's easy to wander off the "official" path, and there are still no signs to tell you what you've found (or missed). Those intent on "seeing the site" should request the help of the English-speaking guard.

XANTHUS RIVER VALLEY

Southeast of Fethiye lies the heartland of ancient Lycia, projecting into the sea in a wide, curving peninsula that marks the transition from the Aegean to the Mediterranean. Drivers should take the main highway heading east from Fethiye 24 km (15 miles) to Kemer, then south toward Kaş through the valley of the Eşen Çayı—the Xanthus river. Yachters sail from Fethiye around the forbidding Seven Capes to Kalkan, where local cabs and minibuses can be hired to travel up the river valley. The "eddying Xanthus" of Homer, the Eşen is the region's largest river, and five of the most important cities of ancient Lycia are to be found in its valley: Tlos, Pinara, Xanthus, the Letoön, and Patara.

Tlos and Pinara

Both Tlos and Pinara lie just off the main road stretching south from Kemer to Kalkan, and their impressive monuments can be reached without undue exertion or athletic ability. The side roads providing direct access by private car are of such recent vintage, however, that it is quite possible to wander through both ancient sites without meeting another tourist.

The new access road, 10 km (6 miles) south of Kemer,

travels a rough 7 km (4 miles) east to Tlos. The **Ottoman castle** at Tlos, brooding on the summit of the acropolis, was still occupied by the local *ağa* in the 19th century and offering hospitality to English travellers. Cut into the slopes below are two groups of Lycian tombs, of both house and temple types. Alongside the path to the western group of tombs is the base of the **monument of Izarza** (late fourth century B.C.), a monolithic pillar carved with scenes of battle. The upper section, broken off and now much battered, has been moved to the storeroom of the Fethiye museum, but casts of the reliefs, made in the 19th century when the base was still in fair condition, are exhibited in the British Museum.

Farther north is the **tomb of Bellerophon**, with an Ionic temple façade like that of the tomb of Amyntas in Fethiye. Carved on the left side of the porch is a relief of the hero Bellerophon mounted on the winged horse Pegasus—most appropriate, since the deeds of the mythological hero and horse took place in Lycia.

On level ground near the present village of Asar Kale are the remains of a stadium, baths, gymnasium, and an Early Byzantine basilica. Across the road is a well-preserved Roman theater.

A visit to ancient **Pinara** used to entail a half-hour climb, and few tourists make the trip even though it is now just a few minutes by car. About 25 km (16 miles) south of Kemer on the highway to Kaş, a paved road leads west 4 km (2½ miles) to the village of Minare. Just before the village, make a sharp left turn onto a signposted dirt road and bounce uphill for 3 km (2 miles) to the site. Visible from afar is a huge mesa "literally speckled all over with tombs," as Fellows observed upon discovering the site. This mesa served as the ancient acropolis; little now remains on the summit, and the path should be attempted only by the nimble.

In the Greco-Roman period, at least, the actual city lay on and around a smaller hill at the foot of the mesa. There is much to see, but the site has not been excavated and you are strongly advised to have the guard, Fethi Parça, take you around (the standard circuit takes about an hour and a half). Pinara has the usual theater, baths, and temples, but most interesting are its elaborate tombs. Among them is the **Royal Tomb** (probably mid-fourth century B.C.); also called the Landscape Tomb, it has panel reliefs depicting Lycian cities carved on the walls of its porch.

These tombs are usually occupied by a black goat or two, snoozing through the heat of the day. Clambering about Pinara during the summer can be hot work, and the only source of liquid refreshment is a spring of cold water (included on the guided tour). The nearest place to purchase food and drink is the tiny restaurant—just a village house with a Pepsi sign and a few tables under the trees—that you pass on the way up, just before the turn onto the dirt road. The young local couple who run it can provide you with cold drinks as well as simple meals made of the freshest of village-grown ingredients.

Xanthus

Twenty-four kilometers (15 miles) south of Tlos, the road passes through the little town of Kınık, nestled at the base of a hill alongside the Eşen Çayı. Make a sharp left at the only intersection onto the dirt road that winds up this hill to the site of ancient Xanthus, noting the Hellenistic gate, the monumental **arch of Vespasian** (first century A.D.), and traces of the ancient road to the Letoön (discussed below) on your left. Stop here to purchase entrance tickets, then drive to the crest of the hill and park near the shaded refreshment stand, where you can usually find the site guard willing to offer his services as guide.

In his journal entry of April 17, 1840, Charles Fellows recorded his pleasure at returning to Xanthus, "my favourite city—the first in which I became acquainted with the remains of the art of the ancient Lycians, . . . embodying their language, history, and poetic sculpture. How might the classic enthusiast revel in the charm of this city and its neighbourhood! With Mount Cragus before him, he might conjure up all the chimaeras of its fabulous history." Xanthus has this effect on most visitors. Founded perhaps in the eighth century B.C., the city had a golden age under its own dynasts, which lasted about two centuries (mid-sixth to mid-fourth centuries B.C., roughly corresponding to the Classical period in Greece). But Xanthus remained one of the principal cities of Lycia well into Byzantine times, and the monuments erected by the Lycian dynasts were preserved, rather than swept away, by later inhabitants. Here are, or were, the most elaborate of Lycian funerary monuments, many embellished with statues and reliefs.

Fellows had most of the sculpture from these tombs carted off to the British Museum ("As I anticipated, the centre fell in pieces, but the sculptured parts did not receive more injury than they probably would have done from a more scientific operation," he wrote), where they have been pieced together and now fill an entire hall. Occupying much of this hall is the Nereid Monument, for only the foundations were left behind at Xanthus, on the steep slope opposite the arch of Vespasian. The monument, assumed to be the mausoleum of the Lycian dynast Arbinas, who ruled about 390 B.C., resembled an Ionic temple on a high podium and takes its name from the statues of the Nereids (sea nymphs) set between the columns. The walls of both temple and podium were ornamented with sculptured reliefs depicting battles, the siege of cities, hunting, banqueting, and sacrifice, and a man and woman seated on thrones. The sculpture is now thought to have been produced by two different workshops, one local and the other Greek.

Two other Lycian monuments stand alongside the Roman theater across the road from the parking lot. Both are "pillar tombs," a distinctive Lycian type in which the actual grave chamber is set on top of a square shaft. The taller is the famous **Harpy Tomb**, probably the funerary monument of an early fifth-century B.C. dynast. The 17-foot-high pillar supports a rectangular grave chamber, faced now with concrete copies of the original marble reliefs. (Fellows left the pillar but took the sculpture.) The reliefs depict enthroned men and women receiving homage and, on two sides, strange bird-women clutching children in their arms. In Fellows's time these creatures were identified as Harpies—the "Storm-Fiends who snatched up the daughters of Pandareus and gave them to the hateful Erinyes to serve their beck and call," as Penelope relates in the *Odyssey*. Nowadays most scholars associate them with sirens carrying off the souls of the dead.

In recent years French excavators have begun clearing the stage building and orchestra of the **Roman theater**. This work has revealed the orchestra of a smaller, Hellenistic predecessor as well as later Roman alterations for the staging of gladiatorial contests. On the hill immediately behind the theater is the Lycian **acropolis**; a guide is useful here, to point out the excavated remains of the palaces and monuments of the dynasts, a temple, and a much later Byzantine monastery and its basilica. From the western edge of the acropolis there is a fine view of the valley and the "eddying Xanthus."

One of the charms of Turkey is being able to stand in the exact spot where some historical event occurred. Herodotus records a particularly notable event that took place on this Lycian acropolis about 60 years before his birth. After conquering the Lydians in 546 B.C., Cyrus the Great sent an army led by Harpagus to bring both Caria and Lycia into the Persian Empire. When this army reached Xanthus, "the Lycians came out to meet Harpagus and did valorous deeds in their battle against odds; but being worsted and driven into the city they gathered into the citadel their wives and children and goods and servants, and then set the whole citadel on fire. Then they swore each other great oaths, and sallying out they fell fighting, all the men of Xanthos."

Having conquered Lycia with such difficulty, the Persians yet allowed it internal freedom under the rule of its native dynasts. While the Greek cities of the Aegean coast may have been happy—at least at first—to join the Delian League, the Lycians preferred the light and distant rule of Persia to the bossy tribute collectors of Athens.

On the north side of the agora in front of the theater stands the monument known as the **Xanthian Obelisk**, or **Inscribed Pillar**. It is, in fact, the shaft of the pillar tomb of the dynast Kherei; originally it supported a burial chamber topped by a statue, perhaps of the dynast himself. Engraved on this shaft is the longest extant inscription in the Lycian language, together with a 12-line summary in Greek verse. The Lycian alphabet is similar to the Greek, but some letters are unique and the language (and thus the inscription) has still not been completely deciphered. The dynast boasts of his youthful athletic prowess and of glorious feats of arms, including the killing of seven Arcadian hoplites in a single day. This last probably occurred during the Peloponnesian War, the dynast having sided with the Persians and the Spartans against Athens—not at all surprising, if indeed the Athenian general Cimon was responsible for the (archaeologically attested) sack of Xanthus about 470 B.C.

If we are to believe the historian Appian, the citizens of Xanthus preferred self-immolation to submission not once, not twice, but three times. Besieged by Alexander in 333 B.C., they again reportedly destroyed both selves and city in a vain attempt to preserve their freedom. Under the rule of Alexander's successors, the native language was at last replaced by Greek, but the Lycian character seems to have remained unchanged: In 42 B.C. Xanthus again resorted to this ultimate defense against the Roman legions of Brutus and Cassius. This time their sacrifice was eventually rewarded, for these murderers of Caesar were defeated by Antony and Octavian, who in gratitude allowed Lycia to remain free.

Most visitors to Xanthus see only the Roman theater and nearby monuments, ignoring the large, and largely unexcavated, **Hellenistic and Roman city** on the other side of the road. So even in the height of summer, when two or three buses crowd the parking lot and their passengers the theater, this part of Xanthus can be explored in delightful solitude. A path heads east from the parking lot toward the eastern city wall, bringing you close to the foundations of a large Byzantine church with fine mosaic floors and—with luck and sharp eyes—upon the tumbled lid of a sarcophagus with reliefs of a boar hunt and dancers. At the wall the path turns north (left) toward a group of well-preserved tombs at the base of the hill that served as the Roman and Byzantine acropolis. The path then climbs the hill on its way back to the road, providing easy access to the ruins of a Byzantine monastery on top and a great view of the Lycian acropolis and its monuments.

The Letoön

One kilometer (about half a mile) north of Kınık, a signposted road leads 4 km (2½ miles) southwest to the Letoön. This sanctuary of Leto and her children was the main religious center of Xanthus, and probably of all Lycia. Various—and conflicting—legends describe the wanderings of Leto, pregnant with Apollo and Artemis and driven from place to place by Hera, the jealous wife of Leto's erstwhile lover, Zeus. According to one legend Leto avenged herself on some ill-mannered Lycian shepherds by turning them into frogs. True or not, the Letoön is now home to numberless croaking amphibians, for most of the excavated remains lie below the present water table.

Within the sanctuary are the remains of three **temples** built during the Late Classical and Hellenistic periods. The largest was dedicated to Leto, the others to her children Apollo and Artemis. The French excavators of the site have removed the fallen blocks to expose the foundations and, in the **temple of Apollo**, a fine floor mosaic of a lyre, bow, and quiver.

Immediately south of the temples was a large Hellenistic **nymphaeum**, an elaborate fountain house associated with a sacred spring. Enlarged during the reign of the Roman emperor Hadrian and partially covered by a Byzantine church, it is now filled with water and inhabited by frogs. A sacred road lined with statues passed alongside the nymphaeum to the temple of Leto. In book 6 of his *Description of Greece,* written in the second century A.D., Pausanias tells of his visit to Olympia and the statues erected there of victors in the games. Among those honored was "Hermogenes of Xanthus, a Lycian, who won the wild olive eight times at three Olympic festivals" during the reign of the emperor Domitian. The discovery of an **inscribed monument** at the gateway to the Letoön proves that Hermogenes was equally honored in his own land—his statue would have been the first seen by every visitor to the sanctuary.

North of the temples is a complex of Hellenistic and Roman **stoas** and another sacred spring. A number of Hellenistic marble statues were found here, broken into thousands of tiny fragments. Several have been painstakingly pieced together for exhibition in the museum at Antalya.

The archaeologists have now begun working in and around the small, well-preserved **theater** nearby—to the consternation of the villagers, who use the ancient structure for their spring Tomato Festival. The theater was entered by two vaulted passages, one on the south side near the stoas and one on the north. Above the outer entrance of the northern passage is a frieze of theater masks, now believed to be Roman rather than Hellenistic. On the hillside behind this passage the excavators have uncovered traces of the ancient road to Xanthus and a number of tombs. Only a few steps from the passage is an exceptionally fine **sarcophagus**, perhaps late Hellenistic or early Roman. Carved in relief on its base, which has been cut from the living rock, is a man reclining on a couch fitted with mattress and pillow, holding a cup in his hand. The lid, carved separately, has two lion-head bosses on each side.

When leaving the Letoön, you might turn left instead of right and drive 10 km (6 miles) to **Gavur Ağlı**, ancient **Pydnae**. Here you will find an almost complete Hellenistic fortress, its 30-foot-tall towers still standing, and an almost tourist-free beach.

Patara

Eight kilometers (5 miles) south of Kınık a branch road covers the 6 km (3½ miles) from the highway southwest to the archaeological site of Patara, the ancient port of the Xanthus valley. Barely a mile from the site the road passes the village of Gelemiş (or Kelemiş), hidden in the pines. This once-tiny spot is now a jumble of hotels and pensions favored by European backpackers who come here not for the ruins of Patara but for its sandy beach, the largest on this stretch of the coast.

Patara was famed in antiquity for its oracle of Apollo. This oracle functioned only six months of the year, the god traditionally spending winters in Patara and summers in Delos—a wise move, for in summer Patara is *hot*. Until a few years ago, not just the gods but the people themselves abandoned the coastal cities and towns for summer homes in the *yayla,* the cool, green pastures high in the mountains. The twin benefits of modern transportation and tourism having been conferred upon them, most must now remain to labor through the summer heat in fields and hotel kitchens.

By the first century A.D. Patara may have replaced Xanthus as the principal city of Lycia, for the archives of the Lycian League were kept here. This league of Lycian cities, which functioned from at least the early second century B.C. until well into Roman times, was described in some detail by the ancient geographer Strabo: "The largest of the cities control three votes each, the medium-sized two, and the rest one. In the same proportion, also, they make contributions.... Likewise, judges and magistrates are elected from the several cities in the same proportion. And since they lived under such a good government, they remained ever free under the Romans, thus retaining their ancestral usages." This was clearly a federal system, with government by proportional representation; very different from the Greek city-states, where each citizen had his say—and at length. When drawing up the U.S. Constitution, the American founding fathers studied the workings of the Lycian League and found its system of proportional representation to be both democratic and practical.

When the Romans formed the joint province of Lycia-Pamphylia (roughly the coastal strip from Fethiye to Alanya) in the latter part of the first century A.D., the governor had his residence in Patara. This is further proof of the city's importance, resulting from the commerce that passed through its harbor, one of the largest along this coast. When this harbor silted up, perhaps as late as the 15th century, Patara finally died along with it. The former harbor is now a marsh, cut off from the sea by huge sand dunes and a beach more than four miles long.

While few today have even heard of Patara, one of its native sons is familiar to almost everyone in the world—Nicholas, bishop of Myra. Born in Patara about A.D. 300, he was canonized soon after his death as Saint Nicholas and, by the 20th century, commercialized as Santa Claus.

Just past the ticket booth the newly asphalted road runs immediately atop its ancient predecessor. This makes it both difficult and a bit dangerous for the Turkish archaeologists who have been uncovering the tombs that lined both sides of this roadway (burials were forbidden within the city limits). Still standing at the entrance to the city proper is the triple **arch of Mettius Modestus**, governor of Lycia-

Pamphylia in A.D. 100. The excavators have cleared the base of this arch, as well as the sixth-century Byzantine harbor church nearby.

The paved road then passes the remains of other baths, churches, and a temple, and ends at a new parking lot. Beyond lies the beach, so long and wide that camels are sometimes used to purvey cold drinks to the sunbathers scattered along it. By the parking lot are two restaurants, the **Patara**, for many years the only establishment here, and its new rival, the **Harabe**. Each offers outdoor service (complete with scratching chickens) and homemade *mantı* (Turkish "ravioli") as a speciality, but the Patara's much larger menu and nicer setting give it a definite edge. On summer weekends the waiters at both places dash frantically about, trying to supply meals, cold drinks, and ice cream to hordes of beachgoers, both foreign and local.

From the parking lot you can see the **Roman theater** built into the small hill behind the sand dunes. Don't make the mistake of heading straight for the theater over the dunes unless you want a serious workout before the next marathon. Instead, backtrack just a bit and take the path leading from the road. The theater is in a good state of preservation, but romantically half covered by drifting sand. From its upper tiers several paths lead through the shrubs to the crest of the hill and the remains of a tower and what was probably a large cistern with a central pillar.

Your reward for making the short scramble up the hill is a marvelous view of the beach and mountains and a panorama of the ancient site. The hill itself marks the eastern entrance to the former harbor. Across the present marsh are the remains of the buildings that lined the western side, notably the **granary of Hadrian** (second century A.D.), complete except for its roof—worth the walk if you are seriously interested in both archaeology and exploring.

KALKAN

From Patara, return to the main road and follow it south through pine-covered mountains. After 25 km (16 miles) the road suddenly comes out onto a high cliff above the little town of Kalkan, nestled in the curve of a small bay. Kalkan possesses nothing visibly older than its stone houses and a small Greek church converted to a mosque. It has recently become popular with Europeans desiring a (comparatively) quiet seaside vacation and a base for visits to the nearby ancient sites.

Many of the old houses have been converted into pensions, and the rest are being restored to pristine quaintness by Europeans, particularly the British, who have succumbed to the town's charm. And Kalkan does have the charm of an isolated fishing village, despite the yachts tied up in its harbor. Amid the touristy souvenir stands are real shops that serve the locals, including tailors who can whip up copies of your favorite baggy pants or jams while you tour Xanthus and Patara. Taxis and minibuses congregate at the harbor, soliciting passengers for trips to the ancient sites. Facing the quay is the only true hotel in town, the **Hotel Pirat**, with an unexciting, rather dowdy exterior. But on the hillside across the street is the hotel's new extension, the **Pirat 2**, built to resemble a double row of traditional Kalkan houses painted in pastel shades. Its simple but very pleasant rooms look down onto a terrace with large swimming pool, open to the public for a fee. An alternative is a pension in one of the restored houses. **Pasha's Inn Pansiyon**, the first—and for many years the only—place to stay in town, has rooms decorated with local handcrafts and equipped with private baths and free antimosquito devices, as well as a rooftop bar that's a popular place to watch the sun drop over the yardarm.

Just east of the harbor is a line of restaurants with outdoor dining on one long, covered terrace, which may lead to confusion as to exactly which restaurant you are in. All offer buffet tables loaded with *meze* (appetizers) and basically the same menu. All are good but rather expensive, presumably because of Kalkan's relatively isolated location on the coast. An attractive and somewhat less expensive alternative is the **Doydoy** (whose name means "really full," i.e., satiated), with a large terrace overlooking the harbor. The Doydoy's food is just as good—again, buffet tables of meze plus fish and meat—and the view is wonderful. Best of all is the atmosphere, relaxed and friendly rather than deliberately "quaint," perhaps because the owner is a local rather than an *İstanbullu* only in town for the tourist season.

Across the bay is the new Club Patara, a year-round holiday community terraced down the steep slope from the highway to the sea. Here are privately owned villas and apartments (some for rent when not in use), swimming pools, tennis courts, seaside restaurants, and the 100-bed **Hotel Patara Prince**. Everything has been strictly planned, down to the vines and flowers on each terrace, but the Club, like all of Kalkan for that matter, may require more "step exercise" than heart or knees can take.

Kalkan is, however, well prepared to handle any medical

emergency. Set up on the harbor quay is a fully equipped mobile health unit with two ambulances and specialists in internal medicine, cardiology, gynecology, pediatrics, and general surgery on call (and on holiday). Right beside it is the new **Yacht Club**, with self-service laundry, showers, and a rooftop snack bar.

KAŞ

Twenty-seven slow, twisting kilometers (17 miles) farther east along the coast is Kaş; the name, which means "eyebrow," recalls the sweeping curve of the town's bay. Though it is larger and livelier than Kalkan, it is still a small town: Kaş has only 4,000 permanent inhabitants, of which fully one-quarter still move with their flocks to the *yayla* each summer. The present town covers the site of ancient Antiphellus, and a few remains of that Lycian city can still be seen. Just off the harbor are a waterfront park and the central square, its Atatürk statue proudly mounted on a pedestal carved in imitation of a Lycian house tomb. A block up the street to the right is the ancient article itself, perhaps the largest and finest **Lycian sarcophagus** (late fifth/fourth century B.C.) still in existence. A few other sarcophagi are scattered about near the harbor, and many tombs are cut into the cliff above the town.

West of the central square, the main street, Hastane Caddesi (Hospital Avenue), passes the foundations of a **temple**, probably constructed in the later first century B.C. Glance up the side street leading off to the right a few steps ahead, and you will see a large whitewashed mosque, converted from a 19th-century church, with charming black-and-white pebble mosaics in its courtyard. Farther west along the main street, past the hospital, is a small, almost intact **Hellenistic theater**. Its size and simplicity make it especially appealing, for unlike most theaters it escaped remodeling during Roman times and seems never to have been given a permanent stage building. From its upper seats there is a wonderful view of the bay—and of Greece, in the form of the island of Megisti (also called Kastellorizo), startlingly close to shore. Leave the other tourists ogling the view and walk five minutes up the hill behind the theater to the fourth-century B.C. **Doric tomb**. A line of tiny dancers carved in relief is still visible on the interior wall. West of the theater the ground is rocky and covered with scrub, and there are few good places to swim (and watch out—you might flush a wild boar).

Kaş is at least trying to control development, so accommodations in town are restricted to pensions and small hotels. Just past the bus station as you enter the town by car is the **Mimosa Hotel**, with 20 simple, pleasant rooms, a tiny swimming pool tucked alongside the ground-floor dining terrace, and the neighbor's rooster to serve as alarm clock. At number 15 Hastane Caddesi, a block past the temple, is the **Kaş Otel**, with clean, basic accommodations and "beach" on the rocks below. East of the central square, the main street (here called Hükümet Caddesi) climbs abruptly to a whole district of pensions and small hotels on a ridge overlooking the sea. One block up to your left is the fanciest hotel in Kaş, the **Hotel Club Phellos**. The Phellos has comfortably furnished rooms, all with magnificent views of the bay and the island of Megisti plus individual air-conditioning units and a large swimming pool. Just across the street is the **Ekici Hotel**, also with air-conditioning and a swimming pool, but a bit older, simpler, and less expensive. Among the family-run hotels bordering Hükümet Caddesi and the sea is the **Hotel Likya**, which caters to scuba divers by providing all the necessary gear, its own boat, and German instructors. The Likya has a pleasant staff and large front rooms that open onto balconies and an expansive view of the bay—as well as dark and blessedly quiet cubbyholes at the back.

Tucked into a narrow cleft in the ridge is the tiny municipal **Küçük Çakıl Plajı** (Little Pebble Beach), a charming spot with a refreshment stand and free access to the sea. A swim here is guaranteed to revive even the most travel-weary: The short walk to the water's edge is so painful ("little" refers to the beach, not the size of its pebbles) that the unwary hastily leap into a sea chilled by an underground stream.

Five kilometers (3 miles) out of town, at the very tip of the long, narrow peninsula (Çukurbağ Yarımadası) that forms the western arm of the harbor, is the **Hotel Sunset Club**. Set right at the water's edge, the Sunset Club has both standard rooms and fully equipped apartments (sleeping two to five people), a swimming pool, and surprisingly moderate rates.

Near the yacht harbor and central square are two of the best restaurants in town. The **Eriş Restaurant**, with outdoor tables shaded by an old tree, serves excellent meze, meat, and fish. The much larger **Mercan**, right on the harbor, is almost as good and has a wide selection of seafood—but check the prices before ordering. Right behind the Mercan are several discos, which can fill the entire harbor with rock music late into the night. (The local fishermen have their revenge at dawn, when the roar of their engines as they head out to sea echoes across the water and throughout the town.)

A few steps up Hükümet Caddesi on the left is the **Antik Restaurant**, most notable for the recently cleared Lycian house tomb at the back of tis small garden. A bit farther on and to the right is the **Gökkuşağı Restaurant, Cafe and Bar**, on a large terrace overlooking the harbor entrance. The emphasis here is on Turkish cuisine and seafood. Leading off the northern side of the square is Çukurbağlı Sokak, a narrow covered street lined with tiny restaurants, a boisterous jumble of busboys, tables, street hawkers, and pedestrians, where only the waiters are certain which customers belong to which *lokanta* (try the **Derya** or the **Çınar Restoran**).

On the west side of town is the **Kas Otel Restaurant**, on a cool, breezy platform above the sea. The narrow stairway at the left of the restaurant will lead you to the **Elite Bar**, a small, rather classy spot with tables set in little balconies and live music.

Around Kaş

A visit to the church at **Dereağzı** is a perfect day's outing for those eager to discover things for themselves—your chance of meeting another traveller is close to zero. At the main intersection 11 km (7 miles) east of Kaş, head north on the road to Elmalı for 12 km (7½ miles). At the town of Kasaba follow the road east for 8 km (5 miles) to Dirgenler, where the villagers will direct you another 3 km (2 miles) southeast to the church. Here in solitary splendor is a late ninth- or early tenth-century Byzantine church, its walls rising in places to a height of 42 feet. A cross-domed basilica with towers, the church was joined by tunnels, now collapsed, to two octagonal buildings. This was no ordinary provincial church: The building plans, perhaps even the architects, must have been brought from Constantinople and the bricks and granite transported from the southern coast of the Sea of Marmara. The church was carefully investigated in the late 1960s and early 1970s by James Morganstern (*The Byzantine Church at Dereağzı and Its Decoration*), who noted, "We may never know its name or the name and nature of the settlement. But the complex was and remains to this day one of the most impressive monuments of the whole Middle Byzantine period."

Visits to the Greek island of **Megisti** depend upon the political situation between Turkey and Greece. Normally, designated boats carry foreigners (with passports) from Kaş to the island. As Megisti is not an official port of entry to Greece, you may only stay long enough for a leisurely lunch and a stroll about town.

KEKOVA BAY

An entire navy of small boats makes day trips from Kaş to Kekova bay, probably the most scenic area along this coast, if not all Turkey. These boats tend to be overloaded with the young and beer-drinking, more interested in sunning and swimming than antiquities. Take a stroll along the harbor and check out the boats, their itineraries and prices, and the maximum number of passengers; if possible, rent one for yourself and move in comfort and at your own pace. The standard trip lasts an entire day and includes stops at Tersane on Kekova island and the little towns of Kale and Üçağız on the mainland.

Kekova Island

Kekova island, about two hours by boat east of Kaş, is uninhabited but for a goatherd or two. At its northwestern end is **Tersane**, another of the numerous "dockyards" along this coast, its beautiful, tiny cove among the day-trippers' regular stops. But these boats stay only an hour, and most of their passengers limit themselves to swimming and a quick look at the stone apse of a presumed Byzantine church right on shore, sadly ruined by campfires. Snorkelers can patrol the shoreline and study the foundations of buildings now beneath the water—but watch out for stinging *deniz kestanesi* (sea urchins). The slopes are covered with the remains of many more buildings, half-hidden in the prickly shrubs (long pants and sturdy shoes are required for serious exploration). The remains of the so-called **sunken city** line the northern shore and continue down beneath the waters, which have risen since antiquity. These ruins are so accessible that swimming and even anchoring here are forbidden; you must be content with a slow cruise along the shore. Both Tersane and the sunken city are assumed to be Byzantine sites, but neither has been excavated or even scientifically investigated.

Kale and Üçağız

Until a few years ago, Kale and Üçağız, the two villages on the mainland opposite Kekova island, could be reached only by boat, and even now not many drive the winding 20 km (12 miles) of newly paved road from the main highway. The towns' inhabitants thus take to the sea at a very early age and use boats as casually as suburbanites elsewhere use their cars. There's a Lycian sarcophagus in the shallows of the harbor of Kale (Castle), ancient **Simena**; the sarcophagus is close to the shore, but, once again, watch out for the sea urchins. Urchins of a much more charming species— village children—maneuver rowboats about the harbor and are likely to pull alongside your yacht and swarm over the sides like tiny pirates, selling colorful headscarves with fancy edging tatted by their mothers—the local, and only, industry.

Kale rises from the harbor up a steep slope, its stone cottages mixed in with Lycian and Roman remains, to a tiny, ancient rock-cut theater and a medieval castle on the summit. An old stone stairway threads its way up between the cottages, the ruins of a Roman bath, several sarcophagi, and groups of village women industriously tatting headscarves, to the castle and a magnificent view of the entire bay of Kekova.

Kale is so picture-postcard perfect that some find it unnerving and prefer nearby **Üçağız**—the "Three Mouths," referring to the triple sea lanes leading to it—built, sensibly enough, on a small patch of level ground. The charm of Üçağız lies in its stone cottages, its tiny lanes, and its exceptionally friendly villagers. At the eastern edge of town are the remains of ancient **Teimiussa**, now a remarkable jumble of Lycian tombs—one still bearing a fourth-century B.C. relief of a young athlete—and sarcophagi. While Kale and Üçağız have only the simplest of village accommodations, both have excellent locally run restaurants along their harbors.

DEMRE

At the traffic circle 11 km (7 miles) east of Kaş the road leaves the coast to cut across the mountains for 36 km (22 miles) to ancient **Myra**, known as Demre to the locals but Kale to the highway department (here the road signposted "Kale" will take you to Demre, not the village of Kale on Kekova sound). It's a wild and beautiful drive, and among the few places where you are likely to pass a camel or two still serving the villagers as beasts of burden. Just before Demre the mountains come to an abrupt end, and the road winds down the face of a cliff in a series of dramatic switchbacks.

Demre lies between the mountains and the sea on rich, fertile land deposited by the Demre river. Most of ancient Myra lies buried beneath the alluvial soil and the modern town, but backed up against the base of the cliff is a huge **Roman theater**. Visitors pass through its double-vaulted corridors and climb the stairs to the seats like fans entering a football stadium. Cut into the rock immediately behind the theater is a large group of **Lycian tombs**, some with decoration in relief. The recent addition of an exceptionally sturdy metal staircase provides access to two levels of tombs; from here many others can be reached by the mildly energetic and reasonably surefooted. Few visitors are aware of a second group of tombs barely a mile away, cut into the northeastern face of the cliff, as there is still no sign pointing the way. When leaving the theater area, turn left onto Ilk Okul Sokak (Grade School Street). Continue past the grade school and then, opposite the middle school (Orta Okul), turn left down the narrow lane now fronted with plastic hothouses. The villagers working here will cheerfully lead you to the second group, which includes the **Lion Tomb** and the **Painted Tomb** (fourth century B.C.), possibly the most famous in all Lycia. It is not far up the cliff and the climb is not difficult, but the acrophobic may well blanch at the narrowness of the rock-cut stairs. Make the climb if you can, for carved on the tomb and the surrounding rock are 11 life-size figures, presumably representing the deceased and his family. Fellows was able to note the colors with which these figures were painted, but only a few traces are visible today.

At the western edge of Demre is a monument that *is* seen by every visitor: the **church of St. Nicholas**. Born about A.D. 300 in Patara 95 km (59 miles) to the west, Nicholas served as bishop of Myra and was buried in or near his church, which soon became a goal of pilgrims. Because the medieval pilgrimage enabled people of all ranks to combine religious devotion with the mundane pleasures of modern tourism, the church and town—fortunate enough to possess the bones of a popular saint—were assured both material prosperity and heavenly protection.

Divine protection saved the tomb of Saint Nicholas during an Arab raid in A.D. 808, but proved inadequate against fellow, albeit Latin, Christians. In 1087 Italian merchants "reverently" smashed the tomb and carried off the saint's relics to Bari, where the large church constructed to house them still draws pilgrims as well as tourists. Understandably, the clergy of St. Nicholas in Myra claimed that several relics had been overlooked. Encased in a reliquary lined with red velvet, these fragments of jawbone and skull are now safely housed in the Antalya Museum (see the Central Mediterranean Coast chapter, below), where each year the Turkish government sponsors a Saint Nicholas symposium. Attended by both scholars and clerics, the symposium begins on December 6, the feast day of the saint, with a religious service in the church of St. Nicholas here in Demre.

Visitors may be disappointed upon first sight of the church, a very ordinary looking white structure with a flat roof and a bell tower. But just beyond the ticket booth is a ramp that takes you to the original floor, some 24 feet below the present ground level and 1,500 years back in time.

It is assumed that the original church, built not long after Saint Nicholas's death, was replaced in the eighth century by a basilica with a central nave, a side aisle on the north, and two side aisles on the south. In the 11th century this church was rebuilt with materials from its eighth-century predecessor, and on the same lines. The processional way that led directly to the second south aisle was perhaps for pilgrims visiting the tomb. Cloisters, courtyard, second entrance portal, and a third south aisle were added in the early 12th century.

The modern ramp, like the processional way, brings visitors directly to the south aisles at the side of the church. In the niches of these aisles are a number of marble sarcophagi. All are Roman (second century A.D.), taken from the ancient necropolis of Myra and reused for the entombment of church dignitaries. The **Column Sarcophagus** in the middle aisle was too big for its niche and had to be reworked. This was done sometime in the 11th or 12th century as a replacement, it has been suggested, for the original sarcophagus of Saint Nicholas smashed by the Italian merchants. In the apse of the central nave is the *synthronon,* semicircular tiers of seats for the clergy, with a special place for the bishop's cathedra and a walkway underneath. This central nave is separated from the side aisles by arcades. The roof, originally domed, has been restored in modern times with a groin vault.

Nicholas became, as everyone knows, the patron saint of children. He also became the patron saint of sailors (appropriate for a native of Lycia) and of imperial Russia. Czar Nicholas I, in his self-proclaimed role of protector of the Ottoman Empire's Christian subjects, began financing the reconstruction of the church, which by the 1860s had fallen into ruinous condition and become partly silted by the Demre river. This rebuilding, as opposed to restoration, was finally completed by the Turkish government in 1963. In preparation for a new, accurate restoration, the Turks have recently begun excavations in and around the church. Work to date has concentrated on the cloisters at the north and east. One question the excavators hope to answer is exactly where Nicholas was buried (or at least where the early Christian pilgrims *thought* he was buried), for none of the spots that has so far been proposed completely matches contemporary descriptions.

Andriace

The site of Andriace, the port of Myra, is just 3 km (2 miles) to the southwest. For much of the way the road leading from the church of St. Nicholas borders a stream that enters the sea at the ancient port. It is this stream, which has given the place its modern name, Çayağzı (Mouth of the Stream), that accounts for the silting of the ancient harbor and the creation of the present sandy beach.

On the far side of the stream are many tombs and the foundations of a few large buildings and the aqueduct, which had lined the north shore of the ancient harbor. On the same side as the road, but separated from it by a scrub-filled and often marshy waste, are the unexcavated remains that had stood on the south side of the harbor—a line of warehouses marking the ancient quay, a market and residential area, and the **granary of Hadrian** (A.D. 117–138), still standing complete with a bust of the emperor over the door.

The present harbor is so shallow that yachts must anchor offshore and hail motorboats to ferry their passengers to the beach, where taxis to Demre can usually be found. The beach itself is clean, and it's popular with local Turkish families. There are no accommodations, just a tiny campground, but the sole restaurant, the Çalpan, is excellent. Locally owned, it serves a wide range of meze and fresh fish at reasonable prices.

Finike

From Demre east to Finike the road follows the twists and turns of the coast for 27 km (17 miles). In addition to a few thrills (more than one monument between Demre and Antalya commemorates workmen who died building this road), each hairpin bend presents the traveller with a tantalizing view of another tiny cove far below. These are deserted except for a yacht or two, their passengers swimming or lunching on deck. Don't envy them too much, for they are merely delaying as long as possible the inevitable end of their Blue Cruise: Most boats travel from west to east, and Finike's large harbor is one of the best places to disembark.

The harbor now has facilities for yachters, including snack bar and souvenir shops. Near the entrance is the pleasant **Petek Restaurant**, where you can enjoy a full range of Turkish food, from meze and seafood to soup and stuffed peppers, on its breezy outdoor terrace. The rest of Finike's waterfront is, unfortunately, a solid line of modern concrete buildings; as a result, most travellers barely give Finike a glance—and the disembarking yachters are too gloomy to care. But this concrete strip is little more than a façade. Those making the short side trip to ancient Limyra will turn north just past the harbor onto the Elmalı road and drive 5 km (3 miles) to Turunçova, discovering along the way the old stone houses of Finike, their walled gardens filled with citrus trees and covered with bougainvillaea.

Limyra

At Turunçova, turn right onto the former main road, which after 3 km (2 miles) passes right through the site of ancient Limyra, separating its acropolis hill from the walled lower city.

At the top of the hill are the remains of fortifications, a Byzantine monastery, and the **mausoleum of Pericles**, a Lycian dynast. A contemporary of the fourth-century B.C. satrap Mausolus, Pericles resisted the expansionist attempts of his Carian neighbor. The competition between the two dynasts seems to have extended if not beyond, at least up to, the grave. While the funerary monument of Mausolus is so famous that it gave his name to the type, that of Pericles was only discovered during excavations in the 1960s. Like the Mausoleum at Halicarnassus and the Nereid Monument at Xanthus, the tomb of Pericles took the form of a temple raised on a high podium, ornamented with statues and reliefs. The "temple" roof was supported not by columns but by majestic statues of females (caryatids) revealing, like the dynast's very name, the influence of Athens and of the Erechtheum on that city's acropolis. (These caryatids and the style and subject matter of the reliefs, however, also show a strong Persian influence.)

On the slopes below are hundreds of tombs, some, such as the fourth-century B.C. **sarcophagus of Xñtabura**, embellished with reliefs. Near the base of the hill the excavators have been uncovering a residential district, its streets neatly laid out in a grid plan. One of the houses, built of wood and stone in the late Classical period (fourth century B.C.), corresponds to the native Lycian house depicted on reliefs and imitated in the house tombs. Cut into the very base of the hill is a fairly well preserved **Roman theater**, known from inscriptions to have been built in A.D. 140.

The **lower city**, on level ground across the road, consists of two separate, walled districts. The remains of baths, a church, an episcopal palace, and a colonnaded street, eight yards wide, have been uncovered in the eastern section. Half of the western part is still enclosed by a sixth-century Byzantine wall with towers; excavators have found built within it a Lycian gate. The residence of Pericles may have been in this western district, and it continued to be occupied by local dignitaries into the Byzantine period. Its importance is emphasized by two spectacular monuments erected within its walls.

The recently discovered **Ptolemeion** consisted of a round, temple-like structure (*tholos*) on a large, square podium, adorned with sculptured reliefs (one depicting a Celtic shield), marble lions, and enormous marble statues of a man and a woman. Constructed in the first half of the third century B.C., the structure is assumed to have served a Hellenistic ruler cult. The rulers most likely to have been worshiped here were Ptolemy II Philadelphus and his wife/sister/queen Arsinoe II, for these offspring of Alexander's general Ptolemy claimed Lycia as well as Egypt. The Celtic shield may refer to an actual event, Ptolemy's protection of Limyra from the Galatians, Celtic tribes that caused much havoc in western Anatolia in the third century B.C.

Also in this western district are the remains of the **cenotaph of Gaius Caesar**, grandson and heir of the Roman emperor Augustus, who died here on February 21, A.D. 4. Sent on an imperial grand tour at the age of 19, Gaius had progressed as far as Syria when he was ordered across the Euphrates to crown a vassal king of Armenia. Caught up in civil war and treacherously stabbed, the young man was able to reach the coast and board ship for Rome, but both his journey and his life ended at Limyra. Augustus's dream of founding an imperial dynasty ended as well. "Bereaved by Fortune," as he states in the account of his life inscribed on the walls of his temple in Ankara, Augustus was forced to name his hated stepson Tiberius as heir. Some fragments of the beautiful reliefs that had adorned the cenotaph can be seen in the Antalya Museum.

Arycanda

From Turunçova, continue north on the road to Elmalı another 30 km (19 miles) as it winds into the mountains. At the little truck stop at Arif are a few simple trout restaurants and the beginnings of the track to the archaeological site of Arycanda. It's a rough five-minute drive or an easy 15-minute walk, but well worth it, for over no other site in Lycia did Fellows wax as lyrical: "I feel as if I had come into the world and seen the perfection of its loveliness, and was satisfied." Turkish archaeologists have devoted many years to the excavation of Arycanda and to the restoration of some of its buildings, adding immeasurably to the visitor's understanding of the site, while its relative isolation has protected the unspoiled natural beauty of its setting.

The city lies on a series of terraces cut into a steep slope in the valley of the Aykırıçay, presumably the ancient Arycandus river. On the lower terraces are the remains of a Roman temple converted into a Byzantine basilica, with traces of wall paintings and floor mosaics, and a large bath-gymnasium complex. Immediately above the latter is the **east necropolis**. While clearing and restoring some of its monumental Roman tombs, the excavators discovered later Byzantine rooms with stucco decoration and mosaic floors. Farther up the slope is an agora enclosed on three sides by stoas, an odeon, a Hellenistic theater (its Doric-style stage building added in Roman times), and a stadium. West of the stadium is a stoa with shops and the *bouleterion,* the meeting house of the city's council. On the terrace below is a Roman villa with mosaic floors.

One kilometer (about half a mile) south of Arycanda are the remains of a small Early Byzantine fortified town. A main street runs between the eastern and western gates in the towered wall of the city; at least one of the four north–south streets was partially vaulted. Within the walls are the remains of houses, some with fireplaces; what was probably a large, vaulted cistern; and four churches.

Olympus

A visit to ancient Olympus will enable you to enjoy both the pleasure of discovery and the beauty of nature, for this coastal site has never been excavated. From Limyra return to Finike and take the coastal road east for 22 km (14 miles), where there is a yellow sign pointing to the right for Olympus. Loop down toward the sea for 5 km (3 miles) on this paved road, then keep a sharp lookout for another yellow sign pointing left through the pines. From here a rough track follows a dry streambed for part of the 4 km (2½ miles) to the site. This track improves as it goes along and can usually be negotiated by ordinary vehicles, but if it has recently rained you may prefer to walk. At the entrance to the site, just beyond the ticket booth, a second stream enters the same bed and flows through the center of the ancient city into the sea. This second stream is perennial and accounts for the lush greenery that smothers most of the unexcavated remains. Nothing is known of the city's foundation or of its history until the second century B.C.; most of the visible ruins date to the Roman and Byzantine periods.

A path follows the stream to a pebble beach, passing the substantial remains of stone buildings and quays, the stump of an ancient bridge, and—hidden off in the vegetation— the remains of a temple and bath. On the far side of the stream, crossed either at the beach or over the stepping-stones near the bridge stump, are several Byzantine churches and a theater.

Until 1992, those few who visited Olympus were happy to find the site guard, a local man who would lead them like jungle explorers through the vegetation. The authorities have now completely cleared the main path and hacked minor ones through the undergrowth to the major remains. They have also added some amenities to the once-deserted beach; it now attracts yachters and day-trippers. Lovers of solitude may not find all this an improvement, but clearance of the main path has exposed two large, handsome **sarcophagi** near the beach, one of them bearing a relief of a large ship, carved in great detail.

By 100 B.C. Olympus was important enough to possess the maximum three votes in the Lycian League, but soon there-after the city was captured by pirates and became the stronghold of their chief, Zenicetes. Human beings were the most valuable of the captured booty; the pirates sold them in slave markets such as that at Delos, which was large enough to handle 10,000 transactions a day. In 78 B.C. the Roman governor Publius Servilius Vatia defeated the pirate fleet at sea, took Olympus, and besieged Zenicetes in his nearby fortress. Seeing that all was lost, the pirate chief set fire to his stronghold and in true Lycian fashion immolated himself and his family. Among the governor's subordinates on this campaign was the young Julius Caesar, who four years later was himself captured by Carian pirates while sailing to Rhodes to study philosophy. Freed upon payment of a 50-talent ransom, Caesar raised his own ships, defeated the pirates, and on his own authority had them crucified. But this was merely a limited act of private vengeance, and the pirates along this coast were not fully routed until the campaign waged by the Roman general Pompey the Great in 67 B.C.

An even more infamous resident of Olympus was the

Chimera, a monster that according to Homer was in the form of "a lion in front, a snake behind, and in between a goat." The slaying of this monster was one of the tasks assigned to the hero Bellerophon by the king of Lycia, and with the help of the winged horse Pegasus he succeeded. The exact lair of the Chimera is not specified in the *Iliad*; the fire-breathing monster probably came to be associated with Olympus because of the perpetual flame (*yanar*) issuing from a nearby mountainside. While not large, this natural phenomenon—a vent of natural gas, issuing from the earth in one or more small jets—is clearly visible to sailors at night. Ask at the ticket booth for village transport to the base of the hill. From here it is an easy 30-minute climb to the flame and to the nearby remains of a sanctuary of Hephaestus, the Greek god of fire, replaced in Byzantine times by a church. There is also a road to the *yanar*, but to reach it you must return to the main highway and it won't save you the half-hour walk up the hill.

Once back on the main road and heading east, keep a sharp lookout for a small sign on the right-hand side pointing to Ulupınar. Follow the narrow, paved road for less than a mile to the **Çınar Restaurant**, with an outdoor dining terrace sheltered by plane (*çınar*) trees and cooled by a mountain stream. Try the trout, plucked live from their pen below the terrace, and, in late summer, the Çınar's special dessert, melon with ice cream.

Phaselis

Just 30 km (19 miles) northeast of Olympus is the site of ancient Phaselis, set on a low headland jutting into the sea. On the very border of Lycia, Phaselis did not become a full member of the Lycian League until the first century B.C. Though originally colonized by Greeks from Rhodes, the city, like its Lycian neighbors, had to be forcibly enrolled in the Delian League of Athens against the Persians. The wealth of the city was based on trade, and by the winter of 334/333 B.C. the amenities it offered were impressive enough that Alexander the Great chose to pass the winter here. Nowadays Phaselis attracts many visitors—including the citizens of Antalya, less than 60 km (37 miles) away; see the Central Mediterranean Coast chapter, below—simply because it is so beautiful: The ancient remains stand among the pines, its three ancient harbors are excellent for swimming, and some of the highest mountains in all Lycia, snowcapped even in April, form a dramatic backdrop.

A signposted road leads from the highway a few kilometers

through the pines to a large, well-equipped visitors' center and tiny **museum** (ask at the snack bar if you wish to see it). The actual site is more than a kilometer farther on, and those with private cars may drive to a paved parking lot behind the arches of the city **aqueduct**. Just beyond are the old **north harbor**, more an open strand where boats were pulled up on the shore, and the small **central harbor** sheltered by the headland. In antiquity the natural arms of this harbor were extended by moles, leaving only a narrow entrance that could be closed off with a chain. Substantial portions of these moles remain, just under the surface of the water, making the harbor perfect for swimming—and potentially disastrous for any boater not aware of their existence. The ancient paved main street still leads from the harbor quay across the neck of the headland to the **south harbor**, now rimmed by a sandy beach.

The bases of the statues that lined the ancient main street have been put back in place by Turkish archaeologists. The inscriptions on these bases have been partly eroded by water, for in late antiquity they were reused to build a harbor quay. On both sides of the main street are important Roman and Byzantine public buildings—several agoras, baths, a theater, and churches—most of them clearly identified by signs. The partially excavated baths on the seaward side of the main street present visitors with a textbook illustration of the standard Roman hypocaust heating system. The elaborately decorated floor is supported by rows of brick columns in the low basement. Hot air from the furnaces passed through the basement, then up tubes within the walls to the chimneys, heating floors and walls as it went. At the southern end of the main street lie the carved marble blocks of the **gate of Hadrian**, built in honor of that emperor's visit here in A.D. 129.

Kemer

Beyond Phaselis the coast is lined with enormous resorts, such as the **Ramada Renaissance Resort Hotel**, the **Iberotel Kiris World**, the **Grand Phaselis Princess Hotel**, and the **Club Salima**, the last known for its truly fabulous buffet meals. Hidden among the pines and fenced off from the outside world, all offer full sports facilities plus nightly entertainment in outdoor theaters. These hotels cater mostly to Europeans on package holidays, but travellers can sometimes find a room, and at bargain rates. The one break in this coastal chain is the town of Kemer, 18 km (11 miles) northeast of Phaselis. Kemer used to be a simple village amid orange groves, its only visitors a few İstanbullus seeking the bucolic on their summer holidays. It is now the proud possessor of many hotels and restaurants, a main street lined with fancy, air-conditioned shops and boutiques, and a yacht harbor with a tennis court and swimming pool. Near the yacht harbor is the four-star, 60-room **Otem Hotel**, where students at the vocational tourism school receive on-the-job training. The Otem staff is thus almost overwhelmingly eager to please—their grades depend upon the service they provide.

With so many hotels, pensions, and villas right in town, Kemer has lavished much care and attention on its municipal beach. On a cove at the southern end of town, the beach is spotlessly clean, bordered by an immaculate, grassy park shaded by trees, and dotted with modern shower and changing rooms operated by tokens. Facing the beach on the far side of the cove is the **Club Méditerranée Kemer Holiday Village**, for many years the only large hotel on this stretch of the coast.

Places to eat in Kemer are numerous and varied, ranging from the restaurants in the large hotels (the Otem's is good) and at the municipal beach to street vendors purveying sandwiches and corn on the cob. For "home cooked" Turkish meals, the **Tuna Lokanta** in the center of town is the definite favorite of local residents.

Beyond Kemer the new highway goes where no road has ever gone before, snaking around and tunneling through massive, rocky headlands before making its final descent to the plain. At the base of the mountains is Antalya, with plenty of luxury hotels to pamper all who have traversed this southwest corner of Turkey.

GETTING AROUND

The Turquoise Coast is served by major airports at İzmir, Dalaman, and Antalya. The İzmir airport, 220 km (136 miles) north of Bodrum, has international connections plus daily Turkish Airlines (THY) flights from Istanbul and Ankara. Dalaman, the only airport actually within the region, is 200 km (124 miles) east of Bodrum, 110 km (68 miles) east of Marmaris, and 55 km (34 miles) west of Fethiye. From March through October there are numerous direct flights to Dalaman from Europe, many of them charters, plus daily flights via Turkish Airlines from Istanbul. The airport at Antalya, 150 km (93 miles) northeast of Kaş, has many regularly scheduled and charter flights direct from the major cities of Europe, as well as Turkish Airlines flights from Istanbul (several daily) and from Ankara (one or two per week). In addition, two private companies—Green Air and Istanbul Airlines—offer flights from Istanbul to Dalaman and to Antalya. At present no private carriers are offering regularly scheduled flights from Istanbul, İzmir, or Ankara to the airstrip at Bodrum. For information on such occasional flights as do exist, contact either of the following Istanbul travel agencies: Setur (Tel: 1/230-0336) or Kefeli Turizm (Tel: 1/230-3568).

Within the region, there is efficient public transportation by bus between the larger towns, minibus dolmuşes elsewhere. A better way to travel, however, especially if you plan to visit some of the more out-of-the-way places, is by car. A wide range of vehicles, including the popular mini-jeep, can be rented at the three major airports, which are served by Avis, Hertz, Eurocar, and Budget, among other car-rental agencies. The only road likely to be crowded, even at the height of the season, is the stretch from Milas to Bodrum. While traffic is not a problem, the narrow, twisting coastal road requires alertness and caution. The section from Demre to Finike, in particular, is cut into the cliff fronting the sea, leaving little room for error and none for guardrails. Drivers subject to vertigo might give serious consideration to reversing the route described here and travelling from Antalya west to Bodrum in order to be on the inside lane. The main and side roads are well marked, but don't waste time learning the official route numbers, as they almost never appear on highway signs. Instead, the signs will refer to the major city at the end of the route plus the next town along the way. At the traffic circle just east of Kaş, for example, one fork is signposted "Antalya Elmalı," the other "Antalya Kale." While both lead to Antalya, one heads north and east through the central plateau and the town of Elmalı, the other hugs the coast and passes through Kale (Demre).

A Blue Cruise can be organized in advance, even from abroad, by writing to the tourism information bureau in the harbor town where you intend to embark—usually Bodrum (Eylül Meydanı 12; Tel: 6141/7694), Marmaris (İskele Meydanı 39; Tel: 612/210-35), or Fethiye (İskele Meydanı 1; Tel: 615/115-27). Tell them how many people will be in your party, the approximate dates, and the general itinerary (the Bodrum peninsula, for example, or the coast from Fethiye to Demre). If you have access to a fax machine, include that number in your letter. The bureau will then send you information provided by a number of charter agencies with specific details on their boats and prices. Make your selection, then fax or write directly to the agency, stating the exact dates you would like to charter a boat (be sure to mention that your information came from the tourism information bureau). Once you have reached an agreement, the agency will give you the account number of a bank (in the United States or Europe) in which you must make an advance deposit of 20 to 25 percent of the total cost in order to hold your reservation. A simpler, and cheaper, method is to proceed directly to the coast, walk along the quay at any of the harbor towns, and pick the best of what's available.

ACCOMMODATIONS REFERENCE

Rates given below are, unless otherwise noted, for double rooms, double occupany, and are projections for 1993. Where a range in rates appears, this reflects the difference in price between the low season (November through March) and the high season (April through October). Some hotels list prices in deutsche marks only; these have been converted to approximate U.S. dollars in the list below. All prices are subject to change and should be checked before booking. Some hotels and pensions include breakfast; others offer half or full board at significantly higher cost. When telephoning between cities in Turkey, dial 9 before entering the city code.

▶ **Antik Hotel.** 48840 **Dalyan**, Muğla. Tel: (6116) 1136 or 1137; Fax: (6116) 1138. $41–$59.

▶ **Baba.** Gümbet, 48400 **Bodrum**, Muğla. Tel: (6141) 2307 or 6697; Fax: (6141) 3231. $30.

▶ **Belceğiz Holiday Village.** Ölüdeniz, 48340 Fethiye, Muğla. Tel: (6156) 4030 or 3993. No rates available.

▶ **Club & Hotel Letoonia.** P.O. Box 63, 48300 **Fethiye**, Muğla. Tel: (615) 149-66; Fax: (615) 144-22. $70–$80.

▶ **Club Kadıkale.** Peksimet Köyü, Kadıkalesi, **Turgut Reis**, 48960 Bodrum, Muğla. Tel: (6142) 1271, 1821, or 1891. $90.

▶ **Club M.** Gümbet, 48400 **Bodrum**, Muğla. Tel: (6141) 4690, 6100, or 6101; Fax: (6141) 2581. No rates available.

▶ **Club Mediterranée Kemer Holiday Village.** 07980 **Kemer**, Antalya. Tel: (3214) 1009; Fax: (3214) 1018. No rates available.

▶ **Club Monakus.** Yalıkavak, 48960 **Bodrum**, Muğla. Tel: (6144) 1392; Fax: (6144) 1411. $35 (open May–Oct. only).

▶ **Club Salima.** Beldibi, **Kemer** 07981, Antalya. Tel: (3184) 8361; Fax (3184) 8083. Prices not available.

▶ **Dedeoğlu Hotel.** İskele Meydanı, 48301 **Fethiye**, Muğla. Tel: (615) 140-10; Fax: (615) 163-39. $52.

▶ **Ekici Hotel.** Arısan Sokak 1, 07581 **Kaş**, Antalya. Tel: (3226) 1824 or 1825; Fax: (3226) 1823. $72 (includes half-board).

▶ **Gazan Motel.** Tatil Köyü Kavşağı, 48702 **Marmaris**, Muğla. Tel: (612) 131-89 or 117-87. $75 (open Apr. 25–Oct. 15 only).

▶ **Grand Phaselis Princess Hotel**. Tekirova, 07983 **Kemer**, Antalya. Tel: (3214) 3200; Fax: (3214) 2079. $150.

▶ **Hotel Begonya**. Kısayalı/Hacı Mustafa Sokak 101, 48700 **Marmaris**, Muğla. Tel: (612) 140-95; Fax: (612) 115-18. $39.

▶ **Hotel Club Phellos**. Doğru Yol Sokak, 07581 **Kaş**, Antalya. Tel: (3226) 1953 or 1326; Fax: (3226) 1890. $77.

▶ **Hotel Kemal**. Kordonboyu–Gezi Yolu 1, 48301 **Fethiye**, Muğla. Tel: (615) 150-09 or 150-10; Fax: (615) 150-09. $30 (includes breakfast).

▶ **Hotel Lidya**. Siteler, 48700 **Marmaris**, Muğla. Tel: (612) 129-40; Fax: (612) 114-78. $38–$50.

▶ **Hotel Likya**. Hükümet Caddesi, 96571 **Kaş**, Antalya. Tel: (3226) 1270; Fax: (3226) 1370. $38 (includes breakfast)–$50 (includes half-board).

▶ **Hotel Manastır**. Kumbahçe Mahallesi, Barış Sitesi, Manastır Mevkii, 48400 **Bodrum**, Muğla. Tel: (6141) 2854, 2858, 2775, or 2776; Fax: (6141) 2772. $55–$90 (no view); $99–$170 (sea view); all prices include breakfast.

▶ **Hotel Patara Prince**. Club Patara, **Kalkan**, Antalya. Tel: (3215) 2338; Fax: (3215) 2337. $95–$125 (includes half-board).

▶ **Hotel Pirat** and **Pirat 2**. Kalkan Marınası, 07960 **Kalkan**, Antalya. Tel: (3215) 1178–1182; Fax: (3215) 1183. $33–$44 (includes breakfast).

▶ **Hotel Sami**. Gümbet, 48400 **Bodrum**, Muğla. Tel: (6141) 1048, 1848, or 1662; Fax: (6141) 3838. $42.

▶ **Hotel Sunset Club**. Çukurbağ Yarımadası, 07580 **Kaş**, Antalya. Tel: (3226) 1444; Fax: (3226) 1980. $26–$41.

▶ **Iberotel Kiriş World**. P.O. Box 99, 07980 **Kemer**, Antalya. Tel: (3214) 3300–3307, 3334–3343; Fax: (3214) 3344. $100–$120 (no view)–$130–$270 (sea view); all prices include breakfast and dinner buffet.

▶ **Kaş Otel**. Hastane Caddesi 15, **Kaş**, Antalya. Tel: (3226) 1271; Fax: (3226) 2170. $10.

▶ **Letoon Motel**. Çalış Plajı, 48301 **Fethiye**, Muğla. Tel: (615) 310-55; Fax: (615) 318-08. $26.

▶ **Merih Hotel**. Ölüdeniz, 48340 Fethiye, Muğla. Tel: (6156) 6060; Fax: (6156) 1482 or 6456. $54.

▶ **Milta Torba Holiday Village**. **Torba**, 48400 Bodrum, Muğla. Tel: (6141) 2343; Fax: (6141) 3451. $46.

▶ **Mimosa Hotel**. Elmalı Caddesi, 07580 **Kaş**, Antalya. Tel: (3226) 1272, 1472, or 2192; Fax: (3226) 1368. $14–$38 (includes breakfast).

▶ **Motel Kaktüs Çiçeği** (Cactus Flower). **Türkbükü**, 48483 Bodrum, Muğla. Tel: (6147) 5253 or 5254. $50–$60.

▶ **Otem Hotel**. Yat Limanı, 07980 **Kemer**, Antalya. Tel: (3214) 3181; Fax: (3214) 3190. $84.

▶ **Pasha's Inn Pansiyon**. 10'üncü Sokak, 07960 **Kalkan**, Antalya. Tel: (3215) 1077. $28 (open Apr.–Nov. only).

▶ **Ramada Renaissance Resort Hotel**. P.O. Box 654, Beldibi, 07983 **Kemer**, Antalya. Tel: (3214) 3255–3257; Fax: (3214) 3256. $207.

▶ **Turban Marmaris Tatil Köyü** (Holiday Village). Boynuz Bükü Mahallesi, 48700 **Marmaris**, Muğla. Tel: (612) 118-43; Fax: (612) 135-76. $48–$58.

THE CENTRAL MEDITER- RANEAN COAST

PAMPHYLIA AND CILICIA

By Scott Redford and Dorothy Slane

Scott Redford is director of Georgetown University's McGhee Center for Eastern Mediterranean Studies in Alanya, Turkey. Dorothy Slane has lived in Adana, Turkey, for six years, first as a Fulbright scholar and then as a lecturer for the University of Maryland extension at İncirlik air base. Her doctorate is in Hittite archaeology of the Adana region.

Turkey's central Mediterranean coast can be divided into two geographical regions. To the west, between the cities of Antalya and Alanya, the coastline is flat, the beaches are sandy, and tourism reigns. East of Alanya the mountains come down to the sea, and a rougher, more unspoiled beauty prevails. These two regions correspond respectively to the ancient Roman provinces of Pamphylia and Cilicia Trachea ("Rough" Cilicia). The plain of Pamphylia, as rich in produce as it was poor in harbors, gave rise to some of the wealthiest cities of the Roman world. Today's traveller can enjoy the sands that bedeviled Pamphylia's ports and visit

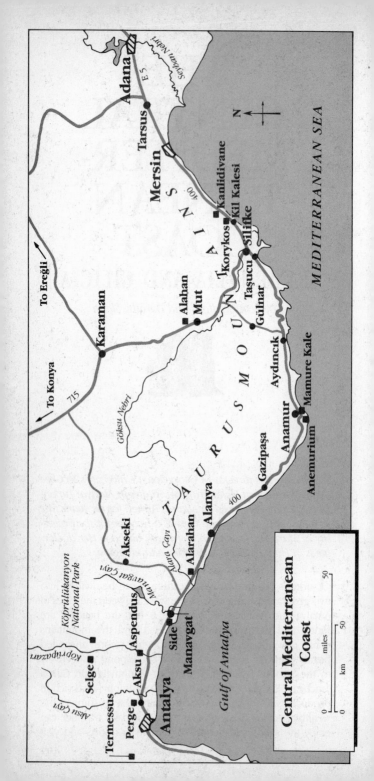

Central Mediterranean Coast

MEDITERRANEAN SEA

Gulf of Antalya

TAURUS MOUNTAINS

Adana
Tarsus
Mersin
Seyhan Nehri
E 5
Kanlıdivane
Kız Kalesi
Korykos
Silifke
Taşucu
Gülnar
Aydıncık
Mamure Kale
Anamur
Anemurium
Gazipaşa
Alanya
Alarahan
Akseki
Side
Manavgat
Aspendus
Aksu
Antalya
Perge
Termessus
Selge
Köprüpazarı
Köprülükanyon National Park
Karaman
Alahan
Mut
Göksu Nehri
To Ereğli
To Konya
715
400
400
N
Manavgat Çayı
Alara Çayı
Aksu Çayı

0   50 miles
0   50 km

some of the best-preserved Roman cities in the Mediterranean. East of Alanya you can enjoy the spectacular mountain- and seascapes of Rough Cilicia and visit castles and ruined cities inhabiting its more remote valleys. In both cases the combination of a favorable climate, warm sea, and abundant natural and archaeological points of interest makes this stretch of Turkey's coastline a justifiably popular destination. This chapter starts in the west with Antalya and proceeds east along the coastal road, only occasionally straying from the coast to suggest detours up into the mountains.

MAJOR INTEREST

Antalya
Roman, Byzantine, Seljuk, and Ottoman old town
Archaeological displays at Antalya Museum
Eating and drinking harborside

Pamphylia's lush plains and sandy beaches
Rough, unspoiled beauty of Taurus mountains
Ruins of ancient mountain towns Termessus and
  Selge
Well-preserved Roman cities of Perge and Aspendus
Beaches and classical ruins of Side

Alanya
Medieval castle
Spectacular setting at meeting of mountains and sea

Roman city of Anemurium and the Mamure castle at
  Anamur
Breathtaking scenery on the roads to Oymapınar
  dam, Alara castle, and between Gazipaşa and
  Anamur

PAMPHYLIA

In 1882 the Austrian count Karl Lanckoronski sailed into Antalya harbor and spent the better part of the next four years in the plain of Pamphylia stretching east of Antalya, measuring and drawing its ruined Roman cities. So taken was he by its architecture, lush vegetation, abundance of water, and snowcapped mountains that he compared Pamphylia favorably to the lake country of northern Italy. In those days Antalya was a small tumbledown port, and the ancient cities of Side, Perge, and Aspendus were overgrown with vines and gorse. Much of the Pamphylian plain was uncultivated, grazed in winter by the flocks of Turkmen nomads descending from the Taurus mountains, and largely abandoned in the heavy summer heat.

Today the climate, scenery, and ancient cities of Pamphylia draw travellers from far and wide, but much has changed since the pioneering expedition of Count Lanckoronski. Antalya is the center of Mediterranean Turkey's tourist industry, and the region's coast, once clear, has been lined with hotels and condominium complexes in the last decade. Indeed, Pamphylia has not seen this much building activity since the early third century A.D. Yet this is still one of the most attractive areas of Anatolia, and its Roman cities are among the best preserved in the world. But you must step carefully to avoid the blandness of package-tour resorts with their generic presentation of sand and sun. The inexpensive, relaxing Mediterranean holiday available in Antalya resorts duplicates the experience available to the traveller in Greece, Spain, or Sicily. But if you set out to avoid tourist traps, it is quite possible to have a comfortable yet singular vacation along this stretch of Turkey's shore.

Four major rivers traverse the Pamphylian plain, each associated with a city in antiquity. The Düden Çayı supplied Antalya (ancient Attaleia) with water; today it furnishes Antalya's residents with picnic areas around two of its three sets of waterfalls. The Aksu river supplied Perge with water and a port; the citizens of Roman Perge acknowledged the importance of the river (called Kestros in antiquity) by placing a marble personification of the river at the head of their main street. Farther east, the Köprüpazarı Çayı served a similar function for Aspendus. Side, the region's only other coastal city apart from Antalya, is hard by the Manavgat Çayı, whose headwaters filled the city's aqueduct and whose outflow brought silt and sand that clogged Side's harbor.

With the exception of Antalya, a later Hellenistic foundation, the histories of the cities of Pamphylia are very similar. Pamphylia means "mixed tribes" in Greek, and both Herodotus and Strabo after him repeated the assertion that this region was settled by the various tribes that the end of the Trojan War loosed on Anatolia. No other evidence exists for colonization this early, however. Several Pamphylian cities are mentioned in accounts of Persian-Greek battles of the fifth century B.C., but the region does not rise to historical prominence until Alexander the Great arrived here in 333 B.C.

Tantalizing traces of the religion and culture of the native Anatolian peoples encountered by the Greeks can be found in the coins and other artifacts recovered from the ancient Pamphylian cities. In Perge, for example, the cult of Artemis was a major institution, but early coins show the cult statue as simply a block of stone, presumably a meteorite, and refer to it as the Queen of Perge. It was only later identified with the Greek moon goddess Artemis. (The temple of Artemis at Perge was famous throughout the Roman world, but intensive searches in recent years have failed to turn it up.) Similarly, the coins of Aspendus and fragmentary inscriptions in a native Anatolian language found at Side point to a strong indigenous culture only gradually supplanted by that of Greek colonists.

ANTALYA

The major city of modern Pamphylia, Antalya is best approached from the north by land or by air. After the largely denuded Central Anatolian plateau, if you use the land route, you pass through the rugged Taurus mountains. But rather than plunging steeply into the sea as they do elsewhere along Turkey's southern shore, here the mountains give way to a broad plain that sweeps in a crescent around the gulf of Antalya. To the west the plain comes to an abrupt end at the Lycian mountains—Beydağları in Turkish—a sharp, steep range whose presence contributes much to the beauty of Antalya. To the east the plain draws to a less dramatic close, broken by ridges east of Aspendus. Finally, the mountains come down to the sea 135 km (84 miles) east of Antalya at Alanya, which classical authors considered at various times the last city in Pamphylia or the first in the adjacent province of Cilicia.

The city of Antalya sits at the head of the gulf and spreads along the cliffs surrounding a tiny, rock-cleft harbor. Here, encased in the concrete shell of the modern city, are narrow streets, citrus gardens, and vine-clad stone, timber, and plaster houses whose tile roofs, high ceilings, and greenery provide a welcome change of scale, scent, and sound. Tourism has made Antalya, and tourism has saved the old town from the wrecker's ball, converting many of the old dwellings of the harbor area into single-house pensions (the word is *pansiyon* in Turkish) or larger complexes of houses strung together to form hotels. And yet old Antalya is far from a museum; Turkish families still live in many old houses, especially in the extensive quarter east of the harbor.

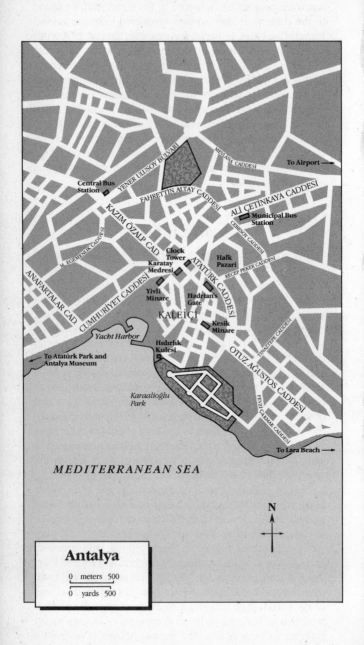

Central Bus
Station

YENER ULUSOY BULVARI

FAHRETTIN ALTAY CADDESI

MEVLANA CADDESI

To Airport →

ALİ ÇETİNKAYA CADDESI

Municipal Bus
Station

KAZIM ÖZALP CAD.

CEBESOY CADDESI

M. EGEMENLIK CADDESI

Halk
Pazarı

Clock
Tower

RECEP PEKER CADDESI

Karatay
Medresi

ATATÜRK CADDESI

CUMHURİYET CADDESI

Yivli
Minare

Hadrian's
Gate

ANAFARTALAR CAD.

KALEİÇİ

Kesik
Minare

TONZTEPE CADDESI

Yacht Harbor

Hıdırlık
Kulesi

To Atatürk Park and
Antalya Museum

OTUZ AĞUSTOS CADDESI

Karaalioğlu
Park

FEVZI ÇAKMAK CADDESI

To Lara Beach →

MEDITERRANEAN SEA

N

Antalya

0 meters 500

0 yards 500

The **Kaleiçi** (literally, "inside the castle"), the old intra-mural settlement, was once protected by stout limestone walls that guarded it from attack from both land and sea and divided it into several quarters. Spurs of these walls can be found in unexpected corners of the old town, bearing the marks of the different masters of the region. Though settle-ment here dates back to Paleolithic times, the city was officially founded by Attalus II, king of Hellenistic Perga-mum, in the mid-second century B.C. The name he gave it, Attaleia, changed little with the succeeding centuries and civilizations: Roman, Byzantine, and Seljuk, and Ottoman Turkish.

The Hellenistic walls of Antalya were expanded to the east and south by the Romans; along one such stretch, to the side of palm-lined Atatürk Caddesi, can be found the most impres-sive remnant of Roman Antalya: **Hadrian's Gate** (Hadrianus Kapısı), a tripartite marble structure built by the citizens of Antalya to commemorate the visit of the emperor Hadrian in A.D. 130. Originally two stories high, the gate consists at present of three arched and coffered entranceways sepa-rated by piers. Above the arches runs an entablature that projects in front of the piers. Supported by columns with composite capitals, it originally formed the basis for a sec-ond story of columns. The ruts in the cobbled road below bear witness to this gate's commercial as well as symbolic importance to the Roman city.

Another Roman edifice, **Hıdırlık Kulesi**, is a solid square building with a round second story located at the junction of the Roman city wall with the sea cliff in the southwest. It was incorporated into Antalya's defenses after it was constructed (about A.D. 100) and is thought to have been the tomb of a Roman senator, presumably a local son who did well for himself.

The Byzantine emperor Constantine VII Porphyrogenitus rebuilt the walls of Antalya in the tenth century, but traces of Byzantine presence in Antalya, aside from inscriptions found in the museum, are confined to one mosque, **Cuma'-nın Camii**, also known locally as **Kesik Minare** (Cut-off Minaret) from its truncated minaret. Located to the east of the harbor in the Kaleiçi quarter, the building was origi-nally a Roman temple, converted into a Byzantine church in the late sixth century. It now stands roofless (it was the victim of fire in 1919) and encircled by a fence, locked except upon application to the Antalya Museum. Despite this barrier it is well worth a visit for what you can see merely by walking around the building and looking in. The carving of the marble pier and column capitals is fine, reminiscent of the best of architectural ornament of the age of Justinian. Note, too, the decorated slabs incorporated into the piers that separate the apse windows. The fine acanthus scroll and floral carving also date from the late sixth century.

Antalya, a major port of embarkation for the armies of the Second Crusade, finally fell to the Seljuk Turks in 1214. The Seljuks expended considerable effort in rebuilding Antalya since it served as the principal southern terminus for the lucrative Anatolian caravan trade that filled Seljuk coffers in the first half of the 13th century. The walls of the town were reconstructed: Many of them still bear Seljuk inscriptions, and three Seljuk monuments also survive.

One of them, the **Yivli Minare**, or Fluted Minaret, located at the main entrance to the Kaleiçi a little below Cumhuriyet Caddesi, is a fine example of early 13th-century brick- and tilework. The minaret, which stands almost 150 feet tall, was built by the Seljuk sultan Alaettin Keykubat I. Unfortunately the mosque and *medrese* (school of Islamic law) complex marked by the minaret are not in their original state; the one oft-rebuilt, the other fallen into disrepair. An equally derelict but charmingly situated Seljuk building, the **Karatay Medresesi**, built in the middle of the 13th century by the Karatay viziers to the Seljuk sultan, is on a side street down the hill from the major entrance to the Kaleiçi (next to the clock tower). Go during the day, when the building, now the Halk Eğitim Merkezi, a school for instruction in playing the *ud* (a lute-like instrument), is easier to find by ear than by eye. The beautifully carved framed doorway is pleasing to behold, and if the school is between classes you can walk into the courtyard.

Wandering the alleys of Antalya's old town you are bound to feel hungry and thirsty; happily, there are many places to stop for a snack or meal. The harborside, restricted to pleasure boats in the summertime, is a natural place to sit and enjoy the view and the passersby, although the throng can be overwhelming late at night and on weekends. Above the fray, perched at the rim of the harbor, is a long, narrow **tea garden** with excellent views of the mountains and harbor and prices a fraction of those you'll pay at establishments below. Just below this lies the cunningly situated honeycomb of vaulted chambers, balconies, and terraces that constitute the **Hisar Restaurant**, built right into the ancient fortification wall on Tophane Yokuşu. In addition to its superior situation and view, the Hisar has a fine wine list and a kitchen that serves excellent grilled meat and fish and fine salads laced with dill. In the evening, to experience pricey new Antalya, try a drink at **Yesterday's**, *le dernier cri,* located in a renovated salt warehouse in the Kaleiçi. There is almost always a tape of 1940s jazz playing here.

Just outside the Kaleiçi quarter is the old market area of Antalya, where small shops selling everything from hardware to kitchen utensils line narrow streets protected from the summer sun. The **Gaziantep Restaurant**, serving traditional Turkish fare, is to be found here, as is another local favorite, the **Parlak**, known for its roast chicken. These two restaurants are a step up from the main source of inexpensive fare in town, the street near the clock tower known either as Arasta Sokak or Kebabçılar Sokak (Street of the Kebap Sellers).

Stretching along the sea to either side of the old town are two well-maintained parks. The public garden to the southeast, **Karaalioğlu Parkı**, is also active by night, with amusement-park rides only for the young and foolhardy, teahouses, and palm-lined plazas.

To the west is **Atatürk Parkı**, with the **Antalya Museum** at its far end. The park is a pleasant place to stroll in good weather. It is hard to overpraise the museum. Essential as a prelude to any archaeological visit in Pamphylia, it also has a well-labeled and well-displayed survey of the region's prehistory, a children's museum, an extensive ethnographic section, and a well-kept sculpture garden that should not be missed. The highlights of the museum are its Roman-period sarcophagi and statuary, most from the excavations at the nearby city of Perge. There are fine Roman copies of Classical and Hellenistic statues of gods, goddesses, heroes, and a bravura dancer, replete with swirling black marble drapery. Among the best-known sarcophagi is that depicting the labors of Hercules, also found at Perge. Its completeness and elegance of proportion exceed the label "provincial art." Another major attraction is the display of artifacts from several Phrygian tumuli recently excavated near Elmalı. In addition to maps and plans detailing the discovery, the display consists of grave goods, including fine silver bowls and a lovely ivory statuette. An excellent array of guidebooks, as well as the museum's own handsome catalogue, are sold in the gift shop by the entrance.

Down the hill from the museum, right on the beach, is an excellent Turkish restaurant, the **Yedi Mehmet** (Mehmet Number Seven), renowned for more than 30 years for its impeccable service and fine menu.

Most visitors to Antalya stay either in small pensions or in the big cliffside hotels, like the **Hotel Antalya Dedeman** or the **Talya Hotel**. Although the former is newer, the Talya still retains the edge in location, service, and food. Both are pricey, but off-season weekend bargains can be arranged. In the old town, the **Marina Hotels and Restaurants**, consisting of three restored old mansions, provides the same level of luxury with a great deal more atmosphere.

Small pensions with good service and gardens are plentiful; in the Kaleiçi the **Atelya Pansiyon**, the **Saray Oteli**, and the **Saraçoğlu Pansiyon** are favorites. The **Tunay Pansiyon** here is bare-bones, but clean, and has a rooftop terrace with a view of the harbor. For those interested in combining a stay in Antalya with a beach holiday, the proximity of **Lara beach** some 10 km (6 miles) east of town offers the best of both worlds. At Lara the **Club Hotel Sera** and the **Hotel OFO Antalya** offer luxury accommodations, while the 75-room **Lara Hotel**, on a cliff above the water and with a lovely pool, is more reasonable. The Sera, which possesses a magnificent garden, a greenhouse, and a pergola-covered bar with live music, is particularly good. Cheaper hotels and pensions abound here as well; the **Şimşek Motel** and the **Bahama Motel** are recommended.

The modern part of Antalya holds little interest for most travellers. However, as a place to make bookings or change airline reservations it is very convenient. And the tourist boom has fueled prosperity, so that Antalya has a wide range of shops of every variety. Although Antalya province was recently rated the fourth most expensive in Turkey, almost all items are cheaper in town than in smaller, more touristy venues along the coast.

To take a look at the Antalya inhabited by Turks, follow the street that turns right off of Atatürk Caddesi opposite Hadrian's Gate. Walk two blocks and you come to the entrance to the **Halk Pazarı** (People's Market), the low-priced shopping center of Antalya. Turn left upon entering and you'll come across ranks of stalls piled with dry goods and local vegetables and fruit. At either end of this market, men with pushcarts sell everything from cassettes to oranges.

Antalya harbor is crowded with pleasure craft in season; docked at the quayside, the most prominent of these are large wooden boats advertising half-day and day-long excursions. The more expensive of these run about $25–$30. Half-day trips to the waterfall of the **Düden Şelâlesi** and to Lara beach are offered for about $8–$10, and day trips across the gulf to the Roman city of **Phaselis** (see the chapter on the Turquoise Coast, above) are also possible.

Termessus

The ancient city of Termessus clings to the sides of a steep mountain valley northwest of Antalya. Although it is only 34 km (21 miles) away, it is far removed from city sights and sounds, in the middle of a pine, laurel, and scrub-oak national park. Follow the main road north out of Antalya about 8 km (5 miles), then make a left on the Korkuteli road, following the signs to the site, about 14 km (8½ miles) farther on. If you arrive at Termessus early enough in the morning, you may catch glimpses of boar, wild goats, partridge, and grouse. Flushing ruins is another sport: The site has never been excavated and has only been partly cleared of its thick underbrush. Part of the considerable pleasure of these ruins rests with the approach to the site, which lies at the end of a seemingly aimless footpath, above a declivity, framed by a view of the distant sea. In summer you'll escape the lowland heat for a few hours, and in fall and spring you'll find crocuses and snowdrops underfoot.

Because of Termessus's location in the mountains above Pamphylia, its history, architecture, and plan are all very different from those of the cities of the plain. In antiquity the mountainous area around Pamphylia was known as Pisidia. The Pisidian mountain peoples were Hellenized later than the Anatolian peoples of Pamphylia, and even though they adopted the Greek language for inscriptions and all the institutions of the Greek city-state, the Solymnians (Termessus lies on the slopes of Mount Solymnus, today's Güllük Dağı) maintained a distinct identity.

Hardiness, a trait common to mountain dwellers, and the boldness engendered by this city's inaccessibility gave Termessus its fame. Termessians derived a good deal of their wealth from duties imposed on goods passing through the valley at the base of their mountain. In fact, you can see remains of the wall erected to enforce this transit tax in the valley when you begin the ascent to Termessus from the entrance to the park. The Termessians attempted to block the passage of Alexander the Great and his armies in 333 B.C.; the Macedonians cleared the pass, but then Alexander decided not to attack, changed direction, and quit the region.

You can get to the site only by taxi or private car. A tour starts at the bottom of the city and entails a fair amount of scrambling. A detailed site guide (available at Antalya Museum and at tourist shops and hotels in town) is useful for its plan—individual monuments are not well marked at the site itself. Or you can hire the site guard, Cemal Bey. He is very pleasant, knows the site intimately, and can explain it in simple English or German. Most impressive is the **agora** area, two-thirds of the way up the slope, with huge cisterns and an adjoining **odeon** and well-preserved **theater**. The theater (with an elevation of more than 3,000 feet and a fine view of Mount Solymnus and, on a clear day, Antalya) is a good example of the adaptation of Greek architectural forms to local conditions. Some of the theater's seats were assigned to families of the town, whose names were scratched in the stone.

Retracing your steps from the agora, rejoin the main path that leads from the parking lot up the middle of the site and walk to the highest point of the city, the **necropolis**. Here, funerary temples and hundreds of massive sarcophagi are littered about the rocky terrain. Their sides smashed and lids pried open by centuries of treasure seekers, these sarcophagi bear eloquent testimony to the wealth of this remote, rocky, and waterless city in its heyday—and not only to its wealth, but to the perseverance of its inhabitants in hewing the rock, making it conform to their will even unto death. Many of the sarcophagi are inscribed with curses against violators of their sanctity and prescribe the exact monetary penalties for such crimes.

Examples of an earlier, native Anatolian form of burial can be observed on the way down the mountain from the necropolis. Take the path that veers off to the left atop the upper fortification wall and then hugs the base of the cliff all the way down to the parking lot at the entrance to the site. As you negotiate the rocks and tree roots, glance up and note three sets of **rock-cut tombs** in the cliff face. These range in form from *arcosolia* (arched burial chambers) to translations of wooden house façades into stone. Such house tombs are also found to the west, in Lycia.

Most of what you see in Termessus dates to the Roman, not the Hellenistic, period. Still, in the finely cut masonry, the elaborate system of cisterns and water canals, the small size (the theater seated only 4,200), and the isolation of Termessus, you gain a sense of earlier ages, when Greek and native Anatolian cultures met on a smaller, but no less significant, scale.

Perge

The ancient city of Perge provides the best example of a complete Roman city in Pamphylia. Its wide range of well-preserved monuments gives the best sense, of all the cities in the region, of the scale, range of activities, and civic institutions of a city of the second and third centuries A.D. In a way that is unique among the cities of Pamphylia, the history of Perge can be traced through its topography—as it developed from a Greek hilltop settlement to a thriving Hellenistic town to a Roman city.

The site of Perge is 19 km (12 miles) east of Antalya. To reach it by car, join the main highway by following signs for the *havalimanı* (airport) and continue east until you see the yellow marker for Perge in the village of Aksu. If you want to reach the site by public transport, go to either the Oto Gar (Central Bus Station) or the Doğu Garajı (Municipal Bus Station) in Antalya; as you enter either area, ask anyone how you can get to Aksu (you'll have better luck if you stick to the name of the village rather than trying that of the site). More than likely, inquiry on your part will not be necessary; in almost every bus station in Turkey there will be men approaching you to find out where you want to go. (Do be careful; you may be misled.) Travelling out of the Doğu Garajı may be quicker (as the minibuses will leave more frequently) and cheaper (maybe as much as 35 cents); travelling out of the Oto Gar will be more comfortable (full-size buses, which leave less frequently) and more expensive (maybe as much as 60 cents). Whichever you choose, tell your driver that you want to get off at Perge; he'll know the site name as this is his territory. At Aksu, walk the fifteen minutes to the site, following posted signs.

In order to understand the history of Perge, it is best to tour the ruins in reverse. Walk past the theater, stadium, and modern site gate. Before you get to the main city gate, walk to the right along a dirt road that takes you beyond the city wall, skirting the ruins. In about ten minutes you will be at the base of the **acropolis** of Perge. Scramble up its rocky slope and you will be rewarded with a panorama of green irrigated fields. Across the plain to the east is the distinctive flat-topped acropolis of Sillyon, and beyond it the outline of Aspendus (both discussed below). These hills are what the first Greek settlers chose as their initial abodes: defensible, close to water and arable land, and accessible from the sea. In the prosperity of the Hellenistic period all these settlements expanded down to the plain.

A view of the topography and layout of Perge from atop the acropolis provides you with a good sense of how Perge grew. (Though there are some cisterns and Byzantine ruins, nothing of the earliest settlement remains on the acropolis.) Standing at the edge of Perge's acropolis, you can see very clearly the checkerboard of streets of the third-century B.C. Hellenistic city, itself surrounded by a wall. Intersecting near

the base of the acropolis are the two main streets of Perge.
The major north–south street is crooked—when the city
was laid out at the base of the hill the main street no doubt
followed the course of an earlier path to the acropolis. As
you descend, the Hellenistic walls are the only pre-Roman
monument you'll see. In Perge, as in all other Pamphylian
cities, the prosperity of the first and second centuries A.D.
erased buildings of earlier epochs. At present, in fact, because of an ongoing program of excavation and restoration
by Istanbul University, Perge imparts a sense of what it was
like to live in a Roman provincial city. The sense of Perge's
urban fabric comes not only from its magnificent main
street, but also from the full range of civic architecture
preserved along with it, from *nymphaea* (fountain houses)
and baths to marketplaces and the aforementioned theater
and stadium.

At the base of the acropolis is the **nymphaeum**, which
served as the visual anchor for the end of the main street
(Romans loved to enclose a vista). The main north–south
street was lined on both sides with shops (some of which
have only recently been excavated) fronted by a wide,
roofed colonnade. All of these features are common to other
Roman-era cities, but at Perge a broad, stepped canal was
added to the middle of the street. Neither for drinking nor
draining, this liquid median was meant only to cool the heat
of the summer months and, through the play of light on
moving water, provide delight to the senses. Water was
brought by aqueduct to the west gate of the city (outside
which were found most of the spectacular sarcophagi in the
Antalya Museum) and on to the northern nymphaeum. From
there the water flowed the length of the street.

At the entrance to Perge lies a cluster of buildings excavated and restored in recent years: an agora, baths, and a
curved court that served as the ceremonial entrance to the
city in the Roman period. The smallish, symmetrical **agora** is
unremarkable save for a gaming board carved into a stone
outside a shop in the northeast corner of the square. For
those accustomed to the sight of bored Turkish shopkeepers
slapping backgammon counters outside modern rug and
leather shops, this board provides a sharp reminder of the
continuity of commerce. As the Turkish saying translates:
"Same bathhouse, same bowl"—the more things change,
the more they stay the same.

The **ceremonial court** is interesting for its elegant shape
and proportions, for the manner in which it conducts you
naturally onto the main street, and for its iconographic
program. Along the curving walls of the court, statues of the

"founders" of Perge were displayed, including Trojan War heroes as well as prominent citizens of the time. The frequency with which civic benefactors and building patrons such as M. Plancius Verus and his son are displayed (as is the case here) is characteristic of all Pamphylian cities in the Roman period.

The south **bath** at Perge is notable for its size and good state of preservation. It was preceded by a palaestra (exercise courtyard), along the west side of which ran a stoa (colonnaded portico) that served as a sort of art gallery full of statues that are now in the Antalya Museum. The original sumptuous decoration of the baths can be divined from the pieces of marble revetment and paving affixed to the walls and floors. This is the largest bath in Pamphylia and brings to mind the architectural contributions the Romans made to the Hellenistic East, from which they had borrowed so many forms.

First to be seen but last to be visited on this trajectory are the stadium and theater, which lay outside the city walls. The **stadium** is well preserved, including its substructure, composed of tilted barrel vaults used to hold up the stands. Shops located in the vaulted spaces around the stadium sold goods to spectators who came here for, among other things, the games held to honor the Pergean Artemis. The stadium seated the same number as the theater, approximately 14,000.

One of the great revelations of recent years has been the careful clearing of the stage building of the **theater** at Perge. Walking the length of the stadium, you encounter finely carved and drilled marble blocks and fragments of entablatures, coffers, door frames, and friezes from the theater's stage building. Animals and birds climb through the scrolls of acanthus leaves; masks and Medusa heads stare sightlessly ahead. Mentally recladding the stage building with these marbles, you can well imagine the richness of the original structure. At the base of the building a series of reliefs depicting scenes from the life of Dionysus adds to the effect. A peculiarity of the theater at Perge is its excellent circulation. Entrance and exit were effected not only through the *parodoi,* the vaulted passages to either side of the stage building, but also through passages at the median level, the *diazoma,* of the *cavea* (the concave auditorium of a theater). These passages, affording quick exit, were called by the Romans *vomitoria* for the expulsive speed they afforded.

The wealth of Pamphylian cities in the first and second centuries can be inferred from one simple observation: Pamphylia has no marble quarries. All of the marble you see at Perge and elsewhere was imported, mostly by sea from the Marmara region near Istanbul. Roman Pamphylia by and large exported raw materials, not manufactured goods. This area was famous for its olive oil and goat and sheep wool. The Pamphylian plain possessed large estates that the Romans had inherited from the Hellenistic states. The geometric field patterns that still mark old irrigation networks and the olive groves that surround ancient sites testify to the presence of these estates.

After visiting Perge, rejoin the main road at Aksu. The road passes through flat fields where wheat and cotton are grown; the greenhouses scattered about produce tomatoes and cucumbers. To the left you will see a turnoff to the ancient city of **Sillyon,** located atop and below a sheer-sided mesa visible from the road. Sillyon's is an impressive location, but it has neither the spectacular individual monuments of Aspendus nor the sense of urban order and artistic wealth derived from a visit to the excavated sites of Perge and Side. Those with a healthy appetite for Roman ruins should visit Sillyon, but beware of farm dogs with healthy appetites of their own.

As if dividing your attention into academic and recreational halves, the signs along the road from Aksu to Manavgat, some 75 km (47 miles) to the east, point left and right to different purposes. Yellow signs to the left note historical sites inland (Perge, Sillyon, Selge, Aspendus) while the signs to the right in increasingly assertive voices summon you to the shore. There, a plethora of communities of concrete condominiums and hulking hotels offer all the creature comforts under the sun. This chorus of signs rises to a clamor around Side, a favorite Teutonophone destination (over 80 percent of the tourists who visit this region are German, Austrian, or Swiss).

Aspendus

After passing through the town of Serik, you come to the turnoff for Aspendus, another of the major cities of Roman Pamphylia, 4 km (2½ miles) beyond. Shortly after you turn off the highway to the left, you will see Aspendos Jewelry and Bazaar 54 above you on the left. **Aspendos Jewelry** is well worth a visit. As you enter, an attendant will hand you a clip-on pass and you are then free to wander. On the first floor of this large building, dozens of jewelers work behind secure glass barricades. You can watch work being done with gold and various colored gemstones as well as cloisonné. After watching the production of these craftspeople, go upstairs to the sales floor. Here much gold and silver jewelry as well as other more mundane objects (such as fountain pens) are for sale. All prices are in German marks, but you can pay in dollars or Turkish liras if you choose to buy something. Even if you don't (and the prices are high), you are still welcome.

Bazaar 54 is one of the largest rug manufacturers and merchants in Turkey. The outlet at Aspendus can give you a glimpse of the wares that they have available. Again, even if you don't choose to pay the tourist prices here, the store is well worth a visit and the visitor is welcomed warmly.

As you continue on your way to Aspendus, you will pass on the right the remains of the huge Roman bridge between whose piers the Seljuks strung a series of pointed arches, resulting in the present arrangement of humps and turns. Shortly after this site, you pass through the village of Belkis, the closest habitation to Aspendus. Just a few hundred yards east of the village runs the river, on whose bank you'll find a most pleasantly situated restaurant, the **Belkis**. An old mill that's been renovated, the Belkis offers cooling views of the river with the ancient acropolis in the distance and a decent, if overpriced, menu. Try the *güveç,* a lamb and vegetable dish cooked in a clay pot, or *menemen,* a simple egg, tomato, and pepper dish.

Belkis means "Queen of Sheba" in Islamic societies; the original Turkish settlers in this area must have likened the ruins of Aspendus to that queen's splendid palace, mentioned in the Koran. However, by the time Count Lanckoronski arrived in the 1880s, the name Belkis had been transmuted into Bal Kız (Honey Girl), identified with the rather androgynous depiction of Dionysus in a relief on the pediment of the stage building of the Aspendus theater. This Honey Girl, as the story goes, was wooed and won by the Serpent King from the mountains, who built for her a palace, recognized today as the best preserved Roman theater in the world.

Like Perge, Aspendus was founded on a hilltop near a river and later spread down to the plain. The city has yet to be excavated systematically, and it is visited today principally for its theater. It is a mistake to depart Aspendus, however, without looking at the aqueduct, one of the best preserved in the ancient world and of unique design. The stadium, gymnasium, and baths, though impressive in outline, await clearing, but the aqueduct (discussed below) is worth visiting.

Roman Aspendus, which used the river as a port, was, with Side, a principal port of Pamphylia. In addition to exporting the agricultural produce of the region, Aspendus served as a way station for products transported across the Taurus mountains from the interior of Anatolia. Wheat, salt, and saltpeter from the area around present-day Konya and Burdur were among the principal exports. Commerce was in the hands of locals—in fact, there were so many merchants from Aspendus living in Roman Alexandria that a whole quarter was named after them.

As with the other cities of the plain, Aspendus fell prey to the mountain brigandage that started in the late third century A.D. and continued intermittently for the next two centuries. There was a brief period of prosperity under the Byzantines, but Aspendus succumbed with the rest of Pamphylia to the ravaging of the coast by Arab fleets that began in the seventh century A.D.

As you approach the site from the road, the first thing you'll notice is the famed **theater**. With buses disgorging deafening throngs of tourists from Easter through October, it is all too possible to experience the excellence of ancient acoustics. Still, the aesthetic power of a near-complete Roman theater is hard to deny, even in the din. The stage building stands to its full height, complete with the alternating rounded and triangle-topped *aediculae* (miniature temple-fronts) that give rhythm and variety to its appearance. In the mind's eye it is easy to replace the missing columns and imagine the complex play of light and shadow over the projecting *aediculae* and recessive niches, which once held statues. The doors at the base of the stage building, once concealed by a wooden stage, served to release wild animals into the orchestra when the theater was used for such displays. The *cavea,* too, is well preserved; indeed, the theater has been used in summer for everything from plays by the Comédie Française to concerts by Joan Baez, though in recent years most of the performances have been by Turkish entertainers. At the more popular events, the theater's original capacity of 20,000 is exceeded.

In the mid-13th century the theater was used as a residence by the Seljuk sultans on their way to their winter residence in Alanya. The sultan resided in the southern stair-tower of the *scena* (scene building), and the arcade at the top of the *cavea* was rebuilt at that time. The Seljuks covered the stage-building towers with plaster painted with red zigzags and filled the niches with turquoise and black tiles, some of which can be seen in the Antalya Museum. The theater has indeed had a long life since it was built in the second century A.D. by two brothers, who dedicated it, according to an inscription over the entrance, "to the gods of the country and to the imperial house."

A path leads up to the **acropolis** hill from the right side of the theater (if you are facing it from outside). Once on top, turn to the left and you'll come to the ancient city's **agora**. An open square surrounded on three sides by *nymphaeum,* basilica, and shops, the agora demonstrates that the acropolis remained at the heart of civic life in Aspendus even when most of the city had moved down to the plain.

If you turn to the right atop the acropolis you'll be looking across the valley spreading to the west of the site. At the base of the acropolis hill is the nearer of the two towers that are the most interesting features of the **aqueduct** at Aspendus. The far tower rises on a hunch of arches across the valley, and a flat-topped arcade stretches in between. This central section functioned both as a water conduit and as a highway across the valley. The towers at both ends lessened the friction on the stone piping. At the top of the two towers are open basins that allowed air bubbles to escape the water. Re-entering the closed pipes, the water, relieved of much of its drag, flowed more freely up to outlets on the acropolis.

The road that leads up to the theater skirts the perimeter of the acropolis hill past the outlines of the **stadium**. It continues across the valley and up over a pine-covered hill. Here, at the edge of a small village, is the far tower of the aqueduct. The beauty of the landscape and the chance to escape the tour-bus groups are the rewards of making this trip. In addition, you can climb this tower. While the view is pleasant, the climb is recommended more for a firsthand experience of the massiveness of the enterprise, and to give you an idea of the lengths to which the Romans went to ensure a pure and plentiful supply of water.

Selge

Retracing your route through Aspendus and Belkis, rejoin the main road and head east again. Soon (about 5 km/3 miles), after passing through rolling fields of wheat, sesame, and cotton, you come to another yellow sign pointing north, this time to the historical site of Selge. Don't be put off by the relatively long distance (55 km/34 miles) posted. If you have an extra day, a trip to Selge is highly recommended, not only for archaeology buffs but also for nature lovers. The road takes you through the pine forests of the **Köprülükanyon national park** and out of sight, you might think, of all civilization. And yet, at a point beyond the reach of most modern conveyances, on a saddle high in the Taurus, lie the extensive remains of this classical city.

The road toward Selge winds through fields and orchards

before starting its slow climb. Leaving behind villages and cultivation, it enters the pine forests of the park, playing tag with the rushing upper reaches of the Köprüpazarı Çayı. The asphalt road turns to gravel and becomes potholed. Although Selge is accessible by automobile, cautious driving is recommended. Köprülükanyon means "canyon with a bridge." Sure enough, after the road departs the river valley at a trout restaurant, it climbs to pass over a single-arch Roman bridge, thrown across a narrow section of the chasm; this bridge remains the only way to cross the canyon. Once you are on the other side (it's better to cross first), look down and see how far below the stream courses.

Selge, with the ramshackle village of **Zerk** built in and around it, is higher still, much higher. Termessus (discussed above), another rock-bound antique city and Selge's ancient rival, is remote, but nothing like this. At last the road levels out amid terraces and other signs of cultivation and comes up over a final rise and into a small sheltered valley. On the far side of the valley lie the best-preserved remains of Roman Selge. Follow the road around as it crosses atop one edge of the ancient stadium, and park just below the theater.

Strictly speaking, Pamphylia has been left far below. Like Termessus, Selge was located in Pisidia, the mountainous crescent that surrounds Antalya. The peoples of Pisidia made their living by trade with the wealthier flatlanders to the south, and much of Selge's income must have derived from the transit trade from Central Anatolia, as at Aspendus. It is hard to see how the small valley and surrounding hillsides could have contributed much beyond subsistence fare, although during the Roman period Selge exported a resin used for incense and a type of iris prized for its oil.

The **theater** is easily Selge's most complete building, but a ramble through the ruins should also include a visit to the **agora**, whose open square can be traced on a hilltop to the southwest of the theater. Tumbled blocks bearing carved scrollwork and inscriptions are underfoot everywhere. The villagers of Zerk are very poor, but they do not ask for handouts, a welcome change from more touristic areas. Some "mountain tourism" has, however, started in Turkey in recent years, and Zerk has been used for several summers as a base camp for treks farther up into the Taurus.

Side

Return from Aspendus to the main road and continue in a southeasterly direction. Although the plain is flat and rich, the mountains and sea draw near on either side. Indeed, the proximity of Side (pronounced SEE-day) is announced by the silhouettes of large beach hotels hunkering on the southern horizon.

The turnoff for Side comes on the outskirts of Manavgat (discussed below), the market town for this region. If you're on a bus that doesn't stop in Side you should get off in Manavgat and take a minibus there: Minibuses leave from Manavgat's bus station every 15 minutes and cost about 20 cents for the 15-minute ride. For those interested in staying in Side, there are many hotels lining the road to the site. In addition, the peninsula housing the ancient city itself has been built over in the last 15 years, so it is possible to find a small hotel or pension smack dab in the middle of ruins.

Side: classical ruins at the beach's edge. In an interesting concession to its tourist appeal, the site's ancient name has everywhere superseded its official Turkish name, Selimiye. The town is living through a period of unbridled mercantilism the likes of which it hasn't seen since the mid-first century B.C., when the Romans put an end to its traffic in slaves acquired from the pirate fleets of Cilicia. True, the beach, which stretches out and under limpid shallows, is exceptional, but the ruins are ill maintained. If you can see through the trash, the faded and fallen signs, the beaten-down vegetation, the camel boys, and the crowds, Side can still summon up considerable charm.

In ancient times Side's twin harbors were the only seaside anchorage between Alanya and Antalya. It was a flourishing port until the Arab invasions of the seventh century. The last of its dwindled population was transferred to Antalya by the Byzantines in the tenth century A.D. Great commercial glory, here as elsewhere in Pamphylia, had occurred during the Hellenistic and Roman periods, with most of the major monuments dating to the second and third centuries A.D. However, the city retained its importance in the early Byzantine period, when it was the seat of a metropolitan, the overgrown remains of whose palace lie near the city walls.

Today's visitor will be attracted first to the theater, which looms large over the site. Essential monuments are clustered around it: the agora, a colonnaded street, and the museum, fashioned out of a fifth-century A.D. bath and filled with treasures unearthed during more than 20 years of excavation by Istanbul University. Those with more time will want to walk down the shop-lined streets leading to the harbor, and from there around the point to the left, the site of the **twin temples of Apollo and Athena** (one of which has been spectacularly restored) as well as a **Byzantine basilica**. A seat in a simple seaside kebap restaurant near the basilica, with a view of the sea washing over column drums and blurred classical moldings, does much to restore the spirits—a dip at the beach that stretches east of Side completes the visit.

Separate admissions are charged at the museum and the **theater**, although the latter fee can easily be avoided by walking along the outside arcade and up through an opening at the theater's rear. This method of entrance, if undignified, has the advantage of revealing the most remarkable technical feature of Side's theater: the solid system of stone arcades, piers, and tilted barrel vaults used to prop up the *cavea*—a hill engineered for a flat city. The theater is not as well preserved as others in Pamphylia, but it is still impressive as a monument of wealth and civic pride. The stage building preserves some weathered reliefs, but perhaps the most interesting part is the orchestra wall built to protect spectators from wild beasts—it is only six feet high! This wall also served to hold in water when the orchestra was flooded for a staged naval battle (naumachy).

Immediately behind the stage building of the theater and across the street from the museum is the main **agora** of Side. A large, open square surrounded by colonnades and shops, this area was the commercial heart of the city. A circular temple to Lady Luck—the goddess Tyche—stood in the middle. (The goddess Nemesis, who ensured that everyone got his just deserts, was another favorite of Pamphylian merchants.) Do not miss the elegant marble curve of the pissoirs tucked in the southwest corner of the agora.

Just past the modern sanitary facilities located beyond the northwest corner of the agora is a series of courtyard houses that illustrate the domestic architecture of the upper middle class at Side, something missing from other Pamphylian cities.

The **museum** houses a fine collection of statuary, sarcophagi, architectural sculpture, and inscriptions, including one in the native language of the region that was supplanted by Greek. Only a handful of short inscriptions in this tongue, called Sidetan, exist, none of them long enough to allow any but the most preliminary determinations concerning its morphology. Notable statues include Hercules, the three Graces, Aphrodite, and a head of Apollo.

If you are planning to stay in Side, your options are limited. Within the town itself there are various small, undistinguished pensions and motels that are rented on a yearly basis by Turkish families. Even if you could find a room within the village, you would be better advised to look elsewhere, as the noisy crowds make it unlikely that you will get any sleep. After leaving Side, you don't have to go far to find pleasant if pricey accommodation. Drive back out of town until you see the signs for **Kumköyü** leading you to the left. Once you have turned here, you will find one hotel entrance after another for miles. Unfortunately, these hotels, each with its own strip of beach and invisible from the road, have to be viewed by separate exitings from the road.

The first hotel to be reached is the two-story **Turtel Side Holiday Village**. The earliest of the modern hotels built at Side, it has lovely, mature gardens and rooms right on the beach. Walk along this same beach to the east and you will come to the ancient site. Next to the Turtel is the **Asteria Hotel**, which resembles a transplanted Aztec pyramid and is done up in high-tech plush. Its enormous swimming pools are wonderful. If you find these hotels too expensive, you can get a nearly equal degree of comfort by travelling further down the road to Kumköyü. There, you will find the **Hane Hotel**, beautifully decorated and well maintained with gardens and a pool. Along this whole stretch of what are essentially back entrances to beachfront hotels, there is not a single restaurant. According to Side locals there is nothing to recommend any one restaurant in the area over any other. There are several along the harbor in Side itself; most of the Kumköyü hotels provide dinner to their guests as part of the room price.

Manavgat

Manavgat was the medieval successor to Side in the region. Today it is a market town of little distinction, notable mostly for the adamantine green of the waters of the Manavgat Çayı, which flows through the middle of town. Take a boat trip from the Paradise restaurant (next to the bus stop) to Side and back. But do it soon: There's a rumor that there are plans to export the Manavgat Çayı's waters by tanker to thirsty Israel—even though there's no evidence of this happening, yet.

Manavgat proper has only one good restaurant, the **Develi**, in the middle of town on the north bank of the Manavgat Çayı; Tel: (321) 61977. Housed in an attractive Ottoman-style building with a huge, high-ceilinged salon, the Develi features a number of superb entrées (all under $5), including 20 different varieties of *kebaps*. The desserts—including baklava and *künefe* (fried shredded wheat stuffed with cheese and drizzled with sugar syrup)—are terrific, too. The restaurant has a bar at each end and has live music nightly during the winter.

For those intent on a trout meal, the best choice lies a few kilometers out of town. At the western edge of Manavgat a sign points left (north) to the *şelale* (waterfall). Follow it, and just beyond the outskirts of town, turn and park. (Or take a *dolmuş* from Manavgat town.) You will find yourself next to the river at the point where it breaks over a ledge. Old plane trees and the cooling roar and greenish turquoise of the water make an attractive setting. A large area has been outfitted here with terraces, paths, and crowded trout pens where you can select your lunch. As you look around, you wil feel surrounded by cool-looking restaurants; don't be deceived. There is only one **restaurant** here with its single cash register set up in the middle of the terrace. Sit where you like; service and quality will not vary. The specialties of the cook are *alabalık* (trout) and *kızarmış piliç* (roast chicken). Surprisingly, considering that there is only one restaurant, the food is not overpriced and you can have a nice lunch for only a few dollars.

Further escape from the crowds of the seashore is possible by continuing on the same northbound road, which follows the valley of the Manavgat Çayı up into the mountains. It is from the high mountain gorges of the river that the inhabitants of Roman Side got their water, and along the road you can spot sections of the Sidetan aqueduct in arches marching across fields or in troughs carved out of the mountain rock.

On the eastern edge of Manavgat, opposite the high school, is the **farmers' market**, held every Monday and well worth a visit in this productive farm region. A few kilometers east of Manavgat is the turnoff north for Akseki and Konya, the fastest and most scenic route through the mountains to the Anatolian plateau. The road has been widened recently but is still full of sharp curves.

Alara

After passing through a blight of new construction, the coastal road from Manavgat crosses the Alara Çayı. A few kilometers farther on, a sign points to Alarahan. Follow this road for 9 km (5½ miles) through pine forests and wheat fields to the 13th-century caravansary of **Alarahan**. From both an architectural and scenic standpoint this is an exceptional site. Situated near the cold, fast-running river as it breaks out of the mountains, the caravansary was protected by nearby Alara castle, which hangs by its fingernails from a neighboring crag.

By no means the largest of the caravansaries built by the

Seljuks, Alarahan is nevertheless one of the most original. The open courtyard for merchants is surrounded on three sides by vaulted halls for beasts of burden. The courtyard itself illustrates a graceful solution to changes in weather: It contains alternating closed and open vaulted rooms around its periphery, plain except for fine limestone masonry and an occasional carved lion's head. This arrangement is best seen from the roof, which you can reach by a staircase to the left of the entrance. As you climb, you pass through a small projecting chamber that served as the caravansary's mosque.

There are two tea gardens close to the caravansary. The nearer is run by a man who pretends to be an official guide and halts cars with ferocious toots on a whistle. Avoid him at all costs—literally; he overcharges wildly. Instead head to the farther teahouse, where you can go for a dip in the river and find a guide for the climb to the castle.

Alara Kalesi, like the castle in Alanya, is a Seljuk rebuilding of an earlier fortification. The best route to the top follows the old water tunnel that runs up the western slope of the rock. It's easy to lose your way, and a guide is recommended (along with a water bottle, sturdy legs, and sneakers) for the climb. Clinging so precariously to the face of a cliff, Alara exerts an almost irresistible appeal on a climber, but in actuality, apart from the water tunnel, there is little to entice the less adventurous, save the spectacular view from the top. If you do go up, remember also to carry a flashlight to investigate the ruins. And beware of snakes and scorpions! The summit is crowned by a two-domed miniature bath of Seljuk construction.

About 15 km (9 miles) outside Alanya is another caravansary, **Şarapsa Hanı**, a long gray stone building at the road's edge. Built in 1246, it is a lesser work than Alarahan, especially now that it has been turned into, of all things, a discotheque.

CILICIA

The ancient province of Cilicia was divided into mountainous and flat areas. The coast east of Alanya is mountainous until just before Taşucu, the start of the Cilician plain. Present-day visitors usually pass through Cilicia, stopping only at Alanya. For the unhurried traveller, this region has much unspoiled natural beauty to offer. Besides Alanya, Anamur and environs combine beautiful topography and superb beaches with good food and interesting historical remains.

ALANYA

Alanya marks the end of Pamphylia and the beginning of mountainous Cilicia to the east. In its present incarnation, the city of Alanya belongs very much to the untrammeled touristic spirit of Antalya. Its classical heritage, unlike that of the cities of Pamphylia, has been obscured by later building. The medieval castle dominates Alanya, whose Gibraltar-like rock makes for one of the most spectacular natural settings in Turkey.

From a fair distance you can spot the humped silhouette of Alanya projecting high and far into the sea. If you arrive in the afternoon you can easily make out the castle wall, a thin line clinging to the carapace, snaking along the edge of steep, pine-covered limestone slopes. Alanya is easy to envisage—the rock, rising emphatically from the sea, bracketed by two crescents of beach. Behind these bend the Taurus mountains, capped with snow until early June.

The modern town of Alanya lies between sea and mountains, spreading around the landward base of the rock. Habitation moved down from the castle rock in the early years of this century, but until 20 years ago Alanya was a sleepy town of 7,000 people living off the sea and surrounded by banana and citrus groves. The expansion of tourism in the last decade has covered most of the greenery with squat six-story buildings: pensions, hotels, and apartment houses. Today Alanya unabashedly lives off tourists. The better, western, beach is lined with hotels, while the eastern beach road is a strip lined with bars and restaurants catering to the evening crowds. Alanya is awash in shops that sell leather, carpets, and gold (more than 150 gold shops in a town of about 60,000), all open in season until late at night. Prices are high, but the shops are crowded, full of vacationers seeking distraction from relaxation and Alanya's daytime routine of sunning and swimming.

World monoculture, as the anthropologist Claude Lévi-Strauss has called it, has come to Alanya, and shops and restaurants are named for comparable resorts in Spain and France. *Simit*s, the delicious round Turkish sesame-coated savories, are sold on the beach as "sesam Kuchen."

Were it not for the castle, then, Alanya would be another

victim of the phenomenon the Turkish press calls *beton-laşma,* the "concreting" of the coast that has taken place in Turkey since the early 1980s. Luckily, the castle rock has been spared development. A ten-minute bus ride or a five-minute car ride will transport you if not back to the 13th century (when the castle was built) then at least away from the concrete and bustle below. Most visitors wishing to walk to the castle take the heavily trafficked road. This is a mistake: It is far safer and more interesting to walk up the streets of old Alanya. Start from the harbor and take Tophane Caddesi, next to the Bayırlı Hotel, to the lower gate of the castle. Enter the walls and take a series of right turns: Mahperi Sultan Sokak to Kargı Sokak to Galip Dede Sokak to Çakırlar Çıkmazı. By now you are almost through the wooden houses of the old town; the rest of the walk up to the main road is through ruins of the old Greek quarter, fragrant with thyme bushes and unfragrant with goats.

Ancient Alanya was called Korakesion (Greek for "rookery") and Kalonoros (Greek for "beautiful mountain"). In antiquity Cilicia was notorious for pirates, and it was just off Alanya that a decisive battle between combined pirate fleets and the Roman navy in 65 B.C. led to the pacification of the eastern Mediterranean. Traces of the Hellenistic walls of the city are preserved; they are on the eastern crest of the hill near the road and are today the foundation of the Ehmedek (lower citadel). Remains of a Doric temple have been incorporated into the Red Tower next to the jetty, but the original site of the temple is unknown. Except for these and a few pieces of statuary and *osteothekes* ("bone containers," stone funerary receptacles) in the Alanya Museum, nothing remains of the Hellenistic and Roman city. The museum is well worth a visit to see these and other antiquities. Well organized and beautifully kept, the museum also has an ethnographic section and a garden with a variety of exhibits to match the scope of those inside.

The city was renamed Alaiyye after its conquest in 1221 by Seljuk sultan Alaettin Keykubat I; the name survives in its present form of Alanya. The **Kale** (castle) as it appears today is almost entirely Seljuk. The harbor is on the western edge of the rock cape that dominates the skyline of Alanya, and the fortification system was developed with the harbor as its focus. The walls of the Dişkale (Outer Fortress) were built up and along the edges of the cliffs towering over the harbor. For hundreds of yards they extend north and south before turning to the east and the interior of the rock. After following the topography across this peninsula, they turn to meet each other at the İçkale, or Inner Fortress. In all, these walls climb from about 30 feet in elevation to about 750 feet at the İçkale. Within these walls, the Dişkale, Ortakale (Middle Fortress), and İçkale are each separated from the others by more walls. The site entrance is today in the south wall of the İçkale, though in medieval times it was in the east.

There are three main areas you will want to visit. At the harbor are the Kızıl Kule, the Tersane, and the Tophane. The **Kızıl Kule**, or Red Tower, is today the symbol of Alanya. A four-level octagonal tower, its name derives from its orange brick superstructure. This sophisticated piece of military architecture was built in 1227 for the Seljuk sultan by an architect from Aleppo, Syria. Today it houses a museum of folk art. The Red Tower protected the harbor, which extended south to the shipyard, also from the 13th century. Known as the **Tersane**, the shipyard is a five-minute walk to the right or west along the seawall from the Red Tower. Descend from the wall by means of the staircase of the last tower and exit seaside through a hole at the base of the wall. From here it is a short walk to the Tersane, a long, low, five-bayed structure half in and half out of the water. Here, in its vaulted pebble-washed halls, ships were built and repaired into Ottoman times. Just to the south of this is the **Tophane**, or Arsenal. Originally, in Seljuk times, this tower defended the harbor on its southern extremity, but during the Ottoman period it may have been used as a cannon factory (hence its name, "ball house").

Any ascent to the citadel, or inner fortress, passes through gaggles of women selling doilies and handsome locally made silk scarves. The old silk looms, still in use, were originally used to weave cummerbunds for the local baggy trousers called *şalvar*. Silk production is partly to blame for Alanya's ferocious mosquitoes: Silkworms are so sensitive that they can be killed by automobile exhaust, let alone pesticides. So, even though the fumes from tour buses have limited local silk spinning to only four or five houses, the municipality rarely sprays for mosquitoes.

The chief objective of a visit to Alanya castle is its citadel, or **İçkale**. Those with more time will enjoy a detour to the 16th-century Süleymaniye mosque, a single-domed brick building constructed from the remains of an earlier Seljuk mosque, and the **Ehmedek**, or lower citadel, which has beautiful views down over the town. A sign points off to these monuments about two-thirds of the way to the top. By the mosque are the 17th-century remains of the han (hostel). This has been converted into the **Bedesten Hotel**. The rooms are spartan but the setting is beautiful.

Continue up the road to the present-day entrance to the

İçkale, which is besieged by camels, taxis, and sellers of orange juice. Pull over at a teahouse—**Muhtarın Yeri** has the best view, the lowest prices, and no music—to catch your breath and enjoy the view across leagues of shifting sea spreading east toward Cyprus.

Current excavations by Ankara University are revealing remains of a palace built by Sultan Alaettin in the northeast corner of the citadel. Alanya was his winter capital, but, these remains notwithstanding, it appears he spent more time down by the sea, hunting and fishing and staying in pavilions like the one that still survives outside town in the village of Gülefşen.

The inner keep of the citadel contains several mammoth cisterns to supply the inhabitants of the waterless rock. You pass two of them as you proceed across the citadel toward the west. Here, too, is a small Byzantine church from the 10th or 11th century, in whose shell you can still make out the outlines of haloed saints in the church's faded frescoes. Beyond, the western wall of the citadel gives way to a steep slope and the sea, 800 feet below. A short walk to the southwest corner of the citadel reveals a view across the sea to the gnarled finger of Cilvarda point, where the ruins of a Byzantine monastery perch on one rocky knuckle.

The modern harbor of Alanya is a very pleasant place to spend time. Boat trips around the rock and down the coast depart from the foot of the Red Tower. Day trips include spectacular views and good food for about $25–$30 per person. Also available from here are horse and buggy rides around the harbor and the center of the town.

It is possible to find any kind of food harborside in Alanya, from pizza and hamburgers to Chinese food prepared by a mainland Chinese cook. Two old-line restaurants on the harbor, **Yönet** and **Mahperi Sultan**, offer fish with the Alanya specialty, *tarator,* a tasty walnut sauce—but at stiff prices. For a more modest, but simpatico, Turkish meal harborside, try **Café Korakesion** or, on the main road near the Atatürk monument, **Güven Restorant**. On the other side of town, near Damlataş cave and the museum, the **Damlataş** restaurant and **Ocakbaşı 65** also offer reasonable Turkish meals. For the homesick tourist **Café Stop**, opposite the museum, offers European-style cakes and American-style deep-dish pies.

Alanya is chockablock with new and old hotels. Two favorites next to the harbor are the three-star **Kaptan Oteli**, with a swimming pool and rooftop restaurant, and the **Blue Sky Bayırlı** Oteli, which also has a rooftop restaurant. At the corner where you turn off Atatürk Caddesi (the highway) to reach the museum, you will find the **Alanya Divan Hotel**, a converted old house with tantalizing patches of molded ceilings that greet one through each arched doorway. Along the strip of hotels to the east of the rock, there is little to differentiate one from another. The **Hotel Wien**, however, has ceiling fans to keep mosquitoes away in this screenless land, while the **Eftalia-Aytur Hotel** next door offers air conditioning for the same price. Wherever you choose to stay, always make sure you will not have to endure mosquitoes. For a beach vacation the **Alaaddin Oteli** has yet to be equaled by newer, fancier hotels. More luxurious is the **Alantur Oteli**, modeled on Club Med–type resorts, 5 km (3 miles) east of town.

Off season, Alanya is a pleasant town, but in July and August the population doubles, and the heat, noise, crowds, and pollution turn it into a swollen simulacrum of itself.

ALANYA TO ADANA

After Alanya the density of hotels and condos gradually decreases, and by the time you reach Gazipaşa, 45 minutes to the east, you've slipped 20 years into Turkey's past. Accommodations and food are simpler and cheaper, and the people you meet are likely to be natives of the region.

About 11 km (7 miles) west of Gazipaşa (5 km after you pass the blue "Gazipaşa—16 km" sign) is an ideal picnic and swim spot: the harbor and acropolis of the Roman-period city of **Iotape**. The site is unmarked, but if you watch for a hump-backed peninsula on the right, you should be able to find the ruins with no trouble. The cape is bracketed by a sand beach on the west and a steep rock harbor on the east. Scramble down to the beach for a picnic and a swim. You will have to climb back up to the road before you can safely climb across to the ruins. The site was originally founded by the Seleucid emperor Antiochus IV Epiphanes in the second century B.C., but most of the visible remains are, once again, Roman. On the saddle between the road and the cape are the remains of the main street, lined with masonry steps and inscribed statue bases. The best remains are to be found on the east side of the rock harbor. The arches of the bath building are easily visible from the road and, moving counterclockwise from this structure, the remains of a church, a basilica, and the **Church of Hagios Georgios**, identified by the poorly preserved fresco in the nave, can be found. If you have the energy, climb the hills behind Iotape to the north and east to see the necropolis and the view.

Continue on the short distance to Gazipaşa. This town is situated in a well-watered plain surrounded by mountains. On your right as you enter the town, the **Güven Oteli** offers very basic accommodations (but private bath) for a very inexpensive price. Gazipaşa is today inland from the classical and medieval city of **Selinus**, a coastal site worth a visit. Take a right at the main intersection (the modern town is inland, to the left); the road leads straight to the beach, where you'll find a few low-key restaurants. The river empties into the sea at the east end of the beach, above which rises a steep hillside crowned with castle walls. The slope and the far bank of the river constitute the site of the ancient city, the ruins of which clutter the fields. The outlines of two agoras can be traced here, as well as the city aqueduct leading to a large basilica, probably the municipal baths. The trek to the **castle** takes half an hour along thistle-bound goat paths. The view from the top is striking: The hill falls steeply to the sea below, and to the east another long valley glints brightly with greenhouses. Surf crawls along a long expanse of rock and sand.

After Gazipaşa the road climbs far above the sea. With the exception of the town of Anamur, from here to Taşucu (some 205 km/127 miles) the view of the landscape is all in one direction, tied to the curving road, which affords spectacular glimpses of mountain and sea, jutting headlands, filigrees of foaming surf, and screes of pine forest, tinder-dry in summer and sparked with wildflowers in spring and autumn. For the passenger this is an ideal drive, full of movement, color, and light. For the driver it is a battle with curves, eroded shoulders, sudden drops, and lumber trucks lumbering along under clouds of diesel smoke and burdens of pine logs. The forest is speckled with admonitory homilies: "The forest is an emerald," says one sign; another advises us that "From the cradle to the coffin we all need WOOD." On this road, which runs almost due east and west, you are very conscious of the sun, either at your back or in your eyes, but creating spectacular vistas. Throughout this drive the ghost of Cyprus lingers on the horizon, the Kyrenia mountains of that island now looming clear, now fading under a pall of sea haze.

The road is intensely involved in the landscape, in repose as in movement. In the most isolated place in the woods, a patient soul waits roadside, with a basket or a pile of produce, often a child nearby. The truckers who travel this road, too, use the rest stops actively. You see them piled out of their overladen, bright trucks, washing their feet before prayer, drinking at a spring of cold mountain water. There's always a spreading plane tree at these stops—as at Tenzile (just before Anamur) and Şayvana—and a tea garden and cafeteria built into a crook in the road.

Occasionally the road dips into a small valley like Kaledran, whose river constitutes the border between the provinces of Antalya and İçel. Kaledran produces the best bananas in Turkey. In the Melleç valley you'll see boats and the ruins of a caravansary on a pebbly beach, and pines bowed under the prevailing southwest wind. Population is sparse; outside of these valleys there is an occasional village high on a slope, stone and cinderblock houses with *çardak*s, raised wooden platforms that are half pavilion, half arbor for sleeping out of doors in the hot weather.

Anamur

Anamur is about two and a half hours east of Alanya by car. Here the mountain road winds down into an open plain that fingers back into the mountains. Settlement is diffused across the plain. The main part of Anamur is set several miles inland. Seaside is the İskele (port) quarter, with a small settlement, a jetty, and fishing boats. On the water at opposite ends of the plain are the two historical attractions of Anamur, the Roman and early Byzantine city of Anemurium to the west, and the 14th- to 15th-century Mamure castle to the east.

The bus stop in Anamur is located at the base of the main town, a 15-minute walk from the center. Anamur is a pleasant, laid-back provincial town, catering to the tourist, but without pretense or fuss. The tourist bureau in town is more often closed than open, and hotels are not gussied up—that is, except for new development along the beach. Anamur has a fine produce market and numerous restaurants and beer halls. A favorite restaurant is **Kismet**, offering fish and kebaps at reasonable prices. The best hotel in town is the **Anahan Oteli**, a modern structure with swimming pool and screens. A bit up the street from the Anahan is the **Takıl** ("Hang Out") bar, with cheap beer, an authentic local clientele, and unimaginable decor.

The İskele, too, has its charms: seaside fish restaurants, cheap and clean pensions—the ten-room **Eser Pansiyon** (six have private baths), with a shady garden and a roof terrace overlooking the sea, and the **Yakamoz Pansiyon** (13 double rooms with private baths), across the street from the Eser and just 60 yards from the sea, are two favorites—and, for the more conventional, the **Dragon Motel**, at the water's edge, with a restaurant and disco. Several new hotels have been built here. The nicest is the **Hotel Hermes**, with air conditioning, sauna, and private beach for a very reasonable price.

Most of the finds of 20 years of excavation by the University of British Columbia at **Anemurium**—pottery, glass, coins, and fine mosaics—have been transported to a new museum next to the jetty in the İskele quarter. A visit to Anemurium is worthwhile both for the ruins themselves and their situation. A yellow sign points off to the south just as the main road descends onto the plain of Anamur. Because the ruins are extensive, it is advisable to engage, for a nominal sum, the site guardian (*bekçi,* in Turkish) or his son to show you around. They will also have keys to the best preserved of Anemurium's **frescoed tombs**, a highlight of the visit.

Less prosperous than Side or Perge to the west, Anemurium nevertheless shared in the same fortunes as its Pamphylian neighbors, flourishing in the late Roman and early Byzantine periods and going into steep decline with the raids of Arab fleets in the late seventh century. All the features of a Roman town are here: theater, odeon, baths (two sets), aqueduct, and agora. The baths, upper and lower, are well preserved, as is the odeon, the small concert and assembly hall. Half the city, the part climbing the hill, is devoted to the dead: mortuary chapels and other sepulchers. These vaulted, multichambered structures were family tombs, and many were furnished with mosaics and frescoes. Some have been removed to the museum, but the guardian will unlock the best of the remaining ones for you.

In the medieval period Anemurium retreated into the fortress above the site, but, aside from a view east across the plain and west across the jagged Cilician coast, there is little to recommend the long trek to the summit. For a better-preserved castle, proceed 13 km (8 miles) or so to the other edge of the plain. Here, on a rock by the beach, is **Mamure Kalesi**, built on earlier foundations in the late 14th century by the Karaman Turkish dynasty, rivals of the early Ottomans (and not, as is often stated, by the Crusaders). Today it is used by Turkish film companies as a backdrop for costume dramas about the Assyrian king Nimrod, for instance, or Attila the Hun. Near the castle, not a thousand-yard walk away from it, are two modest but comfortable motels: The **Motel Karan** is modern and on the beach; the **Star Sonarex Motel** is across the highway from the beach. The Star Sonarex is less pristine than the Motel Karan, but its proprietress is a charming woman from Istanbul, Jale Hanım, who, with the aid of her mother and sisters, turns out international cuisine to be enjoyed in the slightly overgrown garden that fronts her establishment. This latter motel has screened windows, while the staff of the Karan deny the existence of mosquitoes and so don't feel screens are necessary. Whichever you choose, be assured that the beach here is clean and uncrowded.

From Anamur to Taşucu, some 128 km (79 miles) to the northeast, the road continues to climb and dip between mountain, valley, and sea. Shortly after Anamur you come to **Softa Kale**, a Byzantine castle presiding over a narrow coastal plain and harbor. On the headland next to the harbor, side by side with new condos, are the ruins of the medieval town. Just beyond is the southernmost point along the coast, although the road veers inland at this point. After passing through the long plain of Tekeli, the road mounts again through reforested pine slopes, descending again to the towns of **Yeni Kaş** (the **Taylan** restaurant, next to the stream of Soğuk Su, offers a refreshing rest) and the larger **Aydıncık**, with its harbor (often filled with recently felled logs) and its seaside restaurants the **Arsinoë** (be careful: they may try to serve you frozen fish) and **Le Pêcheur**. At Aydıncık it's easy to find a room with bath for next to nothing.

After Aydıncık there is a turnoff north to Gülnar and Mut (the latter is on the main road from Silifke to Konya), an interesting shortcut through the *yayla*—the high-summer pasture favored by nomads—into the interior. (This area is still frequented by *yörük* nomads and their flocks.) You may wish to venture inland here to visit the fifth-century **monastery of Alahan**, astonishing for its architecture, situation, and fine degree of preservation. The monastery lies just beyond the town of Mut.

The coastal road continues past Aydıncık through mountains until it pulls down to the edge of the Cilician plain near **Liman Kalesi**, site of a spectacular beach, just outside Taşucu. The bucolic, sylvan splendors of "rough" Cilicia come to an abrupt end here. (In antiquity, the Cilician plain was called Cilicia Platea, "smooth" Cilicia, in contrast to the mountainous terrain to the west.) From this point on you encounter man-made wonders: large pulp mills and seaside developments, spillover from the free-trade zone the Turkish government has established at Mersin in an effort to encourage development in the southeast.

Taşucu is a new port and a point of departure for ferries to **Northern Cyprus**. There are currently two companies operating ferries Sunday through Thursday. The Ertürk and Fergün companies are located on the harbor in Taşucu; just follow the signs to the Şehir Merkezi (city center) and the Liman (harbor) and you cannot miss them. Services and fares are nearly identical between the companies; Fergün's ferries leave at 11:00 P.M. while Ertürk's leave at midnight. Round-trip fare for a single person is about $29; for a car, $54. (You cannot take a rental car on the ferry; leaving one in the town square is safe.) At present, the trip to Girne in Cyprus takes five hours (there are rumors that a *deniz otobüsü* (sea bus) will be starting up soon; then the trip will only be three hours but the fare will be higher).

After Taşucu the road slices inland to **Silifke**, where the road (route 715) to Karaman and Konya forks to the left. Silifke was founded in the third century B.C. but no pre-Roman remains have been found here. Follow the yellow signs to the remains of the Roman Seleukia in the modern town: a theater, a second-century A.D. temple, and a necropolis. West of the city, at an elevation of about 550 feet, are the remains of a largely 12th-century Crusader castle. Here, at Silifke, the Göksu river comes rushing, milky jade in color, out of the dolomite fastness to the north. Just north of here Holy Roman Emperor Frederick Barbarossa fell into the icy river on a hot June day in 1190 and drowned, bringing German participation in the Third Crusade to an abrupt end.

The museum at Silifke is well worth a visit; don't miss the **Hoard of Gülnar**, a cache of silver coins of Hellenistic date discovered in 1980. And keep an eye peeled for the occasional amphora (wine/oil jar); most of these date to the classical period, as early as the sixth century B.C. They're not labeled, but if the jar has a pointed toe, chances are it is Greek of the classical period.

From Silifke, follow the yellow signs to **Uzuncaburç** (ancient Olba or Diocaesarea) 30 km (19 miles) to the northeast of the city over poorly paved road. There are some of the best preserved ruins in Turkey, including the earliest known example of a temple where the Corinthian order was used. The **temple of Zeus Olbius** was built in the third century B.C., probably by the founder of the city of Seleukia, Seleucus I. Also well worth seeing are the **Tycheum** (Temple to Good Fortune); the colonnaded street with columns still standing, a monumental arch at one end and the main entrance to the ancient city on another; a theater dated to the co-reign of Marcus Aurelius and Lucius Verus (A.D. 161–169); a large Hellenistic tomb; and remains of the fortification walls, including a Hellenistic tower more than 60 feet tall.

Just about 15 km (9 miles) beyond Silifke is the first and nicest resort hotel in this area, the **Altınorfez**. This beautiful hotel takes full advantage of the ideal weather and coastline to create a luxurious interlude. The majority of the guests here (and farther along the coast as far as Mersin) will be affluent Turks rather than German tourists, long ago left behind at Alanya. Just 3 km (2 miles) beyond this resort is the bay called Narlıkuyu. The turn is well marked with a yellow sign. This bay once was the site of a Roman villa, which took advantage of the cold-water spring that makes swimming here so pleasant. There is a one-room museum that houses a mosaic of the Three Graces. The edge of this small bay is ringed with **fish restaurants**. There is no need to recommend any one over another as they are all owned by the same family, descendants of the grandfather who originally owned this land. The food here is excellent, with the most popular fish being *lagos,* a large white-meat fish served as deep-fried steaks, and a close runner-up being *barbunya* (red mullet), fried whole and eaten with one's fingers.

If you turn left instead of right at the Narlıkuyu turning, you will come to **Cennet-Cehennem** (Heaven and Hell). You can climb down into Heaven to see the fifth-century church dedicated to the Virgin Mary. It was supposedly placed there in order to ensure that the Titan Typhoeus would not be able to return to the place where he had imprisoned the Greek god Zeus. It is also said that if you place your ear on the wall at the very end of the descending path, you will be able to hear the River Styx as it flows past.

Strung out along the road about 25 km (16 miles) east of Silifke are the remains of the classical and medieval city of **Korykos**, a main port of western Cilicia Platea. Guarding the harbor of Korykos are twin land and sea castles, once linked by a causeway. The land castle is built in the form of a double trace (with concentric inner and outer walls) and incorporates in one of its gates part of a Roman triumphal arch. The sea castle, reachable by rowboat, has masonry of Byzantine, Crusader, and Armenian types.

The modern town of **Kız Kalesi**, just opposite the Maiden's Castle, looks like a tourist trap of the worst sort when seen from the road. Persevere and you will find some pleasant places to stay for a day or two on a beautiful white-sand beach with a spectacular view of the castles. The oldest of the good hotels here, the **Barbarossa**, is the most expensive of the three but still less than you may have paid at Antalya or Side. This hotel, as well as the even less expensive but hardly less elegant **Otel Kilikya** and **Admiral Hotel**, has a swimming pool, redundant with such a stretch of sand and surf to detract from its appeal.

A few miles beyond Kız Kalesi, turn left to drive up the limestone ridge 3 km (2 miles) to the site of **Kanlıdivane**. Here you will find a limestone sinkhole similar to those at

Cennet-Cehennem. While not associated with myth, the pit at Kanlıdivane was obviously important. It is ringed by churches of various dates and there is a honeycomb masonry tower of the Hellenistic period on its southern edge. This tower is the oldest structure here; the inscription on one corner (on the seventh and ninth courses of masonry) says that this site was under the protection of the priests of Olba (see above, Uzuncaburc). There are five churches in various states of preservation; the last of these on the far side of the pit is very well preserved to two stories. Within the pit itself, look carefully for two Late Roman or Early Byzantine reliefs, one, of an unidentified family, on the south wall, and the other, of a soldier in full armor, on the west wall. Most of the other remains here are funerary in function except for the cistern to the west of the pit. The function of this site is unknown; it was obviously religious through both the pagan and Christian eras but was never mentioned by ancient or medieval authors, and there is only the one inscription here to give any information about the site. Nontheless, it is a fascinating place and very well worth a visit.

As you leave the site, venture off to the right on the dirt road immediately outside the parking area. This will lead you to a fork about 550 yards on where you descend to the left to find a series of **rock-cut tombs** of Roman date. These tombs exhibit a form typical of the area: a rock-cut room with a sculpture of the deceased carved out of the wall above the entry.

Mersin, 84 km (52 miles) east of Silifke, is a busy port city. The harbor area has recently been landscaped and is a pleasant place for a stroll. There are several good hotels in the city, mainly catering to businesspeople connected with the free port at Mersin. The **Mersin Oteli** is the oldest, and is located opposite the older, eastern part of the harbor. The **Ramada Hotel** and the **Mersin Hilton** are brand new and offer every modern convenience. Along the harbor are a number of fish restaurants, all good and many specializing in shrimp dishes.

The main road (E 5) skirts Mersin and heads inland for Tarsus and Adana. This is the heartland of the Cilician plain, a wide expanse of farmland ringed by the Taurus mountains. Infernally hot in summer, the climate of the Cilician plain (called Çukurova, "sunken plain," in Turkish) allows for bountiful crops of citrus, winter wheat, and cotton. Almost as soon as you leave the heavily warehoused, unattractive area which borders Mersin in the east, you will start to notice individual small domed or conical **mounds** at long intervals to either side of the four-lane highway. These mounds date to various archaeological periods from as early as the Neolithic through the Islamic eras. The predominant building material of the region, mud brick, is responsible for these artificial accumulations of human debris. There are a total of 168 of them in the Cilician plain. Watch for small groups of modern houses along the road; some today are still built of this ubiquitous material.

As you approach the modern town of **Tarsus**, you will see a large mound (the largest in the plain), which was the site of the ancient city. Familiar as the birthplace of Saint Paul, Tarsus today bears little trace of its former prominence as an ancient city. Drive to the center of the town to visit **Cleopatra's Gate** (so named for the visit that the Egyptian queen made to Tarsus when it was a port city to meet with Antony), the ethnographic museum, and Gözlü Kule, the mound excavated in the 1930s by a team from Bryn Mawr College (remains are in the Adana museum) but today converted into a pine-tree-covered park. As you exit Tarsus to the east, you will pass the remains of the **Roman stone bridge** on the left. Supposedly built during the reign of Justinian, this bridge spanned the Tarsus river in antiquity just as the Hadrianic bridge in Adana and the Roman bridge in Misis today span the Seyhan and Ceyhan rivers respectively. The latter two bridges are still in use (see The Southeast, below). These three rivers formed the delta that is today the Çukurova plain; however, the Tarsus has changed its course since antiquity, abandoning this stone bridge to a lonely fate by the side of the road.

Beyond Tarsus the highway (E 5) heads northwest through the mountains and, follows the traditional invasion route used by Alexander the Great and others, through the Cilician Gates. As you drive east, if the air is clear, you can see the water gap formed by the Tarsus Çayı very easily from Yenice. There is also a clearly visible mound here if you want actually to explore one. Turn right onto the dirt road directly opposite the very visible outdoor furniture store, Captain's Hobby Center, just beyond Yenice. (Don't pick anything up at the mound; that's illegal.)

As you proceed farther east toward Adana, watch for hand-lettered signs at small roadside eateries advertising *çilek suyu* (strawberry juice). This is only available for a couple of months in the early summer but is very good. While you're drinking it, watch the proprietor's mother or aunt (it is invariably one or the other) make *sıkma* over an open fire. This potato-and-cheese-filled roll-up is normally eaten as breakfast or a snack and is a local specialty.

Adana (discussed in more detail in the chapter on the

Southeast, below) is at the center of the Çukurova plain. Commercial hub for southeast Turkey, Adana today is a boomtown. Many companies have set up their regional head-quarters here, and a new central mosque and high-rise hotel and chamber of commerce building testify to newfound wealth. Natives of Adana are wont to say that the Seyhan river, which flows through the center of town, divides Adana in two, both physically and mentally. The left bank, they say, is a poor Middle Eastern village, the right bank a dynamic, westward-looking metropolis. Whether this is true or not, the pressures of rapid urbanization and industrialization are everywhere evident.

The excesses of encroaching modernity aside, Adana is a convenient way station for connections to the south and east. (The culinary and classical pleasures of Antakya and the Hatay are two hours farther on, to the southeast, and are discussed below.) From Adana there is also a good, if heavily trafficked, road east to Gaziantep and Şanlıurfa.

The region around Adana can be enchanting in spring, when the fields are green, the mountaintops white, and the weather mild. It offers much to see in the way of castle archi-tecture, including the spectacular medieval Armenian castles of Yılan Kalesi and Toprakkale (see the chapter on the Hatay, below), just off the main road east.

GETTING AROUND

The central Mediterranean coast is accessible by air at either end. Daily flights link Adana and Antalya with Istanbul, Ankara, and points in Europe and the Middle East. In sum-mer many European cities are connected by direct service to Antalya. In addition to this added service, summer brings myriad European charter flights to Antalya airport.

Antalya airport lies five miles to the east of town. A tan USAŞ bus meets every scheduled flight, taking passengers into town for about $2. Taxis from the airport cost a flat rate, approximately $8. Taxi service is also available at the airport for resorts up and down the coast as far away as Alanya, two hours distant (approximate fare $50).

Major car-rental firms have offices in Antalya, Side, Alanya, Mersin, and Adana. The easiest way to get around is by car, although driving can be hair-raising, especially between Antalya and Alanya (because of heavy traffic) and east of Gazipaşa (because of hairpin turns and guardrail-less drops).

Bus travel is the best and cheapest alternative. Many bus lines offer service along the coast; in general service is cheap, clean, and courteous. Buses run between Alanya and Antalya almost every half hour; the two-hour trip costs under

$4. Other service is less frequent, but bus companies have offices in larger towns where tickets can be bought and schedules obtained. There are also minibuses that run from these in-town offices to the bus station half an hour before scheduled departures.

A word of caution: Bus companies, especially those at Antalya's bus station, employ men to guide you to their firm's buses. They may misstate the departure time of their next bus in an effort to get your business. Double-check departure times before paying for your ticket. Akdeniz, the largest company operating along the south coast, is notorious for this practice.

Bus connections with the rest of Turkey—Konya, Istanbul, and Ankara—are frequent, although trips of more than eight hours of duration are often scheduled overnight. From Adana's bus station frequent connections operate to Central Anatolia, Antakya and the Hatay, and Gaziantep and Sanlıurfa to the east.

Taxis are plentiful in all cities and towns. All in-city travel is governed by taxi meters. Make sure the meter is on when your trip starts. In addition to taxis, shorter-distance travel can be effected by minibuses (dolmuşes), which follow fixed routes. For a minimal fare, rarely exceeding 60 cents (and often much less), you can travel fairly long distances in and around major towns. These dolmuşes are marked, but don't be afraid to ask if you're unsure; drivers will tell you whether or not you are on the right route.

In season, major towns and hotels house agencies offering day tours of major sites with guides and lunch thrown in. Preferable to group tours in terms of mobility and to short-term car rentals in terms of cost is the hire of a car and driver. With a little haggling and a little luck you can hire a congenial driver to take you where you would like to go at your own pace. Although it's always best to look around first (prices quoted in deutsche marks instead of Turkish lira are likely to be higher), often the fare doesn't amount to much more than that of a bus tour.

Day tours by boat are also available at Alanya, Side, Manavgat, and Antalya.

ACCOMMODATIONS REFERENCE

Rates given below are for double rooms, double occupancy, and represent projections for 1993. Where a range in rates appears, this reflects the difference in price between the low season (November through March) and the high season (April through October). All prices are subject to change and should be checked before booking. Some hotels and pensions include breakfast; others offer half or full board for an added cost. When telephoning between cities in Turkey, dial 9 before entering the city code.

▶ **Admiral Hotel.** Kızkalesi, **Mersin.** Tel: (7584) 1158 (Fax, same number). $22–$29.

▶ **Alaaddin Oteli.** Saray Mahallesi, Atatürk Caddesi, 07400 **Alanya.** Tel: (323) 126-24; Fax: (323) 236-84. $20–$45.

▶ **Alantur Oteli.** Dimçayı Mevkii, **Alanya.** Tel: (323) 119-24; Fax: (323) 144-19. $91–$122.

▶ **Alanya Divan Hotel.** Atatürk Caddesi 111, 07400 **Alanya.** Tel: (323) 112-01; Fax: (323) 117-69. $28.

▶ **Altınorfez. Silifke.** Tel: (7596) 4211; Fax: (7596) 4215. $87.

▶ **Anahan Oteli.** Tahsin Soylu Caddesi 109, **Anamur.** Tel: (757) 4512; Fax: (757) 4045. $42.

▶ **Asteria Hotel.** Kumköyü, **Side,** 07330 Antalya. Tel: (321) 31830 (Fax, same number). $92–$127.

▶ **Atelya Pansiyon.** Barbaros Mahallesi, Civelek Sokak 30, Kaleiçi, 07100 **Antalya.** Tel: (31) 11-64-16. $16–$24.

▶ **Bahama Motel.** Lara Yolu, **Lara,** 07100 Antalya. Tel: (31) 23-15-53. $25.

▶ **Barbarossa.** Kızkalesi, **Mersin.** Tel: (7584) 2089; Fax: (7584) 2090. $55.

▶ **Bedesten Hotel.** İçkale, **Alanya.** Tel: (323) 212-34; Fax: (323) 179-34. $34–$54.

▶ **Blue Sky Bayırlı Oteli.** İskele Caddesi 66, 07400 **Alanya.** Tel: (323) 164-87; Fax: (323) 143-20. $25–$45.

▶ **Club Hotel Sera.** P.O. Box 44, **Lara,** 07100 Antalya. Tel: (31) 23-11-70; Fax: (31) 23-12-79. $130.

▶ **Dragon Motel.** İskele Caddesi, 33640 **Anamur.** Tel: (7571) 1572. $31–$36.

▶ **Eftalia-Aytur Hotel.** Keykubat Caddesi, **Alanya.** Tel: (323) 139-55; Fax: (323) 141-77. $29.

▶ **Eser Pansiyon.** Yalı Evleri 3, İskele, 33640 **Anamur.** Tel: (7571) 2322. $10–$14.

▶ **Güven Oteli.** Turistik Yol Üzeri, **Gazipaşa,** 07900 Antalya. Tel: (3236) 1938 or 1497. $13.

▶ **Hane Hotel.** Kumköyü, **Side.** Tel: (321) 32445; Fax: (321) 32449. $65.

▶ **Hotel Antalya Dedeman.** Lara Yolu, 07100 **Antalya.** Tel: (31) 21-79-10; Fax: (31) 21-38-73. $90–$125.

▶ **Hotel Hermes.** İskele Mevkii, 33006 **Anamur.** Tel: (7571) 6180; Fax: (7571) 3995. $22.

▶ **Hotel OFO Antalya.** P.O. Box 717, **Lara,** 07100 Antalya. Tel: (31) 23-10-00; Fax (31) 23-10-16. $50–$75.

► **Hotel Wien.** Keykubat Caddesi 1, **Alanya.** Tel: (323) 200-37 or 136-17; Fax: (323) 200-37. $29.

► **Kaptan Oteli.** İskele Caddesi 62, 07400 **Alanya.** Tel: (323) 149-00; Fax: (323) 120-00. $42.

► **Lara Hotel.** Lara Yolu, **Lara,** 07100 Antalya. Tel: (31) 23-14-60; Fax: (31) 23-19-33. $48–$60.

► **Marina Hotels and Restaurants.** Mermerli Sokak 15, Kaleiçi, 07100 **Antalya.** Tel: (31) 47-54-90; Fax: (31) 41-17-65. $100–$200.

► **Mersin Hilton.** Gümrük Meydanı, **Mersin.** Tel: (74) 26-50-00; Fax: (74) 26-50-50. $79.

► **Mersin Oteli.** Gumruk Meydanı, **Mersin.** Tel: (74) 32-16-40; Fax: (74) 31-26-25. $69.

► **Motel Karan.** Bozdoğan Köyü, 33640 **Anamur.** Tel: (7571) 1027 or (7577) 1333; Fax; (7577) 1349. $15.

► **Otel Kilikya.** Kızkalesi, **Mersin.** Tel: (7584) 1117; Fax: (7584) 1084. $32–$42.

► **Ramada Hotel.** Kuvayi Milliye Caddesi, Metropola İş ve Alis-Veris Merkezi, **Mersin.** Tel: (74) 36-10-10; Fax: (74) 36-10-30. $54.

► **Saraçoğlu Pansiyon.** Tuzcular Mahallesi, Karanlık Sokak 12, Kaleiçi, 07100 **Antalya.** Tel: (31) 11-33-58. $15–$26.

► **Saray Oteli.** Tahil Pazarı Mahallesi, İsmet Paşa Caddesi 62, Kaleiçi, 07100 **Antalya.** Tel: (31) 11-85-83. $18–$25.

► **Şimşek Motel.** Dinç Sokak, **Lara,** 07100 Antalya. Tel: (31) 23-19-33. Fax: (31) 23-19-35. $25–$35.

► **Star Sonarex Motel.** Mamure Kalesi Yanı, 33640 **Anamur.** Tel: (7577) 1219 (Fax, same number). $15.

► **Talya Hotel.** Fevzi Çakmak Caddesi 30, 07100 **Antalya.** Tel: (31) 26-68-00; Fax: (31) 21-54-00. $88–$132.

► **Tunay Pansiyon.** Selçuk Mahallesi, Mermerli Sokak 7, Kaleiçi, 07100 **Antalya.** Tel: (31) 12-81-43. $13–$16.

► **Turtel Side Holiday Village.** Selimiye Köyü, **Side,** 07330 Antalya. Tel: (321) 12225 or 12828; Fax: (321) 12226. $50–$72.

► **Yakamoz Pansiyon.** İskele Mahallesi 34, 33640 **Anamur.** Tel: (7571) 2308. $14.

THE HATAY

By James Ruggia

Associate editor at Travel Agent *magazine, James Ruggia has contributed articles on Turkey to such magazines as* MD *and* Pan Am Clipper. *He lived in Turkey for a year and has travelled there extensively.*

The outline of the map of Turkey makes sense: It *looks* like a country. Its rectangular shape runs a few hundred miles north to south and just over a thousand across. It would fit like a well-laid mason's brick between Europe and Asia but for the little trigger of land jutting out from its underside at the far southeast and following the curve of the Mediterranean. This little strip, 70 miles long and rarely more than 30 miles wide, is known as the Hatay.

The Hatay became part of Turkey on June 23, 1939 by agreement between Turkey and France, after Turks in the region had secured a majority in a plebiscite the previous year. The annexation brought to a close a long struggle among nations about who owned the Hatay. Before World War I the region had been the Ottoman province (*sancak*) of Alexandretta. With the collapse of the empire after the war, the victorious allies tried to carve up Anatolia and the Ottoman provinces like so much meat on a plate.

The Greeks were to have had Turkish Thrace and many of the Aegean islands as well as the the Aegean coast around Smyrna (İzmir) and its hinterland. The Italians were to get the Antalya area and some Aegean islands. And the French were to receive the Mediterranean coastal area known as Cilicia as far east as Gaziantep and Maraş. The Ottoman *sancak*s of Syria and Alexandretta were placed under French mandate. It wasn't long before Turkish forces defeated the Greeks, and they and the other European claimants gave up their demands on modern Turkey. Syria and the Hatay,

443

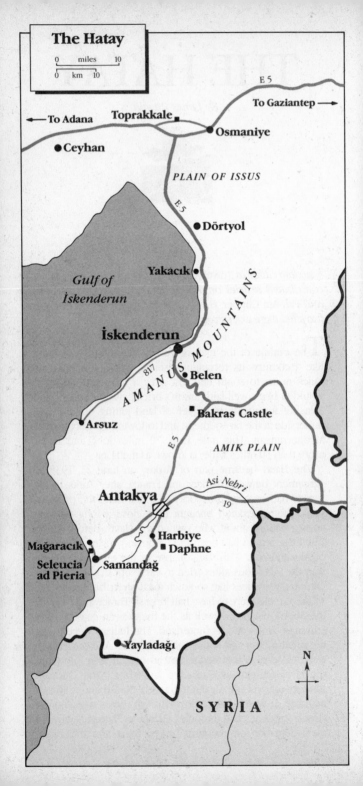

however, remained under French control, with France keeping the Hatay separate from Syria in order to protect the interests of its Turkish population. In the modern sector of the region's main town, Antakya, a vague soupçon of the French presence still lingers in a few of the buildings.

The city of Antakya, ancient Antioch-on-the-Orontes, is the region's most provocative attraction. The city lies about two-thirds of the way into the Hatay, about 80 km (50 miles) from the province's northern border. Sadly, the reality of modern Antakya does not live up to the historical resonance of its name. Precious little remains of the ancient town, one of the greatest of Hellenistic and, later, Roman cities and once revered along with Rome, Constantinople, Jerusalem, and Alexandria as one of the chief centers of early Christianity. But imaginative visitors equipped with a sense of history can bring the ancient city back to life.

A well-trod crossroads, the birthplace of religious cults, and the scene of countless battles and sieges, the Hatay is a quilt of contending cultures. The lovely mountain setting of Daphne, castles such as Bakras and Toprakkale, the beach at Arsuz, and the seaside promenade at İskenderun are among the many elements that combine to make the Hatay well worth a visit.

MAJOR INTEREST
Toprakkale castle
Plain of Issus, site of battle between Alexander the
    Great and Darius III
İskenderun (Alexandretta) and seaside Arsuz
The curative waters of Belen
Eerie Bakras castle

Antakya, ancient Antioch-on-the-Orontes
Church of St. Peter

Harbiye, ancient Daphne
Seleucia ad Pieria, Antioch's port

FROM ADANA TO ANTAKYA

About 70 km (43 miles) east of Adana, at the northeastern corner of the Mediterranean coast, the E 5 highway forks. One road heads for Gaziantep, and the other turns south toward Antakya. The 12th-century **Toprakkale** (Earth Castle) marks the spot, squatting on a mountain overlooking the crossroads. Dating from the Middle Ages, Toprakkale was passed back and forth among the Byzantine, Armenian, Crusader, and Mameluke forces that controlled the region until the mid-14th century, when it lost its strategic importance. A newly paved road leads right up to the foot of this once-impressive fortress, and it's an easy stroll into the castle interior. Inside, much of the ground is overgrown, but you'll have a commanding view of the Plain of Issus to the south of the battlements. A note of caution: Clambering about the castle can be dangerous as it hasn't been restored.

The **Plain of Issus** is situated west of Erzin, just before you reach the modern town of Dörtyol, about 25 km (16 miles) south of Toprakkale. Here (or somewhere nearby), in 333 B.C., Alexander the Great caught up with his great Persian adversary, Darius III. According to the estimates of various ancient historians, the size of the Persian host ranged anywhere from 100,000 up to 600,000. Alexander's triumph in the battle was so complete that Darius just barely escaped, driving his chariot away at full speed until the ground became too rough for its wheels, then dropping his armor and mounting a horse, leaving his wife and three children behind. For Alexander the victory was sweet. According to Plutarch, when Alexander entered the tent of his vanquished foe, "full of splendid furniture and quantities of gold and silver," he removed his arms and entered Darius's private bath, saying, "Now, let us cleanse ourselves from the toils of war in the baths of Darius."

When he entered the battle, Alexander's only goal was to defeat the Persian army, but after his two convincing victories over Darius, at Issus and later at Gaugamela, about 400 miles to the east (in what is now northern Iraq), he decided to conquer all of Persia. Within two years of his victory here he had occupied the Persian capitals—Babylon, Susa, Persepolis, and Ecbatana—and captured the vast treasures of the empire, while Darius, because of his military failures against Alexander, was murdered by his own men.

Driving south on the E 5, look for the yellow historical sign pointing right (west) for the so-called "Issus Ruins." The side road actually leads you just a few kilometers west of the main highway to the rather desolate site of **Epiphaneia/Oiniandos**. Today about all that remains of antiquity on the plain are the ruins of a Roman aqueduct from this town. The ancient aqueduct juts out of the farmland like the vertebrae of a brontosaurus. Wild poppies, sacred to the memory of fallen warriors, are scattered about.

The next stop along the road to Antakya is **Yakacık**, formerly known as Payas, just 10 km (6 miles) south of Dörtyol. A few hundred years ago this now-industrialized town was the area's primary port. A few buildings still stand from those heady days, including the **Selimiye complex**, which contained a mosque, a caravansary, a school of Islamic law (*medrese*), a bath, and a covered market. A caretaker keeps a post in what was one of the long caravansary's stalls. For a pittance he'll lead you through this magnificent complex, empty but for the birds.

Built in 1573 by Sokollu Mehmet Paşa, who secured Cyprus for the Ottoman Empire during the reign of Sultan Selim II (hence the complex's name, "Selimiye"), the complex was restored in the early 1980s and is a fine example of an early Ottoman mercantile foundation. The complex includes a mosque that may have been designed by Sinan, the great Ottoman architect; the classical columns in the mosque's courtyard attest to the much earlier history of the site. The mosque and bath are still in use, and the municipality hopes to lure shopkeepers to set up businesses in the restored covered market.

The **Genoese castle** that stands adjacent to the caravansary adds an Italian touch to Yakacık's harbor. Expanded by the Ottomans and used during the 19th century as a prison, the castle is in wonderful condition. Today flowers bloom so beautifully in the moat that it seems to have been created for them. Of special interest is the conical dungeon. Although a passage has been worn into its side, the original dungeon's only opening was a hole at the top. Prisoners were just dropped in and forgotten. The castle is but one of a number of garrisons built by the Genoese to protect their mercantile posts along the eastern Mediterranean. Another Genoese castle, now called **Cin Kulesi**, sits about half a mile farther down the same road on a hill overlooking the sea. Just beyond Cin Kulesi is a small, walled-off sand beach, and alongside it the **Plaj Restaurant**, with outdoor dining on a covered terrace right on the water and a menu of good (and very cheap) fish and *meze* (appetizers). You can reach the castles by taking the yellow-signposted road to the right as you enter Yakacık on the E 5.

Ruins around Yakacık are scattered but plentiful. A few hundred yards south of the village a handful of fallen columns lie silently in an olive grove, all that remains of the Seleucid city of Baiae. Nine kilometers (five and a half miles) south of Yakacık is **Sarıseki**, where according to legend the great biblical traveller Jonah was disgorged from the whale. A tower by the sea, built by the Romans, marks the supposed spot of Jonah's arrival and is appropriately named **Baba Yunus**, or Father Jonah. The ruins of a castle, the **Kız Kulesi**

(Maiden's Tower), can also be seen here. The castle is probably of Crusader origin but today shows mostly rebuilding performed by the Ottomans.

Payas's fortunes ebbed with the silting of the city's harbor, forcing the region's maritime trade to shift to nearby İskenderun (Alexandretta), a city founded by Alexander after his victory at Issus. In recent years, oil moving in through a pipeline from far-off Iraq made this city, 21 km (13 miles) south of Yakacık, an even more crucial Mediterranean port, but it has long been a significant harbor—as evidenced by the French seizure of the city in 1918. Until the Turkish government cut off the Iraqi pipeline after Iraq's invasion of Kuwait in August 1990, the horizon was usually filled with tankers awaiting their loads of oil. The tankers are fewer nowadays.

İskenderun, one of 16 cities throughout the ancient world named for Alexander (İskender being the Turkish form of his name), is a fine place to pass a night. Evenings on the waterfront promenade present a homey parade of people enjoying their time off. Along the harborfront several open-air taverns play music and serve beer beneath strings of multicolored lights. It's a mixed crowd that gathers here—sprinkled with Tunisians, Syrians, Saudi Arabians, and Libyans. A good, though somewhat expensive, fish restaurant is the **Doğan**, a few blocks east of the main seafront park (the one with the Atatürk statue). The **Kıyı Otel** on the waterfront has clean rooms at low prices. Rooms have ceiling fans and balconies that face the bay.

An even better option is what might be the best hotel in the entire Hatay, in **Arsuz**, a fishing village 30 km (19 miles) southwest of İskenderun. The village of Arsuz itself, with a sandy beach, sits on the site of the Hellenistic city of **Rhosus**. A few years ago, during the oil boom, Arsuz was popular among Syrians; these days you might find a few Europeans vacationing here. The charming **Arsuz Turistik Otel** opened in 1965 and has been growing slowly but steadily since. Guests are given personal, caring attention. Located right on the beach, the Arsuz Turistik features big public spaces and possesses the slow tempo of hotels of a bygone era. (Note that road signs refer to the village as Uluçınar, a name the locals do not use.)

If you make the detour to Arsuz, you must return to İskendurun to pick up the E 5 for your journey farther south. The land rises steeply as you head inland toward Antakya, culminating in the Belen pass in the Amanus mountains, which bisect the Hatay into northern and southern halves. In 333 B.C. Alexander required a few days to move his entire army through this pass, known in antiquity as the Pylae Syriae (Syrian Gates). Today the water of the village of **Belen** (13 km/8 miles south of İskenderun) is famous throughout Turkey for its curative powers. You can sample the water and some fine food as well at the **Kurtoğlu Restaurant** at the side of the E 5 in Belen.

As you look south from the pass, the **Amık plain** spreads out before you, its wealth of mounds bearing witness to the unbroken presence of human beings in this region over thousands of years. When you reach the plain, look for a sign directing you to the village of Ötençay, where stands the evil-looking **castle of Bakras**. This eerie structure towers over the little village like something out of one of Mary Shelley's nightmares. The present castle was constructed from the ruins of a fortification built by Byzantines in the tenth century. Bakras was seized in 1097, during the First Crusade, by a largely Frankish army of Christians seeking to establish a foothold for the attack on Antioch. Their leader, Bohemond of Tarentum, later named prince of Antioch by the pope, was characterized by the Byzantine princess and historian Anna Comnena as having "something savage and horrible in his glance." Not to mention his home.

The castle was captured by a series of invaders, including Saracens, Armenians, and Mamelukes, before Sultan Selim I took it in 1516 for the Ottoman Empire. As for modern invaders, none but experienced climbers should venture to scale it; it takes a steep vertical climb to penetrate its mysterious keep.

ANTAKYA

From Bakras the road (still the E 5) continues south across the plain for 30 km (19 miles) to Antakya. Although Antakya's site has been an urban center of sorts for almost 6,000 years, the city proper was founded by Seleucus I Nicator in 300 B.C. after the battle of Ipsus, which gave the Seleucid dynasty control of Syria. After Alexander's death in 323 B.C., his newly won empire was split into a number of pieces by his successors, known as the *diadochoi,* who founded the various dynasties (the Seleucids and the Ptolemies being the most famous) that ruled the eastern Mediterranean world until the rise of Rome. When Seleucus defeated the Macedonian Antigonus I at Ipsus he merged two of the divisions that had rent Alexander's empire. Seleucus named his capital after his father, Antiochus. As the capital of the Seleucid Empire for more than 200 years,

Antioch was the center of a dominion that included all of Anatolia and stretched east to modern Pakistan.

As an imperial capital Antioch expanded dramatically. Its prosperity derived in part from its being situated on the Silk Road, and its wealth increased until, with a population of approximately half a million, it became the third-largest city in the Roman world, after Rome and Alexandria. (In 64 B.C. the Roman general Pompey brought the city under Roman hegemony and named it capital of the province of Syria.) Archaeologists have shown that the main thoroughfare of modern Antakya, Kurtuluş Caddesi, was once the site of a long, colonnaded Roman boulevard with triumphal arches at both ends. This grand avenue was built by Herod the Great two millennia ago. The arches commemorated the emperor Augustus's defeat of Antony at Actium.

Testimony to its glorious past can be found in Antakya's fine **Archaeological Museum** (open 8:00 A.M. to 12:00 noon and 1:30 to 5:30 P.M., except Mondays, when it is only open during the afternoon), located in the center of the city where Atatürk Caddesi, Cumhuriyet Caddesi, and Gündüz Caddesi intersect near the bank of the Asi Nehri (the ancient Orontes River). The museum's mosaics, taken from Roman villas in the region (first through sixth centuries A.D.), are among its most beautiful treasures—and among the most important works of art in all Turkey. (In fact, the museum is also known as the Mosaic Museum.) The stolid artists of Rome rarely achieved the delicacy of execution accomplished by their counterparts in the Latinized colonies of the Middle East. The good life of old Antioch is illustrated in the relaxed poses of the figures portrayed in these mosaics. The pieces are excellently displayed in large, high-ceilinged rooms that allow ample space for viewing. In one case you can actually mount a spiral staircase to behold one particularly fine example from the ceiling's vantage. While the mosaics are undoubtedly the work of a Latin or Mediterranean sensibility, they show a gradual abandonment of the naturalistic illusion of depth of field in favor of a geometric patterning of figures. The fifth-century *Megalopsychia Hunt,* for example, shows hunters and prey distributed symmetrically around the central figure of Megalopsychia, the personification of all virtues. In addition to its exceptional collection of mosaics, the museum features artifacts recovered from nearly 200 of the mounds that dot the Amık plain, and it possesses an excellent collection of ancient coins. The sarcophagi and stelae displayed in the museum garden are also worth your attention.

With a reputation similar to that of old Hong Kong, ancient Antioch was known throughout the Roman world as a somewhat chaotic conglomeration of wealth, ethnicities, and sin. The Romans and the Byzantines after them embellished the town with beautiful architecture, but earthquakes, perennial sieges, and a few devastating fires—not to mention the unceasing deposit of silt by the Orontes—prevented the glory of this once-beautiful capital from surviving in all its grandeur.

In the late 11th century Frankish Crusaders took Antioch from the Seljuk Turks, who had previously captured it from the Byzantines, who had themselves recaptured the city from the Arabs, who had held dominion here from 636 to 969. The Crusaders established the Principality of Antioch, which lasted 170 years until overrun by the Egyptian Mamelukes, who sacked the city in 1268. In 1516 Antioch was brought into the Ottoman Empire. Unfortunately, the modern city lacks the charisma of its heritage. The past does remain in traces, but the spirit of this great Levantine capital has been choked with a gag of concrete and electric cable. Indeed, the ruins at Ephesus (see Aegean Turkey, above) give a better idea of what ancient Antioch must have been like than does anything you can see here.

In fact, a strong argument could be made that, in sensibility, the Antioch of antiquity was more modern than the Antakya of today. The city familiar to Saint Paul in the first century A.D. was one of carefree consumers. Old wealth and new flocked here to enjoy the empire's finest climate. And Antioch's citizens were great lovers of the theater, the racetrack, and the music hall.

Today Antakya, which lies on both sides of the Asi Nehri, occupies just under a third of the ancient city's area. On one side of the river the new city offers logical modernity; on the other bank, the **old quarter** provides a fine example of a Middle Eastern town, with blank façades that enclose inner courtyards and gardens. With its arched doorways, shuttered windows, and second stories that jut out over the street, the old quarter's charm is undeniable. Occasionally you'll note a Roman decorative frieze at the top of a doorway, built right into the side of a house of much later date. At the corner of Saran Caddesi and Hürriyet Caddesi you'll see a perfect remnant of the French occupation: a building whose rolled wrought-iron balconies would fit in on Bourbon Street in New Orleans. (Some of Antakya's inhabitants still speak French.) Much of the old quarter's population is Syriac Orthodox Christian (the church is in a whitewashed courtyard off Hürriyet Caddesi). The northern section of the old city is commercial, with small shops and a larger market beyond the 11th-century Habib Neccar Camii, a converted Frankish church.

Though you may prefer to stay in Harbiye (see below), just a few kilometers out of town, than in Antakya itself, you can pass a satisfactory night in the **Büyük Antakya Oteli**, a relatively new hotel near the Archaeological Museum. For comfortable, 1930s-style ambience, try the one-star **Atahan Hotel**, at Hürriyet Caddesi 28, which has recently installed air-conditioning units in its rooms. Antakya has a brand new hotel, the **Orontes Oteli**—too new to judge, but worth mentioning to increase your accommodations options in the city. A particularly good restaurant, with a fine garden and serving excellent Adana kebap, grilled chicken, and hummus, is the **Anadolu**, at Saray Caddesi 50/C (about two blocks south of the Atahan Hotel). One small difference between the Hatay and the rest of Turkey is that restaurants here serve mint as a garnish, rather than parsley.

For a truly spectacular view of Antakya and the surrounding plain, go to the top of Mount Sipylus. To get there, take the road (Kurtuluş Caddesi) that exits the city from the northeastern corner of the old quarter; it's the same road you take to reach the church of St. Peter (see below). After about 5 km/3 miles, turn right at the sign for Altıözü. The road is in poor condition, but it's passable and the panorama at the summit makes it worth attempting. At the top (about 10 km/6 miles from the turnoff), there's a modest teahouse offering refreshments.

The Church of St. Peter

According to Christian traditions dating back at least as far as the third century, Saint Peter chose Antioch as the place for his first mission among the gentiles. In seven years of evangelizing, before he moved on to Rome, Peter established the church's first ecclesiastical organization here, composed of both pagan and Jewish converts to the new religion. The term *Christian* was coined in Antioch to denote the new sect. No one knows for sure who first used the word. Jews referred to the followers of Jesus as Nazarenes, and among themselves the early Christians went by terms such as "brethren" and "believers." It's likely that a Roman official, accustomed to calling Caesar's followers "Caesariani" and Pompey's followers "Pompeiani," first sneered the word "Christiani."

St. Peter's church (Sanpiyer Kilisesi in Turkish) is actually a grotto tucked into the face of a cliff a little more than a mile northeast of Antakya. From the church's cliffside terraces you can view the entire city. To get to the church, take a taxi (the fare will amount to a few dollars).

The caves behind the church façade housed some of Christianity's earliest liturgies. Indeed, this may be the oldest working church-site in existence. Services are still held here, where locals believe that Peter himself preached in the first century. It's possible he was here, but the current church building was begun in 1098 by the Crusaders, and the present façade was only added in 1863. The mosaic floors inside, though, date back to the fourth or fifth century. The cave to the left of the altar leads into a labyrinth of tunnels lacing through Stauris mountain (Habib Neccar Dağı in Turkish). These served as a handy escape route during times of persecution. The religious importance of this site probably predates Christianity. On a cliff face about a hundred yards to the left of the church and 50 feet up the face of the mountain is a large relief (a bit difficult to find) showing a veiled woman with a small figure on her shoulder. The origin of this relief is uncertain, but some hold that it was commissioned by Seleucid emperor Antiochus IV (r. 175 to 164 B.C.) to relieve a plague.

Antakya Environs

With a history reaching back to the Neolithic Age, the environs of Antakya offer quite a few worthwhile sites. Many of the beautiful mosaics in the Antakya Archaeological Museum hail from the villas built in the forest around ancient **Daphne**, about 11 km (7 miles) south of Antakya. Though no ruins of ancient Daphne remain, the site is significant in both myth and history. Here, according to local traditions, Paris made his fatal judgment, choosing Aphrodite over Hera and Athena and setting off the Trojan War. It was here that the nymph Daphne, pursued by Apollo, was transformed into a laurel tree. The Seleucid royalty made this the location of a garden sanctuary to Apollo and filled the place with hundreds of enslaved women purchased in Eastern markets. These were then given into the hands of an elite group of priestesses/prostitutes who oversaw the pious rituals enacted in the grove. It may have been here that Antony married Cleopatra in 40 B.C., and the Roman games held here rivaled the ancient Greek Olympics in fame.

The village of **Harbiye** sits where ancient Daphne stood. Though it's a few miles outside the city, Harbiye is by far the best place to stay during your visit to Antakya. The drive here from Antakya is beautiful, with cypress-pointed hills and rolling green mountains more reminiscent of Tuscany than of Turkey.

Harbiye is a lovely spot for picnics. Its mountain locale and springs and waterfalls make it consistently cooler than Antakya. There's a pagan feel to this area, a constant breeze moving through the tables of Harbiye's alfresco restaurants, where you can have your chair set in a few inches of water to keep your feet cool while dining! The restaurants here serve unusual fare: Try the *kakıç*, a kind of salad made from the leaves of mountain shrubs mixed with parsley, tomatoes, olive oil, and a unique pomegranate sauce (pomegranates grow wild here). The **Hidro** restaurant is particularly good. Across the ravine on the hilltop are a string of basic but wonderful hotels with views over the valley. Especially recommended is the **Hotel Çağlayan**, which has modest but clean and airy rooms at reasonable prices. And before you leave Harbiye, be sure to purchase a bar of the locally made bay-laurel soap, whose fragrance will continue to remind you of the place.

Return to Antakya and then follow the road that leads southwest to the seaside town of Samandağ for about half an hour and you'll come to the remains of Antioch's port city, **Seleucia ad Pieria**. Originally built by Seleucus I Nicator in 300 B.C. as a port for Antioch, it now lies inland near the small village of Mağaracık. The sea withdrew from the port as, over the centuries, silt was deposited at the mouth of the Orontes. The old waterfront now lies behind harbor walls amid a stand of mulberry trees. From here Saints Paul, Barnabas, and Mark set out for their mission to Cyprus.

Seleucia ad Pieria now consists of a few ruined walls and a water tunnel, so it's difficult to imagine this as one of antiquity's most bustling ports, with houses scaling the side of a mountain that ran down to the sea. The water tunnel, cut from the rock during the reigns of Roman emperor Vespasian (A.D. 69 to 79) and his son Titus (79 to 81) to divert a mountain stream, runs for 1,400 yards. A path leads between its 20-foot-high walls. With lizards darting about, it feels more like a canyon than a ruin, but it's certainly a remarkable feat of ancient engineering.

Along the road to Samandağ you'll spot a yellow sign for the **monastery of St. Simeon Stylites the Younger**. The sign says 8 km, but it's more like 18 km (11 miles). Don't even attempt the trip from the highway to the monastery without a four-wheel-drive vehicle. After passing through some very primitive villages, you'll spot a small white mosque atop a mountain. From there you can see the monastery, which is a good two-hour hike farther on.

Saint Simeon Stylites the Younger perfected the religious practice of column-sitting (*stylos* is the Greek word for "pillar"). In A.D. 528, at the age of seven, the saint first mounted a column to pray and fast. He made two more ascents, on progressively higher columns. This ascetic practice had been initiated a generation earlier by Saint Simeon Stylites the Elder, who ascended a column some 30 miles east of Antioch. The younger Simeon founded this monastery in 541; the column on which he sat was placed in an octagonal court in the center of the church's main nave. In 551 Simeon ascended his third, and highest, column, which may have been as high as 30 feet. Excavations have revealed the column's base. Both stylites, elder and younger, attracted pilgrims from all over Christendom. The stylites were given to delivering long speeches and sermons from atop their marble pillars. The mountain on which the monastery sits—known as the "Wondrous Mountain" in Saint Simeon's day—now bears the saint's name (Samandağ means "Mount Simeon").

GETTING AROUND

The Hatay is somewhat off the beaten path, but buses bound for the Hatay do depart from Istanbul and Ankara. Be sure to arrange your passage in advance. Bus service from Adana is more frequent; Jet Turizm's services are particularly good, with in-coach video movies. The nearest airport is located at Adana and is served by Turkish Airlines (THY). From Antakya you can visit most of the surrounding sites by minibus, and all of the city's sites are within easy walking distance from one another. Minibuses also run from Antakya to Harbiye, where you'll find some of the best hotels. There are daily buses to Yayladağı at the Syrian border. Likewise, it's easy to catch minibuses to Arsuz from İskenderun. Other destinations, such as Toprakkale and the Plain of Issus, are accessible only by car. If you intend to continue on to Syria from the Hatay, there are frequent buses from the station in Antakya to Latakiah (Turkish, Lazkiye) and Aleppo (Turkish, Halep). You must obtain a Syrian visa beforehand as these are no longer available at the border.

ACCOMMODATIONS REFERENCE

Rates given below are for double rooms, double occupancy, and represent projections for 1993. All prices are subject to change and should be checked before booking. Some hotels include breakfast. When telephoning between cities in Turkey, dial 9 before entering the city code.

▶ **Arsuz Turistik Otel.** Uluçınar, **Arsuz**, Hatay. Tel: (881) 217-82; Fax: (8873) 1448. $60.

▶ **Atahan Hotel.** Hürriyet Caddesi 28, 35869 **Antakya.** Tel: (891) 110-36; Fax: (891) 180-06. $33.

▶ **Büyük Antakya Oteli.** Atatürk Caddesi 8, 35869 **Antakya.** Tel: (891) 358-60; Fax: (891) 358-69. $38.

▶ **Hotel Çağlayan.** Ürgen Caddesi 6, **Harbiye,** Hatay. Tel: (8983) 1011 or 1269. $17.

▶ **Kıyı Otel.** Atatürk Bulvarı 63, 31200 **İskenderun.** Tel: (881) 136-80 or 136-81. $22.

▶ **Orontes Oteli.** İstiklâl Caddessi 58, **Antakya.** Tel: (891) 459-31; Fax: (891) 459-33. Prices not available.

ANKARA
AND ENVIRONS

By Patricia Tarbell Leiser

Patricia Tarbell Leiser did graduate work in Islamic art and architecture and is fluent in French, Arabic, and Turkish. She lived in Ankara for eight years, where she coedited the American Embassy newsletter, The Ankara Scene, *and wrote various articles on the culture and history of Turkey. She has lectured for, managed, and guided numerous tours in Turkey and is a specialist in Turkish weaving.*

Ankara, Turkey's capital since 1923, is a microcosm of past and present, so that even a short stay here lends insight into many facets of the country's heritage and culture. The city was capital of the Roman province of Galatia, then became the site of an important medieval fortification, and in Ottoman times it prospered with the production of mohair from the Angora (i.e., Ankara) goat. With the decline in the mohair trade during the 19th century, Ankara stagnated. Yet after World War I, when Mustafa Kemal was galvanizing Anatolian efforts for the Turkish War of Independence, he chose Ankara, located on the railroad at a strategic central crossroads, as his base. Four years later it became the capital of the new Republic of Turkey. On the upswing ever since, it is today a city with a split personality: Ancient and medieval monuments dot the engaging older quarters, whose inhabitants still follow traditional ways, while distinctive Nationalist and Republican structures, wide boulevards, grand national monuments, parks, and new buildings highlight the modern city, which has seen unrelenting growth as the country's political center.

Much of the city's population is only first- or second-generation Ankaran. People have flocked here from all over Anatolia in hopes of realizing the dreams of the new republic; the resulting population is 100 times greater than what it was 70 years ago. Today Ankara is a city of Europeanized politicians, diplomats, members of the military elite, bureaucrats, businesspeople, professionals, and academics all caught up in the debate over the course of the nation's future. At the same time it is home to a small entrepreneurial "middle class" of merchants and craftspeople, many of them the descendants of the city's pre-Republic inhabitants. Finally, there is a large element of new arrivals from the countryside who come here seeking a better life but often find themselves caught between traditional values and the lure of new ways. Binding these various elements together is a traditional ethic of personal honor and hospitality. The city's inhabitants, who call themselves *Ankaralıs*, are proud of their country's heritage and accomplishments and want the visitor to appreciate them as well.

For the traveller, Ankara and its environs form the gateway to Central Anatolia, providing an exceptional introduction to the complete span of Turkey's past through a combination of archaeological sites (Hattic and Hittite Alacahöyük and Hattuşaş and Phrygian Gordion, discussed below), monuments, and museums, in addition to a wide spectrum of Turkish society.

MAJOR INTEREST

Old Ankara
Museum of Anatolian Civilizations
Temple of Rome and Augustus
Roman baths
Citadel (Kale/Hisar)
Ahi Şerafettin Camii (Aslanhane Camii)
Bazaar area
Sulu Han
Turkish baths

Modern Ankara
First and Second National Assembly buildings
Ethnographic Museum
Atatürk's mausoleum and museum
Atakule (Turning Tower)
Sakarya promenade
Atatürk's Farm
Shopping for carpets and jewelry

Day Trips from Ankara
Hattic site of Alacahöyük

Hittite site of Hattuşaş (Boğazkale)
Phrygian site of Gordion
Ottoman town of Safranbolu

ANKARA

Ankara is situated at the northern edge of the great Central Anatolian plateau in an area of barren hills and fertile plains. Here, within a horseshoe of hills on the northwestern flank of Elmadağ (where there is a small ski facility), a number of streams converge around a massive igneous outcrop in a small plain, creating a perfect site for fortification.

According to Greek legend Ankara was founded by Phrygian King Midas. The apparent derivation of the city's name from a Phrygian–Indo-European root, *ank* (meaning "gorge" or "rocky valley"), plus the discovery of Phrygian pottery on the western side of the low spur in the old city and Phrygian burial mounds to the west—some on the hill where Atatürk's tomb stands today—indicate that a Phrygian town developed here by the seventh century B.C. First recorded as "Ancyra" by Herodotus in a list of resting places along the Achaemenid Persian Royal Road, which connected Anatolia and Persia, the city next appears, described as a sizable town, in an account of Alexander the Great's march east after he cut the famous Gordian knot.

Following Alexander's death in 323 B.C., numerous factions vied for control of Central Anatolia until 278 to 277 B.C., when the king of Bithynia, to the northwest, allowed Galatian (i.e., Celtic) tribes from the Danube area into Asia Minor, using them as mercenaries. They rampaged through western Anatolia until confined to the central plateau, where they acted as a buffer between the Hellenized kingdoms of Bithynia and Pergamum to the west, the dynasties of Pontus and Cappadocia (within the Persian sphere) to the east, and the Seleucid Empire to the south. One of these Galatian tribes was centered around Ancyra and built a fortified position here, traces of which have been found beneath the present citadel's foundations.

The nomadic Galatians proved a constant threat to Anatolia's more settled inhabitants, and wars were a common occurrence. Attalus I, king of Pergamum, commemorated his

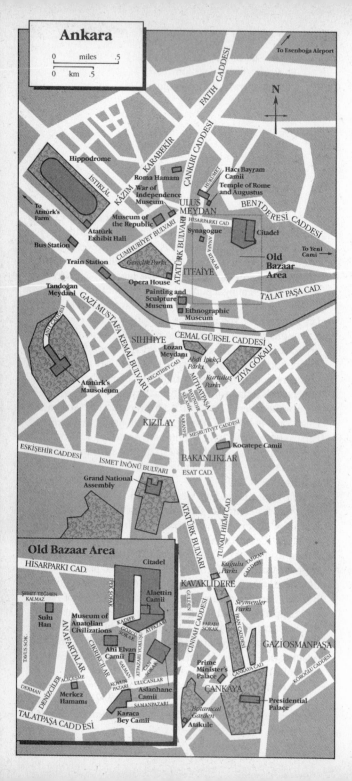

victories over the Gallic tribes in 229 B.C. with a series of bronze sculptures; the famous statue the *Dying Gaul* is a Roman copy of one of these. Subdued by the Romans in 189 B.C., Ancyra and all of Galatia were finally annexed by Emperor Augustus in 25 B.C. Formerly a fortress and market town, Ancyra now began to acquire the trappings of a Roman city. The temple of Rome and Augustus, the earliest and most important building to survive from the Roman period here, stands atop the low spur that faced the road to Rome via Byzantium. Coins minted in the city displayed an anchor, probably adopted because of the resemblance between the city's name and the word for anchor in Greek, which had become the common language.

Saints Peter and Paul may both have visited Ancyra in their travels through Asia Minor. Paul apparently founded a church here, to which he later addressed his blistering Letter to the Galatians, chastising those who questioned his authority. Emperor Nero designated Ancyra capital of the province of Galatia, and Vespasian began the construction of an ambitious network of roads in Central Anatolia, with Ancyra at its center. These roads established a vital system of communications that is roughly paralleled by the highways that radiate from the city today.

During the first several centuries of the Common Era Ancyra prospered and grew: Excavations have uncovered a large bath-gymnasium complex and, quite recently, a small theater, or odeon. No trace survives of any Roman acropolis or city walls. The great citadel walls seen today were built by the Byzantines, who used many of the Roman monuments as quarries for material for the new fortifications. Ankara's citadel stands today as one of the finest extant examples of Byzantine fortification, a testament to the constant threat of incursion into Asia Minor from the east. Between the seventh and tenth centuries the region was invaded, first by the Sassanid Persians, who destroyed the city in 620, then by the Muslim armies of the Umayyad and Abbasid caliphates, which besieged and occupied the city on several occasions.

In the late 11th century the Seljuk Turkish invasions of Anatolia began, and by 1143 Ankara had become part of the Seljuk Sultanate of Rum ("the land of the Romans," i.e., Anatolia), whose capital was at Konya. After the defeat of the Seljuks by the successors of the Mongol leader Genghis Khan in 1243, the Seljuk sultan briefly took refuge in Ankara's citadel. The Seljuks then became a puppet regime under the Mongols, whose successors, the Ilkhanid dynasty of Iran, ruled directly in Anatolia by the beginning of the 14th century. Coins minted in Ankara were inscribed

"Ankuriyya," or "Enguriye" (in popular usage, Enguru). The Ilkhanid hold soon weakened, however, and a series of *beyliks* (Turkish principalities), emerged, splitting Anatolia into numerous independent states that were only reunited with the rise of the Ottomans in the second half of the 14th century. During Seljuk, Mongol, and Ottoman times Ankara remained a provincial center whose citadel was kept in good repair but whose affairs were largely in the hands of local notables. During the Islamic period the city developed mainly on the slopes that extended south, outside the citadel gate facing the road to Konya. Most of its interesting monuments—mosques, *hans* (inns), and baths—are found there, in the area of the old bazaar. Many buildings from the Ottoman era survive on the western slopes and the northwestern spur, oriented toward Istanbul.

Ankara saw its last major military action in 1402, when the great Turkic conqueror Tamerlane (Timur) besieged the city to draw out the Ottoman armies from the west. In the famous battle of Ankara, which took place on the plain near today's Esenboğa airport, Tamerlane's forces smashed the Ottomans and captured Sultan Bayezit I (who died in an iron cage, as Christopher Marlowe's play *Tamburlaine the Great* has it). It took the Ottomans fifty years to regroup. They then expanded into eastern Europe, conquered Constantinople, gained control of Anatolia, and took Syria and Egypt—so that, aside from some internal struggles, Ankara was free to prosper in its position along the main east–west caravan route. Walls built around the Ottoman town—perhaps in the 17th century by, or in defense against, a local brigand who held the city for a year—were restored and mapped in the 19th century but do not survive today.

According to the census of 1522, Ankara contained more than 2,200 houses (180 of them in the citadel), of which more than 2,000 belonged to Muslims, about 120 to Christians, and nearly 30 to Jews. From this the population can be estimated at between 10,000 and 12,000. The 17th-century Ottoman traveller Evliya Çelebi described Ankara as a city of white stone, with a total of nearly 7,000 houses. He also recorded that many of the people of Ankara were Turkmen and that the city's few Greeks were outnumbered by Armenians and Jewish residents. The surrounding plains produced excellent cereals, fruit, and livestock in abundance, and there were well-developed local industries in leather, *pastırma* (cured beef), wine, and dried fruit.

By far Ankara's most important industry was the famous Angora goat, which took its name from the city. Its hair (*tiftik,* or mohair) was highly praised as being "white as milk and soft as silk." Processed and worked into yarn in the city and surrounding towns, it was dyed and woven into a cloth called *sof* or *şalı,* which became the major source of income for the town. The best Ankara cloth was sent to the Ottoman court, while the rest went by caravan to the markets of Istanbul and İzmir and found a growing market in Egypt and Europe. The city was also known as the center of production of a yellow dye made from buckthorn.

During the 19th century the mohair industry in Ankara declined because of a decrease in domestic demand, competition from producers in Kashmir and Iran, the development of mechanized looms in Europe, overbreeding of the local goats, government restrictions, and successful breeding abroad. Consequently, the price of Ankara mohair fell by 80 percent at the beginning of the 20th century, when only a few looms remained in the area (near Ayas, where socks and mittens are still knitted from hand-spun mohair). In addition, production of the local buckthorn dye virtually disappeared in the face of competition from European synthetic dyes.

With the decline of the mohair trade Ankara soon stagnated, even though it remained one of the most populous towns in Anatolia. Houses constructed of sun-dried brick fell into disrepair, and neighborhoods that succumbed to fire were not rebuilt. Furthermore, a great malarial swamp to the west forced a large part of the population to retire to the vineyards and orchards in the surrounding hills during the summer months. (Ironically, although the swamp has long since been drained, attempts to escape Ankara's winter smog have led to the modern redevelopment of these same areas.)

The city's rejuvenation began after World War I, when Mustafa Kemal, later to become Atatürk, made Ankara the headquarters of Turkish nationalist forces during the War of Independence. While the victorious Western allies attempted to apportion the defeated Ottoman Empire, whose sultan in Istanbul offered no resistance, this young general, hero of the Gallipoli Campaign, led the Turkish forces in Anatolia to drive out the British, Italians, French, and Greeks. The citizens of Ankara supported the cause even during the most difficult days of the war. Ultimately, their city became the capital of the new Republic of Turkey, symbolizing the country's break with the Ottoman past. This isolated, undeveloped provincial town—which in the early 1920s had no sewer system, sidewalks, or street lighting and contained fewer than 30,000 inhabitants—grew quickly into a modern city marked by Atatürk's indelible spirit. In 1924 initial efforts for the new capital focused on cutting a few streets and squares into the existing urban fabric and designating a government sector in the open area to the west between the commercial district and the train station on the Baghdad Railway, which ran south of town. These now-older areas together constitute the district of Ulus. Housing for bureaucrats was planned for the area beyond the railroad tracks in the former swamp.

Ankara's principal urban plan, adopted in 1932 at the beginning of the Republican era, sought to preserve the integrity of the old city while laying out new districts (called Yenişehir, "New City) for government, commerce, industry, and culture. A system of broad boulevards was constructed, and new residential quarters of individual homes and garden apartments arose. But the planners underestimated the city's potential for growth: The original plan foresaw a population of only 300,000 and was obsolete by World War II. It was finally revised in 1954, but the city's expansion continued to outstrip even the new planners' vision. An original three-story limit on new buildings was rescinded, and large commercial structures and apartment blocks began everywhere to eliminate the pleasant Republican-era garden residences (a few do survive as restaurants). This second generation of planners predicted that the city's population would peak at a million and a half.

Today the population has climbed to more than three million, and the continuing rapid growth puts enormous pressure on the city. Among the casualties of development have been the Ottoman-era summer houses, with their vineyards and orchards, that used to dot the surrounding hills.

After a period of neglect during the political unrest in Turkey during the 1970s, and since the military coup of 1980 and the restoration of civilian rule in the mid-1980s, Ankara has enjoyed an economic boom, with new hotels, shopping centers, restaurants, and parks springing up throughout the city. This has continued into the 1990s despite the negative economic impact of the Gulf War. In fact, Murat Karayalçın, Ankara's mayor since 1989, is investing $3 billion in Ankara's infrastructure to upgrade the city for the 21st century.

Ankara's inhabitants have long complained of living in a gigantic construction site. Atatürk's biographer, Lord Kinross, reports that in the early days of the republic, Ankara's harassed mayor told his constituents, "You clamour for roads to be built, but at the same time you don't want dust." Today the city's residents demand a solution to the traffic jams and winter smog, but they, like their forbears, bewail the dust and disruption caused by the recent installation of natural-gas pipelines (blessedly reducing wintertime pollution caused by the burning of soft coal) and the construction of the city's first subway line. This subway line won't be completed for another two years or so and presently strangles the city center. It, plus innumerable water, road, and park projects produce a situation that's very much in flux.

Why visit Ankara? Until recently, it has been relatively neglected by tourists, perhaps in part because of the Turks' own negative bias. While the city is not favored by exceptional natural beauty or by the more glamorous ruins and exotic monuments found elsewhere in Turkey, its combination of historical sites and museums and its particular mix of European and Middle Eastern elements make it an especially good place to get an introduction to Turkey.

Ankara's inland location and high elevation (3,000 to 3,500 feet) make for cold, damp winters. (The winter of 1991–1992 was particularly harsh, with nearly three months of subfreezing temperatures.) In foggy conditions, vehicle emissions trapped by the semicircle of hills around the city may still produce some smog. But the summers are warm and dry, with low humidity and pleasantly cool evenings, and the fall is usually a delightful Indian summer, or *pastırma mevsimi* (season for curing pastırma), as the Turks say.

AROUND IN ANKARA

Ankara's Esenboğa airport lies almost 30 km (19 miles) northeast of the city. As you head into town you pass through an open plain and travel over the rim of hills that surrounds the city, where you encounter the outlying *gecekondu* districts (where villages of "overnight houses" have been thrown together by new arrivals from the countryside).

Crossing the Konya–Samsun "ring road" you enter the city proper, passing through urban neighborhoods of three- and four-story apartment blocks built to cope with the rapid increase in population after World War II, and come to a new cloverleaf intersection at what was once the outer gate (Dişkapı, now Yıldırımbayezit Meydanı) at the north end of the old, formerly walled city. Bentderesi Caddesi, to the left, follows the bed of the Hatip Çayı in the great ravine between Ankara's hills. Continuing straight (south) on Çankırı Caddesi you skirt the spur on the northwestern edge of the old city to arrive at Ulus Meydanı, the main intersection near the former Istanbul gate. The Roman monuments are just to the north, and the citadel (called the Hisar, or Kale), which you will glimpse on the hill to the east, crowns the old city above. The district of Ulus encompasses the old city and its western flank, where Ankara's first modern development took place in the decade following World War I.

From Ulus Meydanı and the old downtown of the National- ist and Republican eras, Atatürk Bulvarı, Ankara's main north– south artery, follows the line of the now-gone Ottoman walls, running the length of Ulus along the base of the hill where 20th-century construction begins its invasion of the old city above. The old walls once circled east around the south end of the hill where Ankara and Hacettepe universities stand today. At this point Atatürk Bulvarı continues south, passing under the train tracks and east–west Cemal Gürsel Caddesi, and runs through the modern core of the new city, the down- town Yenişehir/Kızılay (now partly choked off by metro con- struction) and uptown Kavaklıdere districts, to end after four miles in the southern heights of Çankaya, where Atatürk established his residence. Here are the newer public build- ings, the smart shops, and the finer restaurants and hotels. For the purpose of touring, we have divided the city into two parts, old Ankara (i.e., the part of the city that existed prior to 1923; located entirely in Ulus) and modern Ankara (the capi- tal of the Republic, which lies both in Ulus and in the newer sections to the south).

Museums in Ankara are generally open from 8:30 or 9:00 A.M. to 5:00 or 5:30 P.M. A few are closed for lunch, and most museums are closed on Mondays. In general, schedules do not change from summer to winter. Mosques can be visited before or after midday and midafternoon prayer. (Check with your hotel for exact times.) At other times you may have to inquire to find the person with the key, who is not always available.

Museum of
Anatolian Civilizations

If you like to keep your history straight, it is recommended that you begin your stay in Ankara with a full-day tour to the Hattic and Hittite sites at Alacahöyük and Hattuşaş. On the second day make the four- or five-hour round trip to the Phrygian site of Gordion (all three are discussed under Day Trips from Ankara, below). On the day you go to Gordion you'll have an hour or two to spare in Ankara in the morning or afternoon—time enough to see Ankara's **Museum of Ana- tolian Civilizations** (open 8:30 A.M. to 5:30 P.M., except Mon- days). If you have only one day in Ankara, you'll want to include a visit to this museum as part of a tour of the old city (see below).

Possibly the city's greatest attraction, this museum contains the best of the preclassical finds from all over Anatolia, including Hattuşaş and Gordion. (It was originally established by Atatürk as the "Hittite Museum" because of the importance of these materials.) The museum, housed in a restored 15th-century Ottoman *bedesten* that was once Ankara's main covered bazaar, is located near the citadel on Kadife Sokak; to get there from Ulus Meydanı, take Hisarparkı Caddesi to the top of the hill. The han adjacent to the museum to the north once contained lodgings and storage depots for caravan merchants; it now provides offices, laboratories, and storage rooms for the museum.

The museum's collection of artifacts is arranged chronologically, going counterclockwise around the perimeter of the bedesten, where the merchants' stalls were originally located (a few of these at the end have been preserved). A central, multidomed hall also provides exhibition space. A map at the entrance shows the locations of the 57 archaeological excavations in Anatolia—ranging from Paleolithic through Roman sites—from which the museum's priceless holdings were collected. Highlights in the first section include finds from one of the earliest known major urban settlements, Neolithic Çatalhöyük (sanctuary room, wall paintings, and mother goddess statuettes); the Chalcolithic site of Hacılar (fine zoomorphic and painted pottery); and the Early Bronze Age site of Alacahöyük (exquisite Hattic royal tomb treasures and ritual items). In the rear section are finds from Kültepe, where there was an Assyrian trading colony of the Middle Bronze Age (cuneiform tablets and the earliest fine wheel-thrown pottery), as well as the Late Bronze Age Hittite collection (large decorative pottery vessels, cuneiform and hieroglyphic stone seals, clay tablets, a monolith with Late Hittite hieroglyphics, and a unique bronze treaty-tablet found in 1986). From here you should retrace your steps to enter the one-time bedesten's large central hall, which is filled with Bronze Age and Iron Age (Late Hittite, or Neo-Hittite) monumental stone orthostats, carved with reliefs, and large statues. (One of the finest of the relief figures—from the King's Gate at Hattuşaş—stands outside the south door in the first section.)

In the last section of the museum are finds from Gordion, including Phrygian tomb treasures (bronze vessels, decorative pottery, and exquisite wood marquetry); a rich collection of Urartian ivory and metalwork (the Urartians exported caldrons to the Etruscans, Greeks, and Phrygians); and coins—from the most ancient (Lydian electrum pieces) up through the medieval period. There are a few classical items as well.

The museum also has a snack bar, rest rooms, and a small gift-and-book shop. The rose garden in front, a pleasant spot to rest, also contains large pottery and stone artifacts.

THE OLD CITY

The Roman, Byzantine, Seljuk, and Ottoman sights in the old city can best be seen in a full-day tour. If you have only half a day you can still see something from each period by visiting the Roman temple, the citadel, and the Aslanhane Camii, with a stroll through the old bazaar area in upper Samanpazarı. This can be supplemented by a visit to the Museum of Anatolian Civilizations, lunch in one of the restored houses in the citadel, and a last stop at the Ethnographic Museum, which makes a nice transition to a quick tour of the modern city (see below).

Ancient Ankara

A full-day tour of the old city can begin with the Roman bath and gymnasium complex known as **Roma Hamamı**, north of Ulus Meydanı on Çankırı Caddesi. The baths were excavated after their foundations were discovered in 1926 when ground was broken for the construction of new government buildings; subsequent excavations also unearthed Phrygian finds. The square exercise ground outlined by the foundations of the *palaestra*'s portico is now used as a depository for many Roman and medieval carved-stone fragments found around the city, including Roman milestones from the network of roads that radiated from Ankara.

The excavated foundations of the large baths on the west side of the *palaestra* include the standard *frigidarium* (with pool) and a very large *tepedarium* and *caldarium,* recognizable by the extensive system of tunnels and hypocausts that allowed hot air to circulate below the floors. Inscriptions and coins found at the site indicate that the baths were built under the emperor Caracalla—attesting to the city's prosperity in the early third century—and that they were used and restored over the next 500 years.

From the baths you can walk up to Ankara's Roman temple following new signs on a tourist walk via Hükümet square, where stands a 45-foot column with capital thought to have been erected in A.D. 362 on the occasion of a visit of the emperor Julian the Apostate. Moved from its original site nearby, it is known locally as **Belkis Minaresi** (Minaret of the Queen of Sheba) and sports a stork's nest whose residents return each year to raise a family. Proceed to the temple by following the signs off Hükümet Caddesi.

On the knoll of the spur at the base of the citadel, next to the mosque of Hacı Bayram, stand the remains of the **temple of Rome and Augustus** (open daily, 9:00 A.M. to 5:00 P.M.). The space in front of the mosque and temple is being transformed into a kind of plaza mall, and minibus traffic has, mercifully, been rerouted. The temple area is enclosed by a fence. A guard in a kiosk at the gate to the left provides tickets and access to a weed-choked jumble of blocks. The moderate-size sanctuary is a roofless shell fronted by a portal carved with classical decoration; it is now encased in scaffolding.

Indeed, little more than the cella walls of the temple remain, yet chiseled on them is the most important Roman inscription surviving from antiquity, preserving one of the greatest literary treasures of the classical world. Inscribed here is the most complete copy of Emperor Augustus's auto-biographical account of his deeds and accomplishments, the *Res Gestae*. Added to the building after the emperor's death in A.D. 14, this is a priceless source for the history of the early Roman Empire. The official Latin version is carved on the inner walls of the front porch, beginning high on the left side, in large letters, "RERUM GESTARUM DIVI AUGUSTI, QUIBUS ORBEM TERRARUM IMPERIO POPULI ROMANI SUBIECIT . . ." ("The achievements of the divine Augustus by which he brought the world under the rule of the Roman people . . ."). Some of the nearly 3,000-word text is lost due to deterioration of the stone, but, fortunately, around to the right and low on the exterior south wall is a Greek vernacular paraphrase carved for the benefit of the local populace of the day.

These inscriptions, well known to classicists as the *Monumentum Ancyranum,* together with the help supplied by two other fragments found elsewhere in Anatolia (one of which now lies encased in slabs stacked inside the temple), have enabled modern scholars to piece together a nearly complete rendition of the original text, which initially stood before the emperor's tomb in Rome, inscribed on bronze tablets. Ghislain de Busbecq, the Hapsburg ambassador to the Ottoman court, discovered the *Res Gestae* on the Ankara temple in 1555. William Hamilton, secretary of the British Geological Society, transcribed the Greek version during the first half of the 19th century after obtaining permission to enter—and even to demolish—some of the houses that had been built up around the south wall, obscuring the inscription.

With all the attention devoted to the inscriptions, understanding of the actual structure itself has been confused. Excavations now show that the temple originally consisted of a sanctuary (cella) with a front porch (*pronaos*) having four columns and a back porch (*opisthodomos*) with two columns, apparently in the Corinthian order. The actual date of the building is unknown, but its decoration points to the early part of Augustus's reign, most probably soon after he annexed Galatia in 25 B.C. Because the temple faces west, as did temples for the Anatolian fertility goddess Cybele, it may have replaced an earlier sanctuary (stones of the Phyrigian god Men were also found in the neighborhood) or have been initially intended for her. In any case, according to a Greek inscription on the front of the arms of the porch, it came to be dedicated to the goddess Roma (the spirit of the empire) and the emperor. Sometime in the second century an outer colonnade was added, possibly in the Ionic order, judging from the image of the temple on coins.

The walls of the sanctuary and front porch may owe their survival in part to the inscriptions themselves and to the continued use of the building for religious purposes. The Byzantines converted the temple to a church by removing the wall separating the cella from the *opisthodomos,* adding an apse of red and white tufa blocks, and cutting windows high in the cella wall. Early in the Ottoman period, Hacı Bayram Veli (d. 1420), a local religious figure and founder of the Bayramıyya religious fraternity, constructed a mosque whose southeastern corner directly abuts the north side of the *pronaos.* At this time the temple was transformed into a *medrese* (school of Islamic law) with ten cells for the occupants, as described by Busbecq's travelling companion in 1555. Early in the 19th century part of the cella wall was taken to build a bath. Efforts are now underway to conserve the temple and its inscriptions, which have suffered from the effects of air pollution and vibration damage caused by heavy vehicular traffic nearby.

Hacı Bayram's mausoleum, a square building supporting the mosque's minaret, is built against the south exterior wall of the mosque, where it would receive the double blessing of prayers directed toward Mecca and the religious studies of medrese classes very likely held in the adjacent *pronaos.* The reuse of ancient stones in the walls exemplifies medieval recycling. The mosque, altered by 18th- and 20th-century restorations, remains important in the life of the local community: Newlyweds come for blessing after the civil marriage ceremony, and last rites for the deceased are performed here.

The Citadel Area

From a small park area across the street you'll get a fine view of the ravine that gave the city its name and the citadel high above. This is a good perspective from which to distinguish the four levels of fortification: the upper, original inner citadel proper, enclosed by walls with pointed towers; the lower outer walls, added later by the Byzantines to protect the west and south slopes; then the Seljuk Turkish–period bastions protecting the steep slope at the north end; and, at the highest point, the Seljuk keep (Akkale), atop which flies the Turkish flag.

From the temple, walk or take a taxi up to the **citadel**, which has recently been the scene of a good deal of renovation. You might wish to stop on Hisarparkı Caddesi, a block below the lower walls of the citadel, to view on the left the current excavations of the recently discovered **Roman odeon**, or theater, which faced the temple, on the hill opposite. The way up by taxi skirts the late outer walls with their square towers and, at the top, follows Kadife Sokak past the Museum of Anatolian Civilizations. (Gözcü Sokak to the right leads directly up to the outer citadel's south gate, Hisar Kapı, at the top of the bazaars.) Continue straight through a break in the outer fortifications. To the left below, İnönü (formerly Hisar) Parkı fills the area of an old Christian quarter destroyed in a great fire after World War I. The remains of this old quarter of Dış Hisar (Outer Citadel) climb the slope to the right above, followed by the walls of the inner citadel proper, pierced by a western gate (Genç Kapısı). Alternately, a steep walk up from Hisarparkı Caddesi by way of steps leads from the lower walls up through the park to Genç Kapısı. Set among the trees near the top of the park is a new restaurant, **Ankara Evi**, a modern version of a traditional residence. The restaurant offers fine terrace dining plus a view. In the evening, horse-drawn carriages (*faytons*) bring diners from the Kadife Sokak parking area.

The original Galatian citadel fortifications here were restored by the Romans, but what we see today is a reconstruction by the Byzantines, who added the outer walls and made various restorations (including a major rebuilding in the tenth century following the citadel's destruction by Arab forces). The citadel was held briefly by the initial wave of Turks in 1073 and then by Crusader forces for the Byzantines

25 years later, before finally falling to the Turks by the mid-12th century. The impressive walls of the Byzantine citadel (İç Kale or İç Hisar, meaning "Inner Citadel" or "Inner Fort") are defended by massive pentagonal towers that jut out like the prows of ships. These were built according to the theories of ancient military strategists, who advocated such obtuse angles to resist the missiles of siege warfare. The lower portion of the "recycled" walls is constructed largely of ancient material—marble blocks, architectural fragments, columns, and capitals—while the upper portion consists of standard Byzantine masonry, which uses alternating brick-and stonework. The western gate, which faced the city, displays some decorative use of stonework, but it cannot compare with the original main gate on the south. After passing up through the western gate, take the upper lane to the left, which passes between the old houses to come out opposite an old-fashioned fire station. From the open area and small park to the left at the north rim of the fortifications you can look up a lane to the right to see the inner keep (now closed) built by the Seljuks, and, below, the outerworks they added to the northern slopes in a futile attempt to resist the Mongols. Here are said to lie the remains of a Byzantine tunnel that once led down to the Hatip Çayı's ancient waterworks (hence Bentderesi, "stream with barrage"). Atop the high hill (Altındağ, meaning "Mount Gold") across the ravine once stood the tomb of some legendary figure. Squatters' *gecekondu*s now cover the slopes. The fine view west over Ulus below encompasses the temple, surrounded by old wooden houses, the artificial lake and fountain of Gençlik Parkı, and, off to the left, set on a hill, in the western part of the new city, the mausoleum of Atatürk.

Now follow the paved lane (İç Kale, or İç Hisar, Sokak) in front of the fire station south through the **old quarter** of mud-brick houses, some plastered and brightly painted, where life follows traditional patterns. Women crochet in their doorways while chatting with neighbors, boys play soccer wherever they can, and young girls fill water containers at the local fountain. In 1885, Thomas Stevens, in his *Around the World on a Bicycle,* described passing through Ankara's narrow and twisted lanes. Swarms of donkeys burdened with jars endlessly transported water up the steep incline of crooked, stony streets from the stream at the foot of the hill to supply the community clustered about the fortress. Although Stevens found Ankara forlorn, he noted that he liked the people, who smothered him with kindness.

Just before the gate in the south wall of the İç Kale, steps up the slope to the left allow you to explore the circular battlements of the southeastern bastion (Şark Kalesi) above, which buttressed this corner of the original fortifications and was later expanded when the outer wall was added. A somewhat hazardous climb atop the unrestored walls affords a splendid 360-degree view. (There have been plans to turn this into a *gazino* —i.e., an outdoor refreshment area.) Below to the south, where the medieval Turkish quarter developed, you can see the Aslanhane Camii and the bazaars.

Tucked against the wall to the right of the south gate is the city's oldest mosque, the **Alaettin Camii**. This small mosque is significant for its dynastic associations, which are unique in Ankara. It is named for the great 13th-century Seljuk sultan Alaettin Keykubat I; however, it is not known to what degree he was actually responsible for the original structure. The recently restored building sits above sloping ground on a high foundation, which, as there is a fountain below, may well contain a cistern. The façade is distinguished by the odd reuse of old marble columns in its porch and an early cylindrical brick minaret.

Inside the simple mosque are a wooden balcony for women that's reached from stairs in the minaret, some fine old weavings in the layers of carpets on the floor, and a beautiful wooden marquetry *minber* (pulpit) that is signed by the artist and dated 594 A.H. (A.D. 1197) in the name of the Seljuk prince Mesut. Did Mesut, who held Ankara as a principality when his father divided the Seljuk realm among his sons, establish a Friday mosque here, commissioning this *minber* from whose steps the *imam* (community prayer leader) would have proclaimed Mesut's authority by pronouncing the weekly sermon in his name at communal Friday noon prayer? Perhaps the mosque was not yet completed when Mesut and his sons were killed four years later, after Mesut's older brother finally took Ankara to reunite Seljuk lands under one sultan (he died only three days later, himself). The name of a third brother, and the next sultan, Keyhusrev (Kay-Khusraw), appears on a wooden *maksure* (royal prayer screen) from Ankara, probably also from this mosque.

At Keyhusrev's death in 1212, his son Prince Alaettin ('Ala' ad-Din, i.e., Aladdin) held out for a year in the Ankara citadel during the subsequent struggle for succession. Despite his capture, Alaettin eventually became sultan himself in 1219, reigning until 1236, the height of Seljuk rule in Anatolia. Alaettin was a prolific builder—in Ankara he restored the citadel and may have been responsible for the construction of the Akköprü (White Bridge) over the Ankara river (the bridge is best viewed to the north of Istanbul Caddesi about a quarter mile beyond the Samsun–Konya ring road). However, it is not clear if his name is attached to this mosque because he completed its construction or because he and his entourage, Seljuk officials and garrison housed in the citadel, used it for their Friday mosque. The inscriptions over the door only refer to later restorations—one in 1361, shortly after the Ottomans gained control of the city. A *mihrap* niche cut into the fortress wall and numerous marble pieces unearthed in the small side-yard cemetery by the gate raise more questions about the architectural history of this site.

The İç Kale's great south gate (Zindan Kapı, "Prison Gate") comprises a large defensive tower with inner portal and outer portal constructed at right angles. This prevented ramming of the inner portal, forced attackers to approach with their unshielded right sides exposed to the defenders, and, if they broke through the outer portal (Parmak Kapı, "Barred Gate"), trapped the attackers in a confined space at the mercy of the defenders. The massive exterior bastions on the south display an especially imaginative reuse of classical stonecarving: a collage of the past, with Greek and Latin inscription fragments, faces, altars, and statuary, as well as numerous crosses to ward off enemies.

One of the finest of the numerous old Ottoman houses inside the citadel area (Kale İçi) to be restored recently stands opposite this bastion. **Kınacılar Evi** (House of the Henna Merchants) has a distinctive façade with a double stairway and an upper balcony with especially fine woodwork. Five rooms upstairs are used for a cozy restaurant. Its Turkish menu lists typical Turkish fare, including *meze,* but also includes some difficult-to-find specialties such as *hünkâr beğendi,* an eggplant-purée dish. On the ground floor a small courtyard is used for a café that serves light meals, omelettes, and sandwiches. The rooms of the lower floor are occupied by the **Eski Sanatlar Çarşısı** (Old Arts Bazaar), a set of small shops where traditional crafts are produced and offered for sale—leatherwork, fine jewelry, imaginative hand-painted pottery, and Turkish miniatures, as well as reproductions of clay and glass artifacts from the Hittite and classical periods. There is also an antiques shop, an outlet of an exclusive clothing boutique, and a delightful wine bar that hosts wine-tasting parties. It opens at 2:00 P.M. daily.

The **Dış Hisar** (Outer Citadel) quarter was inhabited by the well-to-do a century ago. The central lane (here Kale

Kapısı Sokak) continues to the outer citadel's south gate (Hisar Kapı) past more homes of traditional construction; the slantwise patterns of mud bricks within their wooden frames once would have all been covered with stucco. Upper floors are often cantilevered out over the street in search of light, air, and space. These houses usually have courtyards where daily tasks could be performed in the sunlight and where flowers could be grown and fowl kept. At the end of the lane, inside the Hisar Kapı, is a small new park and, nearby, a number of restored old houses. A lane around to the right takes you to an Ottoman house recently opened as **GESAV Culture House** (Geleneksel El Sanatları Vakfı, closed Mondays). Upstairs, a reception space, nicely furnished and decorated in the Ottoman manner and available for special functions, displays the traditional arrangement of a raised floor with cushioned benches lining the walls. The next room houses an outlet of the Turkish Ministry of Tourism's store, **Döşim**, which sells fine fabrics, pottery, and musical instruments. There is also a small room set aside displaying a fine *oya* (needlework edging) collection. Downstairs you can have Turkish coffee (*Türk kahvesi*) in the courtyard café.

If you return a few steps to the park, the left fork leads down to less rigorous restorations housing the picturesque restaurant **Zenger Paşa**, where you can dine on simple fare in a charming setting with a lovely view. The restaurant features local women in traditional garb making *bazlama* (country bread) and performances of the Turkish popular music known as "Arabesque." It has become an "in" spot for young Turks. Farther on, left then right, at Berrak Sokak 9, a similar, slightly more refined restaurant, **Boyacızade Konağı**, features live music played on a *kanun,* a dulcimer-like instrument, and a pleasant garden café around a fountain. Both can also be reached from off Gözcü Sokak or Kadife Sokak, a short walk from the Museum of Anatolian Civilizations.

Hisar Kapı (sometimes called Kale Kapısı), now the main gate to the citadel, bears an Ilkhanid inscription of 1330 (it's in Persian and concerns Mongol taxes). The gate was restored during the Ottoman period with an arch of black and white stones. A 19th-century clock tower (Saat Kulesi) atop one of the bastions gave the street in front its old name (Saat Kulesi Sokak), but the open area here is known as **Atpazarı Meydanı** (Horse Market Square). Today there is a small open-air market of dried foodstuffs: sacks filled with dried lentils, beans, and grains and all sorts of enticing foods to munch on, such as dried figs, dates, and apricots; mulberries; pumpkin and sunflower seeds; nuts; and chickpeas. The restoration in and around the citadel area has attracted new shops to the streets running from Atpazarı west down to the Museum of Anatolian Civilizations and east down around to the Aslanhane Camii and the old bazaar area.

Old Bazaar Area

The most interesting descent into the bazaar follows the steep cobbled lane called Atpazarı Yokuşu, on the south side of the Atpazarı Meydanı. Here on the right there are two old Ottoman hans. **Çengel Han**, the one on the left, with an old wooden door (note the smaller door cut into it), is a two-story stone-and-brick structure with arches around a courtyard where sheepskins are treated (the smell can be pretty ripe). Next door is the less interesting mud-brick Çukur Han, with columns supporting the arcades around its courtyard.

As you enter the *yokuş* (steeply graded street) you'll see beads and bird cages, flutes, spoons, and spices—a hint of things to come. At this point a detour via the first lane to the left leads to the **Aslanhane Camii** (or Arslanhane Camii; both variants mean "Mosque of the House of Lions"), known officially as the **Ahi Şerafettin Camii**, Ankara's finest Seljuk monument. The mosque faces uphill along Can Sokak curving down from Atpazarı. It served as the Friday mosque for this quarter, which developed during the Seljuk period outside the citadel's south gate in the direction of Konya and inner Anatolia. The open area in front of the mosque formed a kind of forecourt where a number of (possibly) Roman stone lions stood, giving the mosque its popular name. Two of these lions are now sticking out of the wall next to the steps leading up to the entry of an undistinguished building to the left. If open, it leads into an inner courtyard containing the tomb of Ahi Şerafettin and his father. Father and son were leaders of the quasi-religious and civic fraternal society of the city's merchants and tradesmen that governed local affairs as Seljuk authority waned under the Mongols. The small, square tomb structure incorporates a motley admixture of recycled marble and is topped by a stone-and-brick drum supporting a pyramidal roof. The latter, typical of Seljuk tombs (*türbe*s or *gümbet*s), was actually added in 1947 to replace an incongruous wooden roof of uncertain age. An Arabic inscription over the south window of the tomb refers to an *imaret* (a "soup kitchen," that is, a benevolent foundation for the indigent) established in association with the tomb. The father's cenotaph is still inside (the deceased would have been placed in a crypt below), but the finely carved wooden cenotaph of Ahi Şerafettin is now in the Ethnographic Museum. Ahi Şerafettin died in 1350, shortly before the Ottomans annexed the city.

The mosque itself has undergone a face lift and may still be covered with scaffolding. Most of the local andesite stone exterior was once masked by the the bazaars, leaving only the grand entryway visible. One of the last mosques in the High Seljuk style, its brick minaret with inset glazed tiles stands atop an unusual large stone plinth (also incorporating recycled marble fragments) beside a handsome marble stalactite-corbeled portal set slightly left of the north axis. This portal, which may have been left unfinished, bears no dedicatory inscription. It is primarily an architectural formality since, because of the slope, it leads into the second-floor gallery reserved for women. The ablution facilities are down below, and the door on the west side is the functional entry (note the 15th-century ceramic pieces set in above the door).

The mosque's cool, peaceful, two-story interior has a wooden construction that survives in a few early Turkish mosques. "Tree-trunk" columns incongruously sporting classical stone bases and capitals support an intricate wood-beam ceiling. The *mihrap* on the south wall is an excellent example of 13th-century carved and molded plaster with turquoise blue, black, and yellow glazed and mosaic tilework. The wooden minber, significant because it is signed and dated (1289), is one of the finest examples of this genre of exquisitely carved tongue-and-groove construction, with a geometric star pattern developed during this period. It was commissioned under one of the last Seljuk sultans by the leader of the fraternal orders, persumably the father of Ahi Şerafettin, who then apparently completed the complex, which took his name. The main floor now has green wall-to-wall carpeting with lines to indicate the rows for prayer, but there is still a selection of colorful carpets and kilims upstairs. These pieces, traditionally donated to the mosque by the weaver, are a compendium of local rug styles.

Now, using the lane opposite the mosque, return to **Atpazarı Yokuşu**, perhaps the most fascinating street in Ankara. This pedestrian way is lined with small hardware and spice shops and stands catering to Ankaralıs' traditional needs and to foreigners seeking a bit of exotica. Among myriad items you'll find wooden utensils (look for the fine, smooth, hand-carved boxwood spoons); a plethora of spices, including cinnamon (sticks or powder), saffron (a bargain by the gram), and henna (a green powder); sheepskins; wool (raw and spun); heavy felt shepherds' cloaks; seersucker sheeting by the bolt; regional patterned bath wraps (*peştemals*), which when cut in two serve as head coverings; hand-blocked table linens and scarves (*yazma*); tools of all kinds, from metal adzes to wooden pitchforks; sieves; protective *nazarlık*-beaded birds for your vehicle and blue-glass amulets in all sizes for warding off the "evil eye"; worry beads (*tesbih*) for reciting the 99 names of God; gum arabic (looking like white larvae soaking in water); chunks of tar; mousetraps; spiked collars for protecting sheepdogs from wolves; ropes; chains; and all-weather shoes made from tires. There's an antiques shop tucked halfway down to the left as well.

This steep lane is also known as Koyunpazarı (Sheep Market) Yokuşu after the small square at the bottom, the hub of the old market area, now lined with a curious combination of traditional shops (some delicatessens selling goat cheeses and *pastırma*) and tourist-oriented gift shops. On the left are a number of basket shops that carry woven, wicker, and wooden items.

The first lane to the right (Salman Sokak), with the 14th-century Ahi Elvan Camii on the corner (take a peak at the wooden interior), leads into "Copper Alley," the **Copper Bazaar** (Bakırcılar Çarşısı), full of big and little shops with old and new copper, brass, and bronze wares (rice pots, plates, "lunchbox" sets, soap holders, cups, Turkish coffee pots, mortars, and more). There are also shops selling various wooden items (coffee boxes and assorted paraphernalia, spinning wheels and weaving accessories, and carvings), and silver and beaded jewelry—both old and reproduction—as well as odd collectibles and carpets and kilims, all mixed in with practical housewares stores selling new aluminum, plastic, glass, and enamelware. There are also recently built public lavatories—much to the relief of tea-drinking shoppers.

Tragically, a devastating fire swept through the Saraçlar Çarşısı and Çırıkçılar Çarşısı (Saddlers Market and Spinners Market) in the summer of 1992, destroying a hundred shops, including some in Copper Alley. The splendid view the fire opened up can't compensate for the loss of the traditional housewares and cloth bazaar (affectionately referred to as "Cloth Alley" by expatriate residents of Ankara).

At this point, decide how to spend the rest of the day: whether to see Ottoman buildings engulfed in 20th-century Ulus off Anafartalar Caddesi or Ulucanlar Caddesi or perhaps to go directly to the Ethnographic Museum off Talat Paşa Caddesi (see Modern Ankara, below).

Down from Koyunpazarı the jarring new City Hall complex occupies what was the original Samanpazarı (Straw Market), which name now applies to the old bazaar area in general. East on Ulucanlar Caddesi at Samsun Sokak, the **Karaca Bey Camii**, built as part of a complex (*külliye*) by Ankara's *beylerbeyi* (governor) from 1440 to 1489, provides an example of a "reverse T" plan mosque, much like the early Ottoman mosques of İznik and Bursa (see Istanbul Environs, above). The domes, which fell in the earthquake of 1892, unfortunately were replaced by a wooden roof. The complex also included the founder's tomb nearby and a fine double bath below on Hamamönü Sokak (Street in Front of the Bath). These baths have been nicely restored (women on the north, men on the south), and are a wonderful place to relax and swap tales or contemplate your navel.

· In the Islamic tradition every town must have a mosque, a market, and a bath. Especially under the Ottomans, baths were elaborate structures hearkening back to their classical ancestors. Each side has a two-story changing area covered with a wooden cupola, an intermediate "cool" room (*soğukluk*), and an interior domed bath hall lined with marble. If you just want to peek, the attendants will lead you into the steamy interior so that you can see what you're missing. Light filters in through the glass bubbles in the dome, illuminating a heated marble platform where clients get scrubbed and massaged. Men wear towels; women may or may not bother with drawers. Along a raised marble ledge around the central room and in side rooms are individual stone basins for washing and rinsing (unless it's a facility at a therapeutic hot spring, a Turkish bath doesn't usually include a pool for submerging). The complete bath ritual costs about $10—a bargain for a bit of paradise.

Farther down Ulucanlar Caddesi is Yeni Cami, a central-domed 16th-century Ottoman mosque of the Sinan school built by another *beylerbey,* Cenabi Ahmet Paşa. The mosque is the prototype for the ubiquitous two-story, domed, cube-shaped mosques now dotting the country.

Alternatively, you can make your way down to Anafartalar Caddesi. The back end of Copper Alley leads into (if it's still passable) Çırıkçılar near the bazaar's original access to the south door of the former *bedesten*. Built by Mehmet the Conqueror's grand vizier, it served as a major emporium in the important international trade in fine textiles. English and Italians were among the merchants who came here seeking local angora stuffs plus silk and cotton fabric coming by caravan from the east. The Museum of Anatolian Civilizations is now housed there; you can reach it by taking the first right as you head down Çıkrıkçılar. This straight descent to lower Ulus proper was probably the Ottoman-period Uzun Çarşı (Long Market), once a covered bazaar. At the bottom it runs into Anafartalar Caddesi, one of the modern streets created in the old town after 1924 and dominated by 20th-century buildings.

Anafartalar Caddesi is lined with jewelry shops glittering with gold—the investment of choice in a traditional society. Prices are set by gold content and weight and the workmanship involved—and are open to bargaining. If you go straight on Anafartalar, up İşiklar Caddesi is the old St. Thérèse church—under the French flag with services in Turkish (on Sundays) while on the left at the next light (Şehit Teğmen Kalmaz Sokak) you can visit the restored Ottoman **Sulu Han**, a two-story commercial structure housing a variety of new shops around two courtyards. Ankara's largest carpet store, **Şark**, located farther down Şehit Teğmen Kalmaz Sokak on the left, has three floors and just about everything in the way of new rugs as well as some older pieces. Şark is a good place to find out what is available on the market—especially if you go on a Saturday afternoon and watch what others are buying.

Across the street from Sulu Han, you can wander up through the **Hal**, the farmers' market, with a mix of plant and pet shops and street vendors. If you continue through the market you'll come out on Hisarparkı Caddesi. Alternatively, you can exit the han through the lower west door and stroll down the narrow lanes of an old quarter to come out on Yenice Sokak near Atatürk Bulvarı. From here you could go a few blocks south on Tavus (a.k.a. Kosova) Sokak to reach the *döner* restaurants in the İtfaiye section of Ulus off Derman Sokak (see Shopping and Dining, below).

If you go left on Anafartalar Caddesi instead, across the street at Birlik Sokak number 8 is the old **synagogue** (open only on the High Holy Days). Continuing on past Denizciler Caddesi, you will see steps on the right that go down to Acıçeşme Sokak. These lead to another of Ankara's old Ottoman baths, aging but authentic, its sign proclaiming "Histrotical [*sic*] Bath" and its domes studded with bubbles of glass. The Merkez Hamamı is another double bath with separate facilities for men and women. If you have the time and the inclination, this is a great place to relax. If not, it's at least worth a look (men enter the door facing the stairs, women through a door down the right side at the back).

A visit to the Ethnographic Museum (see Modern Ankara, below) might be an appropriate finale to this tour of medieval and Ottoman Ankara (follow Anafartalar Caddesi south to cross busy Talatpaşa Caddesi at the Hasırcılar Sokak overpass). Or you can head for the *döner* restaurants in İtfaiye by going south on Denizciler Caddesi.

MODERN ANKARA

The main features of the city built after World War I deserve a full-day tour to be appreciated. If you have only an afternoon, visit the First National Assembly Building in Ulus, which houses the War of Independence Museum, then, in the newer city, Atatürk's mausoleum (Anıt Kabir), with its museum of Atatürk memorabilia, and, if the evening is nice, dine alfresco at Atatürk's Farm or perhaps at a traditional restaurant in Kızılay or at the new Atakule complex in Çankaya. If you have just a little time for shopping you might want to squeeze in a stop at one of the Turkish Ministry of Tourism's outlets in Kızılay, which have a special selection of Turkish handcrafts, museum reproductions, and other items not available elsewhere.

If you have a full day to devote to exploring 20th-century Ankara, visit one or both of the museums in the old parliament buildings for a look at Turkey's modern history, then the Ethnographic Museum and maybe the Fine Arts Museum (stopping afterward for lunch at a *döner* restaurant). Next see Atatürk's mausoleum, and then drive south through the new city up to the heights of Çankaya to take in the view. This could be combined with shopping in Ulus, Kızılay, Kavaklıdere, or the newer districts at the southern end of town, perhaps having tea or cocktails at Atakule in Çankaya.

Ulus

Atatürk's equestrian statue at today's busy Ulus Meydanı recalls his arrival here in 1919 and that it was here that his dream of a new Turkish nation (*ulus* means "nation") began to take shape in the succeeding decade. Many buildings nearby are landmarks of this first Nationalist-period style in which new Western structural designs combined with mock-Ottoman or pseudo-Islamic decoration, an indication of the national identity crisis at the time. Across the traffic circle, wide eaves and arched windows distinguish the First National Assembly Building, now known as the **War of Independence Museum** (Kurtuluş Savaşı Müzesi). Begun in 1917 as a regional center for the Union and Progress party, the building served a short stint as a school before housing the early sessions of the Turkish Grand National Assembly, or parliament. Here, in 1923, after the building's hasty completion by the citizens of Ankara, the National Assembly's first elected deputies ratified the Lausanne treaty establishing Turkey's borders after the War of Independence, and proclaimed their country a republic, with Ankara as its capital. The school desks used by the deputies recall the meager resources of the young nation. The modest displays of photographs and maps transport the visitor back to the stirring era of the Turkish nation's struggle for birth.

Down Cumhuriyet Bulvarı, which leads to the train station and was the street originally designated as "government row," on the right is the Second National Assembly Building, which now houses the **Museum of the Republic** (Cumhuriyet Müzesi; open 9:00 A.M. to 12:30 P.M. and 1:30 to 5:00 P.M., except Mondays, when it is only open in the afternoon). Conceived during its construction as the headquarters for the Republican People's party, the building was deemed more suitable for the National Assembly, which met here from 1925 to 1960. It was subsequently, until 1977, the headquarters of CENTO, the now-defunct Central Treaty Organization established for military defense of the Middle East. Arches and glazed tiles relieve the rustic local-stone façade, which is actually the end of the structure. A second-story loggia served as a tribunal during public rallies in the open courtyard. The interior's elegant woodwork and painted ceiling resemble the decoration in a traditional Turkish *konak* (mansion). The Museum of the Republic presents the dramatic transformation of the country from the Ottoman Empire to the modern Republic of Turkey. A brief look through the museums in the two National Assembly buildings is enough to get a good idea of the Turks' reverence for Atatürk, whose creative spirit and driving personal force produced the metamorphosis of this city and the nation.

Facing the Second National Assembly Building across Cumhuriyet Bulvarı stands its contemporary, the Ankara Palas. Built as the city's first grand hotel, it has been refurbished as a government guest house and reception hall. Despite its nostalgic "Oriental" façade, with towers, cupola, and ornate portal, when it opened in 1927 its Western plumbing, central heating, and electric generator were the height of modernity in a town still dependent on kerosene lamps. For the next 30 years its ballroom, restaurant, and lounge were *the* center of high society. Here, diplomats intrigued, officials maneuvered, and the new elite aped Western fashions.

South of Ulus Meydanı in the commercial district along Atatürk Bulvarı numerous financial institutions were constructed. Opposite the central post office and next to the Central Bank (Merkez Bankası), the flamboyant Agricultural Bank (Ziraat Bankası) also exemplifies early eclectic Nationalist architecture. At the next traffic circle, bordering on İstiklâl Caddesi, is Gençlik Parkı. Built on the site of a former swamp, it is the first and largest of the city's parks. Its boating lake is overlooked by a hall where civil-ceremony marriages are performed. Outdoor eateries border the lake, and behind these is an old-fashioned amusement park. Beyond the park's main entrance on Atatürk Bulvarı is the pink Opera House, the 1930s National Exhibition Hall converted in 1948 to host ballet performances as well as opera. (Performances, from October through May, are traditionally in Turkish; tickets are very reasonably priced but difficult to obtain— ask at your hotel.) Across the street, the elaborate façade of the first Ministry of Foreign Affairs (built 1927; now the Ministry of Customs) displays an arched portico and windows and decorative pediments that are echoed in the design of the Ethnographic and the Painting and Sculpture museums, looking down from the next hill.

At this point Atatürk Bulvarı is crossed over by Talat Paşa Caddesi, which to the east goes up toward Samanpazarı and takes you to the Ethnographic Museum and Painting and Sculpture Museum, both housed in ornate Ottomanesque buildings. The first right off of Talat Paşa onto Türk Ocağı Sokak and then a driveway to the right leads to the museums' front entrances. Two of the last monuments designed in the romantic Nationalist style, which was soon judged inappropriate for buildings of the new republic, the two museums sit strategically between old and new Ankara as if linking the past to the future.

The smaller domed building on the left is the **Ethnographic Musem** (open from 8:30 A.M. to noon and from 1:00 to 5:30 P.M., except Mondays), which features a collection of Anatolian folk art that recaptures the life of times gone by in costumes, embroidery, rugs, kilims, copper, brass and glassware, Sufi religious artifacts, calligraphy, and wooden doors and *minber*s. This charming structure, whose ornamental marble façade is augmented with glazed tile, was also built in 1927 at Mustafa Kemal's direction, as Turkey's first national museum. Lately, a traditional Turkish nomadic "yurt" (*topak evi*) has been set up out front.

Next door, the **Painting and Sculpture Museum** (Resim ve Heykel Müzesi; same hours as the Ethnographic Museum), also dates from 1927 and was originally built for the Türk Ocağı (literally, "Turkish Hearth"), a national center for cultural activities that Atatürk supervised to promote European and new Turkish theatrical, literary, and plastic arts. The Turkish Historical Society and Turkish Language Association founded by him were also first located here. After 1931 the building was used as the Ankara People's House—a political/cultural center for inculcating the ideals of the Kemalist revolution. Today it houses a small but interesting collection of late 19th-century Romantic and Impressionist paintings of genre scenes by Turkish artists, many of whom studied in France, as well as Turkish art of the 20th century. Downstairs a shop sells cards and posters. (Now might be the time to stop for lunch at a *döner* restaurant in Itfaiye, across Talat Paşa Caddesi.)

Talat Paşa Caddesi west of Atatürk Bulvarı passes on the left the Ankara Symphony concert hall and the train station (Gar). Built in the 1930s, these buildings typify the drab, functional Modernist architecture introduced during the depression years. The official buildings of the new city constructed in the decade before World War II are plagued by unadorned massive blocks with strong horizontal and vertical lines and impractical flat roofs relieved only occasionally by rounded elements. Before the intersection of Talat Paşa and Kâzim Karabekir, a pagoda memorializes the Turkish soldiers who fought and died in the Korean War. (Beyond, on the left, is the main intercity bus station—the former Otogar, now termed A.S.O.T.—which will be moving this year to Soğutözü; see the Getting Around section, below.) A left here, at Kâzım Karabekir Caddesi, leads through Tandoğan Meydanı to Anıt Caddesi and Anıtkabir, Atatürk's mausoleum.

Atatürk's mausoleum stands surrounded by a park atop Rasattepe (Observatory Hill), on the site of a Phrygian necropolis where several tumuli were unearthed. Approached by a long promenade flanked by stone lions, this monumental modern temple stands before a grand esplanade. Special military guards stand stiffly at attention and ensure proper etiquette. The complex was built between 1944 and 1953 and is the grandest example of an all-too-brief second revival of interest in a national architecture. During neutral Turkey's isolation in World War II, indigenous inspiration was sought in the diverse cultural roots of Anatolia's long past. Besides materials from all over Turkey and decoration from many periods, new forms were introduced in bas relief and statuary. Atatürk's cenotaph is a 40-ton marble monolith where officials and visiting dignitaries come to lay wreaths. At one side is a museum devoted to Atatürk's life and times; Atatürk's collection of automobiles is displayed nearby.

This impressive monument is a fitting tribute to Atatürk, who was truly the Father of His Country, having saved it from foreign domination and then molded it into a modern nation-state. After the military victories of the War of Independence he led his countrymen in the great task of transforming the devastated heartland of the Ottoman Empire into the demo-cratic, secular Republic of Turkey. The reforms initiated by Atatürk encompassed all aspects of society, from changing the system of government and establishing equal rights for women to the adoption of the Latin alphabet for written Turkish and of Sunday as the official day of rest.

Directly opposite Atatürk's tomb is the cenotaph of his prime minister, İsmet İnönü, who succeeded him as presi-dent. On the southeastern side, stairs lead down to a small area providing a view out over the old and new sections of the city. (Light refreshments are available here, and there are rest rooms as well.) In summer the mausoleum is open daily from 10:00 A.M. to 5:00 P.M.; in winter it closes at 4:00 P.M. It puts on sound-and-light performances on summer evenings.

Return to Atatürk Bulvarı via Gazi Mustafa Kemal Bulvarı, a major bus route lined with aging nightclubs (*gazinos*) and wedding parlors (*doğun salonus*). Past Maltepe Camii, until recently the new city's main mosque, you'll find the Ministry of Tourism's bureau and shop, on the right at number 33.

Yenişehir and South

South of Talat Paşa Caddesi, Atatürk Bulvarı passes through the district of **Sıhhiye**, where various institutions built largely during the 1930s create an interlude between the older and newer sections of the city. A set of overpasses carries the rail lines and a crosstown express route, Celâl Bayar Bulvarı, which continues to the east as Cemal Gürsel Caddesi, essentially divides the city in half. Beyond is Abdi İpekçi Parkı and Sıhhiye's Lozan Meydanı traffic circle, where a statue of three stags in the Hattic "sun" symbol heralds the beginning of Yenişehir (New City), the official name for modern Ankara's downtown. This square may still be closed for the construction of the metro line under Atatürk Bulvarı.

From here Atatürk Bulvarı passes through the usually crowded central shopping district, with many small shops located in multistory *çarşı*s or *pasaje*s (arcades), the modern incarnation of a covered bazaar. (A shopping and restaurant tour of this area is provided below.) The urban plan of 1932 had maintained Ulus as the commercial center, reserving Yenişehir primarily for official structures and housing for bureaucrats. But in the liberalism of the 1950s the city's economic center shifted here.

The next traffic circle, Kızılay, at the heart of the city, has been its busiest intersection. Construction on the main subway terminal below it at the juncture of the metro and the light rail (AnkaRay, under construction along Ziya Gökalp Caddesi and Gazi Mustafa Kemal Bulvarı) closed the square last year, seriously disrupting traffic and downtown commercial life.

"Kızılay," a term that has now virtually replaced "Yenişehir" as the popular name for this central area of the new city, means "Red Crescent," the Turkish equivalent of the Red Cross, whose headquarters was once located here. At the southeast corner rises Turkey's first office skyscraper, marking the country's adoption in the 1950s of the rational, prismatic International style based on rectangles and squares and increased use of glass curtain walls. A prominent landmark, the building's lower floors house GİMA, the city's first modern department store. Some of the city's more exclusive shops occupy the next block. Now that Kızılay circle has reopened, the main stops for buses going south are across Atatürk Bulvarı alongside Güven Parkı.

The district of government ministries (Bakanlıklar) begins before the next traffic circle, beyond which the **Grand National Assembly**, the new parliament building, constructed between 1939 and 1960, sits above İsmet İnönü Bulvarı surrounded by gardens. Its simple monumental horizontal design retains the spirit of the unpretentious functional cubist period, harmonizing with the other official buildings of this period nearby. A left turn up Akay Yokuşu (Esat Caddesi) and another left at the top takes you to the city's newest and largest mosque, Kocatepe Camii. Built in the classical Ottoman style after a more modern and controversial plan was found unacceptable by religious conservatives, the mosque was finally finished in 1987 after 20 years of construction. Its huge dome and minarets are lit up at night, vying with Atatürk's tomb for attention.

South along Atatürk Bulvarı the district of Kavaklıdere features a park-like "embassy row" on the right, beginning with the United States's embassy and followed by that of Germany. Here during World War II the Albanian valet to the British ambassador, portrayed by James Mason in the classic film *Five Fingers,* sold secrets to the Nazis under the code name Cicero. To the left, before Kavaklıdere circle, the small but charming Kuğulu Park (Swan Park) marks the beginning of a shopping area along Tunalı Hilmi Caddesi, which runs north from the other side of the park. Here is also a charming private residence built in the early 1940s, displaying the interest in rural vernacular architecture.

From the Kavaklıdere circle Atatürk Bulvarı angles to the left to ascend the hill. To make a circuit through the southern heights, continue straight instead (along with most of the traffic) on Cinnah Caddesi, a steep street that leads up to the residential area of Çankaya, once covered in vineyards.

At the top on the left the **Botanical Garden** fills a ravine; overlooking it rises Ankara's newest "monument," a shopping complex and tower. Officially named **Atakule**, it is also called Dönerkule (Turning Tower) since it is topped by a revolving restaurant and bar, which together with the observation deck enjoy excellent views of the city.

Çankaya Caddesi runs east along the top of the Botanical Garden, a favorite promenade that now pastures statues of Ankara's famous Angora goats—the symbol of the city—and passes the grounds of the **Presidential Palace** on the right, where there is a changing of the guard (with a small band) on Sundays at sunset. Also on the grounds is Atatürk's home, which is preserved as a museum, **Çankaya Atatürk Müzesi**. This symbolic residence is open to visitors on Sunday afternoons; inquire at the main gate of the Presidential Palace grounds for an escort to the museum. On the left at the corner of Atatürk Bulvarı is the **Prime Minister's Palace**, one of the most aesthetically successful buildings of the 1930s, where Turkish sheepdogs protect the grounds.

At the next circle, İran Caddesi descends back to Tunalı Hilmi Caddesi; near the top the U.S. ambassador's manorial residence can be glimpsed up a driveway to the right. At the bottom of the hill you are back at Kuğulu Park and Atatürk Bulvarı. The continuation of Çankaya Caddesi follows the rim of the hill through a newer residential area, Gaziosmanpaşa, where the street's name changes to Köroğlu Caddesi and where orchards and old summer villas have been replaced by apartment blocks.

STAYING IN ANKARA

Accommodations in Ankara have come a long way since the first days of the Republic, when there were no hotels and the U.S. representative to the new government stayed in a han. The Ankara Palas, now a government guest house, was built to remedy that situation. Although today the best places to stay are in the newer part of the city, there are still some accommodations in Ulus that are convenient to the historical sites, museums, and the old bazaar area. Two moderate but satisfactory hotels here are the **Turist Oteli**, on Çankırı Caddesi between Ulus Meydanı and the Roman baths, and the **Hitit Oteli**, off Hisarparkı Caddesi on the way up to the citadel. For travellers on a tight budget, the Hitit is a small, older, basic—but friendly and helpful—family hotel haunted by museum scholars, who make an interesting addition to the dining room. The larger Turist Oteli is nicer and well maintained, with a cozy atmosphere, accommodating staff, Turkish bath, sauna, and parking (the latter available at all the hotels listed here), but Çankırı Caddesi has heavy traffic.

Yenişehir has been the best bet for accommodations, both for its central location and because here you'll find two old favorites, each medium-size and each with a longstanding reputation for excellent personal service (the ongoing metro construction, however, may negate this advantage). Off Lozan Meydanı at the beginning of Mithatpaşa Caddesi, the pleasant **Kent Hotel**, the classier of the two, backs onto Atatürk Bulvarı, meaning that rooms at the front are somewhat quieter. It is known for its good food—especially its excellent Sunday brunch consisting of a smorgasbord of Turkish dishes. The vintage **Bulvar Palas Oteli**, on Atatürk Bulvarı in Bakanlıklar, may be past its prime, but on the other hand it retains the atmosphere of another era. It is run by an old Laz family and takes good care of its clientele. One noted archaeologist once spent the night in its dining room when there was no vacancy, rather than going elsewhere. The grand dining room with its romantic miniaturist murals illustrating Turkey's past has been a favorite lunch spot with businesspeople, professionals, and bureaucrats. The hotel also has a front terrace where you can have breakfast or a beer and watch the world go by, imagining yourself a secret agent during World War II, when Ankara was a hotbed of intrigue. Sadly, this hotel may soon succumb to urban renewal. If atmosphere is not important, try the small **Eyuboğlu Oteli** on the street behind; it's clean and modern, with phones in the bathrooms and refrigerators in the rooms. Or you might check out the **Hotel Metropol**, around the corner on Olgunlar Sokak.

For more modern but pricier surroundings there is the low-rise **Büyük Sürmeli Oteli** to the west of Lozan Meydanı. With attractive decor and a small outdoor pool, it has had a few years to work out the kinks. One of the newer luxury high-rise hotels, the **Merit Altınel**, with a rooftop pool, is favored by those on expense accounts because of its full breakfasts and Japanese restaurant. Located more than half a mile west of Kızılay at Tandoğan Meydanı, it's rather isolated, but it is the closest hotel to the train station and is near Atatürk's mausoleum.

Above Bakanlıklar are two nice, large, older hotels and a small new one. The comfortable **Ankara Dedeman Oteli**, up the hill east of İnönü circle, has a pool and a rooftop restaurant with a Turkish floor show. It is frequented by many Americans attached to the U.S. military installation west of town. On Atatürk Bulvarı looms the **Büyük Ankara Oteli**, the city's first high-rise luxury hotel—a favorite with businesspeople and foreign dignitaries. Government-owned, it recently has been refurbished and offers a pool and somewhat lower rates in the face of new competition. Also on Atatürk Bulvarı, just past the next intersection and opposite the U.S. embassy, is the small but stylish **Best Oteli**.

Finally, the southern heights area offers several hotels in the upper price ranges. The smaller, aging **Tunalı Oteli** on Tunalı Hilmi Caddesi is adequate but low on charm. Farther up, off İran Caddesi above Tahran Caddesi, is Ankara's newest luxury accommodation, the tall, imposing, cylindrical **Sheraton Hotel**, which opened in June 1991. The Sheraton, whose lovely spacious grounds were once the Kavaklıdere vineyard, has a pool and squash court. The lobby and restaurant are decorated with kilims and copper (in an effort to introduce local charm); the hotel also has a well-stocked bookstore, and the upper rooms offer fine views. Food here is expensive and servings perhaps not as good or as generous as at the Hilton (see below) but the new staff is eager to please. Adjacent to the Sheraton, the very upscale, glassed-in and airy shopping mall, **Karum**, is attracting the latest in chic. At the top of the stairs on the uppermost level, **Eskil**, a branch of Galerie Eskil in the Kınacılar Evi in the citadel, has fine old and new silver jewelry.

Two blocks down Tahran Caddesi in a quieter locale on the opposite side of the Iranian embassy from the Sheraton, Ankara's second-newest five-star hotel, the sizable yet inviting **Hilton Hotel** features an indoor/outdoor pool and the convenience of its own post office. This is also where you'll find the tour groups, but note that among its shops downstairs, **Urart Gallery** has elegant jewelry reproductions of ancient art, and **Koleksiyon, A.Ş.**, an auction house here, has fine old prints, embroidery pieces, silver belts, porcelain, jewelry, and an extensive selection of carpets and kilims from Turkey and elsewhere. The atmosphere is friendly and the prices are generally competitive, but catalog pieces are expensive.

SHOPPING AND DINING
IN ANKARA

Prices in Ankara are generally more reasonable for most
articles than in Istanbul or some of Turkey's other touristic
spots. If you don't want to be burdened with souvenirs at
this point in your journey, a little perusing here might help
you with bargaining elsewhere later. Remember, too, that
many rug dealers can mail items home for you. The city
code for Ankara is 4.

Carpets and Kilims

The following brief survey will give you some general guid-
ance in unraveling the mysteries of Turkish weavings. Historically, handwoven textiles, either flatweaves (kilims) or
knotted-pile carpets (*halis*) have been produced in three
different settings: traditional items made by the weaver for
her own trousseau or household and associated with a
tribal, seminomadic, pastoral way of life; cottage-industry
pieces woven by settled villagers in regional patterns for sale
in the local town; and workshop, or commercial, products in
which a merchant provides the weaver with a specific design
and color scheme to reproduce for the urban market. Traditional products generally have bold geometric designs,
while the village weavings usually display a stylized floral
pattern and the commercial pieces more often employ a
refined floral ornamentation descended from the former
Ottoman court style. In the last few years traditional and
village-style pieces have begun to be produced commercially for the urban and international markets. Hand-spun
and hand-dyed wool is the basic material for traditional
weavers, while machine-spun and synthetically dyed wool,
sometimes on cotton warps, is often used by villagers. Commercial weavers almost always use cotton warps and commercial wool for the hand-knotted pile. There are also silk
pieces, though these are generally smaller, rarer, and much
more costly.

Hand-dyeing with natural substances (made from plants,
minerals, or insects) gives traditional weavings a vibrant,
local identity and the charming vagaries of a handmade item.
While synthetic dyes, which originally were harsh and
tended to run and fade, have been perfected, the uniformity
they confer is most satisfactory in standardized workshop

pieces. Cottage-industry rugs often use a mixture of natural (the Turks say *kök,* "root") and synthetic dyes. The rugs are sometimes treated with an acid or bleach to age them artificially. Although this may give them an antique look, it has a deleterious effect on the fabric (wet the fringes and sniff for chlorine). These days many carpets and kilims for the new trade are woven with hand-spun and naturally dyed wool and may be laid out in the sun to soften their colors.

Traditional flatweaves fall into five categories by technique: (1) the slit tapestry, or kilim, where the areas of different colored crosswise wefts create the pattern, similar to Navajo weaving; (2) *cicim,* a sort of "loom embroidery" made with extra pattern-wefts wrapped and brocaded on a plain ground; (3) *zili,* in which extra pattern-weft floats leave warp threads exposed to create a ribbed effect; (4) *sumak,* with pattern weft wrapping that covers the ground threads, which in the finest pieces has no structural weft; and (5) *palas,* a type of weaving in which the alternating lengthwise warp threads create the design. Traditional weavers working on portable ground looms most often weave long, narrow pieces. Kilims are generally made in two sections; *cicim* and *palas* weavings are often done in strips that are then sewn together. These traditional flatweaves were used for floor coverings (*kilim*) and furniture coverings (*örtüsü*), picnic spreads (*sofra*) and curtains (*perde*), cushion and pillow coverings (the rectangular *yastık* and the square *minder*), large storage bags (*çuval,* usually having bands of *sumak* decoration), cradles (*beşik,* in *sumak* or kilim technique), and double shoulder- or saddlebags (the smaller *heybe* for donkeys; larger *hurç* for horses or camels), as well as simple small bags (*torba*). Some of these smaller pieces (*yastık, minder, heybe, torba*) may also be done in knotted pile, but this more costly, time-consuming, and heavy technique is generally reserved for rugs and carpets.

Knotted-pile carpets are now made primarily in village cottage industries or urban workshops for the trade. The fineness of the material and the corresponding density of the knots vary widely: The Turkish (Ghiordes) symmetrical knot is used in nomadic and village weaving (e.g., Kars, Milas, Taşpınar, Yağcebedir, Yahyalı), while the tighter Persian (Senna) asymmetrical knot is used on cotton and silk warps in commercial pieces (e.g., Hereke, Ladık, Kayseri, Kula). Standard sizes for village and cottage-industry vertical loom products are the bedroom-size *ceyrek* (about 4 by 6 feet) and *karyola* (about 5 by 8 feet) and the throw-rug or prayer-rug size (called *seccade* or *namazlık,* about 3 by 5 feet), as well as the small bolster cover (*yastık,* about 1½ by 2½ feet). Only commercial workshops can produce the larger carpets.

Ulus

Ankaralıs are coming to appreciate their old city, and restorations in the citadel have attracted Turks as well as foreigners to this picturesque area, which in turn has attracted more shops, making it easier to combine sightseeing and shopping. Aside from the restaurants and shops in the citadel that are listed above, the bazaar area of the old city boasts a burgeoning number of shops filled with all variety of treasures. **Enda** (Gözcü Yokuşu 9), across from the Museum of Anatolian Civilizations, displays a wide selection of silver items—trays, old Russian tobacco boxes, and nomad jewelry, including headpieces, body ornaments, and bracelets. The merchandise is a bit pricey, but of good quality. Nearby, at number 5, the **Kerim** kilim and carpet shop—owned by younger members of a longtime carpet-dealing family in Anakara—has a fine selection. Shops in "Copper Alley," discussed above, are too many to enumerate; they often carry more than just copperware, and they shouldn't be missed. In Koyunpazarı, **Adem Shop** (Can Sokak 13C) has a small entryway leading to a two-story interior with lots of nooks and crannies crammed with old copper, hand scales, Russian *beşik*s (cradles made of *sumak* fabric), carpets, and wooden decoration from old Ottoman houses, as well as antique furniture. Nearby, **Grand Bazaar Carpet and Kilim** (Can Sokak 14) carries a good selection of new and old weavings, including Russian *beşik*s and Afghan carpets. English is spoken and prices are reasonable.

Higher up and across from Aslanhane Camii, the new shop of Fahrettin Deniz, **Deniz Halıcılık,** at Can Sokak number 29, usually has some special treasures. Another area in Ulus of some interest for the textile treasure-hunter is **İtfaiye,** the secondhand area on and around Tavus Sokak (sometimes labeled Kosova Sokak); take the first left off Derman Sokak above Atatürk Bulvarı just north of Talat Paşa Caddesi. Now only a few small shops and repairers (*tamirci*s) dealing in old weavings remain in and around Fuar Pasajı on the right (Ahmet at **Kopmaz** is the best, but he may be moving). Their stock comes from itinerant peddlers who collect old pieces in the countryside or from villagers who come directly to sell their pieces for cash. Consequently, you never know what might be on hand nor in what state of repair the rugs might be. But, as with bargain hunting anywhere, the special finds make the hunt worthwhile.

Within easy walking distance are three good *döner kebap* restaurants. At the top of Derman Sokak on Denizciler Caddesi is the ever-popular **Uludağ Kebapçısı,** (remodeled with nice rest rooms downstairs), which serves one, one-and-a-half, or two-portion servings of *İskender kebap,* flat *pide* bread covered with slices of lamb cooked on a spit, and which can be accompanied by yogurt, hot melted butter if desired, and tomato sauce (the latter two condiments brought around to the table). They also serve beer, but you might try the more traditional *ayran,* a healthy yogurt-based drink somewhat like buttermilk. A more traditional setting is provided at **Ali Bey** on Derman Sokak (no beer), and in the second block of Tavus Sokak on the right is the small, newish **Akman Restoran,** with pleasant decor.

Downtown Area

The Yenişehir/Kızılay downtown offers a variety of shopping and eating experiences; however, the area currently suffers from the detours, dirt, noise, and smell of metro construction—and those who can afford to go elsewhere, either in the old city or the posher southern sector, do. Starting in Sıhhiye on the east side of Lozan Meydanı: **Abdi İpekçi Parkı** offers light refreshments and people-watching by the ponds; on Saturday a colorful outdoor market is held at the other end. South along Atatürk Bulvarı, on the left near the pedestrian overpass, is the **Büyük Çarşı,** a shopping arcade full of jewelry shops; downstairs at the southern entrance is **Antikite Old Bazaar** (number 39/48; English spoken), which has a good selection of silver nomadic jewelry, old pocket watches, teacup holders, and commemorative pieces. **Zeki,** nearby, deals in modern gems and gold, including puzzle rings and Arabic calligraphy pieces. Farther along Atatürk Bulvarı, at number 85, is an outlet for **Paşabahçe** glassware (a descendant of an Ottoman court glassworks), where you can find the blue spiral vases known as *çesmi bülbül* (nightingale's eye).

Before the end of the block, on the left, is the **Sakarya promenade,** where the streets have been blocked off to create a pedestrian shopping area. An ice-cream stand on the right serves fresh fruit sorbets (the *limon* is excellent). Opposite flower stalls, a small shop, tucked between the fishmongers, specializes in cotton *şile bezi* articles in summer and mohair items in winter. Down Selânik Caddesi to the left the **ABC** bookstore carries English-language books about Turkey. In the next block, on the right, are fine Kütahya ceramics, including copies of Ottoman masterpieces. Nearby, dried fruit and nut shops (*kuru yemişçi*) and herb and spice shops (*baharatçı*) offer aromatic delicacies. **Lokman Hekim** has one store in the central area with a fascinating display primarily of culinary items and another (to the right on Selânik Caddesi) for medicinal herbs and witches' brew.

There are numerous indoor-outdoor eateries on Bayındır Sokak, at the end of the Sakarya promenade. The **Körfez** (Gulf) is a favorite with locals who appreciate its excellent Black Sea fare: lots of fish (try *lagos güveç,* a whitefish stew, or the fresh anchovies—*hamsi*—a traditional specialty) at very reasonable prices. Usually quite crowded, the Körfez is, in fact, a relatively refined *meyhane* (Persian for "wine establishment"), where men traditionally gather to sip *rakı* and linger over a table full of *meze* while they straighten out the affairs of the world. The lack of decor is compensated for by the colorful characters who haunt these establishments, but of course you would need a local's expertise to sort out the politicians from the smugglers. A few women now frequent this once-segregated establishment, especially to enjoy the outdoor seating on a summer evening.

Another restaurant catering mostly to local males (who provide the atmosphere) is **Adana Sofrası Restoran,** across Atatürk Bulvarı at number 30 Necatibey Caddesi. This *ocakbaşı* (hearthside) barbecue specializes in spicy food from the south; it's fun to sit around the grill and watch the chef, an artist at heart, at work. The *içli köfte* is especially good and is included among the *meze* selections. *Şiş kebap* and lamb chops are tender. Again, it's not fancy, but a good value.

If you just want a snack, at the corner of Sakarya and Bayındır Sokak you can sample the deep-fried mussels (*midye*)—a specialty from the Bosphorus—at **Sakarya Gıda Picnic,** which also offers *kokoreç* (sheep's lungs). You might also induldge in baklava or some other gooey delight, washed down with tea or coffee, at a pastry shop (*pastahane*). If you have Turkish-style coffee (*Türk kahvesi*), specify *sade* (without sugar), *az* (slightly sweet), *orta* (medium), or *şekerli* (sweet), and then just sip the strong brew, leaving the grounds in the bottom of the demitasse. (Fortunes used to be told by the pattern the grounds make when the cup is overturned.)

Return to Selânik Caddesi and head south over the pedestrian bridge above Ziya Gökalp Caddesi. **Tarhan** bookstore, at number 19/A, has a good selection of English-language books about Turkey, as well as newspapers, magazines, and cards. Off Ziya Gökalp, just before the GİMA department store, take the steps that now close off the end of Karanfıl Sokak. On the left at number 5/53 on the second floor is **Türk El Sanatlarını Tanıtma Vakfı** (look for the sign in the window), a benefit handcrafts store with traditional knitted socks, embroidered towels, jewelry, hand-painted silk pillows, and wooden boxes. A good bet for dining is up Karanfıl Sokak: the **Karadeniz Lokantası** (closed on Sundays), another favorite Black Sea restaurant, which has an outdoor patio with a fountain for summer dining. Try the *levrek buğlama,* steamed sea bass with mushrooms. One street back is a special *mantı* restaurant, **Hatça Ana** (Konur Sokak 39/D), serving this traditional Central Anatolian dish of diminutive meat-filled pasta in yogurt sauce—try the *sulu* variety (cooked in water). Like the Turks themselves, this dish has its origins in Central Asia; versions of this food are eaten as far away as Korea.

Back on Atatürk Bulvarı, south of GİMA are some of the finer clothing stores in town, including **Beymen** and **Vakko** (Vakko has a noted art gallery in addition to clothing). Here too is Yüksel Pasajı, with more gold-jewelry shops. Around the corner at the next street (Meşrutiyet Caddesi 11/B) is another fine **Ministry of Tourism shop**. In addition to museum reproductions and handcrafts on the main floor, the shop carries publications upstairs, and downstairs there are carpets reproduced from antique pieces as part of a special Ministry of Tourism project (the accompanying catalogs have excellent photographs of the original pieces). Across the street is the publication outlet of **İş Bankası** (Labor Bank), which sometimes has interesting books in English on Turkish handcrafts.

Back on Atatürk Bulvarı, in the next block, at number 107, is the Engürü Pasajı, where you'll find **Lapis Lazuli** and **Agat** (downstairs at numbers 7-14 and 7-15, respectively), shops specializing in costume and silver jewelry set with various stones. Toward the end of the block at number 151A, **Bergama Halı** has a stock of cottage-industry and workshop rugs (ask for Barbaros, who speaks English). Finally, in the block above Esat Caddesi is **Top** (at Atatürk Bulvarı 169/A-B), a shop with fine leather goods.

The Southern Heights: Çankaya and Gaziosmanpaşa

Because Ankara's large foreign community lives mostly in the southern districts, these are where you'll find the majority of the gift and souvenir shops, usually with English-speaking salespeople. Along Tunalı Hilmi Caddesi (closed to traffic on Sundays) near Kuğulu Park are leather shops, art galleries, bookstores with English-language titles, and gift shops specializing in Turkish jewelry. There is also a shop selling antique silver jewelry downstairs to the right inside the new **Kuğulu Pasaj**, opposite Kuğulu Park. In Kuğulu Pasajı you'll also find shops carrying sportswear, hand-knitted Angora sweaters, and leather goods. **Berk**, in the Uğurlu Çarşı complex behind the park, offers high-class traditional arts—ceramics, glass, metalwork, and weavings.

This area also provides a variety of good eateries, including **Pizza Pino**, a popular pizza parlor at Tunalı Hilmi Caddesi 111/B; **Güney Mutfağı**, just beyond, which features spicy fare, and **Yakamoz**, at number 114/J2–3, a favorite for seafood. For a classier setting and continental cuisine, you'll like **R-V**, a short distance off Atatürk Bulvarı above the Polish embassy at number 243/D. It's a favorite among higher-ranking diplomats.

Farâbi Sokak, a one-way street running from Atatürk Bulvarı under Cinnah Caddesi, has several shops—**Elsan**, **Murat**, and **Hoca**—that together carry just about all the standard souvenir/gift items. Murat also has modern rugs upstairs and a good collection of old pieces downstairs. On nearby Çevri Sokak are three good restaurants: **Et Subaşı**, at number 11/A, serves simple *lahmacun* (Turkish "pizza"), *içli köfte,* and grilled meats. The fancy **Marlin Restaurant**, at number 7/A, specializes in seafood, which, as usual, is pricey. A better bargain is **Lagos**, at number 25A, with a charming interior lined with aquariums.

There is also some good eating and shopping off and up Cinnah Caddesi. At Kuloğlu 29, behind a garden wall opposite the back fence of the Russian embassy, is the delightful and popular **Mangal Et Lokantası** (Tel: 440-0959), set in the house and grounds of one of the few surviving old Ottoman summer villas that dotted the vineyards and orchards that once covered these hills. One block off Cinnah at Kırkpınar 5/B, **Gallery Z** has an excellent selection of Kütahya faïence and tiles and some unusual handcraft items. A newer restaurant with truly continental cuisine and decor is **Kasır**, at Cinnah Caddesi 44 in the Saraylı building, which looks like a wooden mansion that's been transplanted from the shores of the Bosphorus. The straightforward **Liman Lokantası**, at number 54, has a fine selection of Black Sea offerings, including *muğlama,* a version of cheese fondue. At the end of Cinnah on the right, **Burç** has a fine selection of Turkish arts and antiques, and across the street in the **Atakule**

(Çankaya tower) complex at number 214–216, **Yörük Hali**, has new and old weavings. To take in the view above, possibly with drinks and dinner, at the nearby Anıtsal Kule Asansör Gişe, pay about $1.50 for a truly uplifting ride on the tower's glassed-in elevator (entry outside the lower level, around to the right).

Another shopping and dining area is along Köroğlu Caddesi in the **Gaziosmanpaşa** neighborhood to the east, the most recently developed residential section of Ankara. The friendly, English-speaking Ersoy family owns **Best Collection**, at number 37/5, handling mainly new handwoven carpets; next door **Selçuk** deals in kilim and carpet reproductions sponsored by the Ministry of Tourism. At the end of the street at number 103/B is another **Kopmaz**, a most congenial shop with an especially nice selection of traditional weavings, chiefly older flatweaves; they also do repairs here (İbrahim speaks English). At number 92 Köroğlu is **La Boheme**, very cozy with a small bar, fireplace, and often a solo instrumentalist. For simpler European fare, try **Pineapple** at number 64/B. About two and a half miles south of town, alongside Lake Mogan at Gölbaşı, are a number of good restaurants; **Chez le Belge** (Tel: 484-1478) is particularly known for its trout and crayfish.

Finally, there is **Atatürk's Farm** (Atatürk Orman Çifliği), about two and a half miles west of town between the Eskişehir and Istanbul highways. The best way of getting there is to hire a taxi. Begun as an experimental farm, today it comprises a plant nursery, forestry station, wooded picnic area, dairy, brewery, charming Republican-era suburban train station, and a zoo where Angora cats are bred. There is also a replica of Atatürk's boyhood home in Thessaloniki in northern Greece. Down the street and just before the gas station, the **Merkez Lokantası**, with its pleasant outdoor garden and fountain, is a delightful place to end the day lingering over a delicious array of Turkish delicacies, including the excellent baked savories known as *börek* (*su böreği* are filled with white cheese, *talaş böreği* with minced lamb). Merkez specializes in grilled and roasted meats; try the *tandır,* lamb roasted in a clay vessel.

DAY TRIPS FROM ANKARA

Three rewarding excursions are possible from Ankara: a one- or two-day trip to the picturesque Ottoman-era town of Safranbolu (treated last, below), a four- or five-hour round-trip visit to the Phrygian site of Gordion, and a full-day trip to Alacahöyük and Hattuşaş. These last two cities, respectively the "lost" capitals of the rich Hattic Kingdom and the mighty Hittite Empire, long-forgotten ancient civilizations that were rediscovered by archaeologists. Excavations at Alacahöyük ("Motley Mound") and Boğazkale ("Gorge Castle") revealed some of Anatolia's finest early metalwork and monumental architecture, and some of its oldest written records.

The 200-km (124-mile) one-way trip to Alacahöyük and Boğazkale (ancient Hattuşaş), northeast of Ankara via the Samsun highway, takes two and a half hours by car. If you get an early start, you will have time to visit Alacahöyük first and then continue on to Boğazkale in time to see the impressive bas-reliefs of the sanctuary of Yazılıkaya (just northeast of Hattuşaş) in the midday sun, when photography is best. The detour to Alacahöyük can be done on the return trip, but because it is an earlier site and is rather less impressive than Hattuşaş, you should see it first. You can also take a bus to Sungurlu, where you can hire a taxi to the sites; or check with one of the many travel agencies in Ankara for tours.

From Ankara travel east on the E 23 through rolling uplands and descend into the gorge of the Kızılırmak, the ancient Halys river. After the city of Kırıkkale, a munitions production center, the road follows the green valley of a meandering stream. After 45 km (28 miles) a left fork heads north toward Çorum as route 41, crossing the Delice river and passing ocher-hued hills. Four kilometers (2½ miles) beyond the town of Sungurlu, a right turn to the southeast toward Yozgat leads through fertile agricultural land heading to both the ancient sites.

About 12 km (7½ miles) later, the road to Alacahöyük appears on the left. Eleven kilometers (7 miles) after you make the turnoff down the road toward the village of Alaca Köy, a road to the left leads the final 10 km (6 miles) to the low ancient mound and small museum.

ALACAHÖYÜK AND THE HATTIS

Excavations carried out at Alacahöyük by the Turks have revealed layers of habitation that go back to the fourth millennium B.C.; the most important finds are from 13 "royal" graves that date to the mid-third millennium B.C. The graves are ascribed to the Hatti people, who inhabited Central Anatolia before the arrival of an Indo-European group that has come to be known as Hittites because they took over the "Land of the Hatti" (more on the Hittites below).

The Early Bronze Age objects found in the graves at Alacahöyük—ornaments, cult items ("solar" disks and bull and stag standards), and weapons of gold, silver, electrum, copper, bronze, and lead—exhibit some of the finest craftsmanship of this period in the Middle East. Nearby excavations of houses have uncovered more remarkable metalwork, which resembles finds from Troy.

A type of so-called transitional pottery found here apparently marked the coming of the Hittites, and it is their royal temple-precinct foundations that are the main features of the site today. The main gate is flanked by two protective sphinxes. The one on the right bears a bas-relief of a Hittite god above a two-headed eagle holding a rabbit in its talons. Along the wall are cast copies of great orthostats, basalt and limestone blocks carved with bas-reliefs. Those on either side of the Sphinx Gate depict Hittite religious ceremonies. On the right is a female deity believed to be the sun goddess of the yet-to-be-located city of Arinna; on the left are a king and queen worshiping in front of a bull, as well as sacrificial animals, priests, and entertainers. The original reliefs have been removed for display in the Museum of Anatolian Civilizations in Ankara.

Inside the walls, within the maze of restored foundations, on the east (right) side of a long central plaza area, there is a building with a large courtyard that is believed to have been the temple proper. On the west side of the central plaza, below the Hittite palace level, are the grave sites where, in 1935, in one of the first excavations carried out by Turkish archaeologists, the first of the Hattic treasures were unearthed just as the excavators' initial funds were exhausted. A tower to the west gives a good view over the small site. A postern tunnel can be explored under the walls some 300 yards to the west.

Some scholars speculate that the Hattic city-state at Alacahöyük became the first capital of the Hittites, whose rulers then defeated the Hattic king of Hattuş. Others also claim that Alacahöyük may have been the city of Arinna, mentioned in the Hittite texts, where the Hittites' important temple to the great sun goddess is said to have been. Arinna was a day's journey from Hattuşaş, as the Hittites later called Hattuş.

Although most of the spectacular Hattic treasures from Alacahöyük are on exhibit in Ankara, the small **museum** here houses representative samples and copies of some of the best pieces as well as various Hittite sculptures, vases, and bronze items and later Phrygian wares from here and the nearby site of Pazarlı, plus a regional ethnographic collection.

Returning to the Yozgat road, turn left and continue another 13 km (8 miles) south along the valley of a tributary of the Delice, which is formed by two streams rising in hills to the south. On the hillside above the present village of Boğazkale (formerly Boğazköy), and within the triangle formed by the confluence of these streams (whose ravines, together with numerous rocky outcrops, served as the basis of a remarkable series of defenses), lies the dramatic site of Hattuşaş with its sprawling ruins of stone foundations and terraces.

HATTUŞAŞ AND THE HITTITES

Although the ruins at **Boğazkale** had been known to Europeans since 1834, excavations at the site were not begun until 1906. The most fortunate discovery was archives of tablets written in two languages: Akkadian, the lingua franca of the period, and "cuneiform" Hittite. Scholars were already familiar with Akkadian, and the discovery of the Hattuşaş archives made possible the decipherment of the cuneiform Hittite. The information on these tablets proved that the archaeologists were unearthing the great Hittite capital and told much about the culture, economics, and history of the site. Subsequent excavations by German archaeologists revealed occupation levels from the third millennium B.C. to Roman times, but the city reached its height in the second millennium B.C., when the Hittites ruled Central Anatolia and northern Syria, vying with the Mesopotamian kingdoms of Assyria and Babylonia and, later, pharaonic Egypt.

The original Hattic city occupied the lower slopes beneath a citadel that sat atop a rocky promontory (Büyükkale) that overlooks the eastern ravine. Just below the Hattic city a colony was established in the 18th century B.C. by Assyrian merchants involved in an international trade network, importing luxury goods and tin (for making bronze from Anatolian copper) in exchange for silver and gold. These merchants also brought to Anatolia the art of writing in cuneiform on clay tablets.

The entire city was destroyed by a great fire around 1720 B.C., probably when the city was conquered by the Hittites. A century later the Hittites made it their capital, and their king accordingly took the name Hattusilis. At about this time the city was fortified with a wall that extended from Büyükkale across to the farther ravine, and Hittite control was extended over much of Anatolia and northern Syria. The Old Hittite Empire reached its height under Hattusilis's heir, Mursilis I, who conquered Babylon in 1594 B.C.

In the next century a change of dynasty initiated the New Hittite Empire. Hattuşaş was attacked and burned sometime later by people from the north. Soon after, the greatest of the Hittite kings, Suppiluliumas, drove them back and expanded Hittite hegemony into Syria. The Hittites then rivaled Egypt, which had been weakened by internal struggles during the reigns of Akhenaton and the boy king Tutankhamen, whose widow wrote to the great Hittite king requesting one of his sons in marriage. It was probably under Suppiluliumas that the Great Temple in the lower city was begun and that the city was expanded onto the upper slopes.

One of Suppiluliumas's sons, Muwatallis, moved his residence to southern Anatolia, either in fear of the northern threat or to be closer to the Syrian front, where he fought the army of Pharaoh Ramses II at the great battle of Kadesh on the Orontes river (ca. 1299; depicted on the pylons of the Luxor Temple in Egypt). Muwatallis's son in turn moved the royal residence back to Hattuşaş, where the palace was subsequently burned, no doubt during the struggles between him and his uncle Hattusilis II, who usurped the throne and sent his nephew fleeing to Egypt. In 1275 (or 1284) B.C. Hattusilis III and Ramses II drew up the peace treaty of Kadesh—the earliest recorded document of its kind (once known only from the inscriptions on the temple of Amun at Karnak in Egypt)—and Ramses II married the oldest daughter of Hattusilis III. The city reached its greatest extent under her brother, Tudhaliyas IV, depicted and named in numerous reliefs and inscriptions, including those at the sanctuary Yazılıkaya across the valley (discussed below). The Great Temple, the palace of Büyükkale, and the many structures of the upper city, including the great stone gates and massive ramparts, took their final form at that time; the remains of these buildings are what the visitor sees today.

A unique **bronze tablet** found in 1986 (now in Ankara's museum) records a treaty between Tudhaliyas IV and his vassal, the son of his deposed cousin. This treaty was apparently only the calm before the storm; a more recently discovered seal calling the latter the Great King of Hatti suggests continued dynastic struggles, and under Suppiluliumas II the last Hittite records speak of disloyalty of subjects and defection of vassals. Soon after 1200 B.C. Hattuşaş was destroyed and the great Hittite Empire broke up. The collapse of the Hittite Empire was roughly contemporary with the fall of Troy and the invasions of the "sea people" in Egypt. An imperial remnant (termed Late Hittite or Neo-Hittite) survived in southeastern Anatolia and northern Syria. It is these post-imperial Hittites who are mentioned in connection with the biblical Abraham, whose grandson had two Hittite wives, and with David, who had Uriah the Hittite killed so he could marry Uriah's wife, Bathsheba.

Although Hattuşaş was occupied in the Phrygian period (eighth century B.C.), it essentially disappeared from history for 3,000 years; only the survival of its great stone monuments and clay tablets preserves the memory of its past glory. A useful study of the excavators' discoveries, *Guide to Boğazköy,* by German archaeologist Kurt Bittel, former director of excavations, is available in English at the archaeological museums in Ankara, Alacahöyük, and Boğazkale itself (on the left before entering the village).

The Site

Your tour of Hattuşaş should begin with the rock sanctuary at **Yazılıkaya** (Inscribed Rock), 2 km (1¼ miles) to the northeast of the actual city site, in order to view the carvings there in the best light. Here in open-air rock galleries low bas-reliefs of the Hittite pantheon and of King Tudhaliyas IV, with identifying hieroglyphics, cover the walls of the first chamber, where rites of the festival of the new year may have been held in the spring. In a smaller "hidden" side chamber, reached by a narrow defile, niches for offerings and images of special gods and of Tudhaliyas IV are carved into the walls of what was apparently a mortuary shrine. The foundations of cult buildings that fronted these galleries can still be seen. From here there is a fine view of Hattuşaş. To the left of the sanctuary is a pleasant place for a picnic (water and rest rooms nearby), and there are now two restaurants at Yazılıkaya. The better one is the **Başkent**, with good local food. You might also try the simple hotel near the site museum in Boğazkale, which has a *lokanta* where you can select your meal from a variety of trays and bubbling pots in the kitchen; or you can buy fresh bread, cheese, and fruit farther on in the village square. The **museum** is worth a brief stop to see the plans and drawings of Hattuşaş in addition to pottery, metalwork, and sculpture found on the site, although the best pieces are in Ankara and elsewhere.

Following the road across the bridge, turn left and then right up through Boğazkale to arrive at the northern tip of the city site, where the remains of a tower indicate the position of the lower defense walls. On the left are the excavations of the well-laid-out *karum* (Assyrian trading colony), where numerous tablets associated with the time of Hammurabi (18th century B.C.) were found.

The road forks to the right along the eastern side of the massive stone foundations of the **Great Temple**, where a great gateway led to an inner courtyard and two granite cellas for the principal deities, the weather god Teshub and the sun goddess identified with the city of Arinna. Surrounding this was a vast complex of cult buildings and storerooms, where thousands of written tablets were found and where giant storage jars can still be seen in the ground. Across a stone paved street (which has partially collapsed on its drainage system) is a row of storerooms, in one of which sits a large green block of nephrite that that matches one recently discovered in a shrine to Tudhaliyas in the upper city.

The road now heads uphill. At the next fork go left; this road follows the remains of the older city walls along a stream bed up to **Büyükkale** (Big Castle) and the fortified **palace**. Under the Hittites these buildings consisted of a series of gates, courts, archives, cult structures, pillared reception halls, and royal quarters. Here were found the annals of King Hattusilis—one of the earliest of cuneiform Hittite texts—and the treaty of Kadesh (the original tablet is now in the Museum of the Ancient Orient in Istanbul, and an enlarged bronze copy hangs in the United Nations headquarters in New York City), as well as the pair of large terra-cotta bull rhytons (ritual vessels) now on display in the Museum of Anatolian Civilizations in Ankara.

The road continues past **Nişantaş**, a rock inscribed with Hittite hieroglyphs, into the **upper city**. Here excavators have uncovered the foundations of more than 28 different temples and several shrines to deified kings. Animal sacrifices and festival ceremonies were performed here. The Hittites "took in" the deities of all the peoples they controlled, and this collection of gods symbolized the vast power of their mighty empire. A vaulted chamber recently uncovered under a Phrygian fortress boasts a relief of the last Hittite Great King, Suppiluliumas II, and an inscription referring to the "surrender to the gods" of the vassal kingdom mentioned in the bronze-tablet treaty.

The strength of the gods was not enough, however, to protect Hattuşaş. A great **rampart**, a masterpiece of military engineering, had to be built along the top of the hill. The road brings you to the first of three gates in this rampart, where two sets of large curved stone blocks form pointed arches; the one on the city side is carved with a large figure now identified as either the weather god or the war god, but once thought to be a king, hence the name **King's Gate**. (The original is in the Museum of Anatolian Civilizations in Ankara; a copy is seen here.)

Next, in the center of the rampart at the top of the hill, is **Yerkapı**, a 233-foot-long corbeled stone passageway beneath the earth fill that supports a system of double walls. This postern, whose exterior door frame (with sentinel's seat) is preserved, provides access to a great ditch dug outside the defenses. A climb up the hill opposite gives a fine view of this restored section of the rampart, which is covered with a stone glacis and has two great stairways on either end leading up to the main gate on top. The bronze tablet mentioned above (now in Ankara) was found near this gate, flanked by sphinxes (the originals of which are in Istanbul's Museum of the Ancient Orient and in Berlin). From here there is a grand view of the surrounding countryside and the ancient city spread out below.

The last gate is known as the **Lion Gate**, after the two menacing feline sculptures carved from the jambs of the outer arch. From this point the road descends back to the Great Temple, from where, if you have the time and an inclination toward adventure, you can take the road branching east down to the stream to explore the gorge behind the rocky outcrop called **Ambarlıkaya**, where there are traces of the Hittites' ingenious fortifications. Follow the stream up to a narrow defile. In the cliff above you can see holes cut for a guard's catwalk around Ambarlıkaya, up the side of which large steps were carved as beddings for the city walls. In the rocks atop the narrows are cuts for the footings of a bridge connecting these walls to those on the next hill, Büyükkaya, where the city expanded in the 13th century B.C. Grooves in the rocks below indicate where a portcullis was let down to block entry.

Before returning to Ankara you might want to drive back up to Yazılıkaya for another view of the Hittite capital in the late afternoon light, musing over its past glory and final plunge into obscurity. If you have lingered too long, there are various eateries along the route back. If it's still light out, try the pleasant back garden of the **Kayadibi** restaurant, west of Kırıkkale on the south side of the Samsun highway.

GORDION

Gordion, the capital of Phrygian king Midas (of the legendary golden touch), is about 100 km (62 miles) southwest of Ankara and can be visited in a five-hour excursion from the capital. University of Pennsylvania excavations at the city's acropolis mound and numerous tumuli have revealed traces of a fascinating civilization previously known only from Greek mythology. Although Gordion is a later site than Hattuşaş, the paucity of Phrygian writing means that there are fewer clues for fitting Gordion's finds into the puzzle of history and traditions, and the site yields as many questions as answers.

It is best to buy the *Gordion* guide by the first excavator of the site, the late Rodney Young, at the Museum of Anatolian Civilizations in Ankara before setting out. You can take a bus to Polatlı and then hire a taxi out to the site, or check with a travel agent in Ankara about tours. If you drive, follow the Eskişehir highway (E 23) southwest through an undulating open plateau; 17 km (11 miles) past Polatlı a sign points to the right for Gordion at the modern village of Yassıhöyük (Flat Mound), another 12 km (7½ miles) down the Sakarya river (the ancient Sangarius). The site's location is along a major east–west route marked in antiquity by the Persian Royal Road and today by the highway and railroad.

The Phrygians

The Phrygians, who apparently came from Thrace, settled here in the western Hittite lands possibly as early as the 11th century B.C. According to Homer, they came before the Trojan War, in which they were allied with the Trojan king, Priam, who had aided them against the "Amazons" (possibly the Hittites), while a Lydian source says they came later. It is not clear whether they played a part in the Hittites' demise, although the coexistence of pottery types here indicates a gradual and peaceful transition. The Phrygians reoccupied Hittite sites between the Sakarya and Kızılırmak, reaching their political and cultural height in the late eighth century

B.C. Homer called Phrygia the "land of the vineyard"; here lived Baucis and Philomene, whose legendary hospitality to Zeus saved them from his vengeful flood.

Greek tradition also speaks of a great king called Gordius, from whom the city that he made his capital took its name. Varying versions of the story lead to some confusion of details. An oracle is supposed to have said that a man in a wagon would come to rule the Phrygians and end discord. According to one tradition, this was Gordius himself, upon whose wagon an eagle landed, whereupon he was prompted by his future bride to sacrifice to Zeus and was subsequently chosen king; in another account, it was Midas, a peasant who arrived at the city gates in a cart and was adopted by the childless Gordius as his heir. Another, contradictory, myth claims that King Midas was the son of Gordius and the goddess Cybele, for whom Midas is said to have dedicated the temple at Pessinus, upriver, when he became king. In any case, the famous wagon was dedicated to the temple of Zeus (or Cybele), and another oracle pronounced that whoever loosed the intricate knot fastening its shaft would become master of Asia—a prophesy to be fulfilled four centuries later.

In myth, King Midas is best remembered for the episode in which Dionysus's companion Silenus was caught and brought to amuse the king. Midas, however, soon returned Silenus to the god, who showed his gratitude by offering the king one wish. Midas foolishly asked for the golden touch, but soon regretted it. Pitying Midas, Dionysus told him how to "wash off" the power in the Pactolus river (today's Sart Çayı), whereupon its sands became laced with gold (the supposed basis of the Lydian king Croesus's wealth). Thereafter Midas was said to have promoted the worship of Dionysus. He was also known for having been the first non-Greek to send gifts to the shrine at Delphi, sacred to both Dionysus and Apollo.

To the Greeks, Midas and the Phrygians represented the exotic East, and it was through Phrygia that they acquired items of Oriental splendor. It is, in fact, from Midas's relations with the East that we have our only true historical record of him. According to Assyrian texts, "Mita of the Mushki" was allied with the Neo-Hittites at Carcemish and had to pay tribute when they were defeated by Sargon II in 717 B.C. Then, just 20 years later, Midas's realm was overwhelmed by Cimmerian tribesmen who swept through Anatolia and burned his city. Although Midas either was killed in the battle or, according to another tradition, committed suicide, Phrygian culture continued at Gordion and the surrounding area of western Anatolia for another hundred

years until, as Herodotus tells us, it came under the hegemony of the Lydian king Alyattes. (See Central Anatolia,
below, for discussion of the impressive late-Phrygian stronghold known as Midas City.)

Next, the Persians of Cyrus the Great destroyed Gordion
on their successful campaign against Croesus at Sardis in 546
B.C. The city was rebuilt under the Persians but again destroyed, this time by an earthquake, around 400 B.C., and by
another, unknown disaster in the following century, possibly
related to the passing of Alexander the Great in 333 B.C.

Here, history meets myth. In his account of Alexander's
campaign against the Persians, the Greek historian Arrian
said that the Macedonian audaciously solved the four-
century-old puzzle of the Gordian knot either by cutting the
knot with his sword or by pulling out the peg that held it,
thus ensuring his destiny. In the following century the Galatians ravaged the region, and by 189 B.C., when the Romans
came through, the site was essentially deserted.

The Site

As you cross the Sakarya river (downstream from a fertilizer
factory and now rather polluted), you will see on the right
the ancient **city mound**, a flat-topped accumulation of some
3,000 years of habitation. A steep climb to the rim allows you
to circle the mound, looking down into the excavations
(entry prohibited) where archaeologists have exposed the
eighth-century level. Alternatively, a walk around the base to
the left brings you to the remains of the monumental stone
city gate flanked by two rectangular towers. These structures (similar to gates at Troy) dominated the narrow approach between them and probably housed a contingent of
guards. The one to the south is unexcavated and supports
the remains of a later gate of the Persian period. The odd
angle of the gateway is caused by the orientation of an
earlier gate on the inside (referred to as "polychrome" from
the multicolored stones used in its walls, now removed).

From the rim of the mound you can see the foundations
of the acropolis's interior walled "royal" quarter, which
consisted of courts lined with *megaron*s (a megaron is a
rectangular building with an antechamber fronting a larger
room with a central circular hearth, often with a support
system and balcony in the late Mycenaean tradition). One
megaron was decorated with a red, white, and blue geometric pebble mosaic floor (removed to the site museum), the
earliest such treatment known to exist and probably based
on a rug design. The largest *megaron,* one of the oldest

buildings of this level, had two rows of posts supporting an upper gallery; in the *megaron* were the charred remains of beautiful ivory-inlaid furniture, fine painted pottery, and exquisite floor coverings. Presumably this was the royal residence or reception hall. The *megaron* next to it, a later structure, was built on a raised terrace reached by a processional ramp and may have been a temple.

Backing onto these at the upper terrace level was a row of eight contiguous *megarons;* another row apparently sat opposite. Finds of millstones, grain, animal carcasses, pottery, spinning and loom paraphernalia, large bronze caldrons, and precious items indicate that these were the kitchens, workshops, and storerooms for the royal quarter, and could have employed some 300 cooks and weavers. The regular arrangement of the buildings is evidence of early town planning, as is also displayed at Aegean sites.

To the southeast, opposite the city gate, is a smaller mound—apparently a "suburb" that was occupied during the Lydian period, probably by a garrison. Here archaeologists found evidence of a siege, no doubt that mounted by Cyrus, after which the garrison was covered up like a burial mound.

Looking out over the plain, you can see many of the nearly 100 burial mounds, or tumuli, built for the Phrygian elite over a period of 175 years. So far 25 of them have been excavated. Typically, a wooden chamber was erected in a shallow pit in the ground; after the deceased and gifts had been placed inside, the chamber was covered with a pitched wooden roof and then with a mound that was off-center to discourage robbers.

The largest burial mound, called the Great Tumulus, is Gordion's greatest mystery; it can be seen on the other side of the village of Yassıhöyük. Before you make your way there, you may want to pause for a picnic lunch (if you've brought along food) in the area between the city mound and the river, which offers some greenery, a few shade trees, and a view of a small burial tumulus downriver. Or, head past the archaeologists' compound on the rise to the right and follow the road through the village to the small museum (open 8:30 A.M. to 5:30 P.M., except Mondays) opposite the great mound. Beside the museum is a small snackbar offering sandwiches and cold drinks, run by villagers and most welcome on a hot summer day. You can also picnic in the museum courtyard—a modest reminder of Midas's renowned sweet-smelling rose garden. If protection from the elements is more important to you than flora, around the left side of the building, under a roof, you can munch while musing over the pebble mosaic taken from the *megaron* in the royal quarter of the city mound.

The museum and the Great Tumulus both make cool retreats from the heat of the day. The **museum** is built like a *megaron,* with the small collection in the main room. Most of the best finds from Gordion are in Ankara, but there is a selection of pottery and terra-cotta decorations, including wall pegs and molded tiles showing a connection with Lydian and Hellenic traditions. The most curious item is the small bust of a figure with long ears. The head of a satyr, it was at first mistakenly assumed to represent Midas, who, according to Greek myth chose Pan over Apollo in a music contest and was awarded ass's ears, which he then hid under his Phrygian cap. Only his barber knew and was sworn to secrecy on pain of death. Burdened by his knowledge, the barber dug a hole by the river and told it his secret. The reeds that grew there then whispered it for all to hear. After the barber had been duly executed, Midas was said to have drunk bull's blood and died himself.

A museum guard will let you into the **Great Tumulus** (Midas Mound) opposite. The opening of this tomb in the middle of this century is one of the great stories of archaeology. The mound is now 174 feet high and 984 feet in diameter (it would have been half again as high before erosion). Oil-detection and -drilling equipment was required to locate the burial chamber, and coal miners from Zonguldak on the Black Sea Coast (see below) were employed to dig a 230-foot tunnel into the mound. Inside, they found a stone wall and rubble fill surrounding a log structure whose interior was finished with wooden planks. The remains of a short male, perhaps 60 years old, were found on a bed in the corner surrounded by grave gifts, which had remained undisturbed for more than 2,500 years. At the tunnel's entrance are photographs of the finds as they were discovered. At the end you can see the ancient log structure and look into the now-empty chamber.

Finds included evidence of textiles, bronze fibulae, utensils, bowls and caldrons, pottery, and exquisite inlaid wooden furniture (now beautifully restored and displayed in the Museum of Anatolian Civilizations in Ankara). The large bronze caldrons may have imported from Urartu in the east and are similar to some found in Greece. The exceptional woodwork here invites speculation about the legendary wagon in the temple and the celebrated throne that Midas dedicated to Delphi. A few rare examples of Phrygian writing in beeswax were also found on some bowls. Although the writing is understood to have derived from the Phoenician alphabet, scholars do not know if the Phrygians got it from the Greeks or passed it on to them. The language is Indo-European but still has not been deciphered.

The question remains, whose tomb is this? Is it that of Midas himself, who died at the time of the Cimmerian destruction? Or is it that of the great king Gordius, who made this his capital? Rodney Young believed it to be that of the latter, since he doubted that the huge tumulus could have been constructed after the Cimmerian disaster. Others note, however, that the style of the items in the tomb would seem to date them to sometime after 721 B.C. and that they seem well used. They therefore suspect the tumulus to belong to Midas because the Cimmerian presence was short-lived and Gordion did recover.

A short distance farther along the road and off to the left, archaeologists uncovered a section of **ancient road**, probably the Roman successor of the great Persian Royal Road that ran from Sardis to Susa. It was used by Xerxes, whose Persian army invaded Greece in the early fifth century B.C., and by Alexander and his Macedonians, who returned more than a century later to put an end to the Persian empire.

In our own century two armies met here to decide the fate of Anatolia once again. The Greek invasion of western Anatolia after World War I was successfully stopped at the Sakarya river in a ghastly battle on August 24, 1921. The struggling Turkish nationalist forces were led by Mustafa Kemal, who then received the title *gazi,* meaning "warrior." Though decisive victory was not to come for another year, the Sakarya battle marked the turning of the tide against the invaders and helped the nationalists negotiate the withdrawal of French and Italian forces from regions in southern Anatolia. On your return to Ankara you can see, rising on the hill above Polatlı, an antiquity of the future, the monument to the Turkish victory at the Sakarya, a line of upward-sweeping marble monoliths marking the last line of defense before Ankara.

SAFRANBOLU

From Ankara a leisurely day trip can be made to the well-preserved Ottoman town of Safranbolu, 210 km (140 miles) to the northwest via the Istanbul Highway (E 5). Make a right after 133 km (90 miles), just east of Gerede, and a left after another 33 km (22 miles), going toward Karabük. Buses to Bartin via Karabük pass here, making it a possible stop on the way to Amasra. A very long day, or preferably an overnight in Safranbolu, would allow a loop by car to include Kastamonu and the scenic İlgaz mountains.

The prosperity from Turkey's iron and steel center at Karabük has enabled Safranbolu, 12 km (8 miles) north, to maintain its 18th- and 19th-century civil architecture. Designated as a national protected urban area in 1976, with modernization restricted to a newer section above, old Safranbolu survives as a functioning open-air museum—a slice of life from Ottoman times.

The town occupies the slopes of a ravine formed by a stream that cuts through the surrounding tableland and winds around a central hill. Atop this hill are foundations of medieval fortification. By 1196 the Seljuks had taken this Byzantine town. During the 14th century the Candar Emirs of Kastamonu held sway here, and the famous traveller Ibn Battuta passed through town, stayed in a fine medrese, and was entertained in the citadel. The Ottomans annexed this area in the 15th century after battling over it for half a century with the Candarids and their descendents, the Isfendiyarids. By the 18th century it was known as Zağfiran-Bolu (literally, "saffron city," after the local production of saffron from a purple crocus that blooms in late fall). From 1826 to 1870 Safranbolu was the county seat. Its large abandoned gendarmerie stands in the area where the citadel was, flanked by a 19th-century clock-tower built by a certain *paşa* who was responsible for numerous clock towers around the country.

Traditional family townhouses (*konak*s) cover the hillsides below, facing this way and that along curving lanes. The houses stand on high stone foundations that adjust for the slope and support one story—or more often two stories—of timber frame and sun-dried brick construction that juts out here and there and may or may not be plastered over. The many windows are traditionally shuttered in dark wood. Among the jumble of tile roofs the newer, brick-red roofs stand out from the older, mottled brown ones. Many of the houses have walled gardens, whose greenery and (in spring) blossoms highlight the subtle variations of the natural building materials.

On the shoulder of the hill below the citadel, the **Havuzlu Eski Asmazlar Konağı**, one of a number of houses belonging to the influential Asmazlar family, has been renovated by the Turkish Touring and Automobile Association as a charming hotel. Off the lobby an original reception room, featuring a shallow pool and tinkling fountain set about with small tables, serves as the hotel's bar. Downstairs you can dine before a large, open-hearth fireplace or lunch outside on the garden terrace, which overlooks more old homes and the poplar-lined stream below. The hotel has only ten rooms (reasonably priced) and may not take reservations far in advance unless you're with a very large party and plan to fill all the rooms, so check one or two days ahead.

Ask at the Havuzlu Konak for the walking-tour map of town. A main cobbled street descends the hill through the commercial center of the old town and leads across the stream to the opposite side. In a small square near the beginning of this cobbled street, sample some of the specialties of a confection shop on the left—the fresh walnut taffy (*ceviz helvası*) is to die for. On the way down and along the side streets, some shaded by vines, small shops offer traditional as well as modern wares and traditional craftsmen and tradesmen hold out: making and selling saddlery and riding equipment, baubles and beads, brooms and baskets, cast-iron pieces, knives, quilts, carved wooden pieces (look for fine boxwood spoons—the traditional serving implement in a land of soups, *pilav*s, and *güveç*), caps, and shoes. Off to the left find the restored **Arasta**. This single-story market (with the tourism office in the center) has wooden cupboard-like shops and was once a center of the leather-footwear trade. It now houses a handcrafts bazaar. Near the bottom of the hill, on the left, a high-arched stone portal leads into the **Cinci Han** (Exorcist Han), whose interior courtyard is surrounded by stone arches. The han once housed travelling merchants trading in saffron; it is presently being readied to become a hotel for modern travellers. Across the square at the bottom of the hill is the main Ottoman mosque. To one side the stream has been bridged to create an open market area that on Saturdays is one of the liveliest in Turkey. (On Sundays the town is dead.)

Up the street on the opposite side, the former *kaymakam*'s (local governor's) house has been restored as a **Turkish house museum** by the ministry of tourism. The gate in the wall gives access to the lower section, with stables, utility area, and back garden, and leads directly to the *hayat* (vestibule), with servants' quarters to one side. The family's private apartments, which traditionally accommodated three or four generations, are reached by stairs up to the *çardak,* a large common hall at the center of the house. Rooms open on either side of the *çardak;* in such a traditional house there was usually at least one room with a space that jutted out for added light, breezes, and views. This was designated as the primary "sitting and sleeping room" or reception area (*selamlık*) for the men of the household and for male guests. Raised floors indicated that outdoor footwear was removed and slippers donned for walking on the room's kilims or carpets. Different rooms served as sleeping areas for various family members. During the daytime, bedding and personal items were stored in built-in wall cupboards and the cushioned benches (*divans*) along the walls provided seating. Meals might be eaten anywhere, the food brought in on large trays and set on low, round portable tables around which family members gathered, sitting on cushions. Arched niches in the wall cupboards held decorative items, and the wooden ceilings were frequently made of decorative joinery and painted.

You can spend some time on pleasant walks along back lanes or down by the stream (a picturesque bridge crosses it near the odiferous tanneries). This dip into the past could end with a splash at the double Ottoman bath (*hamam*), whose squat twin domes are visible on the hillside above the han.

In a separate neighborhood on the higher slopes to the west, large wooden summer residences, many with a characteristic stags' antlers hanging from the eaves (reminiscent of Hattic symbols) are surrounded by gardens and orchards. In the new town the **Uz Oteli** provides adequate accommodations.

Going or coming from Ankara, the 300 km (200 miles), via Kastamonu and Çankırı, takes about five hours. Ruins of a 12th-century Byzantine fortress loom above **Kastamonu**, a provincial center with a few historic buildings and a museum housing a small collection of ancient artifacts and folkloric objects from the region. More noteworthy is a fine 14th-century wooden mosque in the village of **Kasabaköy**, 10 km (6 miles) to the northwest of Kastamonu. The drive through the forest of firs and over the **İlgaz pass** (elevation 5,760 feet) has splendid views as it descends into the valley of the Kızılırmak (the ancient Halys river) toward **Çankırı**, which sits beneath the ruins of another Byzantine fortress. A Seljuk hospital stands on the hillside south of town, and there is a mosque designed by Sinan at the town center. The road to Ankara bypasses Kalecik, which is also topped by a Byzantine fortress, which protected the road from Ankara to Paphlagonia and the Byzantine Empire's eastern flank.

GETTING AROUND

Ankara's **Esenboğa International Airport**, which has been nicely renovated, is served by Aeroflot, Air France, Alitalia, British Airways, Iberia, Lufthansa, KLM, Middle East Air, SAS, Sabena, Swiss Air, Turkish Airlines (THY), and TWA. Most flights make a stop in Istanbul, but there are some direct connections to Europe. THY also has a network of domestic flights (none more than 50 minutes long) that connect

Ankara, Istanbul, and İzmir with Antalya, Adana, Dalaman, Diyarbakır, Erzurum, Kayseri, Malatya, Samsun, Trabzon, and Van. Depending on the destination, the flights may run once per week or daily. There is also a daily flight to Lefkoşa in Northern Cyprus. Two private airlines, Istanbul Air and Kıbrıs Yolu, also operate out of Ankara. If you arrive from overseas, you can change money immediately before passport control or while waiting for customs. A THY airport bus runs every half hour between Esenboğa airport and the downtown terminal at the train station; the fare is about $2; pay when you board. Taxi fare from the airport to downtown Ankara can run to $18 or more.

Trains arrive at and depart from the Gar (or Tren İstasyonu), the railroad station located on Talat Paşa Bulvarı at Cumhuriyet Bulvarı. Overnight sleeper trains (*yataklı tren,* with compartments for one, two, or three, or the less fancy couchets for four) connecting Ankara and Istanbul and Ankara and İzmir make for practical and elegant rail service; they will also transport you to a bygone era. The train to Istanbul has a good dining car (especially delightful at breakfast, when you will be approaching the city along the Marmara shore), but if you depart Ankara by train in the evening, try the restored Republican-period restaurant in the station (off the left-hand platform) to complete the mood. The train station also has a small museum (open 8:30 A.M. to 12:30 P.M. and 1:30 to 5:30 P.M., except Mondays).

Information and reservations for **Turkish Maritime Lines** (with connections to Italy and several Greek islands and along the Black Sea, Aegean, and Mediterranean coasts) can be obtained at Denizyolları Bürosu, Şehit Adem Yavuz Sokak 3/2, Kızılay (Tel: 4/417-1161 or 425-6368; Fax: 4/418-2374).

Intercity buses are quite reasonable and convenient. Many lines run from the main bus station (Otogar, indicated by A.S.O.T.), which is moving this year from its old location to the new terminal west of town on the Konya highway (Bahçelerarası Caddessi) north of the intersection with the Eskişehir highway (İsmet İnönü Bulvarı). There is also the reputable Varan line, which has its own terminal nearby on the Eskişehir highway at Söğütözü Caddesi (as well as a Kızılay office with connecting minibus), serves Istanbul and İzmir, and runs night buses from Ankara to Antalya. The Ulusoy line is equally pleasant—uniformed attendants serve tea on board. It, too, has a new terminal at Söğütözü and operates buses to the Black Sea area as well as to Istanbul, İzmir, and Antalya. For information on intercity buses, Tel: (4) 310-4747.

Day or overnight tours to the archaeological sites near

Ankara are also available from many of the numerous travel agencies in town. Agencies may offer scheduled tours that you can join or may be able to provide you with a car and driver and/or guide. Ask at your hotel or try one of the following agencies: **Alabanda Seyahat (Tour) Acentası,** Cinnah Caddesi 67/B, Çankaya (Tel: 4/446-3305); **Saltur S.A.,** Atatürk Bulvarı 169/9, Bakanlıklar (Tel: 4/425-1333 or 425-5973); or **Setur Turizm S.A.,** Kavaklıdere Sokak 5/B, Şişli Meydanı, Kavaklıdere (Tel: 4/467-1165 through 467-1169).

Taxis are the most practical means of getting around Ankara—traffic patterns, construction detours, and lack of parking make driving a real challenge. Taxis are metered; note that fares increase by 50 percent from midnight to 6:00 A.M., as well as for the airport run. Although tipping is not expected, the fare is usually rounded up to the nearest 1,000 TL, as small change is often hard to come by. Drivers have difficulty breaking large bills, so be sure you have change before starting out. There are taxi stands, but finding a cab on major streets is usually no problem, except at rush hour, when some taxis plying Atatürk Bulvarı convert to shared cabs with set destinations (usually up Cinnah to Çankaya) and charge a flat fee for each passenger. If you want to maximize your touring time, you can hire a taxi for a few hours or for the day; ask at your hotel. Specify your itinerary before you negotiate a price.

Ankara is now in the middle of a **subway** and light rail project, scheduled to open in 1995. Construction of a station and tunnels in Kızılay has forced the rerouting of traffic, creating a real mess. The first metro lines will travel out the Istanbul highway to the suburb of Batıkent (West Town), with stations at Ulus and Sıhhiye, and out the Eskişehir highway, with the first stop at Söğütözü. The light rail (AnkaRay) will run from Dikimev on the east to Soğutözü on the west, crossing the metro at Kızılay.

ACCOMMODATIONS REFERENCE

Rates given below are for double rooms, double occupancy, and represent projections for 1993. All prices are subject to change and should be checked before booking. Some hotels include breakfast. When telephoning between cities in Turkey, dial 9 before entering the city code. The city code for Ankara is 4.

▶ **Ankara Dedeman Oteli.** Büklüm Sokak 1, 06640 Akay, **Ankara.** Tel: 417-6200; Fax: 417-6214. $100.
▶ **Best Oteli.** Atatürk Bulvarı 195, Kavaklıdere 06691, **Ankara.** Tel: 467-0880/86; Fax: 467-0885. $104.

▶ **Bulvar Palas Oteli.** Atatürk Bulvarı 141, Bakanlıklar 06581, **Ankara.** Tel: 417-5020; Fax: 425-2971. $50.

▶ **Büyük Ankara Oteli.** Atatürk Bulvarı 183, 06551 **Ankara.** Tel: 425-6655; Fax: 425-5070. $100–$150.

▶ **Büyük Sürmeli Oteli.** Cihan Sokak 6, Sıhhiye 06551, **Ankara.** Tel: 231-7660; Fax: 229-5176. $120.

▶ **Eyuboğlu Oteli.** Karanfil Sokak 73, Bakanlıklar 06581, **Ankara.** Tel: 417-6400; Fax: 417-8125. $75.

▶ **Havuzlu Eski Asmazlar Konaği.** Hacı Halil Mahallesi, Beybağı Sokak 18, **Safranbolu,** 67700 Zonguldak. Tel; (464) 52883; Fax: (464) 23824. Prices not available.

▶ **Hilton Hotel.** Tahran Caddesi 12, Kavaklıdere 06691, **Ankara.** Tel: 468-2888; Fax: 468-0909. $240.

▶ **Hitit Oteli.** Hisarparkı Caddesi, Firuzağa Sokak 12, Ulus 06040, **Ankara.** Tel: 310-8617; Fax: 311-4102. $44.

▶ **Hotel Metropol.** Olgunlar Sokak 5, Bakanlıklar, 06581 **Ankara.** Tel: 417-3060; Fax: 417-6990. $75.

▶ **Kent Hotel.** Mithatpaşa Caddesi 4-6, 06410 Yenişehir 06441, **Ankara.** Tel: 435-5050/58. Fax: 434-4657. $135.

▶ **Merit Altınel.** Tandoğan Meydanı, 06571 **Ankara.** Tel: 231-7760; Fax: 230-2330. $195.

▶ **Sheraton Hotel.** Noktalı Sokak, Kavaklıdere, 06691 **Ankara.** Tel: 467-2175; Fax: 467-1136. $220.

▶ **Tunalı Oteli.** Tunalı Hilmi Caddesi 119, Kavaklıdere 06691, **Ankara.** Tel: 467-4440; Telex: 42142. $65.

▶ **Turist Oteli.** Çankırı Caddesi 37, Ulus 06040, **Ankara.** Tel: 310-3980/89; Fax: 311-8345. $45.

▶ **Uz Oteli.** Kiranköy, **Safranbolu,** 67700 Zonguldak. Tel: (464) 22215; Fax: (464) 42393.

CENTRAL ANATOLIA

By Gary Leiser

Fluent in Arabic and Turkish, Gary Leiser spent eight years in Ankara as an area specialist and interpreter for the U.S. Department of Defense and as a historian for the U.S. Air Force. He has a doctorate in Medieval Islamic history and has led tours to eastern Turkey for the American Research Institute in Turkey. His translation of M. Fuad Köprülü's classic work The Origins of the Ottoman Empire *has recently been published.*

From Constantinople the Byzantine emperors looked across the Bosphorus to Anatolé, Greek for the "land of the rising sun." Today the Turks use the term *Anadolu* to mean all of Asiatic Turkey and, above all, the great plateau at its heart. This plateau, Central Anatolia, is a vast steppe about the size of Ireland. For the most part it is an island of flatlands and low hills ringed by a sea of formidable mountain ranges. Furthermore, with most of its cities and towns, including Ankara, at the periphery, Central Anatolia is an apparent desert island; you can cross it without encountering any significant urban centers. The few villages along the roads seem isolated, lost. Here and there the open landscape is interrupted by a jagged crag or dormant volcano, and in some places a river or stream has labored to create a spacious valley or picturesque gorge. But these formations seem merely to accent the emptiness. In a depression in the very center of the Anatolian plateau is the enormous Tuz Gölü (Salt Lake). With a salinity greater than that of the Dead Sea, it is the epitome of desolation.

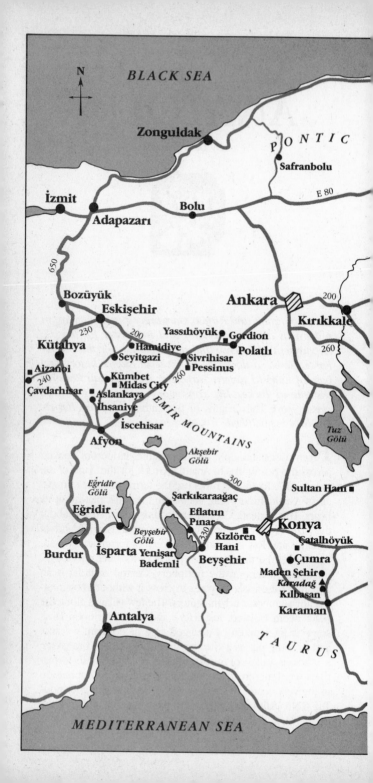

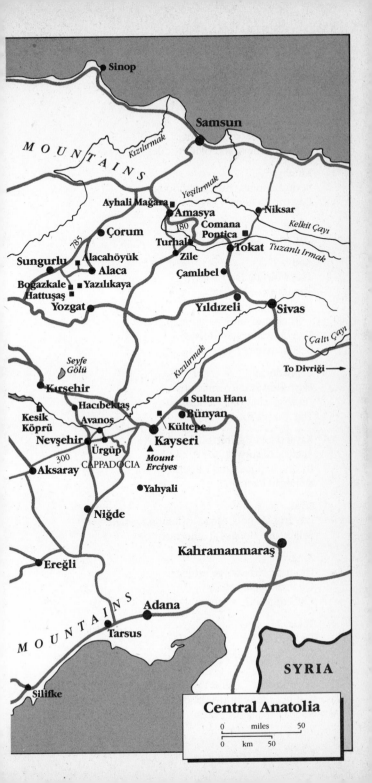

MAJOR INTEREST

Early civilizations
Medieval castles and towns
Medieval Islamic art and architecture
Varied scenery
Fantastic geologic features
Carpets, kilims, and other textiles

Kütahya
Seyitgazi tomb and dervish lodge
Day trip to Roman city of Aizanoi

Afyon
Day trip to Midas City

Konya
The Whirling Dervishes
The tomb of Mevlâna
Day trips to the lake district and the "Valley of a
    Thousand and One Churches"
The caravan route to Kayseri
Seljuk architecture

Cappadocia
Fantastical stone formations
Underground tunnel villages
The Ankara road to Kayseri

Kayseri and Environs
Ancient history
Buying antiques and carpets
Seljuk architecture

Sivas
Day trip to the mosque-asylum in Divriği
Seljuk and Mongol architecture

Amasya
Dramatic river-gorge setting
Ottoman architecture
Cliffside Pontic tombs

Tokat
Old quarter
Day trip to citadel at Niksar

The openness of Central Anatolia makes travel easy. The
fastest, if not the only, overland route between Europe and
Asia is across this great plateau. It is also the natural meeting

point of all Anatolia—from the earliest times it drew travellers of every description. Traders and merchants, pilgrims and preachers, and some of the most renowned armies in history have trod its soil. The soldiers of Alexander the Great, the First Crusade, and the ruthless Turkic conqueror Tamerlane all marched over the dusty steppe on the way to wealth and glory.

The dust, furthermore, is fertile. Despite the walls of mountains that isolate it from the sea, Central Anatolia is *not* a desert. There is sufficient rainfall to grow wheat and barley without artificial irrigation in even the driest districts. At the foot of the surrounding mountains run fast rivulets, and near these sources of water important towns and cities have arisen. Central Anatolia has, in fact, attracted human settlement from the earliest times. At Çatalhöyük, south of Konya, archaeologists have excavated a town dating to 6500 B.C.—one of the oldest urban centers ever discovered. Pigs and cattle may first have been domesticated in or near Central Anatolia, and barley and the ancestors of modern food grains—emmer wheat and einkorn—grew in the Taurus mountains to the south of the plateau.

Over the millennia, scores of states and empires have originated from the Anatolian plateau or were compelled to conquer it. From its rich soil emerged the formidable Hittite Empire (fl. ca. 1380 to 1200 B.C.) and the enigmatic Phrygian state of King Midas (fl. ca. 750 B.C.). For the Greeks, Persians, and Romans, it was a major granary. Even the Gauls found it irresistible. Later, wheat and soldiers from this region were critical to the survival power of the Byzantine Empire. When the nomadic Seljuk Turks arrived in the 11th century, they found the plateau to be ideal for their herds and flocks. Master horsemen and redoubtable warriors, they conquered the plateau and made it the center of a flourishing state, that of the Seljuks of Rum, or Rome. ("Rome" referred to the Roman Empire, as Byzantium long continued to call itself and, by extension, its heartland in Anatolia.) For a short time Central Anatolia became a wealthy province of the Mongol successors of Genghis Khan and then, for almost 600 years, of the Ottoman Turks. In the years following World War I, Central Anatolia played a major role in the formation of the Turkish republic: It was here that Atatürk decisively defeated invading Greek forces, and it was to the modest Central Anatolian farming town of Ankara that Atatürk moved the new, secular nation's capital.

Traces of Central Anatolia's extraordinarily rich historical legacy can be found today in its cities, towns, and villages.

Stone Age settlements, Hittite sanctuaries, Phrygian and Hellenistic tombs, Roman temples, Byzantine churches, Seljuk mosques, 19th-century Ottoman towns, and other historically significant structures dot the landscape. The most common monuments, however, are those erected by the Seljuks and their Turkish rivals and successors, who dominated the area from 1077 up to the time of the Ottoman incursions of the 14th century. Central Anatolia is, in fact, a great treasure house of medieval Turkish architecture. Apart from mosques, the historical buildings that you will encounter most frequently are caravansaries, *medreses*, and *türbes*. Caravansaries, or *hans*, were fortified inns for travelling merchants. They provided food, lodging, stables, storage facilities, and, in some cases, female companionship. Medreses were schools of Islamic law, usually established with endowments that provided scholarships and paid professors' salaries. The Turks were great builders of medreses, which, after mosques, were the most important institution in Islamic society. *Türbes* were mausoleums for members of the ruling elite and important religious figures. Sometimes called tower-tombs, they were cylindrical structures with cone-shaped roofs that originated from pre-Islamic Turkish burial customs. They may have been modeled on Buddhist stupas or, more likely, the yurts of Turkish nomads.

In addition to Central Anatolia's man-made wonders are those created by nature: the fantastic terrain of Cappadocia, the beautiful lakes of the southwestern rim, the great Tuz Gölü, the painted hills of the steppe, the rugged canyons of the Kızılırmak (Red River), and snowcapped Mount Erciyes. In the spring much of Central Anatolia is a waving green carpet of wheat and barley, alternating in places with fields of poppies or sunflowers and flowering fruit orchards. Lambs bleat in the pastures and storks clack their beaks from the tops of minarets and telephone poles.

The Turks in Anatolia

Anatolia has been a melting pot of peoples since ancient times. The coming of the Turks in the 11th century marked the beginning of the last great cultural transformation of this region. Seeking land for his people, Seljuk, the leader of a confederation of Turkish tribes, began to move from Central Asia toward the heartlands of the Muslim Middle East around A.D. 960. Although he and his followers converted to Islam, their progress was opposed by the Muslim Ghaznavid Empire, centered in present-day Afghanistan. In 1040, however,

Toghrıl Beg and Chaghrı Beg, the grandsons of Seljuk, defeated the Ghaznavids and proceeded to conquer most of the Middle East. The state they established became known as the Great Seljuk Empire. Stretching from Central Asia to the Mediterranean, it opened the Middle East—and Anatolia in particular—to massive waves of Turkish immigration. The Great Seljuk Empire subsequently dissolved into various regional states, the most enduring of which was that of the Seljuks of Rum, or Anatolia. As Turks began to stream into Anatolia in the late 11th century, the Greek and Christian Byzantine Empire lost territory to the invaders. The lost lands eventually became Turkish-speaking and Muslim. This gradual process of Turkization and Islamization continued long after Constantinople, the last remnant of the Byzantine Empire, fell to the Ottoman Turks in 1453. Indeed, the last stage in this process occurred in this century, with the exchange of minority populations between Greece and Turkey after the Turkish War of Independence of 1919 to 1922.

Because the Central Anatolian steppe closely resembled the Turks' original homeland in Central Asia, it became a magnet for the early waves of Turkish immigrants. Central Anatolia was the first region of Asia Minor to be thoroughly "Turkized." Even today the Turks of Central Anatolia are considered by other Turks to be the most "Turkish" and to speak the purest form of the Turkish language. And the villagers of Central Anatolia represent to the Turks themselves the backbone of Turkey, as hardy, hardworking farmers and tough soldiers.

Despite centuries of Turkization, the ethnic landscape of Central Anatolia is not completely uniform. Here and there are Kurdish or Circassian villages. Over the years the Kurds have trickled west from their traditional homeland in southeastern Turkey; the Circassians arrived primarily during the 19th century, fleeing the Russian conquest of the Caucasus. Both peoples are Muslim. Except for language differences, there is little to distinguish a Turkish, Kurdish, or Circassian village for the Western visitor. Religious differences among them are even less apparent. Almost all are Sunnis. The inhabitants of a few villages and towns, such as Çorum, are Alawi Muslims, followers of a form of Shi'a Islam. Not all the inhabitants of Central Anatolia are settled. In the mountains to the south and east, you may encounter bands of *yörüks*, nomads who may be descendants of the original Turkish immigrants to Anatolia. They, too, are mostly Alawis. And wagon trains of Gypsies, whose origins are even more obscure, may appear almost anywhere.

The Food and Wine
of Central Anatolia

Despite some industrialization, primarily around Ankara, Konya, and Kayseri, the economic foundation of Central Anatolia is agriculture. Tractors pulling wagons full of vegetables or fruit, groups of women in brightly colored pantaloons working in the fields, and children tending flocks of sheep are common sights. Though cereal grains are the most important crop in this, the "breadbasket" of Turkey, some cities have become associated with a single product: potatoes from Adapazarı, apples from Amasya, and opium and poppy seed from Afyon.

Most of Turkey's beekeepers are to be found along the Aegean and Mediterranean coasts, so Central Anatolia can't really be called the "land of milk and honey," but it could be described with some justification as the "land of wine and cream." In the region around Ankara and in the volcanic earth of Cappadocia, vineyards flourish. Although the Turks do not have a long tradition of wine-making (and sampling Turkish wines can be a bit of an adventure), there is considerable variety. The white Çankaya and the red Yakut from Ankara, both under the Kavaklıdere label, are quite palatable. The wines from Cappadocia are of uneven quality, although the new Nevşah label has a good reputation. Try its *muskat*. During the annual wine festival held the first week in October in Ürgüp, the center of this region, an international jury selects Turkey's best wines.

An older tradition is the making of *kaymak,* or clotted cream—pure cream with the consistency of butter. It is usually spread on pastries such as *tel kadayıf,* which is like shredded wheat soaked in syrup. The smoothest *kaymak* comes from Afyon. (A reason popularly given for its quality is that the stems of opium poppies are the fodder for the local dairy cattle!) Central Anatolia is famous for other dishes as well. Kayseri is well known for its *pastırma*— spice-cured meat, perhaps the original pastrami. Kayseri is also the home of a delicate form of *mantı,* a typical Turkish dish consisting of very small ravioli-like pasta stuffed with ground lamb, boiled, and usually served in a sauce of yogurt and garlic garnished with red pepper. A bowl of *mantı* with a green salad and fresh Turkish bread is an excellent dinner. Roasted chickpeas, called *leblebi,* are a popular snack all over Turkey; the ones from Çorum are the most favored. And in Konya, the religious center of Turkey, try *pişmaniye,* a spun-sugar confection. The word *pişmaniye* derives from *pişman,* meaning "regretful," seeming to suggest that you will regret not having tried it.

Shopping in Central Anatolia

Central Anatolia also has its special crafts. Pipes are carved from the famous meerschaum (*lületaşı* in Turkish) that is extracted from the plain of Eskişehir. A soft white mineral, meerschaum, when polished, has a sensual quality like that of jade. Onyx of many colors—especially pale green, pink, and beige—is found in abundance in Cappadocia, where local artisans carve it into a variety of objects. The town of Avanos in Cappadocia is known for its red-clay pottery. In the 19th century Central Anatolia was renowned for its herds of Angora goats, whose wool was used to make mohair. (The word "Angora" is an anglicization of "Ankara.") Today, however, there are only a few mohair products on the market, mostly from Beypazarı.

Certainly the most important crafts in Central Anatolia, as in other parts of Turkey, are handmade textiles: carpets, kilims (flatweave rugs), saddlebags, pillowcases, grain sacks, and other items. The production of some kinds of carpets and kilims is unique to a few villages in the region, but they all make their way to the carpet shops of Ankara. After the capital, the best cities in which to shop for carpets and kilims are Konya and Ürgüp. Konya is a good place to look for older pieces, in particular kilims from the Konya plain, once a summer pasture for nomads. You can often find especially beautiful carpets in Ürgüp, but prices tend to be higher than elsewhere.

Finally, Ankara, Konya, Kayseri, Ürgüp, and Sivas all have old bazaars or streets of antiques dealers where unusual treasures may turn up: samovars from Russia, old clocks from England, U.S. Navy revolvers from the American Civil War, engraved copper pots from Iran, furniture inlaid with mother-of-pearl from Syria, books from everywhere, and jewelry, utensils, weapons, and sundry items from the time of the Ottoman Empire.

The easiest ways to see Central Anatolia are to start at Ankara (which is covered in its own chapter, above) and drive around the rim of the steppe or to use Ankara as a hub and to drive out along "spokes" radiating from it to selected destinations. The following text moves generally counter-clockwise around the capital, starting at Kütahya, west of Ankara. Except for Divriği, no place is more than a day's drive from the capital city.

Ankara is noted for its archaeology museum, citadel, Roman temple, and shopping, especially for carpets. Easy day trips can be made to the nearby ruins of Gordion, the ancient capital of the Phrygians; to Boğazkale, the site of Hattuşaş, the capital of the Hittites; and to the Ottoman-era town of Safranbolu (see Ankara and Environs, above). Kütahya, southwest of Eskişehir, is the center of Turkey's faience production. South of it are the classical ruins of Aizanoi, among which stands the magnificent temple of Zeus. Near Afyon, about 260 km (161 miles) southwest of the capital and the center of poppy production, are the Phrygian ruins known as "Midas City" and associated monuments. Konya, about 260 km (161 miles) due south of Ankara, is the old capital of the Seljuk sultanate and home of the Whirling Dervishes. The city is virtually an outdoor museum of medieval Turkish architecture. Day trips from Konya lead to grand alpine lakes to the west, a valley of lost medieval churches to the south, and a series of monumental caravansaries along an old caravan route to the east.

The great erosion basin of Cappadocia, southeast of Ankara and roughly bounded by a triangle formed by the cities of Kayseri, Nevşehir, and Niğde, is renowned for its incomparable geologic wonders and early Byzantine art. Kayseri, 284 km (176 miles) southeast of Ankara, and Sivas, 440 km (273 miles) due east of the capital, are, like Konya, treasure houses of pre-Ottoman Turkish architecture. At Divriği, southeast of Sivas, is a combination great mosque and insane asylum, perhaps the most bizarre structure in the history of Islamic art and architecture. Amasya, 338 km (210 miles) northeast of Ankara, boasts a glorious natural setting and an unmatched mixture of historical monuments stretching from the Hellenistic period to Ottoman times. And the old city of Tokat, located midway between Amasya and Sivas, is Central Anatolia's best example of a living medieval Muslim city.

If your time is limited, choose Konya, Cappadocia, and Amasya as your must-see destinations.

KÜTAHYA

Kütahya, the capital of the province of the same name, is 280 km (174 miles) west of Ankara. It is reached by first taking highway 200 to Eskişehir. Known from at least the third century A.D. for its hot springs, Eskişehir is an industrial city that was rebuilt following its virtual destruction during the Greek occupation of 1921. On the wide plain to the north of

Eskişehir, the Byzantine emperors used to mass their armies for campaigns to the east. In 1097, the First Crusade defeated the Seljuk army here, opening the way to the Holy Land. At Eskişehir, turn south on route 230 and then, a few miles later, left onto route 650. (En route to Eskişehir you can turn southwest at Hamidiye to visit Seyitgazi, discussed below.)

Kütahya, known in classical times as Kotiaion or Cotyaeum, is the center of Turkey's faïence industry. At the crossroads in the middle of town is a fountain whose waters splash about a giant multicolored faïence vase. Cotyaeum is mentioned by several classical writers as one of the most important cities of Phrygia. According to Suidas, a tenth-century Byzantine lexicographer, it was the birthplace of Aesop. Christianity arrived early: In 267 Saint Menas is supposed to have testified to the ascension of Christ at "Cotuayio" in Phrygia. In the Byzantine period it was the seat of an archbishopric. Around 1080 the city was captured by the Seljuks, and from 1302 to 1428 it was the capital of the Turkish principality of the Germiyanids, one of many petty dynasties to emerge from the dissolution of the Seljuk sultanate. In the early 1400s Tamerlane briefly made it his headquarters during his conquest of western Anatolia. Finally, in 1429 Kütahya was incorporated into the Ottoman Empire.

Kütahya today is a fairly nondescript city, but some remnants of the town's history can still be seen, the most impressive of which is the great **citadel** (*kale*) crowning the hill above the old city. Entering Kütahya from Eskişehir, turn right at the fountain for the street that runs through the old city, which harbors a few monuments from the Germiyanid and early Ottoman periods, notably, the Kurşunlu Cami (1375/6), Ulu Cami (Great Mosque; 1411), İshak Fakih Camii (1433), Yakub Çelebi Camii (1433/4), and the Karagöz Ahmet Camii (1509). (*Cami* is the Turkish word for mosque.) Next to the Ulu Cami is a Germiyanid medrese (1314) that now serves as the city museum (of marginal interest). The **citadel** is approached from the area behind the Ulu Cami. Although the climb to the top is strenuous, the view is excellent. The walls of the citadel are in a good state of preservation, and inside are the ruins of a Byzantine church.

The production of the glazed polychrome pottery (*çini*) for which Kütahya is famed probably originated in the second half of the 15th century. The tombs of Yakub Çelebi and İshak Fakih, adjacent to their respective mosques, are the earliest buildings in Kütahya that are decorated with glazed tiles. (It is not certain, however, whether these particular tiles are actually a local product.) After İznik, Kütahya was the most important center of pottery and tile production in the Ottoman

Empire. Its ware was in demand throughout the empire and was even exported to Europe. Armenian churches within the empire, most notably the cathedral of St. James in Jerusalem, commissioned Kütahya tiles with figural decoration and Christian iconography. Kütahya ware reached its height in the 18th century, when the last original style of Turkish pottery appeared. New designs were applied with light, free brushstrokes and were composed of small flowers and medallions in blue, red, yellow, purple, and green. The best examples of Kütahya work are to be seen in the museums and Ottoman buildings of Istanbul, particularly the Çinili Köşk (see Istanbul, above).

The heritage of Kütahya's kilns was revived in the early 20th century. The shapes and motifs of today's products are, in fact, based primarily on classical patterns. These products are meant to be decorative rather than utilitarian, and increasing quality control in recent years has resulted in some truly gorgeous pieces. Although Kütahya ware is sold all over Turkey and exported throughout the world, it is popular to make a "buying trip" to the city itself. Most of Kütahya's approximately 30 *çini* factories have showrooms and provide tours of their facilities. The best place to stay is the **Erbaylar Oteli**, at the fountain crossroads, a full-service hotel with a conference center and a good restaurant.

Seyitgazi

A visit to Seyitgazi can easily be incorporated into a trip to Kütahya (though you should note that there are no places to eat in the village). At the small town of Hamidiye, 41 km (25 miles) before Eskişehir, turn left and head southwest. After travelling about 25 km (16 miles) across a barren landscape, you arrive at the village of Seyitgazi. Alone on a low hill next to the village rises a fortress-like complex that supposedly contains the tomb of the village namesake.

Medieval Arabic sources relate that a semilegendary Arab warrior, usually referred to as Abd Allah, gained fame as a champion in the wars between the Arabs and Byzantium in the Umayyad period (661 to 750). His exploits won him the title *al-Baṭṭāl*, "the hero." He died in battle somewhere in western Anatolia. When the Turks conquered Asia Minor, they adopted the local epic traditions, among them the various tales of al-Baṭṭāl's exploits. To these the Turks added elements of their own as well as legends absorbed from Persian traditions. The result was a literary epic, the *Battalname*, a mixture of fact and fantasy whose hero was called Seyit Battal Gazi (Lord Hero Warrior), or simply Seyit Gazi.

In one of the popular tales told of him, Seyit Gazi is given refuge in a convent whose abbess allows him to hide from a Byzantine general. Afterwards he follows his Christian enemy, kills him, and then returns to the convent to carry off all the nuns and marry the abbess, who bears him children.

How the location of Seyit Gazi's burial place was determined is unclear, but the presumed site was on the battle routes of the Byzantine and Seljuk armies at the end of the 11th century. By the second half of the 12th century the site had become a well-known shrine, attracting pilgrims, votive offerings, and precious gifts. The **burial complex** is a rather stark and massive structure of cut stone; it completely dominates the empty surrounding plain. Part of the complex dates from the Seljuk period, but most of it represents restoration work and additions of the 16th century. The entire structure is composed of several tombs, including that of the martyred warrior, a lodge (*tekke*) of the Bektaşi dervish brotherhood, a mosque, and a soup kitchen (*imaret*) for the poor. The cenotaph of Seyit Gazi is enormous, as if to symbolize his superhuman qualities.

Aizanoi

The Roman city of Aizanoi is an easy day trip from Kütahya, or can be a side trip on the way to Afyon, discussed below. Head south from Kütahya on the Afyon road, and after 9 km (5½ miles) turn right on route 240. About 48 km (30 miles) farther you come to the village of Çavdarhisar. In and around this village are the ruins of Aizanoi. In the spring the magnificent remains stand in the midst of a vast emerald pasture, guarded only by flocks of geese.

The real jewel of Aizanoi is the **temple of Zeus**, which was built during the reign of Hadrian (A.D. 117 to 138). A stately Ionic structure, it is one of the best-preserved ancient buildings in Turkey. The city itself dates from the second century B.C., when it was a center for the worship of the goddess Cybele, the "mother of the gods" in ancient Middle Eastern religion. In fact, the remarkable barrel-vaulted substructure of the temple was probably where the worship of this goddess took place.

A short walk north of the temple lie the remains of a stadium and theater, the latter in fairly good condition. From the top extends a fine view of the entire site and the Murat Dağı range. Slightly south of the temple, surrounded by the village and separated from the temple area by a small river, are the remains of the Roman meat market, baths, and other buildings. Spanning the river are two well-preserved Roman bridges that are still in use; the remains of several Roman quays along the banks are used nowadays for flood control. Carved on the lowest course of the stone walls of the meat market is a relatively complete copy of the famous Edict of Diocletian (issued in A.D. 301), which fixed maximum prices for provisions and maximum wages within the Roman Empire. This first attempt at a government-controlled economy, like all similar efforts up to the present, failed.

There's no restaurant in the vicinity of Aizanoi, but it's a good place for a picnic, so pack a lunch.

The Road to Afyon

Afyon is about 260 km (161 miles, or about three hours) southwest of Ankara on the main highway between the capital and İzmir. This road is heavily travelled, and work on widening it to four lanes is progressing slowly. Leave Ankara on route 200, which is also the road to Eskişehir, and follow it through the barren countryside for 139 km (86 miles) to the crossroads near the small town of Sivrihisar. At the crossroads, turn left on route 260 for Afyon. A few miles before this junction are a number of gas station–cafeteria complexes where you can stop for refreshments.

Sivrihisar, meaning "Pointed Castle," is backed against a sawtoothed ridge that can be seen for miles across the Central Anatolian plain. The site of an ancient settlement, the town is mentioned in various early texts. In the 13th century it reportedly had a famous church that could cure animals of disease. Frequent references to Sivrihisar are made in accounts of the campaigns of Tamerlane; for a while it served as his headquarters on his march to the west. In the old part of town are a number of homes from the late 18th and 19th centuries and a medieval "Romanesque" mosque full of local carpets and kilims.

Next to the crossroads at Sivrihisar is a yellow sign pointing south to the ruins of the Phrygian city of Pessinus, 16 km (10 miles) from the junction. Although it had a famous sanctuary of Cybele in the second century B.C., the surviving remains of the city are only of interest to hardened archaeologists. The road to the site does pass a remarkable section of ancient road, however. This road presumably followed the course of the Persian Royal Road, which connected Anatolia with Iran. Built by the Persians after their conquest of Anatolia in the sixth century B.C., this road ran from Sardis to Susa. In a famous passage plagiarized by the U.S. Postal Service, Herodotus described the royal messengers who sped along this highway, saying, "These men will not be hindered from accomplishing at their best speed the distance which they have to go, either by snow, or rain, or heat, or by the darkness of night." The exposed surface of the road on the way to Pessinus probably dates from Roman times.

Some 64 km (40 miles) from Sivrihisar the highway begins to rise and then snake its way over the forested Emir mountains. On the way down it passes some cave dwellings of unknown date at İscehisar and then enters the plain of Afyon. Soon, the great volcanic pinnacle in the heart of that city appears in the distance.

AFYON

Afyon is a busy agricultural city in the midst of Turkey's opium-poppy region. The importance of this crop, which is strictly controlled, is reflected in the very name of the city, which means "opium" in Turkish. The full name of the city, Afyonkarahisar (Opium/Black Castle), incorporates the other distinction of the city, the Late Byzantine fortifications commanding the peak rising above it.

Afyon is a favorite lunch stop on the way from Ankara to İzmir or Antalya. The best restaurant is the İkbal, on the cobblestoned street (Millet Caddesi) leading south from the town square. (At the end of this street is a second square where you can park.) Moderately priced, it serves excellent *tandır kebap* (roast lamb) and desserts topped with the thick Afyon cream called *kaymak*. Two huge branches of İkbal, serving the same excellent food, have recently opened west of Afyon on the main highway at the intersection with the road to Kütahya.

After lunch you should allot an hour or two to visiting the city. Although the site has been settled since Neolithic times, Afyon's only surviving monuments are from the Byzantine and Islamic periods. Most impressive is the great fortress, called **Afyon Kalesi**, albeit more for its dramatic setting than for its actual structure. It can be reached by a steep climb (no railing) up the sheer face of the pinnacle upon which it rests, 600 feet above the plain. The crest of the peak forms a natural redoubt that was virtually impregnable, making Afyon a strategic point in the military history of Central Anatolia. A fortress was first built here by the Hittites, circa 1350 B.C. The present fortress was restored numerous times: The Ottomans used it as a frontier post during their conquest of southern Anatolia, and as late as 1802 it was used as a prison for French prisoners of war brought from Egypt. Little remains standing within the walls today, but the view is spectacular.

A short walk from the İkbal restaurant are several Seljuk and Ottoman buildings. On the southwestern side of the castle rock, on Camii Kebir Sokak, stands the **Ulu Cami**, a Seljuk mosque dating from 1272; the mosque's prayer hall is supported by 40 wooden columns with carved wooden capitals, characteristic of Seljuk architecture. Another Seljuk mosque, the **Kuyunlu Cami**, is located on the southern side of the rock, on Kuyunlu Sokak; its minaret is decorated with medieval faïence. In the market on Kurtuluş Sokak is the town's most noteworthy Ottoman monument, the **mosque-medrese complex of Gedik Ahmet Paşa**, begun in 1477. Gedik Ahmet Paşa, who became grand vizier, erected this complex when he was governor of Anatolia. It was among the first mosques to be built after the fall of Constantinople, and it helped inaugurate a new era in Turkish architecture, though it does possess the inverted-T plan common to earlier mosques in Bursa and Edirne. On the northern edge of the city, behind the sugar factory, is a Seljuk bridge called **Altıgöz** (Six Eyes), named for its six arches.

Finally, if visiting Afyon and, especially, climbing to the fortress prove tiring, you can drive 23 km (14 miles) east of town to the hot springs (*kaplıca*) known as **Gazlıgöl** and try the baths. These springs' curative reputation seems to date back to Phrygian times. Afyon has two fairly comfortable hotels, the plain and basic **Ece Oteli**, on Ordu Bulvarı, and the newer **Oruçoğlu Oteli**, on Bankalar Bulvarı.

Midas City

In addition to the ruins of Gordion (for which see Ankara and Environs, above), the mysterious Phrygians, an Indo-European people who entered Anatolia from the Balkans around 1200 B.C., have left a number of monuments, some rather puzzling, in the wide-open upland between Eskişehir and Afyon. In this treeless area of scattered villages, Phrygian towns and cities flourished in the sixth century B.C. The most important urban settlement was at the site that is now called "Midas City" (Midas Şehri), which can be reached by a dirt road from Seyitgazi (discussed above) or by an asphalt and dirt road from Afyon. In either case, the dirt roads are often intersected by other dirt roads without signs for direction. The local villagers, however, will gladly assist you.

The least confusing approach to Midas City is to take the asphalt road from Afyon north toward İhsaniye; the road

passes several Phrygian monuments on the way. Leaving Afyon, travel about 22 km (14 miles) to a fork in the road; take
the left branch 14 km (8½ miles) to İhsaniye. Near this village
are many Phrygian rock tombs. More interesting is **Aslankaya**
(Lion Rock), between the villages of Döğer and Bayramlılar.
Hewn from the soft volcanic tufa in the sixth century B.C.,
Aslankaya was connected with the cult of Cybele. The site
resembles a grand portal with a façade covered with geometric designs in high relief. In the center is a niche for the statue
of the goddess. The portal is flanked on each side by a lion
standing on its hind legs, and under its peaked "roof" are two
other lions.

After retracing your steps to the fork, take the right branch
to the village of Kümbet. About 20 minutes later you pass the
site of **Aslantaş** (Lion Stone). This block of carved tufa also
dates to the sixth century B.C. and also has a niche in the
center. Above the niche, two lions snarl at each other as if
claiming it as a prized possession. Both of these lion monuments are rather colossal works of art, seemingly in the
middle of nowhere.

At Kümbet, 54 km (33 miles) from Afyon, turn right on a
dirt road for the village of Yazılıkaya (Inscribed Rock).
Rising next to this Circassian village is Midas City. Most
prominent is the upper city, or **acropolis**. Essentially a fortified mesa, the acropolis contains a number of tombs and
altars, the substructures of towers, road cuts, and a few
carved figures, all rather nondescript. The top is a short walk
from the yard of the village hall (*konak*). Apart from the
view and some impressive staircases cut from the living
rock, the most wondrous sight here is the **Midas monument**.
Located below the acropolis and around the entrance to the
right, this massive sculpture, carved from a natural rocky
outcrop, may have been the city's major cult monument of
Cybele. The monument possesses two Phrygian inscriptions,
one at the top and another on the right side. Only the name
"Midas" (in the upper inscription) has been deciphered—
which has sufficed to christen the monument and the site.
Nothing is known of this Midas, however—certainly not
whether he can be identified with the legendary Phrygian
king who was blessed, and cursed, with the ability to turn
everything he touched to gold. More than 50 feet high and
35 feet wide, the Midas monument appears to be another
great portal. Its façade is carved with intricate geometric
patterns, and at the base is a niche for the goddess. Standing
alone, it greets the rising sun at the northern tip of the
acropolis.

From Yazılıkaya, perhaps after being invited for tea in the

village, you can return to Afyon or turn right at Kümbet and head for Seyitgazi and the Eskişehir highway. It is possible in one very long day to make a loop: Ankara, Afyon, Midas City, Seyitgazi, Ankara.

KONYA

"Wander the world, but see Konya!" exhorts an old Turkish saying. And so they do, thousands of tourists and pilgrims travel throughout the year to holy Konya, a city of colorful history and architectural treasures. A three-hour drive directly south from Ankara across the Anatolian plateau, Konya stretches along the edge of a fertile plain at the foot of the Taurus range.

The antiquity of Konya is reflected in a Phrygian legend that claims that it was the first city to be created after a deluge destroyed humanity. It was old even to the early Greeks. A popular etymology for the classical name for the city, Ikonion (Iconium), associated its root, *ikon,* with a likeness of Perseus that was erected in the city in gratitude for his having slain the Gorgon Medusa. In any case, coins bearing the image of Perseus and Medusa were struck in the city. In the late fifth century B.C. the Greek historian Xenophon marched through the city with the Ten Thousand, a force of Greek soldiers on their way to Persia in support of Cyrus the Younger's claim to the Persian throne. Konya was to retain a popular association with ancient Greece that would last until at least the late 12th century. At that time the Arab pilgrim al-Harawi visited the city and took special note of "the tomb of Plato in the church near the great mosque." Saint Paul visited the city on three occasions, in A.D. 47, 50, and 53. It was in Iconium that Paul supposedly became the teacher of Saint Thecla, one of the most celebrated saints in the Greek Orthodox church. The city became an important Christian center, and one of the earliest councils of the Christian church was held here in A.D. 235. A prosperous city during the early Byzantine era, it was raided by the Arabs in the seventh and eighth centuries and was finally captured by the Seljuks toward the end of the 11th century. In 1097 they made it their capital but briefly deserted it during the First Crusade. In 1190, during the Third Crusade, the Holy Roman Emperor Frederick Barbarossa arrived with his army and ravaged the city.

Despite this setback, Konya revived. Indeed, it was as the capital of the Seljuk Sultanate of Anatolia, from 1097 to 1302, that the city reached its golden age. During the two centuries of their rule, the last 60 years of which were under Mongol domination, the Seljuks created a state that controlled about two-thirds of Anatolia. Today the Turks regard the Seljuk state as the precursor of modern Turkey.

The Seljuks encouraged trade and made their capital a major emporium for merchants from as far away as Italy and Egypt. For a while they monopolized much of the commerce between the Black Sea and the Mediterranean and even sent a naval expedition to the Crimea. The stability provided by the Seljuk sultanate also allowed agriculture to flourish. Konya itself became renowned for its gardens. Immense quantities of cotton, yellow plums, and apricots were grown in the surrounding plain. Many of Konya's prized apricots were exported to Syria. Trade and the surrounding fertile fields made the city very rich.

Under Sultan 'Ala' ad-Din Kay-Qubad I (1219 to 1237; called Alaettin Keykubat in modern Turkish), Konya reached the height of its glory. He built a great wall around the city, pierced by 12 gates, each with a castellated entry. Water was brought from the hills and stored in a huge tank from which more than 300 conduits distributed it throughout the city. On the ancient mound in the center of town the sultan built a great mosque next to the palace and court, both of which he expanded considerably. Round about mushroomed other mosques, medreses, dervish lodges, public baths, and various markets.

In order to help construct these buildings and to add artistic and intellectual luster to his court, 'Ala' ad-Din, like many of his predecessors, did his best to attract artisans, poets, historians, theologians, jurists, and dervishes from throughout the Islamic world. His name quickly spread along the trade routes. Soon a small stream of immigrant craftsmen and scholars made its way to Konya—a stream that turned to a flood when the Mongols began their advance westward across Central Asia and Iran. Among the immigrants was Baha' ad-Din Walad, known as the Sultan of Theologians, who arrived in 1228 from Balkh (in modern Afghanistan) with his son, Jalal ad-Din. This young man, who came to be known as Mevlâna, was to change the destiny of Konya forever. But before turning to his story, let's trace the history of the city since Seljuk times.

In 1243, just six years after the death of 'Ala' ad-Din, the Seljuk army was shattered by the Mongols and the Seljuk state became a province of the Mongol Empire. A shadow Seljuk sultanate lasted until 1302. At first the Mongols gave their Seljuk subjects considerable autonomy, but increasing repression led to a revolt. Its failure and squabbles among heirs to the Seljuk throne resulted in the demise of their dynasty. In 1277 the Karamanids, who had established a rival Turkish dynasty to the south, briefly seized Konya. After this the city changed hands several times. It was not until 1465 that the Ottoman army, commanded by Mehmet the Conqueror himself, captured the city once and for all. Under the Ottomans Konya lost most of its political significance, although it remained an important provincial city. When the Republic of Turkey was proclaimed in 1923 and Atatürk decided to move the capital from Istanbul to Central Anatolia, Konya's citizens lobbied for their city to be chosen as the site. The nationalists, however, wanted to make a break with the past and begin a new era, so Konya's rich history proved to be a liability.

After the eclipse of the Seljuks, Konya's prosperity did not immediately wane. Marco Polo, who may have done business here in the late 13th century, mentions it as one of the celebrated cities of Central Anatolia. In the 15th and 16th centuries it served as the residence of various Ottoman princes, sometimes as a place of exile. In 1648 the famous Turkish traveller Evliya Çelebi visited the city and noted that it had 11 medreses, 3 schools of Islamic tradition (*darülhadis*), 40 dervish lodges, 11 public soup kitchens, a covered market, and 900 shops. He praised the skill of the local tanners and spoke enthusiastically of the city's gardens.

Konya's Turco-Islamic heritage is still much in evidence. The city is an open-air museum of architectural masterpieces and Islamic lore. At least two days should be devoted to enjoying the city properly, especially if you go in December when the Whirling Dervishes perform. You can walk to all the places of major interest from the center of town. If you are keenly interested in Seljuk architecture, check with the tourist office (at Mevlâna Caddesi 21) first to see which of the minor monuments are open. The easiest walking tour starts at the corner where the road from Ankara meets Alaettin park (named for the great Seljuk sultan), which is the ancient mound of the city. From there the tour goes counterclockwise a short distance around the park, then through the park and down the main boulevard of the city to the Mevlâna museum.

At the western corner of the Ankara road stands the **Karatay Medresesi**. Built between 1251 and 1252 by the Seljuk vizier Jalal ad-Din Karatay, it is famous for its magnificent marble portal of interlacing geometric panels, stalactites, twisted columns, and raised inscriptions. Only part of the original medrese survives, notably its dome, which rests on tiled pendentives and covers a fountain and the main hall. The interior of the dome is brilliantly decorated with faïence in imitation of the night sky. In one corner is the tomb of the founder. The Karatay Medresesi houses a collection of Seljuk ceramics, including pieces from the Kubadabat palace built by 'Ala' ad-Din on the shore of Lake Beyşehir. Directly across the street from the medrese are the remains of a small mosque built by the same vizier.

Turning right at the corner and walking around the park, you come to the İnce Minareli Medrese (Medrese with the Slender Minaret), erected by Sahib Ata, another Seljuk vizier, between 1264 and 1265. The medrese acquired its name from an elegant three-story minaret built into the façade to the right of the portal. Although the upper two stories crashed to the ground in 1901 after being struck by lightning, the lively, glazed-brick-mosaic patterns of the base remain to give an idea of the minaret's original splendor. The real glory of the building, however, is its monumental portal. Measuring some 25 by 35 feet, this gateway is a spectacular tour de force of sandstone sculpture. A symmetrical composition of writhing bands of bold Arabic calligraphy, delicate columns, floral designs, animals (uncharacteristic of Islamic art), and unusual ornaments, the portal is like nothing else in Islamic art and architecture. The medrese is now a museum of Seljuk wood and stonework; it preserves the only known Seljuk reliefs from the walls of Konya, including a double-headed eagle and a dragon tied in a knot (the last vestiges of the wall disappeared in the 19th century).

From the medrese, cross the street to the park. Trial excavations in the mound turned up remains from 3000 to 2000 B.C. On the northern edge of this small hill, facing the Ankara road, are the ruins of the Seljuk palace and the Alaettin Camii. Of the palace, only a disintegrating kiosk survives, but most of the mosque is intact. (Unfortunately for the sightseer, the mosque is currently closed for restoration.) Although attributed to Alaettin ('Ala' ad-Din), its construction seems to have been started by 'Izz ad-Din Kay-Kavus I (called İzzettin Keykavus I in modern Turkish; r. 1210 to 1219), and alterations and additions were made to it long after the Seljuks. Its most impressive features are its great courtyard wall with two marble portals and the large dome over the front of the prayer niche. It also contains a gorgeous ebony pulpit, made in 1155, a masterpiece of intricate woodwork. This pulpit suggests that the Alaettin Camii may rest on the site of an earlier mosque, perhaps destroyed by Frederick Barbarossa when he sacked Konya in 1190. At the rear of the present mosque is the pyramid-roofed mausoleum of the Seljuk dynasty, containing the remains of eight sultans. In the summer the park is a pleasant place to pause and enjoy a soft drink or tea and a sesame-seed roll.

Across the street from the park to the southwest is a diminutive dark red French church. Two blocks behind it is the **Sırçalı Medrese** (the Medrese with the Glazed Tile). The name derives from the four-colored (turquoise, brown, purple, and black) tile that once covered much of the interior. There is also a splendid faïence prayer niche inside. Although part of the building is in ruins, its wonderful portal survives and more than suffices to capture your attention. The porch is deeply recessed within a frame of delicate geometric designs with the texture of a very busy Persian carpet. These designs transform the heavy stonework into lace and give the building a lightness that distinguishes it from its sisters. The Sırçalı Medrese was built in 1242 by Badr ad-Din Muslih, a tutor of 'Ala' ad-Din. His architect, a Persian from Tus, was evidently quite proud of his work: He left an inscription on the inside, now crumbled away, saying, "What I have created is unrivaled throughout the world. I shall pass away but this shall remain forever and preserve my memory."

Roughly four blocks south of the Sırçalı Medrese is a square containing the **Sahip Ata Camii** and the city's archaeological museum. Nothing remains of the original mosque but its portal, another of the monumental gateways of Konya, and its prayer niche. The vizier Sahib Ata ordered the construction of this mosque in 1258. Judging from its portal, he tried to create an artistic masterpiece to equal other buildings of his time. This portal, the apogee of 13th-century Anatolian stonework, is composed of a rather quirky amalgam of sandstone, interlocking marble, and brickwork. It is embellished with a number of styles of calligraphy, from light and sinuous to heavy and awkward. On either side of the frame of the recessed entrance are decorated vertical panels that mirror each other. The upper portions of the frame contain sharply contrasting forms of calligraphy, and the lower portions are inset with miniature portals that served as fountains. Each of these small portals rests on a Byzantine sarcophagus! Minarets once stood guard at each side of this great gateway; only part of one still stands. The mosque's prayer niche is a beautiful mosaic of blue and black tile.

The **Archaeological Museum** (open 8:00 A.M. to noon and 1:00 to 5:00 P.M.) contains a hodgepodge of antiquities reflecting the many peoples and civilizations that have called Konya home. Its greatest treasure is a large third-century A.D.

sarcophagus brought to life by stunning reliefs depicting the Twelve Labors of Hercules. Also in the museum are several statues of the ubiquitous Phrygian goddess Cybele, who included Konya within her realm, and a statue of Aphrodite that suggests the influence of classical sculpture on depictions of the Virgin Mary.

From the museum you can backtrack to the park circle and go to the right for a few blocks to the main street of Konya, Alaettin Bulvarı. The half-mile stroll along this street to one of Turkey's holiest Muslim shrines, the tomb of Mevlâna (discussed below), will give you a taste of the city's flavor. You'll pass an assortment of flower shops, gold sellers with blazing lightbulbs in their windows, movie theaters, record and tape stores, government buildings, labyrinthine passages of appliance and clothing shops, and pastry and tea salons. Several comfortable hotels are located along this busy avenue. Recommended are the newly refurbished **Selçuk Oteli** and the **Dergah Oteli**, which has a sauna but no restaurant. The **Özkaymak Park Oteli**, which is used by many tour groups and may be the best, is across from the bus terminal, about a mile north of Alaettin park. The best restaurants are in the hotels, although good fare, usually *kebap*s or roast chicken, is available in many eateries in the center of town, such as **Şifa Restoran** or **Hanedan Restoran**, both on Mevlâna Caddesi. The **Fuar Restorant** in the trade-fair park immediately north of İnce Minareli Medrese has a fine Turkish menu. A roasted lamb dish called *kuzu fırın* is a Konya specialty.

A few minutes from the park along Alaettin Caddesi stands the **İplikçi Camii** (Yarn Dealer Mosque). The name of this Seljuk building, which was erected between 1220 and 1230, evokes a time when this part of the city was a wool market. The mosque is notable primarily because of its fine prayer niche and three domes. The accumulated dust of centuries has raised the street above the mosque entrance, so you have to walk down to go inside. Opposite this mosque is the huge **Şerafettin Camii**, originally built in the 12th century and then rebuilt according to a rather standard Ottoman pattern in 1636. The mosque's seven domes are supported by six marble columns.

About halfway down the boulevard on the right is the main **bazaar**, part of which was once a horse market. Like all bazaars, it is teeming with activity and local color. Dry goods, building supplies, furniture, hardware, tools and utensils, books, notions, spices and medicines, and odds and ends fill this warren of stalls and shops. A walk through the bazaar provides a glimpse of the material life of many working-class

Turks. Villagers in particular come to do their shopping here. Leathery-faced farmers and their families are a common sight. The carpet and kilim dealers, mixed with a few antiques dealers, have their stores back on the main avenue two blocks north of the tourist information office. Konya is the hub of an area in which traditional weaving crafts are still strongly pursued. Moreover, dealer connections with the Central Asian republic of Azerbaijan have brought many pieces from the Caucasus to the local market. Closer to the tomb are souvenir shops catering to Muslim pilgrims. Religious texts, framed verses from the Koran, large wooden forks and spoons decorated with Arabic calligraphy, oversized wooden prayer beads, candy, and bric-a-brac are sold as mementos to the faithful.

Mevlâna

When Sultan ʿAlaʾ ad-Din Kay-Qubad met Bahaʾ ad-Din and his son Jalal ad-Din in 1228, he could hardly have imagined that the youth would bring his city undying fame. Jalal ad-Din, known as Celâlettin in Turkish and usually referred to simply as Rumi, "the man from Rum [Anatolia]," was born in Balkh in 1207. By the time he reached Konya he had been trained in Islamic theology by his father. Yet a spiritual hunger gnawed at him and drew him to the Muslim luminaries who came to the Seljuk court. He mixed freely with Konya's cosmopolitan population: Christians, Jews, orthodox and not-so-orthodox Muslims, and perhaps even a few pagans. Although his father had no doubt introduced him to mystical thought, Jalal ad-Din's experience seems to have convinced him that he needed to go beyond theology and attempt to achieve "divine union" by extra-rational means. He became a devoted Sufi, or Islamic mystic, and attracted a circle of disciples.

In 1244 Jalal ad-Din met a wandering dervish from Tabriz named Shams ad-Din, a charismatic figure obsessed with a mystical love of God. The two became inseparable, and Jalal ad-Din turned to poetry. For reasons that are unclear, their friendship angered some of Jalal ad-Din's disciples, who plotted with one of Jalal ad-Din's sons and in 1247 murdered Shams ad-Din. Mourning the loss of his mystical lover, Jalal ad-Din poured himself into poetry, music, and dance.

For a while Jalal ad-Din seemed to find the lost Shams ad-Din in himself. Then, in 1249, he declared that the dervish had reappeared in the form of one of his disciples, Salah ad-Din Zarkub, an illiterate but handsome and congenial man.

Jalal ad-Din appointed Salah ad-Din his successor, but Salah ad-Din became ill and died in 1258 and was succeeded by Husam ad-Din Hasan, the son of the chief of the *akhis* (members of the religious fraternities) in Konya. It was Husam ad-Din who inspired Jalal ad-Din, by then well known as "Mevlâna" ("Our Master"), to compose his immortal poem, the *Mathnawi*.

Written in Persian, the *Mathnawi* consists of six books of about 25,000 rhyming couplets that portray the writer's monistic vision of the universe. It ranges over the entire field of mystical thought, pausing to deliver brilliant anecdotes full of wisdom and humor. For Jalal ad-Din, the poem was "the hope for unity with the One Real Being." A song of passionate love for God and yearning for answers to ultimate questions, the *Mathnawi* is one of the masterpieces of Persian literature. For many Muslims it is second in sacredness only to the Koran and the traditions (*ḥadīth*) of the Prophet.

When Jalal ad-Din died in 1273 he was widely mourned. His compassion, tolerance, and humanity had won him the affection of all Konya, Muslim and non-Muslim. His tomb (today a museum, discussed below) immediately became an object of veneration and pilgrimage.

The Whirling Dervishes

Within a century of Muhammad's death, the Arabs had created a vast empire that brought untold riches to their first great capital, Damascus. For many pious Muslims the sudden preoccupation with earthly rewards came as a shock, and they withdrew from society. Thus began a movement of Muslim asceticism that gradually developed into a sophisticated form of mysticism. Although despised by orthodox theologians, this mysticism became the popular religion of Islam, for it gave believers something the bookish scholars could not, a direct personal experience of the divine. By the 12th century, orthodoxy had capitulated and essentially merged with mysticism.

As mysticism became respectable, it became common for the followers of prominent mystics to create fraternal organizations based on their teachings. Known as *tarikats*, or "paths" to mystical experience, these brotherhoods spread throughout the Islamic world. A main lodge, or *tekke*, was usually established at the founder's tomb, and branch lodges grew up wherever his adherents might live. In the lodges the members held rituals, called *zikirs*, in which they sought to induce in themselves a mystical state. Some brotherhoods used chanting, singing, dancing, music, or other means to produce the desired ecstatic experience.

Upon the death of Jalal ad-Din, his son Sultan Veled, himself a famous mystical poet, established the first branches of the order that would be named after Jalal ad-Din, the Mevleviye. It spread throughout Asia Minor and eventually became the most important urban brotherhood in the Ottoman Empire. Jalal ad-Din had long used music and dance in his own rituals, and the Mevleviye became renowned for its peculiar form of dance. As the ceremonial music plays, the Mevlevi dervish—arms raised, head cocked to the right, his right foot acting as a pivot—begins to whirl. As he turns, he slowly moves in a great circle around the room. His loose vest and long skirt billow as he spins, giving the impression that he is floating above the floor.

The Ottoman sultans showed considerable favor to the Mevleviye, and its lodges sprang up in every major city and town under Ottoman rule. In Istanbul the order became a major political force and, inevitably perhaps, turned to worldly pursuits. In 1925, after Turkey was declared a republic and a secular state, all brotherhoods were outlawed; their lodges were closed and their property confiscated. Only in 1953, on the grounds of promoting Turkish culture, did the government relent ever so slightly on this policy. Henceforth, one brotherhood, the Mevleviye, was allowed to resume its ceremonies in Konya from December 9 through 17 each year. More recently, the Mevlevis have been allowed to perform in the International Istanbul Festival, which is held each summer (see Istanbul Entertainment and Nightlife, above). Somewhat ironically, the dervishes are seen more often while on tour in such bastions of unbelief as North America and Europe than in Turkey. The winter dates in Konya were meant to coincide with the anniversary of Mevlâna's death on December 17 and celebrate his marriage with God. Since 1953, the Ministry of Tourism has sponsored a **Konya Festival** each December, with the emphasis on the dancers. Indeed, the performances of the dervishes, which last about an hour, are a major attraction in Konya. They are held in the Konya Spor Palas, a small basketball gymnasium with limited seating. The interior is equipped with stage lights and decorated with streamers and tent canopies for the event. The hotels in the city are booked solid at this time, so if you intend to spend the night during the festival, reservations are a must. Many travel agencies in Ankara offer special day trips, the most convenient way to enjoy the spectacle.

The Tomb of Mevlâna

After the brotherhoods were abolished, the mother lodge of the Mevleviye was made into a museum (closed Mondays) devoted to Jalal ad-Din and his order. Although the lodge and the great poet's tomb had their origins in the 13th century, the present complex is largely the work of 16th-century Ottoman sultans and their builders.

Crossing the marble courtyard from the entrance and passing on the left a monumental fountain built by Sultan Selim I, you first step into a small chamber where the Koran was recited. This room is now used to display some of the finest calligraphy of the Ottoman period. You next pass through a silver door into the mausoleum proper. Here, in an antechamber, are displayed beautiful early copies of the *Mathnawi* and related works. At the end of this room, on the right, behind a low silver screen are the cenotaphs of Jalal ad-Din and his son Sultan Veled. They rest on a raised dais and are veiled with richly embroidered black satin. At each corner of the dais are piers supporting the drum above the tomb. These piers and their surrounding walls are covered with a dazzling display of brightly colored designs as well as verses from the Koran. The pyramidal vaulting in the ceiling forms a spectacular eight-pointed star. The exterior of the drum and its scalloped, conical dome are covered with blue-green tiles from Kütahya. Together they provide a splash of brilliant color in contrast to the surrounding earth-toned buildings. From the outside, the drum resembles a bunch of reeds—the cry of the reed pipe being a favorite image of Jalal ad-Din's poetry.

Just beyond the saint's tomb, you come to the **dancing room** of the lodge. Flanked by several galleries, this room, and the chapel mosque next to it, were built by Sinan, the architect of Sultan Süleyman the Magnificent. In both the performance hall and mosque are now displayed rare Turkish carpets, clothing, musical instruments, and other objects related to the order. Also on view are several splendid glass mosque-lamps that Selim I presented as prizes from his conquest of Egypt in 1517. And in a gilded case encrusted with bloodstones is perhaps the most precious item of all, a hair from the beard of the Prophet Muhammad. More carpets and kilims are housed in the dervish cells in the annex in the courtyard next to the monumental fountain. Among these carpets are three of Seljuk type taken from the late-13-century mosque at Beyşehir (on which see below). They are among the oldest extant in Turkey.

Immediately north of the poet's tomb complex is a miniature version of the Sultan Mehmet Fâtih Camii in Istanbul. This copy was begun by Süleyman the Magnificent but completed by Selim II. Near the mosque is a library built in 1794. Shams ad-Din's tomb, by the way, survives in an obscure mosque in one of Konya's back alleys.

Toward the end of his life, Jalal ad-Din was revered as a holy man, and upon his death he became a saint. From near and far non-Muslims as well as Muslims journeyed to his tomb in order to seek his intercession with the divinity. Confused students, repentant thieves, debt-ridden merchants, barren women, and crippled children all asked for his help. Even today Turks bring him their problems. Both resembling and differing from the famous Christian shrines of Lourdes, Avila, and Santiago de Compostela, the Konya of Jalal ad-Din represents a special fountainhead of humanism, eternal truths, and oneness with God.

The young man who fled the Mongols gave Konya a character unlike that of any other city in Turkey. It is a conservative, pious city (although stories of raucous private parties do circulate). When the call to prayer is made, Konyans respond. Women commonly wear overcoats and scarves, even in the summer. Now and then a veil is seen. Ramazan is faithfully observed here, so during this month restaurants are closed during the day. Some men have more than one wife, although polygamy is illegal. Alcoholic beverages—beer, wine, and rakı, the anisette liquor that is the national drink—are sometimes difficult to find, even in hotels that cater to Europeans.

THE LAKE DISTRICT

In the summer, a visit to the great lakes west of Konya provides a refreshing escape from the heat of the Anatolian plain. These lakes, Beyşehir and Eğridir, lie in dramatic mountainous settings. Beyşehir, at 3,775 feet, has an alpine flavor, while Eğridir, at 3,034 feet, is surrounded by drier and less heavily wooded country. Both more than 20 miles long, they are the largest bodies of fresh water in Turkey. From Konya a round trip to both, about 564 km (350 miles), can be done in a long day, but two days are better.

Beyşehir Gölü

The town of Beyşehir, on the southeastern corner of the lake, is 102 km (63 miles) from Konya. The road west, route 330, passes through rolling hills and valleys, mostly bare or scrub covered, along what was part of a major caravan route in the Seljuk period. Some 22 km (14 miles) out of Konya you pass, on the left, the ruins of the Kuruçeşme Hanı, a small caravansary built in 1208. A few kilometers farther you pass a second caravansary, Kızılören Hanı, finished in 1206. Although the larger and better preserved of the two, it is a forlorn structure standing alone in the empty fields. Its only visitors are the sheep and goats that sometimes seek its shelter.

Beyşehir, a small town founded by the Seljuks, is known for its Eşrefoğlu Camii, near the lakeshore. Built in 1298 and still in use, this is the largest and most original of the mosques in the Seljuk style, which uses rows of wooden columns in the interior for support. There is beautiful tilework on its *mihrap* and in the dome above. In the center of the mosque is a special cellar in which snow was stored for the making of sherbets in the summer. (Interestingly, the English words *sherbet* and *syrup* both derive from the Arabic word *sharab,* meaning "drink"; hence also the Turkish word for "wine," *şarap.*) The town sits next to the lake's outlet, a small river that rushes toward the Mediterranean, and is notably greener than Konya. Along the river are several pleasant restaurants with basic Turkish cuisine at modest prices. Try the Beyaz Park Restaurant. Across from the restaurant is a shop crammed with an array of costumes, jewelry, and guns. The local park affords fine views of the lake.

From Beyşehir the road continues northwest along the lakeshore, offering splendid panoramas across the dark blue waters to the wall of snowcapped and forested mountains on the other side. Rarely will you spy a boat intruding upon the scene. After travelling about 17½ km (11 miles) from Beyşehir along the lake road, you might make a brief detour to visit the village of Eflatun Pınar, where you will find the remains of a 13th-century B.C. Hittite monument. Turn right just beyond a mill on your right and follow the track for about a mile to the village. Next to it, in a pond, are large blocks of stone partially covered with low reliefs of divinities and other figures. The monument's purpose is unclear, although these blocks may have formed the base for a statue.

Beyond the lake at the large village of Şarkıkaraağaç you can turn left to drive around the lake to the village of Yenişar Bademli, about 51 km (32 miles), adding about a half-day to your journey. The meandering wooded or shrub-lined road to Yenişar Bademli passes several islands bearing the remains of abandoned Byzantine monasteries. The village itself is surrounded by lush orchards, gardens, and pastures fed by alpine streams. Its streets are alive with farm animals and a few tractors. You will surely be invited for tea or have your hands filled with whatever fruit is in season.

Yenişar Bademli stands near the spot at the base of the mountains, on the edge of the lake and far away from the world, where the Seljuk sultan 'Ala' ad-Din built a glorious summer pavilion, the **Kubadabat Sarayı**, in 1226. In the aftermath of the Mongol invasion, the palace was "lost" and not rediscovered until 1949. Excavations performed then revealed mostly foundations and walls and some remarkable glazed tiles. All the ceramics from the site are now on display in the Karatay Medresesi in Konya.

Behind Yenişar Bademli a dirt road winds its way over the 9,000-foot mountains and eventually emerges at the town of Eğridir. If you are a bit adventurous, you might take this track to avoid retracing your steps to the main road at Şarkıkaraağaç. The mountain road has no services and no signs, but it has its delights. A few kilometers above Yenişar Bademli it reaches the hut of a forester who will gladly brew you some tea and take you to a cave from which gushes an amazingly clear and bitterly cold stream—a good place to fill water bottles. The stream itself leads to a fantasy world of subterranean lakes, waterfalls, and speleological wonders. Unfortunately this netherworld can only be visited by experienced spelunkers with special equipment.

Beyond the cave the road enters classic alpine country. Silent granite sentinels watch as you progress through dark forests or break into glorious meadows—the *yayla*s so dear to the hearts of Turks. Villagers from the lowlands bring their flocks here in the summer or come to cut wood. There are remote villages in the mountains that have changed little in the past century; Ankara is far away in a seemingly foreign land. Offer to take someone's photograph with a promise to send him a copy—the locals will understand hand signals and some rudimentary English—and you will never be at a loss for a guide.

Eğridir Gölü

About 32 km (20 miles) from Şarkıkaraağaç, back on the main road to Eğridir, you will pass on your right another caravansary, Ertokuş Hanı, built in 1223 by a Seljuk states-man. Somewhat hidden by poplar trees and farmhouses, this structure is of rather poor workmanship, though it has an attractive doorway composed of carved stones in two colors. Shortly after the caravansary the road begins a long descent into the great basin that contains Eğridir Gölü. The view of this lake from the highway is breathtaking. You can see in the distance the town of Eğridir on a small peninsula that juts into the water from the southern shore. Above the town is a bald peak resembling the Rock of Gibraltar.

As the Byzantine town of Akrotiri, **Eğridir** (also spelled Eğirdir) fell into Seljuk hands at the beginning of the 13th century. At the end of that century, with the passing of the Seljuks, it became the capital of the Turkish principality of the Hamidids. Around 1331 the famous Muslim traveller Ibn Battuta visited the town and described it as "a great and populous city with fine bazaars and running streams, fruit trees and orchards," adding that it possessed "a lake of sweet water on which a vessel plies in two days [to reach the road] to Akşehir." In 1381 it was absorbed by the Ottomans.

Facing each other in the town are a 14th-century mosque and the **Dündar Bey Medresesi**, dated 1302. The latter has a beautiful entry gate that was actually removed from an earlier (1238) Seljuk caravansary and reused here. Ibn Battuta resided in this medrese during his sojourn in Eğridir. Today it is full of small shops.

Just beyond the mosque and medrese and facing the tip of the peninsula are the remains of the town's medieval walls, whose foundations may originate from Lydian times (sixth century B.C.). From the end of the peninsula a causeway connects the mainland with two tiny islands. On the more distant and larger of the two, **Yeşilada**, there was a monastery and settlement with some 1,000 Turkish-speaking Greeks until the end of World War I. The walls of the 12th-century Orthodox church of Ayastephanes still stand. A walk to the islands, mere pebbles in a sea, will impress on you the enormity of the lake.

Yeşilada is dotted with pensions. Some, such as **Adac Pension**, are well appointed, with full facilities and views of the lake. The best pensions can arrange for you to tour the lake in a fisherman's boat, but be warned that many boats are equipped with music systems designed to frighten all wildlife within miles. Also on this island is the new and comfortable **Mavigöl Hotel**, complete with restaurant. On the mainland, the **Köşk Pension**, on a hill on the west side of Eğridir, has a splendid view of both the town and lake. Recommended as well is the **Eğirdir Oteli**, downtown on the shore road. It has a fine view of the lake and full services, including a good restaurant.

Eğridir is renowned for its fish and crayfish; the best place to sample them is on the terrace of the **Eğirdir Restaurant** immediately east of the corniche in the heart of town, or try the family-run **Big Apple Restaurant** on Yeşilada. There is some swimming in town below the corniche, but the most popular spot for swimmers is Altınkum, whose golden sands are about 3 km (2 miles) west of town. Here you can wade out for almost 200 yards. Altınkum has changing cabins, showers, and a good restaurant.

From Eğridir you can return to Ankara or continue west 35 km (22 miles) to the large city of İsparta, the rose-growing capital of Turkey and an important carpet center, and then turn south to Antalya and the Mediterranean (150 km/93 miles). If you wish to linger in Eğridir, you should make a side trip to the small but very pretty **Kovada Milli Parkı** (Kovada National Park), 25 km (16 miles) south of town. Centered around an island-filled alpine lake, the park is a wonderful place to hike amid pine forests. In the spring it is colored by countless butterflies. Taxi and jeep service to the park are available from town.

KARAMAN AND THE VALLEY OF A THOUSAND AND ONE CHURCHES

To get a glimpse of three distinct periods of Anatolian history, make a loop from Konya by going south to Karaman, then due north to the Ereğli highway, and finally back to Konya. The total distance is 260 km (161 miles), a day trip that takes you from the Neolithic to the Seljuk and then back to the middle Byzantine period.

Taking the road out of Konya to Karaman, travel south for 35 km (22 miles) and turn left for the small town of Çumra. About 14 km (8½ miles) north of this town, the British Institute of Archaeology in Ankara excavated two mounds in the early 1960s and discovered one of the most important prehistoric sites in Anatolia, known henceforth by its Turkish name, **Çatalhöyük** (Fork Mound). The archaeologists had unearthed, in fact, one of the oldest known cities. Dating from 6500 B.C., Çatalhöyük reveals a sophisticated and prosperous civilization in the midst of great forests and plains inhabited by red deer, wild boars, stags, leopards, wild asses, and other animals long since extinct in this now-barren region. Perhaps the most remarkable discovery was a series of mural paintings, the earliest to come to light anywhere. Some of them, which seem to relate to religious beliefs, are now on display in the Museum of Anatolian Civilizations in Ankara along with the other significant finds from the site. Since the completion of the excavations, Çatalhöyük has become a victim of the elements, so it is difficult for a layperson to make much sense of the dig. The site guard, however, gives a good tour.

Much easier to ponder, unless you are completely be- guiled by the origins of civilization, are the Islamic monu- ments in **Karaman**, 110 km (68 miles) from Konya. Karaman, the Byzantine Laranda, shared much of Konya's history. Ruled by the Turkish Danishmendid dynasty after the battle of Manzikert, it was seized by the Seljuks in 1165. The Crusader Frederick Barbarossa briefly held it on his ill-fated journey to the Holy Land. Jalal ad-Din settled and married here before moving to Konya. When the Seljuks declined, Karaman became the capital of the powerful principality of the Karamanids, who gave their name to the city. They rivaled the Seljuks, and for a while the Ottomans, for control of central and southern Anatolia.

The Karamanids lavished much wealth on their capital in the form of grand public buildings, which represent the development of Anatolian architecture in the two centuries after Konya reached its artistic zenith. In the old part of town, clustered around the citadel, are mosques, medreses, dervish lodges, soup kitchens, mausoleums, baths, and foun- tains. Many of these structures are in a state of disrepair or have been considerably modified over the centuries. The most important buildings are the **Hatuniye Medresesi** and the **İbrahim Bey İmareti**. The medrese was built between 1381 and 1382 by Sultan Hatun, the daughter of the Ottoman sultan Murat I and the wife of the Karamanid ruler 'Ala' ad- Din Bey. Like its sister institutions in Konya, it has a grand portal, noteworthy for its recessed, elaborately carved, two- colored marble porch. The border decoration around the frame copies patterns found on the Gök Medrese in Sivas and the Çifte Minareli Medrese in Erzurum. The imaret (soup kitchen) of İbrahim Bey, under whose rule Karaman enjoyed its last decades of glory (1424 to 1464), is one of the finest Karamanid works. It has a domed, central courtyard surrounded on three sides by two stories of rooms. A single minaret stands to the right of the entrance. This imaret was, in fact, a complex of soup kitchen, mosque, and probably medrese. The plan of the building, which was completed in 1433, has a number of remarkable features, such as fan- shaped pendentives below the dome that derive from the brick architecture of 13th-century Konya. The beautiful ce- ramic prayer niche is now in the Çinili Köşk in Istanbul. At the southern corner of the imaret is the tomb of the founder and his two sons. Karaman has a one-star hotel, the **Nas Oteli**, in the heart of town on İsmet Paşa Caddesi. It is within walking distance of almost all the monuments of interest. For good Turkish food try the **Dağ Restaurant** on the road that goes south to Mut (Mut Yoluüzeri).

The area around Karaman is rich in Byzantine monastic sites. The largest concentration of churches is in the valley of **Binbir Kilise**—A Thousand and One Churches—37 km (23 miles) north of Karaman. Take the road to Kılbasan, 10 km (6 miles) beyond which turn left for the village of **Maden Şehir**, then continue another 10 km (6 miles) by dirt road. En route you cross a pass on the north side of Karadağ, an extinct volcano.

Maden Şehir is in the heart of the valley of the churches. It occupies the site of a Byzantine monastic center that flourished in the fifth and sixth centuries and again from the ninth century until the Turkish invasion. This may have been a sacred site before the coming of Christianity; later, it may have served as a refuge for heretics. Saint Paul passed through this region on his early missions to evangelize the Jewish communities of Anatolia. The red and black basalt basilicas and chapels scattered about the village were erected between 850 and 1070. For the most part, only the shells survive, although some are of impressive proportions and have a certain majesty as they stand silently in the desolate countryside.

You can easily spend a day exploring the churches outside Maden Şehir, but you will need a local guide. This is especially true if you wish to make the difficult two-hour ascent up a foothill of Karadağ to **Değler**, where a large number of well-preserved buildings are found. A rough track takes a back way to Değler, but again a guide is recommended. (It's best to arrange for a local guide in Maden Şehir, as there is no organized guide service.) From Değler there is an excellent view of the ancient Lycaonian plain. If you are challenged by mountains and are physically well prepared, you might attempt to reach the remains of a ninth-century monastery and a cave containing Hittite inscriptions at the summit of 7,450-foot Karadağ. For those concerned about their blood pressure, it is best to return to the Kılbasan road and then continue north to the Konya–Ereğli highway.

THE CARAVAN ROUTE TO KAYSERİ

The Seljuks' most important trade route with Iran and points east lay directly across the Anatolian plain, connecting Konya

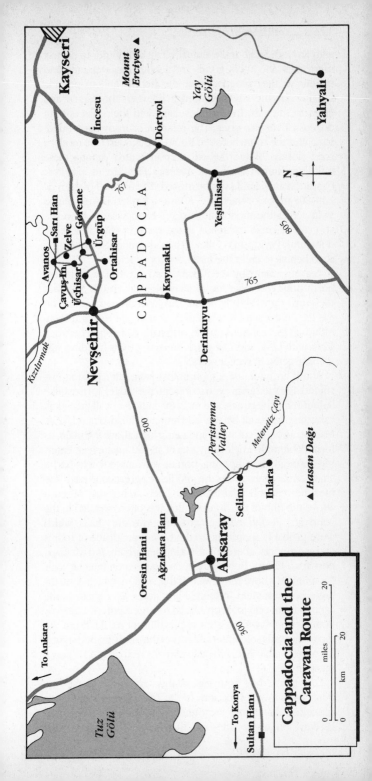

with Kayseri, Sivas, and eventually Tabriz. In order to protect
merchants and their goods from both the elements and
bandits as they plodded over the steppe, and to provide
lodging for the royal entourage between the capital and
cities to the east, the Seljuk sultans and their viziers built
dozens of caravansaries. The remains of many such buildings litter the route between Konya and Kayseri (the modern
road closely follows the old caravan route). Among these
buildings, Sultan Hanı and Ağzıkara Han are in excellent
condition and should not be missed. The first half of the 335-
km (208-mile) journey from Konya to Kayseri is straight and
swift across the monotonous plain. Near Aksaray, however,
you can make an excursion to the rock-cut churches of the
delightful Peristrema valley. Then, beyond Nevşehir, the
road begins to enter the maze of Cappadocia.

Leaving Konya by the Ankara road, go 10 km (6 miles)
north until you meet the Aksaray highway (route 300) and
then turn right. Shortly before this junction you will see on
the left, in the shadow of a tall flour mill, the **Horoğlu Hanı**.
Although this caravansary was originally completed between
1246 and 1249, most of what remains of the building was
reconstructed in recent years.

About an hour (96 km/60 miles) later, after passing two
ruined caravansaries, you confront the huge, fortress-like
Sultan Hanı, the largest and most magnificent of all the Seljuk
caravansaries, built by 'Ala' ad-Din Kay-Qubad around 1230.
Made entirely of cut stone and rising high above the plain, its
formidable walls enclose an area of 48,000 square feet. Entering through the imposing portal, you immediately find a
small, square mosque in the middle of a great courtyard. The
mosque rests on a base of four open arches that raised it
above the filth of the livestock that was often corraled in the
courtyard. To the left is an arcade of two-story halls, which
were probably shops, and to the right is an arcade of rooms
and apartments. There are also a kitchen, a bath, and what was
perhaps a library. Behind the mosque are monumental stalls
for animals. Above the center of this section, which contains
high, barrel-vaulted, cathedral-like aisles, is a small dome
capped by an octagonal pyramidal roof. Certainly no camel or
donkey ever stayed in a more magnificent stable. From the
top of the walls soldiers could survey the unobstructed steppe
for miles. Sultan Hanı has been partially restored and is now a
museum.

Less than a half hour east of this caravansary is the hot,
dusty oasis town of **Aksaray**. In the 14th century Ibn Battuta
remarked that it was surrounded by flowing streams and
gardens on every side and that, in fact, its homes had

running water. He also noted that Aksaray produced carpets without equal that were exported as far away as India and China. The town still has an important carpet industry. Aksaray flourished under the Seljuks and Karamanids. Mehmet the Conqueror, however, transferred most of its people to Constantinople after he captured that city, and the quarter in which they settled took the name of their native town.

Modern Aksaray retains a few buildings from medieval times, but the only one worth seeing is the **Zinciriye Medresesi**, built by the Karamanids in 1336. It has a court-yard enclosed by four arched halls and ovoid domes on each side of the hall that contains the prayer niche. And, of course, it has its own distinct monumental portal.

The road to Kayseri actually skirts the city and turns north toward Ankara. At the corner where you turn right for Nevşehir, there is a very good hotel with a pool, restaurant, and garden, called the **Orhan Ağaçlı Turistik Tesisleri**. This is a good place to have lunch or to spend the night if you wish to devote more time to exploring the area around Aksaray. Also highly recommended is the **Ihlara Oteli**, in Aksaray itself. It's quiet and quite accommodating to tourists.

The major attraction near Aksaray is the **Peristrema valley**. You can make a short visit to this valley on the way to Cappadocia or Kayseri, or spend a full day exploring its wonders. Continue east from Aksaray on the road to Nevşehir for 11 km (7 miles) and then turn right for the village of **Ihlara,** a distance of 34 km (21 miles). Ihlara lies in the shadow of Hasan Dağı, a dormant—but still steaming—volcano whose last eruption was witnessed by the ancient geographer Strabo. Towering more than 9,000 feet, Hasan Dağı forms part of an arc of volcanoes around the eastern rim of Central Anatolia. In a time beyond human memory they spewed fire and ash over a vast area of the central plateau. This ash was mixed with mud and compacted to form a soft stone called tufa. Next to Ihlara the Melendiz Çayı has cut a deep, narrow river gorge—the Peristrema valley—through the tufa. Zigzagging for some 12 miles across the plateau, this hidden valley is a world unto itself, a shaded, well-watered Shangri-la in the desert.

The history of the early settlement of this valley is lost, but by the sixth century A.D. it was a thriving center of Christian monasticism. Not only lone hermits but whole families came here to retreat from the world. From the soft stone they hewed dwellings, churches, and monasteries. The valley is riddled with perhaps 4,500 man-made "caves" and 105 churches and other religious structures. The interiors of many of the churches are decorated with colorful frescoes that, together with those in Cappadocia, represent a great treasure trove of Byzantine art. The churches and paintings are difficult to date, but activity in the area seems to have reached its peak in the eighth and ninth centuries. The paintings are therefore very important for the history of Early Christian art, for during the eighth and ninth centuries much of the religious art of the Byzantine world was destroyed by a movement known as Iconoclasm (from Greek, *eikono-klasma,* "image-breaking"). Fearing that the veneration of images would lead to idolatry, some emperors prohibited the creation of religious art and legislated the wholesale destruction of those images that already existed. The paintings in Cappadocia were among the few images to escape the ravages of the Iconoclasts.

By far the most enjoyable way to explore the now-uninhabited Peristrema valley is to walk through the most spectacular part of it, from the village of **Selime** to Ihlara. You come to Selime, which is at the base of a high rimrock cliff, about 16 km (10 miles) before reaching Ihlara by road. The walk along the babbling Melendiz Çayı in the shade of poplar and willow trees takes three or four hours, depending on the number of churches you visit. Before setting out be sure to arrange return transportation from Ihlara (you can do this at your hotel or with a local taxi service). Take along a picnic lunch and a flashlight (the caves' interiors are often very dark), and be prepared to wade the narrow, shallow river in several places. Then enter an undisturbed, lost world of great natural and artistic beauty. If your time is limited, drive straight to Ihlara, from where you can visit the most remarkable churches in the valley in about two hours.

Approximately one kilometer (about half a mile) before Ihlara, at a rest house at the top of the cliff overlooking the valley, there is an iron staircase that provides steep but direct access down the sheer walls to the valley floor. By walking less than a mile upstream from the staircase, and then about the same distance downstream from the same point, you will encounter several dozen churches of artistic merit as well as other, less interesting churches and countless dwellings and caves. No handy published guide to the valley exists, but the rest house can arrange for someone to lead you through the honeycomb. There is only one path, and the most notable churches are marked. They have all been given Turkish nicknames: Pürenli Seki Kilise (Church with the Pine-Needle Terrace), Kokar Kilise (Fragrant Church), and Eğri Taş Kilise (Crooked Stone Church) are upstream, while Sümbüllü Kilise (Hyacinth Church) and Yılanlı Kilise (Serpent Church) are downstream. These names were inspired by the frescoes in the churches, the shape of the structures, or simple flights of fancy. The five churches just named contain paintings depicting scenes from the life of Christ and related biblical events.

From Ihlara return to the Nevşehir highway and continue east. A few kilometers from the junction, on the right but seemingly in the middle of the road as you approach, is **Ağzıkara Han** (Dark-Mouthed Caravansary). Its name no doubt derives from its dark entrance. This way station, now in the middle of someone's farm and partly shaded by a few stork-inhabited trees, was built sometime between 1231 and 1240. It is a smaller version of Sultan Hanı; the construction stone, however, is of a rosier color and the portal is sited differently. And unlike in most hans, there is a complete absence of figural and floral decoration around the portal. Instead, there are simple repeating geometric forms. Because of its more human scale and feeling of intimacy, Ağzıkara Han is more captivating than Sultan Hanı. Sometimes the local farmers keep their animals in the stalls of this old caravansary and unintentionally bring it back to life.

About 8 km (5 miles) beyond Ağzıkara Han are the non-descript ruins of Öresin Hanı and, 14 km (8½ miles) farther, the decaying walls of Alay Hanı. In less than half an hour you arrive in Nevşehir in the center of Cappadocia. If you wish to continue to Kayseri (discussed below), another 110 km (68 miles) farther, follow the roads to Ürgüp and İncesu.

CAPPADOCIA

Many people come to Turkey just to see Cappadocia (Kapadokya in Turkish). The erosive powers of nature have sculpted this corner of Central Anatolia, a half-day's drive southeast of Ankara, into a geologic wonderland that almost defies the imagination. It is an enchanted labyrinth of natural arches, towers, columns, pyramids, and castles—a terrible place for a farmer to lose a cow, but a photographer's dream.

There are two ways to reach Cappadocia from Ankara. One is to take the road to Kayseri and then, past Kırşehir, turn off for Nevşehir. The other is to go south on the Konya highway until it branches for Aksaray. Then head for Aksaray, from which you turn left for Nevşehir. Both routes are about the same distance, 283 km (175 miles) compared to 295 km (183 miles), respectively. The Kayseri road takes about five hours, which is actually more than the Aksaray road, because of the sights to visit en route. The road to Aksaray, a straight shot across the heart of the Central Anatolian plateau, is the more direct approach.

From Ankara the road to Aksaray surpasses in monotony even the road to Konya—there is nothing in any direction. It seems as if you're driving into oblivion. About halfway, your eye is drawn to a slightly waving sheet of glass, the great **Tuz Gölü**, or Salt Lake. You follow its shore for about 50 km (31 miles). At a number of places you can park and walk down to the crusty edge of the water. Close to 700 square miles in area, the lake changes with the seasons. In the summer there is absolutely no sign of life on its banks except for a bit of scrub brush. If there is a lake in Hades, it must resemble Tuz Gölü in summer. With a certain relief you arrive in Aksaray (discussed above) and immediately order refreshments.

By "Kapadokya" the Turks mean only the erosion basin filled with the famous stone formations known as "fairy chimneys." In ancient times, however, Cappadocia was the name given to a much larger region of Central Anatolia. For Herodotus (ca. 484 to 424 B.C.), it stretched from the Taurus mountain range north to the Black Sea. He claimed, in fact, that this geographical term was first applied by the Persians, who long ruled most of Asia Minor. For Xenophon (ca. 430 to 355 B.C.), Cappadocia was more strictly defined as lying between the Taurus and Pontic mountains to the south and north and the upper Euphrates and the central "salt desert" to the east and west, respectively.

Most of Cappadocia is a high upland tract reaching to more than 3,000 feet above sea level—the highest part of the table-land of Central Anatolia. The western part is an open, treeless plain with good pastures, while the eastern section is more broken up and traversed by mountains. The most important ancient city in the region was Mazaca, near the site of present-day Kayseri. In the centuries before Christ, Cappadocia was sometimes an independent kingdom, usually allied with Rome after about 150 B.C. In A.D. 17 Tiberius reduced it to a province of the empire. Subsequently it remained part of the Byzantine Empire until the late 11th century, when it passed into the hands of the Seljuks. In any case, Christianity came to Cappadocia quite early. In the fourth century A.D. it was an especially thriving center of Christian theology. The Cappadocian Fathers, Basil of Caesarea and the brothers Gregory of Nysa and Gregory of Nazianzus, for example, played a major role in formulating and defending the orthodox conception of the Trinity—namely, that God is one essence in three substances. Much of Cappadocia's population until recent times was Greek and Armenian and, thus, Christian. Most of the remaining Christians left during the exchange of minority populations between Greece and Turkey in 1923, but there are still pockets of Christians in large towns such as Kayseri.

In the last few years, there has been a rush to build hotels in Cappadocia, especially in and around Ürgüp and the featureless city of Nevşehir. You therefore have many choices for accommodations. The new hotels at the lower end of the scale, which are quite pleasant, run about US$50 or less per night for a double. Those at the upper end are full-scale luxury resorts. Among the former are the **Taşsaray Hotel** in the center of Ürgüp and the **Şehir Palas Oteli** and **Şekeryapan Oteli** in Nevşehir. The latter include the **Otel Mustafa, Perissia Oteli**, and **Dinler Oteli** in Ürgüp, the **Dedeman Oteli** in Nevşehir, and the **Yıltok Oteli** between Nevşehir and Avanos. The resort hotels all have swimming pools, tennis courts, and other athletic facilities; Turkish baths and saunas; discos; and restaurants. The older hotels, such as the **Kavas Oteli** on the eastern edge of Nevşehir, tend to be less expensive than comparable new hotels, but they are equally comfortable.

Most destinations in Cappadocia are within a triangle whose corners are Nevşehir, Ürgüp, and Avanos. The longest distance, 20 km (12 miles), is between Nevşehir and Ürgüp. There is no good, detailed guidebook to Cappadocia, but the ones that are available locally can give you an overview. The **tourist office** in the center of Ürgüp (Kayseri Caddesi 37; Tel: 4868/1059) provides assistance and sells many publications. All the major hotels offer tours. Because distances are short and the routes many, you can easily adapt your itinerary to suit your time.

Whether you stay in Nevşehir or Ürgüp, a good way to visit the area is to start by moving generally from west to east. Plan to arrive in Nevşehir in the evening, and in the morning head due south for the underground city at **Kaymaklı** (21 km/13 miles from Nevşehir). Beneath the castle-like promontory in the center of this small town is surely one of the queerest works of engineering to be found anywhere on earth. Perhaps in Hittite times, perhaps as late as the sixth century A.D.—no one knows—the people who lived here began to tunnel into the soft stone. They sank air shafts as deep as 275 feet into the rock and then burrowed laterally at different levels in all directions. They hewed an elaborate system of staircases and corridors to connect all layers to the surface. Along the passages at each level they dug dwellings, latrines, kitchens, dining halls, meeting rooms, storage chambers, wine cellars, chapels, and other rooms. In times of danger they protected their self-contained habitation by rolling huge circular stones across strategic corridors. At the surface the entrances were camouflaged. Some, in fact, have been discovered only recently and others surely remain to be found. Tunneling seems to have continued until at least the tenth century, when several thousand people, all Christians, lived in this subterranean world.

There are no fewer than eight levels at Kaymaklı, the lowest being too dangerous to explore. The top four layers are open to visitors and are well lighted. Nevertheless, it's still a good idea to bring a flashlight, just in case the generator fails. Many passages are low and narrow, with room for only one person—not for the corpulent or claustrophobic. There is no painting, no decoration of any kind. The only color is provided by the green mold that flourishes in the fluorescent light. You can walk and squirm your way through the passageways of Kaymaklı in less than an hour. When you emerge from the depths of the earth, you will certainly have a new appreciation for human ingenuity—or madness.

About 15 minutes south of Kaymaklı is a second troglodyte town at **Derinkuyu** (Deep Well). This underground complex—not completely explored—may actually be larger than the one at Kaymaklı, and the possibility exists that the two may be connected. In the vicinity of Derinkuyu are scores of man-made holes leading to underground passages. Many are under modern houses, whose owners use the passages as cellars. This section of Cappadocia is an enormous human anthill.

Returning to Nevşehir and taking the road to Ürgüp, you start to wind through a geologic fantasy land. The first stop is **Üçhisar** (Three Castles), a village nestled around a pinnacle of tufa that can be seen from a great distance. The jagged crown of this pinnacle gave the village its name. As perforated with chambers as a wheel of Swiss cheese, this natural tower provides a spectacular view of the austere beauty of the northern and eastern parts of the Cappadocian erosion basin. Directly below, in, and about the village, are dozens of pink tufa cones whose carved rooms are, in many cases, still in use. In the distance stretch ridge after undulating ridge of virtually identical rock formations. Scattered among them are clusters of cones, pyramids, and needles that resemble tent camps of a race of giants. The best time to take photographs is in the afternoon, when the sun is in the west. As it sets, the sun highlights the variegated hues of the soft stone—red, yellow, purple, gray, and even green.

A few minutes south of Üçhisar on the main access road is the **Kaya Motel**, which is partially cut into the cliffs and blends with the countryside. In addition to a pool and excellent view, this Club Med motel has excellent buffet-style meals—a cornucopia of French and Turkish cuisine. Next to the Kaya is the underground Bındallı restaurant.

A short distance beyond Üçhisar, back on the main road to Ürgüp, is a turnout on the left from which you can see numerous **fairy chimneys** (*peri bacaları*). Sometimes the tufa was covered by a layer of basalt. Much harder than the tufa, the basalt eroded more slowly and served as a protective cover. Centuries of wind and water wore away the underlying tufa at a more rapid pace, leaving the basalt as a capstone, a natural capital, so to speak, on numerous pillars.

A few kilometers farther, turn right to the village of **Ortahisar** (Middle Castle). It has a narrower, steeper pinnacle than the one at Üçhisar, with its own sweeping vistas to the south and east. In the late summer and early fall, the villagers dry peppers on the roofs of their houses, adding a touch of bright red and yellow to the view. At the base of the pinnacle, to the right of the entrance, is one of the best **antiques shops** in Cappadocia. The only such shop on this street, it has a fine selection of "junk" in the window. On the Kayseri road west of Ortahisar is the **Yeni Yükseller Oteli**, complete with pool and suites.

From Ortahisar, backtrack to the main road and then go north a short distance to **Göreme**, passing on the right the excellent **Ataman** restaurant, which has a wonderful local atmosphere. Göreme is first mentioned, as Korama, in the obscure *Acts of St. Hieron* written around A.D. 600. This work describes the martyrdom of a local villager some 300 years earlier. Göreme consists of a group of monasteries carved into a cliff and several cones surrounding a natural open courtyard on the edge of a narrow valley. The paintings in several of these monasteries, and in the Tokalı Kilise just below them, are the most beautiful in Cappadocia. Unfortunately for the tourist, some of these monasteries have been closed recently for restoration, and it is impossible to predict which ones will be open at a given time. In any case, you can make a circuit of the grounds in about two hours. The most important frescoes are in the Elmalı Kilise, Karanlık Kilise, and Tokalı Kilise, all well marked, but those in the other churches are also worth a look. Just inside the "courtyard" is a Ministry of Tourism shop selling especially fine handcrafts. You should set out from there, flashlight in hand, progressing counterclockwise on the circular path.

The **Elmalı Kilise** (Apple Church), reached by a short, narrow shaft, is burrowed into the face of the cliff where it drops into the valley. This small church is cruciform in plan and has four columns supporting a central dome, one main apse, and two minor apses. On the walls and domed ceiling are a series of paintings probably dating to the 11th or 12th century. As in all the churches of Cappadocia, the paintings depict scenes from the life of Christ. The most hypnotic is the portrait of Christ in the main dome.

Immediately south and to the rear of Elmalı Kilise is **Barbara Kilisesi** (Church of St. Barbara). This cross-vaulted structure with two columns contains cross, bird, eye, and other motifs painted in red, as well as multicolored 11th-century frescoes of various saints. Farther to the south is **Yılanlı Kilise** (Serpent Church). It has two sections, one tunnel-vaulted and the other flat-roofed. It, too, has 11th-century paintings and received its name from one of them, which depicts St. George killing a snake. On the wall opposite the entrance is a standing figure of Christ holding a book.

From Yılanlı Kilise follow the path east until you reach a spiral staircase that leads to **Karanlık Kilise** (Dark Church). Part of a monastery, this basilica, with its central and flanking apses, columns, and cross vaulting, is an excellent example of the attempt to create, inside a mountain of stone, a sanctuary conceived as a freestanding structure of stone or brick. Its frescoes, again dating from the 11th century, are among the best preserved in the region. As the name of the church suggests, you will need a flashlight to see the paintings. To the right of the Karanlık Kilise is a **refectory** with a long table and seats cut from the living stone.

Just beyond Karanlık Kilise is **Çarıklı Kilise** (Sandal Church), with two columns, three apses, and four domes. Its paintings, many still warm and bright, apparently date from the 13th century. In the central apse Christ is enthroned, with St. John the Baptist on his right and Mary on his left. The name of this church derives from a footprint below the fresco depicting the Ascension.

A few minutes on foot below this circle of man-made caverns, to the right of the main road, is the **Tokalı Kilise** (Buckle Church), without doubt the most spectacular of all. Entering this church, which was hewn into a sheer wall of pink tufa in the tenth century, you find yourself standing in a trapezoidal, barrel-vaulted nave facing a broad transept and three apses with horseshoe arches. In front of the apses is a transversal passage with vaulting supported by four large pillars. On the left of the transept is a small chapel. Below the floor is a crypt. In short, the Tokalı Kilise is a tour de force of Cappadocian stonecarving. Furthermore, no other cave church can match the grandeur of its extensive and elaborate murals. Recently cleaned and restored, these paintings, dominated by red, green, and blue, will envelope and dazzle you. On the north wall of the entrance, St. Hieron is depicted as a Byzantine soldier.

Continuing on the road one kilometer past Tokalı Kilise, you reach **Saklı Kilise** (Hidden Church), some 200 yards off to the left. The church features frescoes depicting scenes from the life of Christ, probably dating from the 12th century. A little more than a kilometer farther, turn right for the town of Avanos. After 5 km (3 miles), at the village of Çavuşin, you will see a number of cliff dwellings on the right. At the top of the cliff, reached by an iron staircase, is the **church of St. John the Baptist**. Part of the church has collapsed, but you can still see its carved façade of blind arches resting on columns topped with Byzantine Ionic capitals. The interior bears only traces of the frescoes that once adorned it.

A few minutes past Çavuşin, take the road to the right to **Zelve**, where there is a second major concentration of churches. On the way you wind through a colorful valley of vineyards and clusters of "hatted" cones. At the end of the road, 18 km (11 miles) past the junction with the road from Çavuşin, Zelve consists of three canyons whose curiously eroded walls are pitted with churches, dwellings, dovecotes, and even a mosque. Zelve, in fact, is a relatively new ghost town. Between 1950 and 1955 its inhabitants were forced to leave because of deteriorating living conditions and lack of services. You can easily spend an afternoon exploring Zelve, perhaps after a picnic in the park facing the entrance. The canyons are not very long and have well-worn paths, but many of the cliff dwellings can only be reached by rickety ladders or zigzagging goat tracks. Zelve is the eeriest of all the sites in Cappadocia, especially in the late evening when the bats come out.

From Zelve return to the main road and turn right for the small town of **Avanos**, crossing the Kızılırmak (Red River) as you enter. The longest river in Turkey, it takes its name from the rusty tinge it acquires as it flows through the red clay beds of the region. In addition to cut and polished onyx, the mahogany-colored pots thrown from this clay are an important part of the economy of Avanos. The center of town contains a number of workshops where you can watch the potters at their wheels. One shop, to the right of the square as you enter it from the bridge over the Kızılırmak, resembles a wine cellar with a low, vaulted stone ceiling. The owner has the ghoulish hobby of requesting locks of hair from female patrons and visitors, which he then hangs from the ceiling. The pottery can best be described as folksy and inexpensive.

Avanos is a convenient place to enjoy a meal or escape from the sun with a cool drink. Especially recommended here are Turkey's pure fruit juices: apricot, peach, and cherry. Cherry juice, *vişne suyu,* is more than delicious—it's almost addictive. For a full Turkish meal, try the **Altınocak Restaurant**, located in the Yeni Mahalle (New Quarter) in the Hasankale Mevkii (Hasankale District). Avanos has several good hotels. Near the Altınocak is the **Avanos Irmak Oteli**, which has a view of the river. The new **Grand Avanos Hotel** on Kapadokya Caddesi has a pool, disco, and tennis courts. If you would like to escape from the "ordinary," try the inexpensive **Sofa Oteli**, which is built into an old Turkish house, at number 13 Orta Mahalle (Central Quarter).

From the intersection at the south end of town, take the road to the left for Ürgüp. Shortly thereafter you come to a road on the left to **Sarı Han** (Yellow Caravansary), 6 km (3½ miles) away. It sits forlornly on a knoll overlooking the surrounding plain. Built during the reign of 'Izz ad-Din Kay-Qubad II (Turkish, İzzettin Keykubat II; r. 1246 to 1257), Sarı Han is the last of the Seljuk sultans' hans. Despite its generally ruined condition, it still has pleasing outer and inner portals decorated with geometric motifs. The dominant yellow stone used in its construction virtually glows in the sun.

Continuing on the road to Ürgüp for another 8 km (5 miles) you reach the so-called **Valley of the Fairy Chimneys**. From a turnout on the right you look out over one of the most spectacular eroded ridges in Cappadocia: Here are a forest of cones and sensuously rippling cliffs. A path below the road leads you through the maze. On the left of the road are more cones and a superb view across part of the basin. A photographer could happily spend a day here capturing the tufa's changes of color in the shifting light. Nothing grows in the erosion zones. They are unprotected and naked to the elements. Bring a hat to shield yourself from the ferocious sun.

Just a few minutes to the south of this wondrous sight is **Ürgüp**. The Byzantine bishopric of Hagios Prokopios and an important town in the 11th and 12th centuries, Ürgüp today is the tourist capital of Cappadocia—a description that should be taken in a positive sense. Nestled in a small canyon whose walls are pockmarked with chambers, Ürgüp is a charming town that has slowly emerged from its own cliff-dwelling origins. In the old section of town some of the houses are little more than extensions of their stone-cut predecessors. This was a Christian town before the exchange of populations, and Christian motifs can still be seen carved on the doorways of many old houses.

The main street of old Ürgüp is essentially a row of souvenir, antiques, and carpet shops with a few banks, greengrocers, and maybe a restaurant or two mixed in. The evening is the time to browse through potential heirlooms and the excellent selection of carpets and kilims. After a day of climbing about cliffs, canyons, and caves, relax in a rug shop with tea or a soft drink while the owner patiently unrolls his stock. Not only is this time-honored practice fun, it's also the best way to learn about Turkish textiles.

The restaurants in Ürgüp, such as the **Ar-Saf, Special**, and, above all, **Hanedan Lokantası**, offer inexpensive and basic Anatolian fare. In addition to those mentioned above, good food and lodging in Ürgüp can be found at the **Boytaş Motel**, on the Kayseri road, and the **Turban Ürgüp Moteli**, on the hill above the town. The Boytaş has a nightclub, while the Turban has a large pool and bungalows. One hotel, the **Ürgüp Alfina Hotel**, just inside the western city limits, is actually cut into the tufa like the ancient dwellings and churches of Cappadocia. The façade of the hotel is built against a canyon wall, and the guest rooms have been carved out of the rock. Although they're a bit damp and dimly lit, staying in one of these novel rooms could help complete your Cappadocian experience.

THE ANKARA ROAD TO KAYSERİ

Kayseri is, after Ankara and Konya, the third most important city of Central Anatolia. Highly industrialized and surrounded by bountiful farms, it is one of the most prosperous cities in Turkey. Kayseri's dramatic setting southeast of Ankara in the shadow of Mount Erciyes and its historical buildings and colorful market should make it a magnet for tourists. Yet the city is relatively untouched by tourism. Even many Turks from Ankara have never been there. Partly as a result of this isolation, Kayseri retains the flavor of a traditional Central Anatolian city, which both Ankara and Konya have lost to either political or tourism development. The recommended route from Ankara to Kayseri takes about four hours (328 km/204 miles), plus some time for a brief detour or two on the way.

Leave the capital via the Konya road and, after about 20 km (12 miles), turn left on route 260 for Kayseri. You weave your way through a pleasant countryside of reforested hills and fertile vales and, within an hour, cross the Kızılırmak at a graceful Seljuk **stone bridge**. Probably built in the 13th century, this two-lane, multiarched bridge straddles the now blue-green waters of the Kızılırmak (cleansed of its red silt since leaving Cappadocia) just before the river enters a picturesque rocky gorge. The bridge marks a favorite swimming spot for boys from the nearby village.

The area around the river is prime grazing land for flocks of sheep. You'll see them under the guard of a magnificent, powerful-looking breed of dog called a *kangal* ("coil"). This sand-colored dog with a dark muzzle characteristically coils its tail over its back. Sheepherding *kangals* usually wear thick iron collars studded with long, sharp spikes for protection from wolves. Famed for their loyalty, these dogs are best avoided during lambing season; more than one automobile has acquired souvenir teeth marks. (*Kangals,* by the way, are trained as police dogs in Turkey.) With a keen eye, you may also spy a second, highly prized breed of dog in the village streets: the sleek, fine-haired *saluki,* which is used chiefly for hunting.

Kırşehir

About halfway between Ankara and Kayseri is the city of Kırşehir (City of the Steppe), sometimes also called Gülşehir (City of Roses)—a seemingly inapt name for this dusty and generally colorless town now known for its cultured mushrooms. This was the birthplace of Gülşehri (d. ca. 1317), one of the first Anatolian poets to write in Turkish, helping to make Turkish one of the three great literary languages of Islam. As indicated by the unexcavated mound in the center of the city, Kırşehir has seen much of the ebb and flow of Anatolian history. It reached its heyday between the end of the Seljuk and the late Ilkhanid, or Mongol, period, roughly 1240 to 1340.

It was in this city that the semilegendary Turkish holy man Ahi Evren, who died in the early 1300s, first organized the tanners and leatherworkers into a guild. This association, with its special rites of membership and adherence to Islam, eventually monopolized the leather trade throughout the European and Anatolian provinces of the Ottoman Empire and exerted strong influence on the guilds of most other professions. The organization of the professional trades into guilds and their penetration by members of the Muslim religious fraternities did much to convert the professional classes to Islam. Ahi Evren's tomb in Kırşehir became an important place of pilgrimage, and the income from the leather monopoly brought riches to his city.

Although usually bypassed by tourists, Kırşehir possesses several remarkable buildings from the medieval Islamic period. The most curious is the **Zaza Bey Medresesi** on Ankara Bulvarı next to the main market street. This was probably never really a medrese; built between 1272 and 1273, it was, in fact, originally an observatory. It was transformed into a mosque much later and is still used as a Friday "cathedral" mosque. Its high portal, horizontally striped with stones of two colors, is striking. At the left front corner is the conically crowned tomb of the founder. Behind the medrese towers a minaret that was added when the building became a mosque and that, indeed, looks like an afterthought. Originally the building's dome was open for astronomical observations. Inside the main hall, which is covered with local carpets, is a special platform that was probably used for stargazing. There's also a passage to the rim of the dome. It is unclear exactly how the observatory—one of the few to survive from the medieval Islamic world—functioned.

Artistically, the most unusual structure in Kırşehir is the **tomb of Aşık Paşa**, dated 1322, on the edge of town on Kayseri Bulvarı. A renowned poet and dervish, Aşık Paşa was the grandson of the founder of the Bābā'ī sect, a half-Muslim, half-shamanistic religio-social movement that shook the Seljuk state in 1242. The tomb of Aşık Paşa, which became an object of pilgrimage, is unlike any other in Turkey. Built entirely of marble, it has among its original features an asymmetrical façade and a narrow hall to the side of the entrance. In the center of the façade is a narrow window, to the far left of which is a deep-set narrow porch. The recess of the porch is decorated with a knot-like pattern. The tomb is set in a square space covered by a dome; the narrow hall connects it to the entrance.

Finally, take a look at the **Melik Gazi Türbesi**, also on Kayseri Bulvarı, an excellent example of a traditional Turkish tomb. It was constructed in 1250 by the wife of the local ruler, Melik Gazi of the Mengüchekid dynasty. From a distance it resembles a huge artillery shell pointed toward the sky. The *türbe* is a very harmonious octagonal structure with a pyramidal roof. Large triangles project downward from the upper edge like tent flaps. The tomb is entered by a portal that is richly embellished with carved marble stalactites.

If you have a bit more time, take a short walk northwest of the Melik Gazi *türbe* to the **Lâle Camii** (Tulip Mosque), originally built as a mint under the Mongols. The name supposedly derived from a tulip of great beauty that a student in the Zaza Bey Medresesi gave to the builders. This one flower was then sold to finance the reconstruction of the building as a mosque.

About 20 km (12 miles) south of Kırşehir is **Kesik Köprü** (Truncated Bridge), its 13 arches spanning the Kızılırmak. Built in 1248 by the Seljuk sultan 'Izz ad-Din Kay-Kavus II, it is one of the longest Seljuk bridges in Turkey and a masterpiece of engineering. Next to it, on the east bank, is a restored caravansary originally constructed in 1268. About 40 km (25 miles) northeast of Kırşehir via Mucur is **Seyfe Gölü** (Lake Seyfe), which lies at the center of a large wildlife preserve. This salt lake, resting in a closed basin, is extremely rich in birdlife and hosts one of the world's largest colonies of flamingos.

Should you be inclined to hunt for textiles in Kırşehir, you will probably be disappointed. Its prayer rugs, using two or three shades of red, were quite well known in the early part of this century, but the textile industry here has declined since then.

Kırşehir has a fine hotel, the **Terme Oteli**, complete with swimming pool, tennis courts, thermal bath chambers, and a good restaurant. It is in the center of town at Terme Parkı on Terme Caddesi.

Hacıbektaş

About 20 minutes beyond Kırşehir on the way to Kayseri, the road (route 260) branches to the right for the large village of Hacıbektaş (20 km/12 miles). In the center of this sleepy village is a walled *tekke* belonging to the founder of the Bektaşı order of dervishes, Hacı Bektaş. This complex also contains his tomb. Sometime in the 13th century, Hacı Bektaş appeared in Anatolia from eastern Iran. He attracted a circle of disciples who established a mystical brotherhood that eventually rivaled the Mevleviye in wealth and power. The Bektaşıs were especially associated with the janissaries, the shock troops of the Ottoman Empire, over whom they acquired exclusive authority by the late 15th century. The ritual and teachings of this order, which, like the Mevleviye, had its own special costume, were remarkable for their mixture of Muslim, Christian, and pre-Islamic Turkish elements. Wine, bread, and cheese, for example, were distributed among new members in a ceremony resembling Holy Communion. Bektaşıs also confessed their sins to their spiritual leaders, who granted absolution. Indeed, in many respects they disregarded orthodox Muslim ritual and worship and were thus accused of heresy.

The Bektaşıs frequently settled in, and then made their own, famous places of pilgrimage—even pagan and Christian shrines. In ancient times Hacıbektaş was the site of Venasa, a sanctuary where a god was attended by more than 3,000 temple-servants who were peasants bound to the land "owned" by the god. As late as the 19th century, the Christians in Anatolia believed the tomb of Hacı Bektaş to contain the remains of Saint Charalambos, a local Greek saint.

The Bektaşı brotherhood was dissolved in 1925, along with all the other dervish orders in Turkey. The lodge at Hacıbektaş is now a **museum** (closed Mondays) housing an exhibit of Bektaşı artifacts and donations. Composed of a mosque, bakery, bath, living quarters, and other structures clustered about three courtyards, the lodge dates to about the middle of the 14th century (Hacı Bektaş may have died in 1337) and was frequently remodeled or repaired.

You enter the lodge via the first courtyard, with its refreshing fountain in classical Ottoman style (though built only in 1902), and pass through the "Triangular Gate" to the second courtyard. To the left of this square, with a large pool and attractive lion fountain, is Meydan Evi (Courtyard House), the lodge's oldest dated building (1367). This was where believers applied to join the brotherhood and where initiation ceremonies were held. To the right of this courtyard is Aş Evi (Cook House), a wonderful medieval kitchen with great hearths, caldrons, and cooking utensils. Passing through the "Gate of the Sixes," you reach the third courtyard which leads, via the "White Gate," to the **tomb of Hacı Bektaş**. A dark corridor connects this white marble portal to the saint's tomb. Here, beneath a triangular dome, stands his cenotaph, covered by a green, gold-embroidered shroud.

Outside the main lodge complex, next to the garden, is the **tomb of Balım Sultan**, known as the "Second Master." In the latter part of the 15th century, he spread Bektaşism in the Balkans, where the order is still found.

The sacred soil of Hacıbektaş continues to attract the faithful. Those hoping for the saint's intercession to solve their problems often tie votive offerings to the 700-year-old black mulberry tree in front of the tomb of Balım Sultan. But Hacı Bektaş does not always listen. One recent—and very valuable—offering, a beautiful Persian carpet, went unheeded. It was from the last ruling shah of Iran.

Every year between August 16 and 18 a festival is held in Hacıbektaş to commemorate its namesake's cultural contributions to Turkey. In addition to minstrel contests, there is folk dancing with a dervish flavor. On a hill overlooking the village is the unpretentious, but pleasant, new **Hotel Village House**, complete with bar and restaurant.

By driving north through the village you will again meet the road going east to Kayseri.

KAYSERİ

Located at the junction of several major trade routes, Kayseri has a written history that predates the rise of the Hittite Empire, thanks to a trove of cuneiform tablets left by an Assyrian trade colony that was established nearby (ca. 1950 to 1850 B.C.). Later, as Mazaca, it was the seat of the kings of Cappadocia and then the capital of that Roman province. It was probably the emperor Claudius who renamed the city Caesarea, from which the Turkish name derives. In the fourth century, Basil, bishop of Cappadocia, founded an ecclesiastical center on the edge of the city. The Byzantine emperor Justinian I surrounded part of it with a strong wall in the sixth century. Subsequently, Kayseri grew up mostly within these walls. The city was overwhelmingly Greek Orthodox until the 11th century, when the pressure of the Turkish invasion resulted in a mass migration of Armenians into the area. Kayseri was first captured by the Turks in 1067, but it changed hands several times. (Virtually all of the city's surviving monuments date from the Islamic period.) The soldiers of the First Crusade passed through it in 1097, but it became part of the Seljuk Sultanate of Anatolia in 1168. Under the Seljuks the city enjoyed its golden age: It was the second most important city of the empire and frequently the residence of the sultans. Unfortunately, Kayseri's heyday was short-lived, for in 1243 the inhabitants had the temerity to resist the Mongols, who then stormed the city and massacred much of the population. Kayseri did revive, but until the late 17th century it had a rather turbulent history. The city was coveted by local rival dynasties, was the victim of marauding brigands, and was the object of Egyptian and Iranian military campaigns. All this was testimony to its political and economic importance.

Modern travellers to Kayseri, beginning with Evliya Çelebi in 1649, have praised the city's cereals and many excellent fruits and vegetables. Çelebi also noted that the city's famous *pastırma* was in such demand in Istanbul that none could be found in Kayseri itself. Cotton remains an important product, as it was in Seljuk times, and the making of cotton cloth is still a major industry. This Anatolian metropolis was long renowned for its leather goods (especially footwear) and its carpets and kilims. Its markets, filled with goods from as far away as India, attracted merchants from throughout the eastern Mediterranean and Iran.

Throughout much of its history, Kayseri was a cosmopolitan city of many ethnic groups and religions. At the beginning of this century about 65 percent of the population was Muslim and the remainder Christian. The Muslims included not only Turks, but Kurds and partly settled nomadic tribesmen. In the middle of the 18th century a large number of Circassians migrated from the Caucasus to the pastures of Uzun Yayla, near Kayseri. The Christians in the area were primarily Armenians and Greeks. Events on the eastern front during World War I and the exchange of populations with Greece later reduced the Christian population to about 2 percent.

The people of Kayseri have a reputation throughout Turkey for working hard and being very shrewd businessmen. Indeed, most Turks suspect they will inevitably get the worst of a bargain when dealing with a Kayseri banker, merchant, or salesman. Perhaps because of the commercial importance of the city, it has long had two very good hotels, the **Turan Oteli** and the **Hattat Oteli**. The Hattat has traditionally catered to businessmen. The more relaxed Turan has a rooftop restaurant with a view of Mount Erciyes. More modern facilities are found at the **Konfor Oteli**. All three hotels are near the center of town. Among the best restaurants featuring local cuisine are the **Ekol Turistik Tesisleri** on Sivas Caddesi and the **Demircioğlu Lokantası** on İnönü Bulvarı.

Kayseri has many fine Muslim buildings from the Middle Ages, their interesting architecture in sharp contrast to the architectural monotony modernity has brought. The most important are from the Seljuk and early Mongol periods, although those built from the local gray or black basalt, courtesy of nearby Mount Erciyes, look rather gloomy. Most are within walking distance of the center of the city, now a great open square known as Cumhuriyet Meydanı. (There is an underground shopping mall beneath the square.)

An efficient way to visit the chief monuments of central Kayseri is to walk counterclockwise through the neighborhoods around the square. Begin at the **Mahperi Hunand Hatun Medresesi**, about two blocks southeast of the square. This Islamic law school was built by the wife of 'Ala' ad-Din Kay-Qubad. Adjoining it is a great mosque that was part of the same complex. At the entrance to these two buildings is the attractive tomb of the founder, dated 1238. A public bath built in front of the mosque provided revenue to help fund the foundation. This whole complex was the first of its kind in Anatolia. The medrese is now a museum containing a mixture of objects found in and around the city. It has a typically ornate Seljuk portal and an interior courtyard. Its barrel-vaulted lesson hall, or *iwan*, is now glassed in.

Standing prominently on the southern edge of the city square, and across the street from this complex, is the **citadel**. A quadrilateral structure with many towers of finely cut stone, it was erected by the Seljuks between about 1210 and 1229. You can enter the citadel from its eastern gate and walk through it to its southwestern portal. Inside and opposite the southwestern gate is a small mosque built by Mehmet the Conqueror when he repaired the walls in 1466. The interior of the citadel has recently been turned into a shopping mall. There are several stairways on the inside from which you can climb to the top of the castle walls; you will get a superb view of the city from the ramparts.

Exiting the southwestern gate of the citadel, turn right into the main covered **bazaar** (the Bedesten) and the old merchants' quarters, the **Vizir Hanı**. The bazaar, built in 1497, and han, built in 1727, are lively markets, filled with everyday goods. Here you can also find a few carpet shops with fine selections from Kayseri's looms. Beside the han is the Ulu Cami, the "cathedral mosque" of the town, built in the late 12th century. (It is thought that this mosque was originally a church; much of the stone and most of the columns are from the Byzantine period.)

A few minutes north of this great mosque, in Atatürk park, is **Kurşunlu Cami** (the Lead Mosque, so called because its dome is covered with lead). This appealing, well-proportioned building was erected in 1585 according to a plan of the famous Ottoman architect Sinan. A bit farther north, in a quarter of winding streets and old houses, many of which are being demolished, is the **Çifte Medrese** (Double Medrese), actually two adjoining rectangular buildings connected by a corridor. The plans of the two are very similar; the major distinction is that one side contains a tomb. Historically, this is probably the most significant building in Kayseri, for it is the oldest Muslim hospital in Turkey. The left wing of this complex was built by Jawhar Nasiba, the daughter of the Seljuk sultan 'Izz ad-Din Qılıç Arslan II. The right wing was built by her brother, Sultan Ghiyath ad-Din Kay-Khusraw I, after her death in 1205. He set aside one section for her tomb, one of the earliest in the Seljuk period. Though some say the right wing functioned as a medical school, it was probably simply an extension of the hospital. Much restored, the Çifte Medrese is usually locked. You will have to ask for the watchman *(bekçi)*, who has the key.

Still continuing north you'll come to the brown stone **Hacı Kılıç Camii** on İstasyon Bulvarı. Built in 1249 by a military commander of 'Ala' ad-Din Kay-Qubad, it represents an unusual fusion of a mosque and a medrese. In place of an adjoining wall, there is an arcaded courtyard shared by both institutions. The medrese, with its rows of student cells, is to the right. Inside, the only original architectural decoration is on the stone prayer niche.

The last building of note in the center of town is the **Sahibiye Medresesi** at the opposite end of İstasyon Bulvarı where it enters the main square. It was among the many works of the Seljuk vizier Sahib Ata, who graced Konya with the İnce Minareli Medresesi and other buildings. This law school, however, is much less majestic than its sister in Konya. Erected in 1268, it is simply a courtyard surrounded on four sides by rows of dormitories. Today this medrese is used as a museum to display objects from the Seljuk period.

On the southern edge of Kayseri on the road to Talas, about a kilometer from the square, stands the **Döner Kümbet** (Revolving Tomb, also known as Şah Cihan Hatun Kümbeti). Perhaps the most beautiful of all Seljuk funerary structures, it was built for Princess Shah Jihan Hatun, a daughter of 'Ala' ad-Din Kay-Qubad. The tomb bears no date, but it can be ascribed to roughly 1275. This 12-sided mausoleum of yellow sandstone very closely resembles a monumental tent. Cords of rope are actually carved on the conical roof as if they were attached to supporting stakes. The 12 exterior panels contain rich figural decorations in relief: palm leaves, lions, winged leopards with human heads, a double-headed eagle. Above these figures are tapestries of geometric patterns. At the top and bottom of the cylinder are bands of delicate stalactites. The tomb is a masterpiece of this minor architectural genre.

A little farther beyond the Döner Kümbet is another mausoleum, the **Sırçalı Kümbet** (Faïence Tomb). In sharp contrast to the Döner Kümbet, this tomb is an absolutely bare cylinder. The roof, which has disappeared to reveal the interior dome, was apparently covered with light-blue tiles. The Sırçalı Kümbet probably dates from the middle of the 14th century. It is not known who was buried here.

Kayseri is a treasure house for collectors of Turkish rugs and admirers of Ottoman-era antiques. The town contains numerous carpet and antiques shops, many specializing in regional carpets, especially floss rugs from Bünyan (56 km/

35 miles northeast of Kayseri) and the root-dyed carpets of Yahyalı (dominant colors: sea blue, red, brown, and gray).

Around Kayseri

All around Kayseri you will feel the overwhelming presence of **Mount Erciyes** (Erciyes Dağ), the ancient Argaeus. Surrounded by numerous cinder cones, it looms over the city like a watchful guardian with his servants. Its peak, which rises to 13,100 feet, is rarely free of snow. Directly south of Kayseri (26 km/16 miles) a road leads to a lodge and popular ski runs, partway up the great volcano. If you continue south from the lodge for 58 km (36 miles), you'll reach the village of **Yahyalı**, which has a wonderful carpet market every Friday. Northwest of Yahyalı on the eastern shore of Yay Gölü is a great marsh and bird sanctuary called **Sultan Sazlığı** ("Sultan's Reed-bed"). Some 250 species of birds have been observed here, including flocks of pelicans. There is a banding station that is open to the public.

About 21 km (13 miles) northeast of Kayseri, on the road to Sivas, is **Kültepe** (Ash Hill), the great mound of the ancient city of **Kanesh**. Inhabited from the Copper Age (4000 B.C.) to the Roman era, it is one of the most important archaeological sites in Anatolia. Excavations were begun by French archaeologists in 1893 and have continued under Turkish auspices to the present. The greatest discovery here was an archive of more than 15,000 Assyrian tablets in cuneiform script, the oldest records ever found in Turkey. Around 2000 B.C. Kanesh was the center of an extensive Assyrian trading network in Anatolia. This center was actually a colony of Assyrian merchants established outside the city who directed the export of goods to Mesopotamia. Strolling through the excavation site, which has been opened by the Turkish Historical Society, you can see the mud-brick walls of dwellings, shops, warehouses, archives, a market, and several palaces. In many places you'll see evidence of a great fire that engulfed the city about 1900 B.C.: The heat was so intense that it vitrified many of the bricks. The most important objects found at Kültepe/Kanesh are on exhibit in the Museum of Anatolian Civilizations in Ankara. There is a fine view from the top of the mound, which rises 60 feet above the neighboring plain.

After going another 26 km (16 miles) northeast on the road to Sivas you reach a great castle-like caravansary. Dominating a small village on the right side of the road, this inn, like the one between Konya and Aksaray, is called **Sultan Hanı**. It was also built by the same Seljuk ruler, 'Ala' ad-Din Kay-Qubad, between 1232 and 1236. The two buildings even have the same plan. This one, however, is slightly smaller and its decoration is rather different. Especially noteworthy are the serpent monsters on each side of the supporting arches of the raised kiosk mosque in the center of the courtyard. The serpents squirm and writhe up each side of the arch. At the apex their heads are joined at their open mouths. The entry portal, whose porch projects as much as six feet from the wall, is as monumental as that of its sister han. This building, too, has been considerably restored in recent years.

SİVAS

Sivas is an ancient town northeast of Kayseri whose roots go back to the Hittite era. In 64 B.C. it was refounded by the Roman general Pompey the Great, who gave it the name Megalopolis. According to tradition, Queen Pythodoris, the widow of Polemon, king of Pontus, named the city Sebasteia in honor of Emperor Augustus (*Sebasteia* is the Greek form of the emperor's name). In any case, the Romans of imperial times knew it as Sebasteia, whence the Turkish name. This city, which has some of the finest examples of medieval Muslim architecture in Turkey, is a full day's drive due east from Ankara via Yozgat (448 km/278 miles). Highway 180, which goes north through Amasya, is a slightly longer route (560 km/347 miles) but is much more interesting; it is described below under Amasya.

Situated at an elevation of 4,420 feet in the broad valley of the Kızılırmak, Sivas has grown from a city of about 30,000 people in 1928 to well over 200,000 today. Like Kayseri it is a prosperous center of agriculture and industry. It first became significant in Roman times, when it was the chief town of a military district. Christianity arrived in Sivas in the second century, and the town became the seat of a bishopric under the Byzantines. Although pillaged in the sixth century by the Persians and in the eighth century by the Arabs, it grew to be second only to Kayseri in size and wealth in Anatolia. In 1021 Senekherim, the Armenian king of the region known as Vaspurakan around Lake Van, ceded his lands to Byzantine emperor Basil II and in return received Sivas and its surrounding territory. Some 40,000 of his people then followed him to this new land. Sivas remained an Armenian center for half a century, until it fell to the Turks after the battle of Manzikert in 1071. In 1174 the Seljuk sultan 'Izz ad-Din Qılıch Arslan II incorporated it into his empire. Sivas thrived under the Seljuks. During the reign of

'Ala' ad-Din Kay-Qubad, who rebuilt its walls in 1221, Sivas may have had a population of 100,000. The Persian traveller and geographer al-Qazwini, who may have visited the city in the first half of the 13th century, reported that it was famous for woolens, fruit, cotton, and grain. He noted, however, that the snow was so heavy in the winter that people established special endowments to provide food for the birds during the cold months.

In 1243 the Mongols smashed the Seljuk army near Köse Dağ, 80 km (50 miles) northeast of Sivas, and then plundered the city for three days. Thanks to the efforts of the Muslim judge Najm ad-Din of Kırşehir, the inhabitants were spared the sword. Sivas flourished under the Mongols as well, and some of its most magnificent buildings date from this period. In the late 13th century Marco Polo described this city, along with Konya and Kayseri, as one of the glories of Anatolia. In the following century the Mongol governors of Anatolia usually chose Sivas as their residence, and the Genoese established a consulate there. Around 1331 Ibn Battuta spent a few days in the city, which, he said, had fine buildings, wide streets, and markets choked with people. In 1343 'Ala' ad-Din Eretna, the Mongol governor, declared his independence and Sivas became the capital of his state.

As the Mongol Empire dissolved, Sivas changed hands several times among local chieftains. In 1400 it was struck a blow from which it did not fully recover until modern times. In that year Tamerlane besieged the city for 18 days. The inhabitants finally offered to surrender in return for safe passage. The conqueror agreed, but when the gates were opened he promptly had the defenders buried alive or otherwise slaughtered. Only the commander of the defenders was spared, so that he could take word of the disaster to the Ottoman sultan Bayezit I. The city was sacked and its walls were torn down. Of all the Anatolian cities captured by Tamerlane, Sivas suffered the worst. Its fate was meant to spread terror among the Ottoman Turks, who were defeated two years later. More than 200 years later, in 1649, when Evliya Çelebi visited Sivas, he recorded that the people still spoke with a shudder of Tamerlane's atrocities.

Under the Ottomans Sivas gradually declined to a minor provincial town. Çelebi said it had 44 districts, including Armenian and Greek quarters, and 4,600 houses. He added that there were hans and, around the great mosque, a covered market (*bedesten*) of 1,000 shops. By the beginning of the 20th century, however, Sivas had become little more than a gloomy town of narrow muddy streets and flat-roofed houses built of sun-dried brick.

The revival of Sivas began with the rise of the Turkish nationalist movement. On June 27, 1919, Mustafa Kemal (later Atatürk) went to Sivas during the first stage of his attempt to rally the Turkish people together after the debacle of World War I. Shortly thereafter, on September 4, he convened in a local school a congress that organized the Association for the Defense of the Rights of Anatolia and Rumelia (European Turkey), which became the political instrument of the Turkish nationalist movement. Sivas was put on the political map. But real development began with the coming of the railroad in 1930. Today Sivas is a new city, a bustling agricultural center of undistinguished architecture.

It takes a day to see the half-dozen Seljuk and Ilkhanid buildings in Sivas, most of which can be reached on foot from the town square, Konak Meydanı. The best place to stay is the modest but friendly **Köşk Oteli**, about two blocks southeast of Konak square on Atatürk Caddesi. From the square, on which there is a **tourist office** in the city hall, walk south down Inönü Bulvarı, passing on the right the school in which the Sivas Congress was held. When you reach Selçuk Sokak, turn left into the park for the **Bürücüye Medresesi**.

This school of Islamic law was built under Mongol rule between 1271 and 1272 by the Seljuk vizier Muzaffar Burujirdi. Similar to the Sırçalı Medrese in Konya, the tapestry of intricate geometrical designs around the door frame completely transforms the massive stone into delicate, lacy tracery. This feeling of lightness is further emphasized by the thin miniature columns carved around the frame, which seem to be all that is necessary to support the portal. Passing through the portal you enter a domed vestibule. To one side is the domed tomb of the founder, decorated with faïence, and to the other the domed mosque. Though the plan of the medrese is typical in most ways, it has two stories, which is unusual. The columns around the courtyard to the north and south are Byzantine, as are some of the capitals. This building is used today as an archaeological and ethnographical **museum**, housing a collection of ancient and medieval coins and Seljuk copper eating utensils as well as local folk costumes and dervish artifacts.

About 40 yards south of the Bürücüye, in the same park, stand two buildings that are very famous in the history of Islamic architecture, facing each other across a narrow lane. One is the **Şifaiye Medresesi**, the largest of all Seljuk hospitals, and the other is the Çifte Minareli Medrese (Medrese with Two Minarets). The hospital, whose other name is Darüşşifa (House of Healing), was erected by Sultan 'Izz ad-Din Kay-Kavus I between 1217 and 1218. The entryway, with its stately stalactite porch, has a border of lions' and bulls' heads (symbolizing the sun and the moon) complemented by a braid motif of intersecting hexagons. The plan of this hospital is similar to that of an ordinary medrese, but the rooms are more elaborate and some have fireplaces. The entry hall is also more complex. It is not known how the rooms were used. At the end of the courtyard, at each side of the great hall, now in ruins, are male and female heads also representing the sun and moon. In the center of the row of rooms to the right is the tomb of the founder, who died of tuberculosis. Its decoration is a mosaic of mixed brick and faïence. The effect of the Arabic calligraphy on white, turquoise, and cobalt faïence is stunning. The mausoleum bears an inscription that reads, in part, "My wealth was of no use to me. My sultanate is finished."

The **Çifte Minareli Medrese** was constructed between 1271 and 1272 by the Ilkhanid vizier Shams ad-Din Juwayni. Only the front of this building, a minaret towering above each side of the entrance, survives. Nevertheless, the façade alone is enough to rank the building among the masterpieces of Seljuk art. The gable above the stalactite porch of the monumental doorway is sumptuously carved with interlacing designs in high relief. These designs, which are especially delicate, continue along each side of the entrance. Diminutive columns surmounted by capitals of acanthus leaves accent their fragility. The minarets, woven together with brick and glazed tile, rise above the portal like the horns of a strange beast. Near the top of each is a balcony with stalactite corbeling. Unfortunately, the street between the Çifte Minareli and the hospital is so narrow that it is difficult to photograph the full façade of the medrese. To get the best light you have to come once in the morning to photograph one building and again in the afternoon to shoot the other in order to avoid the shadows the buildings cast on one another.

If you continue south a few blocks and then turn left on Cemal Gürsel Caddesi, you come to the **Ulu Cami** (Great Mosque), the oldest monument in Sivas. (You pass on your right an ancient mound, called Toprak Tepe, where the remains of a Hittite settlement were found in 1946. Today this hill is a city park.) It was long thought that the Ulu Cami was built by the Danishmendids, but an inscription discovered in 1955 declares that it was constructed in 1197 by a certain Kızıl Aslan. Especially impressive is its forest of columns, ten rows of five each, which shield the prayer niche. A large building, the mosque has a flat roof. From the outside the only remarkable feature is a single minaret at the far left corner. This huge beacon, rising 115 feet, is completely out of proportion to the mosque. Wrapped around it is an inscription rendered in turquoise tiles.

Just before the Ulu Cami, a lane to the right leads to the **Gök Medrese** (Blue Medrese), so called because of the turquoise tiles decorating its twin minarets and part of its interior. The Gök Medrese is the most spectacular example of Seljuk medrese architecture. Built in 1271, the same year as the Çifte Minareli, its closest rival, this building represents the height of the architectural megalomania of Sahib Ata, whose works in Konya and Kayseri have already been mentioned. It has generally the same design as the Çifte Minareli but is more elaborate in its decor. The panels on each side of the doorway contain, one above the other, an Arabic inscription in an octagon, a wide palmette leaf surrounded by birds, a large eight-pointed star, and a design that can only be described as enigmatic. The bands of geometric and floral carving in high relief around the door frame are superb. A relief boss on each side of the door depicts the heads of 12 different animals, reminiscent, perhaps, of the pre-Islamic Turkish animal calendar. At each corner of the front wall is an intricately carved buttress. Built into the left side of the façade is the oldest known Seljuk public fountain. It's best to stand back from this building in order to appreciate its full effect and then closely inspect its wonderful decor. Inside to the right is a domed mosque with faïence tiling; in the courtyard is a hexagonal pool. The portico on each side of the courtyard rests on columns decorated with geometric motifs. The Gök Medrese was used as a military depot, a secondary school, and then as a mosque in the early part of this century. It has undergone extensive restoration and is not always open. You may have to ask for the caretaker to obtain the key.

From the Gök Medrese it's best to take a taxi to the final architectural landmark of note, the **Güdük Minare** (Incomplete, or Squat, Minaret). Situated in the northeastern quarter of Sivas, this odd structure is actually a tomb, built by 'Ala' ad-Din Eretna in 1347 for his son Hasan, whose black marble cenotaph can be seen inside. It has a square base of cut stone surmounted by a striking transitional zone of brick triangles from which rises a 30-foot drum. Its original pyramidal roof collapsed long ago, so that from a distance it used to look like the base of a huge truncated minaret—incomplete and squat, as the name indicates. The present roof is a recent addition. The brickwork of the transitional zone and the drum is superb. Around the cylinder, glazed bricks in the style of calligraphy called squared Kufic are used to weave continuously the profession of faith, "There is no god but God and Muhammad is his messenger."

If you have extra time, there are several other mausoleums and a few Ottoman mosques that you can visit. If you would like a taste of modern Turkish history, the building used for the Sivas Congress is now a museum, the **Dört Eylül Atatürk Müzesi** (open Monday through Friday, 8:00 A.M. to noon and 1:00 to 5:00 P.M.). So is the wooden house where Turkey's second president, İsmet İnönü, spent his early childhood, on Kepenek Caddesi in the Ali Baba quarter several blocks northeast of the city square. Called the **İnönü Etnoğrafya Müzesi**, it displays memorabilia from İnönü's life as well as other objects (same hours as Dört Eylül museum).

From Sivas you should by all means make a day trip to Divriği (discussed below), which has what is probably the most outlandish building in the history of Islamic architecture. This excursion will add two nights to your stay in Sivas, but the trip is well worth the extra time. Besides, first-class carpets rivaling those produced in Iran are woven in the Sivas area, so the evenings can be passed browsing in the carpet shops. One place to look is the shopping area in and around the Taş Han, a few minutes south of the Köşk Hotel on the opposite side of Atatürk Bulvarı. The han, built in 1573, now houses the stores of jewelers, shoemakers, and other tradesmen. Carpets and kilims are displayed in windows or hanging outside shops.

For dinner, try the **Şadırvan Restaurant** between the Köşk Hotel and the main square. This well-appointed restaurant may be the best in town; it has an extensive Turkish menu. The **Yeni Ümür Lokantası**, at 88 Sirer Caddesi, also has good local fare.

Divriği

The medieval mosque—in fact a combination mosque and insane asylum—in Divriği might be described as a bad dream of Antonio Gaudí. It is outrageous, flamboyant, grossly overdone. Was it perhaps designed, or at least decorated, by the inmates? Whatever it is, there is nothing quite like it. Historians of Islamic art and architecture are generally at a loss as to how to account for it. To see this phenomenon, you must take a circuitous route (850) south of Sivas; the road later turns east around the mountains at Kangal, which itself has a bizarre sort of fame: In the hot springs 13 km (8 miles) from town swim fish that nibble at the skin of people afflicted with psoriasis, apparently to good effect. The journey is about 185 km (115 miles) one way. Most of the road is paved, and the last section, between Kangal and Divriği, passes through a region of beautiful "painted" hills.

Until fairly recently Divriği was so remote and the roads so bad that the only reliable way to reach it was by train. Today there is "regular" bus service from Sivas. The bus terminal is on Atatürk Caddesi on the southern edge of town.

Divriği is a partly deserted town of several thousand people situated in a fertile valley. Agriculture and iron mines keep the town alive. The only commotion in Divriği is at the railyard, where ancient black steam locomotives herd cars of ore. Dominating the town where the Çaltı Çayı, a tributary of the upper Euphrates, enters the valley is a high bluff crowned by the walls of a fortress. Below it to the right, on a knoll overlooking the valley, is Divriği's most famous landmark.

The town, seemingly in the middle of nowhere, was notorious in the early Middle Ages as a center of the Christian Paulician heresy, which held a dualistic world view similar to that of the Persian Manichean religion and adhered to an iconoclastic christology. In 872 the Byzantine emperor Basil I laid siege to Tephrikè, as the town was then called, captured the citadel, and crushed the sect. Shortly after the battle of Manzikert in 1071, the town was captured by the Turks. Divriği and its surrounding territory were given to a Turkmen officer called Mengüchek, who established a minor independent state here. In 1228 his dynasty recognized the suzerainty of the Seljuks. After the Seljuk period Divriği lapsed into obscurity; in 1516 it was annexed to the Ottoman Empire. The intrepid Evliya Çelebi passed through in 1649 and described it as a city of garden houses stretching to the foot of a formidable castle. Inside were 300 dwellings. Vineyards were everywhere. Divriği also possessed an extensively embellished covered market, numerous mosques, a dervish lodge, and a public bath. And like all travellers who have made their way to Divriği, Çelebi spoke with wonder of its **Ulu Cami** (Great Mosque) of yellow stone.

The Ulu Cami was constructed between 1228 and 1229 by Ahmad Shah, the grandson of the founder of the Mengüchekid dynasty, and his wife, Malika Turan Malik. The mosque is ascribed to Ahmad and the asylum to Malika. The mosque consists of five bays divided by four rows of octagonal piers, which support a complex vaulted ceiling comparable to those of European Gothic cathedrals but much more sophisticated. Everywhere the masonry is massive, almost Cyclopean, an impression that is emphasized by the relatively low ceiling. In the northwest corner a staircase leads to a single minaret. Above the bay before the prayer niche is a great ribbed dome covered by a multisided pyramidal cone. The niche itself has two wide horizontal bands of large palmettes

and "spaghetti" that appear to jump from the wall. An exquisite ebony pulpit stands next to it. Made in 1241, this high
platform is a masterpiece of classical Islamic wood carving. A
number of years ago some rare kilims were discovered on
the floor of the mosque; a few are now on exhibit in the
Vakıflar Kilim Museum below the Sultanahmet Camii (Blue
Mosque) in Istanbul.

The mosque and asylum are connected by a passage to
the left of the niche, which first leads to a tomb containing
several cenotaphs, including those of the founders. The
asylum takes up about 40 percent of the south end of the
building and, like the mosque, has a complicated vaulted
ceiling. It is fairly small, with few rooms and six tiny windows, which provide little light. The stark interior, with
almost no decoration, resembles a dungeon. Some of the
patients were certainly chained to the walls. In the center of
the main hall, however, is a small fountain that may have
soothed the inmates.

The well-deserved fame of this mosque-asylum derives
above all from its fantastic **portals**. A leading Turkish art
historian has described the three mosque entryways as "Baroque" (north), "textile-like" (west), and "typically Seljuk"
(east), and the single asylum gate as "Gothic." The textile-
like portal is an exaggerated version of the conventional
Seljuk gate. The design and decor of the Baroque and Gothic
portals contrast as much with these two entryways as they do
with the plain stone exterior walls of the building. These
strange gates project more than a yard from the façade and
are covered by a symmetrical mixture of floral and geometric designs, a few human faces, various birds, and some
mysterious figures, all in very high relief. It is all rather thick,
like icing on a wedding cake, terribly gaudy but nevertheless
impressive.

While waiting for the sun to cast its most favorable light
for good photographs of each portal, you should follow the
path that leads north of the mosque to the top of the
Medieval **citadel**. The wall and two gates of this fortress, as
well as a few inner buildings, survive. Inscriptions on the
gates give the dates 1236 and 1242; the inner keep was built
in 1252. Within the walls is a small mosque erected by the
Mengüchekid ruler Shahinshah between 1180 and 1181, one
of the earliest dated mosques in Central Anatolia. Compared
to the Ulu Cami, however, it is extremely simple in both plan
and decoration. Only the geometric border, brick arch, and
brick-and-tile design in the spandrels of the porch catch the
eye. Inside, the prayer niche is embellished with a palmette-
lotus frieze and stylized lions' heads.

The real reason to climb to the citadel, though, is not to examine its architecture but to take in the magnificent view. On one side you see the entire valley of Divriği and on the other you look straight down into the rust-colored gorge formed by the Çaltı Çayı. Upstream from Divriği, as far as Kemah and even beyond, are some of the most lovely canyons in Turkey. Unfortunately, only the train (which is very slow and geared to transport cargo, not passengers) closely follows the river for the full distance. There are few villages and no facilities in this seldom-visited region of great natural beauty.

Before returning to Sivas, you might walk about the old section of town below the Ulu Cami. Here are a number of charming but deserted houses dating from at least the last century. Some were once quite grand. There is no hotel or real restaurant in Divriği. You can, however, find some şiş and tea, and fruits, vegetables, and fresh bread are available from greengrocers. The hills and mountains that you passed en route from Sivas will change color in the late afternoon, so the return trip will carry its own reward.

AMASYA

Amasya is the most delightful, and in some respects the most interesting, city in Central Anatolia. Although relatively unknown, it can be challenged only by Konya for touristic appeal. With its mixture of monuments from the Hellenistic to the Ottoman periods and its very special setting at the narrow center of a deep hourglass-shaped canyon, it is unlike any other city of the Central Anatolian plain. Down the middle of Amasya rushes the Yeşilırmak (Green River) on its way to the Black Sea. The two sections of the city, laced together by a series of bridges, are squeezed between the banks of the river and sheer, towering cliffs. The sound of babbling water is always present, and the city is remarkably verdant, with an abundance of trees and flowers.

Amasya lies 338 km (210 miles) northeast of Ankara, about a five-hour drive. Leave Ankara on route 200 heading east, and after about 128 km (80 miles) turn left at Delice on route 785 for Amasya via Sungurlu and Çorum. The road passes through varied countryside: canyons cut by the Kızılırmak, plains full of sunflowers, and red-earth hills covered with vineyards. About 8 km (5 miles) past Sungurlu, a yellow sign on the right indicates the road to the Hittite capital at Boğazkale (discussed under Ankara and Environs, above). Beyond Çorum, as you approach Amasya, passing through the southern reaches of the Pontic mountains, the trees become denser and taller.

Amasya, or Amaseia as it was known in antiquity, first gained fame as the capital of the Hellenistic kings of Pontus (301 to 63 B.C.), who followed in the wake of Alexander the Great. The gigantic tombs that they cut from the rock wall above the northern bank of the river (discussed below) are reminders of their legacy. The last great king of Pontus, Mithradates Eupator, was Rome's greatest foe in Asia Minor. More despotic than enlightened—he murdered his mother, his sons, his sister (whom he had married), and his concubines so they would not fall into the hands of his enemies—Mithradates threw fear into Rome until Pompey defeated him in 66 B.C. and made Amasya a free city. Later, however, Mithradates' son Pharnaces rebelled—only to invite the retribution of an even greater Roman general, Julius Caesar. At the modern town of Zile (discussed below) south of Amasya, Caesar crushed the prince in 47 B.C. and later tersely summed up his campaign in the famous saying "Veni, vidi, vici."

Amasya's most famous son was the geographer Strabo, who was born here in 64 B.C. Strabo wrote the best early account of his native city. He mentions, in particular, its great citadel and the bridge that joined the two parts of the city. The remains of the citadel are still prominent, and the oldest bridge across the Yeşilırmak indeed may date to Strabo's time. In the third century A.D., after the reign of Roman emperor Diocletian, Amasya became the major administrative and religious center of the province of Diospontus. Later, in the eighth century under the Byzantines, it was included in the military district of Armeniakon. How and when the city fell to the Turks is unclear, but by the end of the 11th century it was the seat of the Danishmendid principality. In 1170 the city was annexed by the Seljuks, who subsequently rebuilt it, perhaps after an earthquake. After the Mongols invaded the region, they made Amasya the residence of one of their governors. Ibn Battuta, who visited the city around 1331, praised its spacious streets and bazaars, numerous streams, and luxuriant gardens. He noted, especially, the giant wheels used to lift water from the river to houses and gardens. Amasya thrived under the Mongols and their Ottoman successors; both lavished monuments on the city.

The Ottomans took a special fancy to Amasya, beginning with its successful resistance to Tamerlane's onslaught. Bayezit II was, as crown prince, governor of the town, and Murat II and Selim I were born here. Süleyman the Magnificent often spent time in Amasya: It was here that he received

Augier Ghislain de Busbecq, the Hapsburg ambassador and memoirist. Already an important seat of learning in the Seljuk period, Amasya became one of the most important intellectual centers of the Ottoman Empire, as its many medreses testify. In the 17th century it had so many students and scholars that Kâtip Çelebi, the well-known Ottoman historian and bibliographer, called it the "Baghdad of Anatolia." Others referred to it as the "city of sages." Between the 15th and 17th centuries the city was home to many distinguished theologians, historians, poets, and artisans, including calligraphers, whose art was the most highly esteemed of all. Even as late as the 19th century, a French visitor described Amasya—with its 18 medreses and 2,000 students—as the "Oxford of Anatolia."

In addition to royal and scholarly patronage, Amasya benefited by being on a major trade route between the Black Sea, Sivas, and points east. In the 17th century Evliya Çelebi reported that it had 5,000 homes and 1,060 shops plus dozens of mosques, dervish lodges, public baths, soup kitchens, and hans. Although a large part of the city was reduced to ashes by a great fire in 1915, it still preserves much of its early character. Today a city of more than 60,000 people, Amasya is renowned throughout Turkey for its orchards (especially apples) and textiles. (Silkworms are raised in the surrounding villages.)

Amasya can be explored easily on foot, except for the citadel, which can be reached by taxi. At least two days are needed to see the city properly. Relatively undiscovered by tourists, it has only recently acquired a good hotel, the **Turban Amasya Oteli**, located on the left bank of the river downstream from the central part of town. It is very comfortable, and its bargain-rate rooms come with river views. While the Turban has a fine restaurant, the best place to eat is the **Belediye Şehir Külübü Derneği** (the Municipal City Club Association, at Karşıyaka Mahallesi number 1), at the north end of Hükümet Köprüsü (Government Bridge), the first bridge upstream from the Turban. Part of the restaurant hangs over the river, making for unobstructed vistas up and down stream. The decor is not elegant, but the food is excellent and inexpensive, even including the rakı that you'll certainly want as an accompaniment to your meal. Among the delicacies of Amasya are okra and beef or mutton marinated in lemon juice (*etli bamya*); grape leaves stuffed with spices, rice, and broad beans and cooked in beef broth (*baklalı dolma*); twisted, sweetened bread sticks made with ground poppy seeds (*haşhaşlı çörek*); and rose-hip marmalade (*kuşburnu*). For some Ankarans who regularly travel to the Black Sea, the

Şehir Külübü restaurant alone is worth a detour to Amasya. Indeed, Amasya is a good place to stop for lunch or even spend a day or two on the way from Ankara to the Black Sea coast.

Thanks to the city's peculiar geography, most monuments are next to the river or only a few blocks away, making for very pleasant strolls. Downstream from the Turban hotel, on the left bank and north of Kuş Köprüsü (Bird Bridge), which dates back at least to the 14th century, is one of the most unusual medreses in Turkey, the octagonal **Kapı Ağası Medresesi**. Built in 1488 by the Ottoman palace chamberlain (or chief white eunuch, *kapı ağası*) Abdülmüminoğlu Hüseyin, it was apparently the first, and definitely one of the few, medreses to break the traditional rectangular plan. It has attractive walls of alternating rows of brick and stone. Around its arcaded courtyard are living quarters for students. These rooms are covered with domes and sprout chimneys, indicative of Amasya's cold winters. The Kapı Ağası Medresesi is still used as a religious school.

Directly across the river from the medrese is the **Bayezit Paşa Camii**, completed in 1419 by Necmettin Halil Bayezit Paşa, a governor of Amasya who became the Ottoman grand vizier. It has more minarets than any mosque in town and a complex ceiling of large and small domes. It can be compared to the early Ottoman mosques in Bursa.

Walking upstream a few blocks from Bayezit Paşa, past the Mehmet Paşa mosque, built in 1486 by an advisor to Bayezit II's son when he was governor of the city, you come to the **Darüşşifa**. This was a lunatic asylum constructed between 1308 and 1309 by Ambar ibn Abd Allah, a slave (probably a eunuch) in the service of Yıldız Hatun, the wife of the Mongol sultan Öljeitü. The earliest recorded attempt to treat mental patients with music was carried out in this institution. General medicine was also practiced here—in fact, general practitioners were trained here until 1873. Sharaf al-Din ibn Ali, who prepared a book of miniatures on surgery in 1465, practiced here for 14 years. The asylum has the plan of a traditional Seljuk medrese. Noteworthy is its richly decorated monumental porch with a window at each side. The front wall has a cylindrical tower at each corner. The stone carving around the entrance has various motifs—including some seen at Sivas, Divriği, and Konya. The prominent, high-relief palmettes are especially impressive. On the keystone of the door is a curious carving of a kneeling man. This building was extensively restored in 1945 and again in 1991.

Continuing along the river, cross Hükümet square at the foot of the bridge of the same name and then turn left. After

three blocks you'll find, behind a ruined 17th-century caravansary, which contains some shops, the **Burmalı Minare
Camii** (Mosque with the Twisted Minaret). As is obvious
from its name, the most striking feature of this mosque is its
minaret, which looks like a piece of twisted rope. The
mosque itself was built between 1237 and 1247 by Farruh,
the vizier of 'Ala' ad-Din Kay-Qubad II, and Farruh's brother
Yusuf, who was the treasurer, but the minaret was added
later. Constructed only of cut stone, the mosque has three
aisles perpendicular to its green-glazed prayer niche. The
wide central aisle is roofed by three domes. On each side of
it is a vaulted narrow aisle. At the northeastern corner of the
mosque is a tomb that presumably contains the remains of
the founders. Until 1928 it also contained the mummies of
two Mongol governors, Şehzade Cumudar and İşbuğa Nuyin,
now on display at the city museum.

Walking back toward the river and then turning left on
Ekin Pazarı Sokak, the main east–west artery, you arrive in a
few minutes at the **mosque complex of Sultan Bayezit II**,
who built the first of the great classic mosques in Istanbul
and an impressive mosque complex in Edirne. The mosque
and its neighboring medrese, now a library, were once part
of a much larger complex (*külliye*) that was begun by this
sultan but completed by his son when he was governor of
Amasya, in 1485. This complex was Bayezit's first great work.
The most impressive feature of the mosque is its imposing
roof, consisting of two large domes, one behind the other,
with three smaller lower domes to each side. The domes
unite to create a grand open space in the interior. There are
two minarets, which are beautiful examples of interlocking
stonework in two colors. If you look carefully around the
eaves of the mosque you will discover a delightful
birdhouse in the form of a miniature palace. The mosque's
terrace, shaded by plane trees, cooled by a splashing fountain, and facing the river, is a pleasant retreat.

One block past the sultan's mosque on the opposite side
of Ekin Pazarı Sokak is the **Amasya Museum** (open 8:30 A.M.
to noon and 1:30 to 6:30 P.M., except Mondays, during the
summer; closes at 5:30 P.M. in winter). Its folklore exhibition
includes local carpets, old pistols and rifles, household objects, and a furnished room from a 19th-century house. Also
on display are lots of Pontic, Byzantine, Seljuk, Mongol, and
Ottoman coins as well as the doors from the Mehmet Paşa
mosque and the Gök Medrese-Cami complex, the latter a
masterpiece of woodcarving. The museum's most ghoulish
objects are six stuffed Mongols. In addition to the two taken
from the tomb at the Burmalı Minare Camii there are also

the mummified bodies of the governor, Izzettin Mehmet Pervane, and his wife, son, and daughter. All are on display in the rather unconventional tomb of the Seljuk sultan Rukn ad-Din Mas'ud I (1116 to 1156). This tomb, which looks a bit like a bank vault, stands in the garden outside the museum.

In the next block, a terraced park leads to a lane above the main street where you can see the partly restored **Hilafet Gazi Kümbeti**, the mausoleum of the vizier of the Danishmendid ruler Melik Gazi. According to tradition, it was built between 1145 and 1146, and although it's in a somewhat ruinous state, it has a wonderfully carved main face on the south. Its high-relief moldings and rosettes with foliate and braided designs are exceptional early examples of the Seljuk style.

A little farther on are the last monuments you should see before exploring the left bank. These are the tomb of Torumtay and, behind it, the Gök Medrese-Cami. The **tomb of Torumtay**, a slave who became the master of stables of 'Ala' ad-Din Kay-Qubad I, was built in 1278. Unlike earlier tombs, it is a rectangular vaulted structure that resembles a miniature palace or castle. Its main façade has several large windows and is unusually decorated with rows of palmettes, scrolls, and ornamented pilasters.

As his tomb suggests, Torumtay did all right for a slave. In fact, he managed to become the governor of Amasya. As such he embellished the city with the **Gök Medrese-Cami** (Blue Medrese-Mosque), which received its name from the emerald-green and blue tiles on its façade and central turret. Built between 1266 and 1267, it was used primarily as a mosque but also functioned as a medrese. The plan contains elements of both institutions. Differing from most mosques, on each side of its grand porch it has a high window, which illuminates the rooms that were used by the school. The cylindrical buttressing towers at the corners of the building give it the appearance of a fortress.

If you have followed the general itinerary above, it should be late in the afternoon by the time you reach the Gök Medrese-Cami. You may wish to return immediately to your hotel or to go to the Şehir Külübü for dinner, but if you still have the energy, walk back along the river on the lovely, tree-lined promenade, from which you can admire the old wooden houses hugging and overhanging the opposite bank. One of them, the **Hazeranlar Konağı**, is a restored two-story 19th-century mansion (hours the same as at the Amasya Museum, above). Located just to the left of the third bridge upstream, it is open to visitors as an ethnographic museum. The third bridge, called Alçak Köprü (Low Bridge), once a rustic wooden structure but now replaced by concrete, sits on stone piers supported by the arches of Amasya's oldest bridge, probably the one referred to by Strabo.

The climb to the **Pontic tombs** is best done in the cool of the morning when you are fresh. (But keep in mind that in the morning, when the sun is on these tombs, the best place from which to photograph them will be the opposite bank of the river.) Twelve tombs, which look as if they were stamped into the cliffs by a giant cookie-cutter, can be seen from town, but only the five largest can be visited. High on a cliff above the Alçak and Hükümet bridges is a large terrace with a retaining wall facing the river. This was once the site of the palace of the kings of Pontus and later of residences of the Seljuk and Ottoman sultans, but virtually nothing remains there today. Above the terrace is a group of three tombs reached by a steep path. Next to them is one of three long tunnels that were hewn into the cliffs below the citadel. These tunnels have no exits; their purpose is a riddle. Another path, to the left of the terrace, leads to the two most monumental tombs, which are connected by a remarkable staircase sliced across the face of the cliff. There is no guardrail, so sufferers of vertigo might have second thoughts about the climb; the view of the city, however, is excellent. Each tomb has a high corridor behind its façade, but, like all the others, each is empty and there is no decoration. In the 11th century these tombs were inhabited by Christian monks.

Although a curtain wall of the **fortress** drops down close to the tombs, it is best to get to the top of the cliff by car. A back road north of town leads to the center of the fortress. Inside is a somewhat bewildering array of ruins—towers, walls, cisterns, a medrese, a dervish lodge, baths, and even a dungeon, likened to the "pit of Hell" that Bayezit I used as a prison. Each power to occupy Amasya added something to the fortress. When in good repair and fully manned, it was impregnable, as Tamerlane learned to his regret. Evliya Çelebi ascended to the summit and related that the fortress contained a palace, an armory, and storehouses full of provisions. Abandoned in the 18th century, the citadel commands sweeping views up and down the Yeşilırmak valley and, naturally, of Amasya itself far below. A fine road now leads to the top of the steep hill on the opposite side of the valley from the fortress and tombs. This eagles' nest, Çakallar Mesiresi, has the amenity of a teahouse and modest restaurant from which you can enjoy the grand scene at leisure.

If you have time to linger, Amasya can easily keep you occupied for several days—almost every street has something of interest. Immediately north and south of town are more Hellenistic tombs. Perhaps the easiest to reach is the monumental **Aynalı Mağara** (Mirrored Cave), so called because its polished side walls reflect the sunlight. According to the local office of tourism, one of the Twelve Apostles was supposed to have preached Christianity from its steps! This imposing and well-preserved tomb is about a mile north of town on the left bank of the Yeşilırmak. Within a half-hour drive of Amasya are several **hot springs** whose waters will supposedly benefit your skin and relieve your rheumatism. The one with the best facilities, including a restaurant and modest accommodations, is at **Terziköy**, 32 km (20 miles) to the southwest. These hot springs have been in use since at least Roman times. Check with the kiosk of the Amasya tourist office along the river or at the hotel for directions and recommendations.

TOKAT

Tokat is still almost unknown territory for tourists. The city fathers, however, have been working hard to put Tokat on the tourist map, and today it boasts a four-star hotel, the **Büyük Tokat Oteli** (Grand Tokat Hotel), complete with swimming pool, Turkish bath, sauna, tennis courts, and nightclub. A double room goes for about $40. Tokat also has two one-star hotels, the **Plevne Oteli** and the **Turist Oteli**, both close to the town's major monuments.

Tokat is 116 km (72 miles) southeast of Amasya via Turhal, a drive of about two hours, roughly halfway between Amasya and Sivas (see above). You can also go via **Zile**, reached by a secondary road from Amasya; the distance is about the same. Zile is a quaint town at the base of a ruined citadel that has two stepped tunnels reminiscent of those in Amasya. (Caesar's slogan "Veni, vidi, vici" is carved in the citadel wall.) The road from Zile also passes through **Turhal**, which has its own rocky peak crowned by a castle, again complete with tunnels. From Turhal to Tokat you travel through the lush Yeşilırmak valley, especially beautiful in the spring when the fruit trees are in bloom.

Entering Tokat from the west, you notice right away the gleaming Büyük Tokat hotel across the river on the left. Soon you pass a well-preserved Seljuk bridge and then a major intersection. If you turn left here, and then left again, you will reach the hotel. If you turn right at the major intersection, the road will lead to Tokat's main street, Gazi Osman Paşa Bulvarı.

About the size of Amasya, Tokat has an old quarter of traditional wood and dried-brick houses huddled below a citadel. Among them, mixed in a maze of narrow and twisting streets, are some two dozen buildings—mosques, medreses, tombs, dervish lodges, baths, hans, and others—dating from the 12th to the 18th centuries, some still in use. For the connoisseur of Islamic art and architecture, these structures are not of special note, but together they give old Tokat the feel of a living 18th- or 19th-century town. The clip-clop of horse-drawn wagons, the smell of spices in the bazaar, and the occasional sight of a veiled grandmother transport you to another time.

Rising abruptly like a tall ship from the sea of houses in the old quarter is a jagged saddle-backed cliff that cradles a ruined **fortress**. From this 300-foot perch you have a bird's-eye view of Tokat. This is a good place to get your bearings before plunging into the mass of old buildings below. The fortress is easy to reach by a paved road that leads to its main gate. On Gazi Osman Paşa Bulvarı, just before the tomb of the Mongol Nur ed-Din Sentimur, a yellow sign on the right points to the road to the fortress. Among the famous occupants of this redoubt was the Byzantine emperor Romanus IV Diogenes, who stopped here on his way back to Constantinople following his crushing defeat by the Turks at Manzikert in 1071. In Tokat he received the bad news that he had been deposed. He managed to make his way to Amasya, where he was captured and blinded. Not 200 years later, the equally unlucky Seljuk sultan Ghiyath ad-Din Kay-Khusraw II (1237 to 1246), whose army was smashed by the Mongols, entrusted his family and part of his treasure to this stronghold before attempting to stop the Mongols at Köse Dağ. This fortress was maintained well into Ottoman times. In 1656 Evliya Çelebi described it as having a tunnel cut from the rock and a goat track of 362 steps to the Yeşilırmak.

Tokat's roots actually lie 9 km (5½ miles) to the northeast, at the site of **Comana Pontica**, which, together with Amasya, was one of the great cities of Pontus. Comana Pontica grew up around the temple of the goddess Ma, who possessed vast tracts of land ruled by her priests and farmed by 6,000 temple slaves. Strabo reports that there were great festivals in Comana when the goddess was carried from her temple in solemn procession. He adds that there were numerous temple prostitutes who gladly relieved soldiers and merchants of their money.

The Byzantines moved the city to its present location. Captured several times by the Arabs in the eighth century, it fell permanently into Muslim hands after the battle of

Manzikert, when it was incorporated into the principality of the Turkish Danishmendids. In 1174 it was annexed by the Seljuks. In the middle of the 15th century, under the Ottomans, Tokat became an important cultural and commercial center, rivaling Amasya for several centuries. In the 16th century the Ottoman sultan Süleyman the Magnificent used the city as a staging point in his wars against Iran. The continuity of Tokat's important role in Ottoman history is symbolized, perhaps, by the **clock tower** next to the Behzat Camii (1535). Built in 1909 from local donations, it commemorates the 25th anniversary of the ascension to the throne of the notorious Abdülhamit II.

Returning to Gazi Osman Paşa Bulvarı and continuing for a few blocks, you arrive at the **Gök Medrese** (Blue Medrese) on the right. Erected after 1270 by the Seljuk vizier Pervane Mu'in ad-Din Sulaiman, today it houses the local archaeological and ethnographic museum. The interior courtyard of the medrese was once covered with turquoise and black tiles, from which it acquired its popular name. (Traces of these tiles can be see in the main hall.) Among the objects on exhibit are finds from the nearby Hittite palace at Maşat Höyük and many Byzantine items. The medrese's garden, like those in most Turkish museums, is full of ancient odds and ends, especially tombstones. One unexpected odd object is a memorial to a 19th-century British missionary who died in Tokat on his way home from Iran. At the museum, ask for directions to the nearby **Latifoğlu Konağı**, a newly restored 19th-century Turkish Baroque mansion. Next to the museum is the great **Taş Han** (Stone Inn), sometimes called the Voyvoda Hanı (Governor's Inn). This block-long structure, built in 1631 for all the merchants in the city, is now used as a fruit and vegetable market.

Taking the back streets behind the Taş Han and going around the corner below the cliffs of the citadel, you come to the **Yazma Han** (the Han of Handprinting), where hand-blocked muslins are silk-screened. Enormous stone vats filled with inky dyes sit in the courtyard of this han, while its balcony is lined with rows of cloth put out to dry. Upstairs several men operate a silk screen with lightning speed and precision. About them lie old lindenwood blocks carved with the elaborate floral and geometric designs that are stamped on the cloth. Small shops adjacent to the han sell the products. Scarves and bath wraps are specialties.

If you walk south for several blocks, you reach **Sulu Sokak**, the main artery through the old quarter. Turning west on this street you soon pass in succession the Ali Paşa Camii (built between 1572 and 1573), whose gray marble columns probably came from the ancient temple of Ma; the octagonal tomb tower of Ali Tusi (1234), a governor of ʿAlaʾ ad-Din Kay-Qubad I; the Ottoman han of the edible-oil sellers; another Ottoman han; an 18th-century covered market that is still in use; a 16th-century mosque; and the medrese of Yağıbasan, the Danishmendid ruler of the city from 1151 to 1157. The last was the first medrese covered with a dome, no doubt because of Tokat's climate. Where the dome once stood there is now blue sky, giving this school the nickname Çukur Medrese, "the Medrese with the Hole." Next you come to a 16th-century han for camel caravans, an 18th-century han, and a 15th-century public bath. Hollywood could not have recreated a more realistically "medieval" Turkish city.

As Tokat's many hans indicate, commerce has long been the key to the city's prosperity. Tokat not only benefited from the caravan trade between Amasya and Sivas but also contributed its own products to international markets. In the 17th century it exported wool to Venice. In the following century, when Tokat reportedly had as many different guilds as Istanbul, the French traveller Tournefort visited the city and noted that it was a center of silk production as well as the manufacture of copper utensils and yellow morocco leather. Later, products from Tokat even added to the comfort of the Russian czar's bed: When a commercial treaty was signed between the Ottoman Empire and Russia in 1831, it stipulated that quilt covers from Tokat would be exported to Russia. Today silk and wool carpets of the Hereke type, the highest quality in Turkey, are produced in the vicinity of Tokat. Also, refugees from Afghanistan settled in Tokat province in 1982 and now produce excellent carpets in their own traditional patterns. All these textiles can be found in the local market.

About three blocks south of the Ali Paşa Camii, next to the city hall, is the **Park Restaurant**. Here, amid the shade trees, you can rest your tired feet and satisfy your appetite. Order the city specialty—*Tokat kebap*. Chunks of meat, tomatoes, onions, peppers, and eggplant are arranged on a spit so that the vegetables marinate the meat when grilled. After cooking, everything is pulled off the skewer and rolled up in thin layers of unleavened bread. You might also ask for the local wine, under the Diren label, which has recently begun to make a name for itself. The white Vadi and the red Karmen are quite good.

From Tokat you can make an excursion north to **Niksar**, ancient Neo-Caesareia, in the lovely Kelkit valley. The drive is fairly short, 54 km (33 miles) one way. Once a residence of the kings of Pontus, Niksar's main attraction is its magnificent **citadel**, which rests on a spur at the junction of two ravines. Its dungeon was home to the Crusader Bohemond of Taranto for three years following his capture by the Danishmendid Turks during the First Crusade.

If you continue southeast from Tokat to Sivas you have about an hour's journey (101 km/63 miles). As you head south the road gains altitude. Beyond the village of Çamlıbel, where you can see the ruins of a 13th-century caravansary, you reach the summit of the pass at 5,400 feet. Gradually descending toward the Kızılırmak valley, you pass a 14th-century caravansary in Yıldızeli. A half hour later you arrive in Sivas.

GETTING AROUND

Ankara is the transportation hub of Central Anatolia (see Ankara and Environs, above, for getting to Ankara). An excellent system of fast, efficient, frequent, comfortable, and inexpensive buses connects the capital, from the main terminal in the Ulus district, with all the major cities of the region. Many of these buses carry refreshments and all stop every few hours at roadside cafeterias so that passengers can stretch their legs and have a snack or a full meal.

You can rent a car in the larger cities, but at rates that are usually higher than those in Europe or North America. For the most part, a rented car is useful only if you plan a long trip with many stops. Even for relatively remote places (such as Midas City), it is just as efficient and much cheaper to take a bus to the nearest major town (in this case Afyon) and from there hire a taxi for a day. In Ürgüp taxis are readily available for hire for tours of Cappadocia. Taxi drivers know where they are going and also know how to cope with fellow Turkish drivers. With very few exceptions, all roads are two lanes wide, yet most Turks treat them like the autobahn. Moreover, Turkish drivers do not hesitate to pass other vehicles on curves or over hills—often simply "because they are there." Driving at night can be particularly dangerous because of the many slow, poorly lighted tractors using the roads. In short, unless you are an expert (and calm) driver, the use of rented cars should be kept to a minimum.

If you are headed east, there is air service (Turkish Airlines only) between Ankara and Sivas. There is also train service from Ankara to Kayseri and Sivas, but it is very slow and designed more to carry cargo than passengers.

ACCOMMODATIONS REFERENCE

Rates given below are for double rooms, double occupancy, and represent projections for 1993. All prices are subject to change and should be checked before booking. A few hotels raise their rates during the high season, which in Central Anatolia generally runs from July through September. When telephoning between cities in Turkey, dial 9 before entering the city code.

▶ **Adac Pension.** Yeşilada Mahallesi 1, **Eğridir,** 32500 İsparta. Tel: (3281) 3074. $20.

▶ **Avanos Irmak Oteli.** Yeni Mahalle, Hasankale Mevkii, **Avanos,** 50500 Nevşehir. Tel: (4861) 1317; Fax: (4861) 1530. $40 (includes breakfast).

▶ **Boytaş Motel.** Kayseri Yolu, **Ürgüp,** 50400 Nevşehir. Tel: (4868) 1256. $45.

▶ **Büyük Tokat Oteli.** Demirköprü Mevkii. 60200 **Tokat.** Tel: (475) 168-63; Fax: (475) 131-75. $40 (includes breakfast).

▶ **Dedeman Oteli.** Camicedit Mıntıkası, 50200 **Nevşehir.** Tel: (485) 199-00; Fax: (485) 121-58. $100.

▶ **Dergah Oteli.** Mevlâna Caddesi 19, 42050 **Konya.** Tel: (33) 11-76-61; Fax: (33) 11-01-16. $60.

▶ **Dinler Oteli.** P.O. Box 51 (Kayseri Yolu), **Ürgüp,** 50401 Nevşehir. Tel: (4868) 3030; Fax: (4868) 1896. $42.

▶ **Ece Oteli.** Ordu Bulvarı 2, 03200 **Afyon.** Tel: (491) 160-70. $30.

▶ **Eğirdir Oteli.** 2. Sahil Yolu, Çınar altı Meydanı, **Eğridir,** 32500 İsparta. Tel: (3281) 1798; Fax: (3281) 1219. $40.

▶ **Erbaylar Oteli.** Cumhuriyet Caddesi 16, 43100 **Kütahya.** Tel: (231) 369-60; Fax: (231) 110-46. $55.

▶ **Grand Avanos Hotel.** Kapadokya Caddesi 24, **Avanos,** 50500 Nevşehir. Tel: (4861) 1188; Fax: (4861) 1863. $50.

▶ **Hattat Oteli.** O. Kavuncu Caddesi, 38040 **Kayseri.** Tel: (35) 11-93-31; Fax: (35) 12-65-03. $45.

▶ **Hotel Village House.** Karşıhamam Mevkii, **Hacıbektaş.** Tel: (4867) 1628. $30.

▶ **Ihlara Oteli.** Kılıçarslan Mahallesi, 68200 **Aksaray.** Tel: (481) 118-42; Fax: (481) 135-25. $45.

▶ **Kavas Oteli.** Atatürk Bulvarı 16, 50100 **Nevşehir.** Tel: (485) 217-00; Telex: 49748. $55.

▶ **Kaya Oteli–Club Med Villa.** Germelidağ Mevkii, Üçhisar, **Nevşehir.** Tel: (4856) 1007; Fax: (4856) 1363. $40. (Open in summer only.)

▶ **Konfor Oteli.** Atatürk Bulvarı 5, 38010 **Kayseri.** Tel: (35) 20-01-84; Fax: (35) 22-11-70. $45.

► **Köşk Oteli.** Atatürk Caddesi 11, 58030 **Sivas.** Tel: (47) 11-150; Fax: (47) 39-350. $50.

► **Köşk Pension.** Yazla Mahallesi 37, **Eğridir,** 32500 İsparta. Tel: (3281) 1382. $20.

► **Mavigöl Hotel.** Yeşilada Mahallesi 15, **Eğridir,** 32900 İsparta. Tel: (3281) 1766. $40.

► **Nas Oteli.** İsmet Paşa Caddesi 30, 70200 **Karaman.** Tel: (343) 18-200; Fax: 13-185. $40.

► **Orhan Ağaçlı Turistik Tesisleri.** Ankara–Adana Asfaltı, Nevşehir Kavşağı (E 5), 68200 **Aksaray.** Tel: (481) 149-10; Fax: (481) 149-14. $38.

► **Oruçoğlu Oteli.** Bankalar Bulvarı 3, 03200 **Afyon.** Tel: (491) 201-20; Fax: (491) 313-13. $36 (includes breakfast).

► **Otel Mustafa.** P.O. Box 44 (Tuzyolu), **Ürgüp,** 50400 Nevşehir. Tel: (4868) 3970; Fax: (4868) 2288. $60.

► **Özkaymak Park Oteli.** Otogar Karşısı, 42060 **Konya.** Tel: (33) 13-37-70; Fax: (33) 15-59-74. $60.

► **Perissia Oteli.** Kayseri Caddesi, **Ürgüp,** 50401 Nevşehir. Tel: (4868) 2930; Fax: (4868) 1524. $50 (low season)–$60 (high season; all rates include half board).

► **Plevne Oteli.** Gazi Osman Paşa Bulvarı 83, 60200 **Tokat.** Tel: (475) 12-207. $20 (includes breakfast).

► **Şehir Palas Oteli.** Belediye Caddesi 16, 50100 **Nevşehir.** Tel: (485) 156-13; Fax: (485) 116-42. $60.

► **Şekeryapan Oteli.** Gülşehir Caddesi 8, 50100 **Nevşehir.** Tel: (485) 142-53; Fax: (485) 140-51. $25 (includes breakfast).

► **Selçuk Oteli.** Alaettin Caddesi, 42050 **Konya.** Tel: (33) 11-12-59; Fax: (33) 11-33-78. $71.

► **Sofa Oteli.** Orta Mahalle 13, **Avanos,** 50500 Nevşehir. Tel: (4861) 1489; Fax: (4861) 1489. $15.

► **Taşsaray Hotel.** Mustafapaşa Caddesi 10, **Ürgüp,** 50400 Nevşehir. Tel: (4868) 2344; Fax: (4868) 2444. $25 (low season)–$35 (high season).

► **Terme Oteli.** Terme Caddesi, **Kırşehir.** Tel: (487) 224-04; Fax: (487) 181-48. $25 (includes breakfast and thermal bath).

► **Turan Oteli.** Turan Caddesi 8, 38040 **Kayseri.** Tel: (35) 31-25-06; Fax: (35) 11-11-53. $30 (low season)–$45 (high season).

► **Turban Amasya Oteli.** Helkis Mahallesi, Emniyet Caddesi 10, 05400 **Amasya.** Tel: (3781) 4054; Fax: (3781) 4056. $35.

► **Turban Ürgüp Moteli.** Çimenlitepe Mevkii, **Ürgüp,** 50400 Nevşehir. Tel: (4868) 2290; Fax: (4868) 2299. $49.

► **Turist Oteli.** Cumhuriyet Meydanı, 60200 **Tokat.** Tel: (475) 11-610. $20 (includes breakfast).

▸ **Ürgüp Alfina Hotel**. Karagendere Mahallesi 25, **Ürgüp**, 50400 Nevşehir. Tel: (4868) 1822; Fax: (4868) 2424. $35.

▸ **Yeni Yükseller Oteli**. Kayseri Yolu, Ortahisar, 50650 **Nevşehir**. Tel: (4869) 1450; Fax: (4869) 1642. $50.

▸ **Yıltok Oteli**. Göreme Yolu Üzeri, **Avanos**, 50500 Nevşehir. Tel: (4861) 2313; Fax: (4861) 1890. $60.

THE BLACK SEA COAST

By Anthony Bryer

Anthony Bryer has been haunting the Turkish Black Sea coast for more than 30 years. He is the author of The Empire of Trebizond and the Pontos, Peoples and Settlement in Anatolia and the Caucasus, *and (with David Winfield)* The Byzantine Monuments and Topography of the Pontos. *Professor Bryer is director of the Centre for Byzantine, Ottoman, and Modern Greek Studies at the University of Birmingham, England.*

Turkey's Black Sea coast was divided by the ancients into two great stretches: the western, from the "Holy Mouth" of the Bosphorus to where the cliffs stop falling into the sea short of Sinop, which region they named Paphlagonia; and the Pontus, which is the longer, eastern reach from Sinop (where olive-growing resumes) to the end of the world at what is now the Turkish border with Georgia. The ancients were right: Paphlagonia and the Pontus are quite distinct. Their example is followed below, and the regions are introduced separately; travellers will find that they must retrace ancient footsteps to get to either province.

MAJOR INTEREST

Walled town of Amasra
Sinop: striking site, preserved city walls
Samsun: acropolis and museum
Giresun, second city of the Empire of Trebizond: swimming from fortified islet, dining at Mehmet Efendi's
Promontory castles at Tirebolu and Akçakale

Trabzon
The Meydan (town square)
Walled city
Bazaar and baths
St. Sophia: glorious interior paintings
Atatürk Köşkü museum
Kaymaklı church: Armenian wall paintings

Abandoned monasteries south of Trabzon, especially
  Soumela
Gümüşhane: a Turkish "gold-rush town"
Lazistan
Seven villages of Santa
The Pontic Alps at Hemşin

PAPHLAGONIA

"Paphlagonia" is not a name with many associations for most
people—unless they've read Thackeray's *The Rose and the
Ring*. The ancient province lies along the least-frequented
stretch of the entire Black Sea: its southwestern sector. For
every thousand people sunning themselves on the Black Sea
beaches in Abkhazia to the northeast, there is but one in
Turkish Paphlagonia. Yet the coast is at the back door of both
Istanbul and Ankara, from which there are direct buses to
the towns of İnebolu, Bartın, and Zonguldak (the largest
town). But does even one among the thousands of tourists
who routinely witness sunrise on Nemrut Dağı in the east
even contemplate a trip to Zonguldak? If you want to confront the "real" Turkey, however, do go to **Zonguldak**, which,
though it's the boondocks, is stepped above a busy port with
decent fish restaurants and municipal bandstands.
Zonguldak, about 250 km (155 miles) east of Istanbul along
the coast, had, until a mining disaster in 1992, no troublesome history—you won't have to learn about Antiochus I
Commagene—just an untidy coalfield that enriches
Zonguldak and that, when the soft coal it produces is
shipped there and burned, cloaks Ankara in winter smog.

The Paphlagonian problem is its poor east–west internal
communications, which pivot in the fortress town of Kastamonu. All roads must brave the Paphlagonian Alps (Ilgaz
Dağları), which the indefatigable Turkish traveller/writer
Evliya Çelebi called a "sea of forests," amid which pigs once
rooted. Some kind of road clings to the coast most of the
way, but don't count on it: It is tricky and sometimes washes
away. And count still less on local shipping. Paphlagonia is

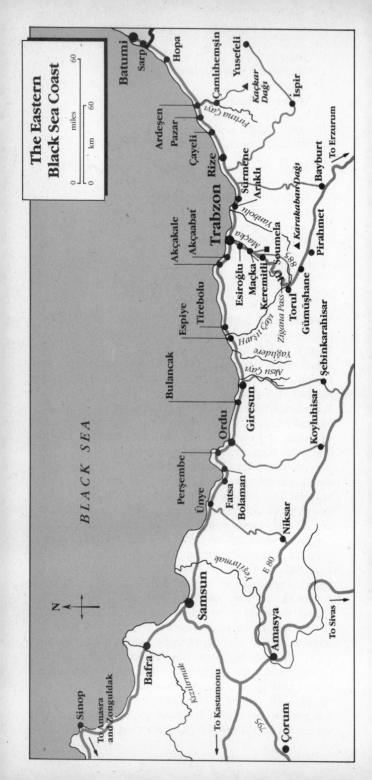

not for travellers with tight schedules, who should stick to the certainties of Nemrut Dağı. There is really only one place here worth visiting whence you can be sure of a quick retreat: Amasra.

Amasra

Amasra (ancient Amastris), located between Zonguldak and Cide, is the exception to the Paphlagonian rule. Major shipping does not call, but buses from Istanbul and Ankara stop at **Bartın**, 15 km (9 miles) inland, with minibuses operating between there and the coast. (You can reach Amasra by bus from Istanbul via either the Özbartın lines, Tel: 1/576-9571, or the Özemniyet lines, Tel: 1/577-1272.) Amasra is being discovered by Ankarans (and the odd astute foreigner) as a holiday place with atmosphere. It is a wholly delightful tiny walled town on a promontory flanked by two harbors (the western one with Roman works overlooked by a medieval beacon), tipped by a great rock **acropolis** (Boz Tepe) and backed by a much larger classical settlement on the mainland.

Originally called Sesamos—the name appears in Strabo—the place was renamed in the third century B.C. after Queen Amastris, wronged wife of the tyrant of Heracleia (Ereğli, west along the coast), who sought solace in planting hanging gardens on Boz Tepe. The landward, classical site is the surprise: Look for the **bedesten** (a massive brick and concrete Roman structure, probably originally a gymnasium, near the inevitable coal mine) and a rather sorry **theater**, probably Roman. But the real pleasure here is in exploring the early Byzantine **town walls** and the ancient bridge to Boz Tepe. The Genoese, who held the place when the Ottomans arrived in 1461, plastered the gates with their coats of arms. The **Fatih Camii** probably began life as a cathedral, and the **Kilise Mesciti** was once a painted Byzantine church.

Amasra has a street of woodworkers, below the castle walls. Hardwood bowls and boxwood spoons can be found all along the Paphlagonian and Pontic coast; the Amasran specialty is carved wooden storks killing snakes.

Life congregates around the west bay, where the bus station, a **museum** with serious classical sculpture, two *pide* bars, a fish restaurant, a café with serious ice cream, and a beach overcrowded in season are found. For a quieter dip, go to the deep bathing spot by the medieval beacon, which the locals claim is Genoese. Meager remains of a Byzantine monastery on the island in the east bay give an excuse to swim to it, but for the finest beach go about 3 km (2 miles) east to Çakraz. Buses connect Amasra and Çakraz, but it is fun to hire a boat from the eastern harbor.

The **Paşa Kaptan Oteli**, near the museum, is the only hotel in town. It's cheap and cheerful; get the manager to light the boiler ahead of time for a hot shower. Two sizable pensions are the **Nur Aile Pansiyonu**, with a noisy disco on the premises, and **Belvü Palas**—failing which there are private rooms and hotels in nearby Bartın and Çakraz.

For a fish treat look for the **Çeşmi Cihan** restaurant on the east bay, where proprietor Yakup Tuş is justly proud of his *çoban salata* (shepherd's salad), commonly a mixture of peppers, tomatoes, and cheese. Yakup Bey's version of this well-known dish also includes crunchy *semizotu* (purslane). The **Canlı Balık** restaurant, next door, is also good.

THE PONTUS

Bordering on Paphlagonia, the ancient Pontus is the south-eastern sector of the Black Sea coast. "Pontus" (Greek, *pontos*) simply means "the sea" and, by extension, its shore. Though its name may seem vague, the Pontus is perhaps the most distinctive region of Turkey. There is no mistaking it: more than 400 miles of coastline from Sinop east to the Georgian border, hemmed by successive ranges of the Pontic Alps that are never more than 60 miles inland. As you travel east the mountains come closer to the glittering black sands of the sea, and climb higher, culminating at 13,000 feet in Kaçkar. The coastal valleys, each nurturing a subculture with its own striped tartan, each with a coastal town that doubles in size on market days, become greener, wetter, and more populous as you go east. The coast east of Trabzon (ancient Trebizond) is almost a rain forest: Batumi (over the Georgian border) just surpasses Rize for the highest annual precipitation in the Black Sea area—an awesome 95-plus inches (French sailors called it *le pissoir de la Mer Noire*). The foliage conceals the densest rural population in Turkey, but the mountain-chalet villages are nonnucleated, in the Caucasian way, and it is quite possible to walk for half a morning through a large settlement without noticing it's there.

Apart from Kaçkar, the Pontic Alps are not great peaks. In the thin air above the treeline at about 6,500 feet lie *yaylas*, boundless summer pastures of breathtaking greenness where summer villages are peopled by migrants from the coast who bring up their flocks from May to September. No Pontic experience is complete without your being wakened before dawn by the bells of sheep leaving for the *yayla;* without tasting the shepherd porridge called *tarhana,* so thick that a boxwood spoon will stand in it; or without dancing the *horon* above the clouds to the relentless strains of the *kemençe,* the three-stringed Pontic lyre. Fiercely local in their loyalties, the Pontic Turks can also be distinguished by the claret and blue colors of the Trabzonspor soccer team and an equal devotion to the *hamsi,* a large anchovy that, when it shoals suddenly in autumn, is welcomed with song and dance and cooked in surprising ways. Evliya Çelebi pronounced the fish a powerful aphrodisiac, which may have something to do with its enthusiastic cult. Unfortunately, the *hamsi* is being depleted, either because of pollution or overfishing. By 1992 the dearth of turbot as well as *hamsi* led to a conference of Black Sea countries in Istanbul, which laid down rules regulating fishing—we shall see how successfully.

Any Pontic traveller can evade the *hamsi,* but you cannot refuse a handful of hazelnuts (*fındık*), which arouse if possible even greater passion. If you are not watching, your boots will be filled with them. Hazelnuts are harvested before *hamsi*-time in August. This little nut has serious antecedents: The first record of its export from the Pontus is to Alexandria in 259 B.C. Diligent Russian excavators have come up with 135 hazelnuts that someone forgot to eat in medieval Novgorod, at a time when the emperors of Trebizond were paying war indemnities to Genoa in shiploads of them. Today hazelnut growing threatens to become a monoculture in some parts. Oregon hazelnutters have managed to limit imports to the United States, though anyone who buys a British nut chocolate bar will crunch on the Pontus.

Other historic imports have faded away, often with the Pontic Greeks who produced them: the alum of Şebin-karahisar, the silver of Gümüşhane, and the wine and olive oil of the coast. These have been replaced by tobacco from Bafra and tea from Rize, both backbreaking to harvest.

The Pontus is distinct not just by geography, climate, and economy, but in its peoples and settlement. Virtually all the major settlements were colonized by the seventh century B.C. by Ionian Greeks from Miletus. The tale of Jason and his Argonauts, who braved the Amazons to row to Batumi and Colchis for the Golden Fleece, is a memory of this commercial lure. The coast passed into Roman hands (Lucullus and Pompey) when Mithradates VI Eupator, the last of the kings of Pontus, died old and in despair in 63 B.C. Successive Roman and Byzantine rule brought Christianity here (Saint Andrew supposedly toured the coast) and spared the Pontus from Arab and Slav raids, but only masked Pontic separatism, which erupted when the Seljuk Turks defeated the Byzantines at Manzikert in 1071, cutting the coast off from the rest of Byzantium. This separatism manifested itself first under local dynasts (this is clan country) and most famously under the Empire of Trebizond, whose emperors, named and titled Grand Comneni, ruled this pocket empire from 1204 to 1461, outlasting Byzantium itself.

In fact it was not with Seljuks but with local Turkmen pastoralists that the emperors of Trebizond struggled for the summer pastures that divided and attracted them, and neither group met the Ottomans until Mehmet II conquered Trebizond and the coast in 1461. This period of prosperity under the Comneni coincided with the opening up of Mongol Central Asia to European traders (such as Marco Polo's family), who planted bases on precisely the same sites along the Black Sea coast as had the ancient Greeks, and for the same reasons. The 15th century saw the drying up of the overland routes for various reasons: the death of Tamerlane, the Turkic conqueror; Ottoman conquest; and the discovery of the Americas and the sea route around the Cape of Good Hope.

From the late 17th century local, and now Muslim, dynasts reemerged on the coast as *derebeys* (feudal lords). Commercially the ancient and medieval heydays of the Pontus were repeated from 1829, when the treaty of Edirne reopened the Black Sea to Western commerce, to 1869, when the Suez Canal opened another route. For the third time Trebizond became the overland entry to Asia. Italian shipping companies and British consuls replaced the medieval Genoese and Venetians and the ancient Milesians and Athenians, using the same ports serviced by Pontic Greeks. Why? Quite simply, until recently transport was infinitely cheaper by sea than by land. Trebizond lies at the easternmost point from which European trade can reach the land routes of Asia by sea, at a break in the Pontic Alps.

Local political or commercial autonomy is expressed in local patronage. There is little sign now, however, of how most patrons spent their surplus. Evidence of the priorities of the past—monks and dervishes—have gone, but medieval endowments of monasteries survive in *vakıf*s (Islamic charitable foundations). The most enduring legacies in the Pontus today are its buildings, roads, or simply an open square here or there filled with history. Therefore virtually everything to "see" in the Pontus comes from one of the three eras of the flourishing of its local patrons: antiquity; the period from 1204 to 1461; and the 40-year period after 1829.

This century has brought galloping changes. First, the Pontic Greeks left their Neoclassical houses, which still line the coast, by 1923, with the exchange of populations between Greece and the fledgling Turkish state. Three generations later those Greeks are scattered all over the world. Although modern Greece was not even their ancient homeland, most went there first. But no suburb of Melbourne, Australia, or Columbus, Ohio, is without its Soumela Club, and there are estimates that from 600,000 to one million Pontic Greeks live in what was until recently the Soviet Union. Stalin deported many of them from southern Russia and the Caucasus to Central Asia, whence thousands began yet another migration to Greece in 1989. What is clear is that they cannot return to the Pontus to live, although you may encounter busloads of them there, well-received visitors in a land where Pontic Greeks and Turks once lived in harmony.

Second, in the last 30 years most coastal towns have tripled in population, and travel along the coast has been transformed by dynamite and bulldozer, which have not just destroyed age-old routes but threaten a singular environment, which, once tasted, lures many back to the Black Sea coast.

Sinop

Sinop (ancient Sinope) is the best place to see the sea. The Black Sea describes a sideways figure 8, with Sinop at its waist. Technically, Cape Kerembe to the west is closer to the Crimea, 140 miles north, but Sinop is somehow more convenient. Test the sea: It has half the salinity of the Mediterranean, for the fresh waters of the Danube, Dniester, Dnieper, and Don pour in at the north and the great "Red" and "Green" rivers (Kızılırmak and Yeşilırmak) of Turkey debouch through deltas to the south, to rotate in opposing but sluggish currents in each of the Black Sea's lobes. The sea is shallow to the north, but its floor tilts south to a 7,365-foot depth quite close to Sinop. The Bosphorus is the sea's outflow pipe rather than its plug, so the sea's depths are lifeless. But near the surface the tunny (Turkish *palamut*) perform an annual clockwise gyration, maturing around Sinop, where in early September men wielding long fishing rods cluster on the headlands, before the fish head down the Bosphorus to winter in the Aegean.

Sinope, daughter of Miletus and mother of Trebizond, was the hub of ancient and medieval Black Sea colonies, none of which is more than 370 miles distant. It lives and dies by the sea, for it has no hinterland. The roads south and west into

Paphlagonia are still abominable: Get here from Samsun (see below).

Sinop's site is striking. It lies, as Strabo says, "on the neck of a peninsula, and has on either side of the isthmus harbours and roadsteads and wonderful tunny fisheries. The city itself is beautifully walled, and is also splendidly adorned with gymnasium and market place and stoas." The walled isthmus points east, its north and south harbors separated by only 400 yards of land but more than four miles of sea. The isthmus develops into a peninsula (Boz Tepe, now festooned with radar installations). In the 14th century the Syrian scholar al-Umari described the then-Turkish Sinub and Christian Boz Tepe more quaintly: It was "commonly called the island of lovers. . . . It has a mountain more beautiful than the buttocks of the houris of paradise, and adjoining it is an isthmus more graceful than the slenderest of loins."

Ancient Sinope was capital of a Black Sea commercial empire. Pericles once inspected the colony, and Diogenes the Cynic and barrel-dweller was born here about 412 B.C. From 183 B.C. the kings of Pontus made it their capital, until Pompey buried the last Mithradates here in 63 B.C. By then the Milesian grid street-plan was established at Sinope, along with its *cardo* (Main, or High, Street, now Sakarya Caddesi) and the footings of its **city walls**, which stride between 43 towers. In the southwest quadrant is the **citadel**, with a vast blocked sea gate. If you *must* see inside, you must go to prison, for that is what it now is.

A bilingual inscription by the land gate of the citadel proclaims the Turkish conquest of Sinub on November 1, 1214, after which the **Büyük Cami** (also called the Alaettin Camii), a dignified mosque, was built on the north side of the cardo, probably on the site of the cathedral of St. Phocas, who himself succeeded Poseidon as patron of Sinope and all Pontic mariners. Behind the Büyük Cami lies the elegant portico of the **Alâiye Medresesi**, which houses the tomb of the Gazi Çelebi, who has some claim to be the first Turkish frogman. Fortified by hashish, he used to dive into the harbor armed with a drill to attack enemy ships, until in about 1324 he scuttled some of the ships of his own Genoese colony. Modern Sinop boasts a less reckless diving school. Happily a more recent local pastime of dynamiting dolphins seems to be dying out, perhaps with the dolphins, who prey on spring turbot (*kalkan*).

Outside the eastern walls at the end of the cardo is a good small **museum**. Walk 300 yards southeast for the vast remains of **Balat**, not a "palace" but perhaps the gymnasium and baths mentioned by Strabo. The Byzantines painted one hall as a church, though hardly in 660, as a notice and guide-books misinform you; a final bilingual inscription refers to a repainting in 1640.

From the 16th century Sinop enjoyed peace, which ended with a bang on November 30, 1853, when a Russian squad-ron sank an Ottoman flotilla in the south harbor, precipitat-ing the Crimean War. The city enjoyed a final period of prosperity after that conflict, as a naval and coaling station. But it has all gone with the steamships. Today Sinop's tunny-fishers watch international shipping hug the coast, but it never calls. Such isolation, and therefore preservation of its walls (last damaged in 1853), gives Sinop great archaeologi-cal importance and incidental charm.

The bus station is outside the northwest corner of the walls. The **Hotel Melia Kasım**, outside the southeast corner, is frequented by NATO personnel. Rooms facing the sea are more expensive than those facing the street. The **117 Oteli**, overlooking the harbor, is cheaper and cleaner, but its seaside rooms, too, are higher in price than those on the street side. All manner of restaurants line the southern sea walls and harbor.

Samsun

From the 1860s this important and unlovely port (ancient Amisos) overtook Trebizond as the sea terminus of the Baghdad road and, from 1891, of the aborted Berlin–Baghdad railway—indeed of any railway to reach the Black Sea coast. Here most coastal traffic turns south to Ankara.

On May 19, 1919, Mustafa Kemal (later Atatürk) launched his national revolution in Samsun, ironically in what had in the previous century become a Greek-dominated city. Four years later, in a neat exchange, Turkish tobacco workers of Kavalla in Greece changed places with the Greek tobacco workers of Samsun and Bafra. The place has not looked back.

The ancient **acropolis of Amisos** (Kara Samsun) is best glimpsed from the air. On the ground it is no injustice to tour Samsun in a couple of hours by horse-drawn buggy, either from the port or the main square, Cumhuriyet Meydanı. Visit the grandiose **museum** (Roman floor mosaics, Atatürk memorabilia; closed Mondays); the pretty **Eski Cami**; the old tobacco warehouses; and the only church now open, which is Capuchin. It is looked after by a kindly and diminutive Chaldean Uniat weight lifter, he says the only one of his kind in town—which may be believed.

Most hotels in Samsun are clustered around Cumhuriyet Meydanı. The **Vidinli Oteli** is a run-down "European" hotel with an echoing dining room, but it's decent. The **Burç Otel** is friendly. A better choice might be the four-star **Turban Büyük Samsun Oteli** on Sahil Caddesi, whose facilities include gardens, a swimming pool, tennis courts, and a nightclub. The **Oskar Restaurant**, on the main square (Saathane Meydanı), is popular with the locals—as are some others on Cumhuriyet Caddesi, including the **Cumhuriyet**, the **Beyaz Saray**, and the **Divan** tea garden. Samsun ice cream, by the way, can be delicious.

SAMSUN TO GİRESUN

The coastal highway along this stretch of the Pontus cuts inland only across the once-malarial deltas of the Kızılırmak and Yeşilırmak, the ancient Halys and Lykos-Iris rivers. Their shifting mouths are lonely places where tortoises copulate in the dunes with much clatter. Inland are misty valleys where Amazons were once endemic.

Ünye (ancient Oinaion) is an attractive place about 80 km (50 miles) east of Samsun. Life here gathers around a square with a great plane tree (under which the Hazinedaroğlu pashas once administered justice), a municipal park, and a city pier. From Ünye you can scramble up to **Çaleoğlu Kale**, 5 km (3 miles) inland by dolmuş, an overgrown castle and rock-cut Pontic tomb off the road that leads south to Niksar (New Caesarea), whence Saint Gregory the Wonderworker evangelized this part of the Pontus. Ünye has a modest motel, the **Çamlık Hotel**, with rocky beach and pool (which is quite likely to be empty of water). Near the pier, eat at the **100. Yıl Tesisi** (Tel: 373/137-97 or 148-99) or, more substantially, under the trees at the edge of the park, at the **Park** restaurant (Tel: 373/130-53).

Ancient Polemonion (now Bolaman), 10 km (6 miles) east of Fatsa, itself just east of Ünye, is remembered in **Bolaman Kalesi**, an enchanting fortified Ottoman *konak* (mansion) by the sea, which encases a Byzantine church (in private hands, indeed descendants of the Hazinedaroğlu dynasty who built it). Twelve kilometers (7½ miles) east of Bolaman, Jason himself is remembered in **Yasun Burnu** (Cape Jason), which is tipped by a 19th-century church on a much older site. On the sheltered east side of Cape Jason the village of **Perşembe** overlooks ancient Vona, the best and best-hidden natural harbor along the entire coast, where yachts now anchor. The **Vona Hotel**, at the east end of Perşembe, is a small, decent hotel with a restaurant and swimming pool.

Ordu (ancient Kotyora) is the next major town. From Kotyora the last of Xenophon's Ten Thousand took ship west. It has an overgrown acropolis, a 19th-century Orthodox cathedral (which has lost its dome) overlooking the corniche, and a wealth of rather decayed turn-of-the-century mansions, such as the **Makrides house** (the family set up the first cinema and department store in Ordu, and since 1923 has been scattered via Athens to Boston and Scotland). One of the finest of such houses (built in 1893) has been admirably restored as the **Ordu Paşaoğlu Konağı ve Etnografya Müzesi**, an ethnographic museum in stately surroundings (open 8:00 A.M. to 5:00 P.M.; closed Mondays). The **Turist Otel** has a decent restaurant, and three others—the **Marina**, the **Midi**, and the **Ayısığı** (all on the seafront)—also offer presentable fare.

You can go south from Ordu over wonderful *yayla* to the great castle of **Koyluhisar**, or press on east to **Bulancak**, the last stop before Giresun. Here the family of the late, much missed Gedik Ali runs a large and splendidly hospitable hotel on the headland just west of the town—the aptly named **Gedik Ali Turistik Tesisleri**. If you want to explore the region further, take the Dereli road south over the summer pastures to **Şebinkarahisar** (ancient Koloneia), a great basalt fortress rock amid alum-streaked mountains, which in spring rises above a sea of flowers.

Giresun

The second city of the Empire of Trebizond, Giresun (ancient Kerasous) is a lively place that should not be missed. Alum is no longer exported through it from Şebinkarahisar, but Giresun remains the world's hazelnut capital (though don't tell that to people from Ordu). The nuts are exported from the harbor west of the promontory on which the city stands. Climb up to the walled classical and medieval acropolis on the promontory itself, now a bosky park with a seasonal restaurant, the **Kale**, where Dursun Ali Tekbaş, Giresun's famed chef, is currently manning the grill. East of the promontory stand dignified Neoclassical houses, a 19th-century school, a Gothic Revival Capuchin chapel (now a library), even a 19th-century Orthodox cathedral (still domed and now a museum). What more could you want?

Why, an island. **Giresun Adası** lies temptingly about four miles to the east. From the eastern shore, get a boatman to take you there. It is a fortified island that once sheltered a monastery to Saint Phocas, where Jason and his Argonauts once had a great to-do with the Amazons, and where today there is refreshing bathing off the rocks. Better still, go there on May 20 of any year, when Giresun is thronged with villagers. Opposite the island, where the Aksu Çayı (White River) debouches into the sea, an annual open-air festival is held, with dancing and picnicking. Participants start the festival's ritual by tossing seven double handfuls and one single handful of pebbles into the Aksu. Then they circumnavigate the island three times—counterclockwise—and, finally, pop a pebble into an aperture in a great black boulder on the island. A rational explanation for such activity may be lacking, but it clearly brings great contentment to the people of Giresun, who end up flat on their backs by the Aksu.

The people of Giresun must also be content with their restaurants. The **Çerkez** is the classiest, set on rocks near the mouth of the Aksu and facing the magic island. Near the beach a few minutes west of the promontory is the **Kerasus**, with fine grilled lamb. In town, on the seaward side of the corniche road, is **Mehmet Efendi's**, a restaurant whose atmosphere compensates for the smartness of the newer places. The recent introduction of a blaring TV is regrettable, but you may persuade them to turn it down—unless, of course, the Trabzonspor soccer team is winning. Indeed, Mehmet Efendi's is quite sufficiently reason to spend a week in Giresun; it would take that long to work through its fish menu systematically. At lunch, in season, watch clouds of migrating quail landing exhausted from Russia across the sea. In the evening, identify the different species of buses migrating west along the coast road as they race through the night to Ankara. During your aperitif (with hot toasted hazelnuts), great Ulusoy coaches from Trabzon lead the procession, followed by such local buses as the Sürmene Birlik and rare strays such as a Bayburtlu or two. Long after dark the Hopa Ekspres limps past, and you know it's time to call for the bill and go to bed, which is easy enough, for the three decent hotels are within yards of Mehmet Efendi's, the town hall, the main square, and a clutch of pubs (almost as numerous as banks). They are the **Giresun Oteli** (on the sea, but dull), the **Otel Kit-Tur** on Gazi Caddesi, and, on Osmanağa Caddesi, the new **Çarıkçı Hotel** in a nicely restored old pink-and-white house.

GİRESUN TO TRABZON

Promontory castles of the Empire of Trebizond punctuate the final stretch of coast before Trabzon. **Tirebolu** (Tripolis), 51 km (32 miles) east of Giresun, naturally has three of them; **Akçakale** (Kordyle), on the Holy Cape (Yoros Burnu) at the bay of Trabzon, was a fortified monastery (Saint Phocas again). At **Tekke**, 23 km (14 miles) up the Yağlıdere river south of Espiye, is a dervish monastery that flourished from the 16th to this century. From Tirebolu, those in a hurry bypass Trabzon by following the Harşit valley 94 km (58 miles) south to Torul. For those with more time, there are two reasons for stopping at **Akçaabat** (Platana), just before Trabzon. First, in the upper town (Orta Mahalle) is the **church of the Archangel Michael**, with a fine medieval mosaic now preserved as the kitchen floor of the private house the church has become; be as courteous as you would expect any unannounced stranger demanding to look at your own kitchen to be. Second, on the seafront are excellent fish restaurants; try the **Sebat**. Akçaabat has even produced a local cookbook, and you might catch one of the best *folklor* groups in the Pontus dancing the *horon* here.

TRABZON

However spelled, Trebizond is to be recited among Milton's legendary names of history—Aspramont and Montalban, Damasco and Marocco. It is the realm whose imperial scepter Don Quixote grasped when transported by his most agreeable delusions. In the seventh century B.C. colonists from Sinope called it Trapezous (accusative "Trapezounta," hence the mellifluous adjective "Trapezuntine"). *Trapezous* happens to mean "table" in Greek, but the name is probably older and Caucasian. Later, but still older than the modern Turkish variant, Trabzon, are the German Trapezunt and French Trébisonde, while the English have called it by their own name since the Middle Ages: Trebizond. Why such fame? To find out, begin with the Meydan (also known as Atatürk Alanı) in Trabzon's eastern suburb, above the commercial harbor. (Trabzon is divided into three parts: the western and eastern suburbs and the walled city in between.)

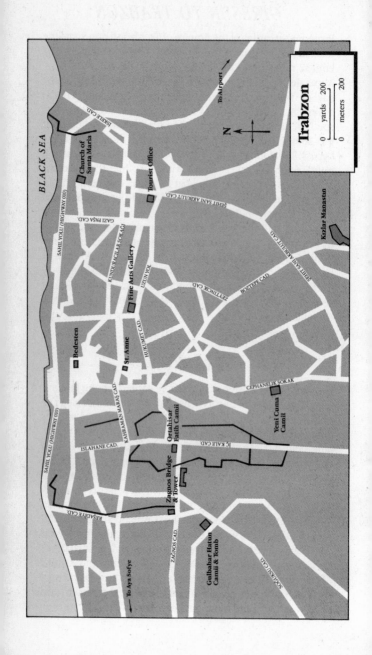

The Meydan

You are going to end up in the Meydan—the name simply means "square"—anyway, if only because it is the terminus of both the airport bus and the Ulusoy buses (their depot replaces the old camel stables off the southeast corner, whence departs the annual package pilgrimage to Mecca: a convoy of green-flagged desert buses). Sit down by the statue of Atatürk, order a glass of tea, get a shoeshine, and look around you.

This square is the oldest living monument in Trabzon, the heart of a classical grid pattern of streets, the place of the ancient agora and later the assembly point for caravans to other parts of Asia. Off the Meydan to the northeast is the fortified Genoese quarter of **Leontokastron** (now Güzel Hisar, a military club, under which the coast road tunnels). Between the Meydan and the sea lies the **church of Santa Maria**, which was consecrated as a Capuchin sanctuary in 1874 and is now looked after by nuns. To the northwest huddle the cacophonous **bazaar** (copper, silver, hardwood, cloth, discounted czarist ruble bills), the **bedesten,** and the site of the Venetians' **castle**. From the west side, the *cardo,* Meraş Caddesi, links the Meydan with the walled lower city. At the Meydan end is the **Şehir Hamamı** (or Meydan Hamamı), civilized Turkish baths that double as an informal stock exchange some mornings—a good place to unwind after a day's hiking while your clothes are pressed. Beyond the banks Meraş Caddesi passes the shell of **St. Anne**, Trabzon's oldest church (rebuilt between 884 and 885). From the southwestern corner of the Meydan, Uzun Sokak runs to the walled middle city, beginning with a historic ice-creamery, *hamsi* parlors, and a bookshop.

In the square itself, the Grand Comneni, emperors of Trebizond, received the diplomatic corps and obeisances of their subjects at Easter. In Turkish heroic poetry, the Meydan witnessed the wooing of a Trapezuntine princess by the Turkmen prince Turalı in about 1352. The emperor made him undergo three labors before he could snatch his bride; the first was to down a black bull (which he disemboweled in the Meydan). Then there was an alarming scene when they brought on a royal lion, who "roared, and every single horse in the square pissed blood." Turalı dealt with that, too, then wrestled down a camel and rode off with his Amazon bride, but not before a final duel with her, in which she "sent the lice in his hair scuttling down to his feet." They lived happily ever after. At that time princesses of Trebizond were already a major export, and the Meydan was already used to wild animals. A leopard presented to Edward I of England seems to have escaped its cage there in 1292, soon after which Marco Polo lost all his luggage in a predecessor of one of the hotels that still line the square—not the last visitor to have done so. Today, you cannot escape the attentions of peddlars from over the former Soviet border in the Caucasus.

The Western Suburb

From the Meydan, where buses and taxis abound, set out to see the city. Take a dolmuş marked "Ayasofya" and start in the western suburb, home of Trabzonspor's soccer stadium—built perhaps on the site of the imperial polo pitch. From the area's western extremity, Ayasofya, work your way back. **St. Sophia** is a fortified monastery, church, and belfry (with 15th-century paintings) overlooking the sea. A great Byzantine monument, the church stands on a platform of vaulted tombs. It was founded by Manuel I (1238 to 1263), the first Grand Comnenus to cash in on his silver mines to the south, which fed the Meydan trade. Peculiar to Trebizond, such centrally planned domed churches have porches on three sides and pentagonal apses (look for the hundreds of votive ship graffiti). Manuel commissioned everything 13th-century money could buy: an Armenian-style Creation relief on the south porch; Seljuk-style stalactite niches; a sixth-century eagle capital from Constantinople in the west porch (its brother is in the porch of San Marco in Venice); and, inside, reused columns and grape capitals supporting a great host of painted angels flapping in the drum of the dome. Manuel ordered everything in his painters' repertoire, so both evangelists and miracles are crammed into the squinches. The result is glorious. The paintings were restored by a British expedition that was here from 1958 to 1964, when St. Sophia became a museum. The staff is gathering the inscriptions of the place in a lapidarium by the church, endeavoring to protect Trabzon's past. But it is an uphill task.

The Walled City

Just how uphill a task it is, you will see by going into the walled city, a wedge between the two suburbs. From the west, enter by the **Zağanos bridge and gate**, just outside which is the pleasing T-shaped **mosque** (1514) **and tomb** (1506) **of Gülbahar**, Pontic mother (reputedly) of Selim, who was Ottoman governor of Trabzon from 1489 to 1512 and sultan from 1512 to 1520. Selim's son, the magnificent Süleyman, was born here.

Many times rebuilt, the **city walls** rise from a still-visible classical harbor mole through a **lower city** (1324), an attenuated **middle city**, up to the **ancient acropolis** and medieval **palace complex** that rises dramatically above the meeting of two ravines at the southern tip. The towers of Trebizond still stand (including three banquet-hall windows), but have, with the best intentions, been so refaced as to destroy their history. But beneath the shambles of the acropolis lies the archaeology of a great administrative center, perhaps as much as 33 feet deep and thousands of years old.

Straddling the middle city, between Zağanos and Tabakhane bridges and probably on the site of an earlier temple, is the **cathedral of the Chrysokephalos** (Golden-headed Virgin), which after 1461 became the **Fatih Camii** (or Ortahisar Camii), Trabzon's chief mosque. (To get there from the Meydan, walk down Uzun Sok to Tabakhane bridge; from Ayasofya, walk east to Zağanos bridge.) The cathedral had been rebuilt by the Grand Comneni after 1222, probably to house the liturgy of their own coronation. Part of the imperial gallery survives; the south porch has been excised for the *mihrap* (niche), but the imperial tombs have gone. Until 1988 the church's wall paintings were safe under whitewash, and a magnificent mosaic floor under floorboards and carpet. But the *vakıf* then smartened the mosque up. The walls were cemented and the Byzantine floor, briefly exposed, was drowned in concrete, amid the protests of Turkish archaeologists, who had worldwide support.

The Eastern Suburb

From the Chrysokephalos, cross the bridge over the eastern ravine along Uzun Sokak back to the Meydan. The eastern, "Frankish," suburb slopes up from the Meydan to the cliffs of yet another Boz Tepe (here Mount Minthrion), site of the painted cave chapels of St. Sabbas, now inaccessible. More prominent at the top of Şehit Sanı Akbulut Caddesi, but sometimes locked, is the abandoned **nunnery of the Theoskepastos** (God-protected Virgin), called **Kızlar Manastırı** (Girls' Monastery), which was refounded by the Grand Comnenus Alexius III (1349 to 1390). Soot protects the medieval paintings of its cave church, and most of the buildings are 19th-century, including the canopied tomb of Metropolitan Konstantios, in which he was buried enthroned. During his formidable reign (1830 to 1879) this bishop was responsible for rebuilding (and so destroying) almost every Byzantine church still in Christian hands. Those that had become mosques, such as St. Eugenios, to the west, were paradoxically in safer hands.

The **monastery church of St. Eugenios**, patron of Trebizond, overlooks the walled city from the east, on Cuma Caddesi. It was rebuilt in the 11th century and decorated under Alexius III, who was (exceptionally) crowned here on January 21, 1350; it retains its north porch. By 1523 the parish had converted to Islam and the church became the **Yeni Cuma Camii** (New Friday Mosque), its painting still safe under whitewash and its mosaic floor of 1291 under boards.

Mistrust the statement in most guidebooks that Alexius III was crowned in Soumela. More imaginative is the common misidentification of the intriguing circular building on the slopes above St. Eugenios as a sort of pleasure dome erected by the empress Eirene in 1340. It is in fact the **Cephane**, an Ottoman arsenal of 1887, blown up in 1919 after the Russian occupation of 1916 to 1918 in an explosion that still reverberates in old men's ears.

Below the Theoskepastos is the mansion (1896) of Osman Nemlizade, Trabzon's deputy in 1908. It was used, for a time, as a girl's high school, and now it's being converted into an institute of tertiary education. It's worth visiting for a look at its Kütahya tiles; though the house isn't open to the public, you'll be welcomed in if you knock. The Franco-Russian tastes of 19th-century Greek bankers and merchants can be savored in the town houses of the Kostakis family (just off Uzun Sokak; scheduled to open in 1993 as Trabzon's museum) and the Phosteropoulos family (near the post office). The most exotic house of all is among other villas at **Soğuksu** (Kryonero), a cool resort above the city, 7 km (4 miles) southwest (take a bus or dolmuş from the north side of the Meydan; watch for Soğuksu signs). It is the house of Constantine Kapayiannides, built in 1903 and happily preserved as the **Atatürk Köşkü** museum, where the first president of the Republic of Turkey wrote part of his will on June 10, 1937, leaving everything to the nation.

Perhaps the most striking monument to Trapezuntine initiative figures in no guidebook, but is impossible not to notice above the coast road northwest of the Meydan. It is the vast 19th-century Greek **Phrontisterion** (College), now the prestigious Anadolu Lisesi, where instruction is in English. Founded in 1683 by Sebastos Kyminites (1630–1702), a luminous forerunner of the Enlightenment, it was until well into this century the most influential center of higher education on the Black Sea. The impressive new Black Sea University (between the airport and city) is Trabzon's successor to the Phrontisterion.

Kaymaklı Church

Kaymaklı is an important site, and it is still inadequately recorded. It used to be the monastery of the All-Savior (Amenap'rkich'), until 1915 the center of Armenian life in Trebizond. The main church may be 13th-century Greek, converted to Armenian use after 1402. It was redecorated around 1700 with perhaps the liveliest Armenian wall paintings that survive anywhere (the rigging of a ship in the awesome Last Judgment dates them). These paintings survive because the church, the hay barn of the farm the monastery now is, has been reroofed. Take a flashlight and do not upset the farmer, his hay, or his dogs. Kaymaklı can be approached from the Meydan over Boz Tepe by car, but it is easier to take the Maçka road 3 km (2 miles) south to the Shell station, from where it is visible, and scramble up a path.

Staying and Dining
in Trabzon

After 1829, when the Meydan again became a hub of world trade, Trebizond's first "Frankish" hotel was opened on its north side, complete with a ballroom in which the city's consular corps once played the great game of diplomacy. George Finlay stayed there in 1850, and it eventually became the Yeşilyurt Oteli, where Rose Macaulay stayed (with the redoubtable "Aunt Dot") when writing *The Towers of Trebizond* a hundred years later. Macaulay's mysterious romance lures droves of discerning travellers to Trabzon, but not to the run-down Yeşilyurt. The opening of its replacement—the Pullman Etap—seems indefinitely postponed. Trebizond's other 19th-century hotel, the Pension Suisse, has, incredibly, survived, though not on the Meydan. It migrated with its owners to Greece in 1923.

And so hotels come and go. At present there is the adequate, clean Özgür Oteli, with a restaurant, next to the tourist office on the south side of the square. To the northeast, near the İskender Paşa Camii (ca. 1530; rebuilt) and the fire station, is the Hotel Usta, whose prices are above its station. Behind the north face of the Meydan, in a street of grocers (tubs of mountain butter and cheese, sides of *pastırma,* barrels of honey), is the **Otel Horon**, one of the first of the newer hotels, a decent, modest place where you get what you pay for.

If you are lucky enough to get to know a member of the Black Sea Club, do not refuse an invitation to eat in its dignified old mansion off the northwest side of the square, but it is as exclusive as any club in London or New York. There you might glimpse Mr. Ulusoy—he of the bus company—playing backgammon. Otherwise, invite yourself to one of at least four good restaurants on the square—which four changes annually. Trapezuntine gastronomes currently recommend the **Kibris**, **Çınar**, **Özgür**, and **Büryan** (in that order). For something classier, get a taxi from the Meydan, going west, to the **Zindan** (on top of the Zağanos tower), or, going east, to the new **Süleyman** (with swimming pool, on the airport road), or, going south, up to the **Boz Tepe** restaurant, which surveys the lights of the city below. A *hamsi* omelet is not to be sniffed at, and if you want Circassian chicken (*Çerkes tavuğu*), order ahead so that they can pound the walnuts.

If during your stay in Trabzon you find yourself in trouble or doubt, check in at the **tourist office** (Atatürk Alanı, Park Köşesi; Tel: 03/21-46-59), where the excellent and reliable Mrs. Sevtap Türko is the person in charge. It was her father, the local historian Cumhur Odabaşioğlu, who looked after "Aunt Dot" in Rose Macaulay's *The Towers of Trebizond.*

SOUTH OF TRABZON
Three Monasteries

South of Trabzon the landscape is dominated by three former great landowning and pilgrim monasteries. Each is poised in a spectacular position and hides a sacred cave church; each claims ancient foundation, of which there is no surviving sign; each was refounded and endowed by the Grand Comneni; each was transformed and rebuilt in the 19th century and in 1923 abandoned. All are wrecked shells today.

To get to the first, **St. George Peristereota** (now Kuştul), from Esiroğlu, 19 km (12 miles) south of Trabzon on the E 885, watch out for a sign on the left and follow the drivable track that leads to the foot of the monastery rock. A steep scramble leads to the massive buildings through orchards unpruned for 70 years. Mostly rebuilt after a fire in 1904, Peristereota once had the most important library of the three monasteries.

To reach the second, the monastery of St. John the Forerunner, **Vazelon**, on Mount Zaboulon (now Ayana), take the new forest road across the valley west from Keremitli, 15 km (9 miles) south of Maçka on the E 885, which crosses the new E 97 highway. Depending on the weather, this is motorable to within a 30-minute ramble through meadows strewn with the ancestors of many European garden flowers. It's best to ask the way at the Keremitli teahouse on the right (west) side of the main road, where there is often someone who will show it to you in exchange for a lift. You'll leave the car behind when it's clear you can drive no farther. The 20th-century façade of Vazelon conceals a 19th-century church, older buildings, and a cave. The fine medieval painted chapel (St. Elias) on a ledge to the right will not survive much more vandalism: Get there while there is time.

With Mount Sinai and the monasteries of Mount Athos, the monastery of the Mother of God, Soumela, was once among the most revered of all pilgrim monasteries in the Orthodox world. The setting of this third and greatest of the monasteries south of Trabzon, on Mount Mela (now Meryemana), never ceases to astonish, which makes it one of the best-known tourist sites in Turkey. Today every taxi driver in the Meydan will try to take you there. You can find a taxi to share in front of the tourist office; rates are posted.

If you're driving yourself, turn left at **Maçka**, 19 km (12 miles) south of Trabzon, up what is now a highway into the forests. Maçka itself has a busy market, restaurants, and good agricultural ironmongers. The Turkish name of its river, the ancient Pyxites, is Değirmendere (Mill River), and the whole valley south is indeed a molinologist's delight, with "two-eyed" horizontal water mills and even water-driven bear-scarers clacking away. The substitution of maize for wheat since 1923 has left threshing floors abandoned; otherwise agriculture cannot have changed much over the centuries in these densely populated and farmed valleys. From the 13th century until 1923 they were largely controlled by the three great monasteries, constituting a monastic economy of almost Tibetan proportions, and so were overwhelmingly Pontic Greek, with hundreds of hidden churches. When your landlord is an abbot, you think twice about turning Turk.

Overlooking Maçka from the northeast is the prominent watchtower of the village headquarters of Soumela's estates at Doubera (Livera, now Yazlık), home of the family of Trebizond's last prime minister in 1461 and of Maria of Doubera, who may have been Gülbahar, the mother of Sultan Selim I. This attractive village became the focus of the "crypto-

Christians" of Stavri and Santa (Orthodox by faith who some-how got registered as Muslim by law), 17,000 of whom declared their faith, or "came out," after Ottoman reforms in 1856, which reaffirmed the religious freedom of non-Muslims. Here they built the cathedral of Rhodopolis in 1863 (now the village mosque).

Until recently pilgrims and visitors faced a six-hour trek through the dripping forests until they came upon **Soumela** (Sumela in Turkish) hanging from its cliff face. Unless there is a landslide (as in 1990) the journey can now be done by car in minutes. The road first deposits you at a café in what since 1961 has been a forestry research station, near a fountain dedicated to its first director, the late Şükrü Köse, who was largely responsible for saving what is left of Soumela. A 20-minute climb (up a path that's easy to find, because of the almost constant procession of visitors) then takes you to the monastery. Enjoy, but please do not pick, the white Soumela crocuses on the way. If the climb daunts you, the new road continues up the valley and doubles back to within a few yards of the gate of the monastery.

Soumela was supposedly founded in A.D. 386; certainly something was there around the sacred cave and fountain by the tenth century. Like the other monasteries, it was patron-ized by the Grand Comneni: Alexius III refounded it in 1364. Apart from some rapidly disintegrating perhaps 13th-century paintings (a Last Judgment on the rock face to the right of the cave church, for example), nothing is visible of this period (there is an inaccessible and, therefore, untouched medieval painted chapel in the vicinity). Most of the visible paintings and main chapel buildings belong to a second period of prosperity, in the 1740s, when the monastery was endowed through the silver mines of Gümüşhane, often by the Phytianos family. In 1864 the present approach, aque-duct, library, and entire façade were built, replacing old wooden cells, which had clung to the cliff. The new build-ings were not for monks (who rarely numbered more than a dozen) but for the hundreds of pilgrims, many of whom came every August 15 to venerate Soumela's icon of the "Virgin Who Answers Quickly," supposedly painted by Saint Luke and a great prophylactic against locusts.

Today many more tourists visit Soumela than pilgrims ever did. Since 1972 its wreckage has been cleaned up, and since 1984 great investment (some of it by UNESCO) has been made in repairing the 19th-century structures; earlier paintings must fend for themselves. The result is a shock. Be warned that until 1995 Soumela will be a construction site, after which it will take its place among the most incongrous of Turkish tourist traps. The insensitivity of the "restoration" must be seen to be believed.

Happily, something of Soumela survives elsewhere. Its treasures, archives, library, and icons and their screens are mostly preserved, if scattered, in museums and public and private collections in Ankara, Istanbul, Athens, Paris, Oxford, Dublin, and New York. Pontic Greeks have built a New Soumela on a less dramatic site near Verria in northern Greece, where they now gather every August 15 to venerate its wonder-working icon.

What remains here is the unforgettable setting—to which the monks may have been quite indifferent. George Finlay (1799 to 1875) gives a glimpse of the monastery in its great days, before the rebuilding, in the entry of his unpublished diary dated June 27, 1850. Expecting little hospitality, he had bought trout on the way (now grilled in rustic restaurants along the valley). He found that the abbot spoke Turkish better than Finlay's Greek, and Finlay excused himself from a welcome mass because his clothes were sodden. But the place overcame him:

> The roar of the waters 3,000 feet below the monastery, the snowy slopes visible to the south over the valley, which is hardly a rifle shot across, the immense wooden pile of buildings with its galleries and cells clinging like swallows' nests to the precipice, the sound of the the convent bell continually announcing the arrival of parties of pilgrims and the nasal chant of the continual masses, was grand, strange, solemn & picturesque.

Three Roads to Gümüşhane

One of the world's great highways runs from the Trabzon Meydan to Tabriz (Iran). Its first leg, to Gümüşhane, was for European merchants and missionaries the most spectacular, if only because it was often their first taste of travel in the East. It drove generations of travellers from exhilaration to despair, yet comprised only the first three days of a 32-day journey, until in 1919 the first Ford motorcar reached Gümüşhane from Trabzon—it was carried. Today Ulusoy buses do it without a tea break. Somewhere along the route Xenophon's Ten Thousand shouted *"Thalassa! Thalassa!"* ("The sea! The sea!"), but it is difficult to see where the sea is until you almost fall into it at Trabzon. From Maçka south, there are now three routes.

If you are in a hurry, join the trucks on their way to Iran and tear up the new highway (E 97) on the west side of the valley. The dynamiting of this road took no account of past roads, and the route takes you through a tunnel more than a mile long, depriving you of the satisfaction of standing on the Zigana pass.

The road that replaced the first (1850s) for wheeled traffic runs from Maçka to **Hamsiköy**, above the valley to the southeast (E 885). All travellers must be grateful to Hamsiköy for bribing the contractors £400 to divert the road to its side of the valley; it is famed throughout Turkey for its rice puddings, for which traffic stops. There is a delightful, if rudimentary, Ottoman *han* (inn) if you want to stay for more (as well as a restaurant and rice-pudding shop just opposite the inn). Beyond Hamsiköy the road runs through forests to the bare *yayla* up to the Zigana pass (6,535 feet), from which you can peer into two worlds: the Pontus and old Armenia.

Finally, just south of Maçka, a modest track, easily missed, starts climbing southeast. (The track begins about 400 yards south of the old Maçka bridge on the E 885.) This is the historic **summer road** that in Roman times led to Satala (headquarters of the Legio XV Apollinaris), carried medieval and later caravans, and was, by the 1850s, burdened with more than half the overland exports of Persia to Europe. After the Trabzon Meydan, it is the most remarkable monument in the Pontus. The trouble is that it was paved for beasts and has not been adapted since for wheeled traffic. Nevertheless, it is perfectly possible to drive along this road the whole way to Gümüşhane in a day, noting the old road as it erupts on the dirt track. By horse or on foot it takes a comfortable three days that you will never regret. (The Trabzon tourist office can advise about walking and, with appropriate cautions, suggest how you can hire mountain horses, which come with their owners.)

The ancient road passes the Roman cohort base of **Hortokop** before crossing east to skirt the Larhan valley, parallel to the Maçka. Once you reach the *yayla* there is no need for paving. Mount Karakaban faces you above the summer pastures, a staging post where the aforementioned English embassy (complete with caged leopard) camped in 1292 and where caravans changed escorts. In summer flocks of sheep, children, teahouses, and even a temporary post office appear out of nowhere. Ask the way to Stavri, and descend through an unassuming pass at 7,477 feet (with teahouse) and through what was anciently known as the **Pontic Gates**. A new world of hidden summer villages opens up—**Stavri** (the most lively), **Kurum** (the least), and **İmera** (with a monastery church preserved as a cow barn, and ruins of the Phosteropoulos summer house)—before you breast a final range down to Gümüşhane.

The western Pontus and Giresun may be carefree, but travellers south and east of Trabzon should be careful. Once you leave main roads and towns here you meet Pontic rural society, which is traditional and conservative. The courtesies of hospitality and the decencies of Islam are observed. All village and *yayla* life is public. Visitors are under friendly but ceaseless observation and comment. Avoid unseemly clothing; drinking is particularly offensive. You should not address, or even make eye contact with, people of the opposite sex. Be equally wary of dogs of any sex.

If you spend any time in a village, introduce yourself to the *muhtar* (headman). Your safety is his responsibility. Given warning, he may find you space in a village *oda* (guest room); otherwise ask permission to camp. Rural hospitality can be protracted; be patient with questions—people have every right to know what you are doing.

Yogurt and all dairy products abound, but bring bread, flashlights (always an acceptable gift), as much Turkish as you can learn—and toilet paper.

The Gümüşhane Basin

From Zigana the first two routes discussed above meet the Tirebolu road to squeeze with the Harşit river through the striking fortified defile at **Torul** (Ardasa); a fascinating valley branches southwest up to Phytianos (now Beşkilise) village. The main road joins the ancient routes at modern Gümüş- hane and beyond. Built in the 1860s on the then "new" road, **Gümüşhane** still has the air of a frontier gold-rush town, where Ulusoy and Bayburtlu buses thread their way among horsemen. At last Gümüşhane has a decent hotel: the **Gümüş**. It is located between the town hall and the Tadlan pastry shop (run by the Ferah family from Rize). Notices outside the town promise travellers a tourist information office in Gümüşhane, which has not yet materialized. Arif Yüce at the Gümüş hotel's reception desk is a mine of information, though. He'll persuade you to linger longer in these parts—so that you can be guided to the newly found stalactites and stalagmites in a cave 17 km (11 miles) away, off the E 390 on the track to İmera and Stavri. (Arif Bey can also obtain the key to the cave's gate.)

Look around the surrounding mountains and spot **Canca Kale**, the castle of Tzanicha, to the northwest. Every peak has its castle, but this one is topped by two painted chapels. (The climb is perilous, but can best be accomplished from the main road beneath.) The Tzanichites family, among others in Torul, held out against the Ottomans for more than 15 years after Trebizond fell in 1461. It is not difficult to see how.

Canca controls the caravan route below and in turn overlooks **Eski Gümüşhane** (Old Gümüşhane), hidden 3 km (2 miles) southwest of the modern town and well worth seeking out. The metaled road to it is signposted to the right (west) just before the bridge that takes you left (east) into modern Gümüşhane. Once a substantial town, Eski Gümüşhane now has all of six inhabitants. From the 13th century this was the silver-mining capital of Anatolia and subsequently an Ottoman mint. The mines (and the concomitant smelting and charcoal-burning economy that has stripped the region of timber) were exhausted when Russian invaders reached Gümüşhane in 1828, at which time they were run by *archimetallourgoi* (Greek, "concessionaries"), often of the Phytianos family, who also endowed Soumela.

Old Gümüşhane (its Greek name, Argyropolis—Silver City—is for once a translation of the Turkish) is today a ghost city of slag-built houses, churches, and kilns. The only life is in the **Süleymaniye Camii** (probably 17th-century), above which lies the **cathedral of St. George** (1726), with its collapsed dome, and the once-handsome **palace of the bishops of Chaldia** (1749). After 1829 the silver miners left to work alum in Şebinkarahisar (in which the Phytianos family also had a hand) and elsewhere. In this region silver was replaced by apples, for which Gümüşhane is now best known.

At Pirahmet, 17 km (11 miles) east, rejoin the easternmost ancient route to head south to Roman Satala (now Sadak), or continue east over two more passes to Erzurum, which replaced Satala as the Anatolian forward military base. The south gate of the Empire of Trebizond is clear: the staggering castle of **Keçi Kale** (Mesochaldia), after which oxen replace horses and firewood gives way to dung cakes (*tezek*) piled high on mud roofs. You leave the red-and-black-striped cloths of the coastlands and meet the first brown sacks favored by the ladies of Bayburt, proclaiming that you have left the Pontus.

SANTA

The seven villages of Santa are among the most breathtaking sights of the Pontus. Settled from the late 17th century in a high, enclosed valley by Greeks seeking isolation from the coastal *bey*s (lords), they lie where tree line and *yayla* meet. Their solid churches and schools were built after the "crypto-Christians" declared their faith in 1856; by the end, in 1923, about 5,000 *Santalı*s had to be winkled out of their smiling valley. Their folklore fills volumes, but their ghost villages are being slowly resettled in summer. Do not count on a bed, but plan to camp.

It is now possible to do Santa in a day by car from Trabzon—if you have strong nerves (the winding dirt track is vertiginous). For example, you might take the Yanbolu river road south from Araklı, which is 27 km (17 miles) east of Trabzon, for 45 km (28 miles). The highest and largest village, **Piştoflı** (Pishtophandon), lies on the map only 15 km (9 miles) due east of Soumela, but is maybe triple that distance across the *yayla* and down to the monastery from the south—a trip well worth doing. There is now a motorable track connecting all the villages on the western side of the valley; the (fewer) settlements on the eastern side can be reached on foot.

FROM TRABZON TO THE GEORGIAN BORDER: LAZISTAN

Lazistan is the wildest stretch of the Pontic shore. The former Greek crust of settlement gives way to the Laz, a west Georgian people separated from their cousins in the Caucasus since Justinian I incorporated them into the Byzantine Empire in the sixth century. He confirmed one of the most enduring borders in the world, near where the tumbling Çoruh river reaches the sea between Batumi and Gonia, the "corner" where empires—some reckon continents—meet. Today the Laz, a term too loosely applied to anyone east of Rize, are firm Muslims, but their language, sense of identity, and clannishness survive, along with a swashbuckling black headgear. Turks elsewhere make Laz jokes, which run along the lines of Polish or Irish jokes and often involve the *hamsi* fish. Nevertheless, the Laz are known all over Turkey as pastry chefs, minaret builders, and general fixers.

Lazistan was a land of clan chiefs, and a bit of their history can be seen at **Sürmene Kastil**, the square, fortified *konak* of a chief named Memiş Ağa Tuzcuoğlu, which stands by the road 5 km (3 miles) east of modern Sürmene (itself 40 km/ 25 miles east of Trabzon). In 1817 Süleyman Paşa Hazinedar-oğlu of Trabzon encompassed the murder of Memiş, precipitating a vendetta that is not forgotten. There was an outright "civil war of Sürmene" from 1830 until Osman Paşa Hazine-daroğlu of Trabzon suppressed the Tuzcuoğlu clan in 1837.

Justinian may have founded the city walls of **Rize** (Rhizaion), 39 km (24 miles) east of Sürmene, but most of the surviving walls are medieval. Like Trebizond, Rize has lower and middle cities and an inland acropolis, much overgrown or overbuilt. From Rize a track leads 125 km (78 miles) south over high *yayla* to İspir, a fascinating place (with a giddy castle) on the Çoruh with a modest but clean municipal hotel. The hotel has no name: Just ask for it. Sometimes it doesn't have any water, either, in which case the village *hamam* (bath) will oblige.

On the coast east of Rize there are good restaurants at **Çayeli** (the **Hüsrev**) and **Ardeşen** (try the place run by Ahmet Gençahmetoğlu). Turkish Maritime Lines boats sometimes venture as far as **Hopa** (which has the basic **Cihan Oteli**), and the road reaches the Georgian border, near Gonia, at **Sarp**. At the moment only Turkish citizens and citizens of the former Soviet republics can cross at Sarp. Visas for European Community and U.S. citizens can be obtained at the former Soviet consulate off the southeastern corner of the Meydan. There is an irregular boat from Trabzon to Batumi. The whole situation, however, is so fluid that you'll probably want to consult the tourist office in Trabzon for the latest information.

In any case, you're going to run into plenty of "Russians"—that is, Georgians, Azeris, Armenians, Caucasians, etc.—who have flooded into Turkey's Black Sea Coast to set up "Russian" bazaars. The Trabzon bazaar alone is half a mile long. These bazaars offer items you never wanted at prices you cannot resist. Signs in Georgian script—last seen in Trabzon in the 13th century—are a bit spooky.

Over the border is **Batumi**. Ottoman until 1878, Batumi was the locale of the young Stalin's revolutionary cell in 1901 and the outpost of the now-forgotten British Army of the Black Sea in 1920. The local people are Adjars, Muslim Georgians, but Pontic Greek can at last be heard. There is a small folkloric **museum**, but make for the nearby **castle of Petra** (Tsikhedziri), Justinian's ultimate Laz outpost.

HEMŞİN AND MOUNT KAÇKAR

Hemşin is a mysterious land; always independent-minded, some Muslim *Hemşinli*s still speak Armenian and used to baptize—just to be on the safe side. To begin with, there are at least two Hemşins. Both are up the Fırtına (Stormy) river, which runs south from a point 6 km (3½ miles) east of Pazar on the coast east of Rize. The river divides at Çamlıhemşin (formerly Mikronkavak). This is a lively place, permanently inhabited, where Savaş Güney and his German wife, Doris, let rooms in their Sisi Pansiyonu at Şenyuva. The Büyük Dere (Big Valley) takes you southwest to the teahouse at Mollaveysi. Thence begins a journey best done on foot, first (half an hour) to Zil Kale (Bell Castle), unmistakable above the track and unmistakably haunted, and then (half a day) to the stunning castle of Varoş, below Baş Hemşin.

The Hala Dere takes you southeast from Çamlıhemşin to Ayder (formerly Ilıca), a once-idyllic and undeniably eccentric summer resort at about 4,600 feet, well used to foreign climbers (who now number about 500 a year). Hotels include the Ayder Hilton Otel & Restoran, named with tongue in cheek, where an indifferent bagpiper will keep you awake until the rakı runs dry. This is not the only snag. Indiscriminate bulldozing of roads to the thermal springs of Ayder, coupled with a massive hydroelectric project downstream, is conspiring to destroy the primeval forest. Go here while there is still time.

From Ayder a track (three hours' walk) takes you to the lower *yayla* village of Kavron, past beehives perched up in trees, out of the reach of bears. Thence you are on your own, blundering in the mist among cattle, until you catch sight of Kaçkar (12,916 feet), or, more often, its glacier below. It is emphatically recommended that you do not climb on your own, but with a group, such as Trek Travel (Aydede Caddesi 10, Taksim 80090, Istanbul; Tel: 1/254-6706; Fax: 1/253-1509) or entrust yourself to Savaş Güney at Şenyuva.

There are two basic routes (by foot) out of Kavron: either straight over the pass, down to Barhal and clean hotels at Yusufeli; or from Kavron west, skirting Kaçkar for about 18 km/11 miles (as the eagle flies) at about 6,560 feet, to Çat (where there is a shelter) and down to Varoş Kale and eventually back to Çamlıhemşin.

GETTING AROUND

Until recent decades, all major communications here were by sea. On land there was little wheeled traffic, and burdens went on the backs of beasts and women. The coast road was broken at most river mouths. The steamship companies that, from the 1840s, established regular services from Trebizond to Trieste or Southampton have long gone, but the Turkish Maritime Lines still runs a service along the coast, now leaving Istanbul late on Monday to arrive in Trabzon on Wednesday, returning to Istanbul early Saturday. It sounds like a good idea to turn it into a "cruise," and it is, for the ship allows you a few (sometimes very early or late) hours on shore at Zonguldak, Sinop, Samsun, and Giresun. You can watch the coast unfold, pick up the local gossip from Rize tea-planters back from shopping in Istanbul, and, indeed, shop yourself. (Sinop is one of the last places in Turkey where you can pick up a decently trained falcon.) The food on the boat is solid. But there are two snags. First, all this applies only to the first-class cabins. On the MS *Truva* (a car ferry) the plumbing is Trojan; the elderly MS *İzmir* is gentler, except in high seas. The first class is relatively inexpensive. Be warned of anything below deck; misery is no economy, and it is cheaper to go by bus. Second, the coastal service is booked months in advance. Booking passage is best done through Turkish Maritime Lines' agencies abroad, which have a certain number of cabins allocated to them, but note that Turkish Maritime has offices in *all* Black Sea ports; in Trabzon, Tel: (03) 11-20-18; Fax: (03) 12-10-04.

Flying is the obvious new alternative. Turkish Airlines (THY) has service to Trabzon from Istanbul and Ankara. THY's subsidiary, Türk Hava Taşımacılığı (THT) flies to Samsun and Rize. From the plane you can glimpse the coast through cloud wrack. It is the most expeditious way to reach the Pontus. But do not overlook a greater innovation.

The old coast road along the entire Pontus from Sinop to the Georgian border is now a great highway, tearing through old towns. Cars can be rented in Trabzon and Samsun, but the road is dominated by every variety of bus, from the busy village mini- or midi-bus (there's always a boy to find you somewhere to sit when you flag it down) to the long-distance coaches that thunder past—from Trabzon to Ankara and Istanbul in under a long day and night. Unquestionably the new kings of the Pontus are the majestic Mercedes coaches of Trabzon's own bus company, Ulusoy. The drivers of these monarchs of the road are liveried like airline pilots, while their cabin crews refresh passengers after every tea stop with eau de cologne—distilled from Rize tea, of course.

There are tourist information offices at Giresun, Gümüşhane, Ordu, Samsun, Trabzon, and Ünye; all are closed on weekends. If you catch one open on other days, you will find friendly service.

ACCOMMODATIONS REFERENCE
Rates given below are for double rooms, double occupancy, and represent projections for 1993. All prices are subject to

change, and you should attempt to check them before book-ing. Hotels on the coast generally charge more for rooms with a sea view, and some hotels raise their prices during the high season (June through September). Note that it may be difficult to reach hotels and pensions in remote areas, as telephone links are often fragile. When telephoning between cities in Turkey, dial 9 before entering the city code.

▶ **Ayder Hilton Otel & Restoran.** Ayder Kaplıcalar, Çamlıhemşin, 53760 Rize. Tel: (0568) 1376. $12.

▶ **Belvü Palas.** Amasra, 67570 Zonguldak. No phone. Rates unavailable.

▶ **Burç Otel.** Kâzımpaşa Caddesi 36, **Samsun**. Tel: (36) 11-54-80 or 11-54-81. $20.

▶ **Çamlık Motel.** Çamlık Mevkii, **Ünye**, 52300 Ordu. Tel: (373) 11-085 or 11-333. $30.

▶ **Çarıkçı Hotel.** 28100 **Giresun**. Tel: (051) 61026; Fax: (051) 64578. $28.

▶ **Cihan Oteli.** Orta Hopa Caddesi 7, **Hopa**, 08600 Artvin. Tel: (0571) 1897; Fax: (0571) 1898. $26.

▶ **Gedik Ali Turistik Tesisleri.** Maden Köyü, **Bulancak**, Giresun. Tel: (0517) 3481; Fax: (0517) 3431. $17.

▶ **Giresun Oteli.** Atatürk Bulvarı 103, 28000 Giresun. Tel: (051) 130-17; Fax: (051) 660-38. $18 (low season)–$20 (high season).

▶ **Gümüş Hotel.** Cumhuriyet Caddesi, **Gümüşhane**. Tel: (0531) 1574; Fax: (0531) 1197. $22.

▶ **Hotel Melia Kasım.** Gazi Caddesi 41, 57000 **Sinop**. Tel: (3761) 4210 or 4211; Fax: (3761) 1625. $25 (street view)–$31 (sea view).

▶ **Hotel Usta.** İskele Caddesi, Telegrafhane Sokak 3, 61100 **Trabzon**. Tel: (032) 121-95, 128-43, or 199-94; Fax: (032) 237-93. $40.

▶ **Nur Aile Pansiyonu.** Küçükköy Çamlı Caddesi 3, **Amasra**, 67570 Zonguldak. Tel: (3895) 1015. $15 (open Apr.–Oct. only).

▶ **117 Oteli.** Rıhtım Caddesi 1, 57000 **Sinop**. Tel: (3761) 5117. $12 (no view)–$16 (sea view).

▶ **Otel Horon.** Sıramağazalar Caddesi 125, 61000 **Trabzon**. Tel: (032) 111-19 or 122-89; Fax: (032) 168-60. $40 (low season)–$43 (high season).

▶ **Otel Kit-Tur.** Arif Bey Caddesi 2, 28000 **Giresun**. Tel: (051) 202-45, 202-55, or 230-32; Fax: (051) 230-34. $34.

▶ **Özgür Oteli.** Atatürk Alanı 29, 61030 **Trabzon**. Tel: (032) 113-19; Fax: (032) 139-52. $26.

▶ **Paşa Kaptan Oteli.** Çamlı Sokak 1, **Amasra**, 67570

Zonguldak. Tel: (3895) 1011. $12 (low season)–$16 (high season).

▶ **Sisi Pansiyonu.** P.O. Box 1, Çamlıhemşin, 53760 Rize. Tel: (0568) 1075. $40 (low season)–$52 (high season; all rates include full board).

▶ **Turban Büyük Samsun Oteli.** Sahil Caddesi 117, 55020 **Samsun.** Tel: (36) 11-07-50 or 11-07-54; Fax: (36) 11-07-40. $57 (low season)–$63 (high season).

▶ **Turist Otel.** Atatürk Bulvarı, **Ordu.** Tel: (371) 14273 or 19115. $18 (low season)–$32 (high season).

▶ **Vidinli Oteli.** Kazımpaşa Caddesi 4, 55100 **Samsun.** Tel: (36) 31-60-50 or 31-60-51; Fax: (36) 31-21-36. $38.

▶ **Vona Hotel.** Perşembe, Ordu. Tel: (3717) 1757 or 1973; Fax: (3717) 1848. $48.

EASTERN
TURKEY

By Gary Leiser

Eastern Turkey is the country's frontier, a sparsely populated transition zone between Central Anatolia and the Caucasus and the Middle East proper. It extends roughly 150 miles from Erzurum east to the border with Georgia, Armenia, and Iran. Covering an area larger than the Netherlands, this region is one of the most renowned marches in history, where mighty armies clashed in great battles that sealed the fate of peoples and empires. Even today the troubles across the border to the north, between Armenians and Azeris, and, to a lesser degree, to the south among Turkey's Kurdish population, reflect the sometimes turbulent history of this general area. A few tourist companies are currently avoiding eastern Turkey because of the difficulties in neighboring regions, but visitors to this region have encountered no problems.

As a gateway to the West, eastern Turkey has been coveted and fought over from ancient times to the present. Early in the second millennium B.C. the mysterious Hurrians streamed into eastern Turkey, apparently from the east, and eventually clashed with the Hittites. In the 13th century B.C. and frequently thereafter, the warlike Assyrians, a Semitic people, invaded this region from northern Mesopotamia. Their major adversaries were the Urartians, the successors of the Hurrians; in the ninth century B.C. the Urartians established the first important kingdom centered in eastern Turkey. Some two centuries later the Indo-European Armenians began to infiltrate this area and merge with the Urartians. They, in turn, were overwhelmed in the sixth century B.C. by invaders from Iran, first the Medes and then their cousins the Persians. Sub-

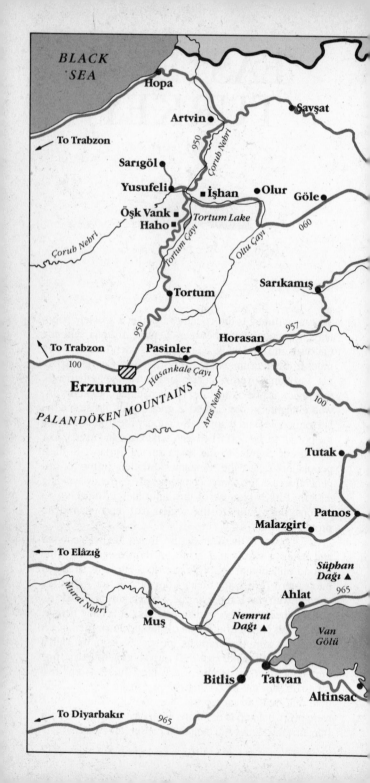

sequently, various Persian dynasties fought for control of eastern Turkey, especially against the Romans and Byzantines, for centuries.

The Arabs first captured this region from Byzantium in the seventh century A.D., and afterwards it changed hands many times. Among the new contenders were the Georgians (an ancient people from the Caucasus mountains), Turks, Mongols, and Russians. The harsh climate and unforgiving geography of eastern Turkey—an endless series of empty valleys, bleak plateaus, and gaunt mountains—accentuate its martial past.

Eastern Turkey's history as a great battlefield does not, however, detract from its sublime natural beauty nor imply an absence of historical and artistic treasures. Here, of course, is the famous Mount Ararat, the goal of Ark-hunters who have not done their homework. Not far away, to the southwest of Ararat, is ethereal Lake Van, stretching to the horizon across a lunar landscape. Next to its shore is the eerie volcanic caldron of Nemrut Dağı (not to be confused with the more famous Nemrut Dağı in southeastern Turkey), whose calm lake belies the violent forces churning beneath it. Eastern Turkey also contains countless lonely valleys and plateaus carpeted by wildflowers in the spring and browned to a trackless desert by the end of summer. These are the haunts of herdsmen and horsemen, who are frequently the only sign of life outside the few oasis towns and villages. Erzurum, eastern Turkey's largest city, possesses a wealth of 13th- and 14th-century Islamic monuments bequeathed by the most notorious of all nomads, the Mongols.

In striking contrast to these, and adding a surreal element to eastern Turkey, are the 19th-century government buildings of imperial Russia in Kars, constructed when this town was the center of a Russian military district. Much less intrusive are the serene churches, jewels of medieval Georgian architecture, tucked away in a few remote mountain valleys. Quiet, too, are the stunning ruins of the medieval Armenian city of Ani, sitting on a desolate bluff overlooking the ancient Silk Road and the modern border with Armenia. At Ani and on a tiny island in Lake Van, Aktamar, you will find masterpieces of Armenian architecture. At Ahlat, near Nemrut Dağı, is a vast medieval Muslim cemetery where for centuries tombstones and cenotaphs of delicate craftsmanship were erected, inadvertently creating a great museum of Islamic stonework.

More recent contributions to the art of eastern Turkey are the ghostly 16th-century fortress at Hoşap, east of the city of Van, and the early 19th-century palace outside Doğubayezit, a kind of latter-day Xanadu. Built by Kurdish chieftains, both command sweeping views from their mountain perches. Compared to the rest of the country, change has come slowly to eastern Turkey. This is typified by Bitlis, a picturesque city south of Lake Van that seems locked in a past era.

MAJOR INTEREST

Undeveloped frontier
Wild, dramatic scenery
Medieval Armenian, Georgian, and Islamic
   architecture
Kilims

Erzurum, Mongol monuments

Kars, imperial Russian buildings

Ani, medieval Armenian city

The route of the Georgian churches

Mount Ararat and Doğubayezit (palace of İshak Paşa)

Lake Van
City of Van
Environs of the city of Van: Hoşap castle, Aktamar
   island
The southwestern shore: Ahlat cemetery, Nemrut
   Dağı, picturesque Bitlis

The special attractions of eastern Turkey are not easily accessible. This part of the country is for the adventurous traveller, the hardy sort who can forgo certain amenities and accommodate the unexpected. In fact, this area has been opened to modern tourism for little more than a decade. Although its roads are improving and it now has a few comfortable hotels, eastern Turkey is not for the timid or, as one experienced tour leader puts it, "for sissies." But if you're the type who's sorry to have missed serving on the Northwest Frontier with the Khyber Rifles, for example, or who sees yourself as a latter-day Sir Richard Burton—or if you are simply captivated by isolated and undeveloped worlds, eastern Turkey will more than reward you for the hardships you endure.

For visitors, eastern Turkey can be conveniently divided into northern and southern sections. The northern section forms a rough triangle whose corners are Erzurum, which is the main point of departure, Kars to the northeast, and Artvin to the north. The southern section contains Mount Ararat and Lake Van and its environs. At least ten days are required to see both sections following the itineraries described below. In order to save time, most tour groups bypass the area north of Erzurum and Kars—which is rather far from Lake Van but which lovers of Georgian church architecture will not want to miss—and concentrate on the south. Within a period of a week, they fly to Erzurum, then go by bus to Kars and Ani, then continue by bus to Mount Ararat and Doğubayezit, and finally arrive at the city of Van, from which they make their return flight.

If you are not travelling with an organized tour, you can rent a car (preferably a sturdy vehicle with good tires, four-wheel drive, and high clearance) in Erzurum (or hire a taxi in Artvin) to explore the north. All the major places of interest in the south can be reached by bus or taxi.

ERZURUM

With a population of more than 350,000, Erzurum is the largest and most important city in eastern Turkey. A two-day journey by train or car from Ankara, it is more easily reached by plane. Erzurum sits at an elevation of 6,250 feet on the northern skirt of the Palandöken mountains, which keep their white crests well into the summer. The city overlooks a broad valley and the Karasu river, which is actually the northern branch of the Euphrates river and which rises in the mountains on the opposite side of the valley. Since ancient times this valley has been the main thoroughfare between Anatolia and the Caucasus to the north and Iran to the east. Moreover, most of the other major valleys in northeastern Turkey are connected with it in such a way that Erzurum lies at the neck of a great funnel. Geography has thus made Erzurum a great emporium from its earliest settlement. Unhappily, it has also made this city the objective of countless military campaigns, resulting in a turbulent history right up to modern times.

Erzurum is an old city. The Armenians, who arrived in the region in the seventh century B.C., referred to it as Karin, a name that may be of Hittite origin. This name was retained until A.D. 387, when Rome (Byzantium) and Iran partitioned Armenian territory and Karin became part of the Roman Empire. It was subsequently renamed Theodosiopolis, probably after Theodosius I, who negotiated the partition with Iran. To the Arabs, who conquered eastern Turkey, including Erzurum, several times between the seventh and tenth centuries, this city was known as Qaliqala—from another Armenian name—and later as Ard ar-Rum, "Land of the Romans." When the nearby trading city of Arzan was destroyed by the

Seljuk Turks in 1049, the Armenians who had lived there moved to Theodosiopolis, which then began to be called Arzan ar-Rum, or "Roman Arzan," whence the Turkish name.

The Arabs first captured Erzurum in A.D. 653 and used it as a base for raids into Byzantine Anatolia. From time to time the city changed hands between them and the Byzantines, with the native Armenian princes in the area playing a role. The Byzantines last held it from 949 until the Seljuk conquest, albeit with some Armenian and Georgian interludes. Not surprisingly, tenth-century Muslim geographers describe Arab Erzurum as a strongly fortified city and a magnet for Muslim warriors who came here from every land and formed war parties that raided as far as Azerbaijan. The booty they brought back to the city did much to account for its throngs of merchants. The same geographers state that the most important household article in the East was made there. They called it *qali,* after their name for the city. This word survives in modern Turkish as *halı,* or "carpet." One geographer, Ibn al-Faqih, says that Erzurum was one of the coldest cities in the world and adds, rather curiously, that soil from the grounds of a certain church in the city was an antidote for any poison. In the 11th century, Byzantine historians refer to the city as being rich and populous, and the famous Armenian historian Matthew of Edessa reports that it had 800 active churches.

Although Arzan fell to Seljuk raiders in 1049, Erzurum was not captured until 1080. It then became the capital of the Turkish principality of the Saltukids. In 1201 it was annexed by the Seljuk Sultanate of Anatolia, which held it until the Mongol invasion of 1242. During this early Turkish period, 1080 to 1242, Erzurum became one of the most important commercial centers in all Anatolia. Major trade routes connected it with Tbilisi, Tabriz, Trebizond, and central and southern Anatolia. The city's most important monuments— the Ulu Cami and the Çifte Minareli Medrese—belong to this period.

Erzurum's prosperity ended abruptly when the Mongols sacked the city and slaughtered or enslaved most of its inhabitants. Although the Mongols erected a number of impressive buildings, their rule initiated a long decline. In 1337 Ibn Battuta described the city as being mostly in ruins; in 1387 it fell to Tamerlane. Not until Sultan Selim I consolidated Ottoman control over eastern Turkey in the early 16th century and incorporated Erzurum into the empire in 1515 was the city revived. It subsequently became the Ottomans' most important marshalling point for military operations against the Caucasus and Iran. The Ottoman traveller and writer Evliya Çelebi visited Erzurum in 1640 and reported that its fortress had two iron gates, each two stories high. Inside the walls were 1,700 houses and outside were 70 Muslim and seven Christian quarters.

A significant boom in trade occurred in the mid-19th century, when steamships began to drop anchor in Trebizond on the Black Sea and that port became a major outlet for Iranian goods, which were brought there via Erzurum. But when Russia built a railroad from Julfa in Azerbaijan to Batumi on the Black Sea, most of this trade was lost. The coming of the Russians, who were expanding their empire south of the Caucasus in the 19th century, proved disastrous for Erzurum in more ways than one.

Since the time of Peter the Great (1682 to 1725), the czars had nibbled away at Ottoman territory. During the Greek War of Independence (1821 to 1829) Russia intervened against the Turks in the Balkans and the Caucasus. In 1829 they captured Erzurum but soon withdrew following the treaty of Adrianople. In 1877 the Russians declared war on the Ottomans again in order to intervene in the Balkans. They beseiged Erzurum for three months in 1877 and 1878. The Turks had built a ring of forts around the city in anticipation of another Russian invasion; the most renowned of them, Aziziye Tabyası, can still be seen 10 km (6 miles) northeast of town. Next to it is a soaring memorial to the soldiers and citizens who fell in the 1877 defense of Erzurum. Behind this memorial is the grave of a young woman, Nene Hatun, who "fought hand to hand like a man against the Russian soldiers."

In the treaty of Berlin, signed in 1878, the Russians agreed to withdraw, but they were allowed to keep Kars and other territory. They were to return once more, however, in one of the saddest episodes in Erzurum's long history. At the outbreak of World War I the city found itself in the middle of the eastern front and the goal of a major Russian offensive aimed at the heart of Anatolia. The Russians captured the city in February 1916 and held it until March 1918, when the treaty of Brest-Litovsk, following the October Revolution, took them out of the war. Before the Turkish army could arrive to secure an orderly withdrawal, Armenian revolutionary forces allied with the Russians massacred the remaining population.

A year later Mustafa Kemal arrived in the city as Inspector of the Third Army. Here he resigned his commission and was elected president of a congress that launched the struggle for an independent Turkish republic. The resurrection of Erzurum came slowly. With Western assistance, a master plan was prepared for a new city to extend west from what remained of the town. It was instituted in 1938. The following year the railroad arrived. Trade with Iran increased and the city returned to life. Erzurum still thrives on commerce with Iran—indeed, Iran's only overland route to Europe begins at Erzurum.

Erzurum Today

As the starting point for visiting eastern Turkey, Erzurum is most comfortable in June or late September. June is a time of bright blue skies, dazzling white mountaintops, and emerald green pastures. By September everything but the sky is brown or gray. The climate in summer is prone to extremes: Temperatures can reach 95 degrees Fahrenheit during the day but then drop to 40 degrees at night. Dust is a constant companion. Winter should be avoided except by very serious and doughty skiers. The cold is numbing, and severe snowstorms can isolate the city from the rest of the world. In the spring Turkey's Olympic ski team trains in the Palandöken mountains just south of town. This almost treeless range is snowcapped well into the summer. The primary skiing season usually runs from the middle of December to the end of April.

Built primarily of cement or gray and black basalt, Erzurum is a drab city, but it bustles with activity. Apart from being a transit center, Erzurum is the hub of a large, rugged farming area. Villagers, animal-drawn carts, and markets bursting with cereals and produce are common sights. Atatürk University in Erzurum, which was founded with help from the University of Nebraska, is famous in Turkey for its agriculture department. You can essentially see Erzurum in one day.

Erzurum has two good hotels, the **Oral Oteli** on the western edge of town near the bus terminal, and the more centrally located **Büyük Erzurum Oteli**. The Oral, the better of the two, was originally built to attract skiers and has a touch of rustic pine decor. Today it caters primarily to tour groups. Its rooms are snug and pleasant and its restaurant offers a fairly elaborate menu. The Büyük Erzurum has a Turkish bath and a rooftop restaurant with a good view of the city. The **Tufan Restorant** on Cumhuriyet Caddesi is run by a transplanted Laz from the Black Sea, which explains the interesting decor: large fish tanks with miniature waterfalls and the like.

The main street through the city, Cumhuriyet Caddesi, begins a few blocks up the street from the Oral. It takes about 30 minutes to walk east from this point to the end of the boulevard. Along this busy street are Erzurum's most famous monuments, its commercial center, and the bazaar. You can shorten your walk by taking a taxi to the first place of interest, the **Yakutiye Medresesi**, about halfway down the boulevard on the left.

This *medrese* (school of Islamic law), which faces a small park, was built in 1310 by the Mongol military governor Jamal ad-Din Yakut in honor of his overlord, the Mongol ruler of Iran, Öljeitü, and Öljeitü's wife. The most striking external features of the medrese are its 20-foot-high portal, which projects from the bare front wall, and its truncated minaret. Mixed with geometric motifs on the intricately carved gate are roses and other plants, stars, and birds. On each side of the portal, in high relief, is a palmette with carvings of two lions below and an eagle above. (Similar figures decorate the earlier Çifte Minareli Medrese down the street.) From the stone buttressing towers at each corner of the façade there originally rose a brick minaret. Only part of one survives, a masterpiece woven of brick and blue tiles. Inside, the remarkable dome drips with architectural "stalactites," which make it resemble the interior of a cave. An inscription in the southern vault gives the names of six villages that provided the revenue for the endowment of the Yakutiye. At the eastern wall of the school is a tomb holding an unknown occupant. The Yakutiye is not always open, so you may have to ask the watchman for the key.

Immediately east of the Yakutiye Medresesi is the **mosque of Lala Mustafa Paşa**. Designed by Sinan and erected in 1562 for the Ottoman conqueror of Cyprus, the mosque has an unusual minaret—short, thick, and built of alternating rows of red and white stone. Inside the mosque are two rows of 14 windows each. The tiles above the second row still bear bullet holes from the occupation of 1916 to 1918.

Walking east, you pass through the city's business hub to its main collection of monuments, the most celebrated of which is the **Çifte Minareli Medrese** (Medrese with Twin Minarets). The largest medrese in Anatolia, the Çifte Minareli sits on a knoll from which it overlooks what remains of the old city, mostly a jumble of dilapidated houses. It is generally dated to 1253 and attributed to Hudavand Hatun, the daughter of the Seljuk sultan 'Ala' ad-Din Kay-Qubad (Alaettin Keykubat). After capturing Erzurum in 1829, the Russians removed some of the inscriptions from this building and sent them to St. Petersburg; among them may have been an inscription giving the foundation date. From the time of the Ottoman sultan Murat IV (1623 to 1640) until 1846, this structure was used as a foundry for artillery pieces. It suffered considerable damage in the various battles over Erzurum. The stately but slightly unfinished façade resembles that of the Gök Medrese in Sivas (see the chapter on Central Anatolia, above) with its vegetal motifs and fountain to the left of the portal. At each side of the entrance is a palmette from the bottom of which emerge two snarling dragons. Above the palmette's leaves is a double-headed eagle. Set in from each side of the façade is a false tower that serves as a buttress. Directly above each side of the portal stands an 80-foot minaret composed of 16 ribs, each rib a mosaic of brick and blue tiles. Some of the columns of the arcade in the interior courtyard are accented with carving. The **türbe** (mausoleum) behind the school is the largest in Erzurum. Though empty now, it was apparently built by Hudavand Hatun. The dedicatory inscription and sarcophagi were removed and carted off in 1829 by the Russians.

To the right of the Çifte Minareli Medrese is the **Ulu Cami** (Great Mosque, also called Atabey Camii), the oldest mosque in the city. According to a now-lost inscription, it was built in 1179 by the local Turkish ruler Nasr ad-Din Muhammad of the Saltukid dynasty, which was subject to the Seljuks. It is an extremely simple stone building; the most interesting decoration is around the prayer niche. The mosque was repaired a number of times over the centuries, sometimes rather poorly. During the reign of Murat IV it was used to store hard biscuits for soldiers.

The narrow street between the medrese and mosque leads to a cluster of **four tombs** standing like great mushrooms in a garden, all dating from the 12th century. Only the one attributed to the Saltukid ruler Nasr ad-Din is of artistic interest. The others are conventional mausoleums built for unknown persons. The style of Nasr ad-Din's tomb is exceptional for this genre of architecture. Its lower structure is an octagon. On each bare, gabled face is a pair of small, blind, arched windows. Each pair of windows is connected by a strip of molding. Altogether the effect is rather Romanesque. Above the octagon is a cylinder capped by a domelike roof. Niches on the entry façade contain reliefs of snakes, bats, rabbits, eagles, oxen, and human heads, motifs that probably derive from the pre-Islamic Turkish calendar.

Across the street from the Çifte Minareli Medrese, curving uphill to the left, a road leads to the surviving walls of the medieval citadel. Inside is a very strange mosque in the shape of a tower-tomb, built by the Saltukids in the second half of the 12th century. A short distance from this mosque is a **clock tower** that was originally the mosque's minaret. The upper part of this brick tower collapsed centuries ago, but some time before the Crimean War (1853 to 1856) it was recapped and a clock was installed. The Russians removed the clock during their occupation at the end of the war of 1877 to 1878. The British, however, presented the Ottomans with a replacement.

A second street across from the Çifte Minareli Medrese leads downhill to a series of jewelry and antiques shops and the **bazaar** in the old city. Jewelry is made here from a local black stone polished to a high sheen and called, logically enough, *Erzurum taşı* (Erzurum stone). Other local products include thick, heavy-duty wool caps and socks. More refined are the women's wool wraps, usually brown or white, called *ehram*s. You will see many women wearing these ultra-light, ultra-soft shawls in the street.

KARS

If eastern Turkey were compared to America's Wild West, Kars would be its Dodge City—albeit with Russian imperial architecture. Horse-drawn wagons are common, and the main source of income derives from livestock and such animal products as cheese, butter, wool, and leather. Until recently Kars had no asphalted streets. A few were cobblestone, the rest dirt. Kars is still a dusty town. Gunfire is no longer heard in the streets, but from 1807 to 1922 Kars was frequently a battleground.

An excellent road connects Erzurum with Kars to the northeast via the town of Horasan, where a branch heads for Iran. The journey of 225 km (140 miles), less than three hours, takes you through a very pretty countryside of pine-covered hills, red, yellow, and gray volcanic ridges, and roadcuts sparkling with obsidian. About 15 km (9 miles) beyond the first town that you come to, Pasinler, there is a magnificent Mongol bridge. Called **Çobandede Köprüsü** (Grandfather Shepherd Bridge), it spans the Aras Nehri where that river forms from the confluence of the Hasankale Çayı and the Bingöl Çayı. This six-arch span dates from the end of the 13th or the beginning of the 14th century and was part of the old road between Anatolia and Iran. The decorative trim on the bridge is similar to that on mosques of the same period in Erzurum and Sivas.

About 62 km (38 miles) before Kars you pass by the small town of **Sarıkamış**, which has a few czarist buildings surviving from the days of Russian occupation. Sarıkamış has the only fairly comfortable hotels within a reasonable distance of Kars, where lodging is very basic. In Sarıkamış, the **Turistik Oteli**, whose restaurant serves simple but filling

Turkish meals, is located on Halk Bulvarı in the center of town. The owner enjoys providing his guests with personal service. In the woods on the hill above Sarıkamış is the **SAR TUR Otelcilik**, a modest but pleasant mountain inn frequented by tour groups. It has the best restaurant in the region.

As soon as you enter Kars, you will be struck by the citadel that looms above the city. This bastion symbolizes much of Kars's history as a fortress outpost. The origins of the city probably go back at least to Urartian times (eighth century B.C.), but it first gained major military and economic significance in the early Middle Ages, when it was fought over by Iranians, Byzantines, Armenians, and Arabs. King Abas (928 to 952) made Kars the capital of the Armenian dynasty of the Bagratids. Under Abas and his successors, medieval Armenia reached the height of its power, prosperity, and cultural achievement. Kars thrived on trade with cities as far away as Baghdad. In 1064 it submitted to the Seljuk sultan Alparslan and subsequently became part of the Saltukid principality centered in Erzurum. Kars remained in Muslim hands until it was captured by the Georgians in 1206, followed by the Mongols in 1239. Leveled by Tamerlane in 1386, the town was rebuilt and eventually became the major Ottoman base of forward operations in the Caucasus and Iran from the 16th through the 18th centuries. By the time Evliya Çelebi visited Kars in 1647, it had 8 cathedral mosques, 47 neighborhood mosques, 200 shops, and 3,000 houses. Many of these buildings were destroyed in a terrible earthquake in 1664.

Kars entered the world of European power politics in 1807, when the Russians marched on the city from Tbilisi, only to be repulsed. In 1828 czarist forces conquered the city and held it until 1830. When they withdrew, the majority of the local Armenian population went with them. Kars was left in ruins. In 1855, during the Crimean War, the Russians took the city again, despite a defense led, in part, by British officers. To commemorate the resistance, special medallions were struck in the Ottoman Empire and Kars was given the honorary title of Gazi, or "Warrior," Kars. As a result of the treaty of Paris, signed in 1856, Russian forces evacuated the city, only to storm it again in 1877 in a major offensive that penetrated beyond Erzurum. In the peace talks that followed, the Russians had to give up Erzurum but were allowed to keep Kars and large sections of Ottoman territory to the north and south. They then turned this region into a special military district, forced out the Muslim population, and encouraged Christians—Armenians, Greeks, Assyrians, and others—to settle here. Indeed, a systematic attempt was made to colonize this region with many people from their empire, including Germans and even Estonians as well as Russians.

Kars remained part of the Russian Empire until the treaty of Brest-Litovsk of 1918, when the Bolsheviks returned the territory to the Ottomans. Fighting over the city among Turks, Armenians, and Georgians did not end, however, until 1920, with the establishment of Soviet power in the Caucasus and the arrival of Turkish forces from other fronts. In 1921 treaties between Turkey and Soviet Russia and then between Turkey and the Soviet republics of Armenia and Georgia established the present border. There was one attempt to change it, in 1945, when Stalin demanded the cession of Kars and Ardahan, a town to the north, along with other concessions from Turkey in return for the renewal of a treaty of friendship signed in 1925. Ankara rejected his demands and began a process of courting the West, which led to Turkey's membership in NATO.

The 40 years that Kars was part of the Russian Empire left an indelible imprint on the city. The Russians, like the French in North Africa, actually built a new city next to the old (the remains of which were on the south side of the citadel) and laid it out on a grid plan. Kars is thus one of the very few cities in Turkey (ancient Greek and Roman sites excepted) whose streets are not a confusion of irregular lanes. As part of a large-scale construction effort, the Russians also gave "New Kars" dozens of "modern" buildings seemingly snatched from St. Petersburg: government offices, banks, shops, hotels, churches, and military quarters. A few of these buildings are still in use, but not for their intended purpose—the Turks are not sentimental about the Russian occupation. The small, attractive, Russian Orthodox cathedral near the stadium is now a gymnasium. The main cathedral in the center of town is a power station. Nearby, what may originally have been a hotel is now the Turkish Officers' Club. Behind the citadel, around the corner from where Kars Çayı flows out from a gorge, is a Russian fairy-tale house that apparently belonged to the Russian military governor. Today it is the residence of the local Turkish army commander and is, unfortunately, off limits.

Kars has two medieval monuments that have managed to survive: the Armenian **church of the Twelve Apostles** (closed to visitors), in the old part of town, and the citadel. The church, which sits next to a ramp that leads to the citadel, was begun by King Abas in 930. Although made of dark basalt, it is a very appealing structure. Its ground floor is in the shape of a cross, from the center of which rises a cylindrical drum capped by a dome that, in turn, is covered with a conical roof. The resemblance between this form of Armenian and Georgian architecture, both of which come from the same tradition, and Turkish mausoleums like the ones in Erzurum is obvious and suggests that Armenian and Georgian stonecutters helped build the Turkish tombs. The Turks themselves call this church the Kümbet Camii, that is, the "Tower-Tomb Mosque." Around the drum are twelve blind arches above which are carved the figures of the Twelve Apostles. The church was apparently converted to a mosque under the Saltukids, but in 1878 it was re-dedicated as an Orthodox church by the Russians, who also made a few additions to the building.

From the door of the church you can see an attractive 18th-century stone bridge and an 18th-century Ottoman bath, İlbeyioğlu Hamamı, that is still in operation. Directly above you is the **citadel**. The Turks treat it as a park and promenade to the ramparts on Sundays. Cattle and sheep sometimes graze inside. The foundations of the castle no doubt go back at least to the ninth century, but most of the present structure was completed in 1579, when the Ottoman general Lala Mustafa Paşa supposedly put 100,000 soldiers to work on it. Various repairs and modifications continued until the end of the Russian occupation. In 1853 it was adapted for artillery. The view to the east is splendid. In the spring you can see for miles across the treeless green plain to the snowcapped mountains on the border.

Before leaving Kars for Ani, you might visit the new **Kars Museum** on the eastern edge of town. Among the items on exhibit are a few finds from excavations at Ani. No hotel in Kars can be recommended with enthusiasm. If you decide to spend the night in town, try the **Yılmaz Oteli** at 14 Küçük Kazımbey Caddesi. It is spartan but functional. On the same street, at number 47, is the **Yılmaz Restorant**, probably the best in Kars. The local rice pudding, *sütlaç,* is delicious.

ANİ

Ani is one of the four or five most spectacular archaeological sites in Turkey, with respect to both its natural setting and man-made structures. It is 45 km (28 miles) east of Kars, right next to the border with Armenia (formerly the Armenian S.S.R.). Because of its location, visitors may be required to obtain a pass from the Directorate of Security in Kars. Inquire at the tourist information office in Kars concerning current regulations; Tel: (021) 323-00 or 384-52. The road to Ani begins at the junction near the Kars Museum.

A few kilometers from the site, the road drops down from a knoll and there, along the horizon, are the massive double walls of the medieval city. The road leads through a village to the main gate. A short distance before the gate is a parking area next to another gendarme post, where you may again have to show your pass. Until recently the Turks did not allow visitors to take cameras to Ani because of Soviet sensitivity about people photographing the border. They have relaxed this restriction but still have the option of asking you to leave your camera in your car. In addition, a gendarme may escort you through the ruins.

Although prehistoric remains have been found at Ani, it first appeared in history in the fifth century A.D. as little more than an Armenian fortress. From the eighth to the tenth centuries it was usually under Arab suzerainty. Its subsequent history largely paralleled that of Kars. When Abas made Kars the capital of the Armenian Bagratids in the early tenth century, Ani was included in their territory. His successor, Ashot III (952 to 977), transferred the capital to Ani in 961. The next ruler, Smbat II (977 to 989), built the great wall. Under Gagik I (989 to 1020) the city reached the height of its prosperity. A wonderful cathedral was erected, and Ani became the seat of the *catholicos* of Armenia. Islamic influence remained strong, however, as evidenced by a statue of Gagik (now in Yerevan) wearing a Muslim-style turban. Civil war and Georgian incursions led to a decline until the Byzantines incorporated the city in 1044. This respite was short-lived, for the Seljuks, under Alparslan, destroyed the city in 1064. The 13th-century Arab historian Ibn al-Athir claimed that Ani had 500 churches at the time of its fall. In 1072 the Seljuk sultan sold the town to the Muslim dynasty of the Shaddadids, who ruled from the city of Dvin to the southeast. In 1124 the Georgians conquered Ani and gave it as a fief to the Armenian family of the Zakarids, who were apparently of Kurdish descent. By the time the Mongols arrived in 1239, Ani was an insignificant town. A disastrous earthquake essentially put an end to it in 1319.

Ani sits on a pointed, triangular bluff at the convergence of two deep gorges. At the bottom of the gorge to the south flows a river, the Arpa Çayı, which forms the border. Across the wide, northern end of the bluff the great wall stretches from gorge to gorge. In this way nature and man have combined forces to create the site for a well-protected triangle-shaped city. Upon passing through the **Lion Gate**, you enter a vast field strewn with rubble. About a dozen freestanding buildings are scattered here and there. From the edge of the bluff you have an unobstructed view of the Armenian side of the frontier.

In addition to the **walls**, with their immense round and square turrets, you should especially take a look at the church of St. Gregory of Tigranes Honentz, the cathedral, and the church of St. Gregory Abugamrentz. A path through the site leads to all the major buildings. The **church of St. Gregory of Tigranes Honentz** lies a bit below the bluff at the eastern corner of town and overlooks the Arpa Çayı. It seems that Tigranes was a wealthy merchant who financed the construction of this beautiful church, which was completed in 1215, and gave it a substantial endowment. Inside are frescoes depicting scenes from the New Testament and the life of Saint Gregory the Illuminator, who brought Christianity to Armenia. On the exterior are carvings of plants and animals.

Following the rim of the bluff to the west, you come to the city **cathedral**. With the exception of the fortress, this is the largest building in Ani. Although its dome has collapsed, it is very well preserved and is one of the most outstanding examples of medieval Armenian architecture. Smbat II began its construction, but the work took a generation; it was finished in 1010 during the reign of Gagik I. The interior is very plain. There are four large supporting piers that form an aisle to a wide apse buffered by two-story side chambers. Around the exterior, which is the same color as the walls of Ani, run blind arches on slim colonettes. The cathedral has a number of serious cracks in it, so a major earthquake would probably bring it down.

Not far from the cathedral, at the edge of the bluff, you can see the octagonal minaret of a partly vanished mosque. The panorama from the top, overlooking Ani and barren Armenia, is wonderful. Far below are the ruins of a medieval bridge that once spanned the rushing Arpa Çayı. To the south, at the tip of the bluff, is the city fortress and beyond it, on an isolated pinnacle at the junction of the gorges, a 13th-century chapel. Both structures are off-limits.

On the western side of the bluff, overlooking the Alaca Çayı gorge, is the small **church of St. Gregory Abugamrentz**. In excellent condition, it is basically a domed cylinder with a conical hat. The interior is unembellished while the exterior decor resembles that of the cathedral. Built in the tenth century, this church was used in the following century as a funerary chapel by one of Ani's leading families. Other structures at Ani include a palace, baths, and, of course, more churches in various states of ruin.

The Russians undertook the first excavations at Ani between 1892 and 1893 and then systematically from 1904 to 1917. Work did not resume at the site until Turkish archaeologists began to dig here in the late 1980s. Before the Russians gave the site back to Turkey, they carted off their finds to Yerevan. The Russians discovered, among other things, that many of the monuments attributed to the Armenian Bagratids were actually much older, some dating from the earliest period of Armenian Christianity. They concluded that the Assyrian church was very important at that time, and that Byzantine, Arab, and Iranian influences were significant only later.

THE ROUTE OF THE GEORGIAN CHURCHES

From Kars you have the choice of going northwest to Artvin and then back to Erzurum, visiting several medieval Georgian churches en route, or going southeast to Mount Ararat and Doğubayezit and then on to Lake Van, which route is discussed later.

The northern route takes two or three days, depending on the number of sites you visit. Tucked away in the ravines and hills of the northeastern corner of Turkey are dozens of churches, monasteries, and castles. The most interesting buildings are the Georgian churches dating from the ninth to the thirteenth centuries, when this region was often part of medieval Georgia. Known to the ancients as Colchis, Georgia first developed as a kingdom in the Caucasus mountains in the fourth century B.C. It reached its greatest expansion and cultural flowering under Queen Thamar (1184 to 1213) and had a significant influence on present-day northeastern Turkey and the Black Sea coast until fairly recent times.

The architectural legacy of Georgia is one of the least-known features of eastern Turkey. A major reason for this has been the relative inaccessibility of the Georgian sites. They are off the main highways on difficult roads or hiking trails. Furthermore, there are virtually no services in the few towns and villages in the region, and the only lodging is in Artvin. Nevertheless, the effort to reach the Georgian churches can be an exciting adventure. In addition to the wonderful buildings themselves, you will see some of the most beautiful scenery in Turkey: forests and canyons frequented by bear, wild boar, and ibex, and charming wooden houses perched on steep hillsides.

For a taste of Georgian architecture accessible from a fairly good road, take the following route: First drive 14 km (8½ miles) north from Kars to the junction at Boğazköy and then take route 060 west to Göle. Follow 060 to Olur and finally to Artvin, a total distance of 269 km (167 miles). Some stretches of this road have many curves where the going is slow. In the spring and early summer the stretch to Göle passes through a carpet of endless green pasture. There are no trees or shrubs to break the wind's flow. In a few places lonely, shallow, glass-like lakes reflect the sky. Otherwise, nothing. You seem to be driving on the roof of the world. This is a horseman's paradise, a place to ride forever. It is, in fact, the only place in Turkey where you will encounter herds of horses.

From Göle to Olur you gradually lose elevation and the geography begins to change. Conifers appear as you enter a zone of greater rainfall. By the time you pass the turnoff for Olur you are following the Oltu Çayı, a tributary of the Çoruh Nehri. When you reach the Çoruh you find yourself at the bottom of a dramatic canyon sliced through hundreds of feet of sandstone by the churning river. You then follow the Çoruh's muddy waters north to Artvin on route 950.

Built on both sides of a road that zigzags up the side of a narrow valley formed by the Çoruh, **Artvin** is a good base from which to visit a number of Georgian churches. The town itself, which, like Kars, was part of the Russian Empire from 1878 to the end of World War I, has no monuments of interest, but it enjoys a refreshing setting among the pine trees and has a good hotel. Located in the center of town, the **Karahan Oteli** is very easy to find, as Artvin really has only one street. The view of the Çoruh valley from its restaurant and from many of its rooms is lovely.

Northeast of Artvin, in the hills north of the road to Şavşat, are many Georgian churches. The most interesting are Dolişhane, Opiza, and Porta, all within 30 km (19 miles) of town. **Dolişhane**, in the village of Hamamlı, is in the best condition of the three and is accessible by car on a rough track. A diminutive and enchanting church built in the tenth century, it has been used as a mosque and as a barn for storing fodder. **Opiza** and **Porta**, both in ruins, require hikes of an hour or two, for which the Karahan hotel can arrange a guide.

There are several other churches to the south of Artvin around Yusufeli. You can see a few of them en route to Erzurum, after getting good directions in Artvin, or you can make a day trip with a guide from the Karahan hotel.

Among the most beautiful buildings in the area are the

tenth-century churches of İşhan and Parhal. **İşhan** is in a village of the same name in the valley of the Oltu Çayı north of route 060 between Olur and Yusufeli, and can therefore be visited while travelling from Kars to Artvin. The village is 7 km (4 miles) into the hills from the main road and can be reached fairly easily by car. The İşhan church was once the seat of a Georgian bishopric. This remarkable structure, a section of which is used as a mosque, is built in the shape of a cross, much like a Western cathedral. Its exterior walls of yellow stone have many molded windows, in blind arches, and are decorated with reliefs of plants and animals, including a lion fighting a huge snake. Above the center of the transept is a domed drum with 16 blind arches. Its conical roof is striped with red and blue-gray tiles. The remainder of the church is covered with terra-cotta tiles. The interior is rather spacious despite four great piers supporting the drum. There are frescoes in the dome and elsewhere, but most were whitewashed when the church was converted to a mosque. A small baptistery stands next to the church.

The **Parhal** church is in the village of Altıparmak, 30 km (19 miles) northwest of Yusufeli, via Sarıgöl, on the Parhal river. Access is by a rough road. This structure, a basilica, known as the church of St. John the Baptist, is a very plain sandstone building. Its chief exterior decorative devices are rows of blind arches on each side. Windows are few and tiny, resulting in a dark interior. The high peaked roof over the nave and the lower roofs of the side aisles are covered with gray tiles. This is the best preserved of all the Georgian churches and is currently used as the village mosque.

On the stretch of the main road to Erzurum from the junction of routes 950 and 060 via Tortum, a distance of 117 km (73 miles) through gorgeous scenery, there are two more churches to visit. Before arriving at the first, you will reach the northern end of Tortum lake. Here its waters plunge 120 feet on the way to the Oltu Çayı, creating the most spectacular waterfall in Turkey. About 12 km (7½ miles) past the falls, turn right for the village of Çamlıyamaç, 8 km (5 miles) west of the main road. Towering above the village is **Öşk Vank**, the largest surviving Georgian church. This impressive structure, with the same plan as İşhan, was built between 958 and 966 by Prince David, who later, as King David the Great, made Georgia the dominant power in the Caucasus. Öşk Vank was the most important monastic complex in this area. The exterior of the church is decorated with very fine carvings of plants, animals, and the archangels Michael and Gabriel. Continuing south for another 8 km (5 miles) on the main road, turn right again for the village of

Bağlarbaşı, also 8 km (5 miles) into the mountains. This village is the site of **Haho**. Built of yellow stone, this church, like its contemporary Öşk Vank, is decorated with reliefs. Haho is currently used as the village mosque.

SOUTH FROM KARS
Mount Ararat and Doğubayezit

If you decide to go south from Kars to visit Mount Ararat and the town of Doğubayezit with its palace of İshak Paşa, a distance of 189 km (117 miles), the most direct way is to take route 070 via Tuzluca. The section between Digor and Tuzluca (54 km/33 miles) is mostly dirt, but quite passable. From Digor you enter a completely barren semidesert region and closely follow the Arpa Çayı, which forms the border with Armenia. The only sign of greenery is along the river and the few oasis villages in Armenia. Just before Tuzluca the Arpa and Aras rivers merge, and the latter henceforth forms the border. From Tuzluca the road runs east, skirting the frontier, and then turns south passing through Iğdır to Doğubayezit.

Taking photographs of the border is prohibited. You may also be stopped by gendarmes who will check your passport. From Iğdır the road ascends to the pass of Çilli Geçidi (6,922 feet), and you begin to have wonderful views of **Mount Ararat**. The great mountain is so high (16,920 feet) that it creates its own weather. Consequently the summit, eternally locked in snow, is frequently covered with clouds. Peeking from behind it is **Little Ararat** (12,880 feet), which is connected to the higher mountain by a narrow saddle. If you wish to climb Mount Ararat, special arrangements must be made with the Ministry of Tourism in Ankara. The point of departure for the ascent is Iğdır. Many companies, such as Trek Travel (see Getting Around, below, for details), now arrange group climbs that save individuals the trouble of getting permission. These climbs are done in the late summer, when there is less snow. The climb takes several days. Groups first hike to a base camp, staying the night in tents. The next day they climb to a second camp (horses carry the baggage), from which they reach the summit early the following morning.

Mount Ararat, whose Turkish name is Ağrı Dağı, is a great volcanic dome more than 60 miles in circumference. It last shook itself to life in 1840, destroying a nearby village in a powerful earthquake. Sulfurous gases continue to escape from numerous vents. The area around the mountain is a starkly beautiful uninhabited desert. In the Middle Ages conditions apparently were quite different: Both Muslim and Christian sources report that the area was wooded and full of game. Even lions prowled in the shadow of the mountain, and there were dozens of villages.

Mount Ararat is renowned, of course, as the landing place of Noah's Ark after the Deluge. In recent years one or two expeditions a year, composed of Turks and people from other countries, have set out from Ankara each summer in search of the elusive Ark, following in a long tradition of such seekers. Some expeditions have returned with tales of exciting discoveries, such as the ship's anchor or parts of the hull. Proof for such claims, however, has never materialized. There is, in fact, no hope of finding the Ark on Ararat (except, of course, for the miniature replica placed at the top by tour companies). This is not because of the harsh environment or numerous volcanic eruptions but because the explorers are on the wrong mountain.

Genesis 8:4 reports that the Ark came to rest "upon the mountains of Ararat." Medieval European Christians interpreted this phrase to mean that the name of the mountain on which Noah landed was Ararat. When they later discovered the highest mountain in the region, they logically assumed it was Ararat and so named it. (They did not realize that *Ararat* was the Hebrew word for the ancient land of Urartu. Indeed, traces of Urartian civilization were not discovered by archaeologists until modern times.) Down to at least the tenth century, Armenian and other Eastern Christians did not connect the present Mount Ararat with the Flood. To the Armenians who lived near the great volcano, it was known as Masik. Not until Eastern Christians came in contact with Europeans, in the 11th and 12th centuries, did they begin to identify Masik with the "Mount Ararat" of the Bible. Prior to the 11th century, Eastern Christians, as well as Jews and Muslims, identified the Ark's resting place as Mount Judi (the Koran specifically gives this name), which is near the Turkish town of Cizre on the Iraqi border. Judi (Cudi in Turkish) was on the northern rim of Babylonia, the region from which the story of the Flood arose. Writing in the 13th century, the Persian geographer al-Qazwini states that during the Abbasid caliphate (749 to 1258) pieces of the Ark still rested there. The Arab Muslim pilgrim al-Harawi (d. 1215), who visited Mount Judi, writes that he met a monk there who shaved him a piece of wood that he claimed was from the Ark. Indeed, Christians, Jews, and

Muslims made pilgrimages to Mount Judi, where today a ruined sanctuary can be seen.

Doğubayezit, near the foot of Mount Ararat and sitting on a barren plain at 6,500 feet next to a tributary of the Aras river, is the last truck stop before Iran. Its economy depends on the transit trade between Turkey and Iran and local agriculture and livestock, especially sheep. Although it's a small, dusty, and rather woebegone town seemingly in the middle of nowhere, Doğubayezit does have several comfortable hotels. **İsfahan Oteli** and **İshakpaşa Oteli** are both on Emniyet Caddesi in the center of town, while **Sim-Er Turistik Tesisleri** is on the edge of Doğubayezit on the transit road to Iran. The İsfahan has a Turkish bath for men, pleasant rooms, and the best restaurant in town. The İshakpaşa has rather plain accommodations, a bit like a dormitory. The Sim-Er ranks with the İsfahan, having a good restaurant and excellent views of Mount Ararat. It is the favorite of mountaineers.

Doğubayezit is a mixed Turkish and Kurdish town. There are approximately ten million Kurds in Turkey, primarily in the southeast, and several million more in the mountains of neighboring Iraq and Iran. Like most Turks, they are primarily Sunni Muslims, but they speak a language closely related to Persian. Their origin is obscure, but they were in upper-eastern Mesopotamia in the fourth century B.C. when Xenophon and the Ten Thousand marched from Babylonia to the Black Sea, and they clashed with him and his fellow Greek mercenaries. In the countryside a traditional trademark of Kurdish men is the wearing of a black-and-white checkered headband or turban. The rug shops on the main street in Doğubayezit are good places to look for Kurdish kilims, which tend to be slightly thicker and more heavy-duty than those made by Turks, and the colors, especially red and brown, often richer.

Doğubayezit's roots go back thousands of years, to Urartian times, but it has never been much of a town. It was first captured by the Ottomans in 1514 and finally incorporated into their empire around 1555. The Russians occupied it in 1828, 1854, 1877, and from 1914 to 1918. Western travellers who passed through in the 19th century described Doğubayezit as a group of houses scattered about in the shape of a theater on the slope of a mountain of red marble southeast of the town's present location.

Visitors today mainly come to see the **İshak Paşa Sarayı**. Visible from the outskirts of Doğubayezit, this palace rests on a rocky outcrop 6 km (3½ miles) southeast of town, above the town's former site. Its construction was probably undertaken by Hasan Paşa, who had been the Ottoman commander-in-chief of Georgia, in the late 18th century. It was completed by his son İshak Paşa II, perhaps at the beginning of the 19th century. By the middle of that century it was abandoned. The palace was actually a complex of many different buildings and had perhaps 360 rooms and halls. It was self-contained, like a small village: There were an audience chamber, barracks, medrese, arsenal, food depots, bakery, baths, harem apartments and other living quarters, a mosque, and even a prison. Architecturally, purists charitably describe it as eclectic, meaning it contains a hodgepodge of elements mostly from Anatolia and the Caucasus. The impression it gives is that İshak visited dozens of buildings over a wide area, picked out the elements he liked, and then had his masons throw them all together in his "dream house." Westerners generally love this palace because it fulfills their romantic notion of what an Oriental pleasure-dome should look like: a structure with the right mix of grand portals and walls, towers and turrets, kiosks and domes in a spectacular but desolate setting. Although Mount Ararat is not visible from the palace, the panorama of the plain and mountains to the north and west is truly magnificent. Sunsets viewed from the palace are glorious.

On a ridge to the northeast, and directly across the road that leads to the palace, are the remains of a **citadel** that can be reached by a path at the west end of its lower wall. The foundations of this fortress apparently date from the Urartian period. Also on this ridge are Urartian rock reliefs, an Urartian tomb, and a 16th-century Ottoman mosque.

LAKE VAN

South of Doğubayezit are the vast azure waters of Lake Van, around whose southern shore are some of the most historically interesting, artistically beautiful, and naturally enthralling sites in Turkey. Mountains block a direct route from Doğubayezit to the lake; consequently, you must go west on the paved but dusty and truck-choked road to Ağrı and then turn left for the town of Tutak. From Tutak a good asphalt road winds around the northern and eastern shores of Lake Van to the city of Van. The total distance is 325 km (202 miles), and, until you reach the lake, the scenery is quite bleak. South of Tutak you pass near Manzikert (near the town of Malazgirt), the site of the famous battle in which the Seljuks, under Alparslan, defeated the forces of Byzantium in 1071 and captured the emperor, Romanus IV Diogenes, opening the way for massive Turkish immigration into Anatolia and changing its fate forever.

You can see the blue and blue-green waters of Lake Van many miles before you reach it. After passing through Erciş, the road closely follows the shore for a considerable distance. Called Bznunik by the Armenians, Arsissa Palus by the Greeks, and the Lake of Ahlat by the Arabs, Lake Van (Van Gölü) is the largest lake in Turkey. At an altitude of about 5,600 feet, it covers 1,443 square miles, more than twice the area of the great Salt Lake (Tuz Gölü) in Central Anatolia. It could swallow Luxembourg with room to spare. There is no outlet, so the water is brackish with high concentrations of sodium carbonate, sodium sulfate, and borax. Everywhere the shore is barren. In a few places the water has evaporated and the residue, called *perek,* is used for washing. Despite the water's high mineral content, a species of fish known as *darek,* related to the carp family, lives in the lake. The 13th-century Muslim geographer Yaqut reported that he found salted *darek* exported as far away as Balkh (in modern Afghanistan). The greatest depths, to 330 feet, are in the southern part of the lake, and the water level frequently fluctuates as much as eight feet. In the middle of the last century, a sudden rise submerged Erciş and forced the construction of a new town.

On the northwestern shore, the peak of Süphan Dağı rises to 13,300 feet, and along the southern shore a steep range of mountains reaches elevations of more than 11,000 feet. Elsewhere around the lake, the land rises fairly gradually. To fully appreciate the beauty of Lake Van and the surrounding country, arrange for a cruise along its shores; you can do this at the Van wharf. Alternatively, take the inexpensive ferry across the lake from Van to Tatvan and back.

The City of Van

Van has one of the longest histories of any city in Turkey. Its creation is credited to the Urartians, an ancient people who are first mentioned in Assyrian sources from the 13th century B.C. Neither Semitic nor Indo-European, they may have emerged from various tribal groups in the area that gradually united to resist the Assyrians, who continually invaded from the south. In any case, around the middle of the ninth century B.C. they established a kingdom centered in the Lake Van basin. It became a major power and flourished until the beginning of the sixth century B.C., when it was destroyed by the Medes from northwestern Iran.

Because of the ever-present threat of invasion, the Urartians often selected rocky outcrops that were easy to defend for the sites of their cities. Records from the reign of Sarduri I (ca. 840 to 830 B.C.) first mention the great citadel rock on the southeastern edge of the lake as the site of the kingdom's capital. Known as Tushpa, it was clearly an important center. The surrounding plain prospered under King Menua (ca. 810 to 781 B.C.), who built a canal 46 miles long to bring fresh water from the mountains. Part of that canal is still used for irrigation. The modern city of Van has its origin in Tushpa but is now located about 5 km (3 miles) east of the citadel rock. (The ruins of the citadel rock are discussed below.)

In the seventh century B.C. the Armenians began to filter into Urartu, apparently from the west, and mix with the local population. Eventually they completely absorbed the Urartians. The Armenians became subject to the Medes and then the Persians. (The latter, in fact, gave them the name "Armenian.") Hellenism came briefly to the region in the late fourth century B.C. with its conquest by Alexander the Great and its rule by his successors, the Seleucids. The Persians returned in the first century B.C., this time under the Parthian dynasty, only to be expelled by Tigranes the Great (ca. 94 to 56 B.C.), who united Armenia in an independent state. This glory was short-lived, however, and within a few generations Armenia was reduced to a buffer state between the Romans and the Parthians.

Around A.D. 300 the Armenians were the first nation as a whole to adopt Christianity. Later, this helped make them an important factor on the eastern border of Byzantium. The partition of Armenia by Byzantium and Persia in 390 made most of Armenia, including Lake Van, part of the Byzantine Empire, albeit with a great deal of autonomy. In 645 the Arabs invaded eastern Anatolia and brought Armenia under their control. Arab suzerainty, with considerable local independence, lasted until the early tenth century. The Armenian Bagratids managed to assert themselves briefly from Kars and Ani, and a rival Armenian dynasty, the Artsrunis, established a kingdom around Lake Van called Vaspurakan. During the reign of Emperor Basil II (976 to 1026) most of Armenia was annexed by Byzantium.

Meanwhile, after Urartian times the town of Van remained in obscurity. Even after the Seljuks took it in 1064, other lake towns, Ahlat and Erciş, were the preferred capitals of local dynasties. Only after Van became part of the Ottoman Empire in 1548 did it become the leading city on the lake. The Ottomans found Van to be a convenient border post and staging point for campaigns against Iran. In the 16th century they set up an artillery foundry there and, in the following century, undertook major construction projects to expand the city. When Evliya Çelebi visited it in 1655, Van was the seat of a military governor. It had a strongly fortified castle (on the citadel rock, discussed below) with 300 janissaries, artillerymen, and armorers; a cathedral mosque; and seven neighborhood mosques. There were three Christian and seven Muslim quarters. When Napoleon's ambassador to Iran passed through in 1805, he guessed that Van had a population of 15,000 to 20,000. In 1835 the British consular officer in the city reported that Van was inhabited by 5,000 Muslim families and 2,000 Armenian families. Many Western visitors came to the city in the 19th century, despite its isolation, and archaeologists began to dig here as early as 1879. In 1895 fighting broke out between Armenian revolutionaries and local Turks and Kurds. In May 1915 the Russians occupied the city and the Muslims were expelled. Van briefly changed hands in savage fighting, but the Russians retook it in August and held the town until 1917. When the Turkish army reoccupied the city in 1918, it was completely ruined. Consequently, a new city was built a few miles to the east. Remnants of the ghost town of old Van can still be seen on the eastern side of the citadel rock.

Modern Van is a large, nondescript city of more than 125,000 people. Its economy is based on agriculture, mostly cereals, truck farming, and livestock. The severe climate, with temperatures that can range from 20 degrees below zero Fahrenheit in the winter to 100 degrees Fahrenheit in the summer, considerably limits agricultural development. Still, despite a fairly short growing season, a surprising amount of fruit is produced.

Most recently Van has enjoyed a booming tourist industry as thousands of visitors come every summer to see the lake and nearby archaeological and historical sites. Van has several of the best hotels in eastern Turkey, the most popular of which are the **Akdamar Oteli** and the **Büyük Urartu Oteli**. Both are in the center of town and have satisfactory restaurants with good service. The Akdamar has a good bar. The Büyük Urartu, one of the city's newer hotels, has the best facilities. The **Büyük Asur Oteli** and **Beşkardeş Oteli** are also comfortable, but neither has dining facilities. No restaurants outside the hotels can be recommended.

Van possesses many carpet shops, especially around the Akdamar Oteli, and is an excellent place to purchase Kurdish kilims. The selection here is wider and the prices lower than in Ankara or Istanbul. Van is also the place to find the Van cat, a special breed with thick white fur and eyes of different colors—one blue and one pink. Its purported love of swimming is probably not true. You may even find a few wandering about the major hotels.

A few blocks east of the Akdamar Oteli is the **Van Museum**, worth visiting for the regional kilims on display upstairs and the Urartian material on the ground floor and in the garden. The Urartians are renowned for their exquisite bronze work, including beautifully decorated armor, caldrons, and figurines. The most important Urartian artifacts, however, are on display in Ankara.

You can take a taxi from your hotel to the **citadel rock** that rises next to old Van. Stretching for about a mile east to west, this mass of limestone reaches heights of 250 feet above the plain. At one time it was at the edge of the lake, which has receded over the centuries. On the northwestern side a path leads to the top (you must walk). Along the crest are the remains of walls and towers that date to the Urartian period but that were virtually rebuilt by the Ottomans. Carved into the rock in several places are Urartian tombs and, more important, cuneiform inscriptions. The Urartian king Sarduri I left such an inscription on one of the towers describing the source of his building material. Argishti I (ca. 780 to 756 B.C.) had one carved around the door of his tomb describing his conquests. On a nearby cliff, the great Persian king Xerxes I (485 to 465 B.C.) placed a cuneiform inscription in three languages—Babylonian, old Persian, and Median—boasting of his achievements. It can only be seen with binoculars. Looking down from the south side of the citadel—from which the city was bombarded in 1915—you can spy the few silent and derelict structures of old Van. The most prominent are one Ilkhanid and three Ottoman mosques. Looking north along the lakeshore, you see long stretches of sandy beach. Watching the sun set over Lake Van from the citadel is a marvelous way to end the day.

Environs of the City of Van

Four sites of interest lie within an hour of Van, but it takes almost two days to see them all at a leisurely pace. The closest and most quickly visited are Toprakkale and Çavuştepe, two Urartian sites. Some 58 km (36 miles) to the southeast is the picturesque Kurdish fortress of Hoşap, and 38 km (24 miles) to the west is the splendid Armenian church on the island of Aktamar in Lake Van, which should by no means be missed. You can plan your itinerary over breakfast in your hotel—local honey on fresh bread, tea, and spicy Van cheese (local herbs are mixed into it).

Toprakkale is 3 km (2 miles) northeast of Van off the Özalp road. Perhaps founded by Rusas I (ca. 735 to 713 B.C.), it was the capital of Urartu from circa 694 to 673 B.C. It was abandoned in the sixth century B.C. after being destroyed by the Medes. Excavating here in 1889, British archaeologists found a temple, a palace, and a wealth of objects, tablets, and inscriptions. They shipped whatever they could to the British Museum. Toprakkale is near a Turkish military installation, so access is often limited. Before going there, it is best to check with the tourism office in Van, Cumhuriyet Bulvarı 127 (Tel: 061/120-18 or 136-75).

Çavuştepe, on a similar site, lies 22 km (14 miles) southeast of Van in the village of Asbaşin. On a narrow ridge overlooking the surrounding plain, this city (actually it was primarily a fortress) was founded in the eighth century B.C. by Sarduri II (ca. 755 to 735 B.C.), under whom Urartu reached its greatest power. Parts of the citadel, palace, and temple have been uncovered by Turkish archaeologists. The ruins are not particularly spectacular, and photography is restricted. The site guard, however, gives a lovely little tour, and the view from the ridge is wonderful.

After visiting Çavuştepe, continue on the road (route 975) to Hakkari to the **castle of Hoşap**. Located near the village of Güzelsu, 58 km (36 miles) southeast of Van, it sits alone in the midst of desolate hills above a stream of the same name. Several miles before reaching this castle, you will see it on your left as you come over a hill. Below the castle is a crenellated outer defensive wall that twists and coils over the broken landscape like an evil serpent. The haunting scene contains no sign of life. The fortress was probably the work of several local Kurdish chieftains. One of them, Sarı Süleyman Mahmudi, left an inscription claiming that he built the impressive entry tower in 1649. A dirt road leads right up to it. Inside are the remains of the keep, two mosques, three baths, a dungeon, and dozens of rooms. A military detachment may have been posted here until late in the 19th century, but the history of this spooky fort has been lost. The view from the walls is superb. Spanning the Hoşap river is a three-arched bridge, made of layers of black and white stone, built by the Kurdish chief Zeynel Bey in 1671.

The jewel of the Lake Van basin, and the goal of every visitor to the area, is the Armenian **church of the Holy Cross** on the tiny **island of Aktamar**. Rather less than half a square mile in area, this speck of land is 4 km (2½ miles) from the southwestern shore of the lake, about 15 minutes by boat. To reach the jetty from which the water taxis depart for the island, take the road to Gevaş via Gümüşdere, a local resort with a fine beach. About 5 km (3 miles) past Gevaş, and 38 km (24 miles) from Van, is the small jetty, opposite a restaurant. You might ask your hotel or the jetty restaurant to prepare a picnic lunch to take to Aktamar. In late July and August you might also take a bathing suit so you can swim in the lake.

The church of the Holy Cross was built between 915 and 921 by Gagik Artsruni, one of the rulers of the Armenian kingdom of Vaspurakan. In addition to this church, the island contained his residence and was surrounded by a wall. The *catholicos* of Armenia had his seat here from 928 to 943. The church functioned primarily as a monastery until modern times; in 1900 it lost its status as a bishop's seat and in 1917 was abandoned.

The slightly dappled stone church, in almost perfect condition, was built according to the traditional Armenian pattern—a cruciform ground floor above which sits a drum topped with a conical roof. Later, a chapel (13th to 14th centuries) and an arcade (14th century) were attached to its northern face; a bell tower (19th century) was added to the south; and a low, wide hall (1763) was annexed to the west. A short distance southeast of the church is a chapel erected in 1293. The church is actually quite small—the main area below the dome is barely 20 feet wide.

The glory of this building, however, doesn't lie in its shape or size but in its delightful and unmatched **exterior sculptures**. Around the church are five bands of decoration in high relief. At the top are animals and human faces, then scenes from everyday life (men and animals) woven into a continuous vine, then a series of isolated animal figures, then a series of large panels primarily depicting scenes from the Old Testament, and, finally, a narrow band of vines. Altogether there are 153 figures, including two cocks fighting, a bear eating fruit, Adam and Eve in the Garden, Jonah and the whale, the giant Goliath, a man working the fields, Saint Sergius killing a panther, and apparently even a portrait of Gagik himself. No other Armenian church has such a wealth of sculpture. Inside are a number of frescoes, mostly illustrating episodes from the life of Christ. None of these paintings, though, compares to the lively, three-dimensional scenes on the exterior.

On the north side of the church is a shady spot where you can eat your lunch while enjoying the history, drama, and frivolity portrayed on the façade and gazing across the waters to Süphan Dağı to the north. Behind the church, to the west, is a small hill. In the spring, the view from the top—a field ablaze with wildflowers, an enchanting church, a vast and deserted blue-green lake, a massive wall of snowcapped peaks swathed at their bases in green—is spellbinding.

The area around Lake Van contains many other Armenian churches; the tourism office in Van can help you reach them. The three largest groups of Vaspurakan monasteries, notably Kanzak in the village of Altınsaç, are in the mountains along the southern shore of the lake. Completely overshadowed by the church of Aktamar, and therefore unknown to tourists and rarely visited, is the 12th-century church on the island of Çarpanak. This island is just off the peninsula that juts out from the eastern shore of Lake Van, but there is no water-taxi service. If you wish to visit it, you will have to hire a boat from the Van wharf for the hour-and-forty-minute trip, one way. The church on Çarpanak, reminiscent of a caravansary, is larger than the one on Aktamar. Though the Çarpanak church is less interesting, you can have it and the island all to yourself.

The Southwestern Shore

Around the southwestern shore of Lake Van, between the island of Aktamar and the city of Ahlat, a distance of 143 km (87 miles), are the stone and mud-brick city of Bitlis, the dormant volcano of Nemrut Dağı with its beautiful crater lake, and an amazing medieval cemetery that is a veritable museum of Islamic stonework. Ahlat can serve as a convenient base for exploring this section of the Lake Van basin. Excellent accommodations are now available there at the new lakeside **Hotel Selçuklu**, complete with restaurant and beach.

Ahlat lies on the site of an Urartian city on the main invasion route from Mesopotamia into eastern Anatolia. As the Armenian town of Khlat', it was captured by the Arabs in 641. Although the Arabs gave the local Armenian princes considerable autonomy and Ahlat was briefly held by the Byzantines in the tenth and eleventh centuries, it was henceforth regarded as part of the Muslim world and an important administrative center. By the middle of the tenth century Ahlat had become a base for Turkish raiders. It was from this city that the Seljuk army of Alparslan set out to meet the Byzantines at the battle of Manzikert. In the 12th century Ahlat became the capital of a Turkish dynasty that ruled most of the Lake Van region. During the next three centuries it was held by various Turkish groups, Egyptians, Mongols, local Kurdish chieftains, and Iranians. In 1548 Süleyman the Magnificent made Ahlat a permanent part of the Ottoman

Empire, but by that time its importance was overshadowed by the city of Van.

From the time of the Arab conquest, Ahlat was a heterogeneous city. The Iranian traveller Nasir-i Khusraw, who passed through in 1046, said the people spoke Armenian, Arabic, and Persian. By the end of the 13th century Turkish had replaced Arabic. Evliya Çelebi wrote that the dialects of the people of Ahlat had a certain resemblance to Mongolian and Central Asian Turkish. At the end of the 19th century Ahlat was about two-thirds Muslim (Turks and Kurds) and one-third Christian (Armenians and Greeks), with a few Yezidis (followers of a syncretic religion composed of Zoroastrian, Manichean, Jewish, Christian, Muslim and other elements). In the 13th century the geographer al-Qazwini described Ahlat as a very populous city. It was, in fact, probably the largest city in eastern Anatolia after Diyarbakır, to the southwest. Following a devastating earthquake in 1246, 12,000 households supposedly emigrated to Cairo. The most convincing physical evidence for the large size and prosperity of medieval Ahlat is its famous cemetery, located between the modern town and the remains of the long-deserted medieval city.

About 2 km (1¼ miles) southwest of modern Ahlat, on a plain overlooking the lake, this **cemetery** is an open-air museum of Islamic stonecarving from the 11th to the 16th centuries. For acres and acres you see nothing but tombstones and cenotaphs plus a few scattered tower-tombs. On many of these monuments, every inch of surface is covered with decoration—vegetal, geometric, and calligraphic—making them small (and not so small) masterpieces of sculpture. Tilting this way and that, weathered and covered with lichen, they bear testimony to the wealth of generations lost to history. A few tombstones are crowned with double-headed dragons, but many have the shape of prayer niches or doors, gateways to the next world. Almost all the inscriptions are in Arabic; the exceptions are in Persian. They generally give the name of the deceased and the date of death, list a few of his or her personal attributes, and ask for God's mercy. Some provide more details. One tombstone belonging to a certain Nur ad-Din Abu 'l-Hasan ibn Shams ad-Din, for example, dated 1314, mentions that he was a warrior who died young, far from his children and loved ones, and asks whomever visits his grave to recite the opening verse of the Koran for him.

Scattered about the cemetery are nine pink basalt **mausoleums**. The most notable are (east to west) the Çift Kümbetler, Bayındır Kümbeti, and Ulu Kümbet. North of the road through the cemetery stand the **Çift Kümbetler** (Twin

Tombs), essentially small replicas of the Ulu Kümbet down by the lakeshore (see below). The smaller of the two was built in 1279 for the Mongols "Hasan Temir, the son of Bughatay Ağa," and "Esen Tekin, the daughter of Hasan Ağa." The larger, dating from 1281, belongs to Bughatay Ağa and his wife Shirin Hatun. On the other side of the village from these two tombs is the most original of all the mausoleums, the **Bayındır Kümbeti**, erected in 1492 to house the remains of Bayındır, a notable of the Turkish tribal confederation known as the Akkoyunlu (White Sheep) Turkmen. Its cylindrical drum is broken by a colonnade of stubby pillars. Finally, south of the road past the little **museum**, which contains Urartian and other objects, is the **Ulu Kümbet** (Great Tomb). Measuring 20 feet in diameter, it is the largest tomb in the lake vicinity. It belonged to a certain Shadi Ağa, probably a leading Mongol, and is dated to 1273.

On a low ridge in the ravine immediately northwest of the cemetery are the remains of an Urartian fortress that was destroyed in the earthquake of 1246. Southwest of this citadel are two bridges that may date from the 15th century. Much more spectacular is the **Ottoman fortress** on the lakeshore due south of the Çift Kümbetler. Begun by Süleyman the Magnificent in 1556 and completed by Selim II in 1568, the fortress is a rectangle, one side of which faces the lake. A moat once protected the other sides. Within the outer walls are two mosques and a smaller citadel enclosing a modern village. The view of the lake from any of the 13 towers in this fortress is wonderful. Another **castle**, with an even better view of the lake, is at Adilcevaz, 26 km (16 miles) north of Ahlat.

Ahlat itself is a featureless city of cement buildings. Its only attraction is the **mausoleum of the Kurdish lady Erzen Hatun**, erected in 1397. A conventional tower-tomb in perfect condition, it stands on the southwest side of town next to the considerably restored tomb of Sheik Najm ad-Din, built in 1222. The tomb of Erzen Hatun is a duplicate of the tomb in the Gevaş cemetery built for another woman, Halime Hatun, in 1358.

Between Ahlat and Tatvan to the south is a mountain called **Nemrut Dağı**, not to be confused with the mountain of the same name near Adıyaman, which is crowned with the colossal funerary sanctuary of Antiochus I of Commagene (see the Southeast chapter, below). Yet this mountaintop has its own special attraction, a volcanic caldron containing a freshwater lake formed after the last eruption in 1441. Although Mount Nemrut is 9,189 feet high, it rises very gradually and its summit is only 2,500 feet from the lake terrace.

The mountain can be climbed in about four hours, though there is a road that goes straight to the top. A taxi from **Tatvan** is the recommended means of ascent. From the rim of the volcano you'll have a view of its crater, five and a half miles across. In the deepest section of the crater, at an elevation of 7,372 feet, is a large crescent-shaped lake. If you decide to go down for a swim, take note of these words from a Turkish geologist: Its deep indigo waters, he says, "cannot fail to make you thrill with fear." Steep cliffs shoot straight up from the lake to the top of the mountain. Elsewhere the surface of the crater is broken by lava flows, cinder cones, crags, and pools; hot and cold springs bubble from the ground. You can easily spend a half day exploring this unspoiled geological spectacle. And, needless to say, on a clear day the rim of Mount Nemrut is an excellent place from which to take the measure of Lake Van. In Tatvan the place to stay is the **ASPA Denizcilik Vangölü Hotel Restaurant**, especially if you are taking the ferry across the lake. This hotel-and-restaurant is run by the same company that operates the ferry between Van and Tatvan.

Bitlis

A final point of interest is Bitlis, a city of about 40,000 people, mainly Kurds, 65 km (40 miles) south of Ahlat and 25 km (16 miles) southwest of Tatvan. Located in a deep narrow valley that connects Lake Van with Mesopotamia to the south, Bitlis has been the beneficiary of trade and the victim of invasions from the earliest times. Xenophon and his Ten Thousand Greek mercenaries passed through this valley on their way to the Black Sea. The origin of the city is unknown, although a legend ascribes its founding to Alexander the Great. An important center in the early history of Armenia, it was captured by the Arabs around 641. The history of Bitlis then paralleled that of Ahlat. After the ninth century the city became increasingly dominated by Kurdish tribes and dynasties. In the 14th century a local Kurdish dynasty, the Sherefids of the Rujeki tribe, made it their seat. By acknowledging the suzerainty of various powers, they managed to maintain autonomy until the Ottomans imposed direct rule in 1847.

Bitlis is at the confluence of two streams that form the Bitlis Çayı, a tributary of the Tigris. Just above the point where the streams meet are the remains of a triangular **castle** whose well-preserved walls and towers, in some places 100 feet high, probably date from the 16th century, although the foundations are much older. When Evliya

Çelebi visited the city in 1655, he observed that the citadel contained the palace of the ruler, a nasty type named Abdal Khan, and 300 houses. The khan liked to dispose of people by lofting them from the high eastern "bloody" tower. The city itself had 17 Muslim quarters and 11 non-Muslim quarters composed of more than 5,000 houses with earthen roofs and spacious gardens. Around the city spread countless orchards. (Even today Bitlis is famous for its pears and mulberries.) Despite the khan, whom he helped drive (temporarily) from the city in a pitched battle with Ottoman forces, Çelebi rhapsodized about the pleasures of the city, such as its wonderful breads and sherbets, and claimed that it produced leather of incomparable quality.

In Çelebi's day, the population was primarily Kurdish, with a large Armenian minority as well as smaller enclaves of Turks, Syrian Jacobite Christians, and Yezidis. The Jesuits established a mission here in 1683. In the following century an Italian priest worked for 18 years among the Kurds. American Protestants arrived to set up a mission in 1858. None of these proselytizing efforts seems to have had any effect on the Muslim population. Eventually the foreign missionaries devoted all their attention to local Christians. Toward the end of the 19th century foreign influence, some from the missionaries but especially promises of help from czarist Russia, encouraged local Armenian nationalist revolutionaries to rise against the Ottomans. The result was anarchy, with one community pitted against the other. When the Russians withdrew from eastern Turkey at the end of World War I, most of the Christians went with them. The loss of population and material damage suffered during the war reduced Bitlis to a small town.

Up to the 20th century, visitors to Bitlis found it a picturesque city. Although the setting has not changed, Bitlis has become a conservative, drab, dour city, somewhat cool to foreigners, and there are no tourist facilities. Yet Bitlis, like a "forbidden city," has a medieval mystique that can be alluring. The old section of town, clustered about the castle, has dozens of rust-colored mosques, medreses, tombs, and bridges from the late Middle Ages.

Two mosques in particular are worth a visit because of their antiquity, the Ulu Cami and Kızıl Cami. The **Ulu Cami** (Great Mosque) is in the market across the bridge below the southeastern corner of the fortress. Built in 1126 by the Artukids, a Turkmen dynasty that ruled from Diyarbakır, it is one of the oldest mosques in Turkey. The Ulu Cami is a simple stone building: a rectangle containing two rows of four heavy columns. It has no courtyard, and its most remarkable feature is the conical roof over the prayer niche. The minaret was built between 1492 and 1493. The **Kızıl Cami** (Red Mosque), on a hill about 50 yards northeast of the Ulu Cami on the site of an Armenian church, and contemporary with the Ulu Cami, is simply a small rectangle covered with an earthen roof and containing two rows of three columns. From Bitlis you can catch a bus to Ankara via Diyarbakır or go back to Van for a return flight to Ankara or Istanbul.

GETTING AROUND

Turkish Airlines (THY) connections link Istanbul and Ankara with Erzurum and Van. There are also THY flights between Erzurum and Van. The trains from Ankara to Erzurum (which continue to Kars) or from Ankara to Van are to be avoided unless you have plenty of time (at least two days each way). Furthermore, the trains to eastern Turkey are not up to the same standard as those travelling between Istanbul and Ankara. These trains, however, can be an adventure, especially the one to Van. At Tatvan it boards a ferry that takes it across the lake.

There is no real need to rent a car in eastern Turkey, although it is possible to do so in Erzurum. All the major towns and cities in eastern Turkey are connected by bus. Service is comfortable and relatively frequent. Local buses connect all the towns around Lake Van. You can reach the Aktamar jetty by taking a bus from Van to Gevaş and then a taxi. Hoşap is a bus ride from Van to Güzelsu, from which you must hire a taxi. In light of the ongoing fighting between guerillas of the P.K.K. (Kurdish Workers Party) and Turkish government forces in the southeastern part of Turkey, you might wish to avoid places off the main roads where tourists are not a familiar sight. Moreover, keep in mind that it is prudent to have a heavy-duty vehicle and that services are almost nonexistent outside the largest cities. Many Turkish travel agencies offer efficient and comfortable package tours to eastern Turkey. One agency, **Trek Travel**, specializes in "adventure" tours and seems to have the best arrangements for climbing Mount Ararat. Contact them at Aydede Caddesi 10, 80090 Taksim, Istanbul; Tel: (1) 254-6706; Fax: (1) 253-1509. Two other good outfits are **Aloha Travel Agency**, Cinnah Caddesi 39/8, Çankaya, Ankara; Tel: (4) 440-1201 or 440-1329; and **InnerAsia Expeditions**, 2627 Lombard Street, San Francisco, CA 94123; Tel: (800) 777-8183; Fax: (415) 346-5535.

ACCOMMODATIONS REFERENCE

Rates given below are for double rooms, double occupancy, and represent projections for 1993. All prices are subject to change, and you should attempt to check them before booking. Some hotels raise their prices during the high season (July through September). Note that it may be difficult to reach hotels and pensions in remote areas, as telephone links are often fragile. When telephoning between cities in Turkey, dial 9 before entering the city code.

▶ **Akdamar Oteli.** Kazım Karabekir Caddesi 56, 65100 **Van.** Tel: (061) 181-00; Fax: (061) 208-68. $50.

▶ **ASPA Denizcilik Vangölü Hotel Restaurant.** İşletme Caddesi 5, 13200 **Tatvan.** Tel: (8497) 1777; Fax: (8497) 4100. $20.

▶ **Beşkardeş Oteli.** Cumhuriyet Caddesi 164, 65100 **Van.** Tel: (061) 111-16. $45.

▶ **Büyük Asur Oteli.** Cumhuriyet Caddesi, Turizm Sokak 126, 65100 **Van.** Tel: (061) 137-53; Fax: (061) 213-10. $35.

▶ **Büyük Erzurum Oteli.** Ali Ravi Caddesi 5, 25100 **Erzurum.** Tel: (011) 165-28; Fax: (011) 228-98. $45.

▶ **Büyük Urartu Oteli.** Hastane Caddesi 60, 65100 **Van.** Tel: (061) 206-60; Fax: (061) 216-10. $60.

▶ **Hotel Selçuklu.** Zübeyde Hanım Caddesi 1, **Ahlat,** 13400 Bitlis. Tel: (8495) 1796; Fax: (8495) 1797. $45 (includes breakfast).

▶ **İsfahan Oteli.** Emniyet Caddesi 26, 04400 **Doğubayezit,** Ağrı. Tel: (0278) 1139; Fax: (0728) 2044. $50.

▶ **İshakpaşa Oteli.** Emniyet Caddesi 10, 04400 **Doğubayezit,** Ağrı. Tel: (0728) 1243. $26 (low season)–$32 (high season).

▶ **Karahan Oteli.** İnönü Caddesi 16, 08000 **Artvin.** Tel: (0581) 1800; Fax: (0581) 2420. $35.

▶ **Oral Oteli.** Terminal Caddesi 3, 25100 **Erzurum.** Tel: (011) 197-40; Fax: (011) 197-49. $45.

▶ **SAR TUR Otelcilik.** Sarıkamış, Kars. Tel: (0229) 1331. $30.

▶ **Sim-Er Turistik Tesisleri.** P.O. Box 13 (İran Transit Yolu), 04000 **Doğubayezit,** Ağrı. Tel: (0278) 2254; Fax: (0278) 3403. $45.

▶ **Turistik Oteli.** Halk Bulvarı 64, **Sarıkamış,** Kars. Tel: (0229) 2151. $20.

▶ **Yılmaz Oteli.** Küçük Kazımbey Caddesi 14, 36100 **Kars.** Tel: (021) 110-74. $38.

THE SOUTHEAST

By James Ruggia

Turkey's southeast remains the most Middle Eastern portion of the country in texture and ambience. Bordered by Syria, Iraq, and Iran, this remote region has the air of an ancient desert crossroads. Its wide-open spaces, dotted by nomad encampments and interrupted by highways travelled by buses and trucks, everywhere suggest the idea of passage. Whether you walk the busy streets of Diyarbakır and Şanlıurfa, hike out into the lonely desert-like spaces between towns, or scale the high mountain pastures of the Taurus range, you will experience simultaneous feelings of otherworldliness and the most intimate familiarity. Indeed the southeast seems to have come out of the pages of an illustrated Bible. Women beat laundry on river rocks, men on donkeys move through market throngs, and the sun bleaches every exposed stone to a brilliant glare and casts the blackest of shadows.

The expansiveness of the terrain tends to isolate and emphasize anything that breaks the monotony of the landscape. A singular castle or a walled city will dramatically dominate its environment, just as a motorcycle or a car can be heard even when it is little more than a dot on the horizon. Here, too, a schism in Western civilization's values comes into sharp relief: A deeply entrenched Judeo-Christian-Muslim heritage confronts modernism head-on.

Until the Persian Gulf War of early 1991 southeastern Turkey had managed to avoid much of the turmoil afflicting the Middle East. Despite the long-running strife between the Turkish government and the P.K.K. (Kurdish Workers Party) in this predominantly Kurdish region, the people here re-

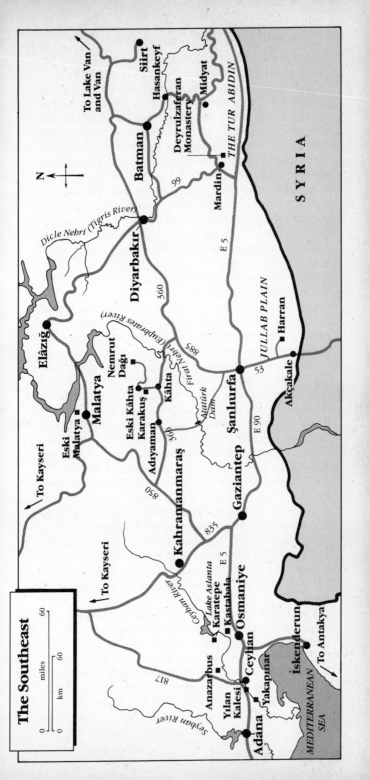

mained very warm toward visitors, interested in their foreignness and quick to invite them for a cup of *çay* (tea).

The city of Diyarbakır traditionally has been the scene of political strife. In recent years most of "the troubles," as they are called, had been centered near Mardin, south of Diyarbakır near the Syrian border, and in Siirt, about 80 miles due east of Diyarbakır. In the past, the routine violence between the P.K.K. guerillas and the Turkish army was of little consequence to the safety of visitors, but today visitors are urged to exercise caution and to avoid remote areas. The Gulf War opened—or exacerbated—many schisms in the community that have yet to heal. Travellers to the southeast are still safe in the cities. It bears mentioning that the vast majority of Turkey's Kurds have continued in their traditional friendliness toward strangers.

That said, travellers who are intimidated by armed soldiers will not enjoy this part of the country. The southeast is best enjoyed by those willing to rough it a bit. Most of the lodgings are spare and basic, fellow travellers rare; the distances between points of interest often necessitate long bus rides. The gain is great for those who can put aside minor annoyances for the chance to experience the landscape, cities, and sights. This part of Anatolia is studded with the remains of great civilizations and of peoples so remote that none but the most erudite scholars even know of their having existed.

But the southeast offers much more than old castles and the ruins of dead civilizations: Southeastern Anatolia is a reserve of communities that continue to live as numberless generations have lived before them. Great as they are, the area's ruins are a minor fascination in comparison to its people and the ways of life they pursue.

This part of the world has always been a petri dish for the development of religion. Monasteries of centuries-old Christian communities still function. Mosques are often built over the ruins of the sites of ancient mysteries, and there are still churches here whose liturgies are spoken in Syriac, a language very close to the Aramaic that Jesus of Nazareth himself spoke.

The southeast has also been a place where invading armies have advanced their various cultures since time immemorial: Assyrian, Persian, Roman, Arab, Seljuk, Artukid, Ottoman, and others. Fortresses and citadels, though spread out, are many, as are the caravansaries and markets that pay homage to age-old paths beaten in the dust between commercial points.

Today, Turkey's largest public-works project, GAP (whose Turkish name means "Southeast Anatolia Project"), near

Şanlıurfa, promises to return fertility to this part of the Fertile Crescent. The series of 22 projected dams (two have been completed) will be the foundation for development in agriculture, industry, and even tourism. Though the project is sure to improve employment prospects for 3.3 million people (the current average annual income is about $650), it's also bound to change it in ways difficult to imagine. The next few years may be the last during which we can peer through this special window on the past. Locals are predicting that in 15 years the population of Şanlıurfa will triple as industries spring up to exploit the dams' electrical potential.

MAJOR INTEREST

History of various civilizations and tribal cultures
Dramatic landscapes, both mountainous and flat
Ancient monasteries and churches
Markets of all major cities
An unspoiled Middle Eastern feel
Ways of life older than the Bible

Nemrut Dağı: colossal statues
Şanlıurfa: Pools of Abraham
Harran: beehive-like homes and ruins
Mardin: citadel and neighborhood of guilds
Diyarbakır: ancient Roman walls, one of the oldest
    mosques in Anatolia, and the Tigris river

There are several ways of organizing a trip to the southeast. You can fly directly into Van or Malatya to the north, Diyarbakır to the east, or Adana to the west. Buses file into these cities from points all over Turkey, but because most travellers will be headed in from the Mediterranean coast, from Antalya and other port towns, we'll follow a route that moves east from the first major city along the way, Adana. East of Adana, we visit a trilogy of sites near Ceyhan, then go on to Gaziantep, from which we head north to the mysterious stone heads of Nemrut Dağı. From there we head south for Şanlıurfa, with its sacred pools and ancient bazaar, before journeying to Mardin—perched above the great Syrian desert. Finally we arrive at the ancient walled city of Diyarbakır.

Many of the attractions in the region require a bit of hiking through underbrush, so be sure to pack hiking boots with thick ankle coverings. The air in summer is blistering in the daytime and cool at night. Bring a visored hat, some high-protection-factor sunscreen, loose-fitting cotton clothing, and a sweater. If you rent a car, be sure to get one with a stick shift (four-wheel drive is best), as many of the sites are on rocky unpaved roads up steep hills and can only be reached in first and second gear. Bring your own film, as it's often hard to procure here, and a good thick book for the hours you'll spend in meager hotel rooms.

ADANA

With more than a million inhabitants, Adana is Turkey's fourth-largest city and perhaps the region's most diverse and busy. It presents a salad of the old and the new: Old mosques crumble alongside newer buildings, also crumbling. Adana, 440 km (273 miles) east of Alanya (for which see the chapter on the Central Mediterranean Coast, above), sits on the abundant plain of the Cilician delta, north of where the Seyhan and Ceyhan rivers empty into the Mediterranean, providing the area with a thick blanket of moist air and rich agricultural bounty. The fields of red earth surrounding Adana yield citrus fruit, bananas, tobacco, sesame, and especially cotton.

Though almost certainly the site of an early settlement, there are no written references to the city until the arrival of Alexander the Great. Adana's history thus lies buried beneath the tangle of wires and slapdash buildings of the modern town. The lone references to premodern Adana are a Roman bridge, a few Roman statues in the Archaeological Museum, and the classic look of the wooden Ottoman-period homes in the old quarter near the Ulu Cami. Much of the charm of the old quarter comes from the two-story scale of its old Ottoman homes, but unfortunately nothing has been done to preserve them.

The **Ethnographic Museum**, housed in a nicely restored church originally built by Crusaders, on a side street off İnönü Caddesi in the center of town, contains a few relics found in the Cilician plain. One exhibit illustrates the lifestyle of the Turkmen nomads who annually wander down out of the cold mountain *yayla* to winter in the lowlands. The museum's collection of kilims and carpets makes it a good stop for those interested in purchasing a carpet on the southeastern swing of their trip. A little knowledge of the traditions involved in the region's carpets will go a long way toward ensuring that your purchase is a good one. The museum also displays funerary monuments, weapons, manuscripts, household items, jewelry, and musical instruments.

Adana's **Archaeological Museum** (open daily 8:00 A.M. to noon and 1:30 to 5:00 P.M.) is on Fuzuli Caddesi, near the Seyhan river and the bus station. The nonspecialist will be able to live without its collection of Hittite, Assyrian, Babylonian, Hellenistic, Roman, and Byzantine artifacts, which are hard to concentrate on anyway, given the barrage of noise that swells the museum's galleries from the buses next door. But if you've gotten this far walk one block south of the museum to the **Roman bridge**, thought to have been built by Hadrian in the second century A.D. and rebuilt by Justinian I. In 1096 Godfrey of Bouillon led his host across the bridge en route to the Holy Land during the First Crusade.

The bridge, called Taş Köprü (Stone Bridge) in Turkish, with most of its original 21 arches still intact, is over 1,000 feet long. Each of the remaining arches seems to march to its own beat: Some are pointed, some rounded, and all are of different sizes. The bridge remains a major thoroughfare, with a steady line of traffic headed east toward Gaziantep. On warm days young boys gather at its base on the Seyhan river to drop a fishing line, as they have surely done for nearly a millennium.

The **Ulu Cami** (Great Mosque), an unimposing structure neatly tucked into the old quarter in the city center, has two entry portals, both striped in black and white marble. The mosque, the largest in Adana, dates back to the Ramazanid Turks. Adana was the capital of the principality of the Ramazanids, one of the many small Turkish states that controlled Anatolia after the collapse of the Seljuk empire in the 13th century. Even after the Ottomans had established their rule throughout much of the rest of Anatolia, the Ramazanid dynasty remained in power here. Built by the Ramazanid ruler Halil Bey during his long reign (1507 to 1541), the Ulu Cami features some of Turkey's most beautiful tilework in the *türbe* (mausoleum) of Halil Bey, in the inner court of the mosque. (The tiles are from the famous ceramics works of İznik and Kütahya.) The stout minaret is topped by a crown with niches carved into each of the tower's eight sides.

Adana's **covered market**, just across the street from the Ulu Cami, features two 16th-century baths, the Çarşı Hamamı and the **Irmak Hamamı**, with daily hours for men and women. The tenders will give you a towel and a chance to sweat out your road weariness—a rejuvenating experience that leaves your skin radiantly clean, fresh, and tingling.

St. Paul's church, built in the early 20th century and tucked away in a neighborhood between the Ethnographic Museum and the bazaar, is the last functioning church in Adana. This remnant of the French occupation, with its distinctive clock tower, serves a small Catholic community. Across the alley from the church is a small sign for the Yeni Görgün Salonu. On Saturday nights this open-air salon is the frequent venue of weddings. If you're lucky enough to stumble into a wedding, don't be bashful; chances are you'll be more than welcome. Turkish weddings are public events. If you get hungry, have a spicy Adana *kebap* with chopped onions and fresh parsley at the **Rose** restaurant on nearby İnönü Caddesi.

Adana has always been a city of transit. We don't recommend that you overnight here, because the area's richness lies ahead, but if you must stay you'll find a full variety of hotels in Adana ranging in price from a few dollars up. The better hotels are in the middle of town—one such is the **Otel Seyhan**, a four-star establishment with a fine pool and a breezy terrace restaurant. The **Zaimoğlu Oteli** is a clean, modern four-star hotel with a relaxing terrace café. The best option, however, is the **Raşit Ener Turistik Tesisleri**, a mile east of the Roman bridge. This reasonably priced combination motel/campground has a large swimming pool as well as cooking facilities and a branch of **Dragon Restaurant**— the Chinese restaurant whose main branch is in the Istanbul Hilton. Though a bit pricey by local standards, the Dragon has an authentic Hong Kong chef whose cooking offers a nice break from standard kebaps and stuffed peppers; Tel: (71) 21-34-63.

EAST FROM ADANA

As you head east from Adana toward Gaziantep on the E 5 highway, you'll see the entrance to the U.S. Air Force base at İncirlik, so much in the news during the past two years. Farther on, there's a turnoff on the right for Yakapınar. This road snakes through some 15 km (9 miles) of fertile flatland at the foot of the Taurus mountains. Though you can't get to the Armenian castle of Yılan Kalesi, the next site discussed, this way, it's a marvelous drive with terrific views of the Medieval castle dominating the landscape from its craggy mount.

To visit the castle continue on the E 5 to **Ceyhan**, a nondescript backwater of a town but a good point of departure for Yılan Kalesi and two other archaeological sites, Anazarbus and Karatepe. The three sites, all difficult to reach, require a car. Visiting Anazarbus and Yılan Kalesi entails some hot, arduous climbs up through rocky and sometimes snake-infested brush. Nonetheless, all the sites are extremely rewarding.

It's up to you to decide where **Yılan Kalesi**, the so-called Snake Castle, got its name. Local legend has it that this was the castle of the King of Snakes, borne out by the coat of arms above the entrance depicting a curling snake. There's also a popular story that a certain Kurdish sheik, named Shah Meran, who had a reputation for saintliness, lived alone in this castle, where he charmed snakes. Or maybe the name simply comes from the snakes that make the castle their home. In any event, a prince, who later became King Leo II of Armenian Cilicia (r. 1198 to 1219), built it some 800 years ago. The castle, among the finer medieval ruins in the region, was briefly occupied by the crusading Knights of St. John.

Though you can drive up to the base of the castle (it's about 9 km/6 miles west of Ceyhan), it's still a relatively rough climb up to the battlements, especially the upward crawl through the tiny passage that leads to the entrance. The castle's eight towers rise over Ceyhan, offering a spectacular view of the lands surrounding the meandering river below.

Many of the homes of the villages on the approach road to ancient **Anazarbus**, about 32 km (20 miles) north of Ceyhan via route 817, are built from the stones of the ancient city. Anazarbus is thought to have been first settled by Assyrians and added onto by Romans, Byzantines, and Arabs. The ancient city, or what remains of it, is scattered across a broad, flat pastureland that butts right up against a towering cliff topped by a fortress. The field at the bottom is a popular site for local shepherds, whose flocks can often be seen munching away at the brush surrounding the lone standing arch, built in the third century A.D.

The site is poorly marked and overgrown, but it does contain the remains of walls, an elaborate gate, churches and baths, two aqueducts, a well-preserved stadium, an amphitheater, and a theater. By locating the theater you can find a set of stone steps to the fortress. The view from the top is staggering, the bronze-colored walls of the ancient city lying below in the felt-green fields. The fortress itself is well preserved and quite impressive. Scale the battlements and watch the local hawks soaring over the Cilician plain below you.

If you set out early you can spend a few hours at Anazarbus and make your way to Karatepe, a couple of hours away, for a peaceful afternoon in a lovely pine forest overlooking a beautiful (albeit man-made) lake. To get to Karatepe from Anazarbus, return to the main road and travel in the direction of Osmaniye; once you reach that town, a yellow road sign points the way to Karatepe.

Karatepe was the site of the Neo-Hittite city of Asitiwanda almost 3,000 years ago. The Turkish archaeologists who excavated the site have laid out in the open air the many sculptures and reliefs they uncovered. The reliefs show a lyric side of Neo-Hittite life. One relief shows King Asiti-wanda enthroned as a group of smiling musicians entertain him. The daily life of the Neo-Hittite world is rendered in scenes depicting families, musicians, merchants, and shepherds. Bring a picnic and figure on spending a few relaxing hours in the shade.

Eighteen kilometers (11 miles) west of Karatepe, near the town of Osmaniye, lies **Kastabala**, also known as Hierapolis, a Roman outpost where a few columns and the remains of an Ottoman castle still stand. The road to Kastabala (now called Bodrum) has no name, so ask the rangers at Karatepe for directions. The castle sits on a knoll surrounded by farmland. It's not worth going out of your way to visit Kastabala, but it is quite impressive from the roadside, set as it is amid rows of yellow wheat.

GAZİANTEP

A *gazi* is a defender of the faith, and this old town (200 km/ 124 miles east of Adana via E 90), known as Antep throughout the Ottoman period, earned the sobriquet "Gazi" in 1920, when the city mounted a staunch ten-month defense against the French, who were trying to lay claim to their slice of Turkey after World War I.

In addition to evidence of a settlement that dates to the middle of the fourth millennium B.C. (the mound on which the fortress sits), Paleolithic caves have been investigated recently. Gaziantep's better-documented history begins nearly 3,000 years ago when a group of small Neo-Hittite states fell to the Assyrian king Sargon II. The Assyrians crumbled under the ruthless Cimmerians, who were themselves fleeing conquest by the same Scythians who were made notorious by Herodotus. In 612 B.C. the Persians took the area, beginning a long succession of domination by conquerors including Alexander the Great and his successors, Romans, Byzantines, Arabs, Seljuks, Mongols, and finally Ottoman Turks, with a brief interruption by the Crusaders.

Nowadays a growing textile industry is giving the city a new life; the hills outside of town are being covered by the homes of laborers who have come to enlist in the mini-boom. The pistachio capital of the nation, Gaziantep also boasts wonderful grapes and olives. The city is famous for the making of a molasses-like grape preserve called *pekmez*. After lunch or dinner wander out to the northern part of town to the city park for a tea or coffee. The park is a popular spot among the local dons for smoking the *nargile* water-pipe.

A **citadel** rises on a mound overlooking the city. Originally built by Byzantine emperor Justinian I in the sixth century, it was captured by the Seljuk Turks some 900 years ago and later refortified by the Ottomans. Presently the castle is undergoing some restoration, but it remains in good repair. The long arched corridor just past the entrance conjures a glimpse of the castle's life at its zenith. There's a fine view of the city from the castle top.

The neighborhoods surrounding the castle are worth walking through. The buildings, clustered around narrow alleyways, are built of the same large stones as the castle. With children running around and women leaning out from second-story windows, neighborhoods like this do more to evoke the lives of medieval people than all the castles combined.

The **Archaeological Museum** (open 8:00 A.M. to 5:00 P.M.; closed Mondays), which is beyond the city park, has a large selection of Hittite artifacts. The museum's eclectic collection includes everything from a stuffed crocodile and the bones of a mastodon (in a pile) to Roman stelae. The highlight of the museum is a frieze of Antiochus I, king of Commagene, shaking hands with the god Helios, or Apollo, who is depicted with a corona circling his head.

Despite its historical interest, Gaziantep is not an especially pleasant place for an overnight stay. If you must stay here, choose the **Kaleli Oteli**, located in the town center on Hürriyet Caddesi. It has large, breezy rooms and a decent rooftop restaurant.

MALATYA

The Anti-Taurus mountain range runs north to south, dividing southeastern Turkey from the area around Lake Van and continuing all the way into Syria. Several hours north of Gaziantep via routes 835 and 850, Malatya is a sort of outpost for nomads who move their sheep into these high mountains for summer pasture. It's one of those largely untouristed parts of the country where a chance encounter might lead an open-minded traveller into close contact with these fascinating and rugged herdsmen.

Malatya is actually two towns—the modern town and Eski Malatya, the old walled city, which is about 10 km (6 miles) north of Malatya proper. Modern Malatya was established during Ottoman times: Every summer residents of old

Malatya would migrate here to escape the heat of the walled city, which is lower in altitude. A military campaign in the mid-19th century forced the Malatyans one year to winter in their summer homes, and the old town—which at its zenith possessed some 60,000 inhabitants—was gradually abandoned.

By regional standards, modern Malatya has a somewhat elegant air, with a few tree-lined boulevards. It's best to seek hotels off the main thoroughfares, however, as teenagers on motorbikes like to cruise them at night and make a great deal of noise in the process. The canal next to the **Archaeological Museum** (with Hittite reliefs and Ottoman weapons) is a pleasant place to enjoy a drink and write postcards.

The ruins of **Eski Malatya** lie crumbling amid wheat fields. Once an important medieval city, Eski Malatya is remarkable for one historical fact: Like other cities in the region it suffered one attack after another and was burned to the ground on more than one occasion, but in 1243, when the Mongols came invading from the east, the city's Christian and Muslim inhabitants actually stopped fighting one another and joined forces to repel the Mongols. (Their success was only temporary; the Mongols did capture the city a few years later.)

Have a look at the **Ulu Cami** (Great Mosque), built in the 13th century during the reign of the Seljuk sultan Allaettin Keykubat I. The architect, a certain Husrev (about whom nothing is known), may have been a Persian; the portal, especially, shows Persian influence on Seljuk architecture.

Just a few miles out of town lie the ruins of **Aslantepe**. For 30 years this mound has undergone a slow archaeological revelation at the hands of academics from the University of Rome. It's always fascinating to visit a dig in progress, and the archaeologists are happy to give the curious a quick tour. Seven different layers of civilization are interred at Aslantepe, ranging in time from 3500 B.C., the early Bronze Age, through 1200 B.C., the end of the Hittite era.

The archaeologists believe that the site is one of the oldest locales of urban life, and that the copper swords found here, which now reside in the Malatya Museum, are perhaps among the oldest metal swords in the world. Two rather terrifying figures, presumably deities, stare back at you like one of Paul Klee's nightmares.

Malatya is making a bid to become the gateway of choice to Nemrut Dağı (discussed below) and is the better option for those visiting the mountain who plan to continue northeast to Van. It's a somewhat cheaper and less touristy option than some of the bases discussed below: For about $35 you can ride in a minibus to the site, where you are assigned a spartan cabin (with cold water and a cot) at the top of the mountain; the price also includes a basic dinner before your departure and an equally basic breakfast on your return.

The brand-new **Malatya Büyük Hotel** features clean, carpeted doubles with private showers at reasonable prices. The hotel also has modest suites with minibars. Budget travellers will find clean rooms for about $13 at the **Merkez Otel**. Both hotels have central locations but are off the noisy main street.

The **Dinçarşlan Carpet Store** (Pak Kazanç İş Hanı, second floor) sells rugs and kilims wholesale to Istanbul retailers, and offers some good bargains.

In late July Malatya stages its annual **apricot festival**. No matter when you visit, be sure to pick up a bag of dried apricots, the best in Turkey.

NEMRUT DAĞI

The dramatic mountaintop site of Nemrut Dağı lies in the highlands between Malatya and Adıyaman. (Don't confuse this Nemrut Dağı with the other mountain of the same name; see Eastern Turkey, above.) The road from Malatya does not connect with the road to Kâhta on the other side of the mountain, so you'll save yourself at least some retracing of steps if you depart Malatya travelling back south along route 850, taking the turnoff at Gölbaşı east toward Adıyaman and the towns of Kâhta and Eski Kâhta. Travel to Nemrut Dağı itself can be arranged from Kâhta or Malatya.

Adıyaman has a good hotel, the **Bozdoğan Oteli**, whose swimming pool gives it the nod over the pensions in Kâhta, farther on. This new hotel does a fair amount of group-tour business and maintains high-quality service at a reasonable price; it features a gracious dining room and clean rooms.

About 6½ km (4 miles) north of Adıyaman sits the village of **Pirin**. In the fields beyond the town are the remains of some 208 Roman graves carved into the rock. A Roman funerary relief of a married couple is cut into the rock face over a tomb on the hill known as Karadağ.

If you like, you can travel direct from Adıyaman to Nemrut Dağı; most hotels offer minibus service. You may also want to consult the friendly tourist office, at Atatürk Bulvarı 41, for information on other interesting sites in the area.

Nemrut Dağı's spectacle—described below—is best enjoyed at dawn. If it's your intention to visit the mountaintop at sunrise, you'll want to stay in Kâhta or in one of the hotels on the road to the mountain. In **Kâhta** itself are a number of suitable pensions whose business is based exclusively on the Nemrut Dağı run; all offer their own minibus services to the summit. These services are highly recommended, as the 72 km (45 mile) drive from Kâhta to Nemrut Dağı is grueling—with the last eight miles or so over a very rough surface. The **Hotel Euphrat**, just 7 km (4 miles) from the summit, is a new property with a good kitchen. The food here and at the other newer hotels in the area is mixed Turkish and Continental. The Euphrat's swimming pool is scheduled to be completed soon.

To facilitate daybreak visits to the mountaintop, an entire system has evolved at the local hostelries that finds you being awakened at 1:00 A.M. so that you can arrive at the summit before the sun rises. The view is, it's true, breathtaking at that hour, but the problem is that every other tourist has the same idea, so in the early morning and again at dusk (another favorite visiting time) the mountaintop terraces resemble city playgrounds, crawling with shutterbugs and tour groups. If you do go early (or late), bring warm clothes; the mornings and evenings are always cold and windy on the mountain. Deep snows make it impossible to visit the site from October through April.

After all this introductory matter about how to get there, you may well be wondering what exactly Nemrut Dağı's sensational attraction is. It is perhaps the most astonishing monument in all of eastern Turkey. The now-toppled heads of the gigantic statues placed here by a truly vainglorious king more than 2,000 years ago stare out from the covers of countless guidebooks (including this one). Impressive enough in their own right, the sculptures might not have drawn so much attention were it not for their setting atop a 6,000-foot-high mountain.

Nemrut Dağı (Mount Nimrod) is topped by an enormous cone-shaped tumulus of apple-sized rocks painstakingly piled there by the worker drones of Antiochus I, king of Commagene from circa 69 to 34 B.C. The king's tomb, as yet undiscovered, may lie somewhere beneath this pile. Two huge terraces, connected by footpaths, are set on opposite (east and west) sides of the site, each holding a host of seated stone gods whose heads have fallen to the ground. (A third terrace, the north, contains the statue of an eagle and is basically the entrance to the end of the processional way from the valley.)

A monument this dramatic should bear witness, one would think, to a great presence in history, but Antiochus I was little more than a petty, megalomaniacal puppet of the Romans. His kingdom, Commagene, was a little "buffer" state that came into independent being during the first century B.C. It comprised territory running from Gaziantep to Adıyaman, and it was able to keep its fragile independence on the border of the much greater Seleucid state only very briefly, until Rome finally annexed it to the province of Syria.

The east and west terraces are basically the same; the minor differences in arrangement are due to the lay of the land: The east terrace has a rectangular layout, while the west is L-shaped. Both terraces hold a row of colossal statues of four seated divinities in addition to Antiochus, flanked at each end by smaller statues of a lion and eagle. The gods depicted are the result of attempts to syncretize Greek and Persian deities: Apollo-Mithra-Helios-Hermes; Tyche/Fortuna or Commagene; Zeus-Ahuramazda; Heracles-Ares-Artagnes.

Along the sides of both terraces are reliefs showing Antiochus's supposed ancestors, both Persian (back to Darius the Great) and Macedonian (back to Alexander the Great). (In front of each relief there would have been an incense altar.) One relief shows a lion with astrological symbols—the earliest Greek horoscope known. Each terrace also holds a large stepped fire-altar in the Persian manner.

Erosion, earthquakes, thunderstorms, and time have caused the colossal heads to fall. The heads have been set upright, and from chin to crown are roughly the size of refrigerators. An inscription on the throne of Antiochus describes the place as the highest point in his kingdom. "I, Antiochus, caused this monument to be erected in memory of my glory and that of the gods," the inscription goes on to boast.

The road from Kâhta to Nemrut Dağı leads you past a few other points of interest. **Karakuş**, about 10 km (6 miles) from Kâhta at the base of the mountain, is where the Commagene queens were interred. Three columns still stand, one with most of a Roman-looking eagle still perched on top. This eagle gives the site its name (*karakuş* means "black bird").

The nearby **bridge** over the Cendere river, rebuilt and dedicated to the Roman emperor Septimius Severus, is a spectacular example of the creative genius the Romans brought to engineering. Set in a steep-sided valley, the bridge is a beautiful structure to behold, its capped columns so surprising here, yet so visually at home.

Eski Kâhta, farther along the well-marked road to Nemrut Dağı, is a small village near Arsameia-on-the-Nymphaios, the some-time capital of Commagene. Above the village stands

Yeni Kale, a medieval castle built by the Mamelukes some 600 years ago. Across the river (the Kâhta Çayı) from Yeni Kale is **Eski Kale**, where lie the remains of the ancient city **Arsameia-on-the-Nymphaios**. There's usually a guide waiting to show you around the ruins here, bothering you for a few liras for the not very informative tour. The most interesting ruins are the remains of the *hierothesion* (sepulchral sanctuary) of Mithradates I Kallinikos, father of Antiochus. The sanctuary is a deep, rather macabre tunnel with steps descending to its eerie depths. The three reliefs here, of Mithradates, Mithra, and Hercules and Apollo, are quite powerful.

ŞANLIURFA

Just a few hours' drive from Kâhta, Şanlıurfa, or **Urfa**, as it was known until recently, is one of Turkey's most compelling cities. (From Kâhta, take the main road east for about 50 km/31 miles until reaching route 885, where you turn south for Şanlıurfa.) Remote as it seems today, "Glorious Urfa" (*şanlı* means "glorious") has found itself at the crossroads of trade, war, and religious activity throughout most of its long history. Şanlıurfa boasts the kind of legend, lore, and history that should place its name among the most renowned towns in the world, and yet it remains outside the standard itineraries of Turkey's growing numbers of tourists.

On first approach the city appears little more than a drab and dusty backwater, the hills at its outskirts clotted with ill-constructed, boxy houses and ragged roads. But as you penetrate the center of town, the cast of Middle Eastern characters in a variety of attires and with sun-wizened faces and clear eyes is startling. A lively banter energizes the street, and vegetables form the theme of the barker's praise and the buyer's derision.

The soon-to-be-completed series of dams on the Euphrates River will change this area forever. The largest, the Atatürk, is the third-largest earth-filled dam in the world and will return this region to the fertility it knew before its ancient irrigation systems were destroyed in the 12th century. Electricity production started up in mid-1991, and in 1992 Şanlıurfa and surrounding towns began receiving water for irrigation. Turkish officials are looking for this project to transform the Şanlıurfa region into the breadbasket of Turkey.

Two tall columns tower from a rise in the southwestern corner of town Known as the **throne of Nimrod**, these columns mark the site of the citadel, the city's oldest ruin. Though these ruins are what remain of a Crusader fortress built on a site that has been fortified for over three and a half millennia, the columns are Late Roman.

In the fourth century B.C. Alexander assumed the area around Şanlıurfa into his empire as he made his way to India. His successor Seleucus changed its name from the native Orhai (Orrhoë to the Greeks) to Edessa, after a city in Macedonia. After 132 B.C., Edessa was the capital of Oshroene, sometimes a Roman client kingdom and buffer state, at others a Roman province.

Christianity came to Urfa very early, in A.D. 200. Christian Edessa had its own patriarch; many of the city's inhabitants later embraced the Nestorian form of Christianity.

Urfa went back and forth between Byzantine and Persian domination until the Arabs arrived in the early seventh century to bring 300 years of relative peace to the area.

The second millennium A.D. dawned on an Urfa that was in a perpetual state of flux between Arabs, the newly arrived Seljuk Turks, the Armenians of the north, and the Byzantine Empire. Between invasions the city maintained its timeless role as a major stop along the way for east–west trade—a role that carries on to this day, with the city remaining a favorite stop for trucks carrying goods between countries farther east and Europe.

At the end of the First Crusade, the so-called Outremer (or Overseas) states were formed by the invading Christians from Western Europe. Urfa was taken in 1098 by Count Baldwin of Boulogne, who established the County of Edessa, the first of the Outremer principalities (the others were Antioch, Tripoli, and Jerusalem). The County of Edessa lasted half a century until 1144, when a Seljuk chieftain named Zengi returned the city to the Muslim fold after a 25-day siege. This so enraged the influential French churchman Bernard, Abbot of Clairvaux, that he vigorously promoted the Second Crusade, which was led by the French king Louis VII and the German king Conrad III. With no support from the Byzantines, who may even have conspired with the Seljuks against the Crusaders, the crusade collapsed in western Anatolia.

The city was later controlled in turn by Muslims under Saladin, followed 200 years later by the Mongols led by Tamerlane, who actually burned it down. The Egyptian Mamelukes twice briefly controlled the city, and the Ottoman Turks, in a campaign led by Murat IV, finally assumed power here in the 17th century.

The historical significance of this city can't be traced

simply by going from one grand site to another. In Şanlıurfa the various cultures are embedded in a mélange: They come at you out of a medieval arched doorway here or an old mosque there. Follow Atatürk Caddesi all the way to the southernmost part of town, for example. There you'll come upon a series of bone-white structures built around an intricate canal system looking like something you might have dreamed after reading yourself to sleep with a tale from the *Arabian Nights*. The **Pools of Abraham**, with their maze of canals covering a few hundred square yards, seem to float a few strata above reality, which takes the shape of tea stands, shaded paths and tables, white mosques, and slow-moving rowboats. The origins of the pools are associated with the prophet Abraham, who is as revered a patriarch in Islam as he is in Judaism.

According to legend, King Nimrod erected a stake at the foot of Şanlıurfa's citadel to burn Abraham, who had condemned the polytheism of the Assyrian tyrant. When the patriarch was thrown to the flames, Jehovah quenched the fire by opening the spring that feeds the pools to this day. The actual origin of these pools and their sacred family of carp is enshrouded, as is so much else in this town, in the mists of prehistory. It has been suggested that the pools were once sacred to the Semitic goddess of love, Astarte.

The thousands of carp living in the pools are all descended from one original school, and they are strictly protected. They are perhaps "the large tame fish that the Syrians regard as gods," mentioned by Xenophon in the fourth century B.C. Through good times and bad, the fish have never been disturbed or eaten. Local children sell plates of chickpeas for feeding them; a few tosses will attract a crowd of ravenous fish, bringing the otherwise tranquil surface of the waters to a boil. Interestingly, the Turkish name for the pools makes no reference to the biblical/koranic patriarch; the Turks simply call the place Balıklı Göl—Fish Pond.

The canals that connect the two main pools of the sanctuary enclose a park where several cafés serve basic food and drink. It's an enchanting place, especially in the month preceding Kurban Bayramı (the Feast of the Sacrifice), when pilgrims stop here along the way to Mecca. Families gather under trees sipping tea and coffee, and the mood of the place combines the relaxed air of a park with the reverent atmosphere of a shrine. Around the pools was built the **Halil ar-Rahman religious complex**, with two mosques, two *medreses* (schools of Islamic law) and tombs and cemeteries.

The waters that feed the pools spring from the base of

Damlacık hill, which is topped by the throne of Nimrod. The face of this hill houses three large **caves**; one of these is reputed to be Abraham's birthplace, another is a reliquary for one of the hairs from Muhammad's beard, and the last is a tomb for a religious figure named Dede Osman.

A cluster of mosques has been built around these caves, which serve as a center for Islamic worship and pilgrimage: the Halil Rahman Camii, a 13th-century structure; the 18th-century Ridvaniye Camii (and its associated medrese); and the Abdurrahman Camii and medrese. You may enter the cave where Abraham is said to have been born. The site is sacred, so you must observe the necessary decorum: Shoes off, and women must cover their heads. It's somewhat cramped inside the cave, and there's always a handful of devotees praying and sipping from the sacred spring.

A similar site, **Eyüp**, can be found 2 km (1¼ miles) south of Şanlıurfa on the road to Akçakale. A taxi ride costing just a few dollars takes you through the suburbs of the city and brings you to a mosque complex with a courtyard occupied by a grove of trees. Also in the courtyard, to the right, is a small kiosk that marks a cave (which you cannot enter) where, according to legend, the prophet Job (Eyüp in Turkish) endured seven years of his trials. Local parents often bring their hyperactive children to this shrine, in hopes that they will acquire the virtue of patience.

Back in the city, just off Atatürk Caddesi, not far from the pools, is the labyrinthine **bazaar**. The covered bazaar in Istanbul might be larger, but no bazaar in the entire country rings as authentic as Şanlıurfa's. It centers in a *bedesten,* at the core of the maze. Sit down and have a drink—you're sure to be offered tea—and watch the bustle about you. This is life in the medieval Middle East: donkeys hauling goods, coppersmiths hammering away at plates and ewers, potters going about their work in tiny cells. Many of the products sold at the bazaar—including, for example, tools and felt—are made using traditional methods. Last year, television and radio stalls made their first appearance. It's to be hoped that this 20th-century incursion does not represent the thin end of a wedge.

Starting from here you can wander around inside the covered bazaar or down any of the surrounding byways. The merchants will invite you to come in, sit, and look at their goods. The best buys in Şanlıurfa's bazaar are probably the copperware and the kilims.

Farther north on Atatürk Caddesi you come to the **Ulu Cami** (Great Mosque), whose broad minaret is topped by a clock. Because of its red stone this mosque is sometimes called the Red Mosque (Kızıl Cami). The mosque's courtyard is a peaceful if somewhat slapdash place. One side is faced by arcades while the other consists simply of the backs of adjacent buildings. A few cats can usually be found sleeping peacefully on the enshrined graves here. The medrese at the mosque's east side was, it is thought, built by the great Muslim leader Saladin in 1191.

After seeing the bazaar and the Pools of Abraham, take a few minutes to explore the residential side streets. Though people in this region lavish most of their attention on the interiors of their homes, they do decorate their doorways with calligraphy and paintings.

The new **Archaeological Museum** (open 8:00 A.M. to noon and 1:30 to 5:30 P.M.; closed Mondays) at the north end of town houses finds from sites along the Euphrates now being flooded by the waters of the new dams. One floor is given over to displays of some fine Ottoman wooden doors, carpets, jewelry, and lamps.

Şanlıurfa's kebaps are among the best in the country, especially the chicken (*piliç*). Try one with a little lemon juice. The *pide* (pita) bread here will make you laugh at those arid little loaves found in Western supermarkets. The **Sümer Lokantası**, on Köprübaşı Kışla Caddesi near the center of town, bakes its own *pide* in a wood-fired oven. With a top-notch staff, this is a warm and comfortable place to eat, frequented by locals and travellers alike.

As the headwaters of the Atatürk dam begin to rise, so will the quality of the hotels. The **Hotel Harran**, which has been the best hotel in town for ten years, has a Turkish bath. The hotel's modern feel and air conditioning provide a relaxing tonic after the sometimes overbearing heat and dustiness of the town. Another option is the air-conditioned **Turban Urfa Oteli**, which has a lovely wood-paneled lobby, clean rooms, and private showers.

The Şanlıurfa **tourist office**, in the center of town right off Sarayonu Caddesi at Asfalt Caddesi 4, can direct you to all the sites in the city or to the minibus tours of nearby Harran. Bus companies in Şanlıurfa also feature daily service to Nemrut Dağı, discussed above.

Harran

The biblical patriarch Abraham, whose footsteps can be traced throughout this region, took his family and left Ur of the Chaldees nearly 4,000 years ago, travelling west to Canaan and then, according to the account in Genesis 11:31, north to a fascinating little community of beehive-like houses about 45 km (28 miles) southeast of Şanlıurfa. The community is called

Harran, and Abraham dwelled here for several years. The region through which you approach Harran, the Colap (Jullab) plain, is dotted with little mounds—the remains of many communities long since vanished under the blistering sun. In this arid terrain the appearance of a brook or a well could bring communities together for millennia; its disappearance could cause them to disperse almost overnight. Harran is the exception that remained.

It's best to visit Harran on a half-day trip out of Şanlıurfa. On the road that heads south from Şanlıurfa (route 53), you will pass a turnoff to the left. This turnoff, which you needn't take, leads to Sultantepe, a mound in the midst of a plain where Assyrian clay tablets containing the text of the Epic of Gilgamesh were found. The epic, which relates the adventures of the Sumerian king Gilgamesh and his friend the wild man Enkidu, is nearly 4,000 years old and one of the most important pieces of ancient literature.

The first sight of Harran is not promising. It's really just a village, an outpost among outposts with a few interesting sights. The distinctive domes of the spare brick houses are made entirely of mud, as the area lacks timber. This domed style is typical of the homes on the border between Turkey and Syria; the domes keep the interiors cool in the summer and warm in the winter.

The little community of Harran is estimated to be 6,000 years old. It is an unusual community in that it remains an entirely Arab village. For the most part only the men speak both Turkish and Arabic; the women, Arabic only. In past years, much of the business here was done by smugglers trading sheep with the Syrians for coffee and other goods. Like Şanlıurfa, however, the area is expected to undergo considerable economic change with the activation of the GAP project.

Harran figured prominently in the age of Assyria's zenith. For the Romans, the city was the scene of a horrible defeat: In 53 B.C. the Roman general, financier, and member of the First Triumvirate, Marcus Licinius Crassus, campaigned against the Parthians in this part of Anatolia. (The Parthian Empire occupied the western part of the former Persian Empire.) At Harran, he unwittingly led his forces into a trap, and Crassus himself was captured and executed. Perhaps most famous for having put down the slave revolt led by Spartacus, Crassus was at his death the wealthiest man in Rome.

Harran was peacefully occupied by the Arabs in A.D. 640; its importance during the early period of Arab expansion is attested to by the fact that the caliph Marwan II (r. 744 to 750) made the town his residence and the capital of the

Umayyad Empire. Harran is surrounded by an old wall. The **Aleppo Gate** in this wall was rebuilt in 1192 by the great Islamic warrior Saladin, the redoubtable infidel foe of many a medieval European romance. The gate actually bears an inscription containing the name of Saladin's brother, al-Malik al-Adil. A Kurd by birth, Saladin achieved a mythical status in the West. Exceptional in war and chivalry, he earned the respect of friends and enemies alike. Compared with the brutish Franks whom he battled, Saladin and his army were members of a highly advanced culture. He was once reported to have called a truce in the middle of a battle to offer his enemies fresh horses and sweetened ices.

Before it was destroyed by Mongol invaders in the 13th century, Harran was home to an early medrese, which today lies in ruins. Standing in the midst of the courtyard of a ruined ninth-century mosque is a large, tower-shaped minaret.

The 10th-century **castle** beyond the wall is in good condition. You can easily scale the steps of the tower to the turret's top or walk through a well-preserved Ottoman caravansary in the castle's interior, its kitchen intact.

Harran was the site of the temple of the moon god Sin, and an important center of moon worship throughout antiquity; the temple was destroyed in the Mongol invasion in the 13th century. Julian the Apostate came here to pay his respects in A.D. 363, and the Sabian cult worshiped here well into the Middle Ages. The Sabians combined Greek philosophy with the star-worship and astrological science of the Babylonians. The planets were sacred to them, and they continued the practice of ritual sacrifice to the planets into the ninth century.

MARDİN

From Harran, return to Şanlıurfa for the night, then set out in the early morning for the town of Mardin. It's just a few hours' drive (187 km/116 miles east), and you can see it—along with one of the monasteries in the region—before heading on to Diyarbakır for a good hotel.

Mardin is perched like an eagle's aerie atop a high mountain on the northern rim of the Syrian desert. This cliff-top position made it virtually impregnable to all invaders except Tamerlane, who came in 1394. At the city's highest point, the ruins of the **citadel** squat alongside three large spheres that look something like large golf balls. These are sophisticated listening devices used to gather intelligence from the air-waves (Mardin is close to several sensitive borders). The interior of the citadel is closed to visitors.

Originally built by the Romans, Mardin was overrun by the Arabs in A.D. 640. It withstood sieges from the Seljuks in the 12th century, the Mongols in the 13th, and though it came into the hands of Tamerlane on his first siege, he failed to take it a second time in 1401 when his brother, whom he set up as ruler here, staged a rebellion.

Mardin is a tiny city stretching along one main road. When you enter Mardin at its western end you'll be in the area of the bus station. The main street, Birinci Cadde, can be walked from one end to the other in under 20 minutes. As you walk east you'll come to the town's only major hotel, the **Hotel Bayraktar**. The hotel is dingy and its staff unpleasant; the rooms on the south side, however, offer marvelous views of the desert. The hotel also has the only full-service **restaurant** in the city.

Continuing a couple of blocks east from the hotel, note on the left side of the street the elegant Arab house whose second-story façade is composed of three arches. The arches are echoed by three more arches set behind the façade. Today this building is divided among five families, making it one of the world's most ornately decorated tenements. The architect used every chance he had to add sumptuous fili-gree in stone around windows and doorways.

Still farther up the street, to the left, a long stairway leads to the **Sultan İsa Medresesi** (1385). This school of Islamic law is an interesting complex that houses both classrooms for religious instruction and the city's archaeological mu-seum. A solemn air pervades the halls of the medrese, with serious young students milling about. In the large class-rooms teachers sit intoning from open Korans to a handful of pupils. The Artukid style of the building makes it a worthwhile place to visit. Most impressive is the large carved portal at the entrance.

After returning to the main street, cross directly over into the maze of streets that contains the 12th-century **Ulu Cami** and the **Latifiye Cami**, built in 1371. The Ulu Cami's minaret was damaged by a bomb during the Kurdish rebellion of 1832; it has been rebuilt since. The Latifiye Cami features a beautifully carved façade of stone stars and a commanding view of the town and the flatland below.

Allow yourself time to wander the small quarter between the two mosques. This working neighborhood of maze-like streets brings the medieval world to life. Donkeys are chained outside many of the working quarters, housed in long rows of cells that open on the street. You won't find plates or vases—the work inside is sundry, not geared to a tourist trade; tanners, pipe fitters, and carpenters toil away at their necessary trades.

Mardin Area

A car or a taxi is needed to visit the **Deyrulzaferan monastery**, just a few kilometers east of town. Mardin has long been a Christian center (the town still contains seven functioning Syrian Orthodox churches), and the monastery's site has been a hub of unbroken religious activity for millennia. Syriac Christians made their home here in the fifth century, and long before that it was the site of a Persian temple to a sun deity. A series of deep caves line the far-off cliffs beyond the monastery. Those caves served as cells for early Christian hermits in the second century.

Deyrulzaferan is a fascinating place. Its name derives from the Arabic *Dair as-Safaran,* meaning "Saffron Monastery," so called because of the yellow stone of which it is built. Upon arriving you will be greeted and offered a tour around the grounds—and shown the phenomenal view south, toward Syria—by Father Abraham or Brother Gabriel. These two jovial men, who serve the 500 remaining Christians in the immediate area, will show you the interior of the monastery. The walls reveal a faded stone relief of the snakes sacred to the ancient god of medicine, Aesclepios. The 300-year-old Bible in the refectory is written in Syriac and Arabic. The Deyrulzaferan monastery has half a dozen rooms in which visitors can spend the night for a nominal donation. (Guests are usually invited to dinner in the refectory.)

A portrait hanging in the refectory is of Jacobus Baradeus, a sixth-century bishop of Edessa (modern Şanlıurfa) and the man for whom the Jacobites, or Syriac Christians, are named. Baradeus fell out with the Orthodox church in Constantinople for believing that Christ's divinity transcended his humanity. This belief, known as the Monophysite doctrine, was declared heretical by the Orthodox church, which held that Christ had a twofold nature, divine and mortal.

When Islamic invaders—Arab, Persian, then Ottoman— conquered the southeastern sector of Anatolia, the split became political as well as religious. From then until now, the Jacobites have existed as a Christian community marooned among Muslims. Today only a few thousand remain.

DİYARBAKIR

Diyarbakır, just a few hours north of Mardin, has been for centuries the strange capital of this strange region. There may have been a Stone Age settlement here. The Romans called the town Amida; for them it was a frontier defense against the (Sassanid) Persians. The emperor Julian the Apostate launched a campaign from here against the Persians; he died nearby in A.D. 363. Diyarbakır often served as a refuge for Christians unsettled by the border wars between the advancing forces of Islam. In 639 the Beni Bakr tribe of Arabs took the city and gave it its modern name, which translates as "the realm of the Bakrs." After the Arabs, the conquerors were many: Persians, Turkmen tribes, Mongols. Sultan Selim I at last conquered the city for the Ottoman Empire in the 16th century, and things quieted down.

The city's distinctive feature is the nearly four miles of Roman walls surrounding it. The oldest sections of the striking black wall, constructed of local basalt, were built by the Romans in the mid-fourth century. Of ancient ramparts, only the Great Wall of China and the walls of Diyarbakır can be seen from space. Of the 72 defense towers that originally stood along the fortifications, 67 remain. The walls were overhauled by the Seljuks in 1088 and the Artukids in 1208. Fundamentally Roman in plan, the city, like a legion encampment, has four major gates at the four compass points, connected by two main roads intersecting at the city's center. Though the city has expanded way beyond these walls, the town inside the gate is divided into four roughly even sectors. The best view of the city can be had by walking south of the Mardin gate about a half mile. From there you have a 360-degree panorama of the verdant banks of the Tigris, the city walls, and the beautifully harmonious medieval bridge crossing the river in the distance.

Though Western eyes may view Diyarbakır as a frontier outpost, its history puts it squarely in the center of Mesopotamia. The plains between the Tigris and Euphrates rivers formed a large wedge of rich land. Out of the life-giving waters here rose the Middle East's earliest civilizations. Unfortunately, Mongol invaders destroyed the intricate irrigation system that kept the area bountiful.

Industrial development in the last few decades has seen the city expand beyond its quasi-rectangle of ancient walls. This "modern" part of the city is a horrible blight of buildings that seem intended to store humanity rather than to house it. It's not uncommon to see young American military men strolling the city, as a NATO radar base where U.S. Air Force personnel are stationed is located just outside of town.

In the last few years the character of Diyarbakır has undergone big changes. A few years ago the city was much sleepier and provincial in its outlook. Today it's a boom town brimming with sharply dressed university students and workers returned from Germany with Western ideas. But those ideas, more and more, are clashing with the growing Islamic fundamentalism in the area and the ever-louder voice of Kurdish nationalism. Ideologically, the city is in a transition largely awakened by the Persian Gulf War.

Walking the neighborhood of the old **bazaar** is a people-watcher's dream. The clothing is the region's most flamboyant: The baggy pants are the baggiest; the women's patterns, bright everywhere in the region, seem brightest here. Drink vendors, looking like a cross between walking junk shops and scuba divers, move up and down the streets clanking cups or ringing bells and wearing large tin tanks on their backs connected via hoses to spigots at their waists.

Next to the bazaar and not far from the main square of the city is one of the oldest mosques in Anatolia still in use, Diyarbakır's **Ulu Cami** (Great Mosque). Built in 1091 by the great Seljuk sultan Malik Shah, this mosque's Friday prayers are among Turkey's most original and fascinating spectacles. When the muezzin calls the afternoon prayer, the whole city seems to converge on the mosque and the courtyard fills with the faithful. The beggars set up early, to get a preferred space at the gate at the mosque's giant courtyard. Vendors sell Korans, caps, and perfumes. The perfume sellers will sometimes appear suddenly out of the crowd and unload a thick mist of scent on you in order to get your attention.

Imagine how the mosque was in its prime, its courtyard green with grass and its fountains bubbling. The south and east walls of the courtyard are arcaded with Byzantine columns supporting the arches. In the center of the courtyard are two fountains and a shade pavilion. Men sit around the faucets of the fountains washing their feet and hands. This cleansing process, so central to Islam, embodies the mosque's appeal to the wandering merchants who refreshed themselves here after long treks across Mesopotamia. Originally the site of a Byzantine church (which in A.D. 639, with the Arab takeover of the region, became the world's fifth mosque), the Ulu Cami contains many details, such as its capitals and columns, that are Roman in origin. The mosque's great rounded portal is carved with two lions attacking two bulls.

Directly across the street from this gate is the arched

gateway of a **caravansary** built in 1550. The original doors remain, with imposing bolts holding the iron scales of the doors in place. Inside the caravansary are various shops. You might have a look in the carpet shops here: Thanks to Diyarbakır's proximity to several borders, these shops have a good selection of styles. You might also compare the deals you're offered here with those you'll find in the bazaar behind the Ulu Cami. A jewelry bazaar can be found one door south.

One of Diyarbakır's most distinctive buildings, the **Nebi Camii**, can be found in the center of town, where most of the hotels are concentrated. Striped in black basalt and white sandstone, this attractive structure was built in the early 16th century.

In early September the city hosts its annual watermelon festival. After the walls, watermelons are the city's most popular symbol, appearing on everything from cigarette packs to postcards. Giant watermelons, weighing as much as 150 pounds apiece, are a local specialty.

You don't have to wait for the watermelon crop to ripen to eat well in Diyarbakır. The city is lucky to have the unusual **Selim Amca Sofra Salonu** restaurant, where only one dish is served: *kaburga,* lamb ribs stuffed with rice and slowly baked for 12 hours. Reservations must be made at least a day in advance; Tel: (831) 216-16. This restaurant, the only one of its kind in Turkey, is a must.

Diyarbakır has a wide variety of hotels to choose from. If you want to try a night in old Diyarbakır, the brand-new *and* thoroughly old **Otel Büyük Kervansaray** is a good choice. The designers renovated a 16th-century caravansary to create this hotel. Try to get a ground-floor room—they are much cooler. The hotel has added what may be the finest swimming pool in the entire eastern part of Turkey. The price is high for Diyarbakır but the pool makes it a bargain.

For a more modest price you can get a clean, if spartan, room in any of a number of hotels along the Kıbrıs Caddesi, such as the **Aslan Oteli** or the **Dicle Oteli**. The prices of these hotels are quite low, making them popular with the merchants travelling through the city. The **Turistik Otel** across the square and around the corner on the Ziya Gökalp Bulvarı is also very nice, but not nice enough to justify its considerably higher prices.

GETTING AROUND

Turkish Airlines (THY) flies into Adana, Gaziantep, Malatya, and Diyarbakır. Every major city in the region has a bus station, and connections are frequent and efficient. Inside the cities you can choose between taxis, which are cheap, and *dolmuş*es, which are cheaper. As the towns in the southeast are relatively small, virtually all of the inner-city sites discussed can be visited on foot.

A rental car is all but compulsory for visiting Karatepe and Anazarbus. From Ceyhan you can visit Yılan Kalesi by taxi for a few dollars.

To visit Harran from Şanlıurfa, hire a taxi or arrange through the tourist office to take a minibus tour, which will also include a visit to the caravansary beyond Harran.

To visit the Deyrulzaferan monastery from Mardin the best bet is to hire a taxi from the city center.

ACCOMMODATIONS REFERENCE

Rates given below are for double rooms, double occupancy, and represent projections for 1993. All prices are subject to change, and you should attempt to check them before booking. Some hotels raise their prices during the high season (June through September). Note that it may be difficult to reach hotels and pensions in remote areas, as telephone links are often fragile. When telephoning between cities in Turkey, dial 9 before entering the city code.

▶ **Aslan Oteli.** Kıbrıs Caddesi 23, Dağkapı, 21100 **Diyarbakır.** Tel: (831) 139-71. $20.

▶ **Bozdoğan Oteli.** Atatürk Bulvarı, 02030 **Adıyaman.** Tel: (878) 139-99 or 127-16; Fax: (878) 136-30. $37.

▶ **Dicle Oteli.** Kıbrıs Caddesi 3, Dağkapı, 21100 **Diyarbakır.** Tel: (831) 230-68. $22.

▶ **Hotel Bayraktar.** 1'inci Cadde 457, 47000 **Mardin.** Tel: (841) 116-45 or 113-38. $15.

▶ **Hotel Euphrat.** Nemrut Dağı, 02030 Adıyaman. Tel: (8795) 2428. $6.

▶ **Hotel Harran.** Atatürk Bulvarı, Şanlıurfa. Tel: (871) 347-43 or 328-60; Fax: (871) 349-18. $30 (includes half board).

▶ **Kaleli Oteli.** Hürriyet Caddesi 50, 27010 **Gaziantep.** Tel: (85) 10-96-90; Fax: (85) 10-15-97. $42 (including breakfast).

▶ **Malatya Büyük Hotel.** Yeni Cami Karşısı, 44000 **Malatya.** Tel: (821) 114-00 or 338-50; Fax: (821) 153-67. $75.

▶ **Merkez Otel.** PTT Caddesi 16, 44000 **Malatya.** Tel: (821) 167-74. $13.

▶ **Otel Büyük Kervansaray.** Gazi Caddesi, Mardinkapı, 21100 **Diyarbakır.** Tel: (831) 430-03; Fax: (831) 377-31. $45.

▶ **Otel Seyhan.** Turhan Cemal Beriker Bulvarı 30, 01060 **Adana.** Tel: (71) 17-58-10; Telex: 62804 SYHO TR; Fax: (71) 14-28-34. $110.

▶ **Raşit Ener Turistik Tesisleri.** İskenderun Yolu Üzeri,

Girne Bulvarı, 01321 **Adana**. Tel: (71) 21-27-58; Fax: (71) 21-27-75. $50.

▶ **Turban Urfa Oteli**. Köprübaşı Caddesi 74, **Şanlıurfa**. Tel: (871) 135-20 or 135-21; Telex: 14314; Fax: (871) 131-04. $30.

▶ **Turistik Otel**. Ziya Gökalp Bulvarı 7, 21100 **Diyarbakır**. Tel: (831) 475-50 through 475-59; Fax: (831) 442-74. $90.

▶ **Zaimoğlu Oteli**. Özler Caddesi 72, Kuruköprü, 01060 **Adana**. Tel: (71) 11-34-01; Telex: 62875; Fax: (71) 11-68-11. $90.

CHRONOLOGY OF THE HISTORY OF TURKEY

Prehistory

The area within the boundaries of modern Turkey was first inhabited by hunters and gatherers during the late Pleistocene epoch, or Ice Age, which lasted from roughly 2,000,000 B.C. to 10,000 B.C. Human bones and implements dating from the Paleolithic era, or Old Stone Age, have been discovered at various sites, such as Karain cave near Antalya and Yarım Burgaz south of Istanbul. They reveal the presence of human beings as early as 200,000 B.C. The ancestors of modern food grains, sheep, goats, pigs, and cattle thrived in the Taurus range. By 7000 B.C., the beginning of the Neolithic period, or New Stone Age, these plants and animals were domesticated and civilization had begun to take root. The earliest evidence of agriculture and the use of hammered metal (ca. 7250 B.C.) has been found at Çayönü, north of Diyarbakır near the Tigris in the southeast. Between 6500 and 5700 B.C., at Çatalhöyük, south of Konya, there developed what may be the world's oldest urban center. Perhaps 1,000 dwellings were uncovered here, a few containing remarkable wall paintings, the earliest known so far.

During the Chalcolithic era, or Copper Age (ca. 5000 to 3000 B.C.), Anatolia entered a period of stagnation compared to Egypt and Mesopotamia, although fine pottery and metal tools were made. Important objects from this period were excavated at Hacılar near Burdur and Can Hasan near Karaman. A cultural revival began in the Early Bronze Age (ca. 3000 to 2000 B.C.), and city-states began to appear. A brilliant Early Bronze Age settlement was established by the first level of habitation at Troy, or Troy I (ca. 3000 to 2500 B.C.). The Early Bronze Age also witnessed the rise of Anatolia's first historic civilization, that of the **Hatti**, who had a major influence on the Hittites. The Hatti were present by 2500 B.C., but their origin is unknown and their language has not been related to any other. Their "state" apparently consisted of a number of small principalities, chiefly in Central Anatolia. Outside Mesopotamia, the Hatti are one of the oldest people known by name. Contemporary with the civilization of the Hatti and their royal tombs of Alacahöyük was the spectacular level II at Troy (ca. 2500 to 2400 B.C.), which archaeologist Heinrich Schliemann mistakenly believed to be the Troy of Homer.

The Hittite Period

The Hittites, an Indo-European people, seem to have descended upon Anatolia from the east and to have been gradually absorbed by the Hatti. Among the first people to perfect the war chariot, the Hittites created one of the greatest powers of the ancient world. Their state and distinct culture developed primarily in the region of the Hatti. The Hittite period as a whole is contemporary with the flowering of Minoan civilization on Crete, the rise and fall of Mycenaean Greece, and the Middle and New kingdoms of ancient Egypt.

- **ca. 2000–1750 B.C.:** Hittites enter Central Anatolia and begin to rule city-states.
- **ca. 2000–1700 B.C.:** Assyrian trading colonies are established in Central Anatolia. Their surviving cuneiform tablets are the earliest written records found yet in Anatolia.
- **ca. 1900–1240 B.C.:** Levels VI and VIIa at Troy, perhaps the Troy of Homer. Troy continues to develop as part of a separate civilization to the west of the Hittites.
- **Early second millennium B.C.:** Abraham, the progenitor of the Hebrews, lives in Harran, in southeastern Anatolia.
- **ca. 1650–1620 B.C.:** Hittite king Hattusilis I founds what is now known as the Old Hittite Kingdom and makes Hattuşaş the capital.
- **ca. 1620–1590 B.C.:** Reign of Mursilis I. The Hittite Kingdom becomes the leading power in the Middle East.
- **ca. 1450 B.C.:** Tudhaliyas I founds a new dynasty that creates the Hittite Empire.
- **ca. 1380–1346 B.C.:** Reign of Suppiluliumas I, the Hittites' greatest ruler. He destroys the Kingdom of Mitanni to the southeast and extends his borders into northern Syria.
- **ca. 1320–1294 B.C.:** Reign of Muwatallis. He clashes with Ramses II in the battle of Kadesh (ca. 1299 B.C.) on the Orontes in northern Syria, and Ramses withdraws.
- **ca. 1265–1240 B.C.:** Reign of Tudhaliyas IV. Reliefs are carved at Yazılıkaya and major building is undertaken at Hattuşaş, but the Hittite Empire begins to disintegrate from internal strife.
- **ca. 1225–1200 B.C.:** Reign of Suppiluliumas II. Naval attacks by mysterious "Peoples of the Sea," Phrygians, and the Kaska tribes, as well as famine and the weakening of the central authority, lead to the collapse of the Hittite Empire (ca. 1193 B.C.). Hattuşaş is destroyed.
- **13th century B.C.:** Assyrian sources begin to mention presence of Urartians in eastern Anatolia.

- **ca. 1200–700 B.C.:** Minor Hittite principalities survive in southeastern Anatolia and northern Syria.
- **ca. 1000 B.C.:** Greeks from mainland colonize Aegean coast of Anatolia—Aeolis in north, Ionia in center, Doris in south. Ionians found 12 major cities, including Ephesus, Priene, and Miletus.
- **ca. 1000–700 B.C.:** Kingdom of Phrygia centered at Gordion. The legendary King Gordius ties the Gordian knot. His son Midas acquires the golden touch.
- **ca. 750–650 B.C.:** The epic poet Homer is born in the region of Smyrna (modern İzmir).

The Kingdom of Urartu in Eastern Anatolia

The Urartians, who were of neither Indo-European nor Semitic stock, established a kingdom that dominated eastern Anatolia and part of Caucasia from about 850 to about 600 B.C. Their civilization was influenced to some degree by the Assyrians, against whom they fought almost continuously, but they developed their own social order and art. They were famed for their horse breeding and metalwork, which was exported to Greece and even to the Etruscans in Italy.

- **ca. 860–840 B.C.:** Reign of Aramu, first known king of Urartu.
- **ca. 840–830 B.C.:** Reign of Sarduri I, who makes Tushpa (modern Van) his capital.
- **ca. 755–735 B.C.:** Reign of Sarduri II. Urartu reaches the height of its power and controls northern Syria.
- **ca. 700–600 B.C.:** Anatolia is invaded by both Cimmerians and Scythians from Russia. Phrygia and Urartu are overrun. Greek colonists from Ionia settle along the Black Sea coast.
- **ca. 650–600 B.C.:** Armenians appear in eastern Anatolia.

Lycia, Lydia, Caria, and the Ionian City States

Lycia, Lydia, and Caria were ancient regions of western Anatolia. The indigenous people of Lycia and Lydia spoke related Indo-European languages. The language of the people of Caria has not yet been definitely classified. The Lycians, first mentioned at the time of the Hittite Empire, disappear and then reemerge in the eighth century B.C. The Lydians, who profoundly influenced the Ionians, founded a large state centered on Sardis (east of İzmir) in the seventh century B.C. They are credited with inventing the use of gold and silver coinage as standard monetary units. The well-travelled Carians, whose graffiti has been found on the temple of Abu Simbel in upper Egypt, claimed kinship with the Lydians and flourished under Lydian rule. The Ionian city-states began to prosper in the eighth century B.C. In the following century their seafarers established colonies along the Black Sea. The achievements of their thinkers and artisans in both the seventh and sixth centuries B.C. had a decisive effect on the development of Greek culture.

- **ca. 680–648** B.C.: Reign of Gyges, first king of the Mermnad dynasty of Lydia. He attacks the Ionian cities.
- **ca. 650** B.C.: Lydia is ravaged by the Cimmerians.
- **625–600** B.C.: Miletus flourishes under the tyrant Thrasybulus.
- **625–585** B.C.: Cyaxares founds the Empire of the Medes in Iran, establishing supremacy over eastern Anatolia.
- **ca. 624** B.C.: Birth of the philosopher Thales (d. ca. 547 B.C.) in Miletus. Thales is the first of the Ionian natural philosophers. He asserts that water is the basis of all things and makes various discoveries in geometry and astronomy, predicting an eclipse of the sun during a battle between the Lydians and Medes.
- **ca. 617–560** B.C.: King Alyattes of Lydia, great-grandson of Gyges, drives the Cimmerians out of Anatolia, conquers and destroys Smyrna (modern İzmir), wages war on the Medes under Cyaxares, and, after attempting to conquer Miletus without success, makes peace with Thrasybulus.
- **610** B.C.: Birth of the mathematician Anaximander (d. ca. 547 B.C.) in Miletus. Anaximander formulates the first systematic philosophical view of the world. He is said to have introduced the sundial to Greece and to have made the first map of the world.
- **ca. 560** B.C.: Birth of the poet and religious thinker Xenophanes (d. ca. 478 B.C.) in Colophon (in Ionia). Xenophanes becomes a student of Anaximander and criticizes the anthropomorphic representation of the gods and attacks the gods' immorality. His philosophy stresses the unity of all things: "The all is one and the one is God."

Persian Rule

The Persians established the first world empire, of which Anatolia was a part for more than two centuries (roughly 547 to 334 B.C.). Herodotus left a detailed account of their complete domination of Anatolia, yet little archaeological material has been excavated from the period of Persian rule. Trade flourished and most of the region prospered.

- **560 B.C.:** Croesus, son of Alyattes, becomes king of Lydia. He conquers Ionia, except for Miletus, and accumulates vast wealth.
- **547 B.C.:** Croesus learns from the Oracle at Delphi that a great empire will fall if he crosses the Halys river (modern Kızılırmak). Croesus interprets this to mean he will be victorious in a war against the Persians. He crosses the Halys to attack Cyrus but is defeated, and his own empire falls. Virtually all of Anatolia is then incorporated into the Persian Empire.
- **ca. 546 B.C.:** Anaximenes of Miletus, the third philosopher of the Ionian school, asserts that air is the primary substance of all things.
- **ca. 540 B.C.:** Temple of Artemis, one of the Seven Wonders of the World, is completed at Ephesus. It is the first monumental sanctuary built of marble and the largest building in the Greek world. Also circa 540 B.C., the philosopher Heraclitus is born in Ephesus.
- **521 B.C.:** Darius I becomes king of Persia.
- **499–494 B.C.:** Encouraged by Athens, Ionians revolt against Persian rule and capture and burn Sardis (498 B.C.).
- **490 B.C.:** After crushing the Ionians, Darius invades Greece. Although he is defeated at Marathon (490 B.C.) and his successor Xerxes is beaten at Salamis (480 B.C.) and at Plataea and Mycale (479 B.C.), Ionia and the rest of Anatolia generally remain under Persian control until Alexander the Great crosses the Dardanelles in 334 B.C.
- **ca. 484 B.C.:** Birth of Herodotus of Halicarnassus (modern Bodrum). Herodotus (d. ca. 430–420 B.C.) travels throughout much of the ancient world and writes the first secular narrative history, primarily an account of the Persian wars.
- **ca. 431 B.C.:** Birth of Xenophon (d. ca. 352 B.C.) in Athens. After becoming a disciple of Socrates, Xenophon joins a force of Greek mercenaries (the Ten Thousand) in the service of Cyrus the Younger of Persia. When Cyrus is killed (401 B.C.), Xenophon helps lead the retreating Greek soldiers from Babylonia back to Greece, recording the journeys to and from Babylon in his *Anabasis*.
- **ca. 412 B.C.:** Birth of the Cynic philosopher Diogenes (d. ca. 320 B.C.) in Sinope on the Black Sea coast. He teaches that the simple life is the virtuous life and, carrying a lantern in broad daylight, searches "for an honest man."
- **ca. 353 B.C.:** The Mausoleum, one of the Seven Wonders of

the World, is erected at Halicarnassus as a tomb for Mausolus, the Persian governor of Caria.

- **350 B.C.:** The Ionian city of Priene is rebuilt on a Hippodamian grid plan. (Hippodamus of Miletus, who lived in the fifth century B.C., was credited by the ancients with inventing the grid town plan.) The city's temple of Athena Polias is dedicated in 334 B.C. Its architect, Pythius, was co-architect of the Mausoleum.
- **ca. 347–344 B.C.:** Aristotle establishes an academy at Assos.

The Hellenistic Age

Alexander's conquest of western and southern Anatolia was followed by a resurgence of Greek culture in Ionia, which spread throughout Anatolia in varying degrees. The mixture of Greek and Eastern cultures resulted in a new civilization, the Hellenistic. After Alexander's death, his generals fought over his empire. Large parts of Anatolia were taken by Alexander's successors, the Seleucids and Ptolemies, while elsewhere in the region local kingdoms emerged. Despite political disunity, science and art flourished. Pergamum (modern Bergama) rivaled Alexandria as a center of learning.

- **334 B.C.:** Alexander the Great crosses the Dardanelles (Hellespont) to invade Asia. He defeats Persian forces at the Granicus river and "liberates" Ionia, Caria, and Lycia from Persian rule.
- **333 B.C.:** Alexander marches to Perge and then turns north for Gordion, where he cuts the Gordian knot. He next heads southeast, defeats the Persian army led by Darius III at Issus (near İskenderun), and continues to Egypt and beyond.
- **323 B.C.:** Death of Alexander. His generals fight each other for a share of his empire. Antigonus takes control of Phrygia (320 to 317 B.C.).
- **310 B.C.:** Work is begun on the temple of Apollo at Didyma.
- **301 B.C.:** Battle of Ipsus in Phrygia in which two of Alexander's generals, Lysimachus and Seleucus, and the Macedonian king Cassander defeat and kill Antigonus. Lysimachus takes western Anatolia, Seleucus takes southeastern Anatolia, while Mithradates I (302 to 266 B.C.), a native dynast, founds the Kingdom of Pontus in northern Anatolia.
- **300 B.C.:** Seleucus I founds Antioch-on-the-Orontes (modern Antakya).
- **281 B.C.:** Seleucus I defeats and kills Lysimachus at the battle of Corupedium in Lydia, becoming master of all

Anatolia, but is then assassinated at the instigation of the son of Ptolemy I of Egypt.

- **278 B.C.:** The Gauls invade Anatolia from the west and settle in Central Anatolia. They are defeated in 275 B.C. by Seleucid emperor Antiochus I, who terrifies them with his elephants.

- **263–241 B.C.:** Eumenes I, nephew of the local governor, makes himself ruler of an independent Pergamum.

- **ca. 262 B.C.:** Birth of the geometer Apollonius of Perge (d. ca. 190 B.C.). His treatise *Conics* is one of the greatest scientific works of antiquity.

- **ca. 250 B.C.:** Apollonius of Rhodes composes his epic poem *Argonautica,* which describes the voyage of Jason and the Argonauts along the Black Sea coast to Colchis in search of the Golden Fleece some time before the Trojan War.

- **246–241 B.C.:** Egyptians under Ptolemy III extend their holdings in Lycia and along the rest of the Mediterranean coast by occupying Antioch.

- **241–197 B.C.:** Reign of Attalus I of Pergamum. He decisively defeats the Gauls (230 B.C.) and establishes his own kingdom in western Anatolia.

- **223–187 B.C.:** Antiochus III restores much of the Seleucid Empire, regaining territory lost to Attalus I as well as other lands, but the Roman army enters Anatolia and defeats him at Magnesia-under-Sipylus (modern Manisa) in 190 B.C.

- **197–ca. 159 B.C.:** Reign of Eumenes II, son of Attalus I. He aids Rome against Antiochus III and is rewarded with western Anatolia. In 190 B.C. he founds Hierapolis (modern Pamukkale) and builds a library in Pergamum to rival that of Alexandria. The altar of Zeus, a masterpiece of Hellenistic art, is built in Pergamum (ca. 166 to 159 B.C.).

- **195 B.C.:** Several years after the Second Punic War, Hannibal flees Carthage for the court of Antiochus III at Ephesus. After Rome defeats Antiochus, Hannibal takes refuge at the court of King Prusias of Bithynia and helps him find a site for the new city of Prusia (modern Bursa). Pursued by Rome, Hannibal finally takes his own life (183 B.C.) in a village west of present-day İzmit.

- **188 B.C.:** Peace of Apamaea; Seleucids abandon all their territory north of the Taurus mountains, which is distributed among the friends of Rome.

- **159–138 B.C.:** Reign of Attalus II of Pergamum, who founds Attalia (modern Antalya).

- **138–133 B.C.:** Reign of Attalus III of Pergamum. At his death he wills his kingdom to Rome; it becomes a Roman province in 129 B.C.

- **120–63 B.C.:** Reign of Mithradates VI, king of Pontus. From his kingdom in the north he conquers much of Anatolia. His attack on western Anatolia in 88 B.C., combined with a large-scale revolt that he encourages, results in the death of thousands of Romans, leading to war with Rome.

- **94–56 B.C.:** Reign of Tigranes I of Armenia, son-in-law of Mithradates, with whom he is allied. He conquers much of eastern Anatolia but is defeated by the Roman general Lucullus (69 B.C.), who takes control of his empire.

- **66 B.C.:** After a series of battles, Mithradates is driven from Anatolia by the Roman general Pompey.

- **65 B.C.** Appearance of the independent petty Kingdom of Commagene, which is centered at Samosata (modern Samsat) on the Euphrates. Its second ruler, Antiochus I (ca. 69 to 34 B.C.), who claims descent from both Alexander the Great and Darius of Persia, builds a colossal funerary sanctuary and temple atop Nemrut Dağı in southeastern Anatolia.

- **ca. 64 B.C.:** Birth of Strabo (d. ca. A.D. 24) at Amasea (modern Amasya). Strabo's *Geographica* is the most important geographical work to survive from ancient times.

- **51–50 B.C.:** The Roman orator, statesman, and scholar Cicero serves as proconsul (governor) of the province of Cilicia in southern Anatolia.

- **47 B.C.:** Julius Caesar defeats Pharnaces of Pontus, the son of Mithradates, at Zela (now Zile, near Amasya). In his report on the campaign, Caesar utters his famous saying, "Veni, vidi, vici."

- **46 B.C.–A.D. 30:** Romans consolidate their power in western Anatolia while Parthians from Iran take eastern Anatolia.

- **41 B.C.:** In the midst of the Roman civil war, which has a terrible effect on Anatolia, Mark Antony meets Cleopatra at Tarsus.

Roman Period

Under the Romans, Anatolia for the first time became part of an empire centered in Europe. The Romans gradually absorbed the different kingdoms in the region, introducing their own administration and law as they progressed east. The *Pax Romana* resulted in considerable building activity in the cities and the development of a remarkable system of roads, which greatly benefited trade. The eastern marches, however, were somewhat insecure, as Rome contested for territory here with a powerful Iran under the Parthian and Sassanid dynasties. The Roman period also witnessed the spread of Christianity throughout Anatolia from the city of Antioch, where the term "Christian" was first used.

- **31 B.C.–A.D. 14**: Reign of Emperor Augustus, the beginning of a period of great prosperity in Anatolia.
- **ca. 25–20 B.C.**: Temple of Rome and Augustus is built in Ankara. Upon the death of Augustus, his own account of his achievements is inscribed on the walls of this temple, the most important Roman inscription to survive from antiquity.
- **A.D. 34 or 36**: Beginning of the Christian mission at Antioch.
- **ca. 47**: Beginning of the missionary journeys of Saint Paul, a native of Tarsus, on the Mediterranean coast. The first journey takes him to Perge in Pamphylia, Antioch in Pisidia, and Iconium (modern Konya); the second (50 to 53) to Galatia; the third (53 to 57) again to Galatia, then Phrygia and Ephesus. In the course of his missions, he writes letters to the Galatians and Ephesians.
- **First century A.D.**: According to one tradition, the Virgin Mary spends her last days in Ephesus in the care of Saint John.
- **ca. 110–112**: The Roman orator, author, and administrator Pliny the Younger serves as imperial legate in the province of Bithynia in northwestern Anatolia.
- **114–116**: Emperor Trajan occupies eastern Anatolia and fights an inconclusive war against the Parthians.
- **117–180**: Romans and Parthians fight for control of eastern Anatolia.
- **ca. 130**: Birth of Galen (d. 200) in Pergamum. Galen serves as the personal physician to Marcus Aurelius and goes on to have an illustrious medical career. His works remain authoritative until the 16th century.
- **161–180**: The theater at Aspendus in Pamphylia is built during the reign of Marcus Aurelius.
- **197–198**: Septimius Severus defeats the Parthians.
- **227**: The Persian Ardashir overthrows the Parthian dynasty in Iran and establishes the Sassanid dynasty.
- **229–260**: Romans and Sassanids fight a series of wars over eastern Anatolia.
- **260**: Emperor Valerian is defeated and captured by the Sassanids at Edessa (modern Şanlıurfa). The Persians advance as far as Caesarea (modern Kayseri) in Cappadocia.
- **ca. 280**: Armenia is Christianized.
- **283**: Emperor Carus invades Iran and captures the Sassanid capital of Ctesiphon, but then dies mysteriously (284).
- **284**: Diocletian succeeds Carus's son as emperor and di-

vides the Roman Empire into eastern and western halves (285), keeping the former for himself.

- **296–376:** Series of wars between Romans and Sassanids over eastern Anatolia.
- **ca. 300:** Birth of Saint Nicholas, bishop of Myra (near Demre, in Lycia). According to legend, he secretly bestowed dowries upon the daughters of a poor citizen, thus originating the custom of giving presents on the eve of the feast of St. Nicholas, a tradition later transferred to Christmas Day.
- **305:** Diocletian and Maximian abdicate as co-emperors, and a struggle begins between their successors for control of the Roman Empire.
- **312:** Constantine becomes sole emperor after defeating Maxentius at the battle of Milvian Bridge near Rome. According to legend, Constantine dreams of a cross in the sky before the battle. His reign is marked by increasing official acceptance of Christianity.
- **313:** Constantine's Edict of Milan recognizes Christianity as a legal religion.
- **325:** Constantine convenes the First Ecumenical Council of bishops at Nicaea (modern İznik), which establishes the divinity and equality of the Son in the Christian Trinity (Nicene Creed). The Arian heresy, which held that God created a Son who was neither equal nor eternal with the Father, is denounced.
- **330:** Constantine founds the New Rome (Constantinople) on the site of Byzantium.
- **361–363:** Reign of Julian the Apostate, who attempts to return the empire to the worship of pagan gods.
- **379–395:** Reign of Theodosius I, who forbids pagan practices, making Christianity the state religion. At his death the empire is partitioned between East and West.
- **451:** The Fourth Ecumenical Council, held at Chalcedon (modern Kadıköy), across the Bosphorus from Constantinople, establishes the foundations of Christian orthodoxy.
- **455:** Rome is sacked by the Vandals. Constantinople becomes the center of the civilized world.
- **457–474:** Reign of Leo I. The western half of the Roman Empire falls away while the eastern half becomes what we now call the Byzantine Empire.

The Rise of Byzantium

Byzantium, or the Eastern Roman Empire, which emerged from the division and collapse of the Roman Empire, was the most enduring state based in Anatolia. Combining Roman political tradition, Hellenic culture (and the Greek language), and Christian beliefs, it produced a civilization that had a profound influence on both Europe and the Middle East. Constantinople, its brilliant capital, was for centuries one of the most important cultural centers of the world. Only Baghdad, after the eighth century the capital of Byzantium's chief rival, the Islamic caliphate, could compare to it.

- **527–565**: Byzantium reaches the height of its power during reign of Justinian I, who recovers lost territory, codifies Roman law, and builds the great church of St. Sophia (Holy Wisdom) in Constantinople.
- **572–591**: Continuous war between Byzantium and Iran. Sassanid Persians ravage Cappadocia.
- **606–608**: War is resumed between Byzantium and Iran. The Sassanids reach the Bosphorus.
- **610–641**: Reign of Heraclius I, who reorganizes the Byzantine army. He drives the Sassanids from Anatolia and decisively defeats them; by the end of the war both empires are exhausted.
- **632**: Muhammad, the Prophet of Islam, dies at Medina in Arabia. Abu Bakr becomes his first successor, or caliph, and Islam spreads throughout Arabia.
- **636–718**: Arabs defeat Sassanids and conquer Iran, capture Egypt and Syria from Byzantium, invade eastern Anatolia, and twice besiege Constantinople but are repulsed with the help of "Greek fire."
- **726**: Emperor Leo III bans "image worship," thus starting the Iconoclasm controversy, which divides the church and the empire.
- **787**: Council of Nicaea abandons Iconoclasm and once again allows the religious use of images.
- **797–802**: Irene, the wife of Leo IV, reigns alone as empress after ruling behind the scenes and working to end Iconoclasm.
- **804–806, 837–838**: Wars between Byzantium and the Arabs.
- **863–885**: Missionary activity of Saints Cyril and Methodius among the Slavs. They invent an alphabet (Cyrillic) for use by the Slavs.
- **871–879**: Emperor Basil I crushes the Christian Paulician heresy and drives the Arabs from Cappadocia and Cilicia.
- **885–1045**: Under the Bagratids, who ruled from Kars and Ani, Armenia reaches the height of its power and culture in eastern Anatolia.

- **907**: Russian forces under Prince Oleg appear at Constantinople and raid suburbs.
- **912–959**: Reign of Constantine VII Porphyrogenitus, whose general, John Curcuas, takes Theodosiopolis (modern Erzurum) (928) and Melitene (modern Malatya) (934) from the Arabs.
- **941**: Prince Igor of Kiev attacks Constantinople without success.
- **ca. 960**: Seljuk, the leader of a confederation of Central Asian Turkish tribes, enters the territory of the caliphate.
- **968**: Emperor Nicephorus II Phocas invades Syria, takes Aleppo and Antioch.
- **976**: Byzantine general and emperor John Tzimisces, who murdered Nicephorus II in 969, takes Damascus and marches to the gates of Jerusalem, then suddenly dies.
- **976–1025**: Reign of Basil II. He expands Byzantine power in Europe and annexes most of Armenia in the east (1021). Byzantine culture reaches its height during the tenth and eleventh centuries, when the art of pictorial painting and the writing of history—among other artistic and intellectual pursuits—flourish.
- **989**: Vladimir of Kiev, who marries a Byzantine princess, is baptized and converts his people to Christianity.
- **ca. 1009**: Seljuk dies in Jand on the Jaxartes river after adopting Islam and laying the foundation of a Turkish empire that would be named after him.
- **1040**: At Dandanqan near Marv in northeastern Iran, Toghrıl Beg and Chaghrı Beg, grandsons of Seljuk, defeat the forces of the Muslim Ghaznavid Empire centered in present-day Afghanistan. Toghrıl is proclaimed the first Seljuk sultan. The first massive immigration of Turks into the Middle East begins.
- **1048**: First major Turkish raid on Anatolia. Theodosiopolis is captured and the Turks penetrate Central Anatolia.
- **1054**: Schism between Constantinople and Rome over papal claim to primacy among bishops.
- **1055**: Toghrıl Beg enters Baghdad, restricts the authority of the caliph to religious affairs, and goes on to establish the Great Seljuk Empire, which ultimately stretches from Central Asia to the Mediterranean.
- **1071**: Romanus IV Diogenes attempts to stop the Turkish advance but is defeated and captured by Alparslan, successor to Toghrıl Beg, at the battle of Manzikert. Eastern Anatolia is now open to large-scale Turkish immigration. The Turks occupy Jerusalem.
- **1072–1092**: Reign of Malik-Shah. The Great Seljuk Empire

is at its height. Upon Malik-Shah's death the empire dissolves into several branches, including that of the Seljuks of Anatolia, also called the Seljuks of Rum (or "Rome," i.e., the lands of the Roman Empire, or Byzantium).

Decline of Byzantium and the Rise of the Seljuks of Anatolia

In the 11th century, as domestic political strife, religious disputes, and attacks from Europeans weakened the Byzantine Empire, the Seljuk Turks swept across the Middle East from Central Asia—adopting Islam en route—and entered Anatolia en masse. Byzantine control of the region was eventually restricted to the west coast. Turkish immigration began the long process of Turkization and Islamization of Anatolia, which resulted in the fusion of Turkish, Islamic, Greek, Christian, and other local traditions into a new civilization, one that began to appear in the Seljuk capital at Konya and later achieved brilliance under the Ottomans.

- **1075**: Süleyman-Shah, a distant relative of Malik-Shah, captures Nicaea and lays the foundation for the future state of the Seljuks of Anatolia. The Turks now control most of Anatolia, which is divided into several principalities.
- **1081–1118**: Reign of Alexius I Comnenus, one of the most brilliant Byzantine emperors. He holds off the Normans and the Pechenegs in the west and asks the Pope for help against the Turks. His daughter, Anna Comnena, writes the *Alexiad,* a biography of her father and a brilliant and comprehensive record of the times.
- **1084–1134**: Amir Gazi establishes the power of the Danishmendid Turks in north-central and eastern Anatolia, rivaling the Seljuks.
- **1089–1213**: The Kingdom of Georgia reaches the height of its power and controls most of northeastern Anatolia.
- **1095**: Council of Clermont. Pope Urban II preaches the First Crusade.
- **1097**: Crusaders capture Nicaea. Qılıch Arslan (Turkish, Kılıç Aslan), the son of Süleyman-Shah, is defeated at the battle of Dorylaeum (modern Eskişehir). Crusaders march across Anatolia and lay siege to Antioch. Qılıch Arslan transfers the Seljuk capital to Konya.
- **1098**: Antioch falls to the Crusaders and Edessa becomes a Crusader county; the next year Jerusalem falls.
- **1107**: Qılıch Arslan dies after overcoming various rivals and consolidating his power in Central Anatolia.

- **1116**: Alexius defeats the Turks at Philomelion (modern Akşehir), forcing them to abandon most of western Anatolia.
- **1137**: John II Comnenus invades Cilicia.
- **1143–1180**: Reign of Manuel I Comnenus. Constantinople again shines as the leading cultural center of the world. The emperor's preoccupation with the West allows the Seljuks to expand their power and influence.
- **1144**: Imad ad-Din Zengi, governor of Mosul in northern Iraq, captures Edessa, provoking the Second Crusade.
- **1147**: The Seljuk sultan Masud I defeats the German army of the Second Crusade at the second battle of Dorylaeum.
- **1171**: Saladin, a Kurd whose family came from eastern Anatolia, establishes the Ayyubid dynasty in Egypt.
- **1176**: Qılıch Arslan II defeats Manuel I at Myriocephalon (near Lake Eğridir) and ends Byzantine hope of ever recovering Anatolia. The following year he annexes the territory of the Danishmendids.
- **1187**: Saladin captures Jerusalem, precipitating the Third Crusade.
- **1190**: Frederick Barbarossa, Holy Roman emperor and leader of the German army of the Third Crusade, crosses Anatolia and captures Konya but later drowns in Cilicia.
- **1195**: Alexius III deposes Isaac Angelus as emperor after considerable dynastic strife.
- **1201**: Isaac Angelus's son Alexius flees to Italy and asks the Venetians for help in regaining the throne.
- **1204**: Venetians divert the Fourth Crusade from Egypt to Constantinople, which is stormed and sacked. Byzantium is partitioned among the Crusaders (who establish the so-called Latin Empire), but Theodore I Lascaris resurrects the Byzantine crown at Nicaea, and the Grand Comneni establish a second Byzantine state at Trebizond.
- **1207**: Birth of Mevlâna Jalal ad-Din ar-Rumi (d. 1273; Turkish, Celalettin Rumi), poet and founder of the Mevleviye order of Whirling Dervishes.
- **1219–1237**: Reign of 'Ala' ad-Din Kay-Qubad I (Turkish, Alaettin Keykubat), the golden age of the Seljuks of Anatolia.
- **1240**: Dervish rebellion of Baba Ishaq shakes the Seljuk state.
- **1243–1310**: Mongols defeat Seljuks at the battle of Köse Dağ in 1243. The Seljuk state becomes a province of the Mongol Empire and gradually disintegrates into a number of Turkish principalities.
- **1261**: Michael VIII Palaeologus, ruler of the Empire of

Nicaea, retakes Constantinople and establishes the last Byzantine dynasty.

- **1276:** The Karamanids, a Turkish dynasty that rivals the Seljuks for control of Central Anatolia, briefly occupy Konya.
- **ca. 1295:** Marco Polo travels through eastern Anatolia.
- **1302:** Osman Gazi, a leader of the seminomadic Turks on the northwestern marches between Byzantium and Seljuk Anatolia, defeats a Byzantine army at Baphaeon near Nicomedia (modern İzmit) and attracts many followers.

The Ottoman Period

With an unmatched dynamism, the Ottoman Turks, the successors of the Seljuks, laid the Byzantine Empire to rest and created a powerful state. The Ottomans enjoyed their golden age in the 16th century, a time of great conquest and artistic achievement. Most of the Middle East and North Africa and perhaps a quarter of Europe were ruled by the sultan. For more than four centuries the Ottoman Empire was the leader of the Islamic world and a major preoccupation of the European Christian powers.

- **1326:** Osman captures Prusa (modern Bursa) and makes it the capital of his newly founded state, which takes the name Osmanlı, or—as it came to be known in the West—Ottoman.
- **1331:** Orhan, Osman's successor, captures Nicaea.
- **1341–1347:** Civil war in Byzantium between John V Palaeologus and rival emperor John VI Cantacuzene. Both sides ask the Turks for help. Orhan marries a daughter of John VI.
- **1354:** Ottomans occupy Ankara and cross the Dardanelles to take Kallipolis (Gallipoli, modern Gelibolu), which serves as their base of expansion into Europe.
- **1361:** Murat I, Orhan's son, captures Adrianople (modern Edirne) and makes it the new capital of the growing Ottoman state. Byzantium is reduced to Constantinople and parts of Thrace and mainland Greece.
- **1363–1400:** Ottomans expand west into Europe and east into Anatolia. Victory at Kosovo (1389) ends the Serbian Empire and firmly establishes Ottoman rule in the Balkans.
- **1400:** The Turkic conqueror Tamerlane invades Anatolia from the east and sacks Sivas.
- **1402:** At the battle of Ankara Tamerlane defeats the Ottomans under Bayezit I, halting Ottoman expansion in Anatolia for half a century.

- **1403–1413:** Civil war among Bayezit's sons until Mehmet I unifies the Ottoman territories.
- **1413–1421:** Reign of Mehmet I. He regains most of western and central Anatolia.
- **1421–1451:** Reign of Murat II. Ottoman expansion continues in Europe and Anatolia. At the battle of Varna in Bulgaria (1444) the last major Christian attempt to stem the Ottoman tide is crushed.
- **1451–1481:** Reign of Mehmet II, the Conqueror, the true founder of the Ottoman Empire.
- **1453:** After a 50-day siege using the largest cannons the world had yet known, Mehmet conquers Constantinople. The Byzantine emperor Constantine XI Palaeologus falls in the heroic defense. The great city becomes the Ottoman capital and the Byzantine Empire is no more.
- **1461–1473:** Mehmet annexes the Empire of Trebizond, conquers Karaman, and defeats Uzun Hasan, the leader of a powerful Turkish confederation centered in Diyarbakır.
- **ca. 1465:** Birth of Piri Reis (d. ca. 1554), navigator and naval commander. In 1517 he presents to Sultan Selim I a map of the world showing the coastline of America. He bases his chart of the New World on a map made by Columbus in 1498.
- **1465–1478:** Construction begins on Topkapı palace (Yeni Saray) in Istanbul.
- **1489 or 1490:** Birth of Mimar Sinan (d. 1578), chief architect of Süleyman the Magnificent.
- **1492:** Tens of thousands of Jews expelled from Spain are given refuge in the Ottoman Empire.
- **16th century:** The production of İznik pottery reaches its height.
- **1512–1520:** Reign of Selim I, called the Grim. The Ottoman Empire enters the period of its greatest power.
- **1514:** Selim defeats Shah Ismail of Iran at the battle of Çaldıran in eastern Anatolia and blunts the spread of Shi'a Islam in Anatolia. Azerbaijan is conquered.
- **1516:** Most of eastern Anatolia submits to Selim. Syria is conquered.
- **1517:** Selim takes Egypt. In Arabia, Mecca and Medina acknowledge Ottoman suzerainty.
- **1520–1566:** Reign of Süleyman I, the Lawgiver, known in the West as Süleyman the Magnificent. The Ottomans reach the height of their power, and the political and social structure of the empire finds its definitive form. The judicial system is reorganized. Art, architecture, and literature flourish. Süleyman's architect Sinan erects 477 (known) buildings. Süleyman's reign witnesses the production of

magnificent ceramics, delicate textiles, beautiful Koran illuminations, miniatures, and bookbindings. Outstanding poets and scholars flock to his court.

- **1529**: Süleyman captures Buda (Budapest) and besieges Vienna.
- **1536**: Süleyman enters an alliance with François I of France against the Hapsburgs of Austria; the alliance becomes the basis of Turkish foreign policy in Europe for three centuries.
- **1548**: Süleyman campaigns against Iran and captures Van.
- **1549**: Süleyman invades Georgia.
- **1555**: Peace of Amasya with Iran.
- **1557**: Inauguration of the Süleymaniye Camii in Istanbul, one of Sinan's masterpieces.
- **1566–1574**: Reign of Selim II. The Ottomans attempt to build a canal connecting the Volga and Don rivers to enable their fleet to enter the Caspian Sea.
- **1570–71**: Ottomans capture Cyprus.
- **1571**: Battle of Lepanto. At great cost, the fleet of the Holy League, commanded by John of Austria, virtually destroys the Ottoman navy and prevents the Mediterranean from becoming an Ottoman lake. (Among the Christian wounded is Miguel de Cervantes.) The Christian victory, however, has little effect on Turkish supremacy on land.
- **1575**: Completion of Sinan's Selimiye Camii in Edirne.
- **1578–1590**: Long campaign in the east, which ends in peace with Iran.
- **1593–1606**: War with the Hapsburgs ends with the treaty of Zsitva-Torok.
- **1609–1617**: Construction of the Sultanahmet Camii (the Blue Mosque) in Istanbul.
- **1611**: Birth of Evliya Çelebi (d. 1679), soldier, traveller, writer.
- **1623–1640**: Reign of Murat IV. He crushes an uprising of the janissaries, the elite—but increasingly corrupt—army units, and attempts to revive Ottoman military power.
- **1683**: Second Ottoman siege of Vienna fails. Fifteen years of war follow in which the Ottomans suffer their first major setbacks in Europe. By the treaty of Carlowitz (1699) the Ottomans cede Hungary and Transylvania to the Hapsburgs.
- **1696**: Peter the Great captures Azov in the Crimea, giving Russia access to the Black Sea.
- **1703–1736**: Reign of Ahmet III, the Tulip Era. First serious attempts to introduce Western reforms.
- **1711**: Peter the Great invades the Ottoman European domains but is defeated.

- **1716–1718**: War with Austria. The Ottomans cede more territory in the Balkans to the Hapsburgs.
- **1727**: İbrahim Müteferrika establishes the first Turkish printing press in Istanbul.
- **1768–1774**: War with Russia, ended by the treaty of Küçük Kaynarca. Russians gain many advantages and henceforth apply relentless pressure on the Ottoman Empire. Their ultimate goal is control of the Bosphorus and Dardanelles.
- **1789–1807**: Reign of Selim III, the period of the first effective reforms in the empire. Selim tries to establish new military and bureaucratic structures but is overthrown by the janissaries.
- **1798**: Napoleon takes Egypt from the Ottomans in order to cut British communications with India. The French later (1802) surrender Egypt to the British, who officially restore it to the Ottomans.
- **1804–1813**: Serbian war of independence, the first of a series of Balkan nationalist uprisings.
- **1805**: After arriving in Egypt with the Ottoman forces to oppose the French, the soldier Muhammad Ali becomes the country's viceroy; he soon founds an independent dynasty and challenges the Ottoman Empire.
- **1808–1839**: Reign of Mahmut II, who centralizes political control and destroys the janissaries.
- **1832–1848**: War with Egypt. The Egyptians invade Anatolia, but the European powers save the sultan and force the Egyptians to retreat. Broad concessions are granted to European merchants.
- **1839–1861**: Reign of Abdülmecit I. Intensified period of westernization known as the Tanzimat (Reorganization).
- **1853**: Abdülmecit builds Dolmabahçe palace in Istanbul.
- **1853–1856**: The Crimean War. Turkey, England, France, and Sardinia defeat Russia. Florence Nightingale tends the wounded in the Crimea and in Istanbul (Üsküdar).
- **1861–1876**: Reign of Abdülaziz. The sultan borrows heavily from Europe, but the empire goes bankrupt. European governments and bankers take control of Ottoman finances. This is followed by the rise of a literary intelligentsia, the spread of Ottoman patriotism, constitutionalism, and Islamic modernism.
- **1876**: Abdülaziz is deposed. The first Ottoman constitution is promulgated.
- **1876–1909**: Reign of Abdülhamit II. He suspends the constitution and rules despotically. He achieves modernization of the education, transportation, and communications systems. Nationalism spreads among the Christian minorities.

- **1877–1878**: War with Russia. The Ottomans lose Bulgaria and northeastern Anatolia. The Russians encourage Armenian nationalists, who hope to create an independent state in eastern Anatolia.
- **1878**: Britain takes administrative control of Cyprus and annexes it in 1914.
- **1894**: Armenian nationalist revolutionaries are ruthlessly suppressed.
- **1908**: Revolution led by the Young Turks, who force Abdülhamit to restore the constitution and reconvene parliament. Turkish nationalism is first articulated.
- **1912–1913**: The Ottomans lose most of their remaining European territory in two Balkan wars.
- **1913**: The Young Turks seize power in a coup d'état. German influence is on the rise.
- **1914**: The Ottoman Empire enters World War I as an ally of the Central Powers.
- **1915–1916**: The Gallipoli Campaign: The allies attempt to capture the Dardanelles, Constantinople, and the Bosphorus and establish direct communications with Russia. Stubborn Ottoman resistance, led in part by an obscure Turkish officer named Mustafa Kemal (later known as Atatürk), results in an allied disaster.
- **1915–1916**: Many Armenians in eastern Anatolia join the Russian army. Thousands die when the Ottomans forcibly evacuate those who remain, regarding them as a potential fifth column. Armenians pronounce it a calculated genocide. Turks claim that the deaths resulted from famine, harsh weather, and anarchy and that a much greater number of Turks and other Muslims died.
- **1918**: World War I ends in defeat for the Central Powers; armistice of Mudros concludes hostilities between the allies and the Ottoman Empire.
- **1919**: The sultan sends Mustafa Kemal to eastern Anatolia as a military inspector to ensure that the terms of the armistice of Mudros are carried out, but upon landing in Samsun he organizes the Turkish Nationalist Party and begins to form an army. Meanwhile, Greek troops land at Smyrna (İzmir) and take the city and its environs as the first step in an attempt to create a Hellenic empire. Kemal launches the Turkish War of Independence.
- **1920**: Treaty of Sèvres between the Ottoman government and the allies (excluding the United States and Russia), which thoroughly humiliates the Turks. The Ottoman Empire is dissolved and apportioned to the victors. The Turks are left with only Istanbul and Central Anatolia. The treaty

is rejected by Mustafa Kemal. In collusion with Britain, Greece invades western Anatolia.

- **1921**: In the savagely fought battle of the Sakarya river, west of Ankara, the Turks halt the Greek onslaught.
- **1922**: In a brilliant campaign, Kemal drives the Greeks from Anatolia. The sultanate is abolished.

Modern Turkey

Plagued by the growth of European imperialism, dynastic troubles, conflicting nationalist movements, economic decline, and various obstacles to modernization, the Ottoman Empire virtually collapsed during World War I. The ambitions of the victorious powers, however, provoked a reaction of Turkish national feeling that was galvanized by Mustafa Kemal (Atatürk). Both general and statesman, he led the Turkish nationalist movement, which succeeded in creating the modern Republic of Turkey. He launched a program of westernization to transform Turkey into a modern secular state. Today Turkey is a member of NATO and the Council of Europe and the largest and most important democracy in the Middle East.

- **1923**: The Turkish republic is proclaimed. Mustafa Kemal is elected president. Ankara replaces Istanbul as the capital. Exchange of populations between Greece and Turkey.
- **1924**: Kemal begins a comprehensive program of westernization. The caliphate, the Muslim leadership that Süleyman had assumed in 1520, is abolished. Civil courts replace religious courts.
- **1925**: Religious brotherhoods are closed. The distinctively Muslim headgear, the fez, is outlawed. A treaty of friendship is signed with the U.S.S.R.
- **1928**: Islam is disestablished and Turkey is made a secular state. The Latin alphabet replaces the Arabic in written Turkish.
- **1933–1935**: As a result of Nazi persecution, some 1,200 European scholars and artists of Jewish origin flee Germany and are given positions in Turkey.
- **1934**: Women are given the right to vote in national elections (suffrage had been extended to women in municipal elections in 1930).
- **1936**: The Montreaux Convention governing shipping in the straits is concluded. Turkey regains military control of this waterway.
- **1938**: Mustafa Kemal, now known as Atatürk (the Father of

the Turks), dies and is succeeded as president by İsmet İnönü.

- **1939**: Turkey annexes the province of the Hatay (Alexandretta) from French-mandated Syria after the Hatay's residents vote for union. Turkey signs a treaty of alliance with Great Britain and France.

- **1939–1945**: Despite the alliance with Britain and France, Turkey remains neutral during World War II.

- **1945**: Stalin denounces the Soviet-Turkish friendship treaty of 1925 and demands the cession of territory in eastern Turkey, military bases on the straits, revision of the Montreaux Convention, and revision of the Turkish border in Thrace in favor of Bulgaria. Ankara rejects his demands.

- **1947**: In response to mounting Soviet pressure on Greece and Turkey, U.S. president Harry Truman pledges military and economic aid to both countries.

- **1950**: Turkey changes from a single-party to a multiparty system. Celal Bayar of the Democratic party is elected president and names Adnan Menderes as prime minister.

- **1950–1953**: Turkey sends a brigade to fight for the United Nations in the Korean War; the brigade receives a U.S. Presidential Citation for valor.

- **1952**: Turkey joins NATO.

- **1954**: Turkey concludes a military defense pact with Yugoslavia and Greece and helps create CENTO (the Central Treaty Organization).

- **1960**: Cyprus, a British crown colony, becomes independent after negotiations among Britain, Greece, and Turkey. The Greek majority and Turkish minority on the island are to share the government. In Turkey the Democratic party's increasingly repressive measures and suspension of many of Atatürk's reforms results in a military coup led by General Cemal Gürsel.

- **1961**: Menderes and two cabinet ministers are convicted of violating the constitution and are executed. A new constitution is adopted by national referendum and elections are held. Gürsel is elected president, and İnönü becomes prime minister.

- **1965**: The Justice Party wins a national election and Süleyman Demirel becomes prime minister. His party is reelected in 1969.

- **1970–1979**: A period of ineffective governments, growing civil unrest, and the rise of political terrorism. A separatist movement grows among the Kurds. The country faces severe economic problems.

- **1973**: The first suspension bridge is built across the Bosphorus. The Turkish consul general in Los Angeles is assassinated by an Armenian, marking the beginning of a campaign of Armenian terrorism that, through 1986, results in the murder of almost 70 Turkish diplomats, members of their families, and bystanders.

- **1974:** Bülent Ecevit becomes prime minister. The military junta in Athens instigates a coup in Cyprus in an attempt to unite that country with Greece. Turkey invades northern Cyprus to protect the Turkish minority on the island. War between Greece and Turkey is narrowly averted.
- **1980:** The military, led by General Kenan Evren, reluctantly seizes power in a bloodless coup. Political terrorism is ended and economic reforms are introduced.
- **1982:** A new constitution is approved in a national referendum; Evren is elected president.
- **1983:** National elections are held; the Motherland party, headed by Turgut Özal, wins the majority of seats in parliament. Özal becomes prime minister. Martial law remains in force in the southeast.
- **1984:** The Kurdish Workers (P.K.K.) party begins a series of terrorist attacks on southeast Turkey from bases outside the country.
- **1987:** Özal is reelected. Turkey applies for membership in the European Community. Tensions flare between Greece and Turkey.
- **1988:** Turkey and Greece agree to work toward a reconciliation.
- **1989:** Tens of thousands of ethnic Turks, fleeing systematic persecution, escape Bulgaria and are accepted by Turkey.
- **1990:** Özal becomes president. At great economic cost Turkey joins UN sanctions against Iraq after its invasion of Kuwait.
- **1991:** Turkey supports the United States and its allies in the Gulf War against Iraq. At war's end, tens of thousands of Iraqi Kurds seek refuge in southeastern Turkey. The True Path party wins the national elections, and Süleyman Demirel becomes the prime minister.
- **1992:** Turkey celebrates the quincentennial of the Ottoman Empire's welcome of the Jews expelled from Spain in 1492. Clashes between Turkish government forces and P.K.K. guerrillas in the remote southeast are frequent and bloody. During military exercises in the Aegean in October, a U.S. ship accidently discharges two missiles, which strike a Turkish vessel, killing its captain and several crew members.

—Gary Leiser

INDEX

Here's what others say...

"As a longtime reader of *Passport*, I trust it as a source of intelligence and ideas on independent travel."

Alan Deutschman
Associate Editor
Fortune Magazine

"The best little newsletter in America."
Crain's Chicago Business

"*Passport* has been appearing for more than 20 years with a brisk, colorful roundup of travel information. Substance prevails over style."
National Geographic Traveler

"In *Passport*, I consistently find the kind of information I want from a travel newsletter—sophisticated, concise and straightforward, without a lot of ego to get in the way."
Travel Editor
Town and Country Magazine

"The first and unquestionably the best luxury travel newsletter."

Alan Tucker, General Editor
Berlitz Travellers Guides

Since 1965, *Passport*, the monthly letter for discriminating travelers, has revealed hard-to-find information about the world's best destinations. Return this card for a free issue or call 800-542-6670. Available worldwide!

Please send a free issue of *Passport* to:

Name _____

Address _____

_____

City _____ State _____ Zip _____

"*This* is the granddaddy of travel letters... *Passport* emphasizes culture, comfort, and quality...it can glow with praise, or bite with disapproval."

Condé Nast Traveler

NO POSTAGE
NECESSARY
IF MAILED
IN THE
UNITED STATES

BUSINESS REPLY MAIL

FIRST CLASS MAIL   PERMIT NO 45660   CHICAGO IL

POSTAGE WILL BE PAID BY ADDRESSEE

Passport Newsletter®
350 West Hubbard Street
Suite 440
Chicago, Illinois 60610-9698